The Video Games Textbook

The Video Games Textbook takes the history of video games to the next level. Coverage includes every major video game console, handheld system, and game-changing personal computer, as well as a look at the business, technology, and people behind the games.

Chapters feature objectives and key terms, illustrative timelines, color images and graphs, in addition to the technical specifications and key titles for each platform. Every chapter is a journey into a different segment of gaming, where readers emerge with a clear picture of how video games evolved, why the platforms succeeded or failed, and the impact they had on the industry and culture. Written to capture the attention and interest of students from around the world, this newly revised Second Edition also serves as a go-to handbook for any video game enthusiast.

This edition features new content in every chapter, including color timelines, sections on color theory and lighting, the NEC PC-98 series, MSX series, Amstrad CPC, Sinclair ZX Spectrum, Milton Bradley Microvision, Nintendo Game & Watch, gender issues, PEGI and CERO rating systems, and new Pro Files and quiz questions, plus expanded coverage on PC and mobile gaming, virtual reality, Valve Steam Deck, Nintendo Switch, Xbox Series X|S, and PlayStation 5.

Key Features

- Explores the history, business, and technology of video games, including social, political, and economic motivations

- Facilitates learning with clear objectives, key terms, illustrative timelines, color images, tables, and graphs

- Highlights the technical specifications and key titles of all major game consoles, handhelds, personal computers, and mobile platforms

- Reinforces material with market summaries and reviews of breakthroughs and trends, as well as end-of-chapter activities and quizzes

The Video Games Textbook
History • Business • Technology

Second Edition

Dr. Brian J. Wardyga

CRC Press
Taylor & Francis Group
Boca Raton London New York

CRC Press is an imprint of the
Taylor & Francis Group, an **informa** business

Cover Image Credit: Shutterstock.com

Second edition published 2023
by CRC Press
6000 Broken Sound Parkway NW, Suite 300, Boca Raton, FL 33487-2742

and by CRC Press
4 Park Square, Milton Park, Abingdon, Oxon, OX14 4RN

CRC Press is an imprint of Taylor & Francis Group, LLC

© 2023 Brian J. Wardyga

First edition published by A K Peters/CRC Press 2018

Library of Congress Cataloging-in-Publication Data
Names: Wardyga, Brian J, author.
Title: The video games textbook : history business technology / Brian J. Wardyga.
Description: Second Edition. | Boca Raton, FL : Taylor & Francis, [2023] |
First edition: 2018. | Includes bibliographical references and index.
Identifiers: LCCN 2022051433 (print) | LCCN 2022051434 (ebook) | ISBN 9781032325804 (Paperback) |
ISBN 9781032325873 (Hardback) | ISBN 9781003315759 (eBook)
Subjects: LCSH: Video games—History. | Video games industry—History.
Classification: LCC GV1469.3 .W464 2023 (print) | LCC GV1469.3 (ebook) |
DDC 794.8—dc23/eng/20221213
LC record available at https://lccn.loc.gov/2022051433
LC ebook record available at https://lccn.loc.gov/2022051434

ISBN: 978-1-032-32587-3 (hbk)
ISBN: 978-1-032-32580-4 (pbk)
ISBN: 978-1-003-31575-9 (ebk)

DOI: 10.1201/9781003315759

Typeset in Minion
by codeMantra

Contents

List of Abbreviations, xvii

Acknowledgments, xxi

Author, xxiii

Introduction, xxv

CHAPTER 1 ▪ The First Video Games   1

    OBJECTIVES   1

    KEY TERMS AND PEOPLE   2

    FIRST-GENERATION TIMELINE   2

    FROM PENNY ARCADES TO PINBALL   3

    THE FIRST INTERACTIVE COMPUTER GAMES   4

    TENNIS FOR TWO   4

    SPACEWAR!   4

    COMPUTER SPACE   4

    MAGNAVOX ODYSSEY   5

    UNDERSTANDING ODYSSEY GAMES   6

    PRO FILE: RALPH BAER   9

    PONG   10

    PONG FOR YOUR HOME TV   12

    COLECO TELSTAR   13

    COLOR TV-GAME SERIES   18

    FIRST-GENERATION MARKET SUMMARY   19

    FIRST-GENERATION BREAKTHROUGHS AND TRENDS   20

    CHAPTER 1 QUIZ   21

    FIGURES   23

    REFERENCES   24

CHAPTER 2 ▪ Behind the Technology   27

    OBJECTIVES   27

    KEY TERMS AND PEOPLE   28

    CHAPTER OUTLINE   28

INTRODUCTION   29

UNDER THE HOOD   29

CPU   29

RAM AND ROM   29

BIOS   30

GRAPHICS AND SOUND CARDS   31

PORTS   31

MAKING THE CONNECTION   31

BITS AND BYTES   32

HERTZ AND FRAME RATE   33

SCANNING SYSTEMS   34

MONITOR TYPES   36

VIDEO FORMATS   36

ASCII AND VECTOR GRAPHICS   37

RASTER AND POLYGON GRAPHICS   38

SHADERS, FLOPS, AND CORES   39

COLOR AND LIGHTING   40

PERSPECTIVE   42

SOUND AND MUSIC   43

SOUND THEORY   45

PRO FILE: SID MEIER   46

CHAPTER 2 QUIZ   48

FIGURES   49

REFERENCES   51

CHAPTER 3 ■ The Atari Generation   53

OBJECTIVES   53

KEY TERMS AND PEOPLE   54

CONSOLE TIMELINE   54

THE GOLDEN AGE   55

THE SECOND GENERATION   56

ATARI VCS (2600)   56

PRO FILE: NOLAN BUSHNELL   58

CONSOLE COMPARISON   59

KEY ATARI VCS TITLES   61

MAGNAVOX ODYSSEY²   61

CONSOLE COMPARISON: ODYSSEY² VS. ATARI VCS   62

KEY MAGNAVOX ODYSSEY² TITLES   63

MATTEL INTELLIVISION   65

HANDHELD SNAPSHOT: MILTON BRADLEY MICROVISION   68

CONSOLE COMPARISON: INTELLIVISION VS. ATARI VCS AND ODYSSEY² 69

KEY INTELLIVISION TITLES 70

COLECOVISION 71

CONSOLE COMPARISON: COLECOVISION VS. ATARI VCS AND INTELLIVISION 72

KEY COLECOVISION TITLES 73

ATARI 5200 74

CONSOLE COMPARISON: ATARI 5200 VS. COLECOVISION 76

KEY ATARI 5200 TITLES 78

VIDEO GAME CRASH OF 1983 78

SECOND-GENERATION MARKET SUMMARY 79

SECOND-GENERATION BREAKTHROUGHS AND TRENDS 80

CHAPTER 3 QUIZ 81

FIGURES 83

REFERENCES 85

Chapter 4 ▪ Early PC Gaming

87

OBJECTIVES 87

KEY TERMS AND PEOPLE 88

EARLY COMPUTER TIMELINE 88

INTRODUCTION 89

APPLE I AND II 89

HARDWARE COMPARISON: APPLE II VS. ATARI VCS (2600) 91

KEY APPLE II TITLES 93

ELECTRONIC ARTS 93

APPLE II SUCCESSORS 93

ATARI 8-BIT FAMILY: 400 AND 800 94

PRO FILE: STEVE WOZNIAK 95

COMPUTER COMPARISON: ATARI 8-BIT VS. APPLE II 96

KEY ATARI 8-BIT TITLES 97

EXTENDED FAMILY: ATARI 8-BIT SUCCESSORS 97

COMMODORE 64 99

COMPUTER COMPARISON: COMMODORE 64 VS. ATARI 8-BIT 100

KEY COMMODORE 64 TITLES 101

COMMODORE 64 SUCCESSORS 101

MADE IN JAPAN 104

NEC PC-98 104

MSX 105

BEST OF BRITAIN 106

ZX SPECTRUM 106

AMSTRAD CPC 107

END OF AN ERA   108

MARKET SUMMARY   110

CHAPTER 4 QUIZ   112

FIGURES   114

REFERENCES   116

CHAPTER 5 ■ The 8-Bit Era   119

OBJECTIVES   119

KEY TERMS AND PEOPLE   120

CONSOLE TIMELINE   120

THE ARCADE SCENE   121

THE THIRD GENERATION   122

NINTENDO FAMICOM   122

COMING TO AMERICA   123

NINTENDO ENTERTAINMENT SYSTEM   123

HANDHELD SNAPSHOT: NINTENDO GAME & WATCH   126

CONSOLE COMPARISON: NES VS. ATARI 2600   127

PRO FILE: SHIGERU MIYAMOTO   128

KEY NES TITLES   129

SEGA MARK III   130

SEGA MASTER SYSTEM   131

CONSOLE COMPARISON: SMS VS. NES   132

KEY SEGA MASTER SYSTEM TITLES   132

ATARI 7800 PROSYSTEM   134

CONSOLE COMPARISON: ATARI 7800 VS. NES & SMS   136

KEY ATARI 7800 TITLES   138

THIRD-GENERATION MARKET SUMMARY   138

THIRD-GENERATION BREAKTHROUGHS AND TRENDS   139

CHAPTER 5 QUIZ   140

FIGURES   142

REFERENCES   144

CHAPTER 6 ■ The 16-Bit Era   145

OBJECTIVES   145

KEY TERMS AND PEOPLE   146

CONSOLE TIMELINE   146

ARCADE REVIVAL   147

THE 16-BIT ERA   147

PRO FILE: YU SUZUKI   148

NEC PC ENGINE   149

TURBOGRAFX-16   149

CONSOLE COMPARISON: TURBOGRAFX-16 VS. NES   152

KEY PC ENGINE/TURBOGRAFX-16 TITLES   152

SEGA MEGA DRIVE   154

SEGA GENESIS   154

HANDHELD SNAPSHOT: GAME BOY   155

CONSOLE COMPARISON: GENESIS VS. TURBOGRAFX-16   159

KEY MEGA DRIVE/GENESIS TITLES   160

HANDHELD SNAPSHOT: ATARI LYNX   161

SUPER FAMICOM   162

SUPER NINTENDO   162

CONSOLE COMPARISON: SUPER NINTENDO VS. SEGA & NEC   165

KEY SUPER FAMICOM/SUPER NINTENDO TITLES   166

SNK NEO•GEO AES   167

HANDHELD SNAPSHOT: SEGA GAME GEAR   168

CONSOLE COMPARISON: NEO•GEO AES VS. GENESIS & SNES   170

KEY NEO•GEO TITLES   170

FOURTH-GENERATION MARKET SUMMARY   172

FOURTH-GENERATION BREAKTHROUGHS AND TRENDS   173

CHAPTER 6 QUIZ   174

FIGURES   176

REFERENCES   178

CHAPTER 7 ▪ Sex and Violence Take Center Stage   181

OBJECTIVES   181

KEY TERMS AND PEOPLE   182

CHAPTER OUTLINE   182

INTRODUCTION   183

WHO PLAYS VIDEO GAMES?   183

SEX AND SOFTPORN ADVENTURE   183

CUSTER'S REVENGE   184

LEISURE SUIT LARRY   184

NIGHT TRAP AND FMV GAMES   185

THE GUY GAME   186

GRAND THEFT AUTO AND MODS   187

GENDER, IDENTITY, AND RACE   188

EARLY VIDEO GAME VIOLENCE   191

MORTAL KOMBAT   192

REGULATION AND THE ESRB   193

PEGI, CERO, AND IARC   193

DOOM AND FIRST-PERSON SHOOTERS   194

PRO FILE: DOUG LOWENSTEIN   195

ROCKSTAR GAMES AND LEGISLATION   197

EFFECTS OF VIDEO GAME VIOLENCE   199

OTHER EFFECTS OF VIDEO GAMES   200

CHAPTER 7 QUIZ   201

FIGURES   203

REFERENCES   204

CHAPTER 8 ■ The 3D Era   207

OBJECTIVES   207

KEY TERMS AND PEOPLE   208

CONSOLE TIMELINE   208

ARCADES IN FLUX   209

THE 3D ERA   210

3DO INTERACTIVE MULTIPLAYER   210

CONSOLE COMPARISON: 3DO VS. 16-BIT SYSTEMS   212

KEY 3DO TITLES   213

PRO FILE: TRIP HAWKINS   214

ATARI JAGUAR   215

CONSOLE COMPARISON: ATARI JAGUAR VS. 3DO   216

KEY ATARI JAGUAR TITLES   218

SEGA 32X   218

SEGA SATURN   219

CONSOLE COMPARISON: SEGA SATURN VS. 3DO AND JAGUAR   221

KEY SATURN TITLES   221

CHANGES AT SEGA   223

SONY PLAYSTATION   223

CONSOLE COMPARISON: SONY PLAYSTATION VS. SEGA SATURN   225

KEY PLAYSTATION TITLES   227

VIRTUAL BOY   228

NINTENDO 64   228

CONSOLE COMPARISON: NINTENDO 64 VS. SONY PLAYSTATION   231

KEY NINTENDO 64 TITLES   232

HANDHELD SNAPSHOT: GAME BOY COLOR   233

FIFTH-GENERATION MARKET SUMMARY   234

FIFTH-GENERATION BREAKTHROUGHS AND TRENDS   235

CHAPTER 8 QUIZ   236

FIGURES   238

REFERENCES   240

CHAPTER 9 ▪ Video Games Become Big Business 243

OBJECTIVES 243

KEY TERMS AND PEOPLE 244

CHAPTER OUTLINE 244

INTRODUCTION 245

GAME INDUSTRY VALUE CHAIN 245

FUNDING 245

PUBLISHING 246

DEVELOPMENT 246

MANUFACTURING 249

DISTRIBUTION 250

PRO FILE: GABE NEWELL 251

RETAIL 252

END USERS 253

DATA RESEARCH 255

BIG BUSINESS 255

VIDEO GAME CONVENTIONS 258

eSPORTS 260

MARKET SUMMARY 262

CHAPTER 9 QUIZ 263

FIGURES 265

REFERENCES 266

CHAPTER 10 ▪ The Sixth Generation 269

OBJECTIVES 269

KEY TERMS AND PEOPLE 270

CONSOLE TIMELINE 270

ARCADE DECLINE AND RESTRUCTURING 271

THE SIXTH GENERATION 272

SEGA DREAMCAST 272

CONSOLE COMPARISON: DREAMCAST VS. FIFTH-GENERATION CONSOLES 275

KEY DREAMCAST TITLES 275

SONY PLAYSTATION 2 276

PRO FILE: KEN KUTARAGI 278

CONSOLE COMPARISON: PLAYSTATION 2 VS. DREAMCAST 279

KEY PLAYSTATION 2 TITLES 279

NINTENDO GAMECUBE 281

HANDHELD SNAPSHOT: GAME BOY ADVANCE 282

CONSOLE COMPARISON: GAMECUBE VS. PLAYSTATION 2 284

KEY GAMECUBE TITLES 285

CHANGES AT NINTENDO 287

MICROSOFT XBOX 287

CONSOLE COMPARISON: XBOX VS. PLAYSTATION 2 AND GAMECUBE 290

KEY XBOX TITLES 291

SIXTH-GENERATION MARKET SUMMARY 292

SIXTH-GENERATION BREAKTHROUGHS AND TRENDS 293

CHAPTER 10 QUIZ 294

FIGURES 296

REFERENCES 298

CHAPTER 11 ■ The Rise of PC Gaming and VR 299

OBJECTIVES 299

KEY TERMS AND PEOPLE 300

COMPUTER MILESTONES TIMELINE 300

INTRODUCTION 301

IBM AND THE RISE OF THE CLONES 301

GAMING IN DOS 303

GENRE PIONEERS OF THE EARLY 1990s 303

WINDOWS 95 AND 3D GRAPHICS 304

THE GOLDEN AGE OF PC GAMING 305

A NEW MILLENNIUM OF MMOs 308

INDIE AND SOCIAL GAMES GATHER [ON] STEAM 309

VIRTUAL ONLINE WORLDS 311

PRO FILE: WILL WRIGHT 313

VIRTUAL REALITY 314

MODERN VR PIONEERS 314

TRENDS OF THE 2010s 316

SUBSCRIPTION AND CLOUD GAMING 318

HANDHELD SNAPSHOT: VALVE STEAM DECK 319

MARKET SUMMARY 320

CHAPTER 11 QUIZ 322

FIGURES 324

REFERENCES 325

CHAPTER 12 ■ The Seventh Generation 327

OBJECTIVES 327

KEY TERMS AND PEOPLE 328

CONSOLE TIMELINE 328

ARCADE APOCALYPSE? 329

THE SEVENTH GENERATION 330

XBOX 360 330

CONSOLE COMPARISON: XBOX 360 VS. SIXTH-GENERATION CONSOLES 333

KEY XBOX 360 TITLES 334

HANDHELD SNAPSHOT: NINTENDO DS 335

SONY PLAYSTATION 3 336

CONSOLE COMPARISON: PLAYSTATION 3 VS. XBOX 360 339

KEY PLAYSTATION 3 TITLES 341

PRO FILE: HIDEO KOJIMA 342

HANDHELD SNAPSHOT: SONY PSP 343

NINTENDO WII 344

CONSOLE COMPARISON: WII VS. PLAYSTATION 3 AND XBOX 360 348

KEY WII TITLES 349

SEVENTH-GENERATION MARKET SUMMARY 349

SEVENTH-GENERATION BREAKTHROUGHS AND TRENDS 351

CHAPTER 12 QUIZ 352

FIGURES 354

REFERENCES 355

CHAPTER 13 ■ Military, Science, and Education Get into the Game 357

OBJECTIVES 357

KEY TERMS AND PEOPLE 358

CHAPTER OUTLINE 358

INTRODUCTION 359

EARLY WAR GAMES 359

MILITARY SIMULATION 359

THE BRADLEY TRAINER 360

MULTIPURPOSE ARCADE COMBAT SIMULATOR 361

MARINE DOOM 361

PRO FILE: JOHN CARMACK 362

AMERICA'S ARMY 363

FULL SPECTRUM WARRIOR 364

DARWARS 364

VIRTUAL BATTLEFIELDS 366

AT EASE 367

VIDEO GAMES IN SCIENCE 367

SERIOUS GAMES 367

SERIOUS GAMES SHOWCASE AND CHALLENGE 370

GAMES WITH A PURPOSE 371

VIDEO GAME RESEARCH 372

NEGATIVE SIDE EFFECTS 372

POSITIVE IMPACT   373

BRAIN DEVELOPMENT   373

FROM SCIENCE TO EDUCATION   374

POPULAR COTS EDUCATIONAL GAMES   376

SCHOOLS SPECIALIZING IN GAMING   377

FINAL EXAMINATION   379

CHAPTER 13 QUIZ   379

FIGURES   381

REFERENCES   383

CHAPTER 14 ■ Mobile and Indie Change the Game   387

OBJECTIVES   387

KEY TERMS AND PEOPLE   388

MOBILE PLATFORMS TIMELINE   388

INTRODUCTION   389

MOBILE AND CASUAL GAMES DEFINED   389

PHONES GET SMART   389

MOBILE GAMING ORIGINS   390

THE NEW MILLENNIUM OF MOBILE   391

NOKIA N-GAGE   391

THE COMPETITION   393

KEY N-GAGE TITLES   394

OTHER MOBILE DEVELOPMENTS   394

GIZMONDO   396

STILL GROWING   397

APPLE IPHONE   397

EARLY iPHONE GAMES   399

MORE PLATFORMS THAN EVER   399

PRO FILE: STEVE JOBS   400

MOBILE MILESTONES   402

NINTENDO GOES MOBILE   404

MOBILE MERITS   405

RECENT TRENDS   405

MOBILE GAMER PROFILE   406

MARKET SUMMARY   407

CHAPTER 14 QUIZ   409

FIGURES   411

REFERENCES   412

CHAPTER 15 ■ Modern Console Gaming   415
   OBJECTIVES   415
   KEY TERMS AND PEOPLE   416
   CONSOLE TIMELINE   416
   THE MODERN ARCADE   417
   MODERN CONSOLE GAMING   418
   WII U   418
   CONSOLE COMPARISON: WII U VS. XBOX 360 AND PS3   421
   KEY WII U TITLES   422
   HANDHELD SNAPSHOT: NINTENDO 3DS   423
   PLAYSTATION 4   424
   CONSOLE COMPARISON: PLAYSTATION 4 VS. WII U   427
   KEY PLAYSTATION 4 TITLES   428
   PRO FILE: MARK CERNY   429
   HANDHELD SNAPSHOT: PLAYSTATION VITA   430
   XBOX ONE   431
   CONSOLE COMPARISON: XBOX ONE VS. PLAYSTATION 4   434
   KEY XBOX ONE TITLES   435
   NINTENDO SWITCH   436
   NO COMPARISON   440
   KEY SWITCH TITLES   440
   NEXT GEN: XBOX SERIES X|S AND PLAYSTATION 5   440
   CONSOLE COMPARISON: XBOX SERIES X|S VS. PLAYSTATION 5   441
   KEY XBOX SERIES X|S AND PLAYSTATION 5 TITLES   443
   MARKET SUMMARY   443
   MODERN GAMING BREAKTHROUGHS AND TRENDS   445
   FINAL THOUGHTS   446
   CHAPTER 15 QUIZ   447
   FIGURES   448
   REFERENCES   450

INDEX, 455

List of Abbreviations

2D	Two-Dimensional	**BIOS**	Basic Input/Output System
3D	Three-Dimensional	**Bit/b**	Binary Digit
3G	Third Generation	**BREW**	Binary Runtime Environment for Wireless
4G	Fourth Generation		
64DD	Nintendo 64 Disk Drive	**CAD**	Computer-Aided Design
AAR	After Action Review	**CD**	Compact Disc
ADF	Australian Defence Force	**CERO**	Computer Entertainment Rating Organization
ADK	Alpha Denshi Corporation		
AES	Advanced Entertainment System	**CES**	Consumer Electronics Show
AFK	Away from Keyboard	**CF**	CompactFlash
AGS	Asia Game Show	**CoD**	*Call of Duty*
AI	Artificial Intelligence	**COLECO**	Connecticut Leather Company
AMD	Advanced Micro Devices	**Compaq**	Compatibility and Quality
ANTIC	Alphanumeric Television Interface Controller	**COTS**	Commercial Off-The-Shelf
		CP/M	Control Program/Monitor
AO	Adults Only (ESRB Rating)	**CPC**	Colour Personal Computer
AoE	Age of Empires	**CPS**	Capcom Power System
APA	American Psychological Association	**CPU**	Central Processing Unit
API	Application Programming Interface	**CRT**	Cathode Ray Tube
APU	Accelerated Processing Unit	**CSSC**	Clinical Skills and Simulations Center
AR	Augmented Reality		
ARM	Advanced RISC Machines	**CTIA**	Color Television Interface Adaptor
ASA	Advertising Standards Authority	**CTR**	Computing-Tabulating-Recording Company
ASCII	American Standard Code for Information Interchange		
		D&D	Dungeons and Dragons
ASIC	Application-Specific Integrated Circuit	**DARPA**	Defense Advanced Research Projects Agency
ASL	Advanced Squad Leader	**DAT**	Digital Audio Tape
ATI	Array Technology Inc.	**DDP**	Digital Data Pack
AT&T	American Telephone and Telegraph Company	**DDR**	*Dance Dance Revolution*
		DLC	Downloadable content
ATSC	Advanced Television Systems Committee	**DLNA**	Digital Living Network Alliance
		DMA	Direct Memory Access
AVS	Advanced Video System	**DOS**	Disk Operating System
BASIC	Beginner's All-Purpose Symbolic Instruction Code	**DPS**	Damage per Second
		DRAM	Dynamic Random-Access Memory
BD-ROM	Blu-Ray Disc ROM	**DRM**	Digital Rights Management
BGS	Brasil Game Show	**DSP**	Digital Signal Processor

DTMB	Digital Terrestrial Multimedia Broadcast	**GDC**	Game Developers Conference or Graphics Display Controller
DTS	Digital Theater Systems	**GD-ROM**	Gigabyte Disc
DVB	Digital Video Broadcasting	**GE**	General Electric
DVD	Digital Versatile Disc or Digital Video Disc	**GFLOPS**	Gigaflops
		GFX	Graphics
DVI	Digital Visual Interface	**GG**	Game Gear or Good Game
DVR	Digital Video Recorder	**GHz**	Gigahertz
DWGE	Dubai World Game Expo	**GMod**	Garry's Mod
E	Everyone (ESRB Rating)	**GoW**	Gears of War or God of War
E3	Entertainment Expo	**GPRS**	General Packet Radio Service
E10+	Everyone 10+ (ESRB Rating)	**GPU**	Graphics Processing Unit
EA	Electronic Arts	**GSM**	Groupe Spécial Mobile
EC	Early Childhood (ESRB Rating)	**GTA**	*Grand Theft Auto*
ED	Enhanced Definition	**GTIA**	Graphic Television Interface Adaptor
EDSAC	Electronic Delay Storage Automatic Calculator	**GUI**	Graphical User Interface
		GWAP	Game with a Purpose
EEDAR	Electronic Entertainment Design and Research	**HDD**	Hard Disk Drive
		HDMI	High-Definition Multimedia Interface
EGA	Enhanced Graphics Adapter	**HDTV**	High-Definition Television
ESA	Entertainment Software Association	**HDV**	High-Definition Video
		HP	Hewlett-Packard or Hit Points
ESL	Electronic Sports League	**HPS**	High-Fidelity Patient Simulations
ESP	Extra Sensory Perception	**HUD**	Heads-Up Display
ESRB	Entertainment Software Rating Board	**Hz**	Hertz
		I/ITSEC	Interservice/Industry Training, Simulation and Education Conference
EST	Engagement Skills Trainer		
EVO	Evolution Championship Series		
F.A.T.S	FireArms Training Simulator	**I/O**	Input and Output
F2P	Free-to-Play	**IARC**	International Age Rating Coalition
FEPA	Family Entertainment Protection Act	**IBM**	International Business Machines
		ICT	Institute for Creative Technologies
FLOPS	Floating Point Operations per Second	**IDSA**	Interactive Digital Software Association
FMV	Full Motion Video	**IEM**	Intel Extreme Masters
fps	Frames (or Fields) Per Second	**IGDA**	International Game Developers Association
FPS	First-Person Shooter		
FPU	Floating-Point Unit	**INTV**	Intellivision Inc.
FSW	*Full Spectrum Warrior*	**iOS**	iPhone Operating System
FTC	Federal Trade Commission	**IP**	Intellectual Property
GAA	Game after Ambush	**ISDB**	Integrated Services Digital Broadcasting
GB	Gigabyte		
GBA	Game Boy Advance	**ISFE**	Interactive Software Federation of Europe
GBC	Game Boy Color		
GBL	Game-Based Learning	**J2ME**	Java 2 Micro Edition
GCC	General Consumer Corporation	**JAMMA**	Japan Amusement Machinery Manufacturers Association
GCN	GameCube (in West) or Graphics Core Next		
		JRPG	Japanese Role-Playing Game

KB	Kilobyte	**NPC**	Non-Player Character
KeSPA	Korean e-Sports Association	**NPD**	National Purchase Diary
kHz	Kilohertz	**NTSA**	National Training Simulation and
LAN	Local Area Network		Association
LCD	Liquid Crystal Display	**NTSC**	National Television Standards
LED	Light-Emitting Diode		Committee
LGBTQ	Lesbian, Gay, Bisexual, Transgender,	**NXE**	New Xbox Experience
	Queer or Questioning	**OLED**	Organic Light-Emitting Diode
LoL	*League of Legends*	**OOE**	Out of Order Execution
LPCM	Linear Pulse Code Modulation	**OS**	Operating System
LTE	Long-Term Evolution	**OST**	Original Soundtrack
LvL	Level	**OTS**	Over-the-Shoulder
M	Mature (ESRB Rating)	**P2W**	Pay-to-Win
MACS	Multipurpose Arcade Combat	**PAL**	Phase Alternate Line
	Simulator	**PAX Prime**	Penny Arcade Expo
MB	Megabyte or Milton Bradley	**PC**	Personal Computer
MFLOPS	Megaflops	**PC/AT**	Personal Computer/Advanced
MHz	Megahertz		Technology
MIDI	Musical Instrument Digital Interface	**PCB**	Printed Circuit Board
MIPS	Millions of Ops per Second	**PCI**	Peripheral Component Interconnect
MLG	Major League Gaming Inc.	**PCM**	Pulse Code Modulation
MMC	MultiMediaCard	**PDA**	Personal Digital Assistant
MML	Music Macro Language	**PDP**	Plasma Display Panel
MMO	Massively Multiplayer Online	**PDP-1**	Programmed Data Processor-1
MMOG	Massively Multiplayer Online Game	**PEGI**	Pan-European Game Information
MMORPG	Massively Multiplayer Online	**PET**	Personal Electronic Transactor
	Role-Playing Game	**PFLOPS**	Petaflops
MMOW	Massively Multiplayer Online World	**PiP**	Picture-in Picture
MMS	Multimedia Messaging Service	**PNAS**	Proceedings of the National
MOBA	Multiplayer Online Battle Arena		Academy of Sciences
MOGA	Mobile Gaming Controller	**POKEY**	Pot Keyboard Integrated Circuit
mono	Monaural	**PPS**	Polygons Per Second
MOS	Metal Oxide Semiconductor	**PS2**	PlayStation 2
MP	Mana (or Magic) Points	**PS3**	PlayStation 3
MRI	Motion Reality Inc.	**PS4**	PlayStation 4
MS	Microsoft	**PSN**	PlayStation Network
MUD	Multi-User Dungeon	**PSP**	PlayStation Portable
MVS	Multi Video System	**PSX**	PlayStation
N64	Nintendo 64	**PTSD**	Post-Traumatic Stress Disorder
Namco	Nakamura Manufacturing Company	**QA**	Quality Assurance
NAOMI	New Arcade Operation Machine	**QTE**	Quick Time Event
	Idea	**RAM**	Random-Access Memory
NEC	Nippon Electric Company	**RAND**	
NES	Nintendo Entertainment System	**or R&D**	Research and Development
NFC	Near-Field Communication	**RCA**	Radio Corporation of America
NFS	*Need for Speed*	**RCP**	Reality coprocessor
NGC	Nintendo Game Cube (Japan)	**RDRAM**	Rambus Dynamic Random-Access
NIS	Nippon Ichi Software		Memory

RF	Radio Frequency		**T**	Teen (ESRB Rating)
RGB	Red, Green, Blue		**TB**	Terabyte
RISC	Reduced Instruction Set Computer		**TBS**	Turn-Based Strategy
R.O.B.	Robot Operating Buddy		**TCG**	Trading Card Game
ROE	Rules of Engagement		**TCI**	Tele-Communications, Inc.
ROM	Read Only Memory		**TES**	Tactical Engagement Simulation
RP	Rating Pending (ESRB Rating)		**TFLOPS**	Teraflops
RPG	Role-Playing Game		**TG-16**	TurboGrafx-16
RRoD	Red Ring of Death		**TGS**	Tokyo Game Show
RTS	Real-Time Strategy		**THQ**	Toy Headquarters
RTT	Real-Time Tactics		**THz**	Terahertz
S-3D	Stereoscopic		**TIA**	Television Interface Adaptor
SAFE	Strategy and Force Evaluation		**TLCTS**	Tactical Language & Culture Training System
SCART	Syndicat des Constructeurs d'Appareils Radiorécepteurs et Téléviseurs		**TRADOC**	Army Training Doctrine and Command
SCE	Sony Computer Entertainment		**TRS**	Tip, Ring, Sleeve
SCI	Sony Computer Interactive		**TRST**	TrustCo Bank
SD	Secure Digital		**TTI**	Turbo Technologies, Inc.
SDT	Self Determination Theory		**TV**	Television
SECAM	Séquentiel Couleur À Mémoire		**UI**	User Interface
SECTER	Simulated Environment for Counseling, Training, Evaluation and Rehabilitation		**UMD**	Universal Media Disc
			USB	Universal Serial Bus
SEGA	Service Games		**USMC**	United States Marine Corps
SFC	Super Famicom		**VBS**	Virtual Battlespace
SGI	Silicon Graphics, Inc.		**VCD**	Video Compact Disc
SHMUP	Shoot 'em Up		**VCR**	Video Cassette Recorder
SI	International System of Units		**VCS**	Video Computer System
SID	Sound Interface Device		**VGA**	Video Graphics Array
SIE	Sony Interactive Entertainment		**VGL**	Video Games Live
SIM	Simulation Game		**VMU**	Visual Memory Unit
SMS	Sega Master System		**VPD**	Video Display Processor
SNES	Super Nintendo Entertainment System		**VPU**	Vector Processing Unit
			VR	Virtual Reality
SNK	Shin Nihon Kikaku		**VRAM**	Video RAM
SOE	Soap Opera Effect		**VRT**	Virtual Reality Therapy
S/PDIF	Sony/Philips Digital Interface Format		**VRU**	Voice Recognition Unit
			WAN	Wide Area Network
SRAM	Static Random-Access Memory		**WAP**	Wireless Application Protocol
SSH	Society for Simulation in Healthcare		**WCG**	World Cyber Games
STEM	Science, Technology, Engineering and Mathematics		**WoW**	*World of Warcraft*
			XBL	Xbox Live
STG	Shooting Game		**XMB**	XrossMediaBar
SVP	Sega Virtua Processor		**XP**	Experience Points
			YLOD	Yellow Light of Death

Acknowledgments

THIS BOOK WAS WRITTEN first and foremost for my students—by supporting the classes for which this textbook was created and for keeping me motivated with your unwavering support and interest in the project. To my family—for your patience and understanding throughout the writing process; you know how much I appreciate you and the sacrifices you have endured for me to complete projects like this. To the video game industry for which this work is a love letter; my hobby, my passion, and my escape. Life is always better with a good video game on the side.

To my students, friends, and colleagues who took the time to review parts of this book and provide me with feedback, especially Marie Franklin for volunteering your valuable time to proofreading every chapter of the first edition and for your words of encouragement; to the Professional Development Committee and administrators of Lasell University for granting my sabbatical in which a substantial portion of this book was written; to the wonderful team at Taylor & Francis; and to God, for providing me with the inspiration, patience, and perseverance to see this through. You made yourself known

to me so many times throughout this entire process. Thank you.

I would also like to acknowledge some of the amazing authors who served as inspirations and foundations for this book. To Steve Kent for covering so much video game history in such great detail! To Damien McFerran for your outstanding coverage of so many vintage game consoles and computer systems; to the writers and producers of the TV show *Icons*; to Evan Amos for your outstanding photography of the majority of console pictures in this text; to Chris Wright for your excellent documentation of early mobile gaming history; and to Jeremy Reimer for your amazing coverage of the rich history of the personal computer market.

To everyone who provided permissions and information pertaining to the figures and tables in this book; to all the key game developers, publishers, and other video game talent who have made contributions to the video game business; and to all video game enthusiasts for supporting video games and helping this industry become the leading form of entertainment today.

Game on!

Author

Dr. Brian J. Wardyga combined his 40+ years' experience with video games with 20+ years in the media industry and 20+ years of teaching in higher education to create The Video Games Textbook. He began playing video games in the early 1980s, beginning with the Atari VCS. Since that time, he has collected games for almost every major system and lived through most of what has been written in this book. An expert on the subject that is both his passion and hobby, Wardyga wrote and designed this textbook to promote student learning and to be the ultimate companion book for all video game enthusiasts. The book's visually rich presentation encourages reading and provides vivid examples of each major platform, its controllers and accessories, along with examples of the print advertisements, game graphics, and box art that was pertinent to each generation of video games.

Wardyga began teaching at the university level in 2002 at Boston University and has taught communication and production courses at Curry College, Fisher College, Lasell University, and University of Massachusetts, Boston. He has been a full-time instructor at Lasell University since 2004, where he began teaching courses on video games in 2009. His array of courses taught includes Advanced Television Production, Communication Research (graduate level), Digital Audio Production, Digital Filmmaking, Digital Video Editing, Effective Speaking, Fundamentals of Communication, Interactive Broadband Television, Life Skills & Video Games, Media Literacy, Oral Communication, Public Speaking, Radio Production, Television Studio Production, Understanding Mass Media, Understanding Video Games, Video Games & Culture, Video Production (graduate and undergraduate), and Writing for the Media.

Wardyga holds a Doctorate in Educational Leadership from Liberty University, a Master of Science in Television from Boston University, and a Bachelor of Arts in Communication from Bridgewater State. His professional vita includes work for organizations such as Bernie & Phyl's Furniture, Borders Books & Music, The Boyds Collection Ltd., GlaxoSmithKline, and Ty, Inc. He has served more than 10 years as the advisor to LCTV—Lasell Community Television and the Lasell University Video Games Club (VGC). His 20+ years of experience in the media industry includes the role of founding General Manager of the award-winning 102.9FM WLAS. His clubs have won Student Organization of the Year on three occasions, and Wardyga has received accolades such as the Broadcast Education Association Festival of Media Arts Award of Excellence, Intercollegiate Broadcasting System winner for Best Television Station Advisor, and the Tom Gibson Award for Outstanding Engineering.

In addition to WLAS, Wardyga worked for another 10 years in the Boston media market as a Stage Manager and Computer Graphics Technician at WCVB-TV ABC5 for programs such as Chronicle, City Line, Commitment 2000, The Evening News, Eye Opener News, Jerry Lewis Telethon, Midday News, Patriots Pregame Show, Patriots 5th Quarter, and the PGA Tour. Prior to WCVB, Brian worked as an Associate Director for WLVI-TV WB56 on programs such as Keller at Large, New England Stories, Patriots SportZone Kickoff, The Sports Zone, and The Ten O'Clock News. He also served as a Postproduction Assistant at WGBH PBS2 on the Building Big documentary series.

Introduction

WELCOME TO *THE VIDEO Games Textbook!* I appreciate your interest in the text and hope that the following chapters teach you all you ever wanted to know and more about video games and the many platforms they've appeared on. My goal for *The Video Games Textbook* was to facilitate learning the history, business, and technology of video games with visually stimulating, comprehensive, and chronological chapters that are relevant and easy to understand for a variety of readers. This book was structured to be a primary textbook for courses on the history, technology, and business of video games. It is also my hope that the book serves every video game enthusiast as a go-to handbook.

There are two main types of chapters in this textbook: (1) "platform chapters," which cover the major platforms from each generation of home video game consoles, as well as PC and mobile gaming and (2) "special topics" chapters that focus on pertinent aspects of video games such as the technology; video game business; sex, violence, gender, and race; and the use of video games in the military, science, and educational communities. Chapters begin with a list of objectives, key terms, and timelines of major releases or chapter subject matter.

Each console-based "platform" chapter reviews the arcade industry for its respective era, which for many generations served as a major influence on the home systems that followed. Consoles and/or computers are then discussed in detail on their history,

key personnel, marketing strategy, technical specifications, breakthroughs and trends, accessories, and important games. Console or computer comparisons are also made between competing systems, including "head-to-head" recommendations in comparing game titles across platforms. Console and computer sections conclude with a review of key games and box art to five of the best titles on each system.

Images and tables are provided for a deeper immersion into the subject matter. Tables highlight each system's launch titles, tech specs, and other information, while images of each console, its controller, advertisement(s), and screenshots of games bring the reader closer to fully understanding each game system. "Pro File" sections include a picture and achievement summary of important industry figures to highlight the most influential people in the business. Each chapter contains "Did You Know" sections that provide additional historical trivia whenever possible. Finally, the chapters conclude with a summary, activity, and chapter quiz to deepen the learning experience.

I hope that this textbook covers everything you expected and more. If it's not in the book, let me know about it in an email! I appreciate your feedback and try to respond to all inquiries. Lastly, PowerPoint presentations should be available on the publisher's website and test banks with correct answers are available to instructors only.

Enjoy the book!

The First Video Games

■ OBJECTIVES

After reading this chapter, you should be able to:

- Describe the types of games found in arcades before video games.
- Discuss the first video games and how they evolved.
- Review the key people who helped pave the way for the video game industry.
- Document the history of *Pong* and how it helped pave the way for the home market.
- Provide a brief overview of Magnavox, Atari, and Coleco.
- Differentiate between the Magnavox Odyssey, Home Pong system, and Coleco Telstar series.
- Identify graphics and general capabilities of first-generation video game consoles.
- Compare the technological differences among first-generation systems.
- Be familiar with the Nintendo Color TV-Game series.
- List important innovations brought to gaming during this period.
- Summarize first-generation market sales and trends.

DOI: 10.1201/9781003315759-1

■ KEY TERMS AND PEOPLE

AC adapter	Connecticut Leather Co.	Joysticks	Prototype
Al Alcorn	Control boxes	Josef Kates	Tom Quinn
Ampex	Copyright infringement	Steve Kordek	Reset button
Amusement hall	Ted Dabney	Alan Kotok	RF switchbox
Andy Capp's Tavern	Dedicated console	Harold Lee	Royalties
Atari	Digital displays	Light gun	Bill Rusch
AY-3-8500 chip	Alexander Douglas	Gene Lipkin	Steve "Slug" Russell
Ralph Baer	Robert Dvorak	Magnavox	Pete Sampson
Baffle Ball	EDSAC	Mitsubishi	Sanders Associates
Bagatelle	Dan Edwards	MOS Technology	Robert Saunders
Bally	Electrotennis/Epoch	MPS 7600-004 chip	Scoring reels
John Bennett	English control	Mutoscope	*Shooting Gallery*
Bertie the Brain	Flipper bumpers	*Nimrod*	SN76499N chip
Brookhaven National Laboratory	Game cards	Nutting Associates	*Spacewar!*
	Bill Gattis	Odyssey	Raymond Stuart-Williams
Brown Box	General Electric	Oscilloscope	*Super Pong*
Bob Brown	General Instrument	*OXO/Noughts and Crosses*	Sync generator
Nolan Bushnell	Martin Graetz	Pachinko	Syzygy Engineering
Cartridge slot	Arnold Greenberg	Penny arcade	Tech Model Railroad Club
Cathode ray tube	Maurice Greenberg	PDP-1 computer	
Circuit boards	David Gottlieb	Philips	Tele-Games
Coleco	Bill Harrison	Pinball	*Tennis for Two*
Coleco Telstar	William Higinbotham	Plastic overlays	Texas Instruments
Color TV-Game	Josh Hochberg	*Pong*	Tilt Mechanism
Combat!	Interchangeable games	*Pong for Your Home TV*	Video game
Computer Space	Peter Jensen	Edwin Pridham	Harry Williams

■ FIRST-GENERATION TIMELINE

Tennis for Two	Spacewar!	Computer Space	Odyssey & Pong	Pong (Home)	Telstar
1958	**1962**	**1971**	**1972**	**1975**	**1976**

■ FROM PENNY ARCADES TO PINBALL

Before video games, the arcade business consisted mostly of mechanical games in venues known as **penny arcades** and **amusement halls**. These games consisted of slot machines, strength and love testers, fortune-telling machines, and peep show machines. The original peep shows were non-pornographic machines where users would insert a coin to view various pictures, flip book-style animations (in machines called **Mutoscopes**), or miniature models (dioramas). Slot machines did not last long because of state laws that prohibited gambling. Soon, pinball would become the next big hit.

The earliest roots of pinball date "back to ***Bagatelle***, a form of billiards in which players used a cue to shoot balls up a sloped table. The goal of the game was to get the balls into one of nine cups placed along the face of the table" (Kent, 2001, p. 2). More than a century later, **pachinko** machines began appearing in Japan and **David Gottlieb** (founder of Gottlieb) introduced the coin-operated ***Baffle Ball*** in the United States during 1931 (Figure 1.1). Players inserted a penny for a handful of balls, which they would launch with a plunger. They would then bump the table to try to land each ball in a number of pockets. The technique of bumping the table would later become known as "tilting." In 1932 **Harry Williams** (founder of Williams Manufacturing Co.) advanced the game further by installing "**tilt mechanisms**," which limited the amount of tilting players could use by penalizing them for overdoing it.

Eventually, companies such as **Bally** and **Williams** released versions of the game that included "pay-outs," which combined pinball with elements of gambling. "As early as 1934, operators, game manufacturers, and distributors argued—most often unsuccessfully—that pinball was a game of skill, and not inevitably connected to gambling" (June, 2013, para. 3). Because early pinball machines did not have a way of controlling the ball, they were deemed games of chance. When politicians caught wind of these devices, pinball games of all kinds were outlawed in the United States—with bans lasting nearly 35 years in major areas such as New York (Kent, 2001, pp. 5–6).

It was not until years later that Gottlieb introduced a new mechanic that would revolutionize pinball forever—**flipper bumpers**. Flipper bumpers (later just called "flippers") first appeared in Gottlieb's *Humpty Dumpty* pinball game in 1947. Besides adding more control of the ball, flippers made pinball into a legitimate game of skill (and less like gambling). **Steve Kordek** further revolutionized the game by placing two flippers at the bottom of the table which the player controlled by pressing buttons on the sides. Advancements such as **electromechanical relays** and **scoring reels** paved the way for pinball in the 1950s and 1960s, followed by **circuit boards** and **digital displays** in the 1970s—the decade when video games first appeared on the arcade scene.

> **DID YOU KNOW?**
> **Josh Hochberg** opened one of the world's first arcade restaurants with Philadelphia's *Cavalier* in 1961 (Kent, 2001, p. 14). Back then arcades consisted mostly of pinball and other electromechanical games—not video games.

FIGURE 1.1 Evolution of pinball: (a) *Bagatelle*, (b) *Baffle Ball* (1931), and (c) *Rapid Transit* (1935).

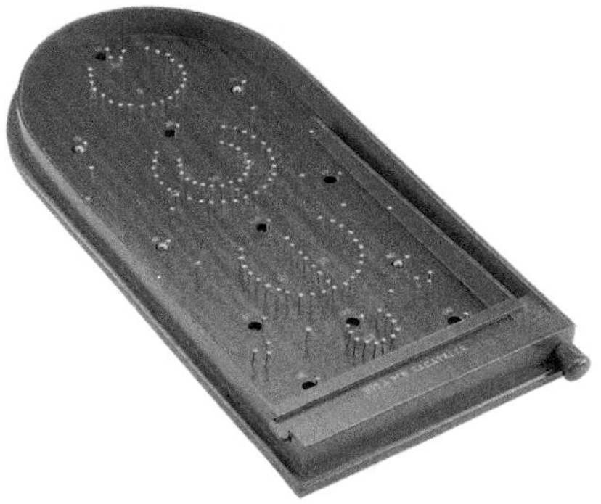

(a)

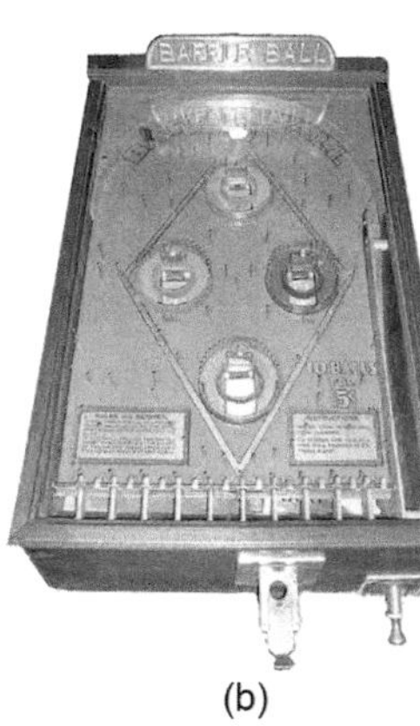

(b)

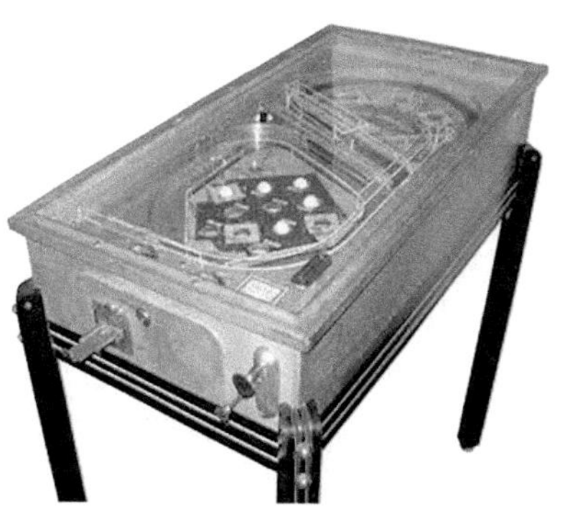

(c)

■ THE FIRST INTERACTIVE COMPUTER GAMES

The earliest interactive computer games premiered in the 1950s on huge, wall-size computers such as Dr. **Josef Kates**'s *Bertie the Brain* (1950, Toronto) and Dr. **John Bennett** and **Raymond Stuart-Williams**'s *Nimrod* (1951, UK). These devices were developed out of academic research labs and played games such as tic-tac-toe, using light bulbs rather than actual monitors with graphics. Dr. **Alexander Douglas**'s *OXO* or *Noughts and Crosses* (1952, UK) was a non-animated version of tic-tac-toe displayed on a **cathode ray tube (CRT)** monitor for the **Electronic Delay Storage Automatic Calculator (EDSAC)** computer. Each of these games provided a level of interactivity with a computer, but it was the additional element of *moving graphics* that led to the concept of a true **video game**.

■ TENNIS FOR TWO

Historians most often credit American nuclear physicist **William "Willy" Higinbotham** with designing the first video game at the Brookhaven National Laboratory. *Tennis for Two* (Figure 1.2) premiered on October 18, 1958, at one of BNL's public exhibitions. Built by Higinbotham and Robert Dvorak, the game was displayed on a small, 5-inch **oscilloscope** (round, monochrome display) and consisted of two custom

FIGURE 1.2 *Tennis for Two* (1958) displayed on a DuMont Lab Oscilloscope Type 304-A.

aluminum controllers. *Tennis for Two* was updated in 1959 with a larger (10–17 inch) screen in addition to variations of the game, including "tennis on the moon, with low gravity, or on Jupiter, with high gravity" (Brookhaven National Laboratory, 2016, para. 10).

■ SPACEWAR!

While attending the Massachusetts Institute of Technology (MIT), **Steve "Slug" Russell** began work on an interactive space combat game with the help of his peers, collectively known as the **Tech Model Railroad Club**. After months of developing the game for the **Programmed Data Processor-1 (PDP-1)** computer, the team completed *Spacewar!* (Figure 1.3a) in the spring of 1962. Russell was the main developer for the game, which originally featured four control switches: (1) rotate the spaceship clockwise, (2) rotate counterclockwise, (3) rocket thrust, and (4) fire torpedoes. To make the game easier to play, **Alan Kotok** and **Robert Saunders** designed separate "**control boxes**"—among the world's first wired video game controllers.

Colleague **Pete Sampson** contributed additional programming to display stars in the background and **Dan Edwards** added the "influence of gravity on the spaceships" (Russell, 2001, p. 19). **Martin Graetz** helped complete the game with his "hyperspace" function, which would cause the player's ship to disappear and reappear in desperate situations (Graetz, 1981). *Spacewar!* appeared in a handful of educational institutions such as Stanford University and the University of Utah. It is therefore one of the first known video games people played in multiple locations.

■ COMPUTER SPACE

One University of Utah undergraduate who became a fan of *Spacewar!* was **Nolan Bushnell**. Bushnell earned part of his tuition money working for Lagoon Amusement Park in Salt Lake City, soliciting quarter games on the midway. He soon worked his way up to maintaining machines in the pinball and electromechanical game arcade (Kent, 2001, p. 29). His work experience and college education led Bushnell to create a coin-operated version of *Spacewar!* called **Computer Space** (Figure 1.3b) with colleague **Ted Dabney**. Released under their company name **Syzygy**

FIGURE 1.3 Screenshots of (a) *Spacewar!* (Steve Russell, 1962) and (b) *Computer Space* (Nolan Bushnell, 1971).

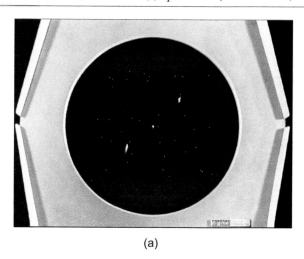

(a)

(b)

Engineering in 1971, players piloted a rocket ship in a space battle with a pair of computer-controlled flying saucers. The game featured four buttons including fire missile, thrust, rotate left, and rotate right.

Since Steve Russell never applied for any copyrights or patents for his game, Bushnell's *Computer Space* never faced any legal trouble for its similarities to *Spacewar!* and coin-op manufacturer **Nutting Associates** produced 1,500 *Computer Space* arcade machines (Edwards, 2011, p. 3). While it may have been too complex for the average consumer, *Computer Space* is renowned for being the first arcade video game and the first commercially distributed video game.

▪ MAGNAVOX ODYSSEY

Electronics engineer **Ralph Baer** was among the first to envision the concept for a home video game console. After more than a decade of working with **Sanders Associates** on military projects, the company gave Baer the green light to begin tinkering with his idea in 1967. With the help of **Bill Harrison** and **Bill Rusch**, Baer worked on **prototypes** (early test models) for years before pitching the seventh iteration to manufacturers. He named his invention the "**Brown Box**," because of "the amount of adhesive tape holding it together, but its crude design didn't stop it from causing a stir among the major television manufacturers of the late 1960s" (Langshaw, 2014, para. 6).

Baer demonstrated the product to multiple companies before electronics manufacturer **Magnavox** picked up the system in January of 1971. Magnavox

was formed in 1917 by **Edwin Pridham** and moving-coil loudspeaker inventor **Peter Jensen**. The company specialized in manufacturing radios, TVs, record players, and other devices (such as the first plasma panel) for the U.S. military. A year after securing the deal with Ralph Baer, Magnavox also became the manufacturer of the world's first home video game system (Figure 1.4).

The newly designed **Odyssey** debuted in the United States in September 1972 for $99.95. It included 12 games on six different **game cards**, two controllers, a **radio frequency (RF) switchbox**/cable to connect it to a TV, game accessories, an instruction manual, and six "C" batteries to power the system, shown in Figure 1.5. Consumers could purchase an optional **AC adapter** to operate the unit on electricity. The system's graphics capability was limited to a few white squares and a vertical line on a black background, so games included **plastic overlays** that would cling to the TV screen (via static electricity) to give each game a unique look and playfield.

The controllers contained flat bottoms that were best suited for placement on a surface such as a coffee table. Each controller had three knobs, including one on the right side and the two on the left side—consisting of a small knob extending from a larger knob. The right knob allowed the player to move the screen dot vertically, the left knob moved the dot horizontally, and the smaller knob allowed the player to exert a small amount of "**English control**" over the console-controlled dot (such as curving the ping-pong ball in *Table Tennis*).

FIGURE 1.4 Magnavox Odyssey, the first commercial home video game console.

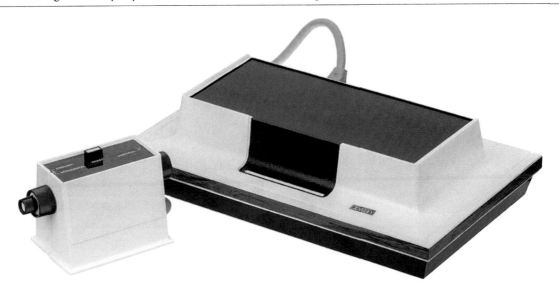

On the top of the controller was a single **"reset" button**. Unlike the modern interpretation of a reset function, the Odyssey's reset button did not actually reset the games. Instead, it served as a function for resetting game *functions*, such as refreshing the placement of the game dot(s). Beyond the controllers, "two additional controls are present on the main unit: a dial to adjust the position of the center line on the screen and a dial to set the speed of the machine-controlled dot" (Smith, 2015, para. 22). Even though video game functions have long since evolved since the Odyssey, its options to adjust screen position and other game settings are still features on modern consoles today.

■ UNDERSTANDING ODYSSEY GAMES

A total of 28 games were made for the Magnavox Odyssey, appearing on 11 different game cards. Six game cards containing 12 games were bundled with the console as listed by card number in Table 1.1. The console was manufactured for Europe in 1973 with different game bundles and eventually imported into Japan. Individual games cost around $6.00 and included screen overlays and game instructions. Game cards with multiple titles played similarly but provided different instructions to the player, which would superficially vary the gameplay.

The game cards were not traditional software like games for modern consoles, but rather printed **circuit boards** that plugged into the console (Table 1.2). The game cards modified the internal circuitry, which directed the console to display different components or react to inputs differently. In other words, "there was no memory or game code on these cards, which merely complete[d] different circuit paths within the hardware itself to define the rule set for the current game. All the game information was contained in the **dedicated hardware**, and inserting a new circuit card was really no different an act from flicking a toggle switch" (Smith, 2015, para. 18).

TABLE 1.1 Magnavox Odyssey U.S. Launch Titles

1. *Table Tennis*
2. *Ski* (Figure 1.6a) & *Simon Says*
3. *Tennis, Analogic, Hockey,* & *Football Part 1* (for passing and kicking)
4. *Cat and Mouse, Football Part 2* (for running), & *Haunted House*
5. *Submarine* (Figure 1.6b)
6. *Roulette, States*

TABLE 1.2 Magnavox Odyssey Tech Specs

Manufacturer:	Magnavox
Launch price:	$99.95
Release date:	September 1972 (US), 1973 (EU)
Format:	"Game Cards" composed of printed circuit boards
CPU:	None (40 transistors and diodes)
Memory:	None
Resolution:	Not applicable
Colors:	2 (black and white)
Sound:	None

FIGURE 1.5   Magazine advertisement for the Magnavox Odyssey in 1973.

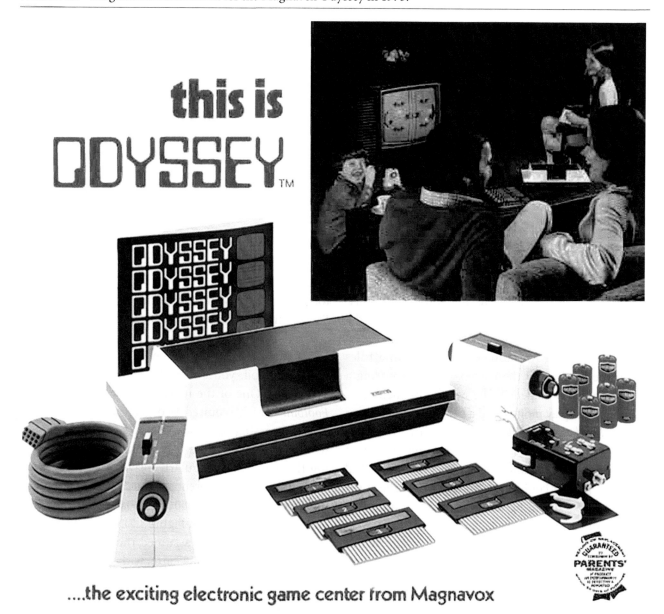

Odyssey, **model TL 200,** is an electronic game center that easily attaches to *any brand TV, 18" to 25"* (diagonal*), *black and white or color.*

The Odyssey Master Control Unit transmits electronic games over your television. To play electronic tennis, simply insert a printed circuit Game Card into the Master Control Unit to activate two player lights and a ball.

There are two Player Control Units. Each player can maneuver his player light vertically and horizontally across the court. An action button on the Player Control serves the ball. A special "English" control puts a twisting curve on the ball to "fake out" your opponent.

Odyssey features 12 games and a Master Control Unit that allows you to play all the optional games too (shown on page 47). In addition to a Master Control Unit, Odyssey also includes two Player Controls, six printed circuit Game Cards, six "C" cell batteries, Game Overlays and everything you need to play the twelve Odyssey games: Table Tennis, Tennis, Football, Hockey, Ski, Submarine, Haunted House, Analogic, Cat and Mouse, Roulette, States, and Simon Says. Odyssey is truly a total play and learning experience, for all ages — young or old! Odyssey — from Magnavox.

All specifications herein subject to change without notice.   * 19" and 26" diagonal in Canada

FIGURE 1.6 Screen overlays of Odyssey launch titles (a) *Ski* and (b) *Submarine*.

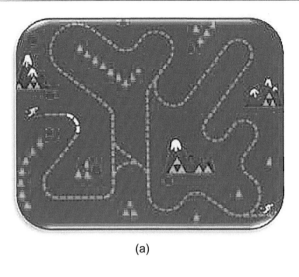

(a)

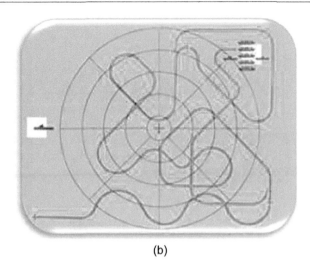

(b)

The Odyssey did not have any sound capability, so all the games were silent. The system also lacked a microprocessor, so it could not keep a score or understand game logic. All scorekeeping and game rules had to be tracked by the players—often requiring a nearby notepad and pencil. The system also included a deck of cards, play money, and a pair of dice for games such as *Football*, *Baseball*, and *Brain Wave*. As primitive as the system was, it did feature an optional light gun accessory called ***Shooting Gallery***. For a handful of games, players could shoot an electronic rifle at the screen to hit a dot of light that moved around under overlays of various cutouts.

Key titles for the Odyssey included *Roulette*, which used an overlay of a roulette wheel and a game board for placing bets with play money and colored chips. *Ski* "required the player to use the dials on the Odyssey controller to follow trails set out on the screen overlay. If you managed to complete a trail without veering too far off, you awarded yourself points" (IGN, 2007, p. 2). One of the most complicated games was *Football*, which required two game cards. Card one was for passing and kicking plays, while card two was for running ground plays. In addition to switching the game cards regularly, players also needed to use a game board, scoreboard, and six decks of playing cards containing various football plays. *Haunted House* (overlay shown in Figure 1.7) was a chase game where player one's dot assumed the role of a detective trying to collect clue cards without being caught

FIGURE 1.7 Plastic screen overlays for Odyssey titles *Haunted House* and *Roulette*.

PRO FILE

KEY FACTS:

Developed the first home video game console, the Magnavox Odyssey

Known as "The Father of Home Video Games"

RALPH BAER

PRO FILE

HISTORY:
- Born: March 8, 1922 in Rodalben, Germany
- Deceased: December 6, 2014 in Manchester, NH

EDUCATION:
- Graduated from National Radio Institute as Radio Service Technician in 1940
- Bachelor of Science in Television Engineering from American Television Institute of Technology in 1949

CAREER HIGHLIGHTS:
- Developed the first multiplayer, multiprogram video game system the 'Brown Box' (1967-69) which became the Magnavox Odyssey in 1972
- Invented first home TV light gun, *Shooting Gallery* (1972)
- Co-created electronic games *Simon* (1978) and *Super Simon* (1979) with Howard J. Morrison and *Maniac* (1979)

RECOGNITION:
G-Phoria Legend Award (2005), Nat'l Medal of Technology (2006), IEEE Masaru Ibuka Consumer Electronics Award (2008), Game Developers Conference Developers Choice Pioneer Award (2008), IEEE Edison Medal (2014), & Academy of Interactive Arts and Sciences Pioneer Award (2015)

TABLE 1.3   Magnavox Odyssey Series Releases

Unit Name	Year	Description
Odyssey 100	1975	Used four Texas Instruments chips; played *Tennis* and *Hockey*; used AC adapter or 6 "C" batteries
Odyssey 200	1975	Used TI single-chip; played *Tennis* and *Hockey* and added a third game called *Smash*; added a scoring system; was the first video game console with two-player or four-player options
Odyssey 300	1976	Used AY-3-8500 chip; simplified to single knobs; same game as Odyssey 200; added three difficulty levels (Novice, Intermediate, and Expert) and on-screen numerical scoring system
Odyssey 400	1976	Same games as Odyssey 300 with the addition of an automatic serving system; three-knob controls returned; added extra Texas Instruments chip to display digital on-screen scoring
Odyssey 500	1976	Paddle graphics were changed into simple human figures (i.e., tennis and hockey players); included a fourth *Soccer* game, which was essentially hockey using squash figures
Odyssey 2000	1977	Added a practice mode of one-player *Squash* (aka *Smash*); programmed to end after a player reached 15 points; returned to single-knob controls found on Odyssey 300
Odyssey 3000	1977	Added *Basketball*, *Soccer*, and *Gridball*; also contained *Smash* and *Basketball* practice modes; added a handicap switch as well as serve, ball speed, and ball deflection options
Odyssey 4000	1977	Used AY-3-8615 (color) chip; played *Tennis*, *Hockey*, *Volleyball*, *Basketball*, *Knockout*, *Tank*, and *Helicopter*; 24 total selectable game modes; included a pause button and detachable joysticks

by the second player's dot who was a ghost. It played much like a board game on TV.

Magnavox was acquired by Dutch electronics company **Philips** in 1974, which released later versions of the Odyssey in Europe. After the acquisition, the company released a total of eight subsequent versions of the Odyssey between 1975 and 1977. See Table 1.3 for descriptions of each unit. All these subsequent Odysseys were **dedicated consoles**, which are systems that only contain built-in games.

■ PONG

Following *Computer Space*, Bushnell and Dabney formed a new company—**Atari**. Bushnell adopted the word "Atari" from the Japanese strategy game *Go*. The term basically means "to hit the target" and is similar to the term "check" in the classic game of *chess*. Atari's focus remained on the arcade market where the manufacturing side of the amusement machine business consisted of around only five important game manufacturers, a handful of pool table manufacturers, and about four major jukebox manufacturers (Adlum, 2001, p. 37). That landscape would begin to change in 1972—the year Atari became incorporated and hired former **Ampex** employee **Al Alcorn** to create the company's next game, *Pong* (Figure 1.8).

To convince Alcorn to develop the game, Bushnell fabricated a story that he had a contract with **General Electric** to design an electronic version of ping-pong. The game was supposed to be a practice project to help

familiarize Alcorn with the process of what would be his first experience in making a video game (Shea, 2008, p. 1). The concept was extremely similar to *Table Tennis* on the Magnavox Odyssey, which hadn't been released yet—however, Bushnell had played it earlier that year at a trade show in Burlingame, CA.

Alcorn went well beyond Bushnell's vision, using less expensive parts, adding deflection angles to the ball when it hit one of eight sections of the paddles, and enhancing the game with ball acceleration. This feature made the game more challenging, where the ball would pick up speed the more times it hit the paddles. He even tinkered with the **sync generator** where he found usable sound effects which were already inside the machine.

Bushnell and Alcorn installed a Pong prototype at a local bar in Sunnyvale, CA called **Andy Capp's Tavern** in September 1972. A couple of weeks later, Alcorn received a call from tavern manager **Bill Gattis** who claimed the machine had stopped working. When Alcorn arrived to fix it, he discovered the problem was that the machine was overflowing with quarters (Kent, 2001, pp. 43–45). Following the game's success at Andy Capp's Tavern, *Pong* was ready for mass production on November 29, 1972.

Atari did not have enough capital initially, so Bushnell and Dabney hired anyone they could find to assemble the *Pong* cabinets. From unemployment office leads to motorcycle gangs, Atari's choice of employees brought along drug abuse and theft. According to Bushnell (2001), "'there was about a

FIGURE 1.8 Vendor print advertisement for *Pong* (1972).

THE NEWEST **2** PLAYER
VIDEO SKILL GAME

PONG

from ATARI CORPORATION
SYZYGY ENGINEERED

The Team That Pioneered Video Technology

FEATURES

- STRIKING Attract Mode
- Ball Serves Automatically
- Realistic Sounds of Ball
  Bouncing, Striking Paddle
- Simple to Operate Controls
- ALL SOLID STATE TV and
  Components for Long,
  Rugged Life
- ONE YEAR COMPUTER
  WARRANTY
- Proven HIGH PROFITS
  in Location After Location
- Low Key Cabinet, Suitable
  for Sophisticated Locations
- 25 ¢ per play

THIS GAME IS AVAILABLE FROM YOUR LOCAL DISTRIBUTOR

Manufactured by
ATARI, INC.
2962 SCOTT BLVD.
SANTA CLARA, CA.
               95050

Maximum Dimensions:
WIDTH -26"
HEIGHT -50"
DEPTH -24
SHIPPING WEIGHT:
   150 Lb.

6-week period [when employee theft was rampant]' … 'We fired a lot of people, and there was still a lot of marijuana use'" (p. 52). While initial manufacturing was slow, *Pong* would become one of the first video games to reach mainstream popularity. It grew into an international success in 1973 and Atari proposed a home version of the game a year later.

Pong's success did not come without a price, however. It was much too similar to *Table Tennis* on Magnavox Odyssey as seen in Figure 1.9. Unlike Steve Russell, who never applied for copyrights or patents on *Spacewar!*, Ralph Baer was meticulous with his recordkeeping and filed numerous patents for his work. "When Atari's *Pong* debuted just months after the Odyssey went to market, Sanders and Magnavox sued them for **copyright infringement**. The case was settled for $700,000 and Atari became an Odyssey licensee" (Mullis, 2014, para. 6). In the end, the deal turned out to be a win–win for both companies. Atari became a licensee for a relatively small amount of money and other companies producing similar ping-pong video games would have to pay **royalties** (compensation for the use of copyrighted or patented works). Magnavox also made out from *Pong*'s success, which helped boost sales of its Odyssey consoles.

■ PONG FOR YOUR HOME TV

Designed by Al Alcorn, **Harold Lee,** and **Bob Brown,** a prototype for the home version of *Pong* was completed in 1974. "With the price of digital circuits constantly dropping, Atari's digital home console ended up costing far less to manufacture than Odyssey" (Kent, 2001, p. 80). Atari had difficulty finding a retailer for the product until VP of Sales **Gene Lipkin** saw an advertisement in a Sears catalog for the Magnavox Odyssey in the sporting goods section. Sears' **Tom Quinn** helped seal a deal with Sears, Roebuck & Company to distribute the system under the Sears **"Tele-Games"** label (Winter, 2013, para. 2). Sears released the *Pong* console (Figure 1.10) for $98.95 in December 1975. See Figure 1.11 for the print advertisement.

Pong's controls were much simpler than *Table Tennis* on the Odyssey. In *Pong*, players had one dial that moved the paddles up and down. The Odyssey featured three dials for moving its square paddles up and down, toward, and away from the net, in addition to applying user-controlled English on the ball. This may seem advantageous on paper—however, it was *Pong*'s simplicity that made this new medium more accessible to most consumers who were experiencing video games for the first time.

☀ DID YOU KNOW?

Shortly before *Pong* landed in U.S. homes, Japan received its first home video game console when *Electrotennis* by **Epoch** released overseas on September 12, 1975. Another ping-pong-style game, its paddle movement and ball English were similar to *Table Tennis*, while its graphics and sound more closely resembled *Pong*.

FIGURE 1.9 Screenshot comparison: Odyssey *Table Tennis* (a) versus *Pong* (b).

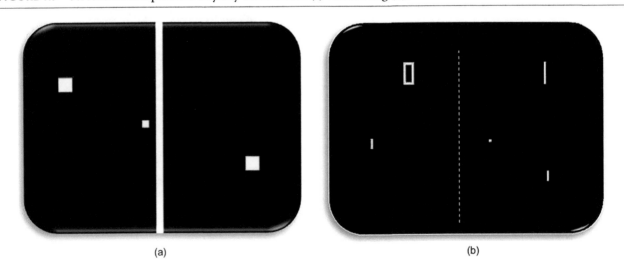

(a)   (b)

FIGURE 1.10 The Sears *Tele-Games Pong* (1975) (a) and Atari's own *Pong* console (1976) (b).

(a) (b)

'Compared to *Table Tennis, Pong* had sharper graphics. The various angles the ball could bounce off the paddles, coupled with the gradual increase in speed, resulted in a more challenging and engaging experience. *Pong* felt more like players were hitting a bouncing ball, whereas the English physics in *Table Tennis* played more like volleying an unpredictable, cartoon-like object. *Pong*'s inclusion of sound also greatly enhanced players' engagement. While the original Odyssey did not have any sound capability, the *Pong* console emitted sound from a built-in speaker at the center of the unit (Table 1.4). Unlike modern consoles, the *Pong* system could not transmit sound through the television speaker.

It was not the first home console on the market, but the home version of *Pong* was a pivotal success for the early video game industry. Sears sold 150,000 *Pong* systems that holiday season. Shortly thereafter, "Atari released its own branded version of the

console [titled '**Pong For Your Home TV**'] starting in 1976, just as an explosion of *Pong* clones saturated the home video game market" (Loguidice, 2009, p. 4). Atari released other *Pong* variations, such as Super Pong, Pong Doubles, and Ultra Pong. These versions added multiple game modes and/or up to four-player simultaneous game play. The collective versions of *Pong* would go on to sell more than a half million units; however, the manufacturer to release the most Western consoles in the late 1970s was a new video game company out of Connecticut.

▪ COLECO TELSTAR

Maurice Greenberg founded **Connecticut Leather Company** in 1932, which began as a shoe supply store. The company shortened its name to **Coleco** in 1961 and expanded to manufacturing plastic molding and wading pools. The company eventually sold off its leather business, and by the end of the 1960s the company became the world's largest manufacturer of above-ground swimming pools (Kleinfield, 1985, para. 21). Under CEO **Arnold Greenberg**, Coleco entered the video game business in 1976 with the **Coleco Telstar** (Figure 1.12), which debuted at just $49.95. The console's release was initially delayed after failing FCC interference tests and Coleco hired Ralph Baer to fix the problem (Kent, 2001, pp. 96–97).

The first Telstar system included single control knobs for each player and came bundled with three internal ping-pong-style games *Tennis, Hockey*, and

TABLE 1.4 Atari Pong Home Console Tech Specs

Manufacturer:	Atari
Launch price:	$98.95
Release date:	December 1975
Format:	Dedicated console (built-in game)
CPU:	None (transistor-transistor logic [TTL] circuits)
Memory:	None
Resolution:	Not applicable
Colors:	2 (black and white)
Sound:	Built-in mono speaker

FIGURE 1.11 Sears Christmas catalog advertisement for *Tele-Games Pong* system in 1975.

FIGURE 1.12 The first Coleco Telstar system, model 6040 (1976).

Handball. The center panel of the unit included an on/off switch, toggle switch for *Tennis, Hockey,* and *Handball,* a reset button, and a beginner/intermediate/pro toggle switch to change the difficulty level of the games. One of the biggest innovations for Coleco's entry system was that it was the first to use the **General Instrument AY-3-8500** chip (Table 1.5). The AY-3-8500 was unique in that it could play up to six selectable games, including two rifle shooting games on systems equipped with a light gun. GI's chip was later adopted by other manufacturers such as Magnavox, for its remarkably similar **Odyssey 300** system.

Like other first-generation systems, the Telstar operated on six "C" batteries or an optional power adapter. And just like Magnavox/Philips, Coleco developed multiple versions of the Telstar—hastily producing 14 different models in just two years. Early models ran on the GI AY-3-8500 chip, such as the Classic, Deluxe, Ranger, and Alpha. The **Telstar Ranger** (1977) was the first Telstar unit to feature a light gun and detachable wired paddles. It also added three more games (*Jai Alai, Target,* and *Skeet*), maximizing the AY-3-8500's six-game capacity. That same year Coleco released the **Telstar Colormatic**, which allowed up to four on-screen colors with the **Texas Instruments SN76499N chip**.

Other Telstar consoles included variations of fixed and detachable controllers, light guns, and updated chips with color graphics. One standout system was **Combat!** (1977) (Figure 1.13a), which was the first Coleco system to include **joysticks**. The system contained four fixed joysticks where up to four players could huddle around the unit together to play *Combat, Night Battle, Robot Battle,* and *Camouflage Combat.* Another significant variation released in 1977 was the **Telstar Gemini,** which was the first Telstar to not include a *Pong*-style game. The Gemini ran on the **MOS Technology MPS 7600-004** chip and was

TABLE 1.5 Coleco Telstar Tech Specs

Manufacturer:	Coleco
Launch price:	$49.95
Release date:	1976
Format:	Dedicated console (built-in games)
CPU:	General Instrument AY-3-8500 chip
Memory:	None
Resolution:	Not applicable
Colors:	2 (black and white)
Sound:	Built-in mono speaker

FIGURE 1.13 Two of the more distinctive Coleco systems: (a) Combat! and (b) Telstar Arcade.

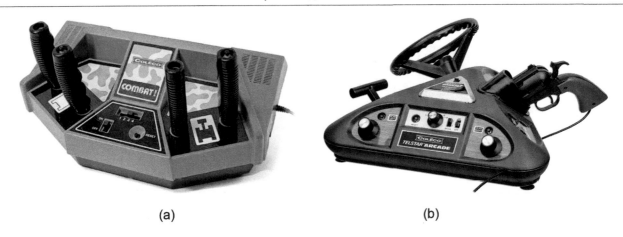

(a) (b)

built to play pinball and light gun games. The console featured red "flipper" buttons on each side of the unit and came with a detachable, wired light gun. One of the most unique Telstar systems released in 1977 was the **Telstar Arcade** (Figure 1.13b). This triangular-shaped console was a three-in-one system, with one side featuring a steering wheel and gear shift section, one side with the *Pong*-like dual paddles setup, and a third side containing a light gun and holster. The Telstar Arcade operated on the same MOS chip as the Gemini; however, this system introduced a triangular **cartridge slot** for **interchangeable games**. Similar to the way the original Odyssey used interchangeable circuit-based games, each cartridge consisted of "a custom programmed MOS Technology MPS-7600 microcontroller with a mere 512 words of program ROM" (Grahame, 2007, para. 3).

> ☀ **DID YOU KNOW?**
>
> Coleco sold its Telstar systems *partially assembled*. In other words, the consumer usually had to attach the paddle knobs and apply the decorative stickers onto the console. Coleco may have done this to reduce assembly costs and is the only major console manufacturer known to release systems this way (Winter, 2013, para. 7).

As interesting as it was, only four different cartridges were ever released for the Telstar Arcade—each containing multiple games. Cartridge 1 was the pack-in game for the system with three games: *Road Race* (Figure 1.14a), *Tennis*, and *Quick Draw*. Cartridge 2 came with four games, including *Hockey*, *Tennis*, *Handball*, and *Target*. The third cartridge included two variations of *Pinball, Shooting Gallery*,

FIGURE 1.14 Screenshots of Telstar Arcade games (a) *Road Race* and (b) *Naval Battle*.

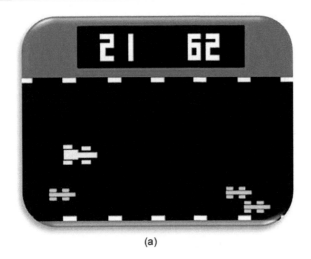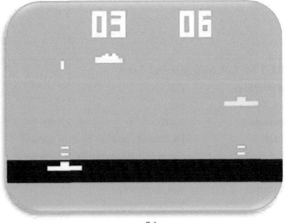

(a) (b)

FIGURE 1.15 Magazine advertisement for the Telstar Marksman (1978).

MARKSMAN™

6136 — TELSTAR MARKSMAN™ The number one selling target game last year. TELSTAR MARKS-MAN™! Two pistol games — Target and Skeet, and four popular sports games — Tennis, Hockey, Handball and Jai Alai. Marksman photo electric rifle, a 3-in-1 combo can be used as a regular pistol, a machine pistol, or a marksman rifle!

Features on-screen digital display scoring, electronic sound effects and variable skill control. The GX-10, a custom chip made for Coleco, makes it all possible at an incredibly low price! Operates on two 9 volt batteries (not included). Full color packaging.

- Six video games: Target, Skeet, Tennis, Hockey, Handball, Jai Alai
- Brilliant color (plays B&W on B&W TV sets)
- Electronic sound effects
- Marksman 3-in-1 photo electric rifle included
- On-screen digital display scoring
- Variable skill control
- Requires two 9 volt batteries or Coleco Battery Eliminator/AC Adapter (neither included)
- FCC approved
- Full color packaging
- Ages 8 to Adult
  Pack: 6   Weight: 21.0 lb. Cube: 2.9'

Manufactured under one or more of the following patents: United States — #3,778,058; #3,829,095; #3,728,480; Re #28,507; Re #28,598; Canada — 1972; 1973; and other patents applied for.

TENNIS   HOCKEY   HANDBALL   JAI-ALAI   SKEET   TARGET

TABLE 1.6 Subsequent Coleco Telstar Series Releases

Unit Name	Year	Description
Classic	1976	Rectangular model of original system with a wood grain case; played *Tennis, Hockey*, and *Handball* on GI AY-3-8500 chip
Deluxe	1977	Same rounded body as original, with a wood grain finish; same three games; manufactured for the Canadian market
Ranger	1977	Silver and black unit; first Telstar with a light gun and detachable wired paddles; added three games: *Jai Alai, Target*, and *Skeet*
Alpha	1977	Simpler silver and black unit; fixed paddles and no light gun; played four games: *Tennis, Hockey, Handball*, and *Jai Alai*
Colormatic	1977	Brown with wood grain; added **on-screen color** with extra Texas Instruments SN76499N chip; removable paddles; same games as Alpha
Regent	1977	Silver and black unit; basically identical to Alpha but added detachable wired paddles; played same four games
Combat!	1977	First Telstar to include **joysticks**—four of them fixed to the unit; played four games; *Combat, Night Battle, Robot Battle*, and *Camouflage Combat*; used GI AY-3-8700 chip
Galaxy	1977	Used AY-3-8600 games chip and AY-3-8615 for color; included paddle controllers, in addition to detachable wired joysticks
Gemini	1977	First **non-*Pong***-style Telstar; played four pinball and two gun games; unit had red "flipper" buttons on sides along with detachable gun; ran on MOS Technology MPS 7600-004
Arcade	1977	Triangular-shaped three-in-one system; with **steering wheel** and **shift** section, dual paddles section, and light gun with holster; same color chip as Gemini; four **triangular cartridge** games
Sportsman	1978	Updated silver and black unit; like Regent but added light gun; played the same six games as Ranger
Colortron	1978	Brown, compact design; used GI AY-3-8510 chip with color; fixed paddles and four games: *Tennis, Hockey, Handball*, and *Jai Alai*
Marksman	1978	Black with silver and red accents; used GI AY-3-8512 chip; wired gun and fixed paddles; same six games as Sportsman and Ranger. See Figure 1.15 for print advertisement

and *Shoot the Bear*. The fourth and final cartridge was bundled with three games: *Naval Battle* (Figure 1.14b), *Speed Ball*, and *Blast-Away*. Coleco released 14 different models of the Telstar. See Table 1.6 for the different Telstar versions released after the original.

■ COLOR TV-GAME SERIES

In Japan, **Nintendo** released a series of five, single-game consoles known as the **Color TV-Game** series (Figure 1.16) between 1977 and 1980. See Table 1.7 for descriptions of the different units. Nintendo was new to manufacturing electronics and so the company teamed up with **Mitsubishi** to produce the original Color TV-Game units. While technically released during the second wave of video game consoles, historians categorize Color TV-Game units as first-generation machines because they were all-in-one "dedicated" systems that did not contain interchangeable software. After working with Mitsubishi

on the first four models, Nintendo developed the latter units on their own with the final three systems' hardware casings designed by soon-to-be *Super Mario* and *Zelda* legendary creator, **Shigeru Miyamoto** (Plunkett, 2011, para. 6–8).

The Color TV-Game series was imperative in Nintendo's beginnings as a video game manufacturer, as well as Miyamoto's entry into the industry. While the original model did not make a profit due to high manufacturing costs, subsequent models were produced at a lower cost and Nintendo estimated to have sold approximately 3 million total units. It would be a stretch to directly compare these sales figures to the other consoles discussed in this chapter since Nintendo only released the Color TV Games in Japan and because the units were manufactured many years after the Odyssey, *Pong*, and Telstar systems. The series earns its place in video game history for its strong success in Japan and for being the first home console from Nintendo.

FIGURE 1.16 Nintendo's first home video game console, the Color TV-Game 6.

■ FIRST-GENERATION MARKET SUMMARY

The Magnavox Odyssey sold just shy of 350,000 units. Odyssey sales were slow early on because a video game system in the home was a new concept that the public had not yet become accustomed to. Sales may have also suffered by how the Odyssey was initially sold. Because Odyssey "distribution was restricted to the Magnavox network of dealers that sold the company's products exclusively … many consumers may well have been left with the impression that the system only worked on Magnavox TVs when they saw it at retail" (Smith, 2015). In 1976, "Magnavox sold 100,000 Odysseys [whereas] Atari sold 150,000 *Home Pong* machines in a single season" (Kent, 2001, p. 94). It can be estimated that the home version of *Pong* and its clones sold at least a half million units. The system became an instant bestseller, earning Atari a Sears "Quality Excellence Award." Atari would go on to become the name synonymous with video games with its next home console in 1977.

A look at the sales figures for the first generation of consoles in Figure 1.17 shows that Coleco dominated the Western market with its Telstar series, although these numbers do not tell the whole story. Coleco did dominate the market in 1976 selling "over $100 million worth of the [Telstar] consoles and rose to the top of the consumer game business" (Kent, 2001, p. 98). However, its *financial* success with the Telstar series would only last for about a year.

By 1978, Coleco nearly went bankrupt as the home video game market progressed "to programmable, cartridge-based game units. With *Pong*-type game manufacturers slashing the price of their dedicated consoles up to 75%, Coleco [was] forced to dump over a million obsolete Telstar machines at a cost of 22.3 million dollars" (Hunter, 2014, p. 1). Coleco may have sold the highest overall volume of video game systems during the first generation, but low returns and major price drops found Coleco barely breaking even with the Telstar series.

As for the pinball industry, it reached a peak of 200,000 machine sales and $2.3 billion revenue in 1979. With electronic video games gaining popularity in the family amusement market, the pinball industry would see a decline to 33,000 machines and a value of approximately $464 million in 1982 (Citron, 1982, p. 13). It was no coincidence that these years would become known as the **Golden Age** of video games in the arcades. Meanwhile, Atari, Coleco, and Magnavox went on to produce cartridge-based game units for a whole new era of video game consoles that would eventually become known as the second generation of video games.

TABLE 1.7 Nintendo Color TV-Game Series Releases

Unit Name	Released	Description
Color TV-Game 6	06/01/77	*Pong* clone with six versions of *Light Tennis (Tennis, Hockey, Volleyball)*
Color TV-Game 15	06/08/77	Contained 15 variations of *Light Tennis*; sold more than 1 million units
Color TV-Game Racing 112	06/08/78	Racing game with steering wheel and gearshift; Shigeru Miyamoto's first video game assignment (casing design)
Color TV-Game Block Breaker	04/23/79	*Breakout* clone, aka "*Karā Terebi-Gēmu Burokku Kuzushi*"; hardware design by Shigeru Miyamoto
Color TV-Game	1979–1980	Home version of Nintendo's first arcade video game *Computer Othello*; hardware design by Shigeru Miyamoto

FIGURE 1.17 First-generation console sales graph.

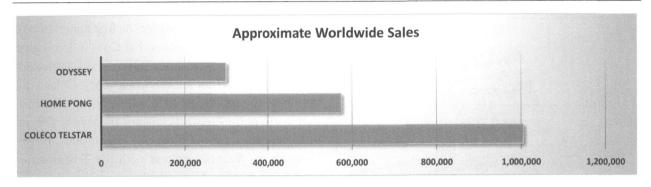

■ FIRST-GENERATION BREAKTHROUGHS AND TRENDS

There were unique breakthroughs and trends that defined the first generation of video games. Here is a list of the top 10 features that defined the generation:

1. Discrete transistor-based digital game logic

2. Mostly dedicated consoles with built-in games, rather than removable media

3. Light gun peripheral and paddle style, analog controllers

4. All first-generation playfields occupied a single screen

5. Most graphics consisted of basic lines, dots, and/or blocks

6. Generally monochrome (black and white) or other dichromatic combination

7. Color overlays provided faux color for Odyssey and arcade games

8. Later games (as seen on Coleco Telstar systems) could display up to four colors

9. Games were limited to single-channel sound or no sound at all

10. No microprocessor logic, flip-screen playfields, or sprite-based graphics

■ ACTIVITY: GAMER PROFILE

What are your earliest memories of video games? What kind of gamer are you? How do your gaming habits and interests compare to other students or your friends?

Name: _____ **Online Name:** _____

Gamer Since (Year): _____ **Why study video games?** _____

First Video Game Memory: _____

I consider my interest in video games: Casual | Moderate | Above Average | Obsessed

Weekly game time: 1–5 hours | 6–10 hours | 11–15 hours | 16–20 hours | 20+ hours

Consoles owned (or played frequently) and number of games completed for each:

_____ # _____   _____ # _____
_____ # _____   _____ # _____
_____ # _____   _____ # _____
_____ # _____   _____ # _____

Favorite console of all time and why:

_____

Favorite types of games (circle or check all that apply):

Action	Fighting	Racing	Simulation
Adventure	First-Person Shooter	Role-Playing	Sports
Board Game	Gambling	Rhythm	Strategy
Dance	Puzzle	Shoot 'em Up	Trivia

Ten favorite games that come to mind:

1. _____
2. _____
3. _____
4. _____
5. _____

6. _____
7. _____
8. _____
9. _____
10. _____

■ CHAPTER 1 QUIZ

1. Which of the following was *not* part of the evolution of games that predated video games?
   a. Bagatelle
   b. Baffle Ball
   c. Pinball
   d. Speedball

2. Often credited for developing the first electronic game called *Tennis for Two* in 1958:
   a. Nolan Bushnell
   b. Steve "Slug" Russell
   c. Willy Higinbotham
   d. Ralph Baer

3. What type of monitor was *Tennis for Two* originally displayed on?
   a. CRT television
   b. Oscilloscope
   c. Movie screen
   d. Personal computer monitor

4. MIT student who developed *Spacewar!*:
   a. Nolan Bushnell
   b. Steve "Slug" Russell
   c. Willy Higinbotham
   d. Ralph Baer

5. The "Father of Video Games" whose Brown Box console game system became the Magnavox Odyssey:
   a. Ray Kassar
   b. Ralph Baer
   c. Willy Higinbotham
   d. Steve Russell

6. Which product was *not* developed for the original Magnavox Odyssey system?
   a. Game card
   b. Joystick
   c. Light gun
   d. Plastic overlay

7. These two gentlemen were the original founders of Atari:
   a. Steve Jobs and Steve Wozniak
   b. Ray Kassar and Ted Dabney
   c. Trip Hawkins and Ted Russell
   d. Nolan Bushnell and Ted Dabney

8. What year was the first *Pong* arcade machine produced?
   a. 1960
   b. 1972
   c. 1978
   d. 1987

9. Which of the following was *not* a feature of *Pong* implemented by Al Alcorn:
    a. Using less expensive parts
    b. Adding deflection angles to the ball when it hit sections of the paddles
    c. Enhancing the game with ball acceleration
    d. Crowd noises such as applause and boos

10. *Pong* led to Atari being sued by _____ for copyright infringement.
    a. Syzygy Engineering
    b. Sanders Associates and Magnavox
    c. Nutting Associates
    d. Brookhaven National Laboratory

11. Atari's first home version of *Pong* was licensed by retailer _____ under the Tele-Games label.
    a. Sears, Roebuck & Company
    b. K-Mart
    c. J.C. Penney
    d. None of the above

12. Which of the following was *not* a business Coleco had a hand in before video games?
    a. asphalt roofing
    b. leather
    c. plastic molding
    d. swimming pools

13. The first home video game system to use the General Instrument AY-3-8500 chip:
    a. Odyssey
    b. Pong For Your Home TV
    c. Telstar
    d. Color TV-Game

14. Subsequent consoles such as Ranger, Combat!, and Gemini were developed by:
    a. Magnavox
    b. Atari
    c. Coleco
    d. Nintendo

15. Which of the following was *not* one of the three sections of the Telstar Arcade?
    a. Joysticks
    b. Paddles
    c. Light gun
    d. Steering wheel and gear shift

16. This company's game systems were sold partially assembled, where the consumer usually had to attach the paddle knobs and apply the decorative stickers onto the console:
    a. Magnavox
    b. Atari
    c. Coleco
    d. Nintendo

17. The first-generation console with removable *cartridges* for different games to be played:
    a. Odyssey
    b. Super Pong
    c. Telstar Gemini
    d. Telstar Arcade

18. Nintendo produced a successful series of single-game home consoles in Japan called:
    a. Game and Watch
    b. Color TV-Game
    c. Game for TV
    d. None of the above

19. Which first-generation U.S. home console series sold the most units overall?
    a. Odyssey
    b. Pong
    c. Super Pong
    d. Telstar

20. Systems with the game(s) built in, rather than using removable media are called:
    a. All-in-one consoles
    b. Dedicated consoles
    c. Solid state consoles
    d. Stand-alone consoles

True or False

21. *Spacewar!* by Nolan Bushnell was the first coin-operated arcade video game in 1971.

22. The original Magnavox Odyssey was not capable of producing sound in its games.

23. The home version of *Pong* only emitted sound from a built-in speaker in the center of the console, which could not be transmitted through the television speaker.

24. The name "Coleco" was derived from the words "California Leather Company."

25. Coleco manufactured 14 different models of the Telstar between 1976 and 1978.

▪ FIGURES

Figure 1.1 Evolution of pinball: (a) *Bagatelle*, (b) *Baffle Ball* (1931), and (c) *Rapid Transit* (1935). (*Bagatelle* photo from Hotel-R. Retrieved from http://www.hotel-r.net/fr/bagatelle; also at http://www.jacqueslondon.co.uk/indoor-games/bagatelle.html. *Baffle Ball* image from Pacific Pinball Museum, 2016, edited by Wardyga. Retrieved from http://pacificpinball.org/articles/baffle-ball. *Rapid Transit* image from Arcade Museum, photo contributed by Clive Godwin. Retrieved from http://www.arcade-museum.com/game_detail.php?game_id=12189.)

Figure 1.2 *Tennis for Two* (1958) displayed on a DuMont Lab Oscilloscope Type 304-A. (*Tennis for Two* come appariva nel 1958, by Brookhaven National Laboratory—Screenshot, public domain. Available at https://commons.wikimedia.org/w/index.php?curid=27864450. Retrieved from https://en.wikipedia.org/wiki/Tennis_for_Two#/media/File:Tennis_For_Two_on_a_DuMont_Lab_Oscilloscope_Type_304-A.jpg.)

Figure 1.3 Screenshots of (a) *Spacewar!* (Steve Russell, 1962) and (b) *Computer Space* (Nolan Bushnell, 1971). (*Spacewar!* and *Computer Space* screenshots by Wardyga.)

Figure 1.4 Magnavox Odyssey, the first commercial home video game console. ("The Magnavox Odyssey, the very first video game console," by Evan-Amos—own work, public domain. Available at https://commons.wikimedia.org/w/index.php?curid=17168362. Retrieved from https://en.wikipedia.org/wiki/Magnavox_Odyssey#/media/File:Magnavox-Odyssey-Console-Set.jpg.) (Part of this image was used on the introductory page of this chapter.)

Figure 1.5 Magazine advertisement for the Magnavox Odyssey in 1973. (Screenshots of Odyssey launch titles *Ski & Submarine* with plastic overlays "Magnavox Odyssey," by Video Game Console Library. Retrieved from http://www.videogameconsolelibrary.com/pg70-odyssey.htm#page=games.)

Figure 1.6 Screen overlays of Odyssey launch titles (a) *Ski* and (b) *Submarine*. ("Plastic television overlays," by Evan-Amos—own work, public domain. Available at https://commons.wikimedia.org/w/index.php?curid=40354387. Retrieved from https://en.wikipedia.org/wiki/Magnavox_Odyssey#/media/File:Magnavox-Color-Screen-Overlays.jpg.)

Figure 1.7 Plastic screen overlays for Odyssey titles *Haunted House* and *Roulette*. (From *The Magnavox High Reliability* magazine, 1973, p. 45. Image scanned and restored by Wardyga. Magazine advertisement for the *Magnavox Odyssey* in 1973.)

Figure 1.8 Vendor print advertisement for *Pong* (1972). (*Pong*, Atari, 1973. Advertisement for Pong. Posted by Jesper Juul. Available at https://www.jesperjuul.net/thesis/2-historyofthecomputergame.html. Restored by Wardyga.)

Figure 1.9 Screenshot comparison: Odyssey *Table Tennis* (a) versus *Pong* (b). (*Table Tennis* image by Wardyga. *Pong* screenshot: "The two paddles return the ball back and forth," by Bumm13 [2]—originally upload at en.wikipedia.org [1], public domain. Available at https://commons.wikimedia.org/w/index.php?curid=799667. Retrieved from https://en.wikipedia.org/wiki/Pong#/media/File:Pong.png.)

Figure 1.10 The Sears *Tele-Games Pong* (1975) (a) and Atari's own *Pong* console (1976) (b). (The Sears *Tele-Games Atari Pong* console, released in 1975, by Evan-Amos—own work, CC BY-SA 3.0. Available at https://commons.wikimedia.org/w/index.php?curid=18298737. Retrieved from https://en.wikipedia.org/wiki/First_generation_of_video_game_consoles#/media/File:TeleGames-Atari-Pong.png. History of Consoles: *Pong*, 1975, posted on June 13, 2012, by Gamester81. Available at http://gamester81.com/history-of-consoles-pong-1975/.) (Part of this image was used on the introductory page of this chapter.)

Figure 1.11 Sears Christmas catalog advertisement for *Tele-Games Pong* system in 1975. (The Atari Home Pong Console Is 40 Years Old, posted August 21, 2015, by MeTV Staff. Retrieved from http://www.metv.com/stories/the-atari-home-pong-console-is-40-years-old.)

Figure 1.12 The first Coleco Telstar system, model 6040 (1976). (Part of this image was used on the introductory page of this chapter.) (Courtesy of Wardyga.)

Figure 1.13 Two of the more distinctive Coleco systems: (a) Combat! and (b) Telstar Arcade. (Telstar Combat! image by Wardyga. Telstar Arcade with cartridge n.1 on top, by Evan-Amos—own work, public domain. Available at https://commons.wikimedia.org/w/index.php?curid=38538814 Retrieved from https://en.wikipedia.org/wiki/Telstar_(game_console)#/media/File:Coleco-Telstar-Arcade-Pongside-L.jpg.)

Figure 1.14 Screenshots of Telstar Arcade games (a) *Road Race* and (b) *Naval Battle*. (Screenshots and edits by Wardyga.)

Figure 1.15 Magazine advertisement for the Telstar Marksman (1978). (Scanned and edited by Wardyga.)

Figure 1.16 Nintendo's first home video game console, the Color TV-Game 6. (Evan-Amos—own work, public domain. Available at https://commons.wikimedia.org/w/index.php?curid=18301347. Retrieved from https://en.wikipedia.org/wiki/Color_TV-Game#/media/File:Nintendo-Color-TV-Game-Blockbreaker-FL.jpg.)

Figure 1.17 First-generation console sales graph. (Graph designed by Wardyga using public data from Magnavox, Atari, and Coleco.)

PRO FILE: Ralph Baer Photo credit: Reddit user Nightwheel (4/9/09). Posted in 2015. Retrieved from http://i156.photobucket.com/albums/t29/nightwheel/RalphHBaerAutograph.jpg.

■ REFERENCES

Adlum, E. (2001). *Interview by Steve Kent from The ultimate history of video games: The story behind the craze that touched our lives and changed the world.* Roseville, CA: Three Rivers Press.

Baer, R. (1998). *Genesis: How the home video games industry began.* R. H. Baer Consultants. Retrieved from http://www.ralphbaer.com/how_video_games.htm.

Bushnell, N. (2001). *Interview by Steve Kent from The ultimate history of video games: The story behind the craze that touched our lives and changed the world.* Roseville, CA: Three Rivers Press.

Citron, A. (1982, December 14). *The rise and fall of pinball.* Pittsburgh, PA: The Pittsburgh Press. p. 13.

Editorial: Odyssey: 35 years later. (2007, May 31). *IGN.* Retrieved from http://www.ign.com/articles/2007/06/01/odyssey-35-years-later.

Edwards, B. (2011, December 11). *Computer Space and the dawn of the arcade video game: How a little-known 1971 machine launched an industry.* Retrieved from http://www.technologizer.com/2011/12/11/computer-space-and-the-dawn-of-the-arcade-video-game/.

Graetz, J. (1981, August). The origin of Spacewar. *Creative Computing.* 6(8), pp. 56–67. Retrieved from http://www.wheels.org/spacewar/creative/SpacewarOrigin.html.

Grahame, J. (2007, October 29). *The terrifically triangular Coleco Telstar Arcade.* Retrieved from http://www.retrothing.com/2007/10/the-terrific-tr.html.

Hunter, W. (2014). *ColecoVision: The arcade in your home!* Retrieved from http://thedoteaters.com/?bitstory=colecovision.

June, L. (2013, January 16). *For amusement only: The life and death of the American arcade.* Retrieved from https://www.theverge.com/2013/1/16/3740422/the-life-and-death-of-the-american-arcade-for-amusement-only.

Kent, S. (2001). *The ultimate history of video games: The story behind the craze that touched our lives and changed the world.* Roseville, CA: Three Rivers Press.

Kleinfield, N. (1985, July 21). Coleco moves out of the cabbage patch. *The New York Times.* Retrieved from http://www.nytimes.com/1985/07/21/business/coleco-moves-out-of-the-cabbage-patch.html?&pagewanted=all.

Langshaw, M. (2014, December 13). *Magnavox Odyssey retrospective: How console gaming was born.* Retrieved from http://www.digitalspy.com/gaming/retro-corner/feature/a616235/magnavox-odyssey-retrospective-how-console-gaming-was-born/.

Loguidice, B. & Barton, M. (2009, January 9). The history of Pong: Avoid missing game to start industry. *Gamasutra.* Retrieved from http://www.gamasutra.com/view/feature/3900/the_history_of_pong_avoid_missing_.php.

Mullis, S. (2014, December 8). *Inventor Ralph Baer, the "father of video games," dies at 92.* Retrieved from http://www.npr.org/sections/alltechconsidered/2014/12/08/369405270/inventor-ralph-baer-the-father-of-video-games-dies-at-92.

Plunkett, L. (2011, March 25). *Nintendo's first console is one you've never played.* Retrieved from https://kotaku.com/nintendos-first-console-is-one-youve-never-played-5785568.

Russell, S. (2001). *Interview by Steve Kent from The ultimate history of video games: The story behind the craze that touched our lives and changed the world.* Roseville, CA: Three Rivers Press.

Shea, C. (2008, March 10). *Al Alcorn interview: The creator of Pong on the birth of Atari, holographic gaming and being paid to not show up to work.* Retrieved from http://www.ign.com/articles/2008/03/11/al-alcorn-interview.

Smith, A. (2015, November 16). *ITL200: A Magnavox Odyssey.* Retrieved from https://videogamehistorian.wordpress.com/2015/11/16/1tl200-a-magnavox-odyssey/.

Winter, D. (2013). *Atari Pong: The home systems.* Retrieved from http://www.pong-story.com/atpong2.htm.

Behind the Technology

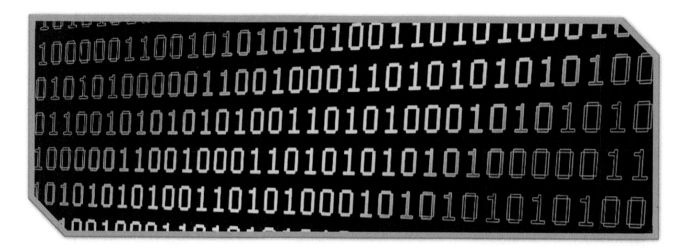

■ OBJECTIVES

After reading this chapter, you should be able to:

- Summarize the main internal components of a personal computer and video game console.

- Translate acronyms such as RAM, ROM, and CPU and explain what each does.

- Understand the basics of how personal computers and video game consoles work.

- Compare types of networks such as LANs, WANs, and the Internet.

- Describe screen display properties such as hertz, frame rate, resolution, and scanning methods.

- Differentiate between video formats such as NTSC, PAL, and SECAM.

- Be familiar with types of graphics such as ASCII, vector, raster, and polygons.

- Review the fundamentals of color and lighting in video games.

- Describe functional characteristics of a game such as perspective, scrolling, and axis.

- Explain how sound and music development have evolved in gaming.

- Name types of surround sound, notable video game music composers, and voice actors.

- Summarize Stockburger's sound objects as they apply to video games.

DOI: 10.1201/9781003315759-2

■ KEY TERMS AND PEOPLE

Achromatic color
Analogous (color)
ASCII
Aspect ratio
ATSC
Audio/sound card
Basic Input/Output System
Binary digit/Bit (b)
Bitmap
Blinn–Phong reflection model
Bloom (lighting)
Bump mapping
Bus/System Bus
Byte (B)
Cache memory
Cathode ray tube (CRT)
Central processing unit
Chrominance/Chroma
Clock rate
Coaxial digital
Color identifiers
Color palette
Complementary color
Component
Composite
Cores
Diegetic sound
Digital Theater Systems
Digital video broadcasting
Digital visual interface
Display port
Dolby Atmos
Dolby Laboratories
DTMB

DTS:X
Effect sound
Ethernet
Expansion cards & slots
F Connector
First-person shooter
FLOPS
Forced progression
Frame rate
Frames per second
Free progression
Gigabyte (GB)
Gigahertz (GHz)
Glyphs
GPU
Graphics (GFX)
Graphics/video card
HDMI
HDTV
Heads-up display (HUD)
Heinrich Hertz
Hertz (Hz)
IEEE-1394/Firewire
Integrated Services Digital Broadcasting (ISDB)
Interface music
Interlaced scan
Internet
Kilobyte (kB)
Kilohertz (kHz)
Johann Lambert
Lambert lighting
Gottfried Leibniz
Light-emitting diode (LED)
Line scrolling

Liquid crystal display
Local area network (LAN)
Luminance/Luma
Megabyte (MB)
Megahertz (MHz)
Memory controller
MIDI
Millions of instructions per second (MIPS)
Modem
Monaural (Mono) sound
Monochromatic color
Motherboard
Network adapter
Non-diegetic sound
NTSC
Organic light-emitting diode
Out of order execution
Parallax scrolling
Parallel processing
PCI
Phase alternate line (PAL)
Bui Tuong Phong
Phong lighting
Pixels
Plasma display panel (PDP)
Polygons
Ports
Progressive scan
Pulse-code modulation
Random access memory (RAM)
Raster graphics
Ray tracing

Read-only memory (ROM)
Region free
RGB color
SCART
Score/Soundtrack
Screen resolution
Scrolling
SECAM
Second-person
Shaders
Shoot 'em Up
Soap opera effect
Sound effects
Sprites
Stereophonic (Stereo)
Stereoscopic 3D
Stockburger's Sound Objects
Strings (Binary)
Surround sound
Texture mapping
Third-person
Toslink/Optical
Ultra HD (4K/8K)
Universal Serial Bus (USB)
Vector graphics
Video Graphics Array (VGA)
Vocalization
Voice synthesis
Wide area network (WAN)
Wi-Fi adapter
X, Y, and Z-axes
Zone sound

■ CHAPTER OUTLINE

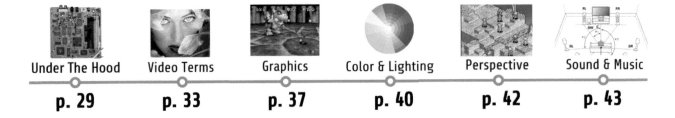

Under The Hood	Video Terms	Graphics	Color & Lighting	Perspective	Sound & Music
p. 29	p. 33	p. 37	p. 40	p. 42	p. 43

■ INTRODUCTION

Computers and video game consoles share many common components that allow these devices to play video games. Comparing this book's "tech specs" charts among consoles is one way to observe the hardware progression over each generation of video games. While it can be interesting to compare these technical specifications, the figures mean very little without a moderate understanding of the technology behind the numbers. This chapter elaborates on the technical lingo used throughout the textbook. It can be revisited whenever a technical term requires further detail, examples, or illustrations. This information is presented as an introduction to common computer and video game components, speed and display types, as well as the basics of graphics and sound. These terms and technologies are also discussed under the respective generations in which they were introduced or became most popular.

■ UNDER THE HOOD

Like personal computers (PCs), video game consoles are made up of various circuits, cards, and other hardware. The main internal component each platform is built on is the **motherboard** (Figure 2.1). "The motherboard gets its name because it is like a mother to all of the other circuit boards." It is "the largest circuit board and has many smaller boards plugged into it"

(Welch, 2002a). Multiple components can be found attached to the motherboard, including one or more of the following basic parts: CPU, RAM, ROM, BIOS, graphics card (GPU), sound card, disk controller, expansion card, and modem/network card.

■ CPU

The **central processing unit (CPU)** is like the brain of a computer or game console. It makes calculations and processes information that tells the other components what to do. The technical specification for "processing speed" usually indicates the speed of the CPU. More powerful CPUs can make decisions more quickly. When starting up a video game, parts of the program (music, levels, characters, etc.) are transferred to the RAM (explained subsequently). The CPU then loads the program data from its RAM by a circuit called a **memory controller**. Finally, the CPU "processes" the program's instructions, such as what information to display on the screen. CPUs can generate high levels of heat and often require a small cooling fan to bring the temperature down. When CPUs overheat, it is common to hear the fan's sound intensify as it speeds up to cool the CPU.

■ RAM AND ROM

RAM stands for **random access memory**. RAM is like the short-term memory of a computer, allowing data

FIGURE 2.1 Motherboards from (a) ColecoVision (1982) and (b) Sega CD 2 (1993).

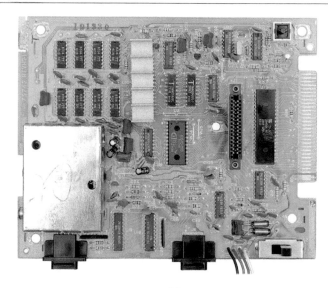

(a)   (b)

FIGURE 2.2 Typical RAM cards (a) and Amic erasable programmable ROM (b).

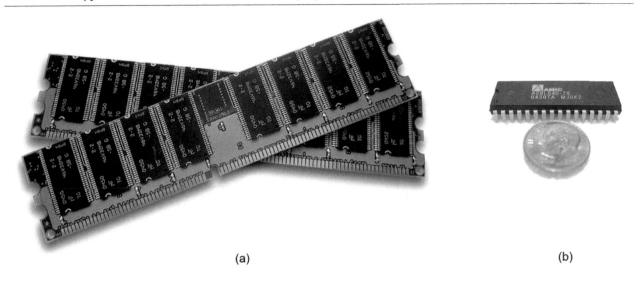

(a)   (b)

to be read, written, and stored—but only temporarily (Le Grange, 2015). RAM chips (Figure 2.2) store and retain information while the system is running but will forget most of this temporary data when the unit is turned off. By storing information in a system's RAM, information such as the layout of a game map can be accessed quickly. The more RAM a system has, the more parts of a game it can load at once. When progressing through a game, the RAM is constantly freeing memory and loading more parts of the game from the hard drive or external ROM media.

ROM stands for **read-only memory**. It is different from RAM in that the information it stores cannot be altered or forgotten. Internally, ROM is primarily used to store the programs required to boot the gaming system. External ROM media includes game software such as cartridges and optical discs like DVD (digital versatile disc) and Blu-ray. Again, ROM media contains information that communicates with the console or computer system, but the content on them cannot be changed or altered. Game information on a ROM disc or cartridge is loaded onto the system's RAM to play the game.

☼ DID YOU KNOW?

The CD-ROM for *Ridge Racer* (Namco, 1995) loaded the entire game onto the PlayStation's RAM, eliminating loading and allowing players to replace the game disc with a music CD, which it would use as the in-game music (GamePro, 1995, p. 37).

■ BIOS

Another important computer component is the **BIOS chip**. BIOS stands for **Basic Input/Output System** and "in very simple terms, the BIOS chip wakes up the computer when you turn it on and reminds it what parts it has and what they do" (Welch, 2002a). The BIOS is usually found on a ROM chip (called the ROM BIOS). It also serves as an important diagnostic tool, as it confirms the configurations and reliability of the system and allows it to use features of hardware by managing all inputs and outputs. The CPU, memory, and BIOS communicate across the **system bus** as illustrated in Figure 2.3.

FIGURE 2.3 Schematic of a personal computer; note how the CPU must go through the system bus to communicate with the other components.

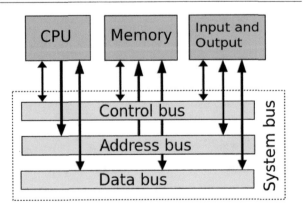

∎ GRAPHICS AND SOUND CARDS

The **graphics card** (or **video card**) is responsible for producing output to the monitor or television. A key component of a graphics card is the **graphics processing unit (GPU)**. The GPU is the muscle behind the image that is displayed on the screen. Modern graphics cards also feature power input connectors and have their own internal cooling solutions.

The **sound card** (or **audio card**) contains special circuits that allow the system to process sound. Sound cards facilitate both the input and output of audio from the system. They have also been included in external devices such as game cartridges that used software to produce or enhance a game's sound. See Figure 2.4 for examples of video and sound cards.

∎ PORTS

Ports (also seen in Figure 2.4) are slots and connectors on the outside of computers and consoles for plugging in additional hardware such as gamepads, keyboards, mice, monitors, speakers, and other peripheral devices. "Ports are controlled by their **expansion cards** which are plugged into the motherboard and [usually] connected to other components by cables" (Welch, 2002a). There are too many types of ports to mention in this chapter; however, two popular ports today include **High-Definition Multimedia Interface (HDMI)** and **universal serial bus (USB)**. HDMI ports can transmit video and audio simultaneously and are the main port for connecting today's consoles to modern TVs and monitors. USB ports are used to connect everything from flash drives to printers, to game controllers, mice, and keyboards. They can even charge devices that run on rechargeable batteries. Like ports, consoles have featured **expansion slots** for connecting add-on units such as the Sega CD for the Mega Drive/Genesis or the Game Boy Player for the Nintendo GameCube.

∎ MAKING THE CONNECTION

PCI or **peripheral component interconnect** is a common means of connecting peripheral devices by providing a shared data path (aka the "bus") between the CPU and peripheral controllers such as graphics and sound cards. This is not to be confused with the **kernel**, which allows software to talk to the hardware. The kernel is a computer program that translates software code into data processing instructions for the CPU.

Modern computers and game consoles can be linked for cooperative and competitive play by networking them together. Common methods of networking computers include **local area networks (LANs)** and **wide area networks (WANs)**. LANs are a network of connected computers in a small geographical area such as in a home, computer lab, or small campus. WANs, on the other hand, cover a much larger geographical footprint between cities, states, countries, and even between nations. Figure 2.5 illustrates how multiple LANs can connect to form a WAN.

The conglomerate of these technologies is the **Internet**, "a worldwide collection of interconnected networks (internetworks or the *Internet* for short), cooperating with each other to exchange information using common standards. Through telephone wires,

FIGURE 2.4 AGP (accelerated graphics port) video card (a) and Turtle Beach sound card (b); note how graphics and sound cards contain external ports for connectors.

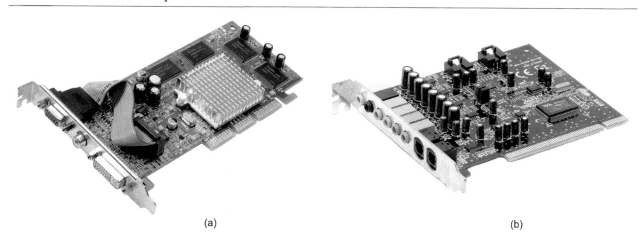

(a)   (b)

FIGURE 2.5 LANs separated by geographic distance connected by a WAN.

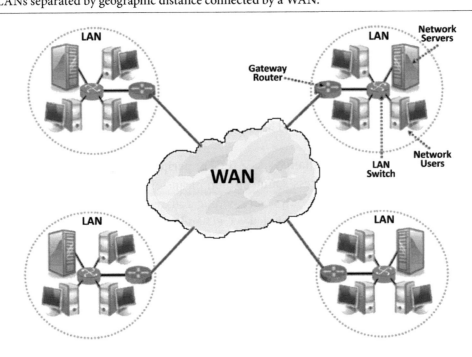

fiber-optic cables, wireless transmissions, and satellite links, Internet users can exchange information in a variety of forms" (Cisco Networking Academy, 2013).

Computers and consoles can be networked in a variety of ways. One method for connecting systems is through an expansion card called a **modem**. "A modem plugs the computer into a phone or cable line so that information can be transferred between computers" (Welch, 2002a). A modem is required to connect to the Internet. Inside most modern PCs and consoles is a **network adapter** (also called a network card, network interface controller [NIC], LAN adapter, or WAN card, among other titles). The network adapter is a small circuit board that allows the system to communicate with other devices. For wireless connections, most devices now contain a **Wi-Fi adapter,** which can provide wireless band connectivity for applications such as multiplayer gaming (Le Grange, 2015).

■ BITS AND BYTES

While not a new term for computer techies, it was not until around the third generation of video games (mid-to-late 1980s) that the average gamer began speaking in "bits" in anticipation of the upcoming "16-bit" consoles. A **bit (b)** is just an abbreviated word for **bi**nary dig**it**. Every bit is either a 0 or a 1, collectively known as **binary code**. The basis for binary

code was discovered by **Gottfried Leibniz** in 1679, illustrated in his article *Explication de l'Arithmétique Binaire*. Binary code is how all computer processing instructions are written using combinations of the binary digits 0 and 1. Zeros represent the command "off" or "no," while ones represent the command "on" or "yes." By themselves, these are only two distinct commands. "The millions of combinations of those two commands given in series are what make a computer work" (Welch, 2002b).

Combinations of bits are called strings. Table 2.1 illustrates the simple formula for writing numbers in binary code. When a 1 is added to a 1 (as it is to make the number 2), the next bit becomes 0 (i.e., number 2 = 10 in binary code). Add another 1 and the next bit becomes a 1 (i.e., number 3 = 11 in binary code). Note how once all 1s are used in a string, another bit is added (with a string of zeros) and the sequence continues.

Eight bits grouped together form a **byte (B)**, and it is this size string that is usually used to represent an

TABLE 2.1 Numbers in Binary Code

0 = 0	7 = 111	14 = 1110
1 = 1	8 = 1000	15 = 1111
2 = 10	9 = 1001	16 = 10000
3 = 11	10 = 1010	17 = 10001
4 = 100	11 = 1011	18 = 10010
5 = 101	12 = 1100	19 = 10011
6 = 110	13 = 1101	20 = 10100

alphabetic character. The letter "A," for instance, is an 8-bit character written like this: 01000001 (Rieman, 1996). "When you type the letter A on your keyboard, electrical signals are sent from the keyboard to the CPU. The CPU turns the signals into binary code. Then, the computer reads the code and sends it on to the monitor to display the letter A" (Welch, 2002b). Larger strings of bytes in metric multiples of 1,000 are given new names. For example, 1,000 bytes is called a **kilobyte (kB)** and 1,000 kB equals a **megabyte (MB)**. See Table 2.2 for these and other common values of bytes.

Bits and bytes can form more than just alphabetic characters. Strings of bits can correspond to a variety of different symbols and processing instructions. For an 8-bit platform, programmers have 256 possible combinations of 0s and 1s to work with. For game consoles and computers, the number of bytes represents the system's **memory capacity**. For instance, "if a computer has 64 MB of RAM, that means that the computer can handle 64,000,000 (64 million) bytes of random access memory" (Welch, 2002b). In addition to RAM, hard drive space and software storage capacity are also measured in bytes.

▪ HERTZ AND FRAME RATE

While memory and storage space are measured in bytes, processor speed and TV/monitor refresh rates are measured in **hertz (Hz)**. Named after German physicist **Heinrich Hertz** (1857–1894), who proved the existence of electromagnetic waves, hertz is the unit of *frequency* in the International System of Units (SI). Quite simply, hertz means "cycle per second." One hertz equals one complete cycle per second, 100 Hz equals 100 cycles per second, and so forth (see Table 2.3 for more information). In other words, a system with a 4.4 GHz processor has a **clock rate** of 4.4 billion times per second! Processor speed alone

is not the only factor in determining how fast a console or computer will operate. Common components that contribute to CPU speed include co-processors, additional **cores** (processing units), and extra **cache memory** (a smaller, faster form of RAM).

For TVs and monitors, "a hertz rating refers to the number of times per second the **pixels** [screen dots] used to display an image are refreshed" (Emigh, 2009). TVs in the United States run at 60 Hz (59.94 Hz), or at a refresh rate of approximately 60 times per second. Newer models can run at refresh rates of 120 Hz, 240 Hz, and even 480 Hz—although most viewers do not notice a major difference once refresh rates reach over 120 Hz. Higher refresh rates were developed for TVs and monitors to reduce motion blur that can occur during fast-moving action as seen in sports broadcasts and video games. Screens with refresh rates of 120 Hz and above typically look great for video games and sports broadcasts—however, this is not always the case when viewing movies or TV shows shot on film. Coined the "**soap opera effect**," high hertz TVs often contain motion smoothing/interpolation or motion estimation/motion compensation (ME/MC) processing that can make films look hyperreal and more like a live broadcast or soap opera. This effect is often in stark contrast to the surreal look most fictional film directors are after and can alter the way such films and shows are perceived. Fortunately, these motion smoothing features can usually be turned off—allowing equal enjoyment for gaming, sports, and movie watching.

While each of these is measured in units per second and can lead to a smoother gaming experience, the speed of the CPU and refresh rate of a monitor are different from the **frame rate** a game is running at. Frame rate is measured by **frames per second (fps)**. The baseline for standard definition video in the United States is 30 fps (29.97 fps to be exact); however, modern games commonly run at 60 fps. So, how does a game running at 60 fps or a movie running at 24 fps display properly

TABLE 2.2 Common Multiples of Bytes (B)

Unit	Abbreviation	Metric Value	Binary Value
Kilobyte	kB	1 thousand bytes or 1,000 kilobytes	1024 bytes
Megabyte	MB	1 million bytes or 1,000 kilobytes	1024^2 bytes
Gigabyte	GB	1 billion bytes or 1,000 megabytes	1024^3 bytes
Terabyte	TB	1 trillion bytes or 1,000 gigabytes	1024^4 bytes

TABLE 2.3 Common Multiples of Hertz (Hz)

Unit	SI Symbol	Value
Kilohertz	kHz	1,000 (10^3) Hz
Megahertz	MHz	1,000,000 (10^6) Hz
Gigahertz	GHz	1,000,000,000 (10^9) Hz
Terahertz	THz	1,000,000,000,000 (10^{12}) Hz

on a TV/monitor with a refresh rate of 120 Hz? In the case of a 24-fps movie, "even with higher refresh rates, there are still only 24 separate frames displayed every second, but they may need to be displayed multiple times, depending on the refresh rate. To display 24 frames per second on a TV with a 120 Hz refresh rate, each frame is repeated 5 times every 24th of a second" (Silva, 2016). Likewise, to display a 60-fps game on a TV with a 120 Hz refresh rate, each frame is repeated 2 times every 60th of a second.

💡 DID YOU KNOW?

Refresh rates of TVs in the United Kingdom and most other countries run at a baseline of 50 Hz and 25 fps (compared to 60 Hz and 30 fps in the United States and a few other countries) due to different base frequencies in their power lines.

■ SCANNING SYSTEMS

Television displays use one of two scanning methods to paint the picture on the screen. "Traditional video systems use an **interlaced scan**, where half the picture appears on the screen at a time. The other half of the picture follows an instant later (1/60th of a second)" (Briere & Hurley, 2008). With interlaced scanning,

each frame is comprised of two fields. The first field is made up of the screen's odd horizontal lines, while the second field contains the even horizontal lines. Interlaced scan was the main scanning system used for analog video displays before the advent of digital TV. Consoles connected to a TV with the yellow **composite** cable (and earlier analog video cables) can only output games using the interlaced scanning display format. Since interlaced video takes two passes to complete a full frame, the term "frames per second" is commonly substituted with "fields per second."

In contrast, a **progressive scan** system paints the entire picture within each field in *one* pass. See Figure 2.6 for a comparison. Like a higher refresh rate, games displayed in progressive scan typically move smoother and look sharper compared to games displayed via interlaced scan. Progressive scan capabilities became popular during the sixth generation of video games when systems such as Dreamcast, PlayStation 2, Xbox, and GameCube were capable of being connected to TVs with optional red, green, and blue (RGB) **component** cables. Of course, the games must be programmed to output progressive scan, so playing interlaced scan titles through component cables will still result in an interlaced picture on screen. See Table 2.4 for these and other common connectors.

FIGURE 2.6 Comparing interlaced and progressive scan on a 60-Hz display.

Interlaced Scan

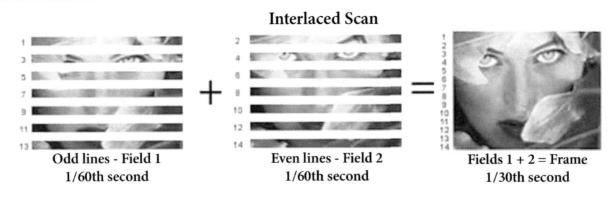

Odd lines - Field 1	Even lines - Field 2	Fields 1 + 2 = Frame
1/60th second	1/60th second	1/30th second

Progressive Scan

All lines - Field 1	All lines - Field 2
1/60th second	1/60th second

TABLE 2.4   Visual Reference Guide to Common Video Game Connectors (Illustrations Not to Scale)

Connector	Name(s)	Audio Specs	Video/Data
	F Connector/coaxial	Analog, mono/stereo	720×576i @ 50 Hz 720×480i @ 60 Hz
	Composite/RCA/phono	Analog, mono/stereo	720×576i @ 50 Hz 720×480i @ 60 Hz
	S-video	Analog, video-only	720×576i @ 50 Hz 720×480i @ 60 Hz
	SCART	Analog, mono/stereo	720×576i @ 50 Hz 720×480i @ 60 Hz
	Component/YP_BP_R	Analog, video-only	up to 1920×1080p @ 50 or 60 Hz
	VGA (Video Graphics Array)	Analog, video-only	Up to 2048×1536p (QXGA) @ 85 Hz
	DVI (Digital Visual Interface)	Video-only	Up to 2560×1600 Up to 144 Hz @ 1080p
	HDMI	Digital, eight channels of 24-bit up to 192 kHz, may also support 8K (7680×4320p)	3840×2160 @ 24, 25, 30 Hz 1920×1080 @ 120 Hz
	Display port	Digital, eight channels of 24-bit up to 192 kHz, may also support 8K (7680×4320p)	3840×2160 @ 60, 144 Hz 1920×1080 @ 144 Hz
	IEEE-1394/firewire	Data cable/varies	50–400 MB/s
	Ethernet	Data cable/varies	Up to 125 MB/s
	USB A B	Data cable/varies	Up to 1280 MB/s (USB 3.0)
	Mini USB Mini-A Mini-B	Data cable/varies	USB 2.0 speeds
	Micro USB Micro-A Micro-B	Data cable/varies	USB 2.0 speeds
	USB-C	Data cable/varies	3.0 to Thunderbolt speeds
	TRS (3.5 mm mini or ¼″ phone)	Analog, mono/stereo	Audio-only
	Coaxial digital	Digital 5.1/7.1 surround	24-bit @ 96 kHz
	Toslink/optical or S/PDIF/ digital audio	Digital 5.1/7.1 surround	24-bit @ 192 kHz

Sources: (Crane, 2016), (Milos, 2013), and (Niridya, 2022).

■ MONITOR TYPES

The round oscilloscope screen that displayed Willy Higinbotham's *Tennis for Two* (1958) and Steve Russell's *Spacewar!* (1962) was a type of **CRT** monitor. CRT is short for **cathode ray tube** and "works by moving an electron beam back and forth across the back of the screen. Each time the beam makes a pass across the screen, it lights up phosphor dots on the inside of the glass tube, thereby illuminating the active portions of the screen" (Beal, 2009, p. 1). CRT was the main type of television and computer monitor throughout the twentieth century until flat panel monitors took over in the early 2000s.

Flat panel monitors became popular due to their thinner depth, lighter weight, higher energy efficiency, and the fact that they emit much lower radiation compared to CRTs. The first major flat panel monitor to be used for computer and television gaming was the **liquid crystal display (LCD)**. As the title suggests, LCD contains a liquid crystal substance. "The molecules of this substance line up in such a way that the light behind the screens [is] blocked or allowed to create an image" (Khan, 2013). Early LCDs often suffered from a poor viewing angle. In other words, the picture would appear faded when viewed from the sides rather than from directly in front of the screen.

Plasma display panel (PDP) was the original competitor to LCD in television sizes 30 inches and above, with the technology initially allowing for deeper shades of black and wider viewing angles. "A plasma display is an array of tiny gas cells sandwiched between two sheets of glass. Each cell acts like a mini fluorescent tube, emitting ultraviolet light which then strikes red, green and blue spots on the screen. These spots glow to build up the picture" (Laughlin, 2016). Early generation plasma displays were susceptible to a phenomenon known as "screen burn-in," where the shadow of a stagnant image could become permanently stuck on the screen if displayed for extended periods of time. This did not bode well for video games, which often contain **heads-up displays (HUDs)** such as timers, life bars, score, and other data that remain on screen for the duration of the games. A plasma's glass screens can also lead to glare from reflected light, and because of their internal makeup, plasmas are often much heavier than other flat screen monitors.

Light-emitting diode (LED) displays are basically LCD monitors that are backlit with tiny LEDs instead of fluorescent tube backlights. LED displays have a more comparable contrast ratio to plasmas, can be thinner, and are usually more energy efficient than both plasmas and LCDs. Newer, **organic light-emitting diode (OLED)** displays use a film of organic compound (rather than a backlight) to emit light and produce an even higher quality picture. The first video game console to use OLED technology was Nintendo Switch OLED Model, launched on October 8, 2021.

■ VIDEO FORMATS

Three main analog video formats were adopted across the globe. **NTSC** or **National Television Standards Committee** has been the format used in North America, Japan, South Korea, and a few other nations (see Figure 2.7). NTSC devices run at a baseline refresh rate of 60 Hz (59.94 Hz) and a frame rate of 30 fps (29.97). Early NTSC screens contained 525 scan lines (of which 483 were used to display the image) and a standard definition **aspect ratio** (width × height) of 4 × 3, which translates to a **screen resolution** of 720 × 480 rectangular pixels (equivalent to 640 × 480 square pixels on a computer monitor).

Phase alternate line (PAL) was the analog format developed for most of Europe, Australia, and sizable portions of Africa and Asia. PAL devices run at a baseline refresh rate of 50 Hz and frame rate of 25 fps. While PAL has a lower refresh rate and frame rate compared to NTSC, standard definition PAL TVs contain 625 scan lines (of which 576 are used to display the image [582 in the United Kingdom]). Like NTSC, the standard definition aspect ratio for PAL is 4 × 3; however, PAL has a higher screen resolution of 720 × 576 pixels.

Séquentiel Couleur à Mémoire (SECAM) is French for "sequential color with memory." This was the first European color television standard and is used in Russia, Eastern Europe, France, and parts of Africa. This format shares many of the same specifications as PAL with a baseline refresh rate of 50 Hz, frame rate of 25 fps, a standard definition of 625 scan lines, and 720 × 576 pixel resolution. It differs from PAL in that SECAM uses a different method of color transmission. See Figure 2.7 for a breakdown of analog television-encoding systems by nation.

FIGURE 2.7 Analog television encoding systems by nation.

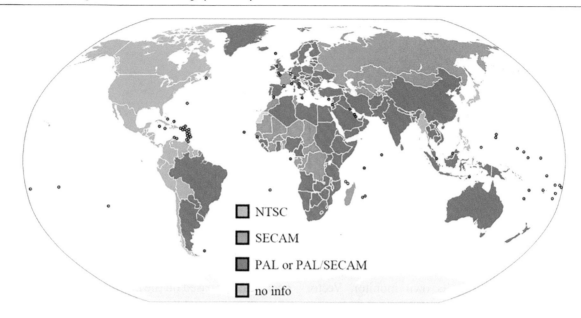

The transition to new digital television standards took place during the early 2000s, with **Advanced Television Systems Committee (ATSC)** replacing NTSC for use in the United States, Mexico, Canada, and South Korea. PAL and SECAM regions converted to **Digital Video Broadcasting (DVB)** or Japan's **Integrated Services Digital Broadcasting (ISDB)** standard, while China and a half dozen other countries adopted China's **Digital Terrestrial Multimedia Broadcast (DTMB)** format.

One of the goals of the introduction of **High-Definition Television (HDTV)** was to unify these formats and eliminate incompatibility issues between countries. For all formats, HDTVs have an aspect ratio of 16 × 9 and share screen resolutions such as 1920 × 1080 pixels. Even lower HD resolution formats such as High-Definition Video (HDV) have resolutions of 1440 × 1080 pixels or 1280 × 720 pixels in every country. Resolution aside, the disparity between hertz remains today, with a broadcasting baseline of 60 Hz for ATSC regions versus 50 Hz for other regions. Frame rate disparities also remain, with ATSC regions running at a baseline of 29.97 fps and other regions running at a baseline of 25 fps.

Despite these disparities, all HDTVs can display a variety of frame rates and refresh rates. It is entirely possible to play a game manufactured for one country's standard on a different region's console and monitor if the game is **region free.** For example, a European PS3 game disc will normally play fine on a U.S. PS3 console and vice versa. **Ultra HD** or 4K monitors can display resolutions of 3840 × 2160 and 8K monitors can display resolutions of 7680 × 4320.

■ ASCII AND VECTOR GRAPHICS

Whatever the display format, all video games are made up of **graphics (GFX)**. One of the early forms of video game graphics is **ASCII (American Standard Code for Information Interchange)**. ASCII graphics are essentially just text character symbols (like fonts in a word processing program). These can be seen in Steve "Slug" Russell's *Spacewar!* (1962) (Figure 2.8a) where text character symbols are used for the two dueling spaceships, missiles, and stars. One of the downsides to early graphics like ASCII was that games could only be displayed on monochrome (single color) displays.

Another form of graphics that became popular around the same time as ASCII is **vector graphics**. Vector graphics are made up of electron beam images—shapes based on mathematical equations of geometrical primitives such as points, lines, and curves. Examples of popular vector graphic arcade games include Atari's *Asteroids* (1979) and *Battlezone* (1980). Like ASCII graphics, vector graphics are entirely monochrome. And like other early arcade games before color, vector-based games often used color overlays to give the illusion of multiple colors on the screen. *Battlezone* (Figure 2.8) used a red and green overlay. The Vectrex home video game console (Western Technologies/Smith Engineering, 1983) was a completely vector

FIGURE 2.8 Screenshots of (a) *Spacewar!* (ASCII GFX) and (b) *Battlezone* (vector GFX).

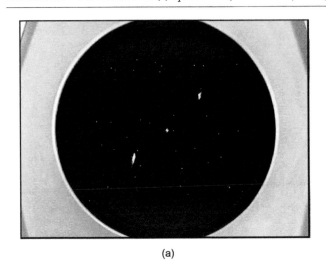

(a)

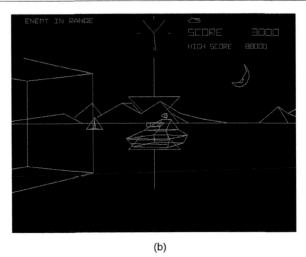

(b)

display-based system with its own monitor. Vector monitors were another type of CRT display. Due to their lack of color and the fact that they could only display a shape's outline, vector-based games began to disappear after around 1985 in favor of raster graphics.

■ RASTER AND POLYGON GRAPHICS

Raster graphics are "made up of a collection of tiny, uniformly sized pixels, which are arranged in a two-dimensional grid made up of columns and rows. Each pixel contains one or more bits of information, depending on the degree of detail in the image" (Encyclopædia Britannica, 2016). Each grid coordinate is called a **bitmap**—a single-bit raster that corresponds with a

specific color based on the number of bits stored in each pixel. To animate bitmaps on the screen without altering the data defining the graphics, most consoles in the 1980s used sprite technology. **Sprites** were invented as a way of combining unrelated bitmaps so that they appear to be part of a larger object, such as an animated character that can move around on the screen. Sprite size and the number of sprites that could be displayed on screen became popular technical specifications in comparing early generations of video game consoles.

The fifth generation of video games popularized polygon graphics. **Polygons** are geometric shapes that are "mapped" onto wireframe models to create 3D graphics. The term "3D" here refers to graphics having multiple sides and depth *within* the screen and

FIGURE 2.9 Screenshots of (a) *Super Mario Bros.* (raster GFX) and *Super Mario 64* (polygons).

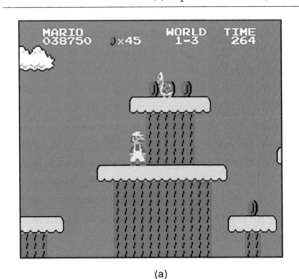

(a)

(b)

FIGURE 2.10 Texture mapping a checkerboard image onto a wireframe face.

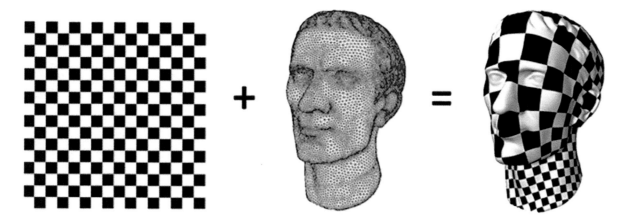

should not be confused with **stereoscopic 3D** technology, which creates the illusion of objects protruding *beyond* the screen. See Figure 2.9 for a comparison between raster and polygon graphics. While all the fifth-generation consoles emphasized polygonal gaming, it was Sony that really pressed developers to focus on 3D polygonal gaming for the PlayStation. This may have been because the PS1 was built specifically for 3D games and, in turn, very few true 2D titles were released for the system.

When reading the tech specs of fifth-generation and later consoles, "polygon count" will refer to the number of polygons capable of being rendered per frame. Another important aspect of polygons is how they are mapped. Two common types of mapping include **texture mapping** (Figure 2.10)—wrapping a 2D "texture map" around a 3D object; and **bump mapping**—adding bumps or wrinkly textures that play off light.

> ☀ **DID YOU KNOW?**
>
> Unlike vector graphics, raster graphics and sprites do not stretch very well—distorting or becoming "pixilated" when zoomed in upon like in *Pilotwings* on SNES.

■ SHADERS, FLOPS, AND CORES

As 3D graphics technology progressed, more attention was given to the number of shaders (Table 2.5) a GPU could produce. While a texture is a 2D image, a **shader** is a program or cluster of instructions for

TABLE 2.5 Types of Shaders

Name	Notes
2D	The only shader for adding textures to 2D pixels
3D	Including primitive/mesh, vertex, geometry, tessellation, and ray tracing shaders
Compute	General purpose; used in graphics pipelines for extra effects
Unity	Can execute any type of shader

drawing a surface. A texture almost always requires a shader, while shaders may or may not utilize textures. The greater the number of shader cores in a GPU, the more levels of contrast and special effects are available. Older graphics cards required separate processing units for each shader type; however, today's GPUs include "unified" shaders, which can execute any type of shader.

In addition to being paired with attributes such as "diffuse," "glossy," or "specular," shaders can be given properties such as "normal," "transparent," "self-illuminated," and "reflective," as depicted in Figure 2.11. Common shaders include "bumped diffuse (normal mapping)" shaders that emulate lighting of bumps without adding any geometry and "parallax specular" for creating displacement (where an object looks different from different angles and distances) (Hergaarden, 2011, p. 9).

With more compute units and stream processors to work from, GPUs took center stage after the turn of the century and polygon count became a secondary technical specification to a system's **floating point**

FIGURE 2.11 Shader examples from the built-in Unity Shaders Matrix (Unity, 2010).

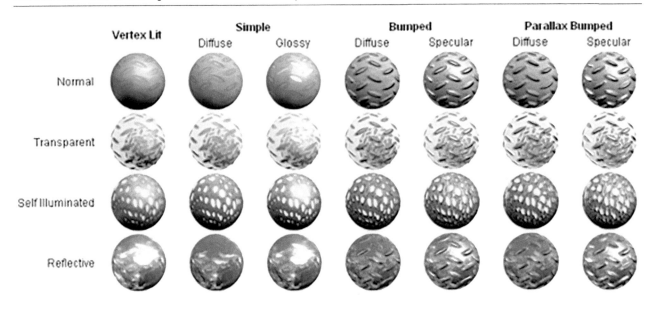

operations per second (FLOPS). A "flop" is a basic unit of computational power that serves as an indicator for graphics processing speeds. For example, GPUs of seventh-generation consoles were clocked between 12 gigaflops or "GFLOPS" (Wii) and 240 GFLOPS (Xbox 360). Subsequent waves of modern consoles contain even faster GPUs that can push multiple teraflops or "TFLOPS" (Table 2.6).

While FLOPS provide a clearer sense of graphics processing speeds for comparing consoles, there are other numbers such as a system's **MIPS (millions of instructions per second)** that go into determining how efficient a console is at processing data in a specific amount of time, often referred to as the "time-to-solution." Then there is technology such as **parallel processing**, which allows for more than one calculation or execution process to be carried out simultaneously—a type of computation that can be expanded by the number of "cores" a processor contains.

Game consoles were introduced with multicore processors starting with the Xbox 360's 3.2 GHz PC Tri-Core Xenon CPU. With a tri-core processor, each core functions as a separate processor, resulting in faster computing and more efficient energy consumption. The PlayStation 3 was built to be even more complex, with a 3.2 GHz multicore cell processor that was "essentially seven microprocessors on one chip, allowing it to perform several operations at once" (Altizer, 2016, para. 8). Note that core architecture can vary from one manufacturer to another, making it difficult to compare them directly.

With the Wii U, Nintendo chose to go with an enlarged cache and a process called **Out of Order Execution (OOE)** (Amas, 2013, para. 3). OOE is a paradigm used by high-end microprocessors. Unlike older processors that executed instructions by their original order in a program, OOE processors can carry out instructions in a nonlinear fashion based on input data as it becomes available. In other words, the processor can preload data in the background (cache), rather than remaining idle until the system calls for something to be processed.

■ COLOR AND LIGHTING

Color or lack thereof—as in *Limbo* (2010)—is a major device in building immersion and triggering an emotional response in the player. The meaning of colors

TABLE 2.6 Common Multiples of FLOPS

Unit	Abbreviation	Value
Megaflops	MFLOPS	1,000,000 (10^6)
Gigaflops	GFLOPS	1,000,000,000 (10^9)
Teraflops	TFLOPS	1,000,000,000,000 (10^{12})
Petaflops	PFLOPS	1,000,000,000,000,000 (10^{15})

can vary between cultures; however, there are commonalities, such as warmer colors signifying daytime and safety, while cooler colors usually suggest nighttime and danger. Early consoles and monitors displayed colors on composite video systems via **luminance (luma),** which is brightness, and **chrominance (chroma),** which doubles for hue and saturation. The **RGB** (red, green, blue) color model became popular in 1987 with the rise of the **Video Graphics Array (VGA)** standard. RGB is an additive color model that combines values of red, green, and blue to create more than 16 million possible colors, with each color having a brightness value ranging from 0 to 255.

Video game characters and environments are designed with a specific **color palette** in mind. Traditional color palettes typically consist of up to five colors within a specific scheme, but this is more of a guideline than a rule. In game design, color palettes can contain any number of colors pertinent to the developer's predefined color scheme (Seitz, 2012). Five sample color schemes include analogous, complementary, achromatic, monochromatic, and custom. **Analogous** palettes include (typically 3) colors that are next to each other on the color wheel, such as red, orange, and yellow (see Figure 2.12). **Complementary** palettes consist of colors opposite to one other on the

FIGURE 2.12 The color wheel is an excellent reference point for selecting color schemes.

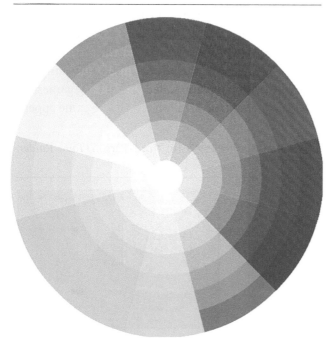

color wheel, like blue and orange. **Achromatic** palettes consist of neutral colors such as black and white, as well as shades of grays, browns, pastels, and other dark colors. **Monochromatic** palettes include different shades or tints of a single color. Finally, palettes that consist of *any* colors are referred to as **custom** color palettes (Seitz, 2012).

Aside from building mood and atmosphere, color is often used in video games to communicate function. **Color identifiers** (also called **glyphs**) are ways of using color to differentiate between complex on-screen objects. Identifiers are commonly used in games to signal which players are part of a particular group, such as placing red markers over players on Team A and blue markers over players on Team B. Another use of color includes **signifiers**, which are used to communicate whether an object or area in the environment can be interacted with and/or how it can be used (Tulleken, 2015). Two blatant examples of signifiers in games include objects with an animated white sheen in *Heavenly Sword* (2007) and red-colored objects in *Mirror's Edge* (2008).

Without light there would be no color, and lighting plays a critical role in modern game development. Like color, lighting can be used as signifiers by illuminating areas and objects of importance to direct the player where to go in complex environments. Just as important as choosing the right color palette, basic lighting decisions should be decided early on—such as whether a game will consist of dramatic, high-contrast lighting or ambient, soft lighting. Other considerations include the intensity of the light (or use of darkness), the light's direction, and whether the lighting will be static or dynamic.

Common lighting models used in video games include **Lambert lighting** and **Phong lighting**. Lambert lighting is among the oldest and is based on the work of Swiss mathematician **Johann Lambert** (1760). "Objects lit in this way are called Lambertian and emit light evenly across all viewing angles. This means that different points on an object will look the same no matter what angle they are viewed from" (Prall, 2012, para. 5). Phong lighting was first proposed by **Bui Tuong Phong** in his dissertation at University of Utah (1973). Phong illumination improved highlights, shading, and reflection of light on objects. This model required an enormous amount of processing power, which led to American computer scientist **Jim Blinn** developing a simplified version in 1977. The updated version was coined the **Blinn–Phong reflection model** and has become "the standard lighting system used today, and is the default method employed by Direct3D, OpenGL, [and] Vulkan" (Evanson, 2020).

Notable lighting effects include **bloom**, which creates a glow around objects that simulates intensely bright light. This effect has been around since before 2000 but became most prevalent during the seventh generation of video games. Intense use of bloom can be found in games such as *Syndicate* (2012) and *BioShock Infinite* (2013). The most talked-about lighting effect in modern gaming is **ray tracing**. Ray tracing is an algorithm that "can trace the path of light, and then simulate the way that the light interacts with the virtual objects it ultimately hits in the computer-generated world." It "allows for dramatically more lifelike shadows and reflections, along with much-improved translucence and scattering" (Thomas, 2019, para. 7–9). Thanks to advancements in GPU capabilities, rendering operations like these allow for lighting effects that make video games more realistic than ever.

■ PERSPECTIVE

Perspective plays an important part in the way a game is played and experienced. In a **first-person** perspective games such as the *Call of Duty* series, the action takes place through the eyes of the player's character. This is the perspective used in **first-person shooter (FPS)** titles, which often requires greater accuracy for shooting and a wider field of view. Seeing through the character's viewpoint in FPS games can be immersive; however, the player is often limited to only seeing the character's hands and arms, but usually little else.

Third-person titles take place *behind* the player's character, where the entire body of the character usually appears on screen. This perspective is popular in action games where player combat and attention to the environment are of equal importance. Third-person games can also be viewed from a closer, over-the-shoulder (OTS) perspective such as in *Resident Evil 4* and *Gears of War*. This is often the case in third-person shooters where shooting is a priority and is not to be confused with second-person games. **Second-person** games include titles where you are viewing the action from afar, but not from directly behind the character like in third-person games. Examples of second-person perspective games include *Double Dragon, Final Fight*, and other "beat 'em up"-style games viewed from more of a side angle.

Isometric games such as *Baldur's Gate* and *Disgaea* take place from a diagonal overhead view. These types of games were made popular by early role-playing games (RPGs) and strategy titles, giving the games a pseudo-3D perspective often referred to as "2.5D." Then there are top-down or overhead games that provide a straight down, aerial view of the action. This perspective has been a popular choice for early generation RPGs, as well as vertical shoot 'em ups like the *Raiden* and *DoDonPachi* series. See Figure 2.13 for examples of common game perspectives.

Isometric and overhead games have their roots in 2D gaming; however, modern variations of these game perspectives often render such graphics using non-fixed angle, 3D polygons for a greater sense of depth. And while first-person and third-person perspective games have their roots in 3D (utilizing the three-dimensional plane called the **Z-axis**), games are only considered true 3D if objects in the game appear

FIGURE 2.13 Common video game perspectives: (a) First-Person (*GoldenEye 007*, 1997), (b) Third–Person (*Tomb Raider*, 1996), and (c) Isometric (*Final Fantasy Tactics Advance*, 2003).

TABLE 2.7 Summary of Video Game Perspective Terms

Perspective	First-Person	Second-Person	Third-Person	Isometric	Top-Down
Dimensions	2D	2.5D	3D	True/S-3D	
Scrolling	Horizontal	Vertical	Diagonal	Multiple	None
Axis	X (left-right)	Y (up-down)	Z (in-out)		
Progression	Forced	Free	Mixed		

Source: (Egenfeldt-Nielsen, Smith, & Tosca, 2012).

to extend beyond the boundaries of the screen, as in stereoscopic 3D video games.

Scrolling is the term used for the direction(s) in which the game plays. Early games such as *Pac-Man* and *Space Invaders* do not scroll at all. Games such as *Super Mario Bros.* that typically scroll from left to right (**X-axis**) are called "side-scrolling" games. Games that scroll vertically and most often upward (**Y-axis**), are called "vertically scrolling" games. Games (including the shoot 'em ups *Zaxxon* and *Viewpoint*) scroll diagonally. Games that move in every direction without constraint are referred to as "free-scrolling" games. Of course, games can also utilize any combination of scrolling methods.

To create a sense of depth in 2D sprite-based games, a common technique for developers was to create separate background (and sometimes foreground) layers in games, which scrolled at different speeds. This is known as **parallax scrolling**, where the furthest background layer scrolls slowest, with each subsequent layer scrolling faster. *Moon Patrol* (1982) is a notable example of an early arcade title that used multiple layers of parallax scrolling. There were also late third-generation games such as *Ninja Gaiden 3* and *Mega Man 6* that used this technique within the software; however, parallax scrolling became most popular during the 16-bit generation. A similar technique to create depth in 2D games is called **line scrolling**. For this effect, numerous horizontal scanlines are scrolled independently at different speeds—such as the floor platforms in *Street Fighter II* (1991) or stage graphics in *Ranger X* (1993).

Beyond the direction in which a game scrolls is the manner in which it encourages the player to progress. Games typically contain two styles of progression. Games with **forced progression** keep the player moving with time limits or forced-scrolling levels like in "endless runner" arcade-style games. Arcade games are more profitable "the more often they're played, so a moving perspective that literally pushes the player forward quickly became the standard"

in these games (Egenfeldt-Nielsen, Smith, & Tosca, 2012, p. 140). In **free progression** games, players can explore and progress through the game at their leisure, without the pressure of a time limit or other constraints. This type of gameplay became more popular as home console technology advanced and could offer more exploration-style games like the *Zelda* and *Tomb Raider* series. See Table 2.7 for a summary of video game perspective terms.

▪ SOUND AND MUSIC

Sound and music play an integral part in the video game experience, setting the mood, conveying emotion, and often providing the motivation to progress forward through a game. In the late 1970s music was stored on physical media such as compact cassettes and phonograph records. These components were expensive and fragile, leading to the development of digital sound where computer chips could change electrical impulses from binary code into analog sound waves. "Some systems could play actual sound recordings while others used **MIDI [Musical Instrument Digital Interface]**-like formats [where the] sound file is simply a series of references to sounds which are then played back by the sound card" (Egenfeldt-Nielsen, Smith, & Tosca, 2012, p. 146). Such early music consumed a lot of memory and so it was usually short and looped or used sparingly at the start of the game or between stages.

Early consoles output **monaural (mono)** sound, which is a single channel of audio. In monaural sound, there is no difference between sound sent to the left speaker or right speaker in a two-speaker setup. Most early household televisions output mono sound because they were manufactured with only one speaker. Even with these technical limitations, there are many early video game jingles that have stood the test of time.

One of the earliest notable melodies in a video game can be credited to Taito's arcade hit *Space Invaders*

(1978). The music consisted of only four looped bass notes, but the pace of the soundtrack would accelerate as the aliens got closer and faster to invading the bottom of the screen—increasing the urgency of the situation (and often the heart rate of the player). As video game technology progressed, composers could program multiple tracks of music in games. Changing musical themes to accommodate the on-screen action was a major part of *Donkey Kong* (1981), which included different melodies for the stage intro, stages, and loss of a life—as well as changing music when Jumpman obtained a hammer or rescued Pauline.

The third generation of video games is where many of the first memorable video game soundtracks were born. The term "chiptune" came to describe the synthesized electronic music of this 8-bit generation. **Pulse-code modulation (PCM)** eventually allowed for the use of sound sampling, such as the percussion sounds in *Super Mario Bros. 3* (1990). This technology led to the sampling of a myriad of instruments to create memorable game soundtracks beginning in the mid-to-late 1980s. Video game composers such as Nobuo Uematsu (*Final Fantasy*), Koji Kondo (*Super Mario Bros., The Legend of Zelda*), and Yuzo Koshiro (*Revenge of Shinobi, ActRaiser, Streets of Rage*) began to receive worldwide acclaim. See Table 2.8 for a sample of gaming's most notable composers.

As the medium progressed, arcade cabinets and home gaming consoles incorporated more and more sound channels. **Stereophonic (stereo)** sound allowed for two separate audio channels. With stereo sound, different sounds could be emitted between two speakers, which provided a sense of directionality when used appropriately. In a video game with stereo sound,

one might hear gunshots from the left speaker when an enemy is firing from the left side of the screen, through both speakers when the enemy is directly ahead, or from the right speaker when an enemy is firing from the right side of the screen. Stereo sound also took game music to the next level. Video game music has now grown to include the same breadth and complexity associated with television and movie soundtracks, allowing for much more creative freedom (Rogers, 2014). Video games have produced such popular music that a separate soundtrack CD is often made available to consumers.

Surround (multichannel) sound would later become available in video games, creating an even richer sound experience—allowing game developers to program sound to appear behind the player for even greater immersion. The leaders in surround sound are **Dolby Laboratories** and **Digital Theater Systems (DTS)**. Surround sound uses between four and eight independent audio channels, which are usually identified with a number. For instance, 5.1 surround means five main channels of sound (front left, front center, front right, back left, and back right), with the .1 occupying a sixth channel for the subwoofer (bass). 6.1 channel surround sound adds a center rear speaker, and 7.1 channel sound (Figure 2.14) adds two additional side speakers. Dolby Labs developed **Dolby Atmos** in 2012, which further improved directionality by projecting sounds onto specific areas of a room. DTS followed with the similar **DTS:X** in 2015.

As game music progressed, so did the use of voice. One of the first arcade games to feature authentic **voice synthesis** was Stern Electronics' *Berzerk* (1980)

TABLE 2.8 Notable Video Game Music Composers

Composer	Game Series Contributions
Harry Gregson-Williams	*Metal Gear Solid* and *Call of Duty* series
Koji Kondo	*Super Mario, Legend of Zelda, Star Fox, Punch-Out!!*
Yuzo Koshiro	*Shinobi, ActRaiser, Streets of Rage*
Yasunori Mitsuda	*Chrono, Xeno, Shadow Hearts*, and *Inazuma Eleven* franchises
Martin O'Donnell	*Myth, Oni, Halo* series, and *Destiny*
Yoko Shimomura	*Kingdom Hearts, Mario & Luigi, Street Fighter II*
Jeremy Soule	*Elder Scrolls, Guild Wars, Total Annihilation, Harry Potter*
Nobuo Uematsu	*Final Fantasy, Chrono Trigger, Blue Dragon, The Last Story*
David Wise	*Wizards & Warriors, Battletoads* series, *Donkey Kong Country* series, *Star Fox Adventures*, and *Viva Piñata: Pocket Paradise*
Michiru Yamane	*Castlevania* series

FIGURE 2.14   7.1 Channel surround sound speaker setup floor plan by Denon.

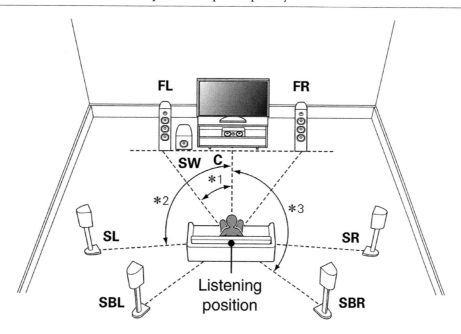

where robots would shout phrases like "Get the humanoid!" and "Intruder alert!" (McDonald, 2004). Mattel's Intellivision was the first to market voice synthesis in a home console with its "Intellivoice" adapter. By adding this side-mounted cartridge to the system, a handful of games could utilize a voice synthesizer to generate audible speech. Until optical media, however, speech in video games was sparse since it consumed a lot of memory. Most early games that featured speech only included short words and phrases. Once this limitation was lifted with CD-ROM and laserdisc, **vocalization** (voice acting for video game characters) became much more conventional. Today, it is common for voice actors to deliver thousands of lines of dialogue in a single video game.

There are dozens of **voice actors** who have made a name for themselves in the video game industry.

Some of gaming's most prolific voice actors (shown in Figure 2.15) include Troy Baker (*BioShock Infinite* and *The Last of Us*), Steve Blum (who holds the Guinness World Record for most appearances in video games), Jennifer Hale (*Mass Effect, Metroid Prime, Metal Gear Solid*, and countless others), Keith David (*Saints Row, Mass Effect, Halo*), and Nolan North (*Assassin's Creed, God of War, Infamous*, and *Uncharted*, among others).

▪ SOUND THEORY

There are two main types of sound in games: **diegetic sound** and **non-diegetic sound**. Diegetic sound comes from *within* the game world and includes both *direct* sounds (guns firing, swords clashing, character dialog) and *ambient* sounds (wind, thunder, whistling birds). Non-diegetic sound takes place *outside* the

FIGURE 2.15   Behind the voices: Faces of five prolific video game voice actors.

Troy Baker   Steve Blum   Jennifer Hale   Keith David   Nolan North

PRO FILE

KEY FACTS:

Pioneer of strategy and simulation games, including the *Civilization* series

Called "The Godfather of Computer Gaming"

SID MEIER

PRO FILE

HISTORY:
- February 24, 1954 in Sarnia, Ontario, Canada

EDUCATION:
- Degree in Computer Science, University of Michigan, 1985

CAREER HIGHLIGHTS:
- Co-founded MicroProse with Bill Stealey in 1982
- Developed 15+ PC games in early 1980s, including flight simulators *Spitfire Ace* (1982) and *F-15 Strike Eagle* (1984)
- Early hits included *Sid Meier's Pirates!* (1987), *Sid Meier's Railroad Tycoon* (1990), and *Sid Meier's Civilization* (1991)
- Co-founder and Director of Creative Development for Firaxis Games since 1996
- Developed a dozen titles for the *Civilization* series

RECOGNITION:
GameSpot's "Most Influential People in Computer Gaming of All Time" (1996), Computer Gaming World's "Most Influential People of All Time in Computer Gaming" (1997), Academy of Interactive Arts and Sciences' Hall of Fame (1999), Computer Museum of America's Hall of Fame (2002) Game Developer's Choice Awards Lifetime Achievement Award (2008), Golden Joystick Awards Life Achievement Award (2017)

TABLE 2.9 Stockburger's Sound Objects

Sound Objects	Definition	Examples in *Civilization IV*
Interface	Sounds heard during set-up or menu options	• Theme song "Baba Yetu" • Music playing while game loads
Speech	Any spoken text	• Narrative by Leonard Nimoy • Phrases spoken by military units
Zone	Sounds that reflect location	• Naturalistic sounds (oceans waves, tree branches falling) • Battle sounds
Effect	Sounds that reflect an action or event	• Sounds accompanying discovering treasure, religion, etc. • Sounds of declaring war or peace
Score	Soundtracks	• Diplomacy themes • Terrain soundtrack

Source: (Donnelly, Gibbons, & Lerner, 2014).

game world, such as mood music and narrative dialog. Scholars such as Karen Collins, Rod Munday, Isabella van Elferen, and Axel Stockburger have deconstructed these sounds "from a theoretical perspective, helping to form vocabularies and modes of investigation that enable discussion of the uses of sound within video games" (Donnelly, Gibbons & Lerner, 2014, p. 168). According to Stockburger, **effect sound** includes sounds that reflect an action or event, such as discovering a treasure, while **zone sound** reflects location, such as sounds in the environment. **Interface music** includes themes heard during game menus or loading screens, while **score** is the background music that plays during the core of the game. See Table 2.9 for Stockburger's sound objects as they apply to the strategy game *Sid Meier's Civilization IV*.

 **DID YOU KNOW?**

Game composers Tommy Tallarico and Jack Wall launched **Video Games Live (VGL)** in 2005. Conducted by Emmanuel Fratianni, video game scores are performed by a live orchestra, along with video game footage, live actors, lighting, and other effects.

■ ACTIVITY: PITCH A GAME

Publishers and developers are always looking for innovative ideas for video games. Do you have a concept for a video game that could revolutionize the industry? Give it a shot!

GUIDELINES

This assignment touches the surface of a full video game proposal, requiring only a pitch and/or logline and a fact sheet. Typically, this would be used to gauge whether there is interest in your idea—which if the case, would be followed by a more detailed proposal called a treatment.

Pitch/logline: In one to two sentences, summarize your game concept as clearly as possible. It often helps to relate it to familiar ideas or existing games; for example, "*Street Fighter* meets *Final Fantasy* in this epic action RPG where random encounters result in real-time 2D battles between one or more opponents."

Fact Sheet: Use the following format to construct your fact sheet with its selling points. Each section should be approximately three sentences.

What:	"What" is the concept and is like the logline.
Why:	"Why" is the purpose; show the game is original and why it will sell.
Who:	"Who" is star(s) of the game. Mention talent or lead voice actors here.
Where:	"Where" is the place of distribution, console(s), and/or online network.
When:	"When" is the production timeline; milestone schedule, release date, etc.
How:	"How" is how it will be funded, developed, and published.

■ CHAPTER 2 QUIZ

1. Acts like the brain of a computer or game console; makes calculations and processes information that tells other components what to do:
   a. CPU
   b. GPU
   c. RAM
   d. ROM

2. Is like the short-term memory of a computer; allowing data to be read, written, and stored—but only temporarily:
   a. CPU
   b. GPU
   c. RAM
   d. ROM

3. The information this device stores communicates with the console or computer system but cannot be altered or forgotten.
   a. CPU
   b. GPU
   c. RAM
   d. ROM

4. A network of connected computers in a small area such as in a home or computer lab:
   a. BIOS
   b. LAN
   c. WAN
   d. Internet

5. Processor speed and TV/monitor refresh rates are measured in:
   a. Bytes (b)
   b. Kilobytes (KB)
   c. Hertz (Hz)
   d. Frames per second (fps)

6. Which of the following is NOT a monitor display type?
   a. CRT
   b. LCD
   c. LED
   d. PCI

7. The baseline frame rate for standard definition video in the United States is:
   a. 15 fps
   b. 24 fps
   c. 25 fps
   d. 30, or 29.97 fps

8. The three analog video formats used around the world include:
   a. NTSC, PAL, and SECAM
   b. NTSC, PAL, and SKYNET
   c. UNLV, PAL, and SECAM
   d. NTSC, PAL, and UNLV

9. What does NTSC stand for?
   a. North To South Coast
   b. National Television Stations Collaboration
   c. National Televisions Standards Committee
   d. National Televised Social Club

10. Which analog television formats use 625 lines at 50 Hz?
    a. PAL & UNLV
    b. PAL & SECAM
    c. SECAM & NTSC
    d. NTSC & UNLV

11. PAL video format has a higher _____ while NTSC has a higher _____:
    a. refresh rate | resolution
    b. frame rate | resolution
    c. refresh rate | frame rate
    d. resolution | frame rate

12. Atari's *Asteroids* (1979) and *Battlezone* (1980) are examples of:
    a. ASCII graphics
    b. Vector graphics
    c. Raster graphics
    d. Polygon graphics

13. These graphics consist of geometric shapes that are "mapped" onto wireframe models to create 3D graphics.
    a. ASCII graphics
    b. Vector graphics
    c. Raster graphics
    d. Polygon graphics

14. Color schemes where the palette's colors are next to each other on the color wheel, such as red, orange, and yellow:
    a. Analogous
    b. Complementary
    c. Achromatic
    d. Monochromatic

15. This lighting effect creates a glow around objects that simulates intensely bright light and is prevalent in games such as *Syndicate* and *Bioshock Infinite*:
    a. Bloom
    b. Luma
    c. Chroma
    d. Ray tracing

16. In this field of view, the player sees through the perspective of character's eyes:
    a. First-person
    b. Second-person
    c. Third-person
    d. Isometric

17. Games such as *Super Mario Bros.* that typically scroll from left to right predominantly utilize the:
    a. X-axis
    b. Y-axis
    c. Z-axis
    d. None of the above

18. What effect gives 2D games a sense of depth by the illusion of a third dimension?
    a. Large sprites
    b. High-resolution pixels
    c. Parallax scrolling
    d. 8-bit sound

19. Early consoles output a single channel of audio where there was no difference between the sound output of a left speaker or right speaker in a two-speaker setup. This kind of audio output is called:
    a. Monaural (mono)
    b. Stereophonic (stereo)
    c. Surround (multichannel)
    d. None of the above

20. According to Stockburger, _____ includes sounds that reflect an action or event, such as discovering a treasure.
    a. effect sound
    b. zone sound
    c. interface music
    d. score

True or False

21. The BIOS wakes up the computer and reminds it what parts it has and what they do.

22. GPU stands for "Gigabyte Polygon Unit."

23. A bit (b) is just an abbreviated word for binary digit.

24. The interlaced scan system paints the entire picture within each field in one pass and provides smoother motion and sharper picture compared to games displayed using progressive scan.

25. LED (light-emitting diode) displays are LCD monitors that are backlit with tiny light-emitting diodes instead of fluorescent tube backlights.

■ FIGURES

Figure 2.1 Motherboards from (a) ColecoVision (1982) and (b) Sega CD 2 (1993). (Evan-Amos—own work, public domain. Available at https://commons.wikimedia.org/w/index.php?curid=34995064. Retrieved from https://commons.wikimedia.org/wiki/File:ColecoVision-Motherboard-Top.jpg#/media/File:ColecoVision-Motherboard-Top.jpg. Game console—Sega CD—motherboard-171-6528C-A, by ZyMOS. Available at http://www.happytrees.org/chips, CC BY-SA 3.0, https://commons.wikimedia.org/w/index.php?curid=9809478. Retrieved from https://commons.wikimedia.org/wiki/

File:Game_console--Sega_CD--motherboard--171-6528C-A.jpg#/media/File: Game_console--Sega_CD--motherboard--171-6528C-A.jpg.)

Figure 2.2 Typical RAM cards (a) and Amic erasable programmable ROM (b). ([a] By Utente: Sassospicco—own work, CC BY-SA 2.5. Available at https://commons.wikimedia.org/w/index.php?curid=860883. Retrieved from https://commons.wikimedia.org/wiki/File:RAM_module_SDRAM_1GiB.jpg. Modified by Wardyga. [b] AMIC EEPROM 512KB 8 bit 32-pin memory chip, removed from a DVD player, by Yanrayaj—own work, public domain. Available at https://commons.wikimedia.org/w/index.php?curid=7389609.)

Figure 2.3 Schematic of a personal computer; note how the CPU must go through the system bus to communicate with the other components. (Courtesy of W Nowicki—own work, based on a diagram, which seems to in turn be based on page 36 of *The Essentials of Computer Organization and Architecture* by Linda Null, Julia Lobur, http://books.google.com/books?id=f83XxoBC_8MC&pg=PA36, CC BY-SA 3.0. Available at https://commons.wikimedia.org/w/index.php?curid=15258936. Simplified diagram of a computer system implemented with a single system bus. This modular organization was popular in the 1970s and 1980s.)

Figure 2.4 AGP (accelerated graphics port) video card (a) and Turtle Beach sound card (b); note how graphics and sound cards contain external ports for connectors. ([a] By Evan-Amos—own work, public domain. Available at https://commons.wikimedia.org/w/index.php?curid=11451358. Retrieved from https://commons.wikimedia.org/wiki/File:AGP-Video-Card.jpg#/media/File:AGP-Video-Card.jpg. [b] By Evan-Amos—own work, public domain. Available at https://commons.wikimedia.org/w/index.php?curid=11960881 Retrieved from https://commons.wikimedia.org/wiki/File:Turtle_Beach_Sound_Card_(Catalina).png#/media/File:Turtle_Beach_Sound_Card_(Catalina).png.)

Figure 2.5 LANs separated by geographic distance connected by a WAN. (Courtesy of Audit3—own work, CC BY-SA 4.0. Available at https://commons.wikimedia.org/w/index.php?curid=49623752. Retrieved from https://commons.wikimedia.org/wiki/File:Lanwan.gif.)

Figure 2.6 Comparing interlaced and progressive scan on a 60-Hz display. (From AnchorBayTech. Editorial: Interlaced vs. Progressive Scan. February 26, 2009. Retrieved from http://www.anchorbaytech.com.)

Figure 2.7 Analog television encoding systems by nation. (By Akomor1—own work; derived from File:BlankMap-World6.svg, public domain. Available at https://commons.wikimedia.org/w/index.php?curid=2314395. Retrieved from https://commons.wikimedia.org/wiki/File:PAL-NTSC-SECAM.svg#/media/File:PAL-NTSC-SECAM.svg.)

Figure 2.8 Screenshots of (a) *Spacewar!* (ASCII GFX) and (b) *Battlezone* (vector GFX). (Courtesy of Wardyga.)

Figure 2.9 Screenshots of (a) *Super Mario Bros.* (raster GFX) and *Super Mario 64* (polygons). (*Super Mario Bros.* courtesy of Nintendo, 1985; *Super Mario 64* courtesy of Nintendo, 1996.)

Figure 2.10 Texture mapping a checkerboard image onto a wireframe face. (From Saboret, L., Alliez, P., & Lévy, B., 2013. Planar parameterization of triangulated surface meshes. Retrieved from http://doc.cgal.org/latest/Surface_mesh_parameterization/index.html.)

Figure 2.11 Shader examples from the built-in Unity Shaders Matrix (Unity, 2010). (Materials and shaders, from Documentation Unity3D, by the Unity Team on September 16, 2010. Retrieved from http://unity.ogf.su/Documentation/Manual/Materials.html.)

Figure 2.12 The color wheel is an excellent reference point for selecting color schemes. (OpenClipart (2020, January 4). Public domain (CC). SVG ID: 113677 "Color Wheel (12 × 7)." Retrieved from https://freesvg.org/1395532509.)

Figure 2.13 Common video game perspectives: (a) First-Person (*GoldenEye 007,* 1997), (b) Third–Person (*Tomb Raider,* 1996), and (c) Isometric (*Final Fantasy Tactics Advance,* 2003). (a) *GoldenEye 007* (Rare, 1997), (b) *Tomb Raider* (Core Design, 1996), and (c) *Final Fantasy Tactics Advance* (Square Product Development Division 4, 2003).

Figure 2.14 7.1 Channel surround sound speaker setup floor plan by Denon. (Courtesy of Denon. Editorial: Speaker installation, 2014. D&M Holdings Inc. Retrieved from http://manuals.denon.com/avrx4100w/na/EN/GFNFSYawzxoxsr.php.)

Figure 2.15 Behind the voices: Faces of five prolific video game voice actors. (Headshots of Troy Baker, http://www.behindthevoiceactors.com/troy-baker/; Steve Blum, http://www.behindthevoiceactors.com/steve-blum/; Jennifer Hale, http://www.behindthevoiceactors.com/jennifer-hale/; Keith David, http://www.behindthevoiceactors.com/keith-david/; and Nolan North, http://www.behindthevoiceactors.com/nolan-north/.)

■ REFERENCES

Amas, A. (2013, February 3). *Wii U: The power of the fox.* Retrieved from http://wiiuconcepts.blogspot.com/.

Beal, V. (2009, August 28). *All about monitors: CRT vs. LCD.* Retrieved from http://www.webopedia.com/DidYouKnow/Hardware_Software/all_about_monitors.asp.

Briere, D., & Hurley, P. (2008, November 17). Interlaced vs. progressive scanning methods. *Home theater for dummies* (3rd ed). Hoboken, NJ: Wiley Publishing, Inc. Retrieved from http://www.dummies.com/how-to/content/interlaced-vs-progressive-scanning-methods.html.

Cisco Networking Academy. (2013, December 19). *Exploring the modern computer network: types, functions, and hardware.* Retrieved from http://www.ciscopress.com/articles/article.asp?p=2158215&seqNum=6.

Crane, K. (2016). *Home A/V connections glossary.* Retrieved from https://www.crutchfield.com/S-b7lDiytxYTv/learn/learningcenter/home/connections_glossary.html.

Donnelly, K., Gibbons, W., & Lerner, N. (2014, February 27). *Music in video games: Studying play.* New York, NY: Routledge.

Editorial: PlayStation proreview: Ridge Racer. (1995, March). *GamePro*, p. 68.

Egenfeldt-Nielsen, S., Smith, J., & Tosca, S. (2012, July 28). *Understanding video games: The essential introduction* (2nd ed). New York, NY: Routledge.

Emigh, J. (2009, December 16). HDTVs: Are more 'hertz' worth more money? *PCWorld.* Retrieved from http://www.networkworld.com/article/2239424/hdtvs—are-more—hertz—worth-more-money-.html.

Encyclopædia Britannica. (2016). Raster graphics. *Encyclopædia Britannica.* Retrieved from http://www.britannica.com/topic/raster-graphics.

Evanson, N. (2020, April 27). *How 3D game rendering works: Lighting and shadows.* Retrieved from https://www.techspot.com/article/1998-how-to-3d-rendering-lighting-shadows/.

Hergaarden, M. (2011, January). *Graphics shaders.* VU Amsterdam. Retrieved from http://www.m2h.nl/files/LiteraturestudyShaders.pdf.

Khan, J. (2013, June 9). *Types of monitors.* Retrieved from http://www.byte-notes.com/types-monitors.

Laughlin, A. (2016). *LED vs LCD vs plasma TV.* Retrieved from http://www.which.co.uk/reviews/televisions/article/led-vs-lcd-vs-plasma-tv.

Le Grange, L. (2015, April 8). *What are the parts found in a game console? What are their functions?* Retrieved from https://www.quora.com/What-are-the-parts-found-in-a-game-console-What-are-their-functions.

McDonald, G. (2004, March 29). *A history of video game music.* Retrieved from http://www.gamespot.com/articles/a-history-of-video-game-music/1100-6092391/.

Milos. (2013). *USB 2.0 and 3.0 connectors.* (By Milos.bmx, CC BY-SA 3.0). Retrieved from https://commons.wikimedia.org/w/index.php?curid=30414864.

Niridya, J. (2022). *USB Type-C icon.* (By Niridya—Own work based on: USB Type-C.svg by Pietz, CC0). Retrieved from https://commons.wikimedia.org/w/index.php?curid=74081486.

Prall, C. (2012, December 4). *Introduction to lighting in games.* Retrieved from http://buildnewgames.com/lighting/.

Rieman, J. (1996, September). *Binary numbers.* Retrieved from http://l3d.cs.colorado.edu/courses/CSCI1200-96/binary.html.

Rogers, S. (2014, April 16). *Level up! The guide to great video game design.* Chichester, West Sussex, UK: John Wiley & Sons Ltd.

Silva, R. (2016, January 09). *Video frame rate vs. screen refresh rate: Understanding video frame rates and screen refresh rates.* Retrieved from http://hometheater.about.com/od/televisionbasics/qt/framevsrefresh.htm.

Thomas, J. (2019, August 20). *What is ray tracing? The games, the graphics cards and everything else you need to know.* Retrieved from https://www.techradar.com/news/ray-tracing.

Tulleken, H. (2015, July 29). *Color in games: An in-depth look at one of game design's most useful tools.* Retrieved from https://www.gamedeveloper.com/design/color-in-games-an-in-depth-look-at-one-of-game-design-s-most-useful-tools.

Welch, C. (2002a). *Computer connections: Lesson 2 – inner hardware.* Retrieved from http://www.mpsaz.org/academy/staff/kmprocopio/class_21/class_21/files/computer-connections-lesson-2-hardware-on-the-inside.pdf.

Welch, C. (2002b). *Computer connections: Lesson 3 – bits and bytes.* Retrieved from http://www.mpsaz.org/academy/staff/kmprocopio/class1/class-20/files/computer-connections-lesson-3-bits-and-bytes.pdf.

The Atari Generation

■ OBJECTIVES

After reading this chapter, you should be able to:

- Discuss the "Golden Age" of the arcade and key arcade titles.
- Describe the climate of video games in homes during this time.
- Review key people behind the video games and consoles.
- Provide a brief overview of the history of Mattel.
- Identify graphics and gameplay capabilities of second-generation video game consoles.
- Compare the technological differences among second-generation systems.
- Discuss the innovations and failures of the Microvision handheld.
- List key video game titles for each second-generation console.
- Illustrate how Atari dominated the second-generation market.
- Explain the reasons for the North American video game crash of 1983.
- List important innovations brought to gaming during this time.
- Summarize second-generation market sales, breakthroughs, and trends.

DOI: 10.1201/9781003315759-3

■ KEY TERMS AND PEOPLE

360-degree joystick
ANTIC
Minoru Arakawa
Asteroids
Atari 2600 (VCS)
Atari 5200
Automatic switchbox
Don Bluth
Ron Bradford
Eric Bromley
Bus
Nolan Bushnell
Chuck E. Cheese
ColecoVision
Color palette
Colors on screen
Computer-controlled opponent (AI)
Console war
Controller ports
Don Daglow
Digital data pack
Directional disk
Donkey Kong
Rick Dyer
E.T. the Extra-Terrestrial

Easter Egg
Expansion modules
Fairchild Channel F (VES)
Fairchild Semiconductor
Galaxian
Manny Gerard
GTIA
Elliot Handler
Home port
Intel 8021
Intellivision
Intellivision II
Intellivoice
INTV Corporation
Toru Iwatani
Joystick
Ray Kassar
Michael Katz
Keyboard component
Steve Lehner
Ed Logg
Master Strategy Series
Harold Matson
Mattel
Microvision
Midway

Milton Bradley (MB)
Jay Miner
Shigeru Miyamoto
MOS Technology
Namco
NEC
Nintendo
Tomohiro Nishikado
Numeric keypad
Odyssey[2]
Overlays
Pac-Man
Philips
George Plimpton
POKEY
Lyle Rains
Radar Scope
RAM
RCA Studio II
RF switch
Warren Robinett
Roller controller
ROM
Steve Ross
SALLY
Kazunori Sawano

Sears Super Video Arcade
Sears Video Arcade
Mario Segale
Shovelware
Jay Smith
Sound channels
Space Invaders
Super Action Controller Set
Taito
TandyVision
Tele-Games
Texas Instruments
Texas Instruments TMS1100
TIA
Trak-Ball controller
Terrence Valeski
Vectrex
Video game crash
Videocarts
The VoiceWarner Communications
Howard S. Warshaw
Yars' Revenge
Gunpei Yokoi

■ CONSOLE TIMELINE

Atari VCS	Odyssey[2]	Intellivision	ColecoVision	Atari 5200
1977	**1979**	**1980**	**1982**	**1982**

■ THE GOLDEN AGE

The Golden Age of the arcades began with the popularity of **Taito**'s *Space Invaders* (1978) (Figure 3.1a) and lasted into 1983, when the market crashed in North America. Part of *Space Invaders'* success was from the world's craze over *Star Wars*, which designer **Tomohiro Nishikado** mentioned to be an influence for the game's theme (Game Informer, 2008, p. 108). The arcade game was known for its four notes of looped music, which sped up as the aliens descended closer to the earth (and the player). It also advanced the concept of a high score, which encouraged gamers to survive for as long as possible. The game's success led to dedicated establishments known as "inbeedaa hausu" (invader houses) across Japan (Ashcraft, 2018).

Atari responded with their hit shooter *Asteroids* (1979) by **Lyle Rains** and **Ed Logg**. Soon there would be an explosion of arcade venues in the West such as Nolan Bushnell's **Chuck E. Cheese's** franchise. Bowling alleys and department store rooftops in Japan became popular video arcade scenes, opening a window of creativity for game publishers. One such publisher, **Namco** (Nakamura Amusement Machine Manufacturing Company) found early global success as a distribution partner with **Atari** and **Midway**. Their hit shooter *Galaxian* (1979) (Figure 3.1b) expanded upon *Space Invaders* with true color graphics and other gameplay enhancements.

A year later, Namco released *Pac-Man* (Figure 3.1c) in 1980. *Pac-Man* became the video game industry's first mascot—a pop culture icon that spawned an animated TV series and a hit music single by Buckner & Garcia called "Pac-Man Fever," among countless ancillary items. *Pac-Man* creator **Toru Iwatani** was successful in his goal to reach the female audience (Purchese, 2010), helping the title become the highest-grossing arcade game of all time. Other hits released in 1980 included Atari's *Missile Command* and *Battlezone*, along with *Berzerk* by Stern Electronics. See Table 3.1 for notable games from each year during the Golden Age.

After *Pac-Man* took the world by storm, **Nintendo** found itself in a fiscal crisis with the commercial failure of its arcade game **Radar Scope** (1980) in North America. With 3,000 units shipped, 2,000 were sitting unsold in its U.S. warehouse. Nintendo president Hiroshi Yamauchi gave visionary **Shigeru Miyamoto** the task of creating a new game that could be installed in the *Radar Scope* cabinets with a conversion kit (Kent, 2001, pp. 157–160). Miyamoto's creation became his first arcade hit with **Donkey Kong** (Figure 3.1d) in 1981. Overseen by Nintendo chief engineer **Gunpei Yokoi**, Miyamoto's *Donkey Kong* pioneered the **platform game** genre, was one of the first to have a substantial narrative, and even provided a sense of humor (Latson, 2015, para. 2). It was the first title to feature Nintendo's iconic Mario character (known then as "Jumpman") and put Miyamoto on course to become arguably the most innovative video game designer of all time. Other hits in 1981 included Namco/Bally-Midway's *Ms. Pac-Man*, Williams Electronics' *Defender*, Konami/Sega's *Frogger*, as well as Atari's *Tempest* and *Centipede*.

FIGURE 3.1 Screenshots of defining arcade games from the Golden Age: (a) *Space Invaders* (1978), (b) *Galaxian* (1979), (c) *Pac-Man* (1980), and (d) *Donkey Kong* (1981).

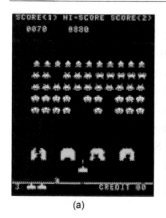 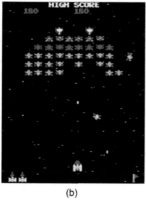 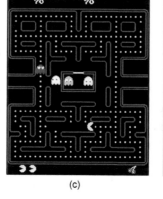 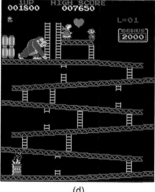

(a) (b) (c) (d)

TABLE 3.1 A Sampling of the Top Arcade Games from the Golden Age by Year

Year	Title	Designer	Publisher	Notes
1978	*Space Invaders*	Tomohiro Nishikado	Taito	Launched the Golden Age of the Arcades
1979	*Galaxian*	Kazunori Sawano	Namco/Midway	Progressed the use of color graphics
1980	*Pac-Man*	Toru Iwatani	Namco/Midway	Highest-grossing arcade game
1981	*Donkey Kong*	Shigeru Miyamoto	Nintendo	Narrative, platformer, Mario's first appearance
1982	*Pole Position*	Toru Iwatani	Namco/Atari	Advanced the arcade racing genre
1983	*Dragon's Lair*	Don Bluth/Rick Dyer	Cinematronics	Popularized LaserDisc games

North American revenue from arcade video game cabinets grew tremendously during this time, from $50 million sales in 1978 to $7 billion in 1981 (Wolf, 2007, p. 105). The Golden Age of arcade games continued through 1982 with chart toppers such as Taito's *Jungle Hunt*, Nintendo's *Popeye*, Gottlieb's *Q*Bert*, Williams Electronics' *Robotron: 2084*, along with Namco's *Pole Position* and *Dig Dug*. A 1982 *Play Magazine* study estimated there to be 24,000 full arcade venues and 400,000 street locations where video games could be found in America—consisting of more than 1.5 million arcade machines (Kent, 2001, p. 152). Game cabinets could be found everywhere—from restaurants and supermarkets to gas stations, and even in doctors' offices. In 1982 the arcade industry grossed $8 billion in the United States alone.

> ### ⌁ DID YOU KNOW?
>
> Jumpman was renamed "Mario" by Nintendo President **Minoru Arakawa** after an intense argument with Nintendo of America's warehouse landlord **Mario Segale** over unpaid rent money (Kent, 2001, p. 159).

■ THE SECOND GENERATION

With the arcade industry booming, more companies took interest in producing video game systems for the home market. There were over a dozen home consoles released during the late 1970s and early 1980s—an era that would later be coined as "the second generation." For most who experienced this time however, it was more aptly remembered as the Atari generation. Atari dominated the market by such a wide margin, the average consumer would only become familiar with a handful of the many consoles released. This chapter focuses primarily on the five systems that sold 1 million units or more.

The system that launched the second generation was the **Fairchild Channel F** in November of 1976. Released by **Fairchild Semiconductor** for $169.95, the Channel F is notable for being the first game console with programmable ROM cartridges (called "**video-carts**"). It was also the first home video game system to use a microprocessor. Only around 26 games were developed for the system and approximately 250,000 units were sold during its first year. Two months later, **RCA** released its **Studio II**. The system lacked color support and did not even have control paddles as games were controlled with its numeric keypads. Only about a dozen games were made for Studio II and it was discontinued in 1978.

■ ATARI VCS (2600)

Knowing that Atari needed a successor to its home Pong system to remain competitive in the home video game market, **Nolan Bushnell** consulted his Grass Valley team to design a microprocessor built off the **MOS Technology 6502** (Kent, 2001, p. 99). The result was a lower-costing 6507 custom chip named "**Stella**," coupled with a display and sound chip called the **Television Interface Adaptor (TIA)** by **Jay Miner**. To raise enough money to manufacture and market the console, Bushnell sold Atari to media publisher **Warner Communications** for $28 million and was allowed to remain on board as chairman. With Warner's funding, the **Atari Video Computer System (VCS)** (Figure 3.2) launched for $199 on September 11, 1977.

The system landed on most store shelves by mid-October. It came bundled with two controllers and the

FIGURE 3.2 Atari VCS, often called "The Atari" with standard, digital joystick controller.

game cartridge *Combat* among its nine launch titles (Table 3.2). A rebranded version of the VCS called the **Sears Video Arcade** was sold exclusively through Sears, Roebuck & Company stores. Sears also rebranded the Atari games they sold, changing the wording from "Game Program" to the Sears "**Tele-Games**" label.

The VCS introduced many innovations to the home video game market. In addition to the traditional **paddle controllers,** the Atari VCS came with a digital "**joystick**" controller, which was better suited for multidirectional games. It also came with built-in switches for selecting game variations and difficulty, as well as a toggle switch for black-and-white or color displays. Another breakthrough for the system was that games included a **computer-controlled opponent,** rather than the standard two-player or asymmetric challenges of previous console games (Monfort & Bogost, 2014, p. 5).

One aspect that began to change at Atari under Warner Communications was the laid back, unconventional ways Nolan Bushnell had originally run the operation. Programmers were used to coming to

work late, staying late, and partying hard. "Bushnell encouraged their laid-back attitude and had no problem with them partying after, and sometimes during, work hours" (Kent, 2001, p. 180). Owner **Steve Ross** and Co-Chief Operating Officer **Manny Gerard** often found themselves at odds with Bushnell, who proposed to discontinue the VCS in favor of newer technology in 1978.

In February of that year, Warner hired executive vice president of Burlington Industries **Ray Kassar** to oversee the consumer division of Atari. A Harvard graduate and East Coast businessman, Kassar was the exact opposite of Bushnell. While Bushnell wanted to discontinue the VCS, Kassar wanted to position the system as Atari's #1 product heading into the 1978 holiday season. Further conflict between Bushnell and Warner ensued until that November when Bushnell was forced to resign and Kassar became Atari's CEO. Bushnell bought back the rights to his Chuck E. Cheese's restaurant, which became the most successful family arcade chain in the United States.

Kassar admittedly knew nothing about video games and approached the business more from a marketing perspective. His high-society lifestyle also clashed with game designers, who often felt underappreciated by him. Despite these conflicts, Kassar achieved what he set out to do and Atari VCS sales eventually skyrocketed. "The year before Kassar became CEO, Atari had $75 million in sales. Under Kassar, Atari became the

TABLE 3.2 Atari Video Computer System U.S. Launch Titles

• *Air-Sea Battle* (Figure 3.3a)	• *Star Ship*
• *Basic Math*	• *Street Racer*
• *Blackjack*	• *Surround*
• *Combat* (Figure 3.3b)	• *Video Olympics*
• *Indy 500*	

PRO FILE

KEY FACTS:

Made first coin-operated arcade video game *Computer Space*

Popularized video games with *Pong* and Atari VCS

NOLAN BUSHNELL

PRO FILE

HISTORY:
• Born: February 5, 1943 in Clearfield, Utah

EDUCATION:
• University of Utah College of Engineering, B.S. in Electrical Engineering (1968), Stanford University Graduate School

CAREER HIGHLIGHTS:
• Formed Syzygy in 1969 to release the first coin-op video game *Computer Space* with Ted Dabney
• CEO and founder of Atari, Inc. with Ted Dabney in 1972
• Hired engineer Al Alcorn to develop *Pong* (1972), the first successful coin-operated video game
• Pioneered Pizza Time Theatre in 1977, which became the popular Chuck E. Cheese's children's arcade chain

RECOGNITION:
ASI Man of the Year (1997), CEA Hall of Fame (2000), Sony Ent. Metreon Lifetime Achievement (2005), British AFTA Fellowship Award (2009), Int'l Video Game Hall of Fame (2010), German Lara of Honor, Lifetime Achievement Award (2010), Newsweek "50 Men That Changed America"

FIGURE 3.3 Screenshots from Atari VCS launch titles (a) *Air-Sea Battle* and (b) *Combat.*

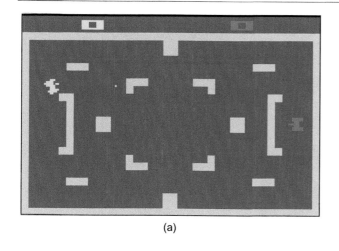

(a)

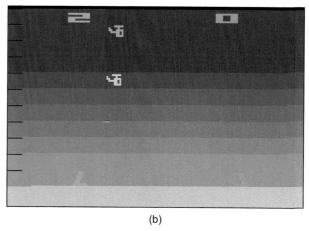

(b)

fastest-growing company in the history of the United States [for its time], as the company's sales exceeded $2 billion within three years" (Kent, 2001, p. 185).

Success did not come without its losses. Kassar's underappreciation of game designers led to several key programmers leaving Atari. One example included a group of Atari's top designers who parted ways with the company after unsuccessful contract negotiations. After leaving the company, programmers David Crane, Alan Miller, Bob Whitehead, and eventually Larry Kaplan formed the first independent developer and distributor of console video games in April of 1980—**Activision**. Activision went on to produce among the console's best titles and eventually became one of the top video game publishers in the world.

💡 DID YOU KNOW?

Designer Howard Scott Warshaw named his 1981 VCS game *Yars' Revenge* after Ray Kassar by reversing the letters of his first name. "Yar"="Ray," that is, "Ray's Revenge" (Campbell, 2015, p. 4). Was this revenge on Activision or just an inside joke?

▪ CONSOLE COMPARISON

The Atari VCS was light years ahead of other systems on the market at the time of its release. While most earlier consoles lacked TV sound output or could only display a monochromatic image, the VCS contained a **2-channel sound chip** and could display multiple colors on screen (Table 3.3). One notable competitor

TABLE 3.3 Atari Video Computer System Tech Specs

Manufacturer:	Atari
Launch price:	$199.95
Release date:	October 1977 (US), 1978 (EU), 1983 (JP)
Format:	Cartridge
CPU:	8-bit MOS Technology 6507 processor (1.19 MHz)
Memory:	128 bytes RAM & 4 KB ROM
Resolution:	160 × 192 pixels
Colors:	4 on-screen; palette of 128 (104 on PAL, 8 on SECAM)
Sound:	2-channel mono

for the VCS early on was the Fairchild Channel F. The Channel F's 1.79 MHz processor ran faster than Atari's **1.19 MHz 6507 processor;** however, Atari's console displayed a higher resolution of **160 × 192 pixels** compared to the Channel F's resolution of 128 × 64.

The VCS had twice the amount of memory with **128 bytes of RAM** (random access memory) and **4 kB ROM** (read-only memory), compared to Channel F's 64 bytes of main RAM and 2 kB of VRAM (video RAM). While both systems were limited to only **four colors per scan line**, Atari had a much larger color palette to choose from—up to **128 colors** compared to just eight colors on the Channel F. Sound was still primitive at this time, but overall, the audio from the VCS was much more capable and diverse compared to the beeps and crackles from the Channel F.

The Channel F controller looked like a handgrip with a triangular, eight-way directional cap that tripled

FIGURE 3.4 Magazine advertisement for the Atari Video Computer System in 1981.

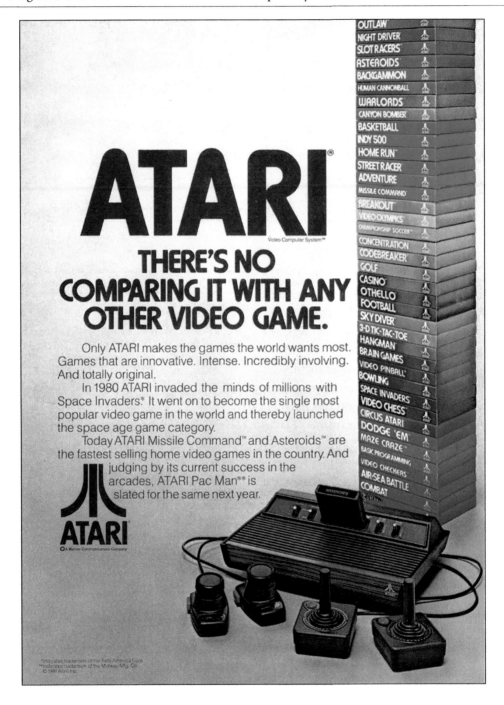

as a joystick, twistable paddle, and button that could be pushed up and down. It was highly innovative but a bit too complex for its time. The Atari joystick was much simpler, consisting of a stick, button, and a base. Since dial controller games were still popular during this time, the VCS could also play certain games with its paddle controllers, as seen in Figure 3.4.

HEAD-TO-HEAD

To compare the graphics and sound between the Atari VCS and Fairchild Channel F, play similar games from each console (or watch video clips of them). Games to compare include *Desert Fox* (Channel F) versus *Combat* (VCS), *Spitfire* (Channel F) versus *Time Pilot* (VCS), and *Pinball Challenge* (Channel F) versus *Breakout* (VCS).

FIGURE 3.5 Box art to five of the best VCS titles including (a) *Adventure*, (b) *Space Invaders*, (c) *River Raid*, (d) *Yars' Revenge*, and (e) *Pitfall II: Lost Caverns*.

(a)　　　　　(b)　　　　　(c)　　　　　(d)　　　　　(e)

■ KEY ATARI VCS TITLES

More than 400 titles were released for the Atari VCS. One of the moves that helped Atari secure its stronghold on the home video game market was when Gerard and Kassar negotiated a deal with arcade rivals Taito and Midway to develop a home port (conversion) of *Space Invaders* (1980) for the VCS (Figure 3.5b). The success of *Space Invaders* (1980) led to Atari licensing other popular arcade hits for its home console, which proved to be a winning formula with consumers (Maher, 2012, para. 2). Other arcade hits seen included *Asteroids, Warlords, Missile Command,* and *Breakout*.

One of the system's notable titles was *Adventure* (1979) by **Warren Robinett**. Adventure was the system's first open world, action-adventure-style game and is often credited as the first video game to include an **Easter egg**—a secret room containing text that credited Robinett for the game's creation. Among the best action-adventure games for the VCS were Activision's *Pitfall!* (1982) and *H.E.R.O.* (1984), as well as *Montezuma's Revenge: Featuring Panama Joe* (1984) by Parker Brothers.

Two titles notorious for their failure included Atari's *Pac-Man* and *E.T. the Extra-Terrestrial*, both released in 1982. *Pac-Man* was a disastrous part of the arcade classic. The maze layout was nothing like the arcade, the ghosts flickered and lacked the original game's vivid colors, the sounds were annoying, and Pac-Man controlled terribly. This highly anticipated arcade port was the best-selling VCS game of all time with more than 7 million units sold but ultimately disappointed serious gamers.

Later that year Atari struck a deal with Steven Spielberg to produce a game based on the hit movie *E.T.* Best-selling game designer **Howard Scott Warshaw** (*Yars' Revenge, Raiders of the Lost Ark*) was given the daunting task of completing the game in under 6 weeks to market the game in time for the holidays (Kent, 2001, p. 238). The game was completed on schedule but ended up being a complete market failure. According to Kassar, about 3.5 million of the 4 million games produced were sent back to Atari as unsold inventory or customer returns (Bruck, 1995, pp. 179–180). Atari infamously buried the unsold games in a New Mexico landfill.

■ MAGNAVOX ODYSSEY²

To remain relevant in the industry it helped to create, Magnavox released the **Odyssey²** (Figure 3.6) in the United States in February of 1979 for $179. The system was released in Europe as the Philips Videopac G7000 (among other names) and in Brazil as the Philips Odyssey. With home computers beginning to gain popularity around this time, Magnavox chose to market the Odyssey² as more of a home computer system with marketing phrases such as "The Ultimate Computer Video Game System" and "A Serious Educational Tool." To expand upon this image, the Odyssey² came with a full, 49-key membrane computer keyboard and released a programming cartridge called *Computer Intro!*. Eleven other cartridges were available at launch, five of which contained more than one game as seen in Table 3.4.

The original build of the system came with joysticks that could be plugged and unplugged from the back of the unit. There were also models manufactured with controllers hardwired into the rear of the unit. The console's biggest strength may have been its speech

FIGURE 3.6 Magnavox Odyssey² with built-in membrane keyboard and updated joysticks.

TABLE 3.4 Magnavox Odyssey² U.S. Launch Titles

- *Armored Encounter/Sub Chase!*
- *Baseball!*
- *Bowling!/Basketball!*
- *Computer Golf!*
- *Cosmic Conflict!*
- *Football!* (Figure 3.7a)
- *Las Vegas Blackjack!*
- *Matchmaker!/Buzzword!/ Logix!*
- *Math-a-Magic!/Echo!*
- *Speedway!* (Figure 3.7b)/ *Spin-Out!/Crypto-Logic!*
- *Take the Money and Run!*

synthesis unit called "**The Voice**," released in the United States in 1982. This add-on peripheral plugged into the top of the system added speech, music, and sound effects enhancement for certain games. Phrases such as "Ouch! Help!" could be heard in *Smithereens* and "You blew it!" in *P.T. Barnum's Acrobats* (Cassidy, 2008, p. 16).

Another achievement the Odyssey² should be remembered for was pioneering the fusion between board games and video games with its **Master Strategy trilogy**. These games included *The Quest for the Rings* (1981), *Conquest of the World* (1981), and *The Great Wall Street Fortune Hunt* (1982). Each title was packed with extended memory, a tabletop game board, and various accessories. The games played like *Dungeons & Dragons* and followed a storyline reminiscent of J. R. R. Tolkien's *The Lord of the Rings*.

Most of the Odyssey²'s first party games were designed and packaged by **Ron Bradford** and **Steve Lehner**. A lot of these titles were clones of other more popular games. For instance, *Armored Encounter!* (1978) looked and played just like *Combat* on Atari. *Alien Invaders—Plus!* (1980) was a blatant clone of

Space Invaders; and *K.C. Munchkin!* (1981) led to a lawsuit from Atari because of its similarities to *Pac-Man*. While the Atari VCS did not start off with independent or third-party developers, it was the support of companies like Activision, Imagic, and Parker Brothers that helped the VCS dominate the second generation with an extensive library of games. Parker Brothers and Imagic eventually released titles for the Odyssey², although many of these games never made it to American shores.

▪ CONSOLE COMPARISON: ODYSSEY² VS. ATARI VCS

Like the Fairchild Channel F, the Odyssey²'s **1.79 MHz** processor ran faster than the VCS's 1.19 MHz 6507 processor (Table 3.5). It also could display a marginally higher resolution at **160 × 200 pixels**, compared to 160 × 192 pixels on Atari's console. On the other hand, its **64 bytes** internal **RAM**, coupled with **128 bytes** of **audio/video RAM** could not compete with processing power of Atari's 128 bytes of RAM and 4 kB of ROM. The Odyssey²'s single channel of sound was less capable than Atari's 2-channel sound chip; however, the games often sounded similar on both systems. The Voice gave the Odyssey² an edge in sound but that was an add-on peripheral.

Furthermore, the Odyssey² had a limited ability to generate graphics because it was challenging for the system to produce custom sprite graphics on the fly. The

FIGURE 3.7 Screenshots from Odyssey² U.S. launch titles (a) *Football!* and (b) *Speedway.*

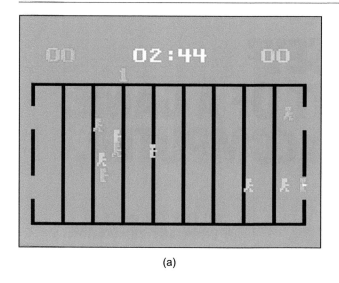

(a)

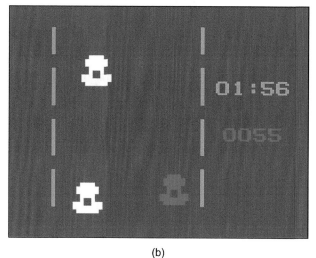

(b)

hardware was designed with a set of **64 built-in characters,** which could be used freely by the programmers, so "most Odyssey² games—particularly the early titles— utilize the built-in character set, giving the games a similar appearance" (Cassidy, 2008, p. 9). Another reason for similar-looking games was a limited color palette of **16 colors**. While this paled in comparison to Atari's 128 color palette, the Odyssey² was capable of **eight on-screen colors** without using software tricks.

As for the controller, the Odyssey² control stick was shaped like the Atari VCS joystick, with a single red action button in the top left corner. The Odyssey² button was square, sat flush, and pushed into the controller, while the round button on the VCS was raised and a bit more accessible. The Odyssey² stick was much more flexible compared to the stiffer VCS joystick. It was comfortable enough to control with a single thumb; however, it was also easy for the stick to get stuck in one of the eight-point slots that surrounded it.

TABLE 3.5 Magnavox Odyssey² Tech Specs

Manufacturer:	Magnavox/Philips
Launch price:	$179.99
Release date:	Dec. 1978 (EU), Feb. 1979 (US), Sep. 1982 (JP)
Format:	Cartridge
CPU:	8-bit Intel 8048 processor (1.79 MHz)
Memory:	64 bytes RAM & 128 bytes Audio/Video RAM
Resolution:	160 × 200 pixels
Colors:	8 colors from a palette of 16
Sound:	1-channel mono

HEAD-TO-HEAD

To compare the graphics and sound between the Odyssey² and Atari VCS, check out similar games released on each console (or watch video clips of them). Popular games for comparison include *Atlantis, Blockout* (Odyssey²) versus *Breakout* (VCS), *Demon Attack, Frogger, Popeye, Q*Bert,* and *Super Cobra*.

▪ KEY MAGNAVOX ODYSSEY² TITLES

Only "49 cartridges were released in the United States during Odyssey²'s initial production run. Some cartridges contained more than one game, so the total number of distinct, original U.S. games is closer to 60" (Cassidy, 2008, p. 9). There were also quite a few games that released exclusively in Europe and Brazil, such as *Air Battle, Chinese Logic, Depth Charge/Marksman, Frogger, Labyrinth Game/Supermind, Loony Balloon, Morse, The Mousing Cat, Neutron Star, Popeye, Q*bert, Secret of the Pharaohs,* and *Super Cobra,* among others. Most game titles released by Philips/Magnavox in the United States ended with an exclamation point (!) to attract attention.

Many of the top titles for the Odyssey² were released late in the system's lifespan, between 1981 and 1983. *The Quest for the Rings!* (1981) was reminiscent of the original Odyssey days with its interplay between screen and board game. In addition to the "Master Strategy" game cartridge, the box included a game board (shown in Figure 3.8), dozens of various tokens,

FIGURE 3.8 Magazine advertisement for the Magnavox Odyssey² from 1981 showing *The Quest for the Rings* title on the TV screen and its unique game board below the console.

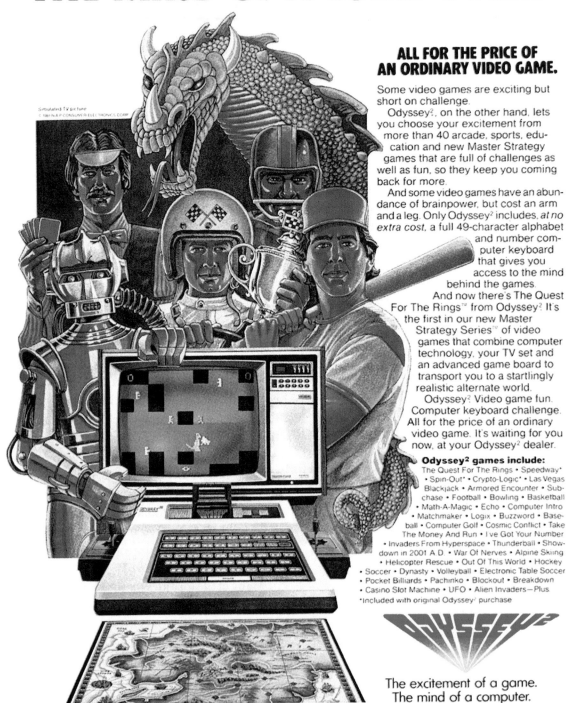

FIGURE 3.9 Box art to five defining Odyssey² titles including (a) *Killer Bees!* (b) *K.C. Munchkin!* (c) *K.C.'s Krazy Chase!* (d) *Pick Axe Pete!* and (e) *Turtles*.

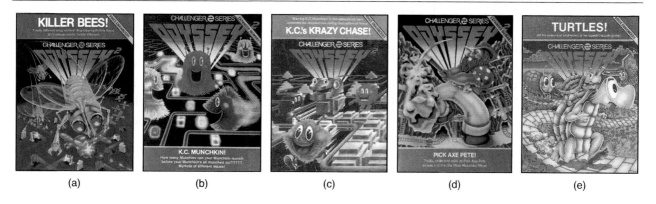

(a) (b) (c) (d) (e)

and a keyboard overlay for the console that utilized the membrane keyboard. The game was named "Most Innovative Game of 1981" by Electronic Games magazine. Popular multiplatform titles worth checking out include *Atlantis* (1982), *Frogger* (1982), *Q*Bert* (1983), and *Turtles!* (1983). Although not all entirely original, the Odyssey² did have a number of fun exclusives, including *K.C. Munchkin!* (1981), *K.C.'s Krazy Chase!* (1982) seen in Figure 3.9, *Pick Axe Pete!* (1982), and *Killer Bees!* (1983).

☀ DID YOU KNOW?

In Europe, Odyssey² "Videopac" games released by Philips contained a number that preceded each game title (such as *5. Blackjack* and *10. Golf*). These numbers were added to create consistency and reduce confusion for games that otherwise had different titles because they were printed in multiple languages.

■ MATTEL INTELLIVISION

Mattel was founded in 1945 by **Harold "Matt" Matson** and **Elliot Handler** as Mattel Creations. A sponsor of the *Mickey Mouse Club* TV series in 1955, the company introduced the *Barbie* doll in 1959, which became its best-selling toy. The following year Mattel released the talking doll *Chatty Cathy*, pioneering the "pull-string talking doll" industry that popularized the 1960s and 1970s. The company then purchased Ringling Bros. and Barnum & Bailey Circus for $40 million in 1971 (Langdon, 1980, para. 15) and launched Mattel Electronics in 1977 to produce electronic handheld games.

With its strong brand recognition and success in the handheld game business, Mattel entered the home video game market with the **Intellivision** (Figure 3.10), released nationwide in 1980 for $299.99. For its high price tag, consumers received the console,

FIGURE 3.10 Mattel Intellivision with its controllers that could be stored inside the unit.

two hardwired controllers, and the pack-in game *Las Vegas Poker & Blackjack*. Only a handful of titles were available at launch (see Table 3.6). Like Atari, Mattel manufactured a rebranded version of the system for Sears called the **Sears Super Video Arcade**, as well as a **TandyVision** model for RadioShack stores.

The Intellivision controllers were innovative in that they contained a 12-button **numeric keypad** that introduced the concept of plastic **overlays** could be slid over keypad. The overlays contained color pictures to help players navigate the buttons of the numeric keypad for each game. Its unique **directional disk** could be pressed as well as rotated, allowing for 16 directions of movement. Four action buttons completed the

controller (two on each side); however, the top buttons functioned identically, so there were actually *three* distinct action buttons.

Intellivision was the world's first **16-bit** home video game system—and the industry would not see another 16-bit home console until the fourth generation of video games in the late 1980s. Mattel is often credited for starting the first "**console war**" when it positioned the Intellivision to go head-to-head with the Atari VCS. It began in 1981 when "Mattel invested $6 million in a national ad campaign in direct competition to Atari that compared the graphic power of the Intellivision to the VCS. For the first time in gaming history, the media was whipped into a frenzy, predicting a bitter war between the two giants" (Slater, 2008, p. 15). Intellivision TV commercials featured well-known sports journalist **George Plimpton** (shown in Figure 3.12) using side-by-side comparisons to demonstrate Intellivision's superior graphics and sound capabilities over Atari's system. One of the slogans used in their ads was "The closest thing to the real thing."

TABLE 3.6   Mattel Intellivision U.S. Launch Titles

- *ABPA Backgammon*
- *Armor Battle* (Figure 3.11a)
- *The Electric Company Math Fun*
- *Las Vegas Poker & Blackjack* (Figure 3.11b)

FIGURE 3.11   Intellivision launch titles (a) *Armor Battle* and (b) *Las Vegas Poker & Blackjack*.

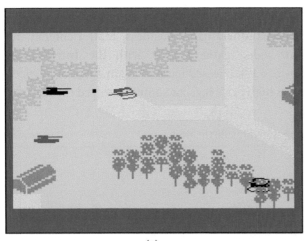

(a)   (b)

FIGURE 3.12   Magazine advertisement for Intellivision with George Plimpton in 1981.

Two pictures are worth a thousand words.

*Atari vs. Intellivision?
Nothing I could say would be more persuasive
than what your own two eyes will tell you.
So compare for yourself. Game for game, feature
for feature, I think you'll find Intellivision
is clearly superior.*

— George Plimpton —

MATTEL ELECTRONICS®

INTELLiViSiON™

Intelligent Television

For the dealer nearest you
Call 1 (800) 323-1715
In Illinois 1 (800) 942-8881

* Trademark of and licensed by
Major League Baseball
Promotion Corp.
© Mattel, Inc. 1981.
All Rights Reserved.

ATARI
HOME RUN™ BASEBALL

INTELLIVISION
MAJOR LEAGUE BASEBALL™

▪ HANDHELD SNAPSHOT: MILTON BRADLEY MICROVISION

The **Microvision** (Figure 3.13) was designed by **Jay Smith** (who later designed the Vectrex console). It was published by board game manufacturer **Milton Bradley (MB)** for $49.99 in November of 1979. Microvision was the first handheld system with interchangeable game cartridges. Its pack-in title was a *Breakout* clone called *Block Buster*. The system was unique in that it did not contain an onboard CPU. The unit itself consisted of an LCD screen, a 12-button rubber keypad, and a paddle dial.

Each game cartridge contained its own CPU and ROM. Two processors were initially available for the system: the **Intel 8021** and **Texas Instruments TMS1100** (Table 3.7). The Intel chip was more advanced but required two batteries and had only 1K ROM (compared to 2K ROM on the 1100, which ran on a single battery). MB would go on to solely use the 1100 and "games that originally ran on the 8021 were also reprogrammed to work on the 1100" (Nobes, 2022, para. 2).

FIGURE 3.13 Microvision featuring *Block Buster*.

TABLE 3.7 Milton Bradley Microvision Tech Specs

Format:	Cartridge/1–2 9-V batteries
CPU:	On cartridges, Intel 8021/TI TMS1100 (100 kHz)
Memory:	64 bytes, 2K ROM (TMS100), 1K ROM (8021)
Resolution:	16 × 16 pixels/2″ diagonal LCD
Colors:	Monochrome
Sound:	Piezo beeper

In addition to containing the CPU and ROM, the game cartridges made up the entire front cover of the unit. Each game included an original marquee title (like an arcade cabinet), a unique screen overlay (like Odyssey and Vectrex), and different sets of buttons. Some games featured only a few buttons, while others used all 12 available functions such as *Sea Duel* and *Mindbuster* (Figure 3.14). Five titles were available at launch, including *Block Buster, Bowling, Connect Four, Star Trek: Phaser Strike* (called *Shooting Star* in Europe), and *Pinball*. Only 12 titles were ever released for the system, with its last game *Super Blockbuster* only seeing a release in Europe.

FIGURE 3.14 Five key Microvision cartridges: (a) *Alien Raiders*, (b) *Sea Duel*, (c) *Super Blockbuster*, (d) *Connect Four*, and (e) *Mindbuster*.

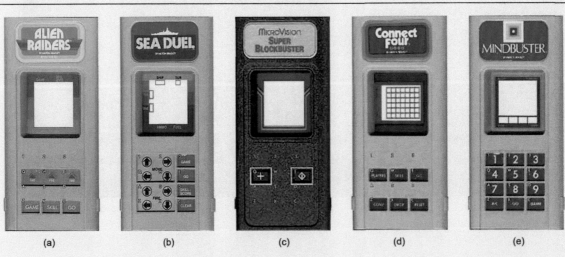

(a) (b) (c) (d) (e)

Intellivision promotions also promised a **keyboard component** add-on unit (Figure 3.15a) in early advertisements, convincing consumers they would be able to turn their system into a full-functioning home computer. Countless delays led to customer complaints and Mattel Electronics was eventually investigated by the Federal Trade Commission (FTC) for fraud and false advertising. A rumored 4,000 keyboard components were made but never received a national release. The units that were sold in test markets or mail order were recalled for technical issues and the product was officially canceled in the fall of 1982.

That same year Mattel released its **Intellivoice** (Figure 3.15b) add-on peripheral for $79–$99. Like The Voice peripheral on Odyssey², the Intellivoice adapter utilized a voice synthesizer to generate audible speech in certain games. The adapter plugged into the cartridge slot of the console and then games plugged into the Intellivoice. Only a handful of games ever utilized the peripheral. The four games that used the Intellivoice could not be played without it and the accessory was phased out in 1983. A sleeker-looking **Intellivision II** (Figure 3.15c) was released in 1982 with detachable controllers but only in North America and Brazil.

☼ DID YOU KNOW?

The original Intellivision programming teams' identities and work location were kept a closely guarded secret to avoid the possibility of competitors snatching them away. Gabriel Baum, Don Daglow, Rick Levine, Mike Minkoff, and John Sohl went by the alias **Blue Sky Rangers**, named after their "Blue Sky" brainstorming sessions.

■ CONSOLE COMPARISON: INTELLIVISION VS. ATARI VCS AND ODYSSEY²

Between Mattel and Atari, "Intellivision had a newer and more powerful CPU than VCS, slightly more memory, and played better-looking games" (Kent, 2001, p. 195). Compared to the VCS and Odyssey², which ran at 1.19 MHz and 1.79 MHz, respectively, the Intellivision's **894.89 kHz** CPU (Table 3.8) was relatively slow—clocking in at about half the speed of the Odyssey². It ran a bit faster at 1 MHz in PAL regions. Intellivision may have had better graphics but the Atari VCS was more adept at handling action games due to its faster processor.

On the other hand, being **16-bit** meant Intellivision could process more information, such as more on-screen objects (sprites). Intellivision also surpassed the competition with its internal memory of **1,456 bytes RAM** and **7,168 bytes (7 kB) ROM**—compared to Atari's 128 bytes RAM and 4 kB ROM and Odyssey²'s 4 bytes RAM with 128 bytes A/V RAM. The console's **192 × 160** pixels screen resolution was about equal to Atari's 160 × 192 pixels and the 160 × 200 resolution of the Odyssey².

Like Odyssey², Intellivision only had a color palette of 16 colors to work with. However, it could display all **16 colors on screen**, compared to eight on the Odyssey² and only four colors per scan line on the Atari VCS. As for audio, Intellivision came equipped with three channels of sound compared to two channels on the VCS and only one channel sound on the Odyssey²—however the games did not always sound better. While some Intellivision games featured background music, the tunes would often cut out during sound effects like in *Carnival* (1982) and *Buzz Bombers* (1983). Like

FIGURE 3.15 The Intellivision keyboard component (a), Intellivoice adapter (b), and Intellivision II console (c).

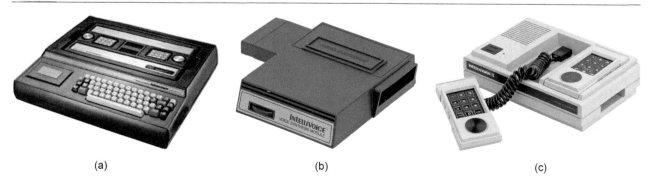

(a)　　　　　　　(b)　　　　　　　(c)

TABLE 3.8 Mattel Intellivision Tech Specs

Manufacturer:	Mattel Electronics
Launch price:	$299.99
Release date:	1980 (US), 1981–82 (EU), 1982 (JP)
Format:	Cartridge
CPU:	16-bit General InstrumentCP1610 (894.89 kHz, 1 MHz in PAL)
Memory:	1,456 bytes RAM & 7,168 bytes ROM
Resolution:	192 × 160 pixels
Colors:	16 from a palette of 16
Sound:	3-channel mono

HEAD-TO-HEAD

To compare the graphics and sound between the Intellivision and VCS, try similar games released on each system (or view clips of them). Popular games to compare include *Night Stalker* (Intellivision) versus *Dark Cavern* (VCS), *NFL Football* (Intellivision) versus *Realsports Football* (VCS), *River Raid, Demon Attack*, and *BurgerTime*.

The Voice accessory on Odyssey², Intellivision added voice synthesis with its Intellivoice, but that was a failed add-on peripheral and only four games were ever released for it.

The Intellivision controller was extremely lightweight, weighing only 2.5 ounces (70 g) compared to the 6-ounce (170 g) Odyssey² controller (not including cord weight). The controller was like the Channel F's, in that the disk could be used for multidirectional movement and could also be rotated for paddle-style games. The gamepad's side action buttons were stiffer and less comfortable compared to the action buttons on the VCS and Odyssey² controllers; however, the Intellivision controller's numeric keypad and overlays set a trend for the next few consoles.

■ KEY INTELLIVISION TITLES

Intellivision was known for its impressive lineup of sports titles. Mattel went out of their way to acquire licenses for every sports-related game they manufactured, "from the American Backgammon Players Association to the U.S. Chess Federation, to Major League Baseball" (Nilsen, 2001, p. 195). Beyond sports games, *Utopia* (1981) by **Don Daglow** is often regarded as one of the first city building/God games, which helped pave the way for the real-time strategy genre. For role-playing game fans, Intellivision was the only console to offer *Advanced Dungeons & Dragons* video games at that time.

Impressive exclusive titles on the system included Imagic's *Dracula* (1982), Activision's *Worm Whomper* (1983), and a late, unofficial sequel to *BurgerTime* (Figure 3.16e) called *Diner* in 1987. While it released more than twice as many games as the Odyssey², the Intellivision library did not contain as many licensed arcade titles compared to the VCS. Mattel eventually obtained arcade ports such as *Pac-Man* and

FIGURE 3.16 Box art to five popular Intellivision titles including (a) *Lock 'N' Chase*, (b) *Astrosmash*, (c) *Night Stalker*, (d) *Bump 'n' Jump*, and (e) *BurgerTime*.

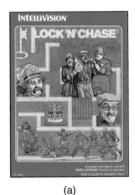

(a)   (b)   (c)   (d)   (e)

Donkey Kong, but these did not release for months after they had already been available on competing systems. Approximately 125 games were released for the Intellivision console, compared to well over 400 games on Atari's system.

▪ COLECOVISION

Appearing late in what would eventually be known as the second generation of video games was Coleco's follow-up to its Telstar series—**ColecoVision** (Figure 3.17). Released in August of 1982, "ColecoVision generally sold for $195. By this time, Atari had cut the price of the VCS to $135" (Kent, 2001, p. 207). To compete with the pre-established consoles on the market, Coleco secured exclusive rights to reproduce Nintendo's arcade classic **Donkey Kong** game, including a tabletop version and a cartridge, which came bundled with every ColecoVision system. Coleco maintained the rights to a home version of *Donkey Kong* beyond the holiday season and sold an estimated 500,000 by that Christmas (Businessweek, 1983, p. 31). Twelve games were available at launch, including arcade ports such as Exidy's *Venture*, along with *Turbo* and *Zaxxon* by Sega (Table 3.9).

If the name "ColecoVision" didn't sound enough like "Intellivision," one look at the console and the influence is obvious. Not only did Coleco design the body of the system with room to store two controllers, but the controllers themselves were remarkably similar to Intellivision's. Aside from reversing the location of the directional stick, each controller included

TABLE 3.9 ColecoVision U.S. Launch Titles

• Carnival	• Space Fury
• Cosmic Avenger	• Space Panic
• Donkey Kong (Figure 3.18a)	• Turbo
• Ken Uston's Blackjack/Poker	• Venture
• Lady Bug	• Zaxxon (Figure 3.18b)
• Mouse Trap	
• Smurf: Rescue in Gargamel's Castle	

a 12-button **numeric keypad** that (like Intellivision's controller) could be fitted with **plastic overlays**. Coleco also followed Mattel's lead by placing action buttons on each side of the controller.

Atari had well over 100 VCS titles on the market when ColecoVision launched in 1982. To superficially inflate the number of games the ColecoVision could play (and to give VCS owners a reason to replace their Atari systems with a ColecoVision), **Michael Katz** and his marketing team developed an adapter known as **Expansion Module #1**. This add-on peripheral (shown in Figure 3.19a) allowed the ColecoVision to play most Atari VCS games—giving it the largest library of game titles at that time. Atari was unable to take legal action against Coleco since the VCS did not contain any patented parts.

The second ColecoVision peripheral called **Expansion Module #2** was a steering wheel (Figure 3.19b) and a gas pedal controller. The package came bundled with a port of Sega's popular *Turbo* arcade game and was compatible with a handful of other titles. **Expansion Module #3** was a console that the

FIGURE 3.17 ColecoVision video game console with two joystick controllers.

FIGURE 3.18 Screenshots from ColecoVision U.S. launch titles (a) *Donkey Kong* and (b) *Zaxxon*.

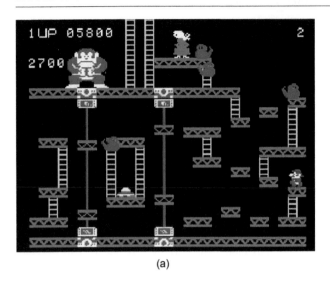

(a)

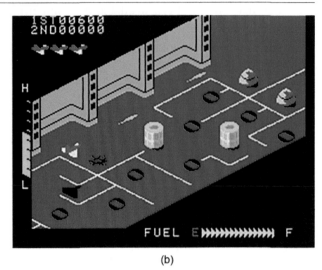

(b)

ColecoVision system plugged directly into to create a piecemeal version of Coleco's **Adam computer**. The device included a separate keyboard, **digital data pack (DDP)** cassette drives, and a printer. Like Intellivision's computer add on, Expansion Module #3 suffered from production problems. Along with the stand-alone Adam computer, Expansion Module #3 was considered a commercial failure.

Other peripherals included the **Roller Controller** trackball, which came bundled with a *Centipede* clone called *Slither*, and the **Super Action Controller Set** (Figure 3.19c), which included two fist-grip joysticks and the game *Super Action Baseball*. The top side of the Super Action controllers included a 12-function keypad, 8-direction joystick, and a two-directional dial called the "speed roller." The handle contained four action buttons mounted in the grip (one for each finger). Like the steering wheel, the Roller Controller and Super Action Controller Set were only compatible with a small number of titles.

■ CONSOLE COMPARISON: COLECOVISION VS. ATARI VCS AND INTELLIVISION

By the time ColecoVision was manufactured, the price of technology had come down so much that Coleco could afford a chip with **memory mapping** and **frame buffers** that Atari left out of Stella, the processing chip in the Video Computer System. These added features gave the ColecoVision smoother animation and more arcade-like graphics than the Intellivision and the VCS (Kent, 2001, p. 206). Engineered by **Eric Bromley**, its top-of-the-line graphics could be credited

FIGURE 3.19 ColecoVision: (a) VCS adapter, (b) steering wheel, and (c) Super Action Controller.

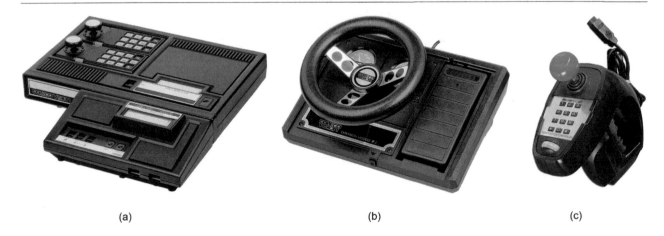

(a)　　　　　　　　　　　(b)　　　　　　　　　　　(c)

TABLE 3.10 ColecoVision Tech Specs

Manufacturer:	Coleco
Launch price:	$195
Release date:	August 1982
Format:	Cartridge
CPU:	8-bit NEC Zilog Z80 A (3.58 MHz)
Memory:	1 kB RAM, 16 kB Video RAM & 8 kB ROM
Resolution:	256 × 192 pixels
Colors:	16 colors from a palette of 16
Sound:	4-channel (3-tone, 1-noise) Texas Instruments SN76489AN

to its **3.58 MHz Zilog Z80A** CPU by **NEC**, in addition to a **TMS9928A video display processor** by **Texas Instruments** (Table 3.10). Its Zilog Z80A ran twice as fast as the Intellivision processor and was three times faster than the VCS.

For internal memory, ColecoVision's **1 kB RAM** and **8 kB ROM** was about equal to Intellivision's 1.46 kB RAM and 7 kB ROM; however, its **16 kB video RAM** gave its graphics an instantly recognizable edge. Atari's 128 bytes RAM and 4 kB ROM landed the VCS in a distant third place in terms of memory. ColecoVision also led the pack with its screen resolution of **256 × 192 pixels**—compared to Intellivision's 192 × 160 and Atari's 160 × 192 pixels. Color capability was a tie with Intellivision, with Coleco's console featuring up to 16 on-screen colors from a color palette of 16 colors.

ColecoVision's sound was superior to Intellivision and the Atari VCS with its **Texas Instruments SN76489AN** sound card, which generated three channels of tone and one for noise. In comparing console

audio, ColecoVision games typically sounded richer and fuller, containing not only better sound—but more of it. Games that appeared on all three consoles sometimes contained musical scores that Mattel and Atari's games lacked altogether, such as in *Donkey Kong* and *Frogger*. One weakness of the ColecoVision was that its games had a 12-second splash screen that players had to sit through before the games would boot up.

The ColecoVision controller was larger than Intellivision's pad, with a more solid feel overall. The side buttons were easier to press, and the higher placement of the joystick felt more intuitive. Unlike the Intellivision disk pad however, the ColecoVision stick did not double as a twistable paddle. Both systems' controllers featured telephone-style, stretchable coiled cables—however Intellivision's pads were hardwired to the unit while ColecoVision's controllers were detachable and easier to replace.

HEAD-TO-HEAD

To compare the graphics and sound between the ColecoVision, Intellivision, and Atari VCS, check out games released on all three consoles (or watch video clips of them). Some popular games for comparison include *Centipede, Donkey Kong, Frogger, Pitfall!, River Raid, Q*Bert,* and *Zaxxon.*

■ KEY COLECOVISION TITLES

A major challenge for ColecoVision at launch was that it did not have anywhere near the number of games as its competitors who had been on the market for years. "Coleco did not have enough money to compete with

FIGURE 3.20 Box art to five defining ColecoVision titles including (a) *Turbo,* (b) *Antarctic Adventure,* (c) *Donkey Kong Junior,* (d) *Jumpman Junior,* and (e) *Venture.*

| (a) | (b) | (c) | (d) | (e) |

FIGURE 3.21 Two-page magazine advertisement for ColecoVision from 1982.

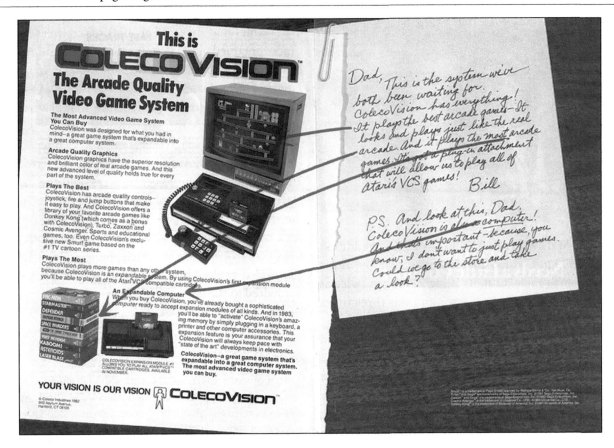

Atari for big licenses, but Coleco's marketers had a knack for selecting small games with strong followings. Coleco secured licenses for *Mr. Do, Lady Bug, Cosmic Avenger,* and *Venture*" (Kent, 2001, p. 207). Other great arcade games included ports of Sega's *Turbo* and *Zaxxon,* Exidy's *Mouse Trap,* and *Antarctic Adventure* from Konami.

In addition to Konami and Sega, Coleco received a healthy amount of third-party support with multiple games from top publishers such as Activision, Epyx, Imagic, Parker Brothers, and Sierra Entertainment. One key title not to be overlooked was *Jumpman Jr.* from Epyx (Figure 3.20d). "It may not be the most jaw-dropping-looking ColecoVision title, but in terms of gameplay it's virtually unmatched and a must for platform fans" (McFerran, 2010, p. 99).

Approximately 145 cartridges were manufactured for the ColecoVision between 1982 and 1984 (Forster, 2005, p. 50). This did not include all the VCS games the system could play with the Expansion Module #1 adapter, which more than doubled that total amount. One interesting business strategy by Michael Katz

and Coleco included manufacturing game cartridges for both the VCS and Intellivision—including *Donkey Kong* the year after it was released on ColecoVision. Atarisoft also made a handful of games for the ColecoVision, including *Centipede, Defender, Galaxian,* and *Jungle Hunt.*

■ ATARI 5200

The **Atari 5200** (Figure 3.22) was marketed as the Atari 5200 "SuperSystem." It was released just 3 months after Coleco's console in November of 1982 for a higher price tag of $269. The system was originally developed

FIGURE 3.22 Atari 5200 with four controller ports and joystick controller.

to compete with the Intellivision, but ultimately ended up in competition with the ColecoVision (Herman, 2003). In retrospect, the systems are considered part of the same generation; however, at that time the 5200 and ColecoVision were viewed as sole competitors during a new wave of video game systems.

Under the hood, "the Atari 5200 had the same processor as the Atari 400 home computer" (Kent, 2001, p. 229) but retailed for much less. Around a dozen games had been produced for the system, but only four were available at launch (Table 3.11). Launch titles included the pack-in game *Super Breakout*. *Super Breakout* hit the arcades in 1978 and was ported to the VCS four years earlier, so it appeared quite dated compared to *Donkey Kong* on ColecoVision. Atari eventually changed the bundled game to *Pac-Man*.

Game cartridges were nearly twice the size of VCS cartridges; however, the 5200 was not backward compatible with 2600 games. Instead, Atari marketed both consoles simultaneously, rebranding the VCS as the **Atari 2600**. Atari continued to support and manufacture games for the 2600, while the 5200 was seen as a more advanced alternative for serious gamers. A 2600 adapter (shown in

Figure 3.24) was eventually released, but it only worked with newer versions of the 5200 console and lacked the VCS's color/black-and-white function.

There were several innovations the 5200 introduced to the home console market in 1982. In place of the manual TV/Game **radio-frequency (RF) switch** of previous consoles, the 5200 included an **automatic switchbox** where the system would automatically switch from a regular TV signal to the game system signal when the console was turned on. The original 5200 model contained **four controller ports** (jacks). The joysticks featured **analog** (touch-sensitive) **control**, four action buttons (two on each side, like Intellivision), as well as **start**, **pause**, and **reset** buttons. Following in the footsteps of Intellivision and ColecoVision, the 5200 controller also included a 12-button **numeric keypad** that plastic **overlays** could be snapped onto for certain games. Like the previous two consoles, the 5200 controllers could be stored inside the console—within a hidden compartment under a panel that flipped open above the cartridge slot.

As state-of-the-art as these features were, the controllers themselves are often regarded as one of the biggest missteps of the 5200. The major problem was that the **360-degree joystick** did not center itself. This made playing most games much more difficult than necessary. Atari's engineering team was aware of this and even filed a petition to have the system dropped until new controllers were designed—however, Ray

TABLE 3.11 Atari 5200 U.S. Launch Titles

- *Galaxian*
- *Pac-Man* (Figure 3.23a)
- *Space Invaders*
- *Super Breakout* (Figure 3.23b)

FIGURE 3.23 Screenshots from Atari 5200 U.S. launch titles (a) *Pac-Man* and (b) *Super Breakout*.

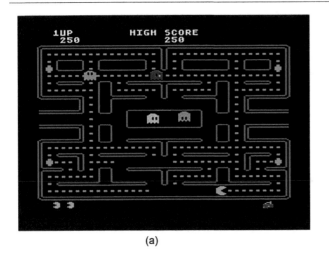

(a)

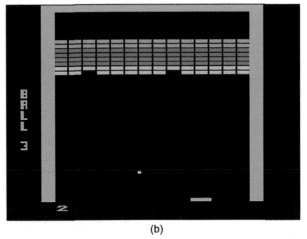

(b)

Kassar ignored their request and moved forward with manufacturing (Kent, 2001, p. 229). An updated version of the console was released in 1983, but it did not address the joystick issue. Instead, the newer model was reduced to two controller ports instead of four and replaced the convenient, automatic switchbox with a manual RF switch. Aside from this, a well-made **Trak-Ball controller** (shown in Figure 3.24) was released for games such as *Missile Command* and *Centipede*.

■ CONSOLE COMPARISON: ATARI 5200 VS. COLECOVISION

Atari's custom version of the MOS Technology 6502 (known as **SALLY**) had the ability to be halted for other devices to control the **bus** (data path). It also included multiple co-processors to assist the CPU. Two custom graphics chips included **ANTIC** (Alphanumeric Television Interface Controller) and **GTIA** (Graphic Television Interface Adaptor) (Table 3.12). Compared to ColecoVision's specs, the 5200's **1.79 MHz** processor appears to be only half as fast as ColecoVision's 3.58 MHz Zilog Z80A CPU. However, while "the Z80 runs faster than the 6502, the latter can do more operations per clock cycle (effectively 2 to 1), so, they are more or less equal" (Molyneaux & Horton, 2016, para. 15).

The 5200's internal memory of **16 kB RAM** was comparable to ColecoVision's combined 1 and 16 kB video RAM but utilized four times the ROM with 32 kB versus 8 kB for Coleco's system. Atari's console had a higher resolution at **320 × 192 pixels**, compared to

TABLE 3.12	Atari 5200 Tech Specs
Manufacturer:	Atari, Inc.
Launch price:	$269.99
Release date:	November 1982
Format:	Cartridge
CPU:	8-bit MOS custom SALLY 6502C (1.79 MHz)
Memory:	16 kB RAM, 2 kB BIOS, 32 kB ROM
Resolution:	320 × 192 pixels
Colors:	16 colors from a palette of 256
Sound:	4-channel sound POKEY chip

256 × 192 pixels on ColecoVision. Both systems could display up to **16 colors** on screen, but the 5200 had the superior color palette with **256 colors** to choose from compared to Coleco's 16 fixed colors. ColecoVision could push more sprites on screen, but overall, the Atari 5200 was a slightly more powerful machine.

Larger cartridge size did not necessarily equal better graphics, but it did allow room for high-quality sounds such as digitized speech to be included in Atari 5200 cartridges as heard in *Berzerk* and *RealSports Baseball* (1983). The 5200's **4-channel POKEY** (Pot Keyboard Integrated Circuit) sound chip produced excellent sound for its time and was about equal to the Texas Instruments SN76489AN sound card inside the ColecoVision. Each machine released an optional adapter that allowed the consoles to play Atari VCS games.

While both standard controllers featured similar layouts, ColecoVision's stick was self-centering, while the 5200 stick was not. Atari's analog joystick worked

FIGURE 3.24   Magazine advertisement for the Atari 5200 and its peripherals from 1983.

HERE'S WHAT MAKES THE ATARI 5200 SUPERSYSTEM SO SUPER.

First off, it really is a system. A family of ATARI 5200™ Super-System components designed together to perform together. Which is what any video gamer should look for. It's also an exclusive system. You can't play its high-resolution, arcade-speed 5200™ Super Games on anything else, not even with an adaptor. And what's coming includes the most popular games, like Joust[1] and Pole Position[2] now in the arcades.

ATARI 5200™ SUPERSYSTEM

It comes with a powerful 16K RAM (memory) built in. Which is 10 times more intelligent than Intellivision.™

It generates 256 colors, compared with Colecovision's 16. And 320 lines of graphic resolution, a good 25% sharper than Colecovision.™

Its circuitry reads signals fast. So with 5200 arcade cartridges, nothing gets lost in translation. Including game speed.

What's more, the controllers actually feel good in your hand. With solid joysticks, not clumsy little disks.

And the action is full-circle, 360° Instead of 16 or 8 positions like other joysticks.

There are left- and right-handed fire buttons. A 12-digit keypad. Plus start and reset all in your hand.

There's even a pause button, in case the phone rings. And it rings a lot when you have an ATARI 5200 SuperSystem.

Everyone wants to come over and play.

ATARI 5200™ TRAK-BALL™ CONTROLLER

If you know video games, you know what TRAK-BALL is. The fastest controller in the arcades.

And now for the ATARI 5200 SuperSystem.

It gives Centipede,™ Galaxian,[3] Missile Command™ and other 5200 SuperSystem games true arcade feel and control.

And turns our new RealSports™ games into real athletic workouts.

ATARI TRAK-BALL is mounted in a hefty base so it won't slip or slide around in heavy use.

All other controls are built right in. With fire buttons and keypads for both lefties and righties.

You just plug it into your ATARI 5200 SuperSystem and let the good times roll.

ATARI VCS™ CARTRIDGE ADAPTOR

This handy device gives you the best of both worlds. It lets you play all the great ATARI 2600™ VCS games—like Asteroids,™ Berzerk,[4] Yars' Revenge,™ the Swordquest™ series—as well as the new 5200™ Super Games, all on one SuperSystem.

ATARI 5200™ VOICE

Speaking of video games, that's exactly what some ATARI 5200 games will do.

Generate a human-sounding voice in response to gameplay.

To guide you. To warn you. Maybe even to scare you a little.

Adding a whole new dimension of video game realism and fun.

ATARI 5200™ SUPER GAMES

Centipede,™ Vanguard,[5] PAC-MAN,[6] Galaxian, Qix,[7] Star Raiders,™ Football, Baseball, Soccer, and Tennis are here now.

Pole Position, Joust, Moon Patrol,[1] Jungle Hunt,[8] Tempest,™ Battlezone,[6] Dig Dug,[9] Xevious,[2] and Pengo[10] are coming soon.

With 5200 graphics, gameplay and sound, in cartridges that no other system, nor their adaptors, can play.

And they're the hottest games now in arcades.

Choose Colecovision or Intellivision and you'll never play them at home.

It's that simple.

So think ahead to the games you'll want to play.

We're pretty certain which system you'll want to buy.

ONLY FROM ATARI

W A Warner Communications Company

well for games that were programmed for analog control, but not as well for non-analog games. Both systems' numeric keypads could accompany plastic overlays for games. The buttons on the ColecoVision controller had a more plastic feel, while the 5200's buttons had a more rubbery feel to them. Atari's controller featured a pause button to its credit; however, the 5200 joystick was more delicate and prone to breakage.

HEAD-TO-HEAD

To compare the graphics and sound between the Atari 5200 and ColecoVision, check out games released on each console (or watch clips of them). Popular games to compare include *Congo Bongo*, *Frogger*, *Jungle Hunt*, *Mr. Do's Castle*, and *Pac-Man*.

■ KEY ATARI 5200 TITLES

Many games released on the 5200 were just upgraded versions of 2600 titles with better graphics and sound. Of course, the 5200 version of *Pac-Man* was leagues above the abysmal 2600 version. Other games only looked marginally better, and the average consumer was not interested in repurchasing slightly enhanced updates of games they already owned. Well over half of the 69 games officially released for the 5200 were also available on the 2600. Notable titles that were superior on the 5200 included *Missile Command* (1982), *Centipede* (1982), *Defender* (1983), *Joust* (1983), *Realsports Baseball* (1983), *Gyruss* (1984), and *Pitfall II: Lost Caverns* (1984).

Among the above titles, all but two were arcade ports since arcade-style gaming was a primary focus. While it did not have a lot of exclusive titles, the 5200 did receive the only home port of the Taito arcade game *Space Dungeon* (Figure 3.25e) in 1983. Another standout title that was not available on the older home consoles was *Robotron: 2084*. This dual-stick arcade game came packaged with a black plastic "dual controller holder" that would secure two Atari joysticks side by side to imitate the dual-stick gameplay at home.

■ VIDEO GAME CRASH OF 1983

The second-generation video game market is well known for what is commonly referred to as the **North American video game crash of 1983**. Total revenues from U.S. video arcades and the home video game market had grown to around $11.8 billion at its peak. This fell by approximately 97% by 1985 when the "console industry that was worth more than $3 billion on its own was estimated to have fallen to just $100 million" (Lambie, 2013, para. 2).

One of the main reasons the market crashed in North America was too many consoles (see Figure 3.26) and poorly made games flooding the market. Atari's *Pac-Man* and *E.T. the Extra-Terrestrial* were just the tip of the iceberg of countless poorly made games (often called "**shovelware**") by independent developers looking to get a piece of the pie. Third-party development was also in its infancy back then, and hardware manufacturers like Atari had not yet developed licensing policies or quality control measures. Other reasons for the crash included competition from home computers, as well as inflation.

FIGURE 3.25 Box art to five defining Atari 5200 titles including (a) *Berzerk*, (b) *Ms. Pac-Man*, (c) *Montezuma's Revenge*, (d) *Robotron: 2084*, and (e) *Space Dungeon*.

(a)   (b)   (c)   (d)   (e)

FIGURE 3.26 A look at the many less-popular consoles of the second generation.

Fairchild Channel VES/F
November 1976

1292 Advanced Programmable
Video System 1976 (Europe)

RCA Studio II
January 1977

Bally Astrocade
October 1977-1978

APF Microcomputer System
(MP1000) January 1978

Interton VC 4000
1978 (Germany)

Epoch Cassette Vision
July 1981 (Japan)

Emerson Arcadia 2001
1982

Vectrex
November 1982

💡 DID YOU KNOW?

The Fairchild Channel F was originally launched as the "Video Entertainment System" or VES but was renamed the "Fairchild Channel F" when Atari released their similarly titled "VCS" the following year. **Vectrex** was the last system released in the second generation and came with its own monochrome **vector monitor**.

▪ SECOND-GENERATION MARKET SUMMARY

The Atari VCS/2600 dominated the second generation by a landslide—selling more than 20 million units by 1986 (Pollack, 1986, p. 1) and eventually selling 30 million units (Figure 3.27) until it was finally discontinued after 1991. Its success could be attributed to acquiring key arcade titles like *Space Invaders* and *Missile Command*, strong third-party support by companies like Activision, Imagic, and Parker Brothers, as well as support from Warner

Communications—even after the release of the 5200. Ironically, it was Atari's poorly made licensed games, too many third-party and independent developers, along with supporting the 2600 simultaneously with the 5200 that contributed to the North American video game crash of 1983.

The Odyssey[2] sold moderately well in the United States and quite well in Europe and Brazil where it was marketed and branded under parent Dutch electronics company **Philips**. It was among the top three consoles leading into 1982, although a distant third after the Atari VCS/2600 and Mattel's Intellivision. "It boasted more CPU intelligence than the Atari 2600, but it lacked the licensed arcade titles and third-party developers to make it competitive over the long run" (Edwards, 2012, para. 17). In fact, no third-party game was even developed for the Odyssey[2] in the United States until Imagic's *Demon Attack* in 1983 (Katz & Kunkel, 1983, p. 40). By then the market had begun to crash, but not before over 1 million Odyssey[2] units were sold in the United States alone.

FIGURE 3.27 Second-generation console sales graph.

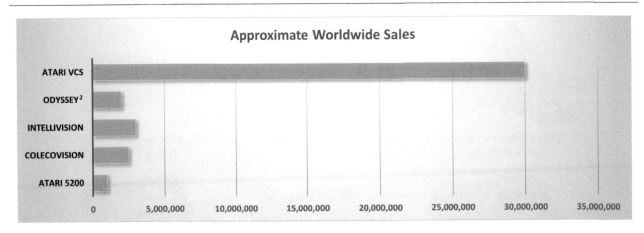

At one point, Intellivision captured approximately 20% of the market. And "despite being twice as expensive as the 2600, the Intellivision sold over 850,000 units [in 1981]. In what was to be Intellivision's finest hour in an industry [then] valued at $1.5 billion, Mattel announced a staggering $100,000,000 profit in 1982" (Slater, 2008, p. 15). When the market began to crash in 1983, Mattel sold Intellivision to Senior Vice President of Marketing **Terrence Valeski** who formed **Intellivision Inc.** (later **INTV Corporation**). While it did not win the console war with Atari, Intellivision was the only console of the second generation to be continuously manufactured and supported with new games well after the video game crash of 1983 (Robinson, 2003).

The last major consoles released in 1982 were the biggest victims of the video game crash. Mattel's ColecoVision sold well over 1 million units by mid-1983 (Johnson, 1983, para. 13) and more than 2 million units by the end of 1984. Between Coleco's console and the 5200, the ColecoVision was the better selling system. However, with all its losses from the video game crash, Coleco officially dropped out of the home console market in October 1985. Had the market not crashed, Coleco may have remained a major player in the following generation of video games.

The Atari 5200 sold approximately 1 million units but was never officially sold outside of North America. Besides its lack of original titles and abysmal, non-centering joysticks, the console's failure can also be attributed to Atari splitting its development and marketing resources between the 2600 and the 5200—rather than putting all its eggs in one basket. Between this, its failings with *Pac-Man* and *E.T.*, and an oversaturation of systems and games on the video game market, "by the end of 1983, Atari had racked up

$536 million in losses. Warner Communications sold the company the following year" (Kent, 2001, p. 240). Stores began liquidating their inventory of games and consoles and many retailers discontinued the sale of video game systems altogether.

■ SECOND-GENERATION BREAKTHROUGHS AND TRENDS

There were unique breakthroughs and trends that defined the second generation of video games. Here is a list of the top 10 features that defined the generation:

1. Microprocessor-driven game logic

2. Interchangeable ROM cartridges for an unlimited number of games

3. Computer-simulated opponents (**artificial intelligence or AI**) for single-player games

4. 12-button numeric keypad controllers with game-specific overlays

5. Non-scrolling, single-screen playfields (most games)

6. Multiscreen playfields spanning multiple screen areas (some games)

7. Blocky, simple sprites with screen resolutions up to 320 × 192 pixels

8. Color graphics, normally between two and 16 simultaneous colors on screen

9. Multiple audio channels (up to four)

10. Digitized speech in games like *P.T. Barnum's Acrobats* and *Berzerk*

■ ACTIVITY: FAILED CONSOLES REPORT AND PRESENTATION

Choose a second-generation console that sold less than 1 million units and develop a report and presentation on the history, business, and technology of that system. Be sure to include (1) the publisher's goals, (2) how the system was marketed, (3) technical specifications and notable game titles, (4) why the system failed, and (5) [conclusion] what might have saved the console from its demise.

The report should contain three main points and a minimum of *two* quotes from expert sources, which you will paraphrase or cite verbally in the speech. The recommended total presentation length is 4–4:30 minutes, not to exceed 5 minutes in total.

CONSOLE SUGGESTIONS

Suggested consoles to report on include Fairchild Channel F/VES (November 1976), 1292 Advanced Programmable Video System (1976, Europe), RCA Studio II (January 1977), Bally Astrocade (October 1977–1978), APF Microcomputer System [MP1000] (January 1978), Interton VC 4000 (1978, Germany), Epoch Cassette Vision (July 1981, Japan), Emerson Arcadia 2001 (1982), or Vectrex (November 1982).

■ CHAPTER 3 QUIZ

1. Part of the success of *Space Invaders* can be attributed to the popularity of:
   a. *Asteroids*
   b. *Star Wars*
   c. *Star Trek*
   d. *Roswell*

2. Credited as the first mascot and/or iconic arcade video game character:
   a. Daisy
   b. Pac-Man
   c. Donkey Kong
   d. Mario

3. The lead character in *Super Mario Bros.* first appeared in which game?
   a. *Popeye*
   b. *Mario Bros.*
   c. *Donkey Kong*
   d. *Defender*

4. The Atari 2600 was originally called the VCS, which stood for:
   a. Video Console System
   b. Vector Computer System
   c. Video Computer System
   d. Video Cartridge System

5. Who took over as the president & CEO of Atari Inc. in 1978?
   a. Ray Kassar
   b. Ralph Baer
   c. Willy Higinbotham
   d. Steve Russell

6. Upon leaving Atari, Nolan Bushnell bought back the rights and grew what franchise?
   a. Pizza Hut
   b. Ground Round
   c. Chuck E. Cheese's
   d. Dave and Busters

7. This company was the first independent developer and distributor of console games:
   a. Electronic Arts
   b. Intellivison
   c. Activision
   d. Nintendo

8. Often credited as the first video game to include an "Easter egg":
   a. Warren Robinett's *Adventure*
   b. Howard Scott Warshaw's *Raiders of the Lost Ark*
   c. Kazunori Sawano's *Galaxian*
   d. Toru Iwatani's *Pole Position*

9. Two poorly received games produced by Atari that damaged the company's reputation:
   a. *Space Invaders* and *Asteroids*
   b. *Asteroids* and *Pac-Man*
   c. *Defender* and *E.T.*
   d. *E.T.* and *Pac-Man*

10. Which second-generation console included a full, 49-key computer keyboard and released a programming cartridge called Computer Intro!
    a. Fairchild F
    b. Atari VCS
    c. Oddessy²
    d. Intellivision

11. These consoles offered add-on peripherals that added speech effects to certain games:
    a. Atari VCS and Oddessy²
    b. Oddessy² and Intellivision
    c. Intellivision and ColecoVision
    d. ColecoVision and Atari 5200

12. This second-generation console was the world's first 16-bit home video game system:
    a. Atari VCS
    b. Odyssey²
    c. Intellivision
    d. ColecoVision

13. Which of the following consoles did not have controllers with 12-button numeric keypads?
    a. Odyssey²
    b. Intellivision
    c. ColecoVision
    d. Atari 5200

14. The well-known sports journalist hired for Intellivision's advertisements comparing their games to Atari's VCS games:
    a. Harold "Matt" Matson
    b. Elliot Handler
    c. George Plimpton
    d. George Harrison

15. The original Intellivision programming team members' identities and work location were kept a closely guarded secret, which became known as the:
    a. Blue Sky Rangers
    b. Red Hawks
    c. Intellivisionaries
    d. Programmers Undercover

16. One of this console's successes was securing exclusive rights to reproduce Nintendo's arcade classic *Donkey Kong* game and bundling it with every system:
    a. Odyssey²
    b. Intellivision
    c. ColecoVision
    d. Atari 5200

17. The first console to develop an adapter to play Atari VCS games:
    a. Odyssey²
    b. Intellivision
    c. ColecoVision
    d. Atari 5200

18. The original version of this console contained four controller ports (jacks), along with start, pause, and reset buttons on its controllers:
    a. Odyssey²
    b. Intellivision
    c. ColecoVision
    d. Atari 5200

19. In what year was the video game crash in the United States?
    a. 1978
    b. 1980
    c. 1983
    d. 1986

20. Which one of the following is *not* a cause of the video game crash?
    a. Floods of new consoles
    b. Renewed interest in going to the movies
    c. Growing number of home computers
    d. Poorly made games by smaller companies

True or False

21. Activision was formed by a group of underpaid, underappreciated Apple employees.

22. Only 49 cartridges were released in the United States during Odyssey²'s initial production run.

23. A sleeker version of the Intellivision called "Intellivision Plus" released in 1982.

24. Motion picture company Paramount/MCA demanded royalties from Coleco and Nintendo—claiming Popeye violated copyrights related to its intellectual property.

25. Vectrex was the last system released in the second generation and came with its own monochrome vector monitor.

■ FIGURES

Figure 3.1 Screenshots of defining arcade games from the Golden Age: (a) *Space Invaders* (1978), (b) *Galaxian* (1979), (c) *Pac-Man* (1980), and (d) *Donkey Kong* (1981). (a) *Space Invaders* (Taito, 1978), (b) *Galaxian* (Namco, 1979), (c) *Pac-Man* (Namco, 1980), and (d) *Donkey Kong* (Nintendo, 1981).

Figure 3.2 Atari VCS, often called "The Atari" with standard, digital joystick controller. (Evan-Amos—own work, public domain. Available at https://commons.wikimedia. org/w/index.php?curid=14517499. Retrieved from https:// upload.wikimedia.org/wikipedia/commons/b/b9/Atari-2600-Wood-4Sw-Set.jpg. An Atari 2600 four-switch "wood veneer" version, dating from 1980 to 1982. Shown with standard joystick.) (Part of this image was used on the introductory page of this chapter).

Figure 3.3 Screenshots from Atari VCS launch titles (a) *Air-Sea Battle* and (b) *Combat*. (a) *Air-Sea Battle* (Atari, 1977) and (b) *Combat*. (Courtesy of Atari, 1977.)

Figure 3.4 Magazine advertisement for the Atari Video Computer System in 1981. ("Ads—Missile Command." Retrieved from http://www.atarimania.com/game-atari-2600-vcs-missile-command_s6870.html and http://www. atarimania.com/pubs/hi_res/pub_no_comparing_2.jpg.)

Figure 3.5 Box art to five of the best VCS titles including (a) *Adventure*, (b) *Space Invaders*, (c) *River Raid*, (d) *Yars' Revenge*, and (e) *Pitfall II: Lost Caverns*. (*Adventure*, courtesy of Atari, 1979; *Space Invaders*, courtesy of Atari, 1988;

River Raid, courtesy of Activision, 1982; *Yars' Revenge*, courtesy of Atari, 1982; and *Pitfall II: Lost Caverns*, courtesy of Activision, 1983.)

Figure 3.6 Magnavox Odyssey² with built-in membrane keyboard and updated joysticks. (Evan-Amos—own work, CC BY-SA 3.0. Available at https://commons.wiki-media.org/w/index.php?curid=17722734. Retrieved from https://upload.wikimedia.org/wikipedia/commons/2/2d/ Magnavox-Odyssey-2-Console-Set.jpg. The Magnavox Odyssey², the 1978 follow up to original 1974 release of the Magnavox Odyssey. The console features two controllers that are wired directly into the system.) (Part of this image was used on the introductory page of this chapter.)

Figure 3.7 Screenshots from Odyssey² U.S. launch titles (a) *Football!* and (b) *Speedway!* (a) *Football!* (Magnavox, 1978) and (b) *Speedway!* (Courtesy of Magnavox, 1978.)

Figure 3.8 Magazine advertisement for the Magnavox Odyssey² from 1981 showing *The Quest for the Rings* title on the TV screen and its unique game board below the console. (From Benj Edwards, May 11, 2012. Available at http://www.vintagecomputing.com/index. php/tag/Magnavox and http://www.vintagecomputing. com/wp-content/images/retroscan/odyssey2_characters_ large.jpg. Retro Scan of the Week. The Magnavox Odyssey², from *TIME*, November 2, 1981, p. 24.)

Figure 3.9 Box art to five defining Odyssey² titles including (a) *Killer Bees!* (b) *K.C. Munchkin!* (c) *K.C.'s Krazy Chase!* (d) *Pick Axe Pete!* and (e) *Turtles!* (*Killer Bees!*, courtesy of Magnavox, 1983; *K.C. Munchkin!*, courtesy of Magnavox, 1981; *K.C.'s Krazy Chase!*, courtesy of Magnavox, 1982; *Pick Axe Pete!*, courtesy of Magnavox, 1982; and *Turtles!*, courtesy of Magnavox, 1983.)

Figure 3.10 Mattel Intellivision with its controllers that could be stored inside the unit. (Evan-Amos—own work, CC BY-SA 3.0. Available at https://commons.wikimedia.org/w/index.php?curid=17891257. Retrieved from https://upload.wikimedia.org/wikipedia/commons/6/66/ Intellivision-Console-Set.jpg. The Intellivision, a second-generation video game console released by Mattel in 1979.) (Part of this image was used on the introductory page of this chapter.)

Figure 3.11 Intellivision launch titles (a) *Armor Battle* and (b) *Las Vegas Poker & Blackjack*. (Courtesy of Mattel, 1979. Uploaded by Scott Decker. Retrieved from http://www. scottdecker.com/video_games/intellivision_armor_bat-tle_screen_2.jpg and http://www.scottdecker.com/video_ games/intellivision_las_vegas_poker_and_blackjack.html.)

Figure 3.12 Magazine advertisement for Intellivision with George Plimpton in 1981. (Retrieved from http://www. intellivisionbrasil.com/.%5Cimagens%5Cadvertising%5CIntellivision-Atari5.jpg.)

Figure 3.13 Microvision featuring *Block Buster*. The back of the Milton Bradley Microvision. (By Evan-Amos—Own work, Public Domain, https://commons.wikimedia.org/w/index.php?curid=18273662. Posted February 5, 2017. Retrieved from https://en.wikipedia.org/wiki/Microvision#/media/File: Milton-Bradley-Microvision-Handheld-FL.jpg.)

Figure 3.14 Five key Microvision cartridges: (a) *Alien Raiders*, (b) *Sea Duel*, (c) *Super Blockbuster*, (d) *Connect Four*, and (e) *Mindbuster*. (a) *Alien Raiders*. (Courtesy of Milton Bradley, 1981.) (b) *Sea Duel*. (Courtesy of Milton Bradley, 1980.) (c) *Super Blockbuster*. (Courtesy of Milton Bradley, 1982.) (d) *Connect Four*. (Courtesy of Milton Bradley, 1979.) (e) *Mindbuster*. (Courtesy of Milton Bradley, 1979.)

Figure 3.15 The Intellivision keyboard component (a), Intellivoice adapter (b), and Intellivision II console (c). ((a) "Skel" (Derek McDonald). Sources of research: Wikipedia, The Dot Eaters, Emperor Multimedia Electronic Archives. Created: January 31, 2012. Retrieved from http://www.old-computers.com/museum/description/mattel/intellivision/component-keyboard_s.jpg. (b) Courtesy of Evan-Amos—own work, CC BY-SA 3.0. Retrieved from https://commons.wikimedia.org/w/index.php?curid=18874849. (c) The Intellivision II redesign was much smaller and cheaper to manufacture than the original. By Evan-Amos—Own work, CC BY-SA 3.0. Retrieved from https://commons.wikimedia.org/w/index.php?curid=18893028. Created: January 30, 2012.)

Figure 3.16 Box art to five popular Intellivision titles including (a) *Lock 'N' Chase*, (b) *Astrosmash*, (c) *Night Stalker*, (d) *Bump 'n' Jump*, and (e) *BurgerTime*. (*Lock 'N' Chase*, courtesy of Mattel, 1982; *Astrosmash*, courtesy of Mattel, 1981; *Night Stalker*, courtesy of Mattel, 1982; *Bump 'n' Jump*, courtesy of Mattel, 1983; and *BurgerTime*, courtesy of Mattel, 1982.)

Figure 3.17 ColecoVision video game console with two joystick controllers. (Courtesy of Evan-Amos—own work, public domain, "A ColecoVision unit." Available at https://commons.wikimedia.org/w/index.php?curid=11421149. Retrieved from https://upload.wikimedia.org/wikipedia/commons/4/4b/ColecoVision-wController-L.jpg.) (Part of this image was used on the introductory page of this chapter.)

Figure 3.18 Screenshots from ColecoVision U.S. launch titles (a) *Donkey Kong* and (b) *Zaxxon*. (Courtesy of Coleco, 1982.)

Figure 3.19 ColecoVision: (a) VCS adapter, (b) steering wheel, and (c) Super Action Controller. ((a) Courtesy of Evan-Amos—own work, public domain. Available at https://commons.wikimedia.org/w/index.php?curid=34985653. Retrieved from https://en.wikipedia.org/wiki/ColecoVision#/media/File: ColecoVision-ExpMod1-Attached.jpg. The Expansion Module #1 allowed the ColecoVision to play any game from the Atari 2600. (b) Courtesy of Evan-Amos—own work, public domain. Available at https://commons.wikimedia.org/w/index.php?curid=34986721. Retrieved from https://en.wikipedia.org/wiki/ColecoVision#/media/File:ColecoVision-Expansion2.jpg. The Expansion Module #2 was a steering wheel for racing games. (c) Retrieved from http://cvaddict.com/images/articles/colecovision-super-action-controller.png and modified by Wardyga.)

Figure 3.20 Box art to five defining ColecoVision titles including (a) *Turbo*, (b) *Antarctic Adventure*, (c) *Donkey Kong Junior*, (d) *Jumpman Junior*, and (e) *Venture*. (*Turbo*, courtesy of Coleco, 1982; *Antarctic Adventure*, courtesy of Konami, 1984; *Donkey Kong Junior*, courtesy of Coleco, 1983; *Jumpman Junior*, courtesy of Epyx, 1983; and *Venture*, courtesy of Coleco, 1982.)

Figure 3.21 Two-page magazine advertisement for ColecoVision from 1982. (Scanned and touched up by Wardyga.)

Figure 3.22 Atari 5200 with four controller ports and joystick controller. (Courtesy of Evan-Amos—own work, public domain. Available at https://commons.wikimedia.org/w/index.php?curid=35179017. Retrieved from https://upload.wikimedia.org/wikipedia/commons/a/a0/Atari-5200-4-Port-wController-L.jpg.) (Part of this image was used on the introductory page of this chapter.)

Figure 3.23 Screenshots from Atari 5200 U.S. launch titles (a) *Pac-Man* and (b) *Super Breakout*. (Retrieved from http://www.atarimania.com/5200/screens/super_breakout_3.gif and http://www.atarimania.com/5200/screens/pacman_3.gif.)

Figure 3.24 Magazine advertisement for the Atari 5200 and its peripherals from 1983. (Retrieved from http://www.atarimania.com/pubs/hi_res/pub_here_s_what.jpg.)

Figure 3.25 Box art to five defining Atari 5200 titles including (a) *Berzerk,* (b) *Ms. Pac-Man,* (c) *Montezuma's Revenge,* (d) *Robotron: 2084,* and (e) *Space Dungeon.* (*Berzerk,* courtesy of Atari, 1983; *Ms. Pac Man,* courtesy of Atari, 1983; *Montezuma's Revenge: Featuring Panama Joe,* courtesy of Parker Brothers, 1983; *Robotron: 2084,* courtesy of Atari, 1983; and *Space Dungeon,* courtesy of Atari, 1983.)

Figure 3.26 A look at the many less-popular consoles of the second generation. (Courtesy of Evan-Amos—own work, CC BY-SA 3.0. Available at https://commons.wikimedia.org/w/index.php?curid=18291554. Retrieved from https://upload.wikimedia.org/wikipedia/commons/3/34/Fairchild-Channel-F.jpg. "The Acetronic MPU 1000, a video game console that was a part of the 1292 Advanced Programmable Video System family." By Evan-Amos—Own work, CC BY-SA 3.0, https://commons.wikimedia.org/w/index.php?curid=18312810. Retrieved from https://upload.wikimedia.org/wikipedia/commons/8/88/Acetronic-MPU-1000.png. "The RCA Studio II, a video game console by RCA introduced in 1977." By Evan-Amos—Own work, Public Domain, https://commons.wikimedia.org/w/index.php?curid=38826714. Retrieved from https://upload.wikimedia.org/wikipedia/commons/c/c1/RCA-Studio-II-FL.jpg. "The Bally Professional Arcade, one of the many names of a 2nd generation video game console released by Bally in the late '70s and early '80s." By Evan-Amos—Own work, CC BY-SA 3.0, https://commons.wikimedia.org/w/index.php?curid=18260687. Retrieved from https://upload.wikimedia.org/wikipedia/commons/5/5d/Bally-Arcade-Console.jpg. "The APF MP1000 (some are also labeled the M1000), a video game console released by APF Electronics in 1978." By Evan-Amos—Own work, Public Domain, https://commons.wikimedia.org/w/index.php?curid=45579767. Retrieved from https://upload.wikimedia.org/wikipedia/commons/8/83/APF-MP1000-FL.jpg. "The VC 4000 with controller. A second-generation video game console released in Germany by Interton Electronics." By Evan-Amos—Own work, CC BY-SA 3.0, https://commons.wikimedia.org/w/index.php?curid=18298292. Retrieved from https://upload.wikimedia.org/wikipedia/commons/3/39/VC-4000-Console-Set.jpg. "The Epoch Cassette Vision, a second generation video game console released only in Japan in 1981." By Evan-Amos—Own work, CC BY-SA 3.0, https://commons.wikimedia.org/w/index.php?curid=18364041. Retrieved from https://upload.wikimedia.org/wikipedia/commons/d/db/Epoch-Cassette-Vision-Console.jpg. "The Emerson Arcadia 2001, a 2nd generation video game console released in 1982." By Evan-Amos—Own work, CC BY-SA 3.0, https://commons.wikimedia.org/w/index.php?curid=17891484. Retrieved from https://upload.wikimedia.org/wikipedia/commons/7/77/Emerson-Arcadia-2001.jpg. "The Vectrex video game console, shown with controller." By Evan-Amos—Own work, CC BY-SA 3.0, https://commons.wikimedia.org/w/index.php?curid=17735830. Retrieved from https://upload.wikimedia.org/wikipedia/commons/7/7a/Vectrex-Console-Set.jpg. The Fairchild Channel F with hardwired controllers. A second-generation video game console released in 1976.)

Figure 3.27 Second-generation console sales graph. (Designed by Wardyga using data from various public sources.)

PRO FILE: Nolan Bushnell Photo credit: By Tech Cocktail Flickr: Tech Cocktail Week: Sessions Speaker Series Downtown Vegas sponsored by Moveline, CC BY-SA 2.0, https://commons.wikimedia.org/w/index.php?curid=31557628.

■ REFERENCES

Ashcraft, B. (2018, October 25). *The birth of Japanese arcades.* Retrieved from https://kotaku.com/the-birth-of-japanese-arcades–1794067285.

Bruck, C. (1995). *Master of the game: Steve Ross and the creation of Time Warner.* Reprint edition. New York: Penguin Books.

Campbell, C. (2015, March 19). The story of Yars' Revenge is a journey back to a lost world of video games. *Polygon.* Retrieved from http://www.polygon.com/2015/3/9/8163747/yars-revenge-is-a-journey-back-to-a-lost-world-of-video-games.

Cassidy, W. (2008, January). *Odyssey²/Videopac faq: The essentials – What you need to know about the O2.* Retrieved from http://www.the-nextlevel.com/odyssey2/faq/essentials/.

Editorial: Classic GI: Space Invaders. (2008, January). *Game Informer,* 177, pp. 108–109.

Editorial: Coleco hits with home video games. (1983, January 24). *Businessweek,* p. 31.

Edwards, B. (2012, May). *Inside the Magnavox Odyssey (40th anniversary).* Retrieved from http://www.vintagecomputing.com/index.php/tag/Magnavox.

Forster, W. (2005). The encyclopedia of consoles, handhelds & home computers 1972–2005. *Gameplan,* p. 50.

Herman, L. (2003, January 19). TV Interview from *Icons Episode #19: Atari.* G4 Network.

Johnson, K. (1983, August 1). Coleco strong in marketing. *New York Times.* G4 Network. Retrieved from http://www.nytimes.com/1983/08/01/business/coleco-strong-in-marketing.html.

Katz, A. & Kunkel, B. (1983, June). Programmable arcade. *Electronic Games,* p. 40. Retrieved from http://www.archive.org/stream/electronic-games-magazine-1983-06/Electronic_Games_Issue_16_Vol_02_04_1983_Jun#page/n39/mode/2up.

Kent, S. (2001). *The ultimate history of video games: The story behind the craze that touched our lives and changed the world.* Roseville, CA: Three Rivers Press.

Lambie, R. (2013, February 19). *The 1983 videogame crash: What went wrong, and could it happen again?* Retrieved from http://www.denofgeek.com/games/24531/the-1983-videogame-crash-what-went-wrong-and-could-it-happen-again#ixzz4IGwiBVV9.

Langdon, D. (1980, May 12). Lord of the Rings' Irvin Feld has made a fading circus the greatest show on earth again. *People,* 13(19). Retrieved from http://www.people.com/people/archive/article/0,20076452,00.html.

Latson, J. (2015, June 2). *How Donkey Kong and Mario changed the world.* Retrieved from http://time.com/3901489/donkey-kong-anniversary/.

Maher, J. (2012, April 8). This game is over. *Digital Antiquaria.* Retrieved from http://www.filfre.net/2012/04/this-game-is-over/.

McFerran, D. (2010). Retroinspection: ColecoVision. *Videogame Hardware Handbook: 1977 to 2001.* London, UK: Imagine Publishing, Ltd.

Molyneaux, M. & Horton, K. (2016). *Head to head: Colecovision vs. Atari 5200: Hardware comparison.* Retrieved from http://www.atarihq.com/5200/cv52/.

Monfort, N. & Bogost, I. (2014). A neuroevolution approach to general Atari game playing. *Racing the Beam.* Retrieved from https://mitpress.mit.edu/sites/default/files/titles/content/9780262012577_sch_0001.pdf.

Nilsen, A. (2001). Interview by Steve Kent from *The ultimate history of video games: The story behind the craze that touched our lives and changed the world.* Roseville, CA: Three Rivers Press.

Nobes, M. (2022, April 7). MB *Microvision handheld game console.* Retrieved from https://www.simplyeighties.com/mb-microvision-game-console.php.

Pollack, A. (1986, September 27). Video games, once zapped, in comeback. *The New York Times,* Section 1, p. 1. Retrieved from https://www.nytimes.com/1986/09/27/business/video-games-once-zapped-in-comeback.html.

Purchese, R. (2010, May 20). *Iwatani: Pac-Man was made for women.* Retrieved from http://www.eurogamer.net/articles/iwatani-pac-man-was-made-for-women.

Robinson, K. (2003, March 23). TV Interview from *Icons Episode #23: Intellivision.* G4 Network.

Slater, J. (2008). Retroinspection: Intellivision. *Videogames Hardware Handbook.* London, UK: Imagine Publishing Ltd, p. 15.

Wolf, M. (2007, November 30). *The video game explosion: A history from Pong to PlayStation and beyond.* Westport, CT: Greenwood Press.

Early PC Gaming

■ OBJECTIVES

After reading this chapter, you should be able to:

- Discuss the history of early computers by Apple, Atari, and Commodore.

- Explore the best-selling Japanese home computer series: NEC PC-98 and MSX.

- Examine important British computer series: ZX Spectrum and Amstrad CPC.

- Review key people behind the video games and personal computers.

- Identify graphics and other capabilities of early home computer games.

- Compare the technological differences among popular home computers.

- List key video game titles and peripherals for each computer series.

- Explain what made each PC unique to the growth of the home computer market.

- Illustrate how each early gaming computer evolved with subsequent models.

- Discuss why Commodore 64 was the best-selling personal computer model of all time.

- List important innovations introduced to gaming during this time.

- Summarize early home computer market sales.

DOI: 10.1201/9781003315759-4

■ KEY TERMS AND PEOPLE

Acorn Computers
Amiga series
Amstrad CPC
ANTIC
Apple II series
Apple III
Apple Computer
Apple Lisa
Apple Music Synthesizer
ASIC
Atari 400/800
Atari 8-bit family
Atari ST series
Atari XL series
AY-3–8910 BASIC
BBC Micro
BEEP sound chip
Bell & Howell
City-building games
Civilization series
Commodore 128
Commodore 16
Commodore 64
Commodore International
Commodore PET
Commodore Plus/4

Control Program/Monitor (CP/M)
Controller ports
Central Processing Unit (CPU)
Colour Clash
CP/M
Will Crowther
CTIA (later GTIA)
Data Cassette Storage
Rick Dickinson
Disk II
Disk Operating System (DOS)
Educator 64
Electronic Arts
Eroge game
Expansion slots
Falling block puzzle games
Richard Garriott
Genlock
God game
Graphical adventure game
Graphical MUD
Graphical User Interface (GUI)

Graphics Display Controller (GDC)
Trip Hawkins
Rod Holt
I/O (input and output)
Steve Jobs
Konami
Macintosh
Sid Meier
MIDI
MMORPG
Mockingboard
Peter Molyneux
MSX series
Multicolor sprites
Multi-User Dungeon (MUD)
NEC μPD7220
Nippon Electric Company (NEC)
Open-ended games
Alexey Pajitnov
Panasonic
PC-98 series
Personal Computer
POKEY
Random Access Memory (RAM)

Read-only memory (ROM)
Role-playing game (RPG)
SID 6581
SimCity series
Clive Sinclair
Sinclair Research
Sound card
Alan Sugar
Teleprinter
Tetris series
Text adventure games
Toggle circuit
Jack Tramiel
Ultima series
VIC-20
VisiCalc
Jim Westwood
Ken and Roberta Williams
Steve "Woz" Wozniak
Will Wright
XE Game System (XEGS)
Yamaha YM2203
Bob Yannes
Zilog Z80
ZX Spectrum

■ EARLY COMPUTER TIMELINE

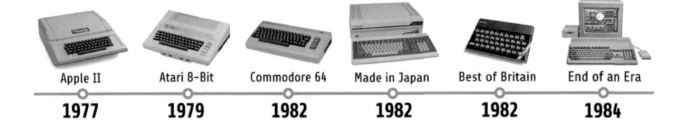

Apple II	Atari 8-Bit	Commodore 64	Made in Japan	Best of Britain	End of an Era
1977	**1979**	**1982**	**1982**	**1982**	**1984**

▪ INTRODUCTION

Before personal computers (PCs), the technological world operated on mainframe computers. Harvard University researcher **Howard Aiken** developed the first mainframe computer in 1936. It was called the **Harvard Mark I** and "was not ready for use until 1943. It weighed five tons, filled an entire room and cost about $200,000 to build" (Tozzi, 2021, p. 1). That is equivalent to more than $3 million today. Add in the expensive networking costs for dedicated data lines and it is no wonder why a "computer" was once something people only talked about.

This chapter reviews the early days of PCs when they began appearing in homes. It will cover key games made popular by the technology, as well as detailed coverage of early breakthrough home computers for gaming by Apple, Atari, and Commodore. The chapter also explores popular systems from Japan and the United Kingdom including the PC-98, MSX, ZX Spectrum, and Amstrad CPC series. The evolution of the technology will be discussed, including the people behind the scenes and the popular genres synonymous with computer gaming during this period.

Coverage of this chapter spans the PC market before and throughout the third generation of console gaming when most computers ran on **CP/M** (Control Program/Monitor, later called "Control Program for Microcomputers") or **DOS** (disk operating system).

▪ APPLE I AND II

While working for Atari, **Steve "Woz" Wozniak** and **Steve Jobs** formed the **Apple Computer Company** in 1976 to sell Wozniak's original **Apple Computer** (later known as the Apple Computer 1, Apple I, or Apple-1). The Apple I was a well-designed circuit board (Figure 4.1) that required users to provide their own cabinet, power supply, keyboard, and video monitor (Dunfield, 2007, para. 1). This meant added costs to the $666.66 launch price, in addition to its users needing to be fairly tech savvy to assemble everything. While the hardware may have been complex, the Apple Computer utilized **BASIC (Beginner's All-purpose Symbolic Instruction Code)** computer language, which, as the name suggests, was quite user-friendly. BASIC also allowed computer games to be programmed and played on the Apple.

FIGURE 4.1 The Apple Computer (1976) circuit board.

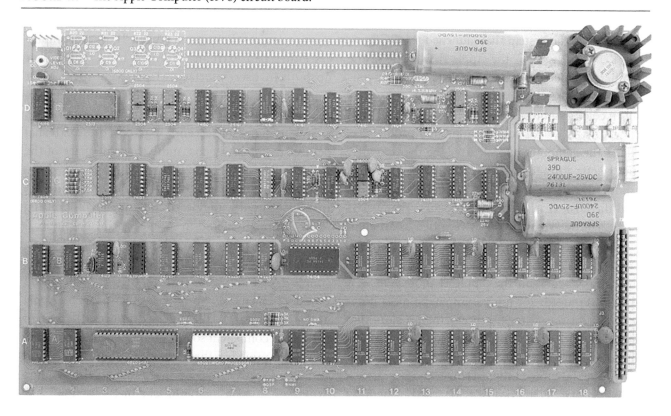

FIGURE 4.2 The Apple II (1977) with two Disk II (1978) floppy disk drives and game paddles.

Steve Jobs was responsible for the marketing and sales of the computers and approximately 200 units were produced—with the majority sold during a span of 9 or 10 months (Williams & Moore, 1984, p. A67). Wozniak managed the customer support side of the business. It was not long before the duo realized they would need to manufacture a more consumer-friendly model of the Apple for mass-market appeal. During the following year, the computer received a refined design with an enclosed cabinet casing designed by Jobs, as well as a keyboard and a power supply developed by **Rod Holt**. The cabinet contained user-friendly connection ports for consumers to attach video monitors, cassette tape storage, and an eventual 5¼-inch floppy disk drive.

The newly remodeled Apple Computer was released and marketed as the **Apple II** (Figure 4.2). Now widely recognized as the system that launched the PC business (Kent, 2001, p. 71), the Apple II was one of the first microcomputers to be accessible to the home consumer. It was also the first commercial PC to include built-in color graphics capabilities with a palette of 16 fixed colors, as well as sound output and paddle controllers. The computer initially used the then-popular **data cassette storage** to save data. A year later, Apple introduced an external 5¼-inch floppy disk drive, called the **Disk II** (shown in Figure 4.2). The Disk II was created by Wozniak and is regarded as an engineering masterpiece for its economic use of electronic components (Freiberger & Swaine, 1985, p. 45).

Wozniak's work on the Apple II pioneered new industry standards for microcomputers, most notably the inclusion of its 50-pin **expansion slots** that allowed users to expand the functionality of the base motherboard. Most Apple II models included at least seven slots for adding peripheral devices such as disk controllers, co-processor cards, memory expansion cards, music and sound cards, as well as standard **input and output (I/O)** devices such as its keyboard and connector ports for a monitor and storage devices. Prior to the Apple II, microcomputers either had extremely limited I/O capability or no built-in user interface whatsoever. These older "mainframes" and "minicomputers" required external **teleprinters** (electromechanical typewriters), as well as separate screens. Together, these external devices could easily cost more than the price of the actual computer.

The Apple II did not contain a dedicated sound chip. Instead, it used a **toggle circuit** capable of emitting "clicks" through a built-in speaker or line output jack. Sounds were generated exclusively by the software, which clicked the speaker at specific times to produce simple beeps and pops—which in succession could produce basic music. Music cards such as ALF's **Apple Music Synthesizer** (1978) helped provide the system with more competent sound in subsequent years. Each ALF card provided three channels (voices) of sound and three cards could be inserted into the system's expansion slots for up to nine channels of sound.

■ HARDWARE COMPARISON: APPLE II VS. ATARI VCS (2600)

A low-end Apple II costs more than six times the price of an Atari VCS/2600 but could do much more than just play video games. Here is a comparison between the two machines. Technically, the Apple II contained the same **1.023 MHz** 8-bit MOS Technology 6502 **CPU (central processing unit)** as the Apple I (Table 4.1), which launched the same year as the Atari VCS in 1977. The VCS ran on an 8-bit MOS 6507 processor at a slightly faster rate of 1.19 MHz.

Beyond processor speed, the units were quite different when comparing **RAM** (random access memory) and screen resolution. The Apple II could utilize **4 kB** (kilobytes) of expandable memory versus the Atari VCS's mere 128 bytes of RAM and **4 kB ROM** (read-only memory). The Apple II displayed a higher horizontal screen resolution of **280 × 192 pixels** (screen dots) for six-color games, compared to the VCS's resolution of 160 × 192 pixels for games displaying four colors per scan line. See Figure 4.3 for examples of the Apple II's graphics and text display capabilities.

While graphically competent for its time, one of the Apple II's biggest weaknesses was its sound. Its software-driven sounds were often comparable to the beeps and noises output from Atari's 2-channel mono sound card. And since the use of sound heavily taxed the **Apple's CPU**, it was customary practice for sound to be used sparingly in games. Eventually, sound cards were developed for the Apple II, such as the **Mockingboard** by Sweet Micro Systems in 1981. Beyond music, these six-channel sound cards could produce general sound effects and speech synthesis. See Figure 4.4 for a look at how the Apple II was marketed.

HEAD-TO-HEAD

To compare the graphics and sound between the Apple II and Atari VCS, play or watch video clips of games released on both systems. Recommended games to compare include *Frogger*, *Jungle Hunt*, *Ms. Pac-Man*, *Pitfall II: Lost Caverns*, and *Tapper*.

TABLE 4.1	Apple II Tech Specs
Manufacturer:	Apple Computer, Inc.
Launch price:	$1,298 w/4 kB RAM, $2,638 w/48 kB, $598 w/4 kB board only
Release date:	April 1977
Format:	Cassette Tape or 5.25″ floppy disk (launched in 1978)
CPU:	8-bit MOS Technology 6502 (1.023 MHz)
Memory:	4–48 kB (3 banks of 4 kB or 16 kB RAM)
Resolution:	280 × 192 or 40 × 48 pixels (text = 40 characters × 24 lines)
Colors:	4–16 onscreen colors from a palette of 16
Sound:	No sound card; software sent "clicks" to built-in speaker

FIGURE 4.3 Screenshots of early Apple II titles: (a) *The Oregon Trail* (1978), (b) *Lemonade Stand* (1979), and (c) *Zork I: The Great Underground Empire* (1980).

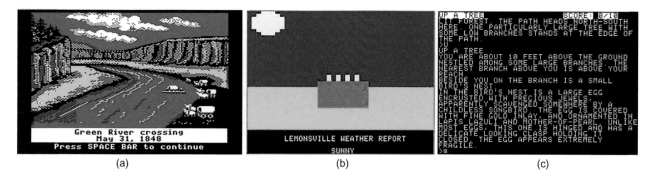

(a) (b) (c)

FIGURE 4.4 Magazine advertisement for the Apple II computer.

How to buy a personal computer.

Suddenly everyone is talking about personal computers. Are you ready for one? The best way to find out is to read Apple Computer's "Consumer Guide to Personal Computing." It will answer your unanswered questions and show you how useful and how much fun personal computers can be. And it will help you choose a computer that meets your personal needs.

Who uses personal computers.

Thousands of people have already discovered the Apple computer—businessmen, students, hobbyists. They're using their Apples for financial management, complex problem solving—and just plain fun.

You can use your Apple to analyze the stock market, manage your personal finances, control your home environment, and to invent an unlimited number of sound and action video games. That's just the beginning.

What to look for.

Once you've unlocked the power of the personal computer, you'll be using your Apple in ways you never dreamed of. That's when the capabilities of the computer you buy will really count. You don't want to be limited by the availability of pre-programmed cartridges. You'll want a computer, like Apple, that you can also program yourself. You don't want to settle for a black and white display. You'll want a computer, like Apple, that can turn any color tv into a dazzling array of color graphics.* The more you learn about computers, the more your imagination will demand. So you'll want a computer that can grow with you as your skill and experience with computers grows. Apple's the one.

How to get one.

The quickest way is to get a free copy of the Consumer Guide to Personal Computing. Get yours by calling 800/538-9696. Or by writing us. Then visit your local Apple dealer. We'll give you his name and address when you call.

*Apple II plugs into any standard TV using an inexpensive modulator (not included).

apple computer™

In California, call 800/662-9238.

CIRCLE NO. 26 ON FREE INFORMATION CARD

■ KEY APPLE II TITLES

Action and arcade games were continually developed for the Apple II, but the games that most differentiated computers from home consoles at this time were adventure games. The first adventure titles were basic **text adventure games**. Also known as "interactive fiction," this genre of games was pioneered by **Will Crowther**'s *Colossal Cave Adventure* (1976) (Figure 4.5a), which he programmed for the PDP-10 mainframe computer. Early text adventure games consisted of just text—where the player would control a character's journey by inputting straightforward text commands such as "climb" or "take." Similar text adventure games appeared on the Apple II such as *Adventureland* (1978) and *Zork I* (1980).

The very first **graphical adventure game** was *Mystery House* (1980) (Figure 4.5b) by **Ken and Roberta Williams** of On-Line Systems (now Sierra Entertainment). Ken was a programmer at IBM and Roberta was the visionary behind writing and designing pictures to accompany the text. "While its simple line graphics were visually primitive in comparison to games released just a few years later on the platform, *Mystery House* established an important precedent" (Barton & Loguidice, 2016, p. 5). The company would go on to develop *King's Quest* (Figure 4.5c), further revolutionizing the graphic adventure game genre with more detailed illustrations and animation.

Another genre that was conceived during this time was the **Multi-User Dungeon (MUD)**. Coined by **Roy Trubshaw** in 1978, early MUDs were text-based adventures that took place in a multiplayer, real-time virtual world. Influenced by the fantasy tabletop **role-playing game (RPG)** *Dungeons & Dragons*, MUDs combined features such as player versus player, interactive fiction, and online chat. Like graphic text adventures, **graphical MUDs** eventually emerged, such as Lucasfilm's *Habitat* (1985).

■ ELECTRONIC ARTS

Trip Hawkins was the Director of Strategy and Marketing at Apple Computer in 1982 when he left the company to incorporate video game publisher **Electronic Arts (EA)**. Aside from becoming one of the largest video game publishers in the world, EA made several important contributions to the business early on. First, the company was notable for promoting its game designers and programmers by including their name or picture on the box and/or in the game's literature. Second, the artwork for each game was extremely important to Hawkins. He believed the packaging for games should be attractive and similar to an album cover. Early EA games such as *Pinball Construction Set* (1983) (Figure 4.6) "were packaged in unique gatefold sleeves, with the designers' names on the front and an elegant graphic design that gave them the hip appearance of rock albums" (Fleming, 2016, p. 2). A third major achievement by EA was that it was the first video game publisher to license athletes for video games, beginning with *One on One: Dr. J vs. Larry Bird* (1983). This pioneered the practice of involving celebrities in the business of video games.

■ APPLE II SUCCESSORS

The **Apple II+** was released in 1979, 2 years after the introduction of the Apple II. This update "included 48 kB RAM, six-color display, and a new BASIC from Microsoft, which established critical base specifications

FIGURE 4.5 Evolution of the adventure game: Screenshots of: (a) *Colossal Cave Adventure* (1976), (b) *Mystery House* (1980), and (c) *King's Quest* (1984).

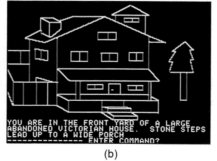
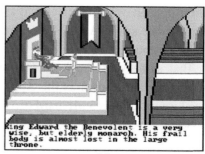

(a)   (b)   (c)

FIGURE 4.6 Box art to five defining Apple II titles: (a) *The Bard's Tale*, (b) *Pinball Construction Set*, (c) *The Oregon Trail*, (d) *Karateka*, and (e) *Ultima I: The First Age of Darkness*.

(a)   (b)   (c)   (d)   (e)

for the computer line" (Barton & Loguidice, 2014, p. 27). Apple also authorized electronics company **Bell & Howell** to manufacture a black Apple II+, which targeted the education industry. A year later, Apple released the **Apple III**, which targeted businesses. The Apple III utilized 128–512 kB of RAM, enhanced audio, and came with the program **Apple III Business BASIC**. The computer had a rough start when technical problems led to a recall of the first 14,000 units. Combined with a high price tag of $4,340–$7,800, the Apple III only sold 65,000–75,000 units and is generally considered a market failure (Linzmayer, 2004, pp. 41–43).

Abandoning all references to the Apple III, the next computer by Apple was released in 1983 under the title **Apple IIe**. The "e" stood for "enhanced," since the Apple IIe came bundled with features that were previously only available as upgrades or add-on peripherals. Codenamed "Diana" and "Super II," the computer included 64 KB RAM (upgradable up to 1 MB) and a custom **ASIC (Application-specific integrated circuit) chip**, which reduced the size and cost of the motherboard. Debuting at $1,395, the Apple IIe eventually came bundled with **DOS (Disk Operating System)**. DOS operated by using the command line and was the innovative operating system (OS) for its time since it ran directly from an internal hard disk. The Apple IIe was manufactured and sold for over a decade, becoming Apple's most successful Apple II series computer.

That same year, Apple introduced another business computer known as the **Apple Lisa** for $9,995. The Lisa included a 5 MB hard drive and a faster processor, but was a commercial failure due to its high cost, insufficient software support, and competing developments at Apple. Part of Lisa's downfall was due to the **Macintosh 128K,** which was released in 1984 for $2,495. Lisa only sold 10,000 units in 2 years. The 128K would be the original **Macintosh**-branded personal computer, which would become the main line of computers from Apple.

Subsequent Apple models included the 1984 **Apple IIc,** which contained 128 KB RAM, as well as a built-in 5¼-inch floppy drive. The "c" stood for "compact" as the Apple IIc was a complete system except for the separate display and power supply. In 1986 "Apple released the 16-bit **Apple IIGS**, the true backwards compatible successor to the original 8-bit II-series of computers. Although Apple was built on the back of the II-series, within a few years the Macintosh [computer line] began to receive most of the company's attention and resources" (Barton & Loguidice, 2016, p. 5).

■ ATARI 8-BIT FAMILY: 400 AND 800

Following the success of the Atari 2600, Atari understood that the computer age was coming and believed its brand was a natural fit for this growing industry. Known as the "**Atari 8-bit family**" computer series, the **Atari 400** and **Atari 800** (Figure 4.7) were launched in November of 1979 for $595 and $999, respectively. Atari management often called the 400 model "Candy" and the 800 model "Colleen," named after two attractive Atari secretaries (Fulton, 2008, p. 4). The official numbered titles for the systems were meant to reflect their RAM—with the 400 originally planned to ship with 4 kB of RAM and the 800 shipping with 8 kB—but falling memory costs allowed Atari to release both computers with at least 8 kB of RAM.

PRO FILE

KEY FACTS:

Co-founded Apple Inc. with Steve Jobs

Pioneered the personal computer revolution with the Apple I and II

STEVE WOZNIAK

PRO FILE

HISTORY:
- Born: August 11, 1950 in San Jose, California

EDUCATION:
- BS in Electrical Engineering and Computer Science, University of California, Berkeley, 1987

CAREER HIGHLIGHTS:
- Designed calculators for Hewlett-Packard in 1971
- Created a circuit board for Atari's Breakout in 1973
- Designed the hardware, circuit board, and operating system for the Apple I in 1976
- Built the Apple II in 1977, which was among the first successful mass-produced PCs and the first w/color graphics and built-in BASIC programming language

RECOGNITION:
ACM Grace Murray Hopper Award (1979), National Medal of Technology (1985), National Inventors Hall of Fame (2000), Heinz Award for Technology (2001), Isaac Asimov Science Award (2011), Hoover Medal (2014), 2015 Alumnus of the Year Award, Legacy for Children Award (2015), and many others, including 10 Honorary Doctor of Engineering degrees

FIGURE 4.7   Atari (a) 400 and (b) 800 computer systems.

(a)   (b)

The Atari 400 computer "was the little brother to the 800. It had a membrane keyboard (to protect against spills from the children who were its target market) and less expansion capability" (Klein, 2014, p. 1). The 400 was also more heavily marketed as a game machine. Both the 400 and 800 had a flip up top that housed a cartridge slot (two slots for the 800) and each computer had four **controller ports (jacks)** that were fully compatible with all Atari VCS/2600 joysticks and paddles. These ports could be used for a variety of functions, such as hard drive interfaces, modems, robot arms, and even a science kit by Atari that could measure light, sound, and temperature.

■ COMPUTER COMPARISON: ATARI 8-BIT VS. APPLE II

The Apple II and Atari 800 could utilize up to 48 kB of RAM and while each computer ran on a MOS 6502 processor (Table 4.2), the Atari 8-bit processor was faster at **1.79 MHz** versus Apple II, which ran at 1.023 MHz. "Both Atari 400 and Atari 800 have multiple purpose co-processors for sound and graphics to

TABLE 4.2	Atari 400/800 Tech Specs
Manufacturer:	Atari, Inc.
Launch price:	$549.95 (Atari 400), $999.95 (Atari 800)
Release date:	November 1979
Format:	Cassette tape or 5.25″ floppy disk + cartridge slot(s)
CPU:	8-bit MOS Technology "Rockwell" 6502 (1.79 MHz)
Memory:	8–16 kB RAM (400), 48 kB RAM (800)
Resolution:	320 × 192 monochrome or 160 × 96 in color (text = 40 × 24)
Colors:	4–16 onscreen colors from a palette of 128 or 256
Sound:	4× oscillators with noise mixing or 2× AM digital

take the load off of the 6502 CPU called **ANTIC**, **CTIA** (later **GTIA**) and **POKEY**" (Bogdan, 2014 p. 79). The POKEY co-processor handled the computer's sound and produced the best sound quality in home computers up to that time. Each system could run up to 16 colors onscreen; however, Atari computers had a much larger color palette to choose from, providing a wider variety to the overall look of their games as seen in Figure 4.8. The main area Apple II bested the Atari computers was in resolution with a color resolution of 280×192 versus Atari's **160×96**. Being overall superior to the Apple II helped Atari computers develop a reputation for games, but there were far fewer business applications to choose from compared to the Apple II.

FIGURE 4.8 Screenshots of Atari 8-bit family titles: (a) *Rainbow Walker* (1983), (b) *Bounty Bob Strikes Back* (1984), and (c) *Rescue on Fractalus!* (1984).

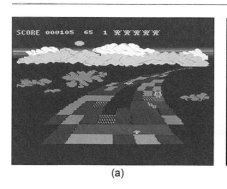
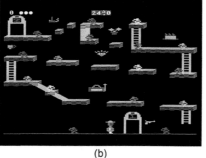
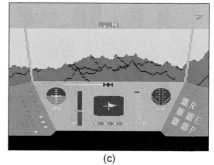

(a) (b) (c)

HEAD-TO-HEAD

To compare the graphics and sound between the Apple II and the Atari 8-bit, play (or research video clips of) games released on both computer systems. Interesting titles to compare include *B.C.'s Quest for Tires*, *Donkey Kong*, *Galaxian*, *Karateka*, and *Pitfall II: Lost Caverns*.

▪ KEY ATARI 8-BIT TITLES

Atari computer games were known for their distinct "graphics look" native to Atari software, including "multiple graphics modes, four directional fine scrolling, [and] colorful modified character-set backgrounds" (Stanton, Wells, Rochowansky, & Mellid, 1984, p. 14). *Star Raiders* (1979) (Figure 4.9) was one of its earliest titles and remained one of the reasons gamers purchased an Atari computer for years. Atari 8-bit computers had the definitive version of *M.U.L.E.*

(1983), which utilized all four joystick ports to allow four-player simultaneous play. For those who owned extra paddles, up to eight players could play together in *Super Breakout* (1979). See Figure 4.10 for more of the computer's highlights.

Despite its virtues, the 400 and 800 were complicated and expensive computers to build and did not prove to be very profitable for Atari. The 400 especially had a tough time competing with technically superior machines appearing in the early 1980s, which typically included more RAM and improved keyboards. Atari would roll out a new generation of 8-bit computers with its **XL series** beginning in 1983.

▪ EXTENDED FAMILY: ATARI 8-BIT SUCCESSORS

Atari launched successors to the 400 and 800 computers (Figure 4.11), beginning in 1983 with the ill-fated **1200XL**. The 1200XL launched for $899 and featured 64 kB of RAM. Due to performance issues such as

FIGURE 4.9 Box art to five defining Atari 8-bit family games: (a) *Star Raiders*, (b) *Rescue on Fractalus!*, (c) *M.U.L.E.*, (d) *Bounty Bob Strikes Back*, and (e) *Boulder Dash*.

(a) (b) (c) (d) (e)

FIGURE 4.10 Magazine advertisement for the Atari 800 computer in 1981.

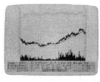

FIGURE 4.11 Evolution of the Atari 8-bit computers: (a) 1200XL, (b) 600XL, (c) 800XL, (d) 130EX, and (e) XEGS Game System.

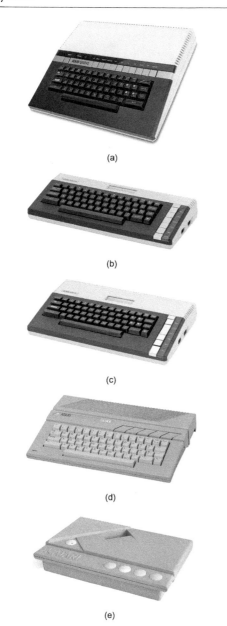

(a)

(b)

(c)

(d)

(e)

poor design and backward compatibility problems with previous Atari systems, the 1200XL was discontinued after less than 6 months in June 1983. It was quickly replaced by the **600XL** and **800XL**.

Aside from improving the design and functionality of the units, Atari's goal for the 600XL and 800XL was to again offer consumers two options at different price points. The 600XL launched at $199 with 16 kB of RAM, while the 800XL shipped for $299 with 64 kB of memory. The 800XL would go on to become Atari's most popular computer of all time.

Following the "XL series," Atari released an "XE series" in 1985 with the **65XE** and **130XE**. The "XE" stood for "XL-Expanded" since the computers contained 64 kB and 128 kB of RAM, respectively. Like the 400 and 800, the XE PCs were given numbers to represent their memory (e.g., the 130XE contained 130,000 bytes of RAM). Beyond additional memory, the XE series was not a substantial improvement over the XL series, as it borrowed technology from previous iterations of XL computers. On top of that, the keyboards had a mushy feeling to the buttons and the white keys would get dirty quickly (RetroIsle, 2015, para. 8).

Atari's final 8-bit release before moving on to its **ST** computer series was the **XE Game System (XEGS)**, which launched in 1987. Essentially a repackaged 65XE with a detachable keyboard, the XEGS was compatible with practically all Atari 8-bit software. A basic and deluxe set was offered, with the deluxe set including a joystick, keyboard, light gun, and two additional games.

■ COMMODORE 64

Commodore International was founded in Toronto by **Jack Tramiel** (pronounced Tra-mel) in 1954 as a typewriter assembly plant. The company expanded to a calculator manufacturing plant in 1969, and Tramiel purchased CPU manufacturer **MOS Technology** for $800,000 in 1976 (Kent, 2001, p. 248). MOS Technology made the 6502-microprocessor chip used by the Apple II, Atari 400 and 800, as well as Commodore's first home computer, the **Commodore PET (Personal Electronic Transactor)** which debuted in 1977. Years later Commodore released a "family" version of the PET, the **VIC-20** computer in 1981. The VIC-20 followed Tramiel's motto for building computers "for the masses, not the classes" and retailed for just $299.95. It was the first computer to retail below $300 and became the first computer to sell more than 1 million units. Tramiel's business model of producing fully functional computers at an affordable price continued with the **Commodore 64** (Figure 4.12), which launched in August 1982 for just $595.

The Commodore 64 was named after its 64 kB of RAM. Its retail price of $595 for 64 kB of RAM was a bargain compared to the Apple II's initial price of $1,298 and Atari 800's launch price of $999.95—and

FIGURE 4.12 Commodore 64 home computer system.

those computers only included up to 48 kB of RAM. In part from acquiring MOS Technology, Tramiel was able to keep the price of the C64 down by manufacturing parts of the computer in-house. Another move that set the Commodore 64 apart from the competition was following in Atari's footsteps by marketing and selling the C64 in retail stores such as Sears, Roebuck and Company.

■ COMPUTER COMPARISON: COMMODORE 64 VS. ATARI 8-BIT

With 20% more RAM at a fraction of the cost of an Atari 800, how did the Commodore 64 hold up in other technical areas? Its screen resolution of **320 × 200 pixels** (Table 4.3) was significantly higher than the Apple II's 280 × 192 display but only marginally better than the Atari 800's 320 × 192. Its improved processing chip allowed for **multicolor**

TABLE 4.3 Commodore 64 Tech Specs

Manufacturer:	Commodore International, Ltd.
Launch price:	$595
Release date:	August 1982
Format:	Cassette tape or 5.25″ floppy disk
CPU:	8-bit MOS Technology 6510 (1.023 MHz)
Memory:	64 kB RAM + 20 kB ROM
Resolution:	320 × 200 pixels (text = 40 characters × 25 lines)
Colors:	16 onscreen colors from a palette of 16
Sound:	3-channel SID 6581 (Sound Interface Device) chip

sprites (two colors per screen dot versus one on the other PCs), which made it "easier to create fast-moving, flicker-free game graphics" (Reimer, 2005, p. 4).

On the flip side, its paltry color palette of 16 colors (see Figure 4.13) paled in comparison to the 8-bit

FIGURE 4.13 Screenshots of early Commodore 64 titles: (a) *Choplifter* (1982), (b) *Spy Hunter* (1983), and (c) *Impossible Mission* (1984).

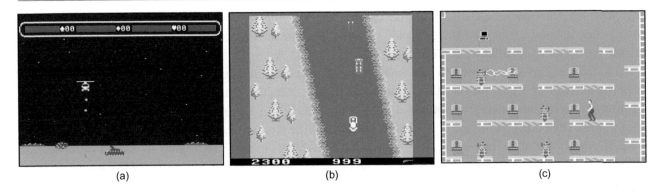

| (a) | (b) | (c) |

Atari computers' hundreds of colors. Furthermore, the Atari computers had a faster CPU, which was evident when comparing games such as *Dropzone* and *Rescue on Fractalus!*. C64 games typically looked and played more smoothly, while Atari's computer games had more vivid color. Sound was another attribute that put the Commodore 64 above the competition. The C64's 3-channel **SID 6581 (Sound Interface Device)** processor by **Bob Yannes** was superior to all home computer sound chips preceding it. See Figure 4.14 for more information.

HEAD-TO-HEAD

To compare the graphics and sound between the Apple II, Atari 400/800, and the Commodore 64, play (or watch video clips of) games that were released on all three computers. Games to compare include *Choplifter, Spy Hunter, Summer Games, World Karate Championship*, and *Zaxxon*.

▪ KEY COMMODORE 64 TITLES

With its superior hardware capabilities and large game library, the Commodore 64 developed a reputation of being a gaming computer more than a business PC. It could play games on cassette tapes, floppy disks, and cartridges, although most of its games were manufactured on tape or cartridge. Impressive third-party cartridge-based games included "*Gyruss* from Parker Bros, *Diamond Mine* by Roklan, *Moondust* by Creative, *Maze Master* by HES and *Jumpman Junior* by Epyx" (Retro Gamer, 2009, p. 57).

Memorable cassette titles included Mastertronic's *Master of Magic, One Man and His Droid*, and *Spellbound*. Other hits included *Boulder Dash, The Sentinel, Archon*, and *Elite*. For those looking for epic quests, there was the *Ultima* and *Bard's Tale* role-playing game series and graphical adventure games *Maniac Mansion* and *Zak McKracken* by LucasArts. MicroProse and Cinemaware also produced classics such as *Sid Meier's Pirates!* and *Defender of the Crown*. Commodore created a few notable first-party titles, including *International Soccer* and an excellent conversion of the arcade hit *Wizard of War*. The C64 had its share of exclusive titles, but most of its top games were multiplatform as seen in Figure 4.15.

An important game genre that made its debut on PCs during this time was the "falling blocks" puzzle game. The pioneer of this type of game was Moscow's **Alexey Pajitnov** with his mega hit *Tetris* in 1984. Published by Spectrum HoloByte for both Commodore 64 and IBM PC, Tetris was the first software title to be exported from the Soviet Union to the United States. The game involves dropping various puzzle-like shapes called "Tetriminos" to form horizontal lines, which disappear and add points to the user's score.

While *Tetris* sold well on PC and was ported to the arcades in 1988, its popularity skyrocketed when it was bundled as the **pack-in** title for Nintendo's Game Boy handheld system, which was released in 1989. It was not long before most major game manufacturers developed their own knockoff of *Tetris*, such as Sega's *Columns* (1990), Taito's *Bust-A-Move/Puzzle Bobble* (1994), and Capcom's *Super Puzzle Fighter II Turbo* (1996), among countless others.

Another pioneer of the early PC generation that debuted on the C64 was *Sid Meier's Pirates!* (1987) by Ontario's **Sid Meier** (Figure 4.16a). These strategy and simulation games would make a name for Meier, leading to titles on other computer platforms such as *Sid Meier's Railroad Tycoon* (1990), and the turn-based **Civilization** series which began in 1991. Meier (with MicroProse co-founder Bill Stealey) redefined the "open-ended" genre. These games fostered features like character creation, plus a multitude of choices and opportunities for players to engage in as they created their own adventures.

💡 DID YOU KNOW?

Partly due to their expensive cost (the Commodore 1541 floppy disk drive debuted at $400), "even at the peak of its popularity, it's said that only around 10% of all C64 owners had a disk drive" (Retro Gamer, 2009, p. 57).

▪ COMMODORE 64 SUCCESSORS

Commodore released successors to the C64, including the **Educator 64** in 1983 and the **SX-64** in 1984. The Educator 64 targeted schools as a replacement for its older PET computers. While it looked like a PET on the outside (using PET casing), its inside contained a

FIGURE 4.14 Magazine advertisement for the Commodore 64 computer in 1982.

WHEN WE ANNOUNCED THE COMMODORE 64 FOR $595, OUR COMPETITORS SAID WE COULDN'T DO IT.

THAT'S BECAUSE THEY COULDN'T DO IT.

The reason is that, unlike our competitors, we make our own IC chips. *Plus* all the parts of the computer they go into.

So Commodore can get more advanced computers to market sooner than anybody else. And we can get them there for a lot less money.

WHAT PRICE POWER?

For your $595,* the Commodore 64™ gives you a built-in user memory of 64K. This is hundreds of dollars less than computers of comparable power.

Lest you think that the Commodore 64 is some stripped-down loss leader, a look at its available peripherals and interfaces will quickly convince you otherwise.

SOFTWARE THAT WORKS HARD.

The supply of software for the Commodore 64 will be extensive. And with the optional plug-in Z80 microprocessor, the Commodore 64 can accommodate the enormous amount of software available in CP/M.®

Add in the number of programs available in BASIC and you'll find that there are virtually no applications, from word processing to spreadsheets, that the Commodore 64 can't handle with the greatest of ease.

PERIPHERALS WITH VISION.

The Commodore 64 interfaces with all the peripherals you could want for total personal computing: disk drives, printers and a telephone modem that's about $100, including a free hour's access to some of the more popular computer information services. Including Commodore's own Information Network for users.

RUN YOUR BUSINESS BY DAY. SAVE THE EARTH BY NIGHT.

At the end of a business day, the Commodore 64 can go into your briefcase and ride home with you for an evening's fun and games.

Because of its superior video quality (320x200 pixel resolution, 16 available colors and 3D Sprite graphics), the Commodore 64 surpasses the best of the video game machines on the market. Yet, because it's such a powerful computer, it allows you to invent game programs that a game machine will never be able to play; as well as enjoy Commodore's own video game cartridges.

ATTACK, DECAY, SUSTAIN, RELEASE.

If you're a musicologist, you already know what an ADSR (attack, decay, sustain, release) envelope is. If you're not, you can learn this and much more about music with the Commodore 64's music synthesizing features.

It's a full-scale compositional tool. Besides a programmable ADSR envelope generator, it has 3 voices (each with a 9-octave range) and 4 waveforms for truly sophisticated composition and playback—through your home audio system, if you

THE COMMODORE 64. ONLY $595.

wish. It has sound quality you'll find only on separate, music-only synthesizers. And graphics and storage ability you won't find on any separate synthesizer.

DON'T WAIT.

The predictable effect of advanced technology is that it produces less expensive, more capable products the longer you wait.

If you've been waiting for this to happen to personal computers, your wait is over.

See the Commodore 64 soon at your local Commodore Computer dealer and compare it with the best the competition has to offer.

You can bet that's what the competition will be doing.

Commodore Business Machines
Personal Systems Division
P.O. Box 500, Conshohocken, Pennsylvania 19428

Please send me more information on the Commodore 64™

Name_____ Title_____

Company_____

Address_____

City_____State_____

Zip_____Phone_____

C= commodore COMPUTER

SIO221

Manufacturer's Suggested Retail Price: July 1, 1982. Disk drives and printers are not included in prices. The 64's price may change without notice.
CP/M® is a registered trademark of Digital Research, Inc.   Canada–3370 Pharmacy Avenue, Agincourt, Ontario, Canada M1W 2K4.

FIGURE 4.15 Box art to five defining Commodore 64 titles: (a) *IK+*, (b) *Zack McKracken and the Alien Mindbenders*, (c) *Impossible Mission*, (d) *Turrican II*, and (e) *Paradroid*.

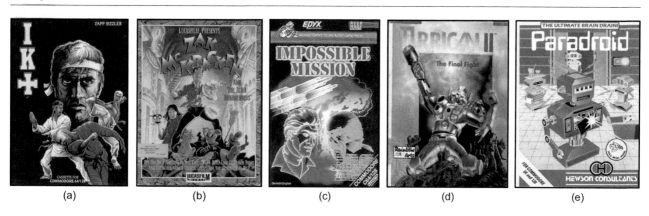

(a)   (b)   (c)   (d)   (e)

C64 motherboard. The Educator 64 included a green monochromatic monitor. Since most C64 games were in color, it did not sell very well. The SX-64 (also known as the **Executive 64**) was an all-in-one portable version of the Commodore 64 and included both a built-in 5-inch monitor and model 1541 floppy disk drive. Released in 1984, this briefcase-size bundle was the first portable color computer on the market and debuted at $995. A unique feature of the SX-64 was that its handle doubled as a stand, which could be rotated to position the angle of the monitor.

Another pair of computers to be released after the Commodore 64 included the **Commodore 16** and the **Commodore Plus/4,** both released in 1984. The $99 Commodore 16 came with 16 kB of RAM and "was designed to replace the Commodore VIC-20, but it was not compatible with the VIC-20, nor with the C64" (Personal Computer Museum, 2016, para. 1). The Commodore Plus/4 contained mostly the same technical specifications as the Commodore 16, with four times the RAM and a price tag of $299. While these PCs could display more onscreen colors than the Commodore 64, they lacked other features such as hardware sprites and the SID sound processor. Better suited for office programs such as word processing and spreadsheet applications, these units did not catch on with gamers and were considered market failures.

The last of Commodore's early 8-bit computers was the **Commodore 128**. Debuting in January 1985 for $299, the C128 came with 128 kB of RAM and contained multiple processors. The inclusion of a **Zilog Z80 CPU** allowed the C128 to run the more powerful **Control Program/Monitor (CP/M)** operating system. It was also backward compatible with most C64 games—one of the best computers of the 8-bit generation. However, the 16-bit generation was just around the corner and gamers would soon be shifting their attention to Commodore's **Amiga** line of computers. See Table 4.4 for a timeline of these and other important computers between 1979 and 1988.

FIGURE 4.16 Screenshots of (a) *Sid Meier's Pirates!* (1987), (b) *Populous* (1989), and (c) *SimCity* (1989).

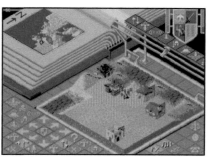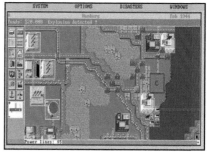

(a)   (b)   (c)

TABLE 4.4 Timeline of Notable Early Home Computer Systems from 1979 to 1988

1979	Atari 400/800, Texas Instruments TI-99/4
1980	Commodore VIC-20, Tandy TRS-80 Color Computer
1981	Osborne 1, TI-99/4A, IBM PC, Sinclair ZX81/TS 1000, BBC Micro
1982	Kaypro II, Sinclair ZX Spectrum, Commodore 64
1983	Atari 1200XL/600XL/800XL, Coleco Adam, Microsoft MSX
1984	Apple Macintosh, Amstrad CPC
1985	Atari 65XE/130XE, Atari ST, Commodore 128, Commodore Amiga
1986	Compaq Portable II, IBM Convertible, Apple IIGS
1987	Atari XEGS (XE Game System), Acorn Archimedes
1988	Apple IIc Plus, NeXT

■ MADE IN JAPAN

Japanese electronics companies Nippon Electric Company (**NEC**), Sord (Toshiba), Hitachi, Fujitsu, Sharp, and others all began releasing single-board microcomputers in the mid-to-late 1970s. NEC revolutionized the computer industry in the early 1980s when the company introduced the first graphics processor chip, the **µPD7220 Graphics Display Controller (GDC)**. The chip incorporated efficient ways for drawing arcs, lines, circles, and special characters with light pen support that "could drive up to four megabits of bit-mapped graphics memory, which was quite a lot for the time. Prior to the µPD7220 every graphics device had its own drawing primitives library, with IBM's 2250 (1974), and Tektronix's

4010 (1972) being the most popular" (Peddie, 2019, para. 5–6). The controller's simple instructions made it incredibly user-friendly, and the chip was used in more than a half dozen Japanese computers into 1987, including NEC's best-selling **PC-9800** computer series.

■ NEC PC-98

NEC's PC-9800 series (commonly shortened to "**PC-98**") and Microsoft Japan/ASCII's **MSX** were the best-selling computers from Japan, selling upward of 18 million and 9 million units, respectively. The PC-9800 series started with the PC-9801 (Figure 4.17a), which was launched in October 1982. The PC-9801 contained two µPD7220 display controllers—one for text and one for graphics. It was a powerful machine with a **16-bit** Intel processor and **128 kB RAM** (Table 4.5). It was originally built for business but quickly became a gaming PC. The original model only contained an internal buzzer for sound. Optional sound cards were made available, including the **PC-9801-26K** featuring FM synthesizer **Yamaha YM2203**. This chip produced sound quality similar to the Sega Mega Drive/Genesis and became a popular PC-98 sound card for video games.

Around three dozen PC-98 models were released over a 20-year timespan—gradually upgrading everything from the sound, memory, speed, and colors—to 32-bit processors in the early 1990s. With so many versions spanning two decades of releases, top games vary drastically in graphics and sound quality depending on when they were released. One aspect the PC-98

FIGURE 4.17 Best-selling computers in Japan: (a) NEC PC-9801 and (b) MSX2 by Sanyo.

(a)

(b)

TABLE 4.5 PC-9801 Tech Specs

Manufacturer:	NEC
Launch price:	¥298,000 (approx. $1,400)
Release date:	October 1982
Format:	Floppy disc
CPU:	16-bit Intel 8086 CPU (5 MHz)
Memory:	128 kB RAM (Expandable to 640 kB)
Resolution:	640 × 400 pixels (initially)
Colors:	16 out of 4,096-color palette
Sound:	Internal buzzer

TABLE 4.6 MSX Tech Specs

Manufacturer:	Various
Launch price:	¥59,800 ($445)
Release date:	October 21, 1983
Format:	Cartridge and cassette
CPU:	8-bit Zilog Z80A (3.58 MHz)
Memory:	8–64 kB RAM (MSX1) + 16 kB TMS9918 VRAM
Resolution:	256 × 192 (Text modes: 40 × 24 and 32 × 24)
Colors:	16 colors (15 + 1 transparent)
Sound:	3-channel, General Instrument AY-3-8910

became known for was **eroge** (erotic game) titles and visual novels featuring adult manga or anime. While eroge titles were common on all Japanese computers, the PC-98 developed a reputation for them. Respectable key titles from the 1990s include the platform adventure games *Popful Mail* (1991) and *Rusty* (1993), Hideo Kojima's graphic adventure *Policenauts* (1994), falling blocks puzzler *Puyo Puyo 2* (1995), and 1996 shoot 'em-ups *Flame Zapper Kotsujin* and *Rude Breaker*.

▪ MSX

The other best-selling computer series to come out of Japan was the **MSX**. Developed by a joint effort between **ASCII Corporation** and the Japanese division of Microsoft, the MSX was built on standardized home computer architecture that guaranteed software and hardware compatibility, regardless of manufacturer. This concept—which predated Windows—helped the MSX become the most popular Japanese PC outside its home country. More than "a dozen other (mostly Japanese) companies participated in the standard, including electronics giants like Canon, Casio, Pioneer, Panasonic, and Sony" (Loguidice, 2017, para. 3–6). Announced on June 27, 1983, the MSX hit Japanese retail shelves on October 21 that year with the **Mitsubishi ML-8000**. It would not reach European stores until the end of 1984 and barely scratched the surface in North America.

The system's **TMS9918** video processor (Table 4.6) produced adequate graphics and colors; however, it lacked hardware scrolling, resulting in slow or choppy

performance by software-driven movement or reduction in colors or sprites (Loguidice, 2017). Like its popular Zilog Z80 CPU, which was used by countless computers and consoles, its 3-channel **General Instrument AY-3-8910** was also a staple sound card in the computer and video game industry. Thanks to its excellent sound, the AY-3-8910 could be found in more than two dozen arcade machines, at least 20 computer systems, as well as home consoles such as Mattel Intellivision and Vectrex.

The MSX was a competent gaming platform. Key Japanese game developers such as **Konami**, **Hudson Soft**, and **Compile** were producing titles for the MSX computer system before making games on Nintendo and Sega's home consoles. Examples of well-known video game franchises that debuted on the MSX series include *Bomberman*, *Metal Gear*, *Parodius*, and *Puyo Puyo*. Konami had a streak of solid titles every year, with hits such as *Vampire Killer* (1986), *Penguin Adventure* (1987), *King's Valley II: The Seal of El Giza* (1988), *Space Manbow* (1989), and *Metal Gear 2: Solid Snake* (1990).

For a quick comparison between the original MSX and PC-9801, check out each computer's version of *Thexder* (1986). Four main versions of the MSX were manufactured over its 10-year lifespan: the original MSX (1982) was released worldwide; **MSX2** (1985) (Figure 4.17b) was released worldwide and could play all games mentioned above; **MSX2+** (1988) was released in select regions; and **MSX TurboR** (1990) released in Japan only. The TurboR added a 16-bit R800 (7.16 MHz) processor.

■ BEST OF BRITAIN

The United Kingdom was the home of notable early PCs in the 1980s. **Clive Sinclair** founded **Sinclair Research** in 1973 as Westminster Mail Order Ltd. and began as a developer of electronics such as radios and calculators. Computer research began in the late 1970s and in 1980 chief engineer **Jim Westwood** launched Sinclair's first home computer, the ZX80 for just £99. This was quickly followed by the ZX81 in 1981 and then the **ZX Spectrum** (Figure 4.18) 1 year later. Another British computer introduced during the early 1980s was the **BBC Micro** (short for "British Broadcasting Corporation Microcomputer System") by **Acorn Computers,** which was launched on December 1, 1981. The BBC Micro sold more than 1.5 million units, while the ZX Spectrum would more than triple that number and become the country's best-selling computer.

■ ZX SPECTRUM

Based on the popular Zilog Z80A CPU (Table 4.7), Sinclair Research released the ZX Spectrum on April 23, 1982, for as low as £125. Often referred to as "Speccy," the affordable system had its share of shortcomings. To keep the price down, there were no hardware sprites nor hardware scrolling to its graphics modes (Vallantine, 2021, para. 8). It had a limited palette with only two shades of blue, red, magenta, green, cyan, yellow, and white, along with one shade of black.

TABLE 4.7 ZX Spectrum Tech Specs

Manufacturer:	Sinclair Research
Launch price:	£125 (16 kB) or £175 (48 kB)
Release date:	April 23, 1982 (UK), 1983 (US)
Format:	Compact cassette, ZX Microdrive, 3-in. floppy disk (Spectrum +3)
CPU:	Zilog Z80A (3.5 MHz)
Memory:	16 kB or 48 kB (later 128 kB)
Resolution:	256 × 192 (Text mode: 32 columns × 24 rows)
Colors:	15 colors (7 colors of 2× shades + black)
Sound:	1 channel, 10-octave BEEP chip (built-in speaker plus output) (3-channel 4-bit sound AY-3–8912 on 128K model)

FIGURE 4.18 (a) The Sinclair ZX Spectrum and (b) screenshot of *Chase H.Q.* (1988) with its limited colors and Colour Clash effect where blue and yellow meet at the horizon.

(a)

(b)

The system was most notorious for its unique "**Colour Clash**" issue, where the colors of moving sprites or character blocks would change to match one other—giving graphics somewhat of a transparent effect (see Figure 4.18). "Some form of Colour Clash can be found in just about every game produced for ZX Spectrum. It caused a graphics style that became synonymous for British computing and gaming of the 1980s" (Paleotronic, 2018, p. 47). If anything, the computer's shortcomings forced programmers to become more creative coders.

Compared to the competition, the Spectrum's "basic **BEEP sound chip** was inferior (especially alongside the Atari 8-bits, Commodore's VIC20 and the BBC Model A and B micros)" (Vallantine, 2021, para. 8). The Spectrum did not even include joystick ports, so an external joystick interface had to be purchased separately to connect game controllers. What made the Spectrum a success was affordability, unique library of games, and its legacy as the machine that brought mainstream computer programming to the United Kingdom. "It was so popular that it spawned magazines like *Sinclair User,* published in the U.K. between 1982 and 1993" (Westaway, 2021, para. 1). It was also small and stylish, thanks to the product design of **Rick Dickinson**. Three versions of the Spectrum were released by Sinclair, including the original 16/48K model, followed by the **ZX Spectrum+** and **ZX Spectrum128** in 1985. Amstrad would acquire the series in 1986 and released a handful of other Spectrum systems in the following years.

Top Spectrum games include the overhead adventure game *Atic Atac* (1983), 3D space trader *Elite* (1984), platformers *Manic Miner* (1983) and *Jet Set Willy* (1984), graphic adventure *Lords of Midnight* (1984), and early sandbox games *Skool Daze* (1984) and *Back to Skool* (1985). Other key titles include isometric action-adventure games *Knight Lore* (1984) and *Head Over Heels* (1987), *R-Type* (1988), as well as Taito's arcade hits *Target: Renegade* and *Chase H.Q.* in 1988.

■ AMSTRAD CPC

The **Amstrad CPC** (Colour Personal Computer) series was another notable computer line from the United Kingdom. **Alan Sugar** (aka "Lord Sugar") founded Amstrad as AMS Trading Ltd. in 1968. The company made a name for itself manufacturing bargain-priced audio and video appliances—a business

strategy they would continue with their home computer systems. Retailing at just £229 with a green, monochrome screen or £329 with a color screen, the Amstrad **CPC464** (Figure 4.19a) debuted at a lower price than the Commodore 64. The machine was built to compete with 8-bit computers like the ZX Spectrum and C64 at a time when Commodore and Atari were already transitioning to more powerful, 16-bit machines. To maintain affordability, the Amstrad contained the same Zilog CPU as the ZX Spectrum, with a slightly higher clock speed and additional RAM (Table 4.8).

Despite its lesser power, the Amstrad saw much success in the United Kingdom and other parts of Europe. One reason for the PC's success was its "all-in-one" package of the computer, monitor and tape deck—all on a single power cord (Crookes, 2018, p. 39). At that time, these components were typically sold separately, with many consumers using their television sets to double as their computer monitors. The Amstrad's "cassette deck (which made available software cheaper than on floppy disk) made it more appealing to home users and gamers. Although future models were designed to appeal to business owners, the 464 was very much a games machine" (Nobes, 2020, para. 5). With its success in the PC arena, Amstrad purchased Sinclair Research for £5 million in early 1986, acquiring the rights to all Sinclair computer products, including the ZX Spectrum.

Six distinct models were released over its 6-year lifespan. The best-selling CPC464, **CPC664**, and **CPC6128** (made for the U.S. market) were manufactured between 1984 and 1985. Things went downhill in 1990 when Amstrad tried to keep the line going with "plus" versions of the systems including the **464plus** and **6128plus**, as well as a failed game console version

TABLE 4.8 Amstrad CPC464 Tech Specs

Manufacturer:	Amstrad
Launch price:	£229 (green screen); £329 (color screen)
Release date:	April 12, 1984 (UK), June 13, 1995 (US)
Format:	Compact Cassette and 3-inch floppy disk
CPU:	8-bit Zilog Z80A (4 MHz)
Memory:	64 kB or 128 kB (Expandable to 576 kB)
Resolution:	160 × 200 (16 colors), 320 × 200 (4 colors), or 640 × 200 (2 colors)
Colors:	2–16 onscreen colors from a palette of 27
Sound:	3-channel General Instrument AY-3–8912

FIGURE 4.19 (a) Amstrad CPC 464 with monitor and (b) screenshot of *Get Dexter!* (1986).

(a)

(b)

of the computer called the **Amstrad GX4000**. The £99 GX4000 ran on outdated technology and most of its games were already available on the Amstrad computer systems at a lower price. This trend of releasing outdated hardware continued into 1993 when Sega licensed Amstrad to produce the **Amstrad Mega PC**—which bundled an Amstrad computer with Sega Mega Drive (Genesis) hardware for a whopping £999.99 (approximately $1,250). Amstrad shifted its focus to the telecommunication industry before closing its doors to the market in 2008.

Key Amstrad game titles include the 1986 isometric action games *Get Dexter!* (Figure 4.19b) and *Spindizzy*, action platformers *Rick Dangerous* (series, 1989–90) and *Prince of Persia* (1990), run and gun shooters *Gryzor* (aka *Contra*, 1987) and *Xyphoes Fantasy* (1991), as well as *Bomberman* clone *Megablasters* (1994). For slower-paced titles, check out puzzler *The Sentinel* (1987) and first-person adventure game *Total Eclipse* (1988). Top British game publishers during this time included Alternative Software, Codemasters, Firebird Software, Gremlin Graphics, Mastertronic, Ocean Software, and U.S. Gold.

HEAD-TO-HEAD

Compare the graphics and sound between the ZX Spectrum and Amstrad by playing or viewing the following games on each system: *Vampire, Future Knight, Dizzy, Marauder,* and *Switchblade*. These games were also available on the Commodore 64 for further comparison.

Two important game genres emerged from Britain during these early PC years. England's **Richard Garriott** (known as alter ego "Lord/General British" in his games) created the *Ultima* series. Launched in the early 1980s, *Ultima* is heralded as the first definitive commercial role-playing game and a major influence on the RPG genre. Garriott is also noted for coining the term **"Massively Multiplayer Online Role-Playing Game" (MMORPG)**, providing a fresh identity to graphical Multi-User Dungeon (MUD) games years later.

England's **Peter Molyneux** created the "God games" genre, where the player uses supernatural powers to influence a population of simulated worshippers. Unlike in strategy games, players in God games do not have the ability to give direct commands to units of people. Gameplay instead revolves around growing and utilizing one's supernatural powers, such as blessing a civilization's crops or destroying them with natural disasters (Rollings & Adams, 2006). Notable God games from Molyneux include *Populous* (1989) (Figure 4.16b), *Dungeon Keeper* (1997), and *Black & White* (2001).

▪ END OF AN ERA

The 8-bit line of computers were succeeded by more powerful offerings from companies such as Apple, Atari, and Commodore in the mid-1980s. Apple led the way with its monochrome, 32-bit **Macintosh** home computer in January 1984. It was the company's first mass-market PC to include a **graphical user interface**

(GUI) and mouse (Polsson, 2009). The GUI provided users with graphical icons and other visual information they could interact with more easily by using a mouse—as opposed to being limited to a strictly text-based user interface and keyboard commands. On the other hand, the first three Macintosh computers lacked color graphics.

The **Atari ST** (Figure 4.20a) line of home computers debuted in June 1985. It contained both 16-bit and 32-bit architecture where the "ST" stood for "Sixteen/Thirty-two" since its Motorola 68000 was a 32-bit processor that communicated through a 16-bit bus (Reese, 1989, para. 2). Following in the footsteps of the ST was the launch of Commodore's **Amiga** family of PCs in July 1985; however, the system was not widely available until early 1986 due to production problems. Like the Atari ST computers, the Amiga also ran on the 16- and 32-bit Motorola 68000 series of microprocessors. Atari and Amiga's systems retailed for over $1,000 with color monitors, while the Macintosh home computer cost twice as much.

It was around this time that the term "**personal computer**" became popular, and most computer companies began avoiding the term "home computer." An article by *Compute!* magazine explained that "home computers" had developed a connotation of being low-end machines primarily used for playing video games. Apple's John Sculley flat out denied that his company was selling "home computers," instead referring to them as "computers for use in the home" (Halfhill, 1986, p. 38). Apple's stance on being a more costly, sophisticated machine may have contributed to

the Atari ST and Commodore Amiga becoming the dominant gaming computers through the end of the 1980s.

While the ST and Amiga began a new era of computer gaming, their high price tags held gamers and developers back on the older 8-bit systems until prices came down later in the decade. Aside from gaming, the Atari ST became the popular platform for audio production due to its built-in **MIDI (Musical Instrument Digital Interface)** ports, while Amiga became a prominent computer for video production applications such as *Video Toaster*. Its **genlock** ability allowed the Amiga to match the refresh rate of incoming video signals, while the computer's transparency setting provided the ability to display graphics over video.

HEAD-TO-HEAD

To compare the graphics and sound between the Atari ST and Commodore Amiga, try games released on both systems. Recommended games to compare include *Shadow of the Beast, Speedball 2: Brutal Deluxe,* and *The Secret of Monkey Island.*

Popular games around this time included action platformers such as *Turrican* and *Zool*, RPG and adventure games *Dungeon Master* and *The Secret of Monkey Island* (Figure 4.21), space shooters *Battle Squadron* and *Xenon 2: Megablast*, and strategy games such as *Lemmings*. The first "city-building" simulation

FIGURE 4.20 End of an era: (a) Atari ST and (b) Commodore Amiga 500 with peripherals.

(a)   (b)

FIGURE 4.21 Screenshots of popular computer titles: (a) *Dungeon Master* (on Atari ST) and (b) *The Secret of Monkey Island* (on Amiga 500).

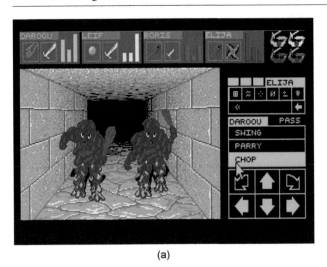

(a)

(b)

game was ***SimCity*** (Figure 4.16c) by Atlanta's **Will Wright**. *SimCity* debuted on Amiga and Macintosh in 1989. Published by Maxis (which became a division of EA), players are provided with tools to develop a city from an overhead perspective. The gameplay involves defining zones (such as residential, commercial, and industrial) and providing adequate power, transportation, and other resources to keep the citizens happy and within budget. *SimCity* led to spin-offs such as *SimFarm, Sim City: The Card Game, SimCopter, Streets of SimCity,* and *SimsVille*—but the series may be most notable for carving the way for *The Sims* games, which pioneered the strategic "life-simulation" genre.

After co-founding the company and helping pioneer the home computer market, "Steve Jobs [was] exiled from Apple in 1985 because of poor sales of the original Macintosh" (Reimer, 2005, p. 7). Apple released subsequent systems in the Macintosh family, including the **Macintosh Plus** in 1986 and a return to color graphics with the $5,500 **Macintosh II** in 1987. These systems were followed by the Macintosh "Classic" series in the early 1990s, with the original Classic being the first Mac under $1,000.

The **Atari STE** (E for "enhanced") succeeded the ST in 1989. The **Atari TT** ("Thirty-two/Thirty-two") followed in 1990, with the final ST computer being the **Atari MEGA STE** in 1991. Atari would release one last computer called the **Atari Falcon** in 1992, before focusing its efforts back on the home console market with its Jaguar console in 1993.

The original **Amiga 1000** would be succeeded by no less than 10 subsequent models and/or upgrades, from the best-selling **Amiga 500** in 1987 (Figure 4.20b), to the **A1200** and **A4000** released in late 1992. Like Atari and Amstrad, Commodore would make a final effort on the home console market when it released the 32-bit **Amiga CD32** in Europe, Canada, Australia, and Brazil in 1993. Even though the Amiga consistently outsold the ST, the CD32 was a market failure. The company went bankrupt in April 1994.

■ MARKET SUMMARY

The initial market for the Apple II consisted only of electronics hobbyists, gamers, and computer enthusiasts. Sales expanded to the business market when the spreadsheet program **VisiCalc** was released in 1979 and Apple grew exponentially over its first 5 years—doubling operations revenues nearly every 4 months. Between September 1977 and September 1980, annual Apple sales grew from $775,000 to $118 million, an average annual growth rate of 533% (Malone, 1999, p. 157). Apple sold close to 5 million Apple II computers by the time it was discontinued.

Atari outsold the Apple II from the beginning, but Atari's machines were expensive to produce. By mid-1981, the company had reportedly lost $10 million on sales of $10 million (Hogan, 1981, pp. 6–7). Then home computer prices plummeted in 1983. Caught between the video game crash and the low-priced Commodore

64, Atari and Apple were forced into a price war. Atari dropped the successor to the 400 and 800 computers (the 1200XL) just months after its release and quickly replaced it with the 600XL and 800XL, which debuted at just $199 and $299, respectively, to only modest sales.

Even at their peak in 1984, Atari's 8-bit line sold less than a quarter of the number of Commodore 64 units, as illustrated in Figure 4.22. According to Commodore, the C64 sold 17 million systems and "the *Guinness Book of World Records* lists the Commodore 64 as the best-selling single computer model of all time" (Griggs, 2011, para. 5). Commodore's Amiga 500 was also a tremendous success, selling close to 6 million units. By 1986, however, the market share shifted to IBM-compatible computers, which would soon dominate more than 75% of the market. Atari

and Commodore computers were eventually discontinued in the 1990s, with only Apple surviving—albeit in a distant second place.

The ZX Spectrum became the best-selling home computer in the United Kingdom, comparable to the Apple II with 5 million units sold. The Amstrad sold approximately 2 million units in total (3 million when including all CPC models). This was twice as many units sold compared to Acorn's BBC Micro, which sold for £349 without a monitor (Nobes, 2020, para. 3). As successful as Amstrad was in Europe, it only sold a third of the estimated 9 million MSX computers, which retailed without a monitor for a higher price tag. Seven million of those were sold in Japan alone. Finally, the NEC PC-98 series sold between 16 and 18 million units—however that series included three dozen models over a 20-year lifespan.

FIGURE 4.22 Early U.S. computer sales in thousands of units by Apple, Atari, and Commodore.

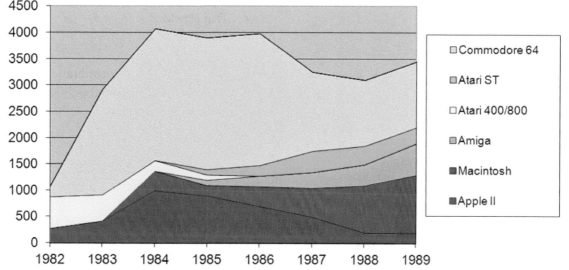

■ **ACTIVITY A: PERSONAL COMPUTER REPORT AND PRESENTATION**

Choose a computer from Table 4.4 that was not covered extensively in this chapter and develop a report and presentation on the history, business, and technology of that system. Be sure to include:

1. the publisher's goals,
2. how the computer was marketed,
3. technical specifications and notable game titles,
4. why the computer was less successful, and
5. conclusion/what might have made the computer more popular.

■ ACTIVITY B: GAME DEVELOPER REPORT AND PRESENTATION

Choose a small-to-medium size game developer (avoid large companies such as EA, Nintendo, Sony, or Microsoft) and draft a report and presentation on the following:

1. Company history and key employees
2. Key games the company created
3. Any breakthroughs, catastrophes, or other major happenings with the company
4. The cultural impact of the company's games (societal trends, influences, lasting appeal, spin-offs)
5. Conclusion/where the company is today and whether the trends their games created will continue to be popular in the future

Reports should contain 3–4 main points and a minimum of *two* quotes, which are to be paraphrased or cited verbally in the speech. The recommended total presentation length is 4–5 minutes, not to exceed 6 minutes total.

■ CHAPTER 4 QUIZ

1. This computer programmer went on to form Apple with Steve Jobs:
   a. Steve Wozniak
   b. Ray Kassar
   c. Nolan Bushnell
   d. Trip Hawkins

2. Apple's first *commercially* produced computer system for the mainstream home PC market:
   a. Apple I
   b. Apple II
   c. Macintosh Core
   d. Core Macintosh

3. Sierra Entertainment Inc. (formerly Sierra On-Line and On-Line Systems) was the company in which Ken and Roberta Williams pioneered the _____ genre of games.
   a. Text adventure game
   b. Spoken adventure game
   c. Graphical adventure game
   d. None of the above

4. Coined by Roy Trubshaw in 1978, these text-based adventures called "MUDs" stood for:
   a. Massively Uber Dungeoncrawlers
   b. Mind-User Development games
   c. Micro Universe Dungeons
   d. Multi-User Dungeons

5. Founded Electronic Arts, with a focus on crediting programmers on its album-like box art; also paved the way for athlete- and celebrity-endorsed games:
   a. Steve Wozniak
   b. Rod Holt
   c. Trip Hawkins
   d. Jack Tramiel

6. This computer had a membrane keyboard to protect against spills from the children who were its target market:
   a. Apple IIe
   b. Atari 400
   c. Atari 800
   d. Atari 1200XL

7. This 1979 exclusive was one of the Atari 8-bit computer's earliest titles and remained one of the reasons gamers purchased an Atari computer for many years:
   a. *Star Raiders*
   b. *Asteroids*
   c. *Rescue on Fractalus!*
   d. *King's Quest*

8. Founded Commodore International in 1954 as a typewriter assembly plant and went on to produce computers "for the masses, not the classes":
   a. Steve Wozniak
   b. Rod Holt
   c. Trip Hawkins
   d. Jack Tramiel

9. The reason(s) for the success of the Commodore 64:
   a. Low price for a fully functional PC with 64 kB of RAM
   b. Commodore manufactured computer parts in-house
   c. Marketing and selling the C64 in retail stores like Sears
   d. All of the above

10. This computer was known for its improved processing chip that allowed for "multicolor sprites," which made it easier to create fast-moving, flicker-free game graphics:
    a. Apple II
    b. Atari 400/800
    c. Commodore 64
    d. VIC-20

11. This computer manufacturer released multiple versions of its 8-bit computer lineup, including the XL series, XE series, and XE Game System (XEGS):
    a. Apple
    b. Atari
    c. Commodore
    d. IBM

12. All three original 8-bit computers by Apple, Atari, and Commodore contained a CPU manufactured by:
    a. Microsoft
    b. MOS Technology
    c. Minolta
    d. Magnavox

13. Known as alter ego "Lord British" and "General British" in his games, this programmer created the pioneering *Ultima* RPG series and coined the term MMORPG:
    a. Richard Garriott
    b. Sid Meier
    c. Will Wright
    d. Alexey Pajitnov

14. Responsible for developing the "falling blocks" puzzle game *Tetris*:
    a. Richard Garriott
    b. Sid Meier
    c. Will Wright
    d. Alexey Pajitnov

15. Created the first "city-building" simulation games, which led to the strategic "life-simulation" genre with games like *The Sims*:
    a. Richard Garriott
    b. Sid Meier
    c. Will Wright
    d. Alexey Pajitnov

16. This computer won the early PC market by a wide margin and is regarded as the best-selling single computer model of all time:
    a. Apple II
    b. Atari 400/800
    c. Commodore 64
    d. VIC-20

17. The last two major gaming computers by Atari and Commodore included the:
    a. ST and Amiga
    b. ST and Macintosh
    c. Amiga and PCJr
    d. Amiga and PC-compatible

18. Became prominent for video applications like *Video Toaster* with its genlock ability:
    a. ST
    b. Amiga
    c. Macintosh
    d. PCJr

19. This best-selling computer series from Japan continued to release models for more than 20 years, resulting in 16 and 18 million units sold:
    a. PC-98 series
    b. MSX series
    c. ZX Spectrum series
    d. Amstrad series

20. Key Japanese game developers like Hudson Soft and Konami were producing titles such as *Bomberman* and *Metal Gear* for this computer system before making games on home consoles:
    a. PC-98 series
    b. MSX series
    c. ZX Spectrum series
    d. Amstrad series

True or False

21. The Apple II was known for its state-of-the-art SID 6581 sound processor.

22. Will Crowther's *Colossal Cave Adventure* (1976) for the PDP-10 mainframe computer pioneered the text adventure genre, also known as "interactive fiction."

23. The abbreviation RPG stands for "Role-Playing Game."

24. Most of the games for Commodore 64 were manufactured on floppy disk.

25. Sinclair Research purchased Amstrad for £15 million in early 1996, acquiring the rights to all Amstrad computer products, including the CPC series.

◼ FIGURES

Figure 4.1 The Apple Computer (1976) circuit board. (Courtesy of Achim Baqué—https://www.apple1registry.com/en/press.html, CC BY-SA 4.0, https://commons.wikimedia.org/w/index.php?curid=109364693. Created: January 1, 2019. Retrieved from https://en.wikipedia.org/wiki/Apple_I#/media/File:CopsonApple1_2k_cropped.jpg.)

Figure 4.2 The Apple II (1977) with two Disk II (1978) floppy disk drives and game paddles. (Courtesy of FozzTexx—Own work, CC BY-SA 4.0, https://commons.wikimedia.org/w/index.php?curid=79580939 Created: June 9, 2019. Retrieved from https://en.wikipedia.org/wiki/Apple_II#/media/File:Apple_II_typical_configuration_1977.png.) Modified by Wardyga. (Part of this image was used on the introductory page of this chapter.)

Figure 4.3 Screenshots of early Apple II titles: (a) *The Oregon Trail* (1978), (b) *Lemonade Stand* (1979), and (c) *Zork I: The Great Underground Empire* (1980). (*The Oregon Trail* courtesy of MECC/Brøderbund, 1978; *Lemonade Stand* courtesy of MECC/Apple, 1979; and *Zork I: The Great Underground Empire* courtesy of Infocom, 1980.)

Figure 4.4 Magazine advertisement for the Apple II computer. ("Apple II 1979 Advertisement: How to Buy" from "The 7 Principles of Apple" by Mike Cane. December 2, 2009. Retrieved from https://ebooktest.wordpress.com/2009/12/02/the-7-principles-of-apple/.)

Figure 4.5 Evolution of the adventure game: Screenshots of: (a) *Colossal Cave Adventure* (1976), (b) *Mystery House* (1980), and (c) *King's Quest* (1984). (*Colossal Cave Adventure,* courtesy of William Crowther and Don Woods, 1976; *Mystery House,* courtesy of On-Line Systems, 1980; and *King's Quest,* courtesy of Sierra On-Line/Sierra Entertainment, 1984.)

Figure 4.6 Box art to five defining Apple II titles: (a) *The Bard's Tale,* (b) *Pinball Construction Set,* (c) *The Oregon Trail,* (d) *Karateka,* and (e) *Ultima I: The First Age of Darkness.* (*The Bard's Tale,* courtesy of Interplay Productions/Electronic Arts, 1985; *Pinball Construction Set,* courtesy of BudgeCo/Electronic Arts, 1983; *The Oregon Trail,* courtesy of MECC/Brøderbund, 1978; *Karateka,* courtesy of Jordan Mechner/Brøderbund, 1984; and *Ultima I: The First Age of Darkness,* courtesy of Richard Garriott/Origin Systems, 1981.)

Figure 4.7 Atari (a) 400 and (b) 800 computer systems. (Courtesy of Evan-Amos—own work, CC BY-SA 3.0. "Atari 400, 1979. Featuring a membrane keyboard and single-width cartridge slot cover." Available at https://commons.wikimedia.org/w/index.php?curid=17758254. Retrieved from https://en.wikipedia.org/wiki/Atari_8-bit_family#/media/File:Atari-400-Comp.jpg. (Part of this image was used on the introductory page of this chapter.) "The Atari 800, an 8-bit computer released by Atari in 1979. Based on the MOS 6502 microprocessor and custom video and sound processors, the Atari 800 was the first in a line of popular home computers." By Evan-Amos—Own work, Public Domain, https://commons.wikimedia.org/w/index.php?curid=53205709. Retrieved from https://en.wikipedia.org/wiki/Atari_8-bit_family#/media/File:Atari-800-Computer-FL.jpg.)

Figure 4.8 Screenshots of Atari 8-bit family titles: (a) *Rainbow Walker* (1983), (b) *Bounty Bob Strikes Back* (1984), and (c) *Rescue on Fractalus!* (1984). (*Rainbow Walker,* courtesy of Synapse Software, 1983; *Bounty Bob Strikes Back,* courtesy of Big Five Software, 1984; and *Rescue on Fractalus!,* courtesy of Lucasfilm Games/Activision, Atari, Epyx, 1984.)

Figure 4.9 Box art to five defining Atari 8-bit family games: (a) *Star Raiders*, (b) *Rescue on Fractalus!*, (c) *M.U.L.E.*, (d) *Bounty Bob Strikes Back*, and (e) *Boulder Dash*. (*Star Raiders*, courtesy of Atari, Inc., 1979; *Rescue on Fractalus!*, courtesy of Lucasfilm Games/Activision, Atari, Epyx, 1984; *M.U.L.E.*, courtesy of Ozark Softscape/Electronic Arts, 1983; *Bounty Bob Strikes Back*, courtesy of Big Five Software, 1984; and *Boulder Dash*, courtesy of First Star Software, 1984.)

Figure 4.10 Magazine advertisement for the Atari 800 computer in 1981. (Atari 800 ad posted in "The Timeless Computer: Remembering the Atari 800" by John Kenneth Muir on December 7, 2015. Available at http://flashbak. com/timeless-computer-remembering-atari-800-47864/. Retrieved from: http://flashbak.com/wp-content/ uploads/2015/12/flashbak800b.jpg.)

Figure 4.11 Evolution of the Atari 8-bit computers: (a) 1200XL, (b) 600XL, (c) 800XL, (d) 130EX, and (e) XEGS Game System. ("Atari 1200XL" by Daniel Schwen, CC BY-SA 3.0. Available at https://commons.wikimedia. org/w/index.php?curid=16255854 and "Atari 600XL." "This machine featured a slightly shallower case than the 800XL." by Evan-Amos—own work, CC BY-SA 3.0. Available at https://commons.wikimedia.org/w/ index.php?curid=17835117. "An Atari 800XL," by Evan-Amos—own work, CC BY-SA 3.0. Available at https:// commons.wikimedia.org/w/index.php?curid=18553927. "Atari 130XE," by Evan-Amos—own work, CC BY-SA 3.0. Available at https://commons.wikimedia.org/w/index. php?curid=18548917. "Atari XE Game System," by Bilby— own work, CC BY 3.0. Available at https://commons.wiki-media.org/w/index.php?curid=10955083.)

Figure 4.12 Commodore 64 home computer system. (Courtesy of Evan-Amos—own work, public domain. Available at https://commons.wikimedia.org/w/index. php?curid=17414886. "Commodore 64.") (Part of this image was used on the introductory page of this chapter.)

Figure 4.13 Screenshots of early Commodore 64 titles: (a) *Choplifter* (1982), (b) *Spy Hunter* (1983), and (c) *Impossible Mission* (1984). (*Choplifter*, courtesy of Dan Gorlin/Brøderbund, 1982; *Spy Hunter*, courtesy of Bally Midway, 1983; and *Impossible Mission*, courtesy of Epyx, 1984.)

Figure 4.14 Magazine advertisement for the Commodore 64 computer in 1982. (From "Commodore Computers" posted on MagazineAdvertisements.com. Retrieved from http://www.magazine-advertisements.com/commodore-computers.html.)

Figure 4.15 Box art to five defining Commodore 64 titles: (a) *IK+*, *Zack McKracken and the Alien Mindbenders*, (b) *Impossible Mission, Turrican II*, and (c) *Paradroid*. (*K+*, courtesy of System 3/Epyx, 1987; *Zack McKracken and the Alien Mindbenders*, courtesy of Lucasfilm Games, 1988; *Impossible Mission*, courtesy of Epyx, 1984; *Turrican II*, courtesy of Rainbow Arts, 1991; and *Paradroid*, courtesy of Graftgold/Hewson Consultants, Jester Interactive Publishing, 1985.)

Figure 4.16 Screenshots of (a) *Sid Meier's Pirates!* (1987), (b) *Populous* (1989), and (c) *SimCity* (1989). (*Sid Meier's Pirates!*, courtesy of MicroProse, 1987; *Populous*, courtesy of Bullfrog/Electronic Arts, 1989; and *SimCity*, courtesy of Maxis, 1989.)

Figure 4.17 Best-selling computers in Japan: (a) NEC PC-9801 and (b) MSX2 by Sanyo. "PC-9801 with 8-inch floppy disk drive unit." (By MH0301—Own work, CC BY-SA 4.0, https://commons.wikimedia.org/w/index. php?curid=106075103. Created: May 20, 2006. Retrieved from https://en.wikipedia.org/wiki/PC-9800_series#/ media/File:PC-9801-1st-001.jpg. Part of this image was used on the introductory page of this chapter. "Sanyo PHC-23J(B)." By Mars2000you. Based on work by Sd snatcher and Sdsnatcher73 and others. November 3, 2021. (c) By the MSX Resource Center Foundation. Retrieved from https:// www.msx.org/wiki/Sanyo_PHC-23J.)

Figure 4.18 (a) The Sinclair ZX Spectrum and (b) screenshot of *Chase H.Q.* (1988) with its limited colors and Colour Clash effect where blue and yellow meet at the horizon. "Sinclair 48K ZX Spectrum computer (1982)." (By Bill Bertram—Own work, CC BY-SA 2.5, https://commons. wikimedia.org/w/index.php?curid=170050. Created: May 29, 2005. Retrieved from https://en.wikipedia.org/wiki/ File:ZXSpectrum48k.jpg#/media/File:ZXSpectrum48k. jpg. Part of this image was used on the introductory page of this chapter. Screenshot of *Chase H.Q.* (Ocean/Taito Corporation 1988) Courtesy of Taito Corporation.)

Figure 4.19 (a) Amstrad CPC 464 with monitor and (b) screenshot of *Get Dexter!* (1986). "Amstrad CPC 464 computer (1984)." (Courtesy of Bill Bertram—Own work, CC BY-SA 2.5, https://commons.wikimedia.org/w/index. php?curid=133247. Created: May 7, 2005. Retrieved from https://en.wikipedia.org/wiki/File:Amstrad_CPC464.jpg#/ media/File:Amstrad_CPC464.jpg. Part of this image was used on the introductory page of this chapter. Screenshot of *Get Dexter!* (ERE Informatique/Personal Software Services 1986) Courtesy of PSS.)

Figure 4.20 End of an era: (a) Atari ST and (b) Commodore Amiga 500 with peripherals. ("Commodore Amiga 500, 16-bit computer (1987) Post Processing: BG, B/C, spot, composite picture." Courtesy of Bill Bertram—own work, CC BY-SA 2.5. Available at https://commons.wikimedia.org/w/index.php?curid=350965. Retrieved from https://en.wikipedia.org/wiki/Amiga#/media/File:Amiga500_system.jpg.) ("Atari 1040STF 16-bit computer (1986) Post Processing: BG, B/C, spot, unsharp mask, composite picture." Courtesy of Bill Bertram, 2006—Own work, CC BY-SA 2.5, https://commons.wikimedia.org/w/index.php?curid=500910. Retrieved from https://en.wikipedia.org/wiki/Atari_ST#/media/File:Atari_1040STf.jpg.)

Figure 4.21 Screenshots of popular computer titles: (a) *Dungeon Master* (on Atari ST) and (b) *The Secret of Monkey Island* (on Amiga 500). (The Secret of Monkey Island courtesy of Lucasfilm Games, 1990; and Dungeon Master courtesy of FTL Games, 1987.)

Figure 4.22 Early U.S. computer sales in thousands of units by Apple, Atari, and Commodore. (Adapted from data by Reimer, Jeremy. "Personal Computer Market Share: 1975–2004" 2012. Retrieved from http://www.jeremyreimer.com/m-item.lsp?i=137.)

PRO FILE: Steve Wozniak. Photo credit: By Gage Skidmore, CC BY-SA 3.0, https://commons.wikimedia.org/w/index.php?curid=63344547 October 12, 2017. Retrieved from https://commons.wikimedia.org/wiki/File:Steve_Wozniak_by_Gage_Skidmore.jpg#/media/File:Steve_Wozniak_by_Gage_Skidmore.jpg.

◼ REFERENCES

Barton, M. & Loguidice, B. (2014). *Vintage game consoles: the greatest gaming platforms of all time.* New York, NY: Focal Press.

Barton, M. & Loguidice, B. (2016). A history of gaming platforms: The Apple II. *Gamasutra.* Retrieved from http://www.gamasutra.com/view/feature/3527/a_history_of_gaming_platforms_the_.php?print=1.

Bogdan, P. (2014, September 22). *Games vs. hardware. The history of PC video games. The 80's (reduced content edition).* Kindle edition. Romania: Purcaru Ion Bogdan.

Crookes, D. (2018). *History of the Amstrad. Retro gamer annual volume five.* Bath, Somerset, United Kingdom: Future Publishing Limited. pp. 36–41.

Dunfield, D. (2007). *Dave's old computers: Apple II.* Retrieved from http://classiccmp.org/dunfield/apple2/index.htm.

Editorial: Atari XL/XE-series. (2015, January). *RetroIsle.* Retrieved from http://www.retroisle.com/atari/xlxe/general.phpe.

Editorial: Colour clash: The engineering miracle of the Sinclair ZX Spectrum. (2018, April–June). *Paleotronic Magazine.* Retrieved from https://paleotronic.com/2018/09/29/loading-ready-run-sinclair-edition-the-zx-spectrum/.

Editorial: Commodore 64. Videogames hardware handbook: 1977–1999. (2009). *Retro Gamer.* Bournemouth, UK: Imagine Publishing, Ltd., p. 57.

Editorial: Atari 800XL. Videogames hardware handbook: 1977–2001. (2010). *Retro Gamer.* Bournemouth, UK: Imagine Publishing, Ltd., p. 142.

Fleming, J. (2016). *We see farther: A history of electronic arts.* Retrieved from http://www.gamasutra.com/view/feature/130129/we_see_farther__a_history_of_.php?print=1.

Freiberger, P. & Swaine, M. (1985, January). Fire in the valley, part two (Book excerpt). *A+ Magazine,* 3(1), p. 45.

Fulton, S. (2008, August 21). Atari: The golden years: A history, 1978–1981. *Gamasutra,* 15(8), p. 4.

Griggs, B. (2011, May 9). The Commodore 64, that '80s computer icon, lives again. *CNN.* Retrieved from http://www.cnn.com/2011/TECH/gaming.gadgets/05/09/commodore.64.reborn/.

Halfhill, T. R. (1986, December). The MS-DOS invasion/IBM compatibles are coming home. *Compute!.* p. 38. Retrieved from https://archive.org/stream/1986-12-compute-magazine/Compute_Issue_079_1986_Dec#page/n33/mode/2up.

Hogan, T. (1981, August 31). From zero to a billion in five years. *InfoWorld.* pp. 6–7.

Kent, S. (2001). *The ultimate history of video games: The story behind the craze that touched our lives and changed the world.* Roseville, CA: Three Rivers Press.

Klein, E. (2014). *Atari 400.* Retrieved from http://www.vintage-computer.com/atari400.shtml.

Linzmayer, O. (2004). *Apple confidential 2.0: The definitive history of the world's most colorful company* (2nd ed). San Francisco, CA: No Starch Press.

Loguidice, B. (2017, April 14). The bright life of the MSX, Japan's underdog PC. *PC Gamer.* Retrieved from https://www.pcgamer.com/the-bright-life-of-the-msx-japans-underdog-pc/.

Malone, M. (1999, February 16). *Infinite loop.* New York: Doubleday Business. p. 157.

Mesa, A. F. (2016). *Apple I.* Retrieved from http://applemuseum.bott.org/sections/computers/a1.html.

Nobes, M. (2020, February 22). *Amstrad CPC 464.* Retrieved from https://www.simplyeighties.com/amstrad-cpc-464.php.

Peddie, J. (2019, December 4). *NEC µPD7220 graphics display controller: The first graphics processor chip.* Retrieved from https://www.electronicdesign.com/technologies/embedded-revolution/article/21122304/

jon-peddie-research-vol-1-no-1-nec-pd7220-graphics-display-controller-the-first-graphics-processor-chip.

Personal Computer Museum. (2016). *Commodore 16*. Retrieved from http://www.pcmuseum.ca/details.asp?id=287.

Polsson, K. (2009, July 29). *Chronology of Apple computer personal computers*. Retrieved from https://web.archive.org/web/20090821105822/http://www.islandnet.com/~kpolsson/applehis/appl1984.htm.

Reese, A. (1989, December). The future of Atari computing: TT and STE unveiled in Germany. *Start*, 4(5), p. 1. Retrieved from http://www.atarimagazines.com/startv4n5/the_future.html.

Reimer, J. (2005, December 15). Total share: 30 years of personal computer market share figures. *Ars Technica*. Retrieved from http://arstechnica.com/features/2005/12/total-share/.

Reimer, J. (2012). *Personal computer market share: 1975–2004*. Retrieved from http://www.jeremyreimer.com/m-item.lsp?i=137.

Rollings, A. & Adams, E. (2006). *Fundamentals of game design*. Berkeley, CA: Prentice Hall.

Stanton, J., Wells, R., Rochowansky, S., & Mellid, M. eds. (1984). *The Addison-Wesley book of Atari software*. Los Angeles, CA: Addison-Wesley. pp. 12–210.

Tozzi, C. (2021, March 5). *Mainframe history: How mainframe computers have changed over the years*. Retrieved from https://www.precisely.com/blog/mainframe/mainframe-history.

Vallantine, S. (2021, September 21). *The A to Z of the ZX spectrum*. Retrieved from https://mancunian1001.wordpress.com/2021/09/21/the-a-to-z-of-the-zx-spectrum/.

Westaway, L. (2021, September 17). *Meet the ZX Spectrum, a breakthrough home computer of the '80s*. CNET. Retrieved from https://www.cnet.com/pictures/zx-spectrum-in-pictures/.

The 8-Bit Era

■ **OBJECTIVES**

After reading this chapter, you should be able to:

- Discuss developments and breakthroughs in arcade industry during this time.
- Provide a brief overview of the history of Nintendo and Sega.
- Review key people behind the video games and consoles.
- Explain the challenges Nintendo overcame to bring the NES to the West.
- Describe how publishers redesigned Japanese consoles for the Western audience.
- Identify graphics and capabilities of third-generation video game consoles.
- Compare the technological differences among Nintendo, Sega, and Atari consoles.
- Discuss the innovations and influence of the Game & Watch and *Nintendo Power*.
- Recognize key video game titles and peripherals for each third-generation console.
- Illustrate how Nintendo dominated the third-generation market.
- List important innovations brought to gaming during this period.
- Summarize third-generation market sales, breakthroughs, and trends.

DOI: 10.1201/9781003315759-5

■ KEY TERMS AND PEOPLE

10NES
Activision
Advanced Video System
Minoru Arakawa
Arcade ports
Atari 2600 Jr.
Atari 7800 Proline Controller
Atari 7800 ProSystem
Atari Corporation
Atari Games (Division)
Backward compatibility
Lance Barr
Capcom
Central Processing Unit
Coleco
Color Game-TV series
Commodore
Consumer Electronics Show (CES)
Control Stick

D-Pad controller
Data East
Digital signature
Easter Eggs
Famicom
Game & Watch
General Consumer Corporation (GCC)
JAMMA
Japanese role-playing game (JRPG)
Ray Kassar
Konami
Licensing policy (NES)
Howard Lincoln
Master System
Mastertronic
Shigeru Miyamoto
Motorola 68000
Multicart
Namco
NES Zapper
Nintendo Co., Ltd.

Nintendo Entertainment System (NES)
Nintendo Power
Parker Brothers
Howard Phillips
Printed circuit board (PCB)
POKEY (chip)
Power Glove
Power Pad
Random access memory (RAM)
Robot Operating Buddy (R.O.B.)
Rosen Enterprises
SALLY
Hideki Sato
Screen resolution
Seal of Quality (NES)
Sega Card
Sega Enterprises
Sega Light Phaser
Sega Mark III
Sega SG-1000

Sega Sports Pad
SegaScope 3D Glasses
Side-scrolling platformer
Super Mario Bros.
Yu Suzuki
System 16
Taito
Technōs Japan
Tecmo
Tectoy
Third-party developer
TIA (chip)
Tonka
Jack Tramiel
Masayuki Uemura
Video cassette recorder (VCR)
Warner Communications
Worlds of Wonder
Hiroshi Yamauchi
Gunpei Yokoi
Zilog Z80

■ CONSOLE TIMELINE

Famicom	SG-1000	Sega Mark III	NES	Atari 7800	Master System
1983	**1983**	**1985**	**1985**	**1986**	**1986**

■ THE ARCADE SCENE

With the end of the Golden Age and the video game crash of 1983 in North America, the arcade market experienced a steady decline during the mid-1980s. Chuck E. Cheese's Pizza Time Theatre filed for Chapter 11 bankruptcy in 1984 and was acquired by ShowBiz Pizza's parent company Brock Hotel Corp. Aside from its VS. arcade systems (which were basically **Nintendo** console games in an arcade cabinet), Nintendo all but pulled the plug on the arcade market to focus on the home console market. **Capcom** entered the arcade scene around this time and large companies such as **Atari, Namco, Sega, Taito**, and **Konami** continued to release strong titles (as in Figure 5.1) to keep arcades afloat. **Data East** sparked arcade interest in the one-on-one fighting game genre when it published *Karate Champ* (1984), which was developed by **Technōs Japan**. Konami expanded the genre with *Yie Ar Kung-Fu* in 1985, introducing a life bar, special attacks, and characters with a variety of fighting styles.

These companies were also developing console and PC titles that were quite profitable. Home ports of arcade hits were still common, but console games that shared the same title as arcade games were often alike in name only. Games such as Capcom's *Bionic Commando* and **Tecmo**'s *Ninja Gaiden* (*Shadow Warriors* in Europe) were completely different games on home consoles and not direct ports of the arcade originals. Countless arcade boards during this time utilized the popular **Zilog Z80** and/or **Motorola** 68000 processors, including Sega's **System 16**, which Sega produced more than three dozen titles in the mid-to-late 1980s.

Prior to 1985, each arcade cabinet had its own **printed circuit board (PCB)**, power supply, and wiring harness. In 1985, **Japanese Amusement Machine Manufacturers Association (JAMMA)** revolutionized the industry when it developed the JAMMA wiring standard for arcade machines. Rather than having to replace or rewire the whole cabinet for a new game, JAMMA compatible cabinets could just swap out the PCB from the JAMMA harness. Namco, Taito, Sega, Capcom, Tecmo, and other companies adopted JAMMA, and it became the arcade standard by the end of the decade.

One game that helped revolutionize the arcade industry was Sega's *Hang-On* in 1985. Developed by **Yu Suzuki** and his Sega AM2 team, the game utilized pseudo-3D, "Super Scaler" sprite-scaling hardware and a motion-controlled hydraulic motorbike cabinet where players controlled what looked and felt like real motorcycle handles. The game even mirrored the angle of the seat, where players would lean left and right to control the motorcycle on-screen. This led to other popular hydraulic titles by Sega such as *Space Harrier* (1985), *OutRun* (1986), and *After Burner* (1987). Coined "Taikan games" in Japan, these ride-on arcade games which employed moving cabinets, were exciting experiences that players could not replicate in the home, prompting Western gamers to return to the arcades.

FIGURE 5.1   Atari still delivered defining arcade games after the video game crash of 1983, including (a) *Paperboy* (1984), (b) *Marble Madness* (1984), and (c) *Gauntlet* (1985).

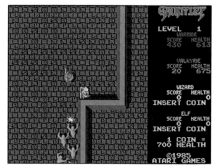

(a)   (b)   (c)

■ THE THIRD GENERATION

The third generation of video games (also called the "8-bit era") began in Japan with video game consoles by **Nintendo** and **Sega**. While these systems continued the tradition of producing ports of arcade hits, the games that brought players back to their TVs during this time were quite different from those in the arcades. Console games during the third generation were often more intricate than their arcade counterparts, containing more elaborate stories, secrets to discover, and a greater time commitment. Home console action-adventure games could now take several hours to complete. Role-playing games could last for 10 hours or longer. Arcade games, however, remained superior in graphics and sound.

■ NINTENDO FAMICOM

Fusajiro Yamauchi founded Nintendo Koppai in 1889. The company's original operation was the manufacturing of Japanese playing cards. It was not until the early 1970s that the newly branded **Nintendo Co., Ltd.** began developing electronic games. Its first major video game success was the *Pong*-like **Color TV-Game** series in the late 1970s, followed by its **Game & Watch** LCD handheld games in 1980. The company reached international success with the arcade hit *Donkey Kong* (1981), before releasing its debut third-generation console, the **Nintendo Famicom** (Figure 5.2a) on July 15, 1983. The name Famicom was a combination of its formal name "**Fami**ly **Com**puter." The system was designed by **Masayuki Uemura** and introduced in Japan for 14,800 yen (around $120).

The Famicom launched with three titles, including arcade ports of *Donkey Kong, Donkey Kong Jr.,* and *Popeye* (Figure 5.3). The Japanese release had several features not included in the West. First, its controllers were hardwired to the rear of the console. The initial model controllers featured square-shaped action buttons like the Odyssey[2] controller, which Nintendo changed to more user-friendly, circular buttons. Controller II lacked a Start or Select button but contained a built-in microphone that players could use in a handful of games. For example, in the Japanese version of *The Legend of Zelda,* players could yell into the microphone to eradicate Pols Voice enemies.

There was also the **Family Computer Disk System** (Figure 5.2b), which cost as much as the Famicom. Debuting on February 21, 1986, the Disk System was a disk drive unit the Famicom sat on top of. It included a RAM adapter cartridge that plugged into the top of the Famicom, which sent information to the system and provided 32 kB RAM for program data, 8 kB for image data, and processor with an extra audio channel. Its double-sided 112 kB "Disk Cards" used "Quick Disk" media format by **Mitsumi** and were smaller than standard 3.5" floppy disks. The Disk System sold 2 million units after first year and Nintendo of Japan supported it by only manufacturing Disk System games for the Famicom between November 1985 and November 1987 (Caruso, 2016). The Disk System became obsolete when it became more affordable to manufacture cartridges. Cartridges were also more reliable, harder to pirate, and soon rivaled the capacity of Disk Cards with 128 kB games and higher.

FIGURE 5.2 Nintendo Family Computer (Famicom) game system (a) and Famicom with Disk System (b).

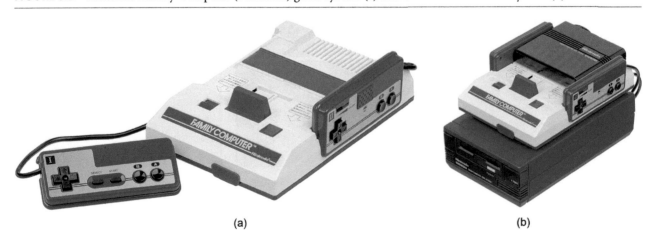

(a)   (b)

FIGURE 5.3 Screenshots of Famicom launch titles: (a) *Donkey Kong*, (b) *Donkey Kong Jr.*, and (c) *Popeye*.

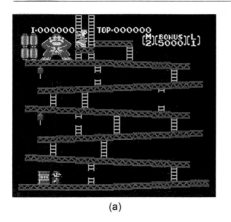

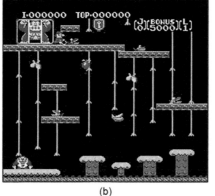

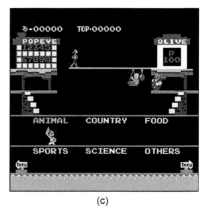

(a)   (b)   (c)

☀ DID YOU KNOW?

The first batch of Famicom systems had a bad chip set, causing a massive recall and reissue with all new motherboards. Once they got over this hurdle, Nintendo went on to sell "more than 500,000 Famicoms within two months" (Kent, 2001, p. 279).

■ COMING TO AMERICA

Despite the recent video game crash in North America, the Famicom sold extremely well in Japan and Nintendo president **Hiroshi Yamauchi** believed the system could succeed in the United States. Nintendo of America President **Minoru Arakawa** and Vice President **Howard Lincoln** offered **Atari** the chance to distribute the system in the United States (or even use the Famicom board inside an Atari-built console). Multiple meetings with **Ray Kassar** and Atari ensued and eventually the two companies appeared to have a deal. Then at the 1983 **Consumer Electronics Show (CES)** in Chicago, Atari learned that Nintendo had licensed *Donkey Kong* to Atari's competitor **Coleco** for play on the Coleco Adam Computer. Kassar claimed this "breached the licensing agreement Atari had made with Nintendo" (Kent, 2001, p. 283) and never completed the deal. Atari forced Kassar to resign that July after allegations of insider trading when he sold 5,000 shares of Warner stock just minutes before the company released its fourth quarter loss report. Besides Atari's fiscal crisis and the declining market in the United States, another culprit for the fallout was the fact that unbeknownst to Nintendo, Atari already had another console in development, the **Atari 7800**.

The Famicom became the best-selling game console in Japan by the end of 1984 with over 3 million units sold. Yamauchi was ready to give America another shot and sent Arakawa to unveil the console at the Las Vegas Consumer Electronics Show in January 1985. Nintendo renamed the console the **Advanced Video System (AVS)**, which displayed at a small booth with around 25 games. The AVS came bundled with a keyboard, cassette data recorder, and BASIC interpreter software cartridge. The redesigned system (displayed in Figure 5.4) looked more like a home computer than a video game console. The CES presentations showed that the U.S. market was quite skeptical of re-entering the video game arena. While the AVS demonstration was not a tremendous success, Nintendo gathered enough data from focus groups to go back to the drawing board.

■ NINTENDO ENTERTAINMENT SYSTEM

In an attempt to appeal to U.S. consumers, Nintendo turned to **Lance Barr** to redesign the look of the system again for what would finally become the **Nintendo Entertainment System (NES)** in the West (Figure 5.5). The company completely abandoned the home computer approach of the AVS and changed the top-loading cartridge slot to a front-loading slot with a dust cover door. This design more closely resembled the then-popular **Video Cassette Recorder (VCR)** than any game system developed up to that time. Nintendo also abandoned the game pad with an internal microphone in favor of standard D-Pad controllers with longer, detachable cords.

FIGURE 5.4 The first redesign of Famicom, called the Nintendo Advanced Video System.

In addition to avoiding the term "video games" in the eyes of retailers, Nintendo was careful to name and market the console as an "entertainment system." To compliment this marketing campaign, the system included the addition of an optional **NES Zapper** light gun accessory and **Robot Operating Buddy (R.O.B.)** (shown in Figure 5.6) developed by **Gunpei Yokoi**. The Zapper only supported a few initial games such as *Wild Gunman, Duck Hunt,* and *Hogan's Alley,* but would see enough releases over the years to warrant its purchase by shooting fans. R.O.B., on the other hand, only worked with two games at launch (*Gyromite* and *Stack-Up*). While the robot gave the system a unique sense of identity, R.O.B. was unpopular in both the West and Japan, and never received a third title before Nintendo discontinued the device altogether. Sparse

software support aside, these peripherals made the NES appear quite advanced in the mid-1980s.

Beyond these peripheral devices, it was the NES controller that truly revolutionized the industry. Prior to the launch of the NES, most video game controllers utilized a joystick to control the on-screen action. Nintendo changed that with its +shaped **directional pad** or "**D-Pad.**" Gunpei Yokoi originally developed the D-Pad for Nintendo's Game & Watch handhelds as a more compact way of controlling a multidirectional video game on a pocket-size device. Its comfort and precision helped the D-Pad become the standard method of controlling video games until Nintendo's touch-sensitive **control stick** for the Nintendo 64 more than a decade later. Even today, most video game controllers still contain a D-Pad in one form or another.

FIGURE 5.5 Nintendo Entertainment System and its restyled D-Pad controller.

FIGURE 5.6 Pages from the 1986 CES NES Brochure showing R.O.B., the Zapper, and newly designed Nintendo Entertainment System.

With the redesigned **Nintendo Entertainment System** ready to go, Nintendo prepared to test the console in the U.S. market. Rather than follow Nintendo of America's test market plans to start in small markets, Yamauchi chose to start directly in New York City for the 1985 holiday season. To help convince retailers to carry their product, Arakawa offered a money-back guarantee for any unsold merchandise and hired Nintendo staff members to set up all the in-store displays (Kent, 2001, p. 297). Among the 500 retailers who took a gamble with the system, Nintendo was able to secure deals with large toy stores such as FAO Schwartz and Toys "R" Us.

Nintendo sold at least **50,000 units** in New York in 1985—about half the number of consoles it shipped to the United States. The test launch was a reasonable success, considering *Super Mario Bros.* had not yet been released. That game would not reach the United States until the national launch in September of 1986, along with an impressive 17 other titles (Table 5.3). That year Nintendo also secured former toy giant **Worlds of Wonder** (Teddy Ruxpin and Lazer Tag) as a distributor.

Nintendo remained mindful of the recent video game crash in the United States and set out to regain the confidence of both consumers and retailers. The company called its cartridges "game paks" instead of "video games." To avoid the problems Atari had with too many poor third-party titles flooding the market, Nintendo instilled a strict **licensing policy**. Under the policy, third-party companies had to order at least 10,000 cartridges up front, and Nintendo would be the exclusive manufacturer (Sheff, 1993, pp. 215–215). Nintendo limited each publisher to five game titles

■ HANDHELD SNAPSHOT: NINTENDO GAME & WATCH

The **Game & Watch** (Gēmu & Uotchi) was a series of dedicated handheld systems designed by **Gunpei Yokoi**. The name came from the fact that the handhelds featured both a video game and a digital clock (aka watch). Nintendo published the first Game & Watch title *Ball* (Figure 5.7) in 1980—a juggling game that sold less than a quarter million units. Nintendo would release a total of 60 different Game & Watch systems through 1991, not including anniversary editions and reissues. Thirty of the main games released after the debut of the Famicom, placing the Game & Watch series in between the second and third generations of video games.

There were ten main hardware designs Nintendo manufactured under the Game & Watch brand, named after their shell color or other defining characteristic. For example, five games released on the original "Silver" system in 1980, including *Ball, Flagman, Vermin, Fire,* and *Judge.* See Table 5.1 for a breakdown of all Game & Watch systems and release numbers.

The first vertical **Multi Screen** game to utilize two screens was *Oil Panic* in May of 1982. One month later, the best-selling *Donkey Kong* (Figure 5.8) became the first game to feature a **D-Pad.** More than 20 years later, the Game & Watch Multi Screen clamshell design influenced the form factor of the Game Boy Advance SP and Nintendo DS handhelds.

FIGURE 5.7 The first Game & Watch, *Ball* (1980).

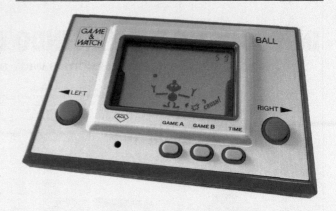

Despite all its releases, the technology never improved beyond its 4-bit Sharp SM5XX series processor with simple black LCD graphics and beeps for sound (Table 5.2). Like Microvision before it, Game & Watch games could have a static color overlay to complement their monochrome displays. Most games were programmed with two modes of play (A and B) with Game B typically beginning at a higher level.

The main competition for Game & Watch were the dedicated handheld games by **Tiger Electronics**, which operated on similar LCD technology and retailed for a comparable price tag. According to Satoru Iwata (2011), "the Game & Watch series sold 12.87 million domestically [in Japan] and 30.53 million overseas for a total of 43.4 million."

TABLE 5.1 Main Game & Watch Releases

Series	Year(s)	Games
Silver	1980	5
Gold	1981	3
Wide Screen	1981–82	11
Multi Screen	1982–89	12 vert/3 horiz
New Wide Screen	1982–91	8
Tabletop	1983	4
Panorama	1983–84	6
Super Color	1984	2
Micro Vs. System	1984	3
Crystal Screen	1986	3

TABLE 5.2 Nintendo Game & Watch Tech Specs

Format:	LR4x/SR4x button cell batteries
CPU:	4-bit Sharp SM5XX series
Memory:	40–160 b LCD driver circuit
Resolution:	Various
Colors:	Monochrome
Sound:	Internal beeper

FIGURE 5.8 Three Game & Watch models: (a) Vertical Multi Screen *Donkey Kong* (1982), (b) Two-player Micro Vs. System *Donkey Kong 3* (1985), and (c) final release New Wide Screen *Mario the Juggler* (1991).

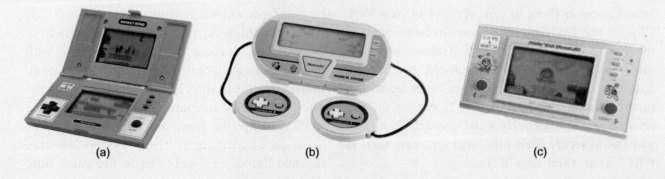

(a)   (b)   (c)

TABLE 5.3 Nintendo Entertainment System U.S. Launch Titles

- *10-Yard Fight*
- *Baseball*
- *Clu Clu Land*
- *Donkey Kong Jr. Math*
- *Duck Hunt*
- *Excitebike*
- *Golf*
- *Gyromite*
- *Hogan's Alley*
- *Ice Climber*
- *Kung Fu* (Figure 5.9a)
- *Mach Rider*
- *Pinball*
- *Stack-Up*
- *Super Mario Bros.* (Figure 5.9b)
- *Tennis*
- *Wild Gunman*
- *Wrecking Crew*

per year and prohibited those titles from appearing on competing game systems. To avoid piracy issues encountered with the Famicom in Asia, Nintendo installed a special lockout chip in every NES console that had to be paired with a counterpart chip installed in every officially licensed cartridge. Known as the **10NES**, if the chip could not detect a cartridge's counterpart chip, the game would fail to load (Sheff, 1993, p. 247).

In addition to these measures, Nintendo created a "**Seal of Quality**" that appeared on the packaging of aptly licensed games and accessories. Players could also mail in a questionnaire to subscribe to the *Nintendo Fun Club News*. This color newsletter featured sections such as "Sneak Peeks" and "Tips and Tricks," further connecting players to their games. Nintendo of America spokesperson and Fun Club President **Howard Phillips** helped change the newsletter into the full-length magazine *Nintendo Power* in 1988. The magazine was full of previews, reviews, game maps, secret codes, high scores, as well as a "Howard & Nester" comic strip that featured Phillips with his iconic smile and bow tie. There was even a 24-hour Nintendo Power Line—a toll hotline where players could call a "game counselor" to receive over-the-phone help with any officially released Nintendo game. At its peak, the call center in Redmond, WA had 200 game counselors fielding around 100 calls per day (Hester, 2022, para. 13).

All these efforts to support their product led to Nintendo becoming the new undisputed king in the North American home video game market. By 1988, Nintendo cartridges were in higher demand than all computer software combined (Computer Gaming World, 1988, p. 50). The marketing phrase "Now You're Playing with Power" became a popular part of their advertising, along with peripherals such as the **Power Glove** and **Power Pad.** Nintendo was in power now, as the NES had single-handedly revived the once-presumed-dead video game market in North America and became the world's leading game console.

▪ CONSOLE COMPARISON: NES VS. ATARI 2600

The NES launched for $199.99 shortly after the video game crash in the United States, when an Atari VCS/2600 was available for less than $50. Compared to the Atari 2600 CPU, the NES's **1.79 MHz** 8-bit **Ricoh 6502 processor** (Table 5.4) did not look much

FIGURE 5.9 Screenshots from NES launch titles (a) *Kung Fu* and (b) *Super Mario Bros.*

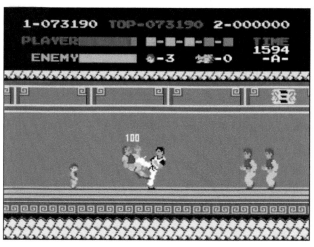

(a)

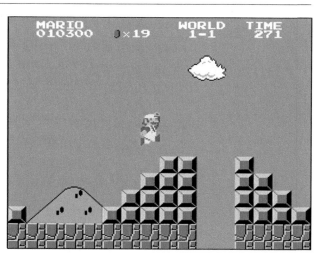

(b)

PRO FILE

SHIGERU MIYAMOTO

KEY FACTS:

Creator of *Donkey Kong*, *Mario*, and *Zelda* series, among many others

More than 760 million *Mario* games have been sold

PRO FILE

HISTORY:
- Born: November 16, 1952 in Sonobe, Kyoto, Japan

EDUCATION:
- Degree in industrial design from Kanazawa Municipal College of Industrial Arts in 1975

CAREER HIGHLIGHTS:
- Creator of *Donkey Kong* series (1981)
- Director and/or Designer for *Popeye, Mario Bros., Baseball, Tennis, Golf, Devil World, Excitebike, Hogan's Alley, Wild Gunman, Duck Hunt,* and *Kung Fu* (1982-1985)
- Producer, Director, Designer for the *Super Mario* series, *The Legend of Zelda* series, and *Star Fox* series (1985-present)
- Producer and/or Designer for *F-Zero, Super Mario Kart, Pokémon Red/Blue, Paper Mario, Luigi's Mansion, Pikmin, Metroid Prime, Nintendogs, Wii Sports, Wii Fit,* and more.

RECOGNITION:
First in Academy of Interactive Arts and Sciences' Hall of Fame (1998), GDCA Lifetime Achievement Award (2007), NAVGTR Award (2016), Person of Cultural Merit (2019), among others

TABLE 5.4 Famicom/NES Tech Specs

Manufacturer:	Nintendo
Launch price:	$199.99
Release date:	7/15/83 (JP), 10/18/85 (US), 9/01/86 (EU/US national)
Format:	Cartridge
CPU:	8-bit Ricoh processor (1.79 MHz)
Memory:	2 kB RAM, 2 kB VRAM
Resolution:	256 × 240 pixels
Colors:	25 on-screen from palette of 54
Sound:	5-channel mono Ricoh 2A03/07

better than Atari's 1.19 MHz 8-bit 6507 processor on paper, but technology had come a long way since the VCS and Nintendo's programmers were able to squeeze a lot more power out of its chip. The NES also had over 15 times more RAM at **2 kB RAM** versus Atari's 128 bytes RAM, as well as an additional **2 kB VRAM** dedicated to graphics.

The NES displayed a screen resolution of **256 × 240 pixels** (screen dots), compared to the 2600's resolution of 160 × 192 pixels. Because NTSC televisions displayed NES games at 256 × 224 pixels, programmers typically reserved the pixels at the top and bottom of the screen for nothing more than background color. Nintendo could also display **25 on-screen colors** (one transparent) from a palette of 54, whereas the 2600 only displayed four colors per scan line. Finally, the NES was able to output **five channels** of **mono sound**, compared to Atari's two channels of mono sound. The difference in sound was just as drastic as the improvement in graphics.

While the Atari mostly outputted beeps and fuzzy noises (save for a handful of well-programmed, single-track theme songs), the NES could produce more intricately arranged music with a separate channel devoted entirely to percussion.

HEAD-TO-HEAD

To compare the graphics and sound between the NES and 2600, play games released on both consoles (or watch video clips of them). Recommended games to compare include *Bump 'n' Jump, Donkey Kong, Ghostbusters, Mario Bros.*, and *Ms. Pac-Man*.

■ KEY NES TITLES

One of the major reasons for the early success of the Nintendo Entertainment System can be attributed to *Super Mario Bros.* (Figure 5.10a), which became the pack-in title with every NES console when Nintendo initiated its national launch in the West. *Super Mario Bros.* was the brainchild of *Donkey Kong* designer **Shigeru Miyamoto**. While games that preceded it commonly took place on a single (often black background) screen, *SMB* transported players to a vibrant, scrolling world filled with secrets (i.e., **Easter eggs**) that gave gamers a sense of exploration and discovery. It distinguished the NES from the previous generation of consoles and showed what the system was capable of. While there *were* side-scrolling games that came out before it, *SMB* was one of the first **side-scrolling platformer** games and set the standard for the genre.

FIGURE 5.10 Box art to five prestigious NES titles baring the Nintendo Seal of Quality: (a) *Super Mario Bros.*, (b) *Contra* (*Probotector* in PAL regions), (c) *The Legend of Zelda*, (d) *Mega Man 2*, and (e) *Metroid*.

(a)   (b)   (c)   (d)   (e)

The NES saw the debut of numerous key titles, many of which are still receiving sequels and reinventions today. The three *Super Mario Bros.* games were the NES's top-selling games of all time (not counting *Duck Hunt,* which was bundled with *Super Mario Bros.* and included with the Action and Deluxe sets). Other notable series that began on the NES included *Metroid* from Gunpei Yokoi and Shigeru Miyamoto's *The Legend of Zelda.* Each of these games placed an emphasis on nonlinear exploration and powering up one's character—setting new standards for action-adventure games. Third-party series such as Capcom's *Mega Man,* Konami's *Castlevania,* Tecmo's *Ninja Gaiden,* and Enix's *Dragon Quest (Dragon Warrior* in North America) all saw at least three titles on the NES. The system was also home to the original *console* versions of *Final Fantasy, Metal Gear,* and *Kirby's Adventure.* Nintendo licensed more than 700 titles for the NES, with more than 1,000 games for Famicom in Japan.

■ SEGA MARK III

Sega Games Co., Ltd. began in 1940 as an American company called Standard Games. The company was formed by Martin Bromley, Irving Bromberg, and James Humpert in Honolulu, Hawaii to manufacture coin-operated games such as slot machines for military bases. Following World War II, the company changed its name to **Service Games** and moved to Tokyo, Japan when the U.S. government began outlawing slot machines. The company merged with competitor **Rosen Enterprises** and using the first two letters in "Service" and "Games" became **Sega Enterprises** in 1965.

With its experience in the arcade business, Sega debuted on the Japanese home console market the same day as the Nintendo Famicom, introducing the **Sega SG-1000** (Figure 5.11a) on July 15, 1983. The machine received an updated model in 1984, which Sega dubbed the "Mark II." It was not a tremendous success but served as a pivotal stepping stone to Sega's next console, the **Sega Mark III** (Figure 5.11b). The Mark III was an improved version of the SG-1000 that Sega specifically designed to be more powerful than the Nintendo Famicom (Parkin, 2014). It was designed by Sega's Away Team, headed by **Hideki Sato** (who also designed the SG-1000). The system was launched in Japan on October 20, 1985, for 15,000 yen (around $120). The Mark III could play both cartridges and **Sega Cards** (credit card-shaped games that publishers could manufacture and sell for less).

Although technically superior to the Famicom and **backward compatible** with SG-1000 games, the Mark III struggled due to Nintendo's firm licensing policy with third-party developers that did not allow companies to port their Famicom games to other consoles. To compensate for the lack of third-party support, Sega had to obtain rights for those developers' titles and produce the games themselves. As difficult as it was to compete with Nintendo in Japan, Sega believed they could be competitive in the West and began planning a U.S. release for 1986. Like Nintendo's Famicom, Sega would redesign the Mark III to appeal to Western gamers.

FIGURE 5.11 Sega's first console, the SG-1000 (a) and the Sega Mark III (b).

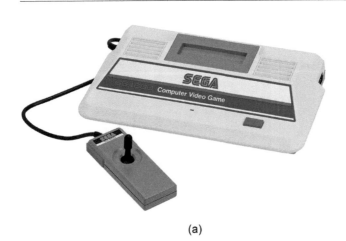

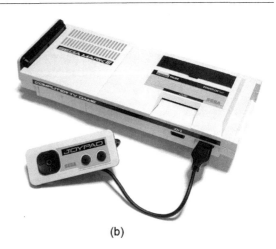

(a)   (b)

FIGURE 5.12 Sega Master System "Power Base" and D-Pad controller with joystick inserted.

▪ SEGA MASTER SYSTEM

Sega redesigned and renamed the Mark III the **Sega Master System** (Figure 5.12) for the West. It first appeared in North America at the June CES but did not officially reach most North American store shelves until September and October of 1986, shortly after the national launch of the NES. It did not reach Europe until a year later. Sega modeled the control pad after Nintendo's, with the addition of an optional small joystick that players could twist into the center of the directional pad. Its initial controller cord was placed on the side of the game pad (like Mark III and Famicom), while later models featured the cord on the top of the controller.

The Master System was released in North America for $199 with only two games available at launch: *Hang-On* and the "Light Phaser" gun game *Safari Hunt* (Figure 5.13). Sega bundled the light gun with the console, along with *Hang-On* and *Safari Hunt* on a **multicart** (multiple games on one cartridge). More than a dozen titles were available by the end of the year. Sega would also release a $99 "Base System," with a single controller and game cartridge featuring *Hang-On* and *Astro Warrior*.

In October 1987 Sega released its "**SegaScope 3-D glasses**" for a handful of 3-D games. Around this time, Nintendo bundled its "Action Set" with a more popular multicart featuring *Super Mario Bros.* and *Duck Hunt*. That same year, Sega released the **FM**

FIGURE 5.13 Screenshots of Sega's two U.S. launch titles (a) *Hang-On* and (b) *Safari Hunt*.

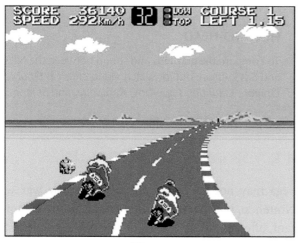

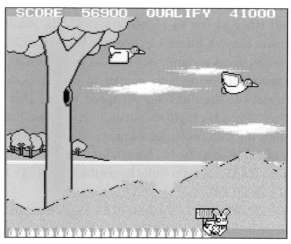

(a)

(b)

TABLE 5.5 Sega Master System European Launch Titles

• *Action Fighter*	• *Hang-On*
• *Black Belt*	• *Transbot*
• *Choplifter*	• *World Grand Prix*
• *Fantasy Zone*	

Sound Unit add-on for the Mark III. The unit contained a Yamaha YM2413 chip that added nine mono sound channels to enhance the sound of roughly 50 compatible games. Unfortunately, Sega never released the unit outside of Japan. Other noteworthy peripherals included the **Sega Sports Pad** trackball controller and **Control Stick** (available with rapid fire).

Like the situation in Japan, the Master System and its meager game library were not nearly as successful as the Nintendo Entertainment System. And because of Nintendo's strict licensing policy, Sega was only able to obtain **Activision** and **Parker Brothers** as consistent third-party developers in the United States. With the market looking bleak in North America, Sega proceeded to distribute the Master System in Europe under **Mastertronic** in 1987 and in Brazil under **Tectoy** in 1989. The system was released for £99 in Europe along with seven launch titles (Table 5.5). It sold well in these regions and maintained a reasonable market share in both Europe and Brazil—even after the release of the more advanced systems in the next generation (McFerran, 2014). Sega continued to market the Master System after the launch of its 16-bit Mega Drive/Genesis console as shown in Figure 5.14.

■ CONSOLE COMPARISON: SMS VS. NES

Sega Master System's processor specs (Table 5.6) topped the NES on paper. Its **3.57 MHz Zilog Z80** looked twice as fast as Nintendo's 1.79 MHz Ricoh processor but was different technology. While the Z80 was faster, it was certainly not *twice* as fast—with the two processors being quite similar in overall clock performance. The difference in speed was as marginal as Nintendo's slight advantage in resolution. For memory, the SMS contained four times the RAM with **8 kB of RAM** compared to Nintendo's 2 kB. Its **16 kB of video RAM** was eight times larger than the NES's 2 kB of video RAM.

With **32 colors** from a **palette of 64**, Sega's machine could also display about 25% more on-screen color compared to Nintendo's 25 colors from a palette of

54. Furthermore, each tile (that makes up a game's backgrounds and sprites) could contain up to 16 colors and any combination from the SMS's color palette. Nintendo was more limited in that it could only use four colors per tile from a combination of four sets of colors. Unlike the NES however, Sega's console could not flip sprite tiles. In other words, programmers would have to draw a character facing left and again facing right on the Master System and this used up video RAM.

Sega's sound was powered by the 4-channel mono Texas Instruments SN76489—the same chip inside the ColecoVision and BBC Micro computer. Nintendo's 5-channel Ricoh 2A03/07 had just one additional channel, but its different types of channels allowed more flexibility for programmers. It processed samples much better than the SMS chip and produced an overall better sound. Sega's Japanese-only FM Sound Unit created superior sound in the games that utilized it—including better sound than the Famicom Disk System, however that technology was only available in Japan.

Overall, Sega's specs were superior. Numbers aside—as history has proven in this and other generations, bigger tech specs do not always translate into bigger sales figures or better games. Sega's games often looked better than NES titles, but overall, the NES library contained more innovative games that were arguably more fun to play. One of Sega's popular slogans for the Master System was "The Challenge Will Always Be There." In retrospect, this slogan was fitting for the company. While this slogan was meant to be for the players, Nintendo's market command in Japan and North America was the challenge that would always be there for Sega.

HEAD-TO-HEAD

To compare the graphics and sound between the NES and SMS, check out (or watch video clips of) *Double Dragon, Gauntlet, Paperboy, Rampage,* and *Shinobi.*

■ KEY SEGA MASTER SYSTEM TITLES

Sega may not have won the 8-bit console war with Nintendo, but the Master System did produce important, often exclusive titles for the video game industry. The role-playing game *Phantasy Star* was one of the

FIGURE 5.14 Magazine advertisement for the Sega Master System in 1990.

WITH A MASTERFUL NEW GAME LINEUP

Summer Sizzle comes to the Sega Master System this May and June with a lineup of HOT new game titles. Look at what's "in-store" for you and you'll agree—the Sega Master System has the hottest new games and prices under the sun!

But that's only the beginning for the Sega Master System. Because starting in September, Sega will "kick-off" a Fantastic Fall by introducing 15 new games. Don't miss any of the great arcade hits, comic book characters and action-packed sports challenges all coming to you this Fall on the Sega Master System.

WATCH FOR OUR NEW 1990 SEGA MASTER SYSTEM RELEASES INCLUDING DICK TRACY, JOE MONTANA FOOTBALL, MICHAEL JACKSON'S MOONWALKER AND MORE!

PSYCHO FOX
You're Psycho Fox, the wily wizard of disguise. Leap and twist your way to the goal as you outsmart your enemies and collect a fortune.

GOLDEN AXE
A sword-swinging romp with fiery dragons, amazing Amazons and elusive magic! Go face to skull with skeleton buccaneers in cliff-edge combat! It's barbaric!

DEAD ANGLE
Blast wall-to-wall gangsters in this inner-city shootout. Step into the alley, dude, where crime meets grime. Get the angle on the street—The Dead Angle.

SLAP SHOT
Slam the puck and slap it into the goal! Pressure 'em into the boards in fast action ice hockey. When the offense is tough, your defense is Slap Shot!

ULTIMA IV
Strive for glory in this powerful medieval quest—as danger beckons! Resist the darkest temptations as you seek to become the Avatar!

Sega's Full Line-up of Games Sizzles Too!

Monopoly	Phantasy Star	Blade Eagle	Montezuma's
Space Harrier II	Kings Quest	After Burner	Revenge
Global Defense	Action Fighter	Miracle Warriors	Great Soccer
Rescue Mission	Sports Pad Football	Rastan	Great Baseball
Power Strike	Great Ice Hockey	Cloud Master	The Ninja
Zaxxon	Lord of the Sword	T's	Captain Silver
Wonder Boy in	Shooting Gallery	Poseidon	Quartet
Monsterland	Gangster Town	R-Type	Zillion
Out Run	Parlour Games	Wonder Boy	Zillion II
Shinobi	Fantasy Zone	Kenseiden	Shanghai
Thunder Blade	Great Golf	Great Basketball	
Great Volleyball	Space Harrier	Spy vs. Spy	

CHECK YOUR LOCAL RETAILER FOR THESE GREAT GAMES. IF GAMES ARE NOT AVAILABLE, ORDER DIRECTLY FROM SEGA BY CALLING: 1-800-USA-SEGA

Great Games At Great Prices

TABLE 5.6 Mark III/Sega Master System: Tech Specs

Manufacturer:	Sega (Service Games)
Launch price:	$199.99
Release date:	10/20/85 (JP), June–Sep. 1986 (US), 1987 (EU), 1989 (BR)
Format:	Cartridge and Sega Card
CPU:	8-bit Zilog Z80 processor (3.57 MHz)
Memory:	8 kB main RAM, 16 kB VRAM
Resolution:	256 × 192 (NTSC) and 256 × 224 pixels (PAL)
Colors:	32 colors from a palette of 64
Sound:	4-channel mono Texas Instruments SN76489

first of its kind and one of the pioneers of the **Japanese role-playing game (JRPG)**. *Golden Axe Warrior* was a shameless but competent clone of *The Legend of Zelda*. Alex Kidd became the de facto mascot of sorts for the Master System but was nowhere near as popular as Nintendo's Mario. The *Alex Kidd* series spawned decent titles such as *Alex Kidd in Miracle World* and *Alex Kidd in Shinobi World*. The *Zillion* and *Wonder Boy* series were among the best side-scrolling action games on the system. See Figures 5.14 and 5.15 for box artwork.

Half of the best games on the console never reached North America. The console's success in Europe led to countless key European exclusives such as the *Castlevania*-like *Master of Darkness*, three different *Asterix* games, the Compile shoot 'em up *Power Strike II*, an exclusive version of *Ninja Gaiden*, as well as *Ultima IV—Quest of the Avatar*. The European market

was also the exclusive home to Hollywood movie titles including *Back to the Future II* and *III*, *Batman Returns*, *Bran Stoker's Dracula*, *Jurassic Park*, *Star Wars*, *The Terminator*, and more. Even Disney games such as *Aladdin* and certain games featuring Mickey Mouse and Donald Duck only released for the Master System in Europe. Sega and its affiliates released barely over a third of the Master System's 300+ games in North America and Japan.

> ### 💡 DID YOU KNOW?
>
> Early versions of the Master System included a secret "Easter Egg" game in the system's BIOS called *Snail Maze*. Players could access the game by turning on the system without a game inserted and holding up plus buttons 1 and 2 together during the Sega startup screen.

■ ATARI 7800 PROSYSTEM

General Consumer Corporation (GCC) developed the **Atari 7800 ProSystem** (Figure 5.16) to replace the unsuccessful Atari 5200 before the Nintendo Famicom became an enormous success. GCC was an experienced company that produced more than half of the titles on the 5200. Atari announced the console in May 1994 but then shelved the system when Warner Communications sold the company to Commodore head **Jack Tramiel**. It sat for 2 years and did not receive a full launch (often called a relaunch) until May 1986 at a competitive price of $139. The console was released in Europe thereafter but never saw an official release in Asia.

FIGURE 5.15 Box art to five standout SMS titles including: (a) *Phantasy Star*, (b) *Shinobi*, (c) *Wonder Boy in Monster World*, (d) *Alex Kidd in Miracle World*, and (e) *Zillion*.

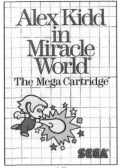
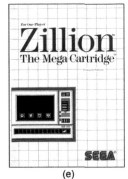

(a)   (b)   (c)   (d)   (e)

FIGURE 5.16 Atari 7800 ProSystem with a Proline joystick controller.

The 7800 looked like a combination of the newly designed **Atari 2600 Jr.** and the Atari 5200. Atari initially called it the "3600" but then renamed it the "7800" because of its 5200 graphics power+2600 **backward compatibility** (ability to play 2600 games). The joystick was a hybrid between the 2600 and 5200 controllers. Gone was the cumbersome numeric keypad from the 5200 controller and the joystick was self-centering again like the 2600's stick. The **Proline controller** had just two buttons but remained comfortable for both right-handed and left-handed players. On the downside, there were no Pause or Reset buttons on the controller. These buttons were located on the console. To keep costs down, the 7800 featured just a quarter of the RAM of the 5200 and used the exact TIA sound chip as the 2600.

Like Nintendo's 10NES lockout chip, the 7800 also contained technology to maintain quality control of its software. "The solution was a unique and encrypted **digital signature** contained in all cartridges, that when not present would automatically lock the system into 2600 mode" (Retro Gamer, 2010, p. 229). Unlike European games, all 7800 games released in the United States required this digital signature code by Atari to operate. Like many of the previous second-generation consoles, Atari originally planned for the 7800 ProSystem to be upgradable to a home computer. Atari even developed a computer keyboard for the system that never came to fruition. The 7800 launched with seven titles (Table 5.7);

however, Atari only released two other games during the remainder of the year with *Galaga* in August and *Xevious* in November. By the end of 1986, Sega had more than twice the number of games on U.S. shelves and Nintendo had more than four times as many games compared to the 7800.

Compared to Nintendo's lineup of exclusive and original titles, most 7800 games were just enhanced **ports** of arcade games that were already playable on the 2600 and/or 5200. The graphics were better than the older Atari consoles, but players were more interested in newer titles they had not experienced yet. Furthermore, Nintendo was providing titles that were exclusive to the home market—games that players could not find in the arcades. Atari's console would never compete with the NES library in terms of quality or quantity. To its credit, the 7800 was among the first U.S. consoles to contain backward compatibility with its ability to play 2600 titles. The system could not play Atari 5200 games, however, because while it included the 2600's **TIA (Television Interface Adaptor)** graphics and sound chip, it did not contain the chips from the less popular 5200.

TABLE 5.7 Atari 7800 ProSystem U.S. Launch Titles

• *Centipede*	• *Ms. Pac-Man*
• *Dig Dug*	• *Pole Position II* (Figure 5.17b)
• *Food Fight*	• *Robotron: 2084*
• *Joust* (Figure 5.17a)	

FIGURE 5.17 Screenshots from Atari 7800 launch titles (a) *Joust* and (b) *Pole Position II*.

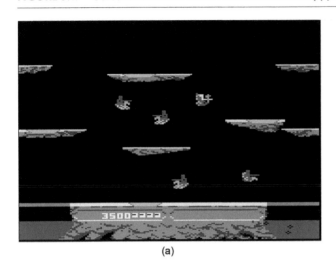

(a)

(b)

■ CONSOLE COMPARISON: ATARI 7800 VS. NES & SMS

The 7800's 8-bit 6502C "**SALLY**" processor clocked in at **1.79 MHz** (Table 5.8), which was identical to the speed of Nintendo's Ricoh processor but not as fast as Sega's. Where the SALLY differed the most was in its custom graphics chip called **MARIA** (combined with the TIA = TIA-MARIA, named after the Jamaican coffee liqueur). This chip was drastically different from the other consoles of the third generation in that it could display a larger number of moving sprites on

TABLE 5.8 Atari 7800 ProSystem Tech Specs

Manufacturer:	Atari
Launch price:	$139.99
Release date:	May 1986 (US), 1987–89 (EU)
Format:	Cartridge (32K)
CPU:	8-bit 6502C "SALLY" processor (1.79 MHz)
Memory:	4 kB RAM, 4 kB BIOS ROM
Resolution:	160 × 240 or 320 × 240 pixels
Colors:	25 from a palette of 256
Sound:	2-channel mono

screen—although doing so would often halt the CPU. And while it could move large graphics around on the screen, it was not as adept at handling side-scrolling games like *Super Mario Bros*.

The 7800 utilized **4 kB of RAM** and **4 kB of BIOS ROM**. Its games were capable of being displayed at **160 × 240** or **320 × 240 pixels**—the latter being higher than the resolution of both the NES and the Master System. Capability aside, most 7800 games ran at the lower resolution to accommodate the processing demands of MARIA. On-screen colors were comparable to the NES with **25 colors** per scan line. However, the 7800 had a much larger color palette to choose from with **256 total colors** versus the NES's palette of 54 and Sega's 64 colors.

It was sound limitations that crippled the 7800 from the beginning more than anything else. Since it used the same, **two-channel, mono sound** chip as the outdated VCS, Atari 7800 games sounded like Atari 2600 games unless the software included the **Pot Keyboard Integrated Circuit (POKEY) audio chip** from the 5200. Adding the POKEY chip inside a cartridge could enhance the sound of a game but doing so made the game more expensive. Only *two* 7800 titles used this technique—*Ballblazer* (1988) and *Commando* (1990). Most of its best games, including *Pole Position II*, did not contain the POKEY audio chip and suffered from poor sound quality. Comparing the technical specifications of major third-generation consoles puts the Atari 7800 in a distant third place behind the competition—and their advertisements (Figure 5.18) did not have much to say about it.

FIGURE 5.18 Comic book advertisement for the Atari 7800 (1990).

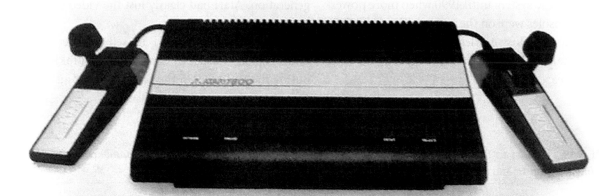

■ KEY ATARI 7800 TITLES

One of the slogans used by Atari to market the 7800 was, "We Reinvented the Video Game." A more appropriate slogan could have been, "We Reinvented *Our* Video Games," as most of the games on the 7800—especially in the beginning—were simply upgraded versions of older titles already available on previous systems. Atari priced their 7800 games competitively at just $15–$20 each—which was half the cost of most Nintendo and Sega games. Updated classics attracted gamers for their nostalgic value and improved graphics, such as notable upgrades of *Joust* and *Centipede* in 1986. *Food Fight* proved that throwing food could be tons of fun, and *Dark Chambers* was a solid dungeon crawler similar to *Gauntlet*.

Other arcade titles such as vertical shoot 'em ups *Xevious* and *Galaga* were welcome additions to the console's library since neither title released on the Atari 5200. The excellent sound and gameplay of *Ballblazer* (1988) and *Commando* (1990) also warranted a look at the system. The 7800 had some late but unique exclusives with target shooter *Alien Brigade,* isometric adventure *Midnight Mutants*, and the mixed action of *Ninja Golf* (Figure 5.19). Like *Commando*, these titles did not reach the system until 1990 when more powerful 16-bit consoles were on the market. The Atari 7800 spawned more exclusive titles than the 5200 but had an even smaller library of games with only 59 titles officially released.

HEAD-TO-HEAD

Compare the graphics and sound between the 7800 and NES by playing or watching video clips of *Donkey Kong, Commando, Ikari Warriors, Xenophobe,* and *Xevious.* To compare the 7800 with both the NES and SMS, check out each system's version of *Double Dragon* and *Rampage.*

■ THIRD-GENERATION MARKET SUMMARY

Atari was in hot water before the release of the 7800, and the company's financial situation only worsened afterward. When Jack Tramiel acquired the company, he divided rights of patents, licenses, and products between the coin-op (arcade) division **Atari Games** and between **Warner Communications**, with Warner maintaining ownership of the 7800 ProSystem. Arguments between Warner and Tramiel over who should pay General Consumer Corporation for their work on the 7800 and its launch titles ensued, with Tramiel reluctantly absorbing the bill in May 1985 (Retro Gamer, 2010, p. 231). The 7800 sold millions more units than the 5200, but by the end of the third generation, Atari had clearly lost the video game market it once dominated.

Sega originally planned to sell between 400,000 and 750,000 Master System consoles (Takiff, 1986), but by the end of 1986 the SMS had sold just 125,000

FIGURE 5.19 Box art to five of the top 7800 titles including: (a) *Alien Brigade*, (b) *Dark Chambers*, (c) *Food Fight*, (d) *Midnight Mutants*, and (e) *Ninja Golf*.

(a)　　　　(b)　　　　(c)　　　　(d)　　　　(e)

consoles—more than the Atari 7800's 100,000 but far less than Nintendo's 1.1 million (Computer Entertainer, 1987, p. 13). Unlike in Japan and North America where Nintendo focused its efforts, the Master System outsold the NES in Europe by a considerable margin (Screen Digest, 1995, p. 61) with more than 6 million units sold. It performed just as well in Brazil and lasted for years in South America where it saw other exclusive titles. It was Sega's home console success in Europe and Brazil, plus a profitable coin-op business in the arcades that helped Sega become a major player in the next generation.

Sega handed the Master System over to **Tonka** for distribution until they reacquired distribution rights for the smaller, redesigned (cartridge-only) **Master System II** in 1990. Nintendo would also release a redesigned, top-loading version of the NES with a game pad in the bone shape of the Super Nintendo controller. The NES sold the most units in the third generation due to its earlier initial release, strong first-party titles, and Nintendo's strict licensing policy with third-party developers. Nintendo supported its system even further with *Nintendo Power* magazine, consumer tip line, and successful marketing strategies. By 1988, Nintendo commanded an 83% share of the North American video game market (McGill, 1988) and at least 90% of the Japanese video game market. Nintendo's effect on American culture was so profound that "a 1990 survey showed that Mario was more recognized by children than Mickey Mouse" (Diski, 2004, p. 4).

Figure 5.20 illustrates the millions of consoles each platform eventually sold. Nintendo's success with the Famicom and NES signaled a significant market shift in the video game industry. "Much development in the arcades had switched to Japan, and with Nintendo's Famicom the clear market leader there, it had a lock on the latest titles" (Retro Gamer, 2010, p. 231). This market change saw Japan as the dominant force in the video game industry—a crown the country would hold for generations.

▪ THIRD-GENERATION BREAKTHROUGHS AND TRENDS

There were unique breakthroughs and trends that defined the third generation of video games. Here is a list of the top 10 advancements that defined the generation:

1. D-Pad game controllers
2. Tile-based playfields with smooth hardware scrolling
3. The "platformer"-style video game
4. Detailed sprite graphics with integer sprite zooming (to double sprite size)
5. Higher screen resolutions (up to 320×240 pixels)
6. Multidirectional scrolling and diagonal scrolling
7. Enhanced sound (up to 5-channel mono audio [more with add-ons])
8. Battery backup save feature (players could save progress on cartridge)
9. Light gun game popularity
10. Active-shutter stereoscopic 3D glasses

FIGURE 5.20 Third-generation console sales graph.

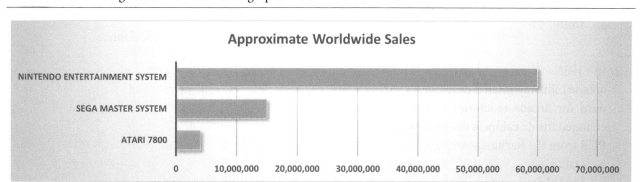

■ ACTIVITY: ARCADE TO HOME PORT COMPARISON

Play or view gameplay from both an arcade title and its home port for at least 30 minutes each. Take notes on the graphical, aural, and gameplay differences and similarities.

SUGGESTED TITLES

Compare the arcade and NES versions of *Ikari Warriors*, *Punch-Out!!*, or *Splatterhouse*; the arcade and Sega Maser System versions of *Space Harrier*, *Double Dragon*, or *Shinobi*; and/or the arcade and Atari 7800 versions of *Pole Position II*, *Joust*, or *Xevious*.

GUIDELINES

Always begin by playing/viewing the arcade version of the game first; then discuss how the home port measures up. Write a 500- to 1,000-word essay comparing the two games regarding:

- Graphics—include size and scale, color palette, resolution (clarity), animation, effects, and presentation.
- Sound—include the quality and accuracy of the games' music and sound effects.
- Playability—include how well the games control and how fun they are to play.

QUESTIONS

1. How do these games compare to arcade ports from the previous generation?
2. Did the home console version add anything to or lack something important from the arcade experience?
3. Do you feel that the console version was close enough to the arcade game that players would want to purchase the game to play from home?
4. Did the arcade version contain any features that would still attract owners of the game to visit a public venue to play the arcade game?
5. What impact do you think this had on the arcade industry, if any?
6. Could the publisher/developer have done anything differently?
7. What are your concluding thoughts?

■ CHAPTER 5 QUIZ

1. Which company was *not* a leading arcade game publisher in the mid-1980s?
   a. Capcom
   b. Cave
   c. Konami
   d. Taito

2. In 1985, _____ revolutionized the arcade industry when it developed a wiring standard for arcade machines that allowed games changed inside cabinets just by swapping out the PCB from the harness.
   a. Data East
   b. JAMMA
   c. Tecmo
   d. Technōs Japan

3. Which third-generation console sold the largest number of units?
   a. Nintendo Entertainment System
   b. Sega Master System
   c. Sega SG-1000
   d. Atari 7800

4. Nintendo's Famicom stood for:
   a. Family Computer
   b. Future Computer
   c. Family Console
   d. Future Console

5. What system launched with a bad chip that caused a product recall and reissue with a new motherboard?
   a. Atari 2600
   b. Nintendo Famicom
   c. Sega Master System
   d. Atari 7800

6. Nintendo initially approached _____ to market and distribute the NES in the United States.
   a. Atari
   b. Coleco
   c. Mattel
   d. Tonka

7. In which U.S. city was the NES first released?
   a. Boston
   b. New York City
   c. Miami
   d. Los Angeles

8. The original mascot for the NES was a robot named R.O.B., which stood for:
   a. Robot Opponent Buddy
   b. Robot Operating Buddy
   c. Robot Operating Bus
   d. Random Operating Bus

9. This dedicated Nintendo handheld released a total of 60 different systems through 1991, not including anniversary editions and reissues.
   a. Microvision
   b. Game Boy
   c. Game & Watch
   d. None of the above

10. What creation(s) is Shigeru Miyamoto famous for?
   a. *Donkey Kong*
   b. *Legend of Zelda*
   c. *Super Mario Bros.*
   d. All of the above

11. SEGA stands for:
   a. Service Games
   b. Sonic Electronic Games of America
   c. Super Electronic Games of America
   d. Solid Electronic Games of America

12. The typical launch price for an NES or a Master System video game console was:
   a. $299.99
   b. $249.99
   c. $199.99
   d. $99.99

13. Which console did publishers *not* redesign for the American audience?
   a. Nintendo Famicom
   b. Nintendo Advanced Video System
   c. Sega Mark III
   d. Atari 7800

14. Which console was technologically superior based on tech spec numbers?
   a. Nintendo Entertainment System
   b. Sega Master System
   c. Sega SG-1000
   d. Atari 7800

15. These two 7800 games included the POKEY sound chip inside the cartridge:
   a. *Dig Dug* and *Ms. Pac-Man*
   b. *Xevious* and *Galaga*
   c. *Joust* and *Centipede*
   d. *Ballblazer* and *Commando*

16. The Atari 7800 failed to obtain long-term market success because of:
   a. Poor hardware sound
   b. Dated initial game library
   c. Divided patents, licenses, and product rights
   d. All of the above

17. One of Sega's marketing slogans for the Master System was:
    a. "The Challenge Will Always Be There"
    b. "Now You're Playing with Power"
    c. "We Reinvented the Video Game"
    d. All of the above

18. The Sega Master System was a commercial failure in most countries, except for:
    a. Japan and Europe
    b. Japan and Brazil
    c. Brazil and Europe
    d. Brazil and the United States

19. The Disk System was a disk drive unit that provided 32 kB RAM for program data, 8 kB for image data, and processor with an extra audio channel for:
    a. Nintendo Famicom
    b. Sega SG-1000
    c. Sega Mark III
    d. Atari 7800

20. Which feature was not part of the major three third-generation consoles?
    a. 16-bit graphics
    b. Battery backup save feature (players could save progress on cartridge)
    c. Light gun game popularity
    d. Active-shutter stereoscopic 3D glasses

True or False

21. The original Nintendo Famicom launch titles were *Super Mario Bros.* and *Duck Hunt.*

22. Nintendo renamed the Famicom the Advanced Video System (AVS), before renaming it again as the Nintendo Entertainment System (NES) for the U.S. market.

23. Nintendo only released two games for R.O.B. including *Gyromite* and *Stack-Up.*

24. The Sega FM Sound Unit featured a Yamaha YM2413 chip that added nine additional mono sound channels to the U.S. version of the Master System.

25. The Atari 7800 contained the same 2-channel sound chip found in the Atari 2600.

■ FIGURES

Figure 5.1 Atari still delivered defining arcade games after the video game crash of 1983, including (a) *Paperboy* (1984), (b) *Marble Madness* (1984), and (c) *Gauntlet* (1985). (*Marble Madness,* courtesy of Atari, 1984; *Gauntlet,* courtesy of Atari, 1985; and *Out Run,* courtesy of Sega, 1986.)

Figure 5.2 Nintendo Family Computer (Famicom) game system (a) and Famicom with Disk System (b). (a) "Nintendo Family Computer." By Evan Amos—Own work, Public Domain, https://commons.wikimedia.org/w/index.php?curid=19135654. July 29, 2016. Retrieved from https://en.wikipedia.org/wiki/Nintendo_Entertainment_System#/media/File:Nintendo-Famicom-Console-Set-FL.jpg. (b) "A Japanese Nintendo Famicom shown with the Disk System add-on." By Evan Amos—Own work, Public Domain, https://commons.wikimedia.org/w/index.php?curid=19135792. August 14, 2017. Retrieved from https://en.wikipedia.org/wiki/Famicom_Disk_System#/media/File:Nintendo-Famicom-Disk-System.jpg. (Part of this image was used on the introductory page of this chapter.)

Figure 5.3 Screenshots of Famicom launch titles: (a) *Donkey Kong,* (b) *Donkey Kong Jr.,* and (c) *Popeye.*(a) *Donkey Kong* (Nintendo, 1983), (b) *Donkey Kong Jr.* (Nintendo, 1983), and (c) *Popeye* (Nintendo, 1983). (Courtesy of Nintendo, 1983.)

Figure 5.4 The first redesign of Famicom, called the Nintendo Advanced Video System (Courtesy of Russell Bernice and Chris Donlan ("Doonvas"), CC BY 2.0, https://commons.wikimedia.org/w/index.php?curid=31293613. Retrieved from https://commons.wikimedia.org/wiki/File:Nintendo_Advanced_Video_System_(retouched).jpg#/media/File:Nintendo_Advanced_Video_System_(retouched).jpg.)

Figure 5.5 Nintendo Entertainment System and its restyled D-Pad controller. "NES-Console-Set." (By Evan Amos. Own work, Public Domain, https://commons.wikimedia.org/w/index.php?curid=11408666. Retrieved from https://commons.wikimedia.org/wiki/File:NES-Console-Set.png#/media/File:NES-Console-Set.png. Part of this image was used on the introductory page of this chapter.)

Figure 5.6 Pages from the 1986 CES NES Brochure showing R.O.B., the Zapper, and newly designed Nintendo Entertainment System. "The Complete 1986 CES NES Brochure For Your Viewing Pleasure." Posted Mon September 3, 2012 by Damien McFerran. Retrieved from http://www.nintendolife.com/news/2012/09/the_complete_1986_ces_nes_brochure_for_your_viewing_pleasure. (Courtesy of Evan Amos—own work, public domain. Available at https://commons.wikimedia.org/w/index.php?curid=11408666. Retrieved from https://commons.wikimedia.org/wiki/File:NES-Console-Set.png#/media/File:NES-Console-Set.png.)

Figure 5.7 The first Game & Watch, *Ball* (1980). "Game & Watch Ball handheld game, sirca 1980." (By masatsu—https://flickr.com/photos/masatsu/4536721793/, CC BY-SA 2.0, https://commons.wikimedia.org/w/index.php?curid=88743631. April 20, 2010. Retrieved from https://commons.wikimedia.org/wiki/File:Game-and-watch-ball.jpg. Part of this image was used on the introductory page of this chapter.)

Figure 5.8 Three Game & Watch models: (a) Vertical Multi Screen *Donkey Kong* (1982), (b) Two-player Micro Vs. System *Donkey Kong 3* (1985), and (c) final release New Wide Screen *Mario the Juggler* (1991). (a) "The Game & Watch system Donkey Kong." By sanrojoga.com, https://www.mariowiki.com/index.php?curid=37278. December 1, 2012. Retrieved from https://www.mariowiki.com/Donkey_Kong_(Game_%26_Watch)#/media/File:G-w-donkeykong.jpg. (b) "A Nintendo Game & Watch (Micro Vs System), this is Donkey Kong 3." By Evan Amos—Own work, Public Domain, https://commons.wiki-media.org/w/index.php?curid=11419633. September 5, 2010. Retrieved from https://en.wikipedia.org/wiki/List_of_Game_%26_Watch_games#/media/File:Game&watch-donkey-kong-3.jpg. (c) "Game & Watch—Mario the Juggler at the National Video Game Museum." By WMrapids—Own work, CC0, https://commons.wikimedia.org/w/index.php?curid=106890548. June 14, 2021. Retrieved from https://commons.wikimedia.org/wiki/File:Game_%26_Watch_-_Mario_the_Juggler.png#/media/File:Game_&_Watch_-_Mario_the_Juggler.png.

Figure 5.9 Screenshots from NES launch titles (a) *Kung Fu* and (b) *Super Mario Bros.* (*Kung Fu,* courtesy of Irem/Nintendo, 1985; and *Super Mario Bros.,* courtesy of Nintendo, 1985.)

Figure 5.10 Box art to five prestigious NES titles baring the Nintendo Seal of Quality: (a) *Super Mario Bros.*, (b) *Contra*

(*Probotector* in PAL regions), (c) *The Legend of Zelda*, (d) *Mega Man 2*, and (e) *Metroid*. (*Super Mario Bros.*, courtesy of Nintendo, 1985; *Contra*, courtesy of Konami, 1988; *The Legend of Zelda*, courtesy of Nintendo, 1987; *Mega Man 2*, courtesy of Capcom, 1989; and *Metroid* courtesy of Nintendo, 1987.)

Figure 5.11 Sega's first console, the SG-1000 (a) and the Sega Mark III (b). (a) "Sega-SG-1000-Console-Set." (By Evan Amos. Own work, CC BY-SA 3.0, https://commons.wikimedia.org/w/index.php?curid=18273359. Retrieved from https://commons.wikimedia.org/wiki/File:Sega-SG-1000-Console-Set.jpg#/media/File:Sega-SG-1000-Console-Set.jpg.) (b) "Sega Mark III." (By Muband. Own work, CC BY-SA 3.0, https://commons.wikimedia.org/w/index.php?curid=9038926. Retrieved from https://commons.wikimedia.org/wiki/File:Sega_Mark_III.jpg#/media/File:Sega_Mark_III.jpg.)

Figure 5.12 Sega Master System "Power Base" and D-Pad controller with joystick inserted. "Sega-Master-System-Set." (By Evan Amos. Own work, Public Domain, https://commons.wikimedia.org/w/index.php?curid=14249084. Retrieved from https://commons.wikimedia.org/wiki/File:Sega-Master-System-Set.jpg#/media/File:Sega-Master-System-Set.jpg. Part of this image was used on the introductory page of this chapter.)

Figure 5.13 Screenshots of Sega's two U.S. launch titles (a) *Hang-On* and (b) *Safari Hunt*. (*Hang-On, courtesy of Sega*, 1985; *Safari Hunt, courtesy of Sega*, 1986).

Figure 5.14 Magazine advertisement for the Sega Master System in 1990. "*The Sega Master System's Hot This Summer*" posted by *Retroist*. (Retrieved from http://www.retroist.com/2011/01/27/the-sega-master-systems-hot-this-summer/.) (*Hang-On,* courtesy of Sega, 1985; and *Safari Hunt,* courtesy of Sega, 1986.)

Figure 5.15 Box art to five standout SMS titles including: (a) *Phantasy Star*, (b) *Shinobi*, (c) *Wonder Boy in Monster World*, (d) *Alex Kidd in Miracle World*, and (e) *Zillion*. (*Phantasy Star,* courtesy of Sega, 1988; *Shinobi,* courtesy of Sega, 1988; *Wonder Boy in Monster World,* courtesy of Westo One/Sega, 1993, published by Sega; *Alex Kidd in Miracle World,* courtesy of Sega, 1986; and *Zillion,* courtesy of Sega, 1987.)

Figure 5.16 Atari 7800 ProSystem with a Proline joystick controller. "Atari-7800-Console-Set." (By Evan Amos. Own work, CC BY-SA 3.0, https://commons.wikimedia.org/w/index.php?curid=18312472. Retrieved from https://

commons.wikimedia.org/wiki/File:Atari-7800-Console-Set.png#/media/File:Atari-7800-Console-Set.png. Part of this image was used on the introductory page of this chapter.)

Figure 5.17 Screenshots from Atari 7800 launch titles (a) *Joust* and (b) *Pole Position II*. (*Joust,* courtesy of Atari, 1986; *Pole Position II,* courtesy of Atari, 1987.)

Figure 5.18 Comic book advertisement for the Atari 7800 (1990). (Retrieved from Atari Age at http://atariage.com/forums/topic/168431-a-few-more-vintage-atari-7800-print-ads/.)

Figure 5.19 Box art to five of the top 7800 titles including: (a) *Alien Brigade*, (b) *Dark Chambers*, (c) *Food Fight*, (d) *Midnight Mutants*, and (e) *Ninja Golf*. (*Alien Brigade,* courtesy of Sculptured Software/Atari, 1990; *Dark Chambers,* courtesy of Sculptured Software/Atari, 1988; *Food Fight,* courtesy of Atari, 1990; *Midnight Mutants,* courtesy of Radioactive Software/Atari, 1990; and *Ninja Golf,* courtesy of Blue Sky Software/Atari, 1990.)

Figure 5.20 Third-generation console sales graph. (Designed by Wardyga using data from Resource Site for Video Game Research, "Console Wars through the Generations." Available at http://dh101.humanities.ucla.edu/DH101Fall12Lab4/graph-console-wars.)

PRO FILE: Shigeru Miyamoto. Photo credit: Shigeru Miyamoto at E3 2013. Photo by Jan Graber via Public Domain CC BY-SA 3.0 de, https://commons.wikimedia.org/w/index.php?curid=57040765.

■ REFERENCES

Caruso, N. (2016, July 16). *Famicom disk system | Gaming historian.* [Video]. YouTube. https://youtu.be/r9PuSrn_H1c.

Comparing the New Videogame Systems. (1987, February). *Computer Entertainer Newsletter,* 5(11), p. 13. Retrieved from http://www.smspower.org/forums/files/computer-entertai01unse_page_0841_154.jpg.

Diski, P. (2004, August). *Nintendo entertainment system documentation.* Retrieved from http://nesdev.com/NESDoc.pdf.

Editorial: The Nintendo threat? (1988, June). *Computer Gaming World,* 48, p. 50.

Editorial: Total 8-bit and 16-bit cartridge consoles: Active installed base estimates. (1995, March). *Screen Digest,* p. 61.

Hester, B. (2022, February 22). Inside the Nintendo Power hotline. *Game Informer.* Retrieved from https://www.gameinformer.com/2022/02/22/inside-the-nintendo-power-hotline.

Iwata, S. (2011, February 26). Interview by Club Nintendo from *Iwata Asks: Super Mario Bros. 25th anniversary.* Retrieved from http://iwataasks.nintendo.com/interviews/.

Kent, S. (2001). *The ultimate history of video games: The story behind the craze that touched our lives and changed the world.* Roseville, CA: Three Rivers Press.

McFerran, D. (2014, July). Hardware classics: Sega Master System. *Nintendo Life.* Retrieved from http://www.nintendolife.com/news/2014/07/hardware_classics_sega_master_system.

McGill, D. C. (1988, December). Nintendo scores big. *The New York Times.* Retrieved from http://www.nytimes.com/1988/12/04/business/nintendo-scores-big.html?pagewanted=all.

Parkin, S. (2014, June). A history of video game hardware: Sega Master System. *Edge.* Retrieved from http://www.edge-online.com/features/a-history-of-video-game-hardware-sega-master-system/.

Retro Gamer. (2010). Retroinspection: Atari 7800. *Videogames Hardware Handbook,* 2, pp. 226–231. London, UK: Image Publishing Ltd.

Sheff, D. (1993). *Game over.* New York: Random House.

Takiff, J. (1986, June). Video games gain in Japan, are due for assault on U.S. *The Vindicator.* p. 2. Retrieved from https://news.google.com/newspapers?id=QBhcAAAAIBAJ&pg=2846,1271636.

The 16-Bit Era

■ OBJECTIVES

After reading this chapter, you should be able to:

- Discuss developments and breakthroughs in arcade industry during this time.
- Provide a brief overview of the history of NEC and SNK.
- Review key people behind the video games and consoles.
- Describe how publishers redesigned Japanese consoles for the Western audience.
- Identify graphics and other capabilities of fourth-generation games.
- Differentiate fourth-generation consoles from their 8-bit predecessors.
- Compare the technological differences among NEC, Nintendo, Sega, and SNK consoles.
- Describe the strengths and weaknesses of Nintendo Game Boy, Atari Lynx, and Sega Game Gear.
- List key video game titles and peripherals for each fourth-generation console.
- Illustrate how and when Sega rose above Nintendo during the fourth generation.
- List important innovations introduced to gaming during this period.
- Summarize fourth-generation market sales, breakthroughs, and trends.

DOI: 10.1201/9781003315759-6

■ KEY TERMS AND PEOPLE

16-bit
32X
3D polygons
Alpha Denshi
    Corporation (ADK)
Arcade Card
Atari Lynx
Backward compatibility
Lance Barr
Blast processing
Capcom
Censorship
Central Processing Unit
    (CPU)
Color layering
Color palette
ComLynx Adapter
Compile
Console war
CPS (hardware)
Data East
Digital Signal Processor
Direct Memory Access
Electronic Arts
Full Motion Video
    (FMV)
Game Boy
Game Gear

Game Link Cable
GEMS
Genesis
Graphics Processing Unit
Ben Herman
HuCard/TurboChip
Hudson Soft
Irem
Masami Ishikawa
Tom Kalinske
Michael Katz
Konami
Yuzo Koshiro
Localization
Master Gear Converter
Mega-CD
Mega Drive
Memory card
Menacer
R. J. Mical
Midway
Mode 7
Mosaic
Motorola 68000
Yuji Naka
Hayao Nakayama
Namco
Dave Needle

Neo•Geo AVS
Neo•Geo CD
Neo•Geo MVS
Nippon Electric Company
    (NEC)
Naoto Ohshima
Parallax scrolling
PC Engine
Power Base Converter
Recreational Brainware
Region protection
Reprogramming
Kent Russell
Satellaview
Hideki Sato
Sega CD
Sega Channel Adapter
Sega R&D Team
Sega Virtua Processor
Shin Nihon Kikaku (SNK)
Shoot 'em up/shmup
Slowdown
Sonic the Hedgehog
Sprite Rotation
Sprite Scaling
St.GIGA
Street date
Street Fighter II

Super Famicom
Super Game Boy
Super Nintendo
Super Scope
Super System Card
SuperFX chip
SuperGrafx
Yu Suzuki
Taito
Tommy Tallarico
Technōs Japan
Tele-Communications, Inc.
    (TCI)
Time Warner Cable
Turbo Technologies, Inc.
    (TTI)
TurboDuo
TurboExpress
TurboGrafx-16
TurboGrafx-CD
TurboPad
TurboTap
TurboVision
TV Tuner
Masayuki Uemura
VRAM bandwidth
Western Electric Company
Zilog Z80

■ CONSOLE TIMELINE

PC Engine	Mega Drive/Genesis	TurboGrafx-16	Super Famicom	Neo·Geo	Super NES
1987	**1988/89**	**1989**	**1990**	**1991**	**1991**

▪ ARCADE REVIVAL

During the mid-to-late 1980s, the graphics and sound of arcade games remained superior to home consoles. Sega's motion-controlled, hydraulic cabinets by director/designer **Yu Suzuki** such as *OutRun* (1986) and *After Burner* (1987) provided an additional level of immersion that players could not experience at home. Following the success of *Double Dragon* by **Technōs Japan**, companies such as **Data East**, **Sega**, and **Capcom** introduced refined titles to the "beat 'em up" genre with the games *Bad Dudes Vs. DragonNinja* in 1988, followed by *Golden Axe* and *Final Fight* in 1989. A slew of similar titles would follow, with **Konami** capitalizing on licensed franchises including *Teenage Mutant Ninja Turtles, The Simpsons,* and *X-Men,* among others. Thanks to the popularity of these beat 'em ups and what would become an explosion of fighting games, the arcade industry would enter a resurgence period around the turn of the decade.

The game that prompted players to return to the arcades more than any other was Capcom's ***Street Fighter II: The World Warrior*** (1991) (Compton, 2004, p. 119). This head-to-head fighting game (shown in Figure 6.1) featured fighters from across the world. Its intricate controls included six buttons (for light, medium, and heavy punches and kicks) and each character had unique special moves and attack combinations for players to learn. As complex as the game was, it attracted players of all ages. Gamers would place their coin on the arcade cabinet's **bezel** (window surrounding the screen) and eagerly await their turn behind a line of other players for their chance to compete in the best-of-three matches where the winner would continue for free.

The success and popularity of *Street Fighter II* helped revive the arcade industry and set the standard for a whole new generation of fighting games. Titles like **Midway**'s *Mortal Kombat* (1992) and a plethora of other fighting

series (including *Fatal Fury, World Heroes, Samurai Shodown,* and *The King of Fighters* by **SNK**) would follow its success. Capcom's **CPS (Capcom Power System)** hardware spawned dozens of popular arcade hits beyond *Street Fighter II,* such as *1941—Counter Attack, Forgotten Worlds (Lost Worlds), Ghouls 'n Ghosts (Daimakaimura), Knights of the Round, Mercs,* and *Strider.* Other popular boards during this time included Konami's TMNT- and TMNT 2-based hardware, **Namco** System 1 and 2, Sega System 18, 24, 32, and X board, as well as **Irem** M72 and M92 and **Taito** B and Z systems.

3D polygon graphics also started to appear more frequently during this time, with games like Atari's *Hard Drivin'* (1989) and Sega's *"Virtua"* series by Yu Suzuki. Along with the innovative technology, market inflation and rising manufacturing costs resulted in arcade cabinets beginning to require two or more coins/tokens (or multiple coins to start the game and one coin for each continue). Like the second generation of video games, consumers wanted to bring the arcade experience home and many of the best-selling console games in the early 1990s were ports of popular arcade games.

▪ THE 16-BIT ERA

Often referred to as the "16-bit era," the fourth generation of video games began once again in Japan, near the end of 1987. Consumers could sense the arcade revival from their living rooms the way publishers were marketing the consoles as bringing the arcade experience home. The concept of playing arcade games from home was popular again and this theme would be a major influence on the games released during this period. Larger sprites, more colorful graphics, stereo sound, and effects such as **parallax scrolling** (multilayered backgrounds), sprite scaling, and rotation would define the fourth generation of video games.

FIGURE 6.1 Defining arcade fighting games in the fourth generation: (a) *Street Fighter II* (1991), (b) *Mortal Kombat* (1992), and (c) *Virtua Fighter* (1993).

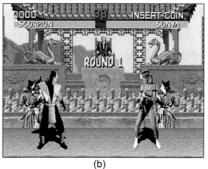

(a)   (b)   (c)

PRO FILE

KEY FACTS:

Pioneered the 'Taikan' trend of motion simulator hydraulic arcade cabinets

Led the 3D polygonal arcade game movement

YU SUZUKI

PRO FILE

HISTORY:
• Born: June 10, 1958 in Kamaishi, Iwate, Japan

EDUCATION:
• Degree in Electronic Science from Okayama University of Science

CAREER HIGHLIGHTS:
• Director/Designer for *Champion Boxing, Hang-On* series, *Space Harrier, Enduro Racer, OutRun* series, *After Burner, Power Drift,* and Producer for *Dynamite Düx* and *Sword of Vermilion* (1984-1988)

• Producer and/or Director for *G-LOC: Air Battle, GP Rider, Strike Fighter, Virtua Racing* series, *Virtua Fighter* series, *Burning Rival, Daytona USA, Virtua Cop* series, *Fighting Vipers* series, *Fighters Megamix,* and more (1990-1998)

• Director, Producer, and Writer of *Shenmue* series

RECOGNITION:
Sixth person inducted into the Academy of Interactive Arts and Sciences' Hall of Fame (2003), Game Developers Choice Awards Pioneer Award (2011), Golden Joystick Lifetime Achievement Award (2019), and NAVGTR Award (2020)

■ NEC PC ENGINE

The first console of the 16-bit era was manufactured by **Nippon Electric Company** (**NEC**). Kunihiko Iwadare and Takeshiro Maeda established the company in 1898 and the following year, NEC teamed up with **Western Electric Company** to become the first Japanese joint venture with foreign capital (Mason, 1987, p. 95). The company began as a telephone and switch manufacturer and over the decades expanded its business to include radio, telecommunications, and computers. Success in the computer industry during the 1980s led to NEC licensing technology from video game manufacturer **Hudson Soft** to create their first video game console, the **PC Engine** (Figure 6.2).

The PC Engine launched in Japan on October 30, 1987, for ¥24,800 (approximately $208). NEC initially developed the system to compete with the Famicom/NES but found its greatest competition with later fourth-generation offerings by Sega and Nintendo. The console featured only one controller port and launched with just two titles: *Bikkuriman World* and *Shanghai*. Like the rarely seen 8-bit Sega Cards, the PC Engine's games (called **HuCards**) were similar in size to a credit card. Hudson Soft originally developed the HuCard as the "Bee Card," which they licensed for use on the MSX computer series. Rumors suggest Hudson Soft may have also pitched the card to Nintendo (Spence, 2020, para. 27) for use on the Famicom Disk System.

The system's casing was also ultra-compact, "with dimensions of $135 \times 130 \times 35$ mm [or $5.3 \times 5.1 \times 1.37$ inches], it remains the smallest home console ever made" (McFerran, 2012, para. 4). Even the controller's cord was small at only three feet in length. Similar to how **Electronic Arts** designed its computer software packaging after vinyl records, its software was packaged in plastic clamshells resembling CD jewel cases, with a modified interior to hold the game cards. Everything was very stylish to Eastern gamers, and the PC Engine performed quite well in Japan. NEC sold more than a half-million units in the first month and "more Japanese consumers purchased PC Engines in 1988 than Famicoms" (Kent, 2001, p. 411). It also outsold Sega's 16-bit console in Japan and in less than 2 years after its Japanese launch, NEC redesigned and launched the system in the United States.

■ TURBOGRAFX-16

The redesigned PC Engine was rebranded as the **TurboGrafx-16** (Figure 6.3) and debuted in the United States on August 29, 1989, for $199. Its redesign featured the "bigger is better" mentality, which NEC

FIGURE 6.2 NEC PC Engine and PI-PD001 controller.

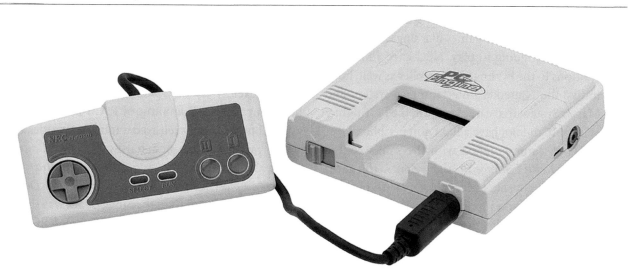

FIGURE 6.3 NEC Turbo Grafx-16 console with TurboPad controller.

believed would be more attractive to U.S. consumers at that time. Even with its larger casing, the TG-16 was still a PC Engine under the hood and only contained a single (albeit larger) controller port. NEC renamed the HuCards "**TurboChips**" and rebranded just about every peripheral to include the word "Turbo" in the title. To play with more than one controller, consumers had to spend an additional $18–$20 for a "**TurboTap**" peripheral. The TurboTap (a precursor to the NES's "Four Score") allowed players to plug up to five controllers into the system.

One unique feature of the **TurboPad controller** was the inclusion of **turbo switches** above the two action buttons. When switched on, just holding down the action buttons would simulate rapid button pressing by the player. This feature (first seen on the NES Advantage joystick) made games like single-fire shooters much less fatiguing to play. NEC later added the turbo buttons to the PC Engine controller as well, however unlike the Nintendo Entertainment System and Sega Master System that came before it, the PC Engine/TurboGrafx-16 did not have a light gun peripheral.

The TG-16 came bundled with the side-scrolling action game *Keith Courage in Alpha Zones*. The game highlighted the console's high color palette but was a mediocre title beyond its graphics. The TG-16 had nine respectable launch titles (Table 6.1), which were of both high quality and variety. One of the biggest struggles for the TG-16 was **localization**—adapting its

TABLE 6.1 NEC TubroGrafx-16 U.S. Launch Titles

• Alien Crush	• Power Golf
• China Warrior	• R-Type (Figure 6.4b)
• Dungeon Explorer	• The Legendary Axe
• Keith Courage in Alpha Zones (Figure 6.4a)	• Victory Run
	• Vigilante

Japanese PC Engine games for U.S. release. Between licensing/copyright conflicts and NEC's focus on the Japanese market, three-quarters of the PC Engine's titles never reached North America. NEC also did not invest the same amount of advertising dollars that Sega and Nintendo would eventually dish out for their 16-bit systems.

Shortly after the TurboGrafx-16 launched in the United States, NEC began to release more powerful versions of the console, including a CD add-on (shown in Figure 6.5). The first new system was an enhanced PC Engine called the **SuperGrafx**, which released exclusively in Japan. The system contained about four times the amount of RAM as the regular system, but NEC only released a total of six titles that took advantage of the new hardware: *1941: Counter Attack, Aldynes, Battle Ace, Daimakaimura* (aka *Ghouls 'n Ghosts*), *Madö King Granzört,* and *Darius Plus*. More successful than the SuperGrafx was the PC Engine's CD-ROM² (pronounced "CD-ROM-ROM").

The CD-ROM² was the first CD-ROM add-on (expansion) unit for a video game console. The CD

FIGURE 6.4 Screenshots from TurboGrafx-16 launch titles: (a) *Keith Courage in Alpha Zones* and (b) *R-Type*.

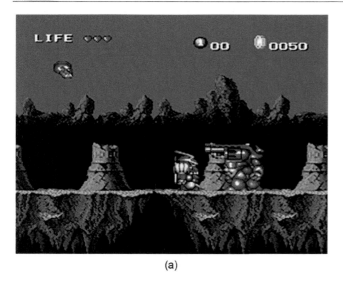

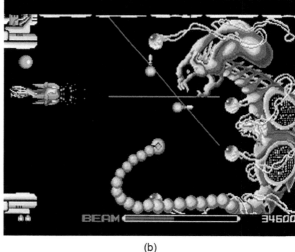

(a)

(b)

expansion unit released as the **TurboGrafx-CD** in the United States on August 1, 1990, for $399 without a pack-in title. Only *Street Fighter* and *Monster Lair* were available at launch. TG-CD games were capable of full speech dialog and high-quality music since CD-ROMs "could store nearly 260 times more data than TurboGrafx [TurboChip] cards" (Kent, 2001, p. 413). Unlike the HuCards and TurboChips (shown in Figure 6.6), there was no **region protection** on TurboGrafx-CD and CD-ROM² games. This meant that games released exclusively in Japan would work on U.S. systems and vice versa. Often, the best CD-ROM² import titles contained all-Japanese text and/or language, making certain imports difficult or impossible for most U.S. consumers to play.

NEC later released a portable version of the TG-16 called the **TurboExpress** for $249, which played all TG-16 games and featured a **TurboVision** TV tuner add-on. There was also the **TurboDuo**, which combined the CD-ROM unit and TurboGrafx-16 into a single system for just $299. NEC produced two

HuCards (called "System Cards") that would upgrade the CD-ROM unit. The **Super System Card** was released in 1991 and NEC would later build that chip into the Turbo Duo. The Super System Card quadrupled the unit's RAM from 64K to 256K and the TG-16 required this card for all "Super CD" branded games (Branagan, 2020, para. 6). A second, Japanese-only **Arcade Card** was released in 1994 and enhanced the CD system even further. By this point, however, NEC was in a distant third place in the U.S. video game market behind Sega and Nintendo and discontinued the North American console altogether.

💡 **DID YOU KNOW?**

NEC manufactured a limited, gray version of the TurboGrafx-16 console for Europe simply called "TurboGrafx." After slow sales in North America, the company quickly discontinued the unit and there was never a European release of the CD add-on.

FIGURE 6.5 The NEC SuperGrafx (Japan) (a), TurboGrafx-CD add-on connected to a TurboGrafx-16 console (b), and the TurboDuo combo system (c).

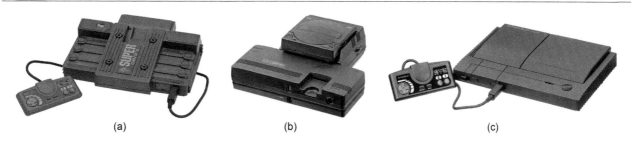

(a)

(b)

(c)

TABLE 6.2 NEC PC Engine/TG-16 Tech Specs

Manufacturer:	NEC & Hudson Soft
Launch price:	$199.99
Release date:	10/30/87 (JP), 8/29/89 (US), 11/22/89 (EU)
Format:	TurboChip (called "HuCard" in Japan)
CPU:	8-bit Hu 6820 processor (7.6 MHz)
Memory:	8 kB work RAM, 64 kB video RAM
Resolution:	256 × 239, 336 × 239, and 512 × 224
Colors:	482 from a palette of 512
Sound:	6-channel wavetable synthesis

■ CONSOLE COMPARISON: TURBOGRAFX-16 VS. NES

Part of the marketing strategy in the fourth generation was to differentiate from the previous generation by emphasizing the newer consoles' technical superiority. The buzzword of the fourth generation was "**16-bit.**" Prior to this generation, most consumers never even spoke about "bits" or other technical specifications of their consoles. One popular dispute was whether the PC Engine/TurboGrafx-16 was a true 16-bit system. NEC marketed the console as a 16-bit system, but it contained an **8-bit central processing unit (CPU)** with a dual **16-bit graphics processing unit (GPU)** (see Table 6.2).

While both systems contained 8-bit CPUs, TG-16's **8-bit Hu6820** processor (7.6 MHz) clocked at a much higher speed compared to the NES's 8-bit Ricoh 6502 processor (1.79 MHz). The TG-16 could display games with a 512×224-pixel resolution; however, developers programmed most titles at **256×239**—about the same resolution as Nintendo's console. This allowed the Hu6820 CPU to work more efficiently, coupled with its **16-bit GPU,** which was better at handling larger sprites. The TG16's vast color palette provided much more detail to its graphics compared to previous-generation consoles. NEC's system could display an extraordinary **482 colors** on-screen, compared to the NES's 25 on-screen color limit. Sound and music packed more punch and voice samples were also cleaner on the TG-16.

■ KEY PC ENGINE/TURBOGRAFX-16 TITLES

The PC Engine catered to the Japanese fanbase with its emphasis on anime, shoot 'em ups, and other Eastern favorites such as RPGs and cute characters. The console produced more than 650 titles, with over half of those releasing on the CD unit. Unfortunately, less than a quarter of those titles ever made it to Western retailers. Third-party games such as Capcom's *1943 Kai, Street Fighter II: Champion Edition,* and *Strider Hiryu* (CD-ROM²) never officially released outside of Japan. Other omissions included Konami's *Gradius* games, as well as CD-ROM² titles *Akumajō Dracula X: Chi no Rondo* (i.e., *Castlevania X: Rondo of Blood*) and *Snatcher.* Even Sega licensed games to NEC for the PC Engine's larger Japanese userbase, including *After Burner II, OutRun,* and *Shinobi* among other popular Sega titles.

The TurboGrafx-16 still had many solid (mostly exclusive) titles that released outside of Japan. Bonk from *Bonk's Adventure* became a mascot for the system, spawning three platforming adventures. Other notable side-scrolling action titles included the *Legendary Axe* games and *Splatterhouse,* which caught gamers' attention with its lead character's resemblance to Jason from the popular *Friday the 13th* movies. Pinball titles *Alien Crush* and *Devil's Crush* had exceptional music and atmosphere and *Military Madness* helped pave the way for real-time and turn-based strategy games.

NEC's system was home to more shooters than any other console. With well over 100 titles, the system became known for its shoot 'em ups (known as "**STGs**" in Japan). Early title *Blazing Lazers* (*Gunhed* in the East) was an amazing vertical shooter developed by **Compile**. The console's *"Soldier"* games were also strong vertical shooters, with *Gate of Thunder* and *Lords of Thunder* being excellent side-scrolling shooters for those who owned the CD unit. For role-playing games, the *Neutopia* titles were competent *Zelda* clones, and the *Ys* series were popular RPGs on CD-ROM. See Figure 6.7 for key title box art.

HEAD-TO-HEAD

To compare the graphics and sound between the TurboGrafx-16 and NES, see each system's version of *Adventure Island, Bomberman,* and *Jackie Chan's Action Kung Fu.*

FIGURE 6.6 Magazine advertisement for the TurboGrafx-16 in November 1992.

TAKE THREE OF THESE AND CALL YOUR FRIENDS IN THE MORNING.

We've got just what the doctor ordered. These three games for your TurboGrafx-16 game system are the perfect cure for the video game blues.

In "Neutopia II", you'll have to battle the Evil Demon Dirth and his band of monsters in order to bring peace back to the land of Neutopia.

"Jackie Chan's Action Kung Fu" challenges your skills as you chop, kick, and fight scores of stupid fu's. Or take on the bad guys in "New Adventure Island", where you'll have to avoid enemies and obstacles on a South Seas island if you want to rescue your bride-to-be.

And while these games can be addicting, they won't harm your system. That's because they were made for play on the TurboGrafx-16 game system, the leader of the 16 bit revolution.

And TurboGrafx is at its lowest price ever, so make an appointment to get one soon. But hurry. This stuff is spreading fast, and your friends might catch it before you do.

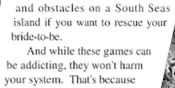

Turbo Technologies, Inc.

Available at Toys "R" Us, Babbages, Electronics Boutique, The Good Guys, Software Etc., Walden software and through Sears catalog.
Neutopia II, Jackie Chan's Action Kung Fu, and New Adventure Island are trademarks of © 1992 Hudson Soft.

CIRCLE #119 ON READER SERVICE CARD.

FIGURE 6.7 Box art to five defining TurboGrafx-16 titles including (a) *Blazing Lazers*, (b) *Military Madness*, (c) *Splatterhouse*, (d) *Bonk's Adventure*, and (e) *Neutopia*.

    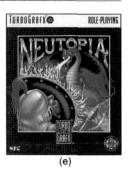

(a)　　　　　(b)　　　　　(c)　　　　　(d)　　　　　(e)

■ SEGA MEGA DRIVE

Shortly after the release of the PC Engine in Japan, Sega released its first 16-bit home system (code-named "Venus") on October 29, 1988. Sega named it the **Mega Drive**, with "Mega" having the subtext of superiority, while "Drive" suggested both power and speed. To compete with the Famicom and PC Engine, Sega built its new machine "around the **Motorola 68000** processing chip, the same chip that Apple used to power the Macintosh computer" (Kent, 2001, p. 401). The Motorola 6800 had also been the main CPU used by popular arcade boards such as the Sega System 16 years prior, making it an ideal processor for arcade-style gaming. The Mega Drive also contained a separate 8-bit processor, the **Zilog Z80**. The Z80 was another popular chip used by computers and arcade machines throughout the early to mid-1980s. Sega used it as a secondary CPU to manage the sound and reduce the load on the main CPU (Sato, 2013).

Sega's R&D (Research and Development) team developed the Mega Drive under the supervision of **Hideki Sato** and **Masami Ishikawa**. The console debuted at ¥21,000 (approximately $168), and while technically superior to the Famicom and PC Engine, it failed to compete with either console in Japan. The system launched without an initial pack-in title and only *Space Harrier II* and *Super Thunder Blade* were available at launch. It also did not help Sega that Nintendo had released *Super Mario Bros. 3* for Famicom just one week earlier. Like with the Master System, the Mega Drive promised to bring the arcade experience home. As the first true **16-bit** console, Sega could now deliver on that promise and the company prepared a U.S. launch of the console for the following year.

☀ DID YOU KNOW?

Sega pioneered an internet-based service for the Japanese Mega Drive in 1990 called **Sega Meganet**. It worked with the **Mega Modem** peripheral and offered about two dozen online games. Sega had planned a "Tele-Genesis" version for North America but canceled it due to the system's commercial failure in Japan.

■ SEGA GENESIS

Where the Mega Drive was released a full year after the PC Engine in Japan, the **Sega Genesis** (Figure 6.10) beat the TurboGrafx-16 to the U.S. market by 2 weeks. Sega changed the name of the system to Genesis to avoid a trademark dispute with U.S. storage devices manufacturer **Mega Drive Systems Inc.** (Sczepaniak, 2006, p. 45). Released on August 14, 1989, for $189, the Genesis came bundled with one controller and a port of the arcade game *Altered Beast*. Unlike the Famicom, Mark III, and PC Engine, which were all redesigned for the West, the Genesis retained the same shell design and black color as the Mega Drive. Its sleek design and action-oriented game library made the Sega Genesis particularly attractive to the male audience, who was the target demographic during this time. The kidney bean-shaped controller accommodated larger hands and was also more ergonomic than the smaller, rectangular pads from previous systems. The original model even featured a headphones jack and volume slider so players (often limited to a single-speaker television at that time) could enjoy the console's stereo sound.

▪ HANDHELD SNAPSHOT: GAME BOY

The **Game Boy** (Figure 6.8) was created by Nintendo's R&D1 team under **Satoru Okada** and **Gunpei Yokoi**. The system was launched in Japan on April 21, 1989, and in the United States on July 31, 1989, for just $89.95. It would reach Europe on September 28, 1990. Five titles were available at launch, including *Alleyway, Baseball, Super Mario Land, Tennis,* and the system's pack-in title *Tetris* by Alexey Pajitnov. *Tetris* was the perfect game for its small, monochrome screen. See Table 6.3 for specs.

Its low cost and excellent battery life were major contributors to the handheld's success (McFerran, 2009, p. 148). Like its would-be competitors, Nintendo produced a **Game Link Cable** that enabled two Game Boy units to link up for head-to-head gaming or cooperative play. Nintendo took the technology a step further, pioneering the process of trading items between linked systems, such as trading Pokémon in *Pokémon Red* and *Blue.*

In addition to its small, monochrome screen, a downside to the Game Boy was its lack of a backlit screen. The system required an external light source to play, and it was not long before various light attachments were released for the system. Some models included a magnifying glass to simulate a larger screen.

What made the Game Boy truly stand out was its games. Its library of more than 1,000 games featured exclusive sequels and spin-offs from the *Castlevania, Super Mario,* and Zelda franchises, along with the introduction of new Nintendo stars such as *Kirby* (seen in Figure 6.9) and *Wario*. It was the only system where gamers could play the lauded sequel to *Metroid, Metroid II: The Return of Samus.*

FIGURE 6.8 Nintendo Game Boy featuring *Tetris.*

Other important titles to appear on the Game Boy included puzzlers like *Mario's Picross* and *Kirby's Star Stacker,* as well as original RPGs such as *Final Fantasy Adventure* (*Mystic Quest* in Europe) and multiple *Pokémon* releases. The Game Boy version of *Donkey Kong* added 97 new levels to the original four!

Nintendo released the **Super Game Boy** cartridge adapter in 1994, which played Game Boy games on a TV through a Super NES console. A smaller version of the handheld called **Game Boy Pocket** was released in 1996. Even with its monochrome display, Game Boy became the most popular handheld system with interchangeable cartridges, selling more than 118 million units (Nintendo Co., Ltd., 2016).

TABLE 6.3	Game Boy Tech Specs
Format:	Cartridge/4 AA batteries (20–30 hours)
CPU:	8-bit Sharp LR35902 processor (4.19 MHz)
Memory:	8 kB SRAM, 8 kB video RAM
Resolution:	160 × 144 pixels/2.6″ diagonal LCD screen
Colors:	4-level grayscale
Sound:	4-channel FM mono speaker with a 3.5 mm stereo jack

FIGURE 6.9 Box art to five top Game Boy titles: (a) *Kirby's Dream Land,* (b) *Super Mario Land 2: 6 Golden Coins,* (c) *Tetris,* (d) *The Legend of Zelda: Link's Awakening,* (e) *Pokémon Yellow.*

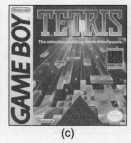

(a)   (b)   (c)   (d)   (e)

FIGURE 6.10 Sega Genesis and three-button controller (U.S.), which was the first console to release outside of Japan with nearly identical casing to its Japanese and European sibling (Mega Drive).

TABLE 6.4 Sega Genesis U.S. Launch Titles

- *Alex Kidd in Enchanted Castle*
- *Altered Beast* (Figure 6.11a)
- *Last Battle*
- *Space Harrier II* (Figure 6.11b)
- *Thunder Force II*
- *Tommy Lasorda Baseball*

The Genesis launched with six available titles (Table 6.4), which was the largest selection of games out of the three Sega console launches. Four more titles became available over the following month, including *Ghouls 'n Ghosts, Arnold Palmer Tournament Golf, World Championship Soccer,* and *Super Hang-On.*

To extend the Genesis library, Sega offered a $35 peripheral called the **Power Base Converter** (Figure 6.12a). The Power Base Converter plugged into the Genesis's cartridge slot and utilized the system's Zilog Z80 to provide **backward compatibility** with both Master System cartridges and Sega cards.

Sega's library of arcade game ports was not enough to push the Genesis to greatness in North America. It still had to overcome an initial deficit of third-party software support due to Nintendo's strict licensing policy that kept top developers such as **Capcom** and **Konami** from developing games for the system in the beginning. Until such third parties could develop titles for the Genesis, Sega would often buy

FIGURE 6.11 Screenshots from Genesis launch titles: (a) *Altered Beast* and (b) *Space Harrier II.*

(a)   (b)

FIGURE 6.12   Two of the many Genesis add-ons: (a) Power Base Converter and (b) Sega CD.

(a)   (b)

the rights to their games and reprogram the games for Genesis under the Sega name. Examples of this include Capcom arcade hits *Forgotten Worlds, Ghouls 'n Ghosts*, and *Strider*.

Sega Enterprises' CEO **Hayao Nakayama** hired **Michael Katz** (Intellivision, Coleco) as President of Sega of America just one month after the console's U.S. release. The directive from Nakayama was clear: *"Hyakumandai!"* (Japanese for *"One million units!"*). To reach this goal, Katz led Sega toward producing games endorsed by popular sports figures such as in early titles *Tommy Lasorda Baseball* and *Arnold Palmer Tournament Golf*. The result was celebrity-endorsed games *Pat Riley Basketball, Joe Montana Football, James "Buster" Douglas Knockout Boxing*, and *Michael Jackson's Moonwalker* (Figure 6.13). Following a similar strategy, **Electronic Arts** licensed games such as *John Madden Football, NHL Hockey*, and its own lineup of original sports titles that really helped the Genesis gain momentum.

Michael Katz made a second contribution that became Sega's most memorable advertising campaign. The first Genesis slogan was "We bring the arcade experience home." For a more aggressive approach, Katz and his team decided to attack Nintendo head-on and produced the slogan "**Genesis Does What Nintendon't**" (Fahs, 2009, p. 4). The phrase became an iconic jingle in Sega's television commercials where a group of female singers chanted "Genesis Does! You can't do this on Nintendo!" The jingle was accompanied by a deep-pitched, male announcer shouting the word "Does!" along with other marketing commentary.

After 14 months, Katz was only able to help Sega sell a half-million units and in 1990 the company replaced him with **Tom Kalinske** from Mattel. Kalinske's four-part strategy for the Genesis involved: (1) lowering the price of the console to $149 (and eventually $99), (2) creating a U.S. development team to make more U.S.-friendly games, (3) continuing to push Sega's aggressive advertising campaign, and (4) replacing *Altered Beast* as the pack-in title with its upcoming game, *Sonic the Hedgehog* (Kent, 2001, p. 427).

For accessories, Sega eventually released a light gun for the Genesis in 1992 called the **Menacer.** Sega created the Menacer in response to the Nintendo **Super Scope,** which debuted for the 16-bit Super Nintendo the same year. In response to the Super Nintendo's six-button controller, Sega released a six-button controller of its own in 1993. Moreover, the Genesis built a reputation (for better or for worse) on its add-on units.

In addition to the Power Base Converter, which allowed the Genesis to play 8-bit Master System games, Sega followed in the footsteps of the TurboGrafx-16 and introduced its own CD-ROM add-on unit called the **Mega-CD** on December 12, 1991 in Japan and on October 15, 1992 in North America. Simply dubbed the **Sega CD** in North America (Figure 6.12b), the $299 optical disc unit provided hundreds of times the storage space of regular cartridges and could output CD quality sound. The add-on also featured the ability to scale and rotate graphics—something that the stand-alone Genesis could only achieve through software tricks or with additional chips such as the **Sega Virtua Processor (SVP)** found in *Virtua Racing*.

FIGURE 6.13 Magazine advertisement for the Sega Genesis in 1990.

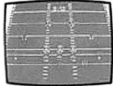

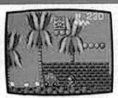

Because the CD unit worked in tandem with the Genesis CPU, Sega CD games were limited to the console's 64 on-screen color limitation. This made **Full Motion Video (FMV)** games that utilized live actors (such as *Sewer Shark* and *Night Trap*) appear washed out compared to the millions of colors displayed on standard television programs. While FMV games offered a new experience and were popular in the beginning, they quickly became nothing more than a fad from their lack of gameplay depth. Still, the company sold more than 2 million CD units. Sega released a smaller, "Mega Drive II/Genesis Model 2" in 1993 that omitted the headphones jack and volume slider—as well as a smaller "Sega CD Model 2" to accommodate the new console.

Other technology Sega produced for the North American Genesis included the 32-bit **32X** introduced on November 21, 1994 (discussed in Chapter 8), and the **Sega Channel Adapter** which debuted on December 14, 1994. The Sega Channel Adapter plugged into the cartridge slot and gamers could temporarily download games to its 4 MB RAM. Rather than "using the Internet (which was in its pop culture infancy in 1994), Sega teamed with **Time Warner Cable** and **TCI [Tele-Communications, Inc.]**—both cable giants in the nineties—to deliver games over regular coaxial cable" (Buchanan, 2012, para. 2). The service cost $15 per month, offered up to 50 rotating titles at any given time, and boasted more than 250,000 subscribers at its peak (Redsell, 2012).

■ CONSOLE COMPARISON: GENESIS VS. TURBOGRAFX-16

Comparing the first two fourth-generation consoles, "TurboGrafx clearly lagged behind Genesis in overall power, though it could display far more colors on the screen" (Kent, 2001, p. 412). It was the Genesis's 16-bit Motorola 68000 processor and Z80 co-processor (Table 6.5) that helped it excel over the TG-16. When comparing similar titles, Genesis games would often contain more **parallax scrolling**, giving a greater sense of depth perception to the stages. Sega's system could display more sprites with **80 sprites** on screen (20 per scanline) versus on-screen 64 sprites (16 per scanline) on the TG-16. The Genesis could produce marginally larger games when comparing cartridge vs. card

storage capacity. Typical games were 2–4 megabits on either system, with larger titles often reaching 8 megs. "No HuCard was larger than 8 megabits, except for *Street Fighter [II]* which was 20. By comparison, the Mega Drive/Genesis version of the same game was 24 megabits" (NFG Games, 2015).

Sound quality for both systems was often a matter of the developer's effort and/or understanding of the sound hardware for each machine. **Yuzo Koshiro** was an expert video game music composer who produced memorable soundtracks for the Genesis, including *The Revenge of Shinobi* and *Streets of Rage* series. *Nintendo Power* magazine regarded Koshiro as "arguably the greatest game-music composer of the 16-bit age" (Nintendo Power, 2006, p. 102). Japanese composers had an edge on Sega's sound due to more experience with its hardware and better documentation compared to Western developers.

This disparity led to Sega of America hiring **Recreational Brainware** programmers Jonathan Miller, Burt Sloane, Chris Grigg, and Mark Miller to produce a program that would simplify the process. The group developed a sound driver program called **GEMS (Genesis Editor for Music and Sound effects),** which allowed Western developers to create sound for games more easily. The program was applauded by composers including **Tommy Tallarico** (*Cool Spot, Mick & Mack as the Global Gladiators*), who used the program with his own original sound samples. Unfortunately, Western programmers often stuck to the program's built-in sounds—resulting in redundant, tinny audio that was not as robust as the sound in most Japanese-developed games.

TABLE 6.5	Sega Mega Drive/Genesis Tech Specs
Manufacturer:	Sega
Launch price:	$189.99
Release date:	10/29/88 (JP), 8/14/89 (US), 11/30/90 (EU)
Format:	Cartridge
CPU:	16-Bit Motorola 68000 (7.67 MHz) Zilog Z80 co-processor (3.58 MHz)
Memory:	64 kB RAM & 1 MB (8 Mbit) ROM
Resolution:	320 × 224 pixels
Colors:	64 from a palette of 512
Sound:	6-channel stereo

■ KEY MEGA DRIVE/GENESIS TITLES

The key title to Sega's 16-bit success was **Sonic the Hedgehog** (seen in Figure 6.14), programmed by **Yuji Naka** (*Phantasy Star, Ghouls 'n Ghosts*). Developed directly for the U.S. market, Sonic's designer **Naoto Ohshima** explained, "his shoes were inspired by the cover to Michael Jackson's *Bad* [album], which contrasted heavily between white and red [which] went well for a character who can run really fast, when his legs are spinning" (Ohshima, 2009, p. 2). Sonic's bad attitude and blue color perfectly symbolized Sega's image at that time. The game was released in the United States on June 23, 1991—more than a month before Sonic's Japanese release and 2 months before Super Nintendo would reach U.S. shores. Sonic's graphics and sound were among the best on the Genesis at that time. Naka and his team were able to squeeze sound and graphic quality out of the system like no

game before it. Controlling the hedgehog as he blazed across the screen, bounced off springboards, and ran 360-degree loops was a refreshingly new experience for gamers.

Other defining titles appeared throughout each phase of the Genesis's history. *Phantasy Star II* was the sequel to the Master System classic and spawned two sequels on the system. Its *Shining* series made Sega popular with both RPG and turn-based strategy fans. *Sonic the Hedgehog* also received two sequels on the system, as well as spin-offs *Sonic & Knuckles* and *Sonic the Hedgehog Spinball*. Sega's console did not have the vast array of shoot 'em ups as NEC's system; however, it did feature classic shooters such as *Gaiares, M.U.S.H.A.*, three *Thunder Force* games, and Japan exclusives *Gley Lancer* and *Eliminate Down*.

Genesis was also a choice system for "beat 'em up" games with its three *Streets of Rage (Bare Knuckle)* titles. Once Nintendo's third-party licensing limitations expired, Sega received excellent games from Capcom and Konami such as *Street Fighter II: Special Champion Edition, Rocket Knight Adventures, Castlevania: Bloodlines*, and *Contra Hard Corps*. One of the most regarded action games on the system was Treasure's *Gunstar Heroes*, a platform shooter that featured special effects once thought impossible on the Genesis. More than 850 games released for the system, plus over 200 Sega CD titles. Most of the console's best games landed on Western store shelves.

FIGURE 6.14 Box art to five defining Genesis titles including (a) *Phantasy Star II*, (b) *Sonic the Hedgehog*, (c) *Streets of Rage 2*, (d) *Shinobi III: Return of the Ninja Master*, and (e) *Gunstar Heroes*.

(a) (b) (c) (d) (e)

■ HANDHELD SNAPSHOT: ATARI LYNX

The **Atari Lynx** (Figure 6.15) was designed by **R. J. Mical** and **Dave Needle**, who originally developed the system for Epyx as the "Handy Game." Atari picked up the unit when Epyx faced bankruptcy and the newly named Lynx launched in the United States on September 1, 1989, for $189.95—about a month after Nintendo's Game Boy. Four titles were available at launch, including *Blue Lightning,* pack-in title *California Games, Electrocop,* and *Gates of Zendocon.*

Lynx was the first handheld system with a color, backlit LCD screen, sported **16-bit** graphics, and the unit could be flipped upside down to accommodate left- or right-handed play. See Table 6.6 for specs. Named after the animal, Atari also chose the word "Lynx" because the system included a **ComLynx Adapter** that provided the ability to link up (typically up to eight) systems together for multiplayer gaming. The handheld also had the ability to flip and scale sprites (well before the SNES released with its Mode 7 effects).

On the downside, the Lynx required six AA batteries (1/3 more than Game Boy) and consumed them 75% faster than

FIGURE 6.15 Atari Lynx featuring *Blue Lighting*.

Nintendo's handheld. An updated "Lynx II" was released in July 1991, featuring better battery life, a sleeker design, and an improved headphones jack that added stereo sound. However, the newer model was still quite large and consumed more power compared to the Game Boy—both of which limited its portability.

Lynx was the only non-PC console (handheld or otherwise) to feature arcade versions of *Ninja Gaiden, S.T.U.N. Runner* (Figure 6.16), and *Rygar* (apart from its Mark III release in Japan). Key adventure titles included *Xenophobe, Shadow of the Beast,* and *Todd's Adventures in Slime World* (the first game to support 8-player co-op). Atari's *Pit-Fighter* was the only fighting game for the system.

While more powerful than its competitors, the Lynx had nowhere near the game library or marketing support compared to Nintendo and Sega's handhelds. The Lynx saw just over 75 officially licensed games, with an estimated 3 million Lynx systems sold.

TABLE 6.6 Atari Lynx Tech Specs

Format:	Cartridge/6 AA batteries (4–6 hours)
CPU:	8-bit WDC 65SC02 (4 MHz); 2 × 16-bit CMOS (16 MHz)
Memory:	64 kB RAM
Resolution:	160 × 102 pixels/3.5″ diagonal LCD
Colors:	16 from a palette of 4096 colors
Sound:	4-channel, 8 bits per channel, with 3.5 mm headphones jack

FIGURE 6.16 Box art to five defining Lynx titles: (a) *Blue Lightning,* (b) *S.T.U.N. Runner,* (c) *Chip's Challenge,* (d) *Todd's Adventure in Slime World,* and (e) *California Games.*

(a)   (b)   (c)   (d)   (e)

■ SUPER FAMICOM

The Famicom remained a strong competitor to the PC Engine and the Mega Drive was not selling well in Japan. Similarly, the NES continued to perform well after the release of the Genesis and TurboGrafx-16 in the West. Nintendo had dominated the last generation by such a wide margin, they were not in a real hurry to enter the 16-bit market compared to their competition. Nintendo finally launched the **Super Famicom (SFC)** (Figure 6.17) in Japan on November 21, 1990—more than *3 years* after PC Engine and over 2 years after the Mega Drive launched. Famicom designer **Masayuki Uemura** was once again at the helm for the console's design.

Its debut price was ¥25,000 yen (about $210) and like its predecessors, only two games were available on launch day—*F-Zero* and *Super Mario World*. According to Steve Kent (2001), "nearly 1.5 million people [in Japan] ordered the console" and "tens of thousands of people lined up in front of department and electronics stores the night before" its release—leading to all of Tokyo being slowed down in the process (p. 431). The Super Famicom quickly became the leading 16-bit system in Japan, followed by the NEC PC Engine in second, and Sega's Mega Drive in a distant third place.

Similar to how Sega released its Sega Channel exclusively in the United States in 1994, Nintendo would go on to release the **Satellaview** satellite modem peripheral exclusively for the Super Famicom in Japan on April 24, 1995. Dubbed the Broadcast Satellaview/Satellite X, or "BS-X," the 512 kB RAM unit retailed

for ¥14,000–¥18,000 ($150–$176) and required a subscription to the **St.GIGA** satellite's BS-5 channel. With the Satellaview and a BS tuner, players could download games and other media to its 8-megabit memory pak, which is plugged in to a Satellaview Cartridge (Bivens, 2011, para. 2). The program streamed daily, weekly, and monthly gaming broadcasts, complete with live radio commentary. More than 100 games were released for the system and "at its height in March 1997, St.GIGA's BS-X service was being broadcast to a total of 116,378 subscribers" (Bivens, 2011, para. 5).

■ SUPER NINTENDO

A year after its debut in Japan, Nintendo released the **Super Nintendo Entertainment System (SNES)** (Figure 6.18) in the United States on August 23, 1991 for $199. Nintendo commissioned **Lance Barr** to redesign the system for North America—the same designer who remodeled the NES. Like the Super Famicom, its controller featured four main action buttons, two unique shoulder buttons, and was more ergonomic than the NES pad. Barr changed the button colors from green, blue, red, and yellow to shades of purple and "changed the controller's X and Y buttons so they had a concave curvature, which offered a better haptic distinction between all four face buttons" (Reeves, 2017, p. 95). The North American system came bundled with the classic hit *Super Mario World* and despite only a handful of launch titles (Table 6.7), more than 30 games were available by the end of December—including *ActRaiser, Final Fantasy*

FIGURE 6.17 Nintendo Super Famicom console and six-button controller.

FIGURE 6.18 The Super Nintendo Entertainment System with a six-button controller.

TABLE 6.7 Super Nintendo U.S. Launch Titles

• *F-Zero* (Figure 6.19a)	• *SimCity*
• *Gradius III*	• *Super Mario World*
• *Pilotwings*	(Figure 6.19b)

II, Super Castlevania IV, and *Super Ghouls 'n Ghosts*. The Super Nintendo released in Europe during spring of 1992 and maintained the design and color scheme of the Japanese Super Famicom.

Unlike the consumer loyalty it embraced in Japan, the video game market was a bit different in North America the way American gamers chose to hop on the Sega bandwagon. By the time the Super NES released, the Sega Genesis was selling for $149 and had established itself as the next-generation market leader in the United States (Sheff, 1993, pp. 353–356). Nintendo also had to compete with Sega's aggressive marketing campaign. Following the "Genesis Does What Nintendon't" advertisements, Sega started a line of commercials that depicted Mario as a slow game for children, with *Sonic the Hedgehog* portrayed as the game that cool people (especially teens) should be playing. Nintendo responded with a lower-priced "Control Set" (Figure 6.20) featuring the console, single controller, and no pack-in title.

When competition grew between the Super Nintendo and Sega Genesis, the TurboGrafx-16 was out of the race and became a clearance item on most

FIGURE 6.19 Screenshots from SNES launch titles: (a) *F-Zero* and (b) *Super Mario World*.

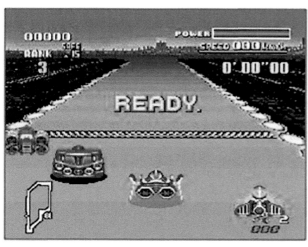

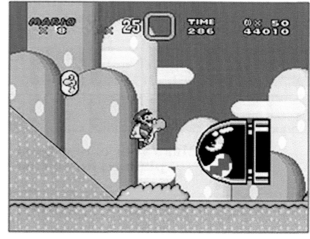

(a)

(b)

FIGURE 6.20 Magazine advertisement for Super Nintendo in 1992.

Puts you in control.

The new SUPER NES CONTROL SET™ gives you the ultimate power of choice. We've given Mario a break by taking the Game Pak out of the package and lowered the price to put the control where it belongs -- with you! So the question arises: Which game will you buy first? How about the arcade sensation Street Fighter II? It's a knock out! Are you into art?

Mario Paint (sold with the new Super NES Mouse) may be just the ticket. How about the new epic Legend of Zelda game? F-Zero? Final Fantasy II? Are your sights set on the amazing Super Scope 6? The choice is yours. And with a price tag of only $99.99* lookin' you in the face, how can you refuse? Exercise your power to choose. CHOOSE CONTROL!

Make your choice from over 125 Super NES games planned for release by the end of the year.

* Suggested retail price.

store shelves. In what became known as the most prominent "**console war**," the rivalry between Sega and Nintendo reigned fierce during this time. Sega coined the term "**blast processing**" in their advertisements to emphasize the system's faster processing speed. The SNES became known for its "**Mode 7**" special effects that allowed for the **scaling** (zooming) and **rotation** of graphics. In short, the SNES contained different graphics modes, labeled zero through seven. The seventh mode [Mode 7] allowed for programmers to scale and rotate background graphics (Ritz, 2013). To complement its hardware strengths, Nintendo's new slogan became "Now You're Playing with Power—Super Power."

Nintendo had originally commissioned **Sony Corporation** to develop a CD-ROM add-on unit for the Super Nintendo. By the time Sony completed a **prototype** (sample model), Nintendo began fearing business conflicts with the company, such as risk and vulnerability in providing Sony access to their technology. "Nintendo executives allowed Sony to announce plans for the drive at the Consumer Electronics Show, then appeared the next day to say they had struck a deal with **Philips N.V.**" (Kent, 2001, p. 452). Neither add-on unit ever released for the console, and the SNES would become the only fourth-generation competitor without a CD-ROM system.

■ CONSOLE COMPARISON: SUPER NINTENDO VS. SEGA & NEC

Nintendo's Mode 7 was one of the biggest features that set the SNES apart from Genesis and TurboGrafx-16.

Its capabilities allowed for unique level design and shifting "camera angles" as immediately noticeable in games such as *F-Zero* and *Pilotwings*. Developers often used Mode 7 effects liberally, whether if doing so was a requirement or if they were simply experimenting with the technology. Examples of Mode 7 usage included warping a game's title text like on the introductory screen of *ActRaiser*, rotating backgrounds in *Super Castlevania IV*, and the 3D flying overview maps in *Secret of Mana*. The system was also capable of **mosaic** (scrambling blocks) effects and true **color layering** where programmers could use "color math" (addition, subtraction, averaging) to make graphics appear translucent and blend them over background colors. Konami's *The Legend of the Mystical Ninja* (*Ganbare Goemon: Yukihime Kyūshutsu Emaki* in Japan) used all of these effects as shown in Figure 6.21.

Another feature that gave the Super Nintendo an edge over its competitors was its **S-SMP** audio processing unit (Table 6.8). The unit consisted of a **Sony SPC700** 8-bit processing core, a 16-bit **digital signal processor (DSP)**, 64 K of **static random-access memory (SRAM)** shared by the two chips, and a 64-byte boot ROM. The sound system operated almost entirely independent of the rest of the console and could produce more realistic sound samples when compared to the Genesis or TurboGrafx-16. Orchestral soundtracks became a common trait in SNES games—particularly in its role-playing titles.

Super Nintendo's highest resolution edged out the TG-16's 512 × 224, but to accommodate its slower processor, most SNES games ran at its lower **256 × 224**

FIGURE 6.21 Screenshots from Konami's *The Legend of the Mystical Ninja* displaying the Super Nintendo's color layering (a) and Mode 7 scaling (b) and rotation (c) effects.

(a)

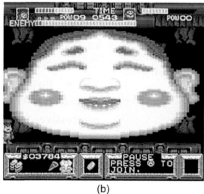

(b)

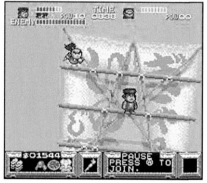

(c)

resolution. One common issue with the SNES was with games that were also designed for Sega's 320 × 224 resolution, which typically resulted in wider sprites and a narrower playfield on Nintendo's console. These games were often easier to play on the Genesis. Examples of this can be seen when comparing games including *Earthworm Jim, Cool Spot,* and *The Lion King.*

The TurboGrafx-16 had the highest on-screen color capacity with 482, compared to Super Nintendo's 256 and Genesis's 64; however, later SNES games (such as *Donkey Kong Country*) were rumored to display thousands of on-screen colors using **scale line blending** tricks. Nintendo also produced enhancement chips for SNES software, such as the **SuperFX** chip, for rendering **3D polygon graphics** in *Star Fox* and *Stunt Race-FX.* The SNES could move **128 sprites** on screen and 32 per scanline, which was exactly double that of the TG-16 and over a third more than the Sega Genesis.

The one feature that Super Nintendo lacked was processing speed. Sega's Motorola 68000 clocked at 7.67 MHz, which was faster than the SNES's Ricoh 5A22 on paper. However, it was Sega's **Yamaha VDP** graphics chip, which provided quicker **Direct Memory Access (DMA)** transfer speeds and **VRAM bandwidth** that really made it faster. Early SNES titles suffered from **slowdown**, where the graphics and gameplay decelerated below regular speed when a high number of sprites occupied the screen. Slowdown did not affect a game's music but was nonetheless distracting. While Sonic was blazing through levels on the Genesis, SNES games such as *Gradius III* would slow down to a crawl when there were too many simultaneous objects moving on the screen.

TABLE 6.8 Super Famicom/SNES Tech Specs

Manufacturer:	Nintendo
Launch price:	$199.99
Release date:	11/21/90 (JP), 8/23/91 (US), spring 1992 (EU)
Format:	Cartridge
CPU:	16-bit Ricoh 5A22 processor (3.58 MHz)
Memory:	128 kB RAM, 64K VRAM
Resolution:	256 × 224 to 512 × 478 pixels
Colors:	256 (more with blending) from a palette of 32,768
Sound:	8-channel stereo S-SMP audio processing unit

HEAD-TO-HEAD

There were a vast number of games that released on both the Super Nintendo and Sega Genesis. To compare the gameplay, graphics, and sound between them, see each system's version of *Aero the Acrobat, Earthworm Jim, Mortal Kombat II,* and *Thunder Force III* (Genesis) versus *Thunder Spirits* (SNES).

■ KEY SUPER FAMICOM/SUPER NINTENDO TITLES

The Super Nintendo released an extensive line of defining titles over its lifespan. Its pack-in title *Super Mario World* is often regarded as the best game in the *Super Mario* series (Shea, 2022). Nintendo's popular exclusives from the previous generation returned with enhanced sequels such as *Super Metroid* and *The Legend of Zelda: A Link to the Past* (shown in Figure 6.22), plus a late sequel to *Super Mario World* titled *Yoshi's Island.* The SNES became the console of choice for RPG fans with hits *Final Fantasy II* and *III* (*IV* and *VI* in Japan) *Chrono Trigger,* and *Secret of Mana,* among others.

Nintendo also introduced new franchises such as *Super Mario Kart* and *Star Fox* on the SNES. And just when gamers thought they had seen everything the system had to offer, *Donkey Kong Country* emerged utilizing pre-rendered 3D graphics (i.e., advanced computer modeling) and other new techniques to produce one of the best-looking games on the console. *Donkey Kong Country* sold out of its initial shipment of 500,000 units in less than a week (Kent, 2001, p. 497) and spawned two SNES sequels. More than 700 games released for the Super Nintendo in the West, with more than twice that number of titles on the Super Famicom in Japan.

Japan saw countless RPG exclusives on the system, such as *Tales of Phantasia* and *Star Ocean.* These were the largest cartridges made for the console, weighing 48 megabits each and featuring voiced narration, character dialog, and music with vocals—quite impressive for the time. Other noteworthy titles included *Rendering Ranger: R2, Secret of Mana* sequel *Seiken Densetsu 3,* and *Terranigma* (also released in PAL regions).

FIGURE 6.22   Box art to five defining SNES titles including (a) *Chrono Trigger*, (b) *Super Metroid*, (c) *Final Fantasy III*, (d) *The Legend of Zelda: A Link to the Past*, and (e) *Donkey Kong Country*.

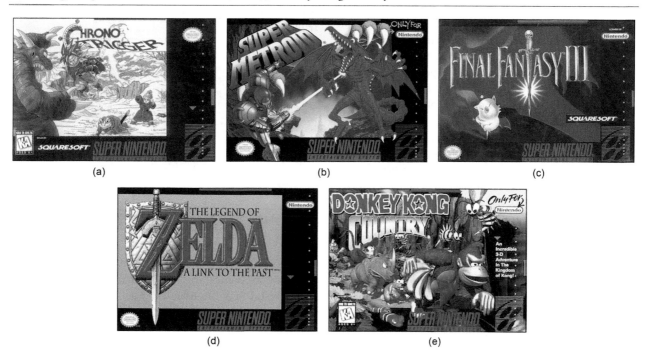

(a)   (b)   (c)

(d)   (e)

■ SNK NEO•GEO AES

Shin Nihon Kikaku ("New Japan Project," shortened to **SNK** Corporation in 1986) would bring one more fourth-generation console to market. SNK was founded by Eikichi Kawasaki as a Japanese coin-op arcade developer in 1978. The company gained popularity from its arcade titles *Vanguard* (1981) and *Ikari Warriors* (1986), as well as its NES games such as *Baseball Stars* (1989) and *Crystalis* (1990). SNK partnered with **Alpha Denshi Corporation (ADK)** in 1987 to create a handful of arcade titles, beginning with *Time Soldiers* (known in Japan as *Battle Field*). The partnership led to the companies' co-development of a new modular arcade cabinet system in 1990.

SNK knew that one of the biggest chores for arcade operators was the practice of swapping out entire arcade cabinets every time they replaced old games with new titles. Even JAMMA-compatible games required operators to swap out the circuit board from the JAMMA harness. To alleviate this issue, the company developed the **Neo•Geo MVS (Multi Video System)** in 1990. The MVS was a single arcade cabinet that featured multiple, selectable titles (up to six but usually between two and four games), which arcade operators could easily change by swapping internal **cartridges** and changing the marquee and bezel on the exterior of the cabinet. In addition to relieving operators from replacing entire cabinets, having multiple titles in one cabinet saved floor space and proved to be more profitable. That same year, SNK developed a home version of the MVS called the **Neo•Geo AES (Advanced Entertainment System)** (Figure 6.25).

■ HANDHELD SNAPSHOT: SEGA GAME GEAR

The **Game Gear** (Figure 6.23) was Sega's answer to Nintendo's Game Boy. Codenamed "Mercury" after the planet, Game Gear launched on October 6, 1990, in Japan. It debuted in the United States on April 26, 1991 for $149.99 and did not officially release in Europe until 1992. To expedite development, Sega used the same technology as the 8-bit Master System, with an expanded color palette of 4,096 colors (Wild, 2009, p. 161). See Table 6.9 for specs.

Six titles were available for the U.S. launch, including *Castle of Illusion starring Mickey Mouse, Columns, G-Loc, Psychic World,* and *Revenge of the Drancon.* Since the system was essentially a portable Master System, Sega released a **Master Gear Converter** accessory, which users could plug into the cartridge slot to play Master System games on the handheld. In addition to the converter, the Game Gear featured an optional **TV Tuner adapter** (similar to TurboVision on Turbo Express) for viewing local broadcast television.

Game Gear followed its competitors with the "Gear-to-Gear Cable" ("VS Cable" in Japan), which allowed users to link together two systems for multiplayer gaming. In addition to these peripherals and its backlit screen, Sega's system featured other advantages over Nintendo's Game Boy, including stereo sound and a more comfortable, ergonomic design.

Where it failed was in overall size and battery life. The system was bulkier than Game Boy (although not as wide

FIGURE 6.23 Game Gear featuring *Sonic the Hedgehog: Triple Trouble.*

as Atari Lynx) and batteries only lasted around 5–6 hours, compared to Game Boy's 20–30-hour battery life. It was less powerful than the Atari Lynx but Game Gear's backlit screen supported twice the number of on-screen colors. Sega released a handful of limited-edition systems in assorted colors but never redesigned the Game Gear the way Nintendo and Atari would reinvent their handhelds.

Like Lynx, Game Gear lacked the third-party support that Nintendo locked down for its system. Beyond its many Master System ports, Sega produced spin-offs of its popular franchises on the system (Figure 6.24). Key titles for Game Gear included two exclusive *G.G. Shinobi* titles, two *Streets of Rage* games, and Sonic exclusives *Sonic the Hedgehog: Triple Trouble,* and *Tails' Adventures.*

Notable exclusive role-playing games included *Shining Force: The Sword of Hajya, Ax Battler: A Legend of Golden Axe, Crystal Warriors,* and *Defenders of Oasis.* More than 350 officially licensed games released for Game Gear (100+ were exclusive to Japan, with a similar number of titles only available in the West). Sega sold about 10 million units globally.

TABLE 6.9	Game Gear Tech Specs
Format:	Cartridge/6 AA batteries (3–5 hours)
CPU:	8-bit Zilog Z80 processor (3.57 MHz)
Memory:	24 kB (8 kB RAM and 16 kB video RAM)
Resolution:	160 × 146 pixels/3.25″ diagonal LCD screen
Colors:	32 from a palette of 4,096
Sound:	4-channel mono speaker with 3.5 mm stereo jack

FIGURE 6.24 (a) *Sonic the Hedgehog: Triple Trouble,* (b) *Shinobi II: The Silent Fury,* (c) *Shining Force: The Sword of Hajya,* (d) *Ax Battler: A Legend of Golden Axe,* and (e) *Super Columns.*

(a) (b) (c) (d) (e)

FIGURE 6.25 Neo•Geo Advanced Entertainment System with its large joystick controller.

The Neo•Geo AES kept its original "Neo•Geo" title and released in the United States on June 18, 1991 for $649. Its "Gold System" came bundled with two joystick controllers and one game: *Baseball Stars Professional* or *NAM-1975*. What made the Neo•Geo unlike any console before it was that the AES was technologically equivalent to its MVS arcade counterpart, meaning its home games were *identical* to the arcade games. Neo•Geo AES truly brought the arcade experience home. The system even featured a **memory card** slot that allowed console owners to save their progress on certain arcade games and continue them at home (or vice versa) if they owned the respective cartridge. The AES released with 10 launch titles (Table 6.10), but the price tag held back the average consumer from even considering the system. Most Neo•Geo cartridges cost between **$199** and

TABLE 6.10 Neo•Geo AES U.S. Launch Titles

- *Alpha Mission II*
- *Baseball Stars Professional* (Figure 6.26a)
- *Cyber-Lip*
- *Ghost Pilots*
- *King of the Monsters*
- *League Bowling*
- *Magician Lord* (Figure 6.26b)
- *NAM-1975*
- *Ninja Combat*
- *Top Player's Golf*

$249 since they were both physically large and could hold over **100 times more data** than other fourth-generation cartridges.

To help move the system, VP of marketing **Kent Russell** launched an aggressive marketing campaign that was often more controversial than Sega's.

FIGURE 6.26 Screenshots from AES launch titles: (a) *Baseball Stars Professional* and (b) *Magician Lord*.

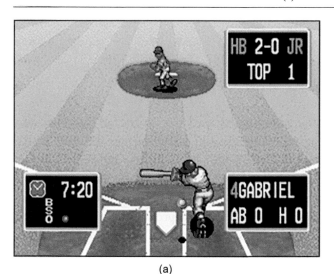

(a)   (b)

One memorable ad claimed, "YOU NEED A SET OF THESE" (with a picture of two steel balls) "TO PLAY ONE OF THESE" (with a picture of a NeoGeo console). Another ad depicted a woman in lingerie with the caption "I Remember When He Couldn't Keep His Hands Off Me!" as her man appeared in the background deeply distracted by the Neo•Geo title *Cyber-Lip*. The print advertisement in Figure 6.27 further illustrates this aggressive marketing campaign.

SNK eventually released a stand-alone, CD-based version of Neo•Geo called **Neo•Geo CD**. The company created the system to play more affordable "CD versions" of its popular cartridges but also produced a few exclusive titles for the console. Neo•Geo CD games retailed for $49–$79, compared to the $300 AES cartridges (GamePro, 1995, p. 30). The console was released in Japan in September 1994 and in the United States in October 1995 for $399. While it sold more than a half-million units, the system's **1X** drive speed suffered from extremely slow load times (where players would often have to wait 30–60 seconds for games to start up). SNK released an updated **2X** version of the unit in Japan called the **Neo•Geo CDZ**, but the system would quickly become overshadowed by the wave of fifth-generation consoles.

■ CONSOLE COMPARISON: NEO•GEO AES VS. GENESIS & SNES

The Neo•Geo AES was in a league of its own with its high price tag and for being the most powerful console of the fourth generation. Some of the advertisements for the Neo•Geo marketed the console as 24-bit, although it was technically a 16-bit system powered by a 16-bit **Motorola 68000**, which ran parallel to an 8-bit **Zilog Z80** co-processor (Table 6.11). On paper, this looks like the specs of the Sega Genesis; however, Neo•Geo's processor was much more powerful. The AES's 65,536 color palette and **4,096 on-screen colors** were leagues ahead of other fourth-gen systems.

When booting up a Neo•Geo game, the intro screen would play a signature jingle while displaying the words "MAX 330 MEGA PRO GEAR SPEC" in reference to the system's original maximum ROM size. This phrase also appeared on the shell of the console as this number was remarkably high compared to the typical Genesis or SNES cartridge that

averaged between 4 and 8 megabits. Later Neo•Geo cartridges would be as large as 716 megabits (or 89.5 MB), which is still only a fraction of the capacity of a CD-ROM. Still, the Neo•Geo's more powerful hardware produced larger sprites and more impressive on-screen action compared to competing consoles. Add nearly double the number of sound channels and most Neo•Geo games also sounded far better than all other fourth-generation cartridges.

The Neo•Geo AES could display six parallax backgrounds simultaneously. The console was designed with support for 380 'line-sprites,' of 16×16 pixels each. Ninety-six of these line-sprites could be displayed on each scan line, and sprites could be chained together for ease of manipulation"(Spence, 2020, para. 52–53). This was three times the number of sprites and background layers typically used on the Genesis and SNES, not including **line scrolling**, which even the TG-16 was capable of rendering. The AES could chain together line sprites to look and move like larger sprites and was also capable of **sprite shrinking**, which mimicked sprite scaling (as seen in the *Art of Fighting* and *Samurai Shodown* series). Unlike the SNES, the AES hardware was not capable of true rotation and so rotation effects were powered by the software.

■ KEY NEO•GEO TITLES

One game that shaped the future for Neo•Geo was Capcom's arcade hit *Street Fighter II: The World Warrior* (1991). *SFII* launched the fighting boom in the early 1990s, which revived the arcade scene for a while (June, 2013, para. 32). SNK joined the cause and became one of the most prolific fighting game publishers, with series like *Fatal Fury* (*Garō Densetsu: Shukumei no Tatakai*), *Art of Fighting* (*Ryūko no*

FIGURE 6.27 Magazine advertisement for Neo•Geo in 1991.

IF YOU'RE STILL PLAYING SEGA, NEC, OR NINTENDO YOU'RE NOTHING BUT A WEENIE!

IF YOU'RE PLAYING THE INCREDIBLY HIGH POWERED NEO•GEO® SYSTEM YOU'RE A REAL HOT DOG!

Tough talk, but think it over. Why fool around with limp, underpowered 16 bit systems when NEO•GEO® now offers the hottest, most advanced video entertainment system in the world!

Fact. NEO•GEO simply out-muscles those guys with the big names. NEO•GEO features a huge 330 meg hardware setup that delivers robust 15-channel real voice stereo sound. Unmatched graphics with over 65,000 vivid colors of amazing detail! Not to mention effects with 4-dimensional realism.

Does NEO•GEO cost more than other video game systems? You bet. Does a Ferrari cost more than a Yugo Does Prime Rib cost more than squirrel burgers? With NEO•GEO you get more than you paid for.

It's simple. Would you rather be a cold weenie? Or a real hot dog!

4096 Simultaneous Colors displayed at one time!		NEO•GEO	4096
	NEC	512	
	SEGA 64		
	NINTENDO		
380 Sprites! (Character Power)		NEO•GEO	380
	NEC	80	
	SEGA	64	
	NINTENDO		
15 Sound Channels! 7 Channels dedicated to real voice speech!		NEO•GEO	15
	NEC	10	
	SEGA	6	
	NINTENDO		

A Quantum Leap Forward In Video Entertainment.

Call: SNK at (213) 787-0990 or Authorized SNK Dealers
• Video Express Inc.   (800) 253-6665
• Premier Electronics Group (800) 783-7344

Anyone else may be a weenie in disguise.

All other product names are trademarks or registered trademarks of their respective holder.

The trademarks of "NEO-GEO"are registered by SNK Home Entertainment, Inc

CIRCLE #114 ON READER SERVICE

TABLE 6.11 Neo•Geo AES Tech Specs

Manufacturer:	SNK
Launch price:	$649.99
Release date:	4/26/90 (JP rental), 6/18/91 (U.S.), 7/01/91 (national)
Format:	Cartridge
CPU:	Motorola 68000 (12 MHz) and Zilog Z80 (4 MHz)
Memory:	64 kB main, 84 kB (total) video, 2 kB audio
Resolution:	304 × 224 pixels
Colors:	4,096 from a palette of 65,536
Sound:	15-channel stereo

Ken), *Samurai Shodown* (*Samurai Spirits*), *The King of Fighters*, and *World Heroes*. Since the Neo•Geo AES library was based on its MVS arcade machine, its games were very action-oriented (Figure 6.28).

The largest part of the AES library consisted of fighting games, followed by run and gun and **shmup** (shoot 'em up) style games such as *Metal Slug, Shock Troopers, Blazing Star,* and *Viewpoint.* Beyond these types of games, the system had a dozen beat 'em up games like *Ninja Combat* and *Sengoku,* two dozen sports titles including *Baseball Stars Professional* and *Football Frenzy,* along with puzzle games such as *Magical Drop.* The console did not have any complex role-playing games and so seasoned players could complete most titles in under an hour. Approximately 148 games released for Neo•Geo, with most titles appearing on the AES.

▪ FOURTH-GENERATION MARKET SUMMARY

The PC Engine was quite successful in Japan, at one point becoming the country's top-selling video game console (Electronic Gaming Monthly, 1995, p. 15) and outselling the Nintendo Famicom in 1988. The system struggled to gain substantial footing in North America and after 2 years, NEC turned over the marketing and publishing rights of TG-16 products to Los Angeles-based **Turbo Technologies, Inc. (TTI).** Despite their efforts, the TurboGrafx-16 took a distant third place in the United States, lagging far behind the better-marketed Sega Genesis and Super Nintendo. The opposite was true of the Sega Mega Drive, which took third place in Japan, but did quite well in the United States. Sega sold more than 30 million Genesis consoles globally, "but less than a tenth of those were to Japanese customers. Meanwhile, the PC Engine moved merely 10 million units during its lifetime—but roughly eight million of those sales happened in Japan (Parish, 2014).

Sega surpassed Nintendo with a **55% share** of the market in 1992 for several reasons. The Mega Drive and Genesis released 2 years before the Super Famicom and Super Nintendo. Its larger library of games (including *Sonic the Hedgehog*), lower price tag, and aggressive marketing campaign provided further leverage. To add to his legacy, Sega of America President Tom Kalinske pioneered the "**street date**" for video game releases with *Sonic the Hedgehog 2.* Called "Sonic Tuesday," Sega air shipped the game to all its retailers in the United States and Europe for a simultaneous, multinational release day (Harris, 2014).

FIGURE 6.28 Box art to five defining Neo•Geo titles including (a) *Samurai Shodown,* (b) *Fatal Fury Special,* (c) *The Last Blade,* (d) *Metal Slug X,* and (e) *The King of Fighters '98.*

(a)   (b)   (c)   (d)   (e)

With Sega marketing the Genesis as the more mature system and the SNES as a child's toy, it did not help that Nintendo also developed a reputation for **censoring** their early titles. For games like the U.S. version of beat 'em up *Final Fight* (1991), Nintendo had Capcom replace blood with flashes and remove all references to alcohol. Among other changes, Capcom completely redrew the sprites of the sexy female characters to heavily clothed, androgynous street punks. When *Mortal Kombat* (1993) released on both consoles, Nintendo's version replaced the blood with sweat and changed the game's **fatalities** (finishing death moves) to less-violent depictions.

One turning point in the console war was when Nintendo secured the first home console port of the popular arcade hit *Street Fighter II*. The Genesis would not see a version of the game until well over a year later. Nintendo also eventually revoked its elevated level of censorship and the SNES version of *Mortal Kombat II* (1994) released with all the blood and fatalities intact. As the system matured and its library grew, the Super Nintendo would go on to outsell the Sega Genesis before the end of the fourth generation.

The Super NES may have outsold the Genesis in the end because of Sega's focus on the next generation of 32-bit hardware, leaving the true winner of the 16-bit console war up for debate—at least in the United States. In the end, Sega sold close to 20 million Genesis units compared to approximately 23 million Super Nintendo systems in North America. Globally, the margin was even wider as shown in Figure 6.29. Even when gamers had moved on to the next generation of hardware, Nintendo released a smaller version of the SNES console in 1997 with the "New-Style Super NES" in North America and "Super Famicom Jr." in Japan, which omitted the S-Video and RGB outputs.

Starting as a rental console for commercial establishments, SNK did not originally plan for the Neo•Geo AES to be a mass market console. SNK USA President **Ben Herman** claimed his goal for the system was a 10% market share; however, the console only reached a **2%** share (Herman, 2004). In the end, the Neo•Geo AES was only available in specialty stores and through mail orders. It would sell barely a million units and the average consumer would mostly recall the fourth generation as a console war rivalry between Nintendo and Sega. Two lesser-known, multifunctional consoles from this generation included the **Philips CD-i** (Compact Disc-Interactive) launched on December 3, 1991 and **Pioneer LaserActive**, which released on September 13, 1993. Philips built the CD-i from technology it had initially created for the SNES CD unit add-on.

■ FOURTH-GENERATION BREAKTHROUGHS AND TRENDS

There were unique breakthroughs and trends that defined the fourth generation of video games. Here is a list of the top 10 advancements that defined the generation:

1. 16-bit microprocessors

2. Expanded multi-button game controllers (between 3 and 8 buttons)

3. Parallax (multilayer background) scrolling

4. True and pseudo-3D sprite scaling and rotation

5. Larger sprites (up to 64×64 [SNES] or 16×512 pixels [Neo•Geo])

FIGURE 6.29 Fourth-generation console sales graph.

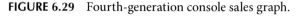

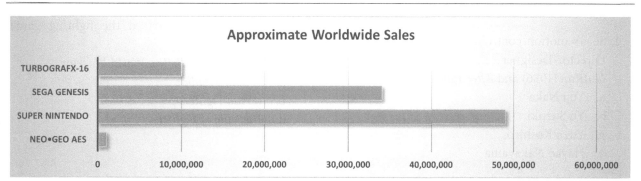

6. More color (64–4,096 on-screen colors from palettes of 512 to 65,536 colors)

7. Color layering (translucent graphics)

8. Flat-shaded 3D polygon graphics

9. CD-ROM add-ons for larger storage space and FMV (full motion video)

10. Stereo sound with digital audio playback and advanced music synthesis (FM synthesis and "wavetable" sample-based synthesis)

■ ACTIVITY: ARCADE TO HOME PORT COMPARISON II

Compare how 16-bit home console ports became closer to the arcade games they were based on. Play or screen gameplay footage from an arcade title and then its home port for at least 30 minutes each. Take notes on the graphical, aural, and gameplay differences and similarities.

SUGGESTED TITLES

Suggested titles to compare include the arcade version and as home console port of: TurboGrafx-16 versions of *Ninja Spirit, Raiden, Splatterhouse, Vigilante,* or *R-Type*; Sega Genesis versions of *After Burner II, Altered Beast, Golden Axe, OutRun,* or *Truxton*; and/or the Super Nintendo versions of *Final Fight, Gradius III, Mortal Kombat, Super Street Fighter II Turbo,* or *Teenage Mutant Ninja Turtles IV–Turtles in Time*.

GUIDELINES

Always begin by playing/viewing the arcade version of the game first; then discuss how the home port measures up. Write a 500- to 1,000-word essay comparing the two games regarding:

- **Graphics:** include size and scale, color palette, resolution (clarity), animation, effects, and presentation.
- **Sound:** include the quality and accuracy of the games' music and sound effects.
- **Playability:** include how well the games control and how fun they are to play.

QUESTIONS

1. How do these games compare to arcade ports from the previous generation?
2. Did the home console version add anything to or lack something important from the arcade experience?
3. Do you feel that the console version was close enough to the arcade game that players would want to purchase the game to play from home?
4. Did the arcade version contain any features that would still attract owners of the game to visit a public venue to play the arcade game?
5. What impact do you think this had on the arcade industry, if any?
6. Could the publisher/developer have done anything differently?
7. What are your concluding thoughts?

■ CHAPTER 6 QUIZ

1. Sega's motion-controlled, hydraulic cabinets by Director/Designer _____ led to games like *OutRun* (1986) and *After Burner* (1987):
   a. Yuji Naka
   b. Yu Suzuki
   c. Yuzo Koshiro
   d. Hayao Nakayama

2. The 1991 game that helped revive the arcade industry and popularized the fighting game genre:
   a. *Street Fighter II: The World Warrior*
   b. *Mortal Kombat*
   c. *Virtua Fighter*
   d. *The King of Fighters*

3. Capcom's CPS hardware powered each of the following games except:
   a. *Street Fighter II: The World Warrior*
   b. *Ghouls 'n Ghosts*
   c. *Strider*
   d. *Hard Drivin'*

4. During its peak success in 1992, this game console gained a 55% share of the U.S. video game market:
   a. Super Nintendo
   b. Sega Genesis
   c. TurboGrafx-16
   d. Neo•Geo

5. Known as the TurboGrafx-16 in the United States, this system fared much better in Europe and Japan than in North America:
   a. Mega Drive
   b. PC Engine
   c. Super Famicom
   d. Neo•Geo

6. The PC Engine was known for being the *first* system to:
   a. have four controller ports built into the console
   b. offer a CD add-on unit to the console
   c. play pixel-perfect ports of arcade games in the home
   d. feature controllers with more than two buttons

7. This was the only fourth-generation system that came with large joysticks instead of traditional variants of the D-Pad (+) controller:
   a. Neo•Geo
   b. Sega Genesis
   c. Super Nintendo
   d. TurboGrafx-16

8. Which of these peripherals did Sega *not* develop for the Genesis?
   a. Power Base Converter
   b. Super Scope light gun
   c. CD add-on
   d. 32X

9. Early on, _____ developed a reputation for censoring blood and sexuality from its games:
   a. TurboGrafx-16
   b. Super Nintendo
   c. Neo•Geo
   d. Sega Genesis

10. Neo-Geo was known for being the *first* system to:
    a. have four controller ports built into the console
    b. offer a CD add-on unit to the console
    c. play pixel-perfect ports of arcade games in the home
    d. feature controllers with more than two buttons

11. Which console was technologically superior based on tech spec numbers?
    a. Neo•Geo
    b. Super Nintendo
    c. Sega Genesis
    d. TurboGrafx-16

12. What video game is Yuji Naka famous for?
    a. *Super Mario World*
    b. *Bonk's Adventure*
    c. *Sonic the Hedgehog*
    d. All of the above

13. Which console was *not* renamed or redesigned for the U.S. market?
    a. Neo-Geo
    b. Super Nintendo
    c. Sega Genesis
    d. TurboGrafx-16

14. SNK stands for:
    a. Shin Nihon Kikaku
    b. Shinto Nippon Kyoto
    c. Super Nintendo Kart
    d. System Network Keyframing

15. This fourth-generation console contained only one controller port and was not considered a true 16-bit system:
    a. Neo•Geo
    b. Super Nintendo
    c. Sega Genesis
    d. TurboGrafx-16

16. This fourth-generation console was unique for its *Mode 7* scaling and rotation graphics effects and Sony sound chip:
    a. Neo•Geo
    b. Super Nintendo
    c. Sega Genesis
    d. TurboGrafx-16

17. GEMS was a sound driver program that allowed Western developers to produce sound more easily. GEMS stood for:
    a. Game Effects for Master System
    b. General Effects for Master System
    c. Genesis Editor for Music and Sound effects
    d. None of the above

18. Sega released the _____ handheld to compete with the Nintendo Game Boy.
    a. Microvision
    b. Game Gear
    c. Lynx
    d. TurboExpress

19. The first handheld system with a color, backlit LCD screen:
    a. Microvision
    b. Game Gear
    c. Lynx
    d. TurboExpress

20. Which console sold the largest number of units by the end of the fourth generation?
    a. Super Nintendo Entertainment System
    b. Sega Genesis
    c. TurboGrafx-16
    d. Neo•Geo

True or False

21. With dimensions of $135 \times 130 \times 35$ mm [or $5.3 \times 5.1 \times 1.37$ inches], the Sega Mega Drive remains the smallest home console ever made.

22. *Altered Beast* was the original pack-in title for the Sega Genesis.

23. The CD-ROM^2 was the first CD-ROM add-on (expansion) unit for a video game console.

24. The Super Famicom/Super Nintendo was the only fourth-generation system *not* to have officially released a CD add-on or stand-alone CD-ROM console.

25. Nintendo coined the term "blast processing" in their advertisements to emphasize the Super Nintendo's faster processing speed.

■ FIGURES

Figure 6.1 Defining arcade fighting games in the fourth generation: (a) *Street Fighter II* (1991), (b) *Mortal Kombat* (1992), and (c) *Virtua Fighter* (1993). (*Street Fighter II*, courtesy of Capcom, 1991; *Mortal Kombat*, courtesy of Midway, 1992; and *Virtua Fighter*, courtesy of Sega, 1993.)

Figure 6.2 NEC PC Engine and PI-PD001 controller. (Courtesy of Evan Amos—own work, public domain. Available at https://commons.wikimedia.org/w/index.php?curid=18269320. Retrieved from https://en.wikipedia.org/wiki/TurboGrafx-16#/media/File:PC-Engine-Console-Set.jpg.) (Part of this image was used on the introductory page of this chapter.)

Figure 6.3 NEC Turbo Grafx-16 console with TurboPad controller. (Courtesy Evan Amos—own work, public domain. Available at https://commons.wikimedia.org/w/index.php?curid=17385690. Retrieved from https://en.wikipedia.org/wiki/Turbo Grafx-16#/media/File:TurboGrafx16-Console-Set.jpg.) (Part of this image was used on the introductory page of this chapter.)

Figure 6.4 Screenshots from TurboGrafx-16 launch titles: (a) *Keith Courage in Alpha Zones* and (b) *R-Type*. (*Keith Courage in Alpha Zones* courtesy of Hudson Soft/NEC, 1989; and *R-Type* courtesy of Irem/NEC, 1989.)

Figure 6.5 The NEC SuperGrafx (Japan) (a), TurboGrafx-CD add-on connected to a TurboGrafx-16 console (b), and the TurboDuo combo system (c). (Left: "The SuperGrafx" by Evan Amos—own work, CC BY-SA 3.0. Available at https://commons.wikimedia.org/w/index.php?curid=18300104. Retrieved from https://en.wikipedia.org/wiki/PC_Engine_SuperGrafx#/media/File:SuperGrafx-Console-Set.jpg. Center: "NEC-TurboGrafx-16-CD-FL" by Evan Amos—own work, public domain. Available at https://commons.wikimedia.org/w/index.php?curid=18874804. Retrieved from https://en.wikipedia.org/wiki/Turbo Grafx-16#/media/File:NEC-TurboGrafx-16-CD-FL.jpg. Right: "NEC-TurboDuo-Console-wController-L" by Evan Amos—own work, public domain. Available at https://commons.wiki-media.org/w/index.php?curid=34581517. Retrieved from https://en.wikipedia.org/wiki/Turbo Grafx-16#/media/File:NEC-TurboDuo-Console-wController-L.jpg.)

Figure 6.6 Magazine advertisement for the Turbo-Grafx-16 in November 1992. (From "Too Little, Too Late?," VintageComputing.com April 21, 2008, by Benj Edwards. Retrieved from http://www.vintagecomputing.com/wp-content/images/retroscan/tg16_three_large.jpg.)

Figure 6.7 Box art to five defining TurboGrafx-16 titles including (a) *Blazing Lazers*, (b) *Military Madness*, (c) *Splatterhouse*, (d) *Bonk's Adventure*, and (e) *Neutopia*. (*Blazing Lazers,* courtesy of Compile/NEC, 1989; *Military Madness,* courtesy of Hudson Soft, 1989; *Splatterhouse,* courtesy of Namco/NEC, 1990; *Bonk's Adventure,* courtesy of Hudson Soft/NEC, 1990; and *Neutopia,* courtesy of Hudson Soft/NEC, 1990.)

Figure 6.8 Nintendo Game Boy featuring *Tetris*. (Courtesy of Evan Amo—Media:Game-Boy-FL.jpg, public domain. Available at https://commons.wikimedia.org/w/index.php?curid=37808150. Retrieved from https://en.wikipedia.org/wiki/Game_Boy#/media/File:Game-Boy-FL.png. Screenshot of *Pokémon Yellow,* courtesy of Game Freak/Nintendo, 1999. Part of this image was used on the introductory page of this chapter.)

Figure 6.9 Box art to five top Game Boy titles: (a) Kirby's Dream Land, (b) Super Mario Land 2: 6 Golden Coins, (c) Tetris, (d) The Legend of Zelda: Link's Awakening, (e) Pokémon Yellow. (Kirby's Dream Land, courtesy of HAL Laboratory/Nintendo, 1992; Super Mario Land 2: 6 Golden Coins, courtesy of Nintendo, 1992; Tetris, courtesy of Nintendo, 1989; The Legend of Zelda: Link's Awakening, courtesy of Nintendo, 1993; and Pokémon Yellow, courtesy of Game Freak/Nintendo, 1999.)

Figure 6.10 Sega Genesis and three-button controller (U.S.), which was the first console to release outside of Japan with nearly identical casing to its Japanese and European sibling (Mega Drive). (Retrieved from http://ecx.images-amazon.com/images/I/512iSU24CdL._SL1280_.jpg.) (Mega drive image used for chapter title page courtesy of Evan Amos—Own work, Public Domain, https://commons.wikimedia.org/w/index.php?curid=17288445.) (Part of these images were used on the introductory page of this chapter.)

Figure 6.11 Screenshots from Genesis launch titles: (a) *Altered Beast* and (b) *Space Harrier II*. (Courtesy of Sega, 1989.)

Figure 6.12 Two of the many Genesis add-ons: (a) Power Base Converter and (b) Sega CD. (a) "Sega-Genesis-Power-Base-Converter" by Evan Amos—own work, public domain. Available at https://commons.wikimedia.org/w/index.php?curid=14230616. Retrieved from https://en.wikipedia.org/wiki/Sega_Genesis#/media/File:Sega-Genesis-Power-Base-Converter.jpg. (b) "Sega-CD-Model1-Set" by Evan Amos—own work, public domain. Available at https://commons.wikimedia.org/w/index.php?curid=14400186. Retrieved from https://en.wikipedia.org/wiki/Sega_CD#/media/File:Sega-CD-Model1-Set.jpg.)

Figure 6.13 Magazine advertisement for the Sega Genesis in 1990. (Posted on *The Requiem*, August 14, 2014. "The Genesis launches its ad campaign." Retrieved from http://www.seganerds.com/2014/08/14/the-genesis-launches-its-ad-campaign/.)

Figure 6.14 Box art to five defining Genesis titles including (a) Phantasy Star II, (b) Sonic the Hedgehog, (c) Streets of Rage 2, (d) Shinobi III: Return of the Ninja Master, and (e) Gunstar Heroes. (Phantasy Star II, courtesy of Sega, 1990; Sonic the Hedgehog, courtesy of Sonic Team/Sega, 1991; Streets of Rage 2, courtesy of Sega, 1992; Shinobi III: Return of the Ninja Master, courtesy of Megasoft/Sega, 1993; and Gunstar Heroes, courtesy of Treasure/Sega, 1993.)

Figure 6.15 Atari Lynx featuring *Blue Lighting.* (Courtesy of Evan Amos—own work, CC BY-SA 3.0. Available at https://commons.wikimedia.org/w/index.php?curid=19709905. Retrieved from https://en.wikipedia.org/wiki/Atari_Lynx#/media/File:Atari-Lynx-I-Handheld.jpg. (Screenshot of *Blue Lightning* courtesy of Epyx/Atari, 1989.)

Figure 6.16 Box art to five defining Lynx titles: (a) *Blue Lightning,* (b) *S.T.U.N. Runner,* (c) *Chip's Challenge,* (d) *Todd's Adventure in Slime World,* and (e) *California Games.* (*Blue Lightning,* courtesy of Epyx/Atari, 1989; *S.T.U.N. Runner,* courtesy of Atari Games, 1989; *Chip's Challenge,* courtesy of Epyx/Atari, 1989; *Todd's Adventure in Slime World,* courtesy of Epyx/Atari, 1992; and *California Games,* courtesy of Epyx/Atari, 1989.)

Figure 6.17 Nintendo Super Famicom console and six-button controller. (Courtesy of Evan Amos—own work, public domain. Available at https://commons.wikimedia.org/w/index.php?curid=17748368. Retrieved from https://en.wikipedia.org/wiki/Super_Nintendo_Entertainment_System#/media/File:Nintendo-Super-Famicom-Set-FL.jpg.) (Part of this image was used on the introductory page of this chapter.)

Figure 6.18 The Super Nintendo Entertainment System with a six-button controller. (Courtesy of Evan Amos—Own work, Public Domain, https://commons.wikimedia.org/w/index.php?curid=13297023. August 28, 2013. Retrieved from https://en.wikipedia.org/wiki/Super_Nintendo_Entertainment_System#/media/File:SNES-Mod1-Console-Set.jpg. Part of this image was used on the introductory page of this chapter.)

Figure 6.19 Screenshots from SNES launch titles: (a) *F-Zero* and (b) *Super Mario World*. (Courtesy of Nintendo, 1991.)

Figure 6.20 Magazine advertisement for Super Nintendo in 1992. (Posted by Tanooki's Stuff on August 16, 2011. Retrieved from https://www.flickr.com/photos/65846913@N02/6052166222.)

Figure 6.21 Screenshots from Konami's *The Legend of the Mystical Ninja* displaying the Super Nintendo's color layering (a) and Mode 7 scaling (b) and rotation (c) effects. (Courtesy of Konami, 1992.)

Figure 6.22 Box art to five defining SNES titles including (a) Chrono Trigger, (b) Super Metroid, (c) Final Fantasy III, (d) The Legend of Zelda: A Link to the Past, and (e) Donkey Kong Country. (Chrono Trigger, courtesy of SquareSoft, 1995; Super Metroid, courtesy of Intelligent Systems/Nintendo, 1994; Final Fantasy III, courtesy of SquareSoft, 1994; The Legend of Zelda: A Link to the Past, courtesy of Nintendo, 1992; and Donkey Kong Country, courtesy of Rare Ltd./Nintendo, 1994.)

Figure 6.23 Game Gear featuring *Sonic the Hedgehog: Triple Trouble*. ("A Sega Game Gear handheld video game system." by Evan Amos—own work, public domain. Available at https://commons.wikimedia.org/w/index.php?curid=12172585. Retrieved from https://en.wikipedia.org/wiki/Game_Gear#/media/File:Game-Gear-Handheld.jpg.) (Screenshot of *Sonic the Hedgehog: Triple Trouble*, courtesy of Aspect/Sega, 1994.)

Figure 6.24 (a) Sonic the Hedgehog: Triple Trouble, (b) Shinobi II: The Silent Fury, (c) Shining Force: The Sword of Hajya, (d) Ax Battler: A Legend of Golden Axe, and (e) Super Columns. (Sonic The Hedgehog: Triple Trouble, courtesy of Aspect/Sega, 1994; Shinobi II: The Silent Fury, courtesy of Sega, 1992; Shining Force: The Sword of Hajya, courtesy of Camelot Software Planning/Sega, 1994; Ax Battler: A Legend of Golden Axe, courtesy of Aspect/Sega, 1991; and Super Columns, courtesy of Sega, 1995.)

Figure 6.25 Neo•Geo Advanced Entertainment System with its large joystick controller. ("Neo-Geo-AES-Console-Set" by Evan Amos—own work, CC BY-SA 3.0. Available at https://commons.wikimedia.org/w/index.php?curid=18260466. Retrieved from https://en.wikipedia.org/wiki/Neo_Geo_(system)#/media/File:Neo-Geo-AES-Console-Set.png.) (Part of this image was used on the introductory page of this chapter.)

Figure 6.26 Screenshots from AES launch titles: (a) *Baseball Stars Professional* and (b) *Magician Lord*. (*Baseball Stars Professional,* courtesy of SNK, 1991; and *Magician Lord,* courtesy of ADK/SNK, 1991.)

Figure 6.27 Magazine advertisement for Neo•Geo in 1991. (Posted by Sebastian Mihai on January 2, 2016. Retrieved from http://sebastianmihai.com/downloads/ngscans/Neo-Geo-Hotdog.jpg.)

Figure 6.28 Box art to five defining Neo•Geo titles including (a) *Samurai Shodown*, (b) *Fatal Fury Special*, (c) *The Last Blade*, (d) *Metal Slug X*, and (e) *The King of Fighters '98*. (*Samurai Shodown,* courtesy of SNK, 1993; *Fatal Fury Special,* courtesy of SNK, 1993; *The Last Blade* courtesy, of SNK, 1998; *Metal Slug X,* courtesy of SNK, 1999; and *The King of Fighters '98: The Slugfest,* courtesy of SNK, 1998.)

Figure 6.29 Fourth-generation console sales graph. (Designed by Wardyga using data from Resource Site for Video Game Research, "Console Wars through the Generations." Available at http://dh101.humanities.ucla.edu/DH101Fall12Lab4/graph—console-wars and GamePro. "The 10 Worst-Selling Consoles of All Time." Retrieved from http://www.gamepro.com/gamepro/domestic/games/features/111822.shtml and Consoles +, issue 73.)

PRO FILE: Yu Suzuki: Photo by Yu Suzuki, Game Developers Conference 2011, Day 3 (2).jpg: Official GDCderivative work: Masem. This file was derived from: Yu Suzuki, Game Developers Conference 2011, Day 3 (2).jpg, CC BY 2.0, https://commons.wikimedia.org/w/index.php?curid=14496549.

■ REFERENCES

Bivens, D. (2011, October 27). "Nintendo's expansion ports: Satellaview." *Nintendo World Report*. Retrieved from http://www.nintendoworldreport.com/feature/27669/nintendos-expansion-ports-satellaview.

Branagan, N. (2020, September 7). *Why did we need an arcade card?* Retrieved from https://nicole.express/2020/why-do-you-need-an-arcade-card.html.

Buchanan, L. (2012, June 14). *The SEGA channel: This Genesis download service was way, way ahead of its time.* Retrieved from https://www.ign.com/articles/2008/06/11/the-sega-channel?page=1.

Compton, S. (2004). *Gamers: writers, artists & programmers on the pleasures of pixels.* Brooklyn, NY: Soft Skull Press, p. 119.

Editorial: 101 secrets of the PC Engine. (2015). *NFG Games.* Retrieved from http://nfggames.com/games/pce/.

Editorial: This month in gaming history. (2002, January). *Game Informer,* 12(105), p. 117.

Editorial: What in the name of Sam Hill is a PC Engine? (1995, May). *Electronic Gaming Monthly* (Ziff Davis), 70, p. 15.

Fahs, T. (2009, April 21). *IGN presents the history of Sega.* Retrieved from http://www.ign.com/articles/2009/04/21/ign-presents-the-history-of-sega.

Guinness World Records. (2008). *Guinness world records: Gamer's edition. Guinness world records,* New York: Jim Pattison Group.

Harris, B. J. (2014). *Console wars: Sega, Nintendo, and the battle that defined a generation.* New York: HarperCollins, pp. 227–228, 273–275, 372.

Herman, B. (2004, August 19). Interview from "SNK" episode. *G4 Icons,* 3(12).

June, L. (2013, January 16). "For amusement only: The life and death of the American arcade." *The Verge.* Vox Media. Retrieved from http://www.theverge.com/2013/1/16/3740422/the-life-and-death-of-the-american-arcade-for-amusement-only.

Kent, S. (2001). *The ultimate history of video games: The story behind the craze that touched our lives and changed the world.* Roseville, CA: Three Rivers Press.

Mason, M. (1987). "Foreign direct investment and Japanese economic development, 1899–1931." *Business and Economic History,* 2(16), p. 95.

McFerran, D. (2009). "Retroinspection: Game Boy." *Videogames hardware handbook: 1977–1999.* UK: Imagine Publishing, Ltd., p. 148.

McFerran, D. (2012, November 2). *The making of the PC engine: With NEC's machine turning 25, we take a look back at the history of the Famicom's biggest rival.* Retrieved from http://www.nintendolife.com/news/2012/11/feature_the_making_of_the_pc_engine.

Neo•Geo CD: The new kid in town. (1995, October). *GamePro, (IDG).* 85(30).

Nintendo Co., Ltd. (2016, April 26). *Consolidated sales transition by region.* Retrieved from https://www.nintendo.co.jp/ir/library/historical_data/pdf/consolidated_sales_e1603.pdf.

Nintendo Power. (2006). *Nintendo Power,* Nintendo of America, 208–210, p. 102.

Ohshima, N. (2009, December 4). "Out of the blue: Naoto Ohshima speaks." Interview with Brandon Sheffield. *Gamasutra.* UBM plc. Retrieved from http://www.gamasutra.com/view/feature/132596/out_of_the_blue_naoto_ohshima_.php.

Redsell, A. (2012, May 20). *Sega: A soothsayer of the games industry.* Retrieved from https://www.ign.com/articles/2012/05/20/sega-a-soothsayer-of-the-games-industry.

Reeves, B. (2017, November). Super powered: The lasting legacy of the Super NES. *Game Informer.* Minneapolis, MN: GameStop Corp, 295, pp. 92–95.

Ritz, E.J.M. (2013, July 15). *An introduction to mode 7 on the SNES.* Retrieved from http://ericjmritz.name/2013/07/15/an-introduction-to-mode-7-on-the-snes/.

Sato. (2013, September 18). "Sega's original hardware developer talks about the company's past consoles." *Siliconera.* Retrieved from http://www.siliconera.com/2013/09/18/segas-original-hardware-developer-talks-about-the-companys-past-consoles/.

Sczepaniak, J. (2006). "Retroinspection: Mega Drive." *Retro Gamer.* London, UK: Image Publishing Ltd, 27, pp. 42–47.

Shea, B. (2022, March 10). *Ranking every game in the Super Mario series.* Retrieved from https://www.gameinformer.com/b/features/archive/2017/10/15/best-super-mario-game-rankings.aspx.

Sheff, D. (1993). *Game over: How Nintendo zapped an American industry, captured your dollars, and enslaved your children* (1st ed). New York: Random House.

Spence, T. (2020, July 13). *The decade of arcade consoles.* Retrieved from https://tedspence.com/the-decade-of-arcade-consoles-3627d149ff86.

Wild, K. (2009). "Retroinspection: Game Gear." *Videogames hardware handbook: 1977–1999.* UK: Imagine Publishing, Ltd., p. 161.

Yang, V. & Slaven, A. (2002). "SNK Neo-Geo AES." *Video Game Bible, 1985–2002,* p. 338.

Sex and Violence Take Center Stage

■ OBJECTIVES

After reading this chapter, you should be able to:

- Present basic demographic data on who plays video games.
- Discuss the history and development of sex, gender, race, and violence in video games.
- Identify gender, race, and identity portrayals and inequities in video games.
- List popular titles known for sex, violence, and other controversies.
- Review key people behind the video games.
- Explain the game industry's challenges and successes with inclusion and diversity.
- Name the key people and companies behind the profiled video games.
- Summarize early political reactions to adult themes in gaming.
- Describe major court hearings, bills, and outcomes on video game regulation.
- Provide details on regulatory organizations such as the ESA, ISFE, and IARC.
- Decipher icons and specific content descriptors of ESRB, PEGI, and CERO.
- Reflect on recent studies about the effects of video game content on society.

DOI: 10.1201/9781003315759-7

■ KEY TERMS AND PEOPLE

#MeToo movement

3DO Interactive Multiplayer

Action Replay

American Psychological Association

Joe Baca

Charles "Chuck" Benton

Birdo

Ed Boon

Brown V. Ent. Merchants Ass'n

Sam Brownback

California Bill Ab 1179

California Law Ab 1793

John Carmack

Catharsis theory

Hillary Clinton

Columbine High School

CompUSA

Computer Entertainment Rating Organization (CERO)

Correlation

Custer's Revenge

Customizable character

Death Race

Whitney Decamp

Demographic data

Desensitization

Digitized graphics

Doom

Entertainment Software Association (ESA)

Entertainment Software Association of Canada (ESAC)

Entertainment Software Rating Board (ESRB)

Eroge

ESRB Ratings

Family Entertainment Protection Act (FEPA)

Fatalities

Federal Trade Commission (FTC)

Christopher Ferguson

First-person shooter (FPS)

Full Motion Video (FMV)

GameStop

Gender discrimination

Grand Theft Auto

Andrew Grizzard

Dave Grossman

The Guy Game

Hack/mod/patch

Hot Coffee (mod)

Hypermasculine

id Software

Interactive component

Interactive Digital Software Association

Interactive Software Federation of Europe (ISFE)

International Age Rating Coalition (IARC)

International Game Developers Association (IGDA)

Henry Jenkins

Kōei

Herb Kohl

Leisure Suit Larry

LGBTQ

Joseph Lieberman

Al Lowe

Douglas Lowenstein

Manhunt

Minigame

Mortal Kombat

Mystique

Night Life

Night Trap

Non-player character (NPC)

On-Line Systems/Sierra

Oversexualized

Pan-European Game Information (PEGI)

Phantasmagoria

Arthur Pober

Poison

Polygon graphics

Postal

Prosocial motive

Protagonist

Racial inequity

Riot Games

Rockstar Games

John Romero

Sandbox game

Arnold Schwarzenegger

Short-term aggression

Softporn Adventure

Soldier of Fortune

Stereotype

Take-Two Interactive

Jack Thompson

John Tobias

Ubisoft Entertainment SA

Video compact disc

Vivid Interactive

Ronald M. Whyte

Roberta Williams

Wolfenstein 3D

Leland Yee

■ CHAPTER OUTLINE

Sex in Games

p. 183

Gender & Race

p. 188

Game Violence

p. 191

MATURE
M
ESRB CONTENT

Regulation

p. 193

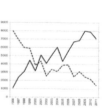

Social Effects

p. 199

■ INTRODUCTION

The early 1990s was the period that video game graphics became more realistic—and along with the gamers, video games matured. Sexual themes and violence began to take center stage in certain games, attracting the attention of lawmakers, the media, parents, and other social institutions. This chapter reviews the history of sex and violence in video games, portrayals of gender and race, in addition to major legislation and regulation as "games grew up." The chapter concludes with subsequent controversy and media coverage, as well as theories and scientific research on the effects of video games on society.

■ WHO PLAYS VIDEO GAMES?

Video games have come a long way since the early days of 8-bit graphics and primitive sound. Once primarily seen as a hobby for kids, those children have grown up and today people of all ages enjoy video games. A recent report by the **Entertainment Software Association (ESA)** lists the average age of a video game player in the United States as 33 years old—with the largest percentage of gamers (36%) being between the age of 18 and 34 years old (ESA, 2022, p. 5). This figure breaks down by age group to 24% of gamers under 18 years old, 36% between 18 and 34 years old, 13% between 35 and 44 years old, 12% ages 45–54, 9% ages 55–64, and 6% ages 65 and over (Figure 7.1). The **Interactive Software Federation of Europe (ISFE)** reported similar findings in 2020, with European players consisting of 18% ages 6–14, 22% between 15 and 24 years old,

20% ages 25–34, 16% ages 35–44, and 23% from 45 to 64 years old (p. 4).

Early generations of video games were primarily played by and marketed to males; however, females now represent almost half of the gaming population. Today, U.S. gamers consist of approximately 52% male and 48% female (ESA, 2022, p. 4). Those figures were 59% male and 41% female just six years prior (ESA, 2016, p. 3). These gender percentages are similar to **demographic data** in other countries as well, with Savanta (2019) reporting gamers in the United Kingdom who play on most days to be 50% male and 50% female (p. 6). These are important figures for the industry to take note of, as the market and types of games that cater to this audience must evolve with it for video games to be successful.

> ### ☀ DID YOU KNOW?
>
> "74% of Americans have at least one video game player in their household" (ESA, 2016, p. 3) and "more than half (54%) of all UK adults play most days" (Savanta, 2019, p. 6).

■ SEX AND *SOFTPORN ADVENTURE*

Sex, nudity, and adult themes in video games have always been more common in Eastern, Asian markets when compared to the West—however, the rest of the world has matured since the early years of gaming. Sexual themes in video games became more accessible when CD-ROM technology emerged in the 1990s. With improved graphics featuring live actors, it was inevitable that more adult themes would begin infiltrating the gaming landscape. Prior to CD-ROM games, developers kept sexuality in games to a minimum—particularly on the home console market. With a larger adult user base, the PC market was exposed to adult themes in video games much earlier.

One of the first titles known for its strong sexual content was *Softporn Adventure* in 1981 by **On-Line Systems** (Figure 7.2). Developed by **Charles "Chuck" Benton** and released for PC, this was a "text adventure game" with no graphics or sound. The game starts off in a sleazy bar with the objective to win the

FIGURE 7.1 Distribution of U.S. gamers by age in 2022.

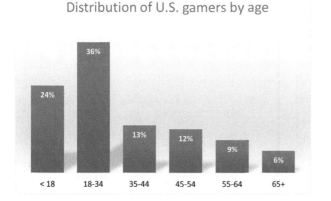

Distribution of U.S. gamers by age

affection of three women. The player reads the story and responds to the text prompts, "WHAT SHALL I DO?" by entering actions such as "BUY WHISKEY" and collecting items like a condom at a drugstore. The game was featured in a *Time* magazine article by Kenneth M. Pierce on October 5, 1981 (Maher, 2012). One of the title's biggest criticisms was not so much the sexual content but that there was no female protagonist version of the game.

■ CUSTER'S REVENGE

The credit to first graphical adult game goes to **Night Life** by **Kōei**, released exclusively in Japan for the PC-8801 in April 1982. It plays more like a tutorial of basic outlines of sexual positions than an actual video game. Later that year, the *graphically* explicit **Custer's Revenge** by **Mystique** was released in the United States in November (Figure 7.2). Developed for the Atari 2600, its graphics were primitive, but the game was no less controversial.

The player assumes the role of a naked General George Armstrong Custer (a historical figure known for his defeat at the Battle of Little Bighorn). The object of the game is "to navigate a battlefield to have sex with [a Native American] maiden who was tied to a post. Although Mystique claimed the sex was just a consensual bondage escapade and not rape, Native American groups as well as the National Organization for Women believed the game promoted sexual violence and staged national protests against it" (GameSpy, 2011, p. 1). Mystique went on to develop two other

adult 2600 titles including *Beat 'Em & Eat 'Em* and *Bachelor Party*.

■ LEISURE SUIT LARRY

During the early 1980s, most adult games featuring sexual content were released in Japan. Companies such as Kōei, Enix, Square, and Nihon Falcom helped create the early demand for what are now known as **'eroge'** titles, or Japanese erotic games (erochikku gēmu) (Ellison, 2014, para. 14). The U.S. PC market had a handful of adult card games such as *Samantha Fox Strip Poker* by Martech in 1986. That same year, On-line Systems approached designer **Al Lowe** to develop an adult graphical adventure game similar to the company's popular *King's Quest* series. The result was an expanded, visual version of *Softporn Adventure*, released in 1987 as **Leisure Suit Larry in the Land of the Lounge Lizards** (Figure 7.3). The game follows a similar story of a 38-year-old virgin named Larry Laffer who is on a quest to get lucky in the fictional city of Lost Wages. Larry encounters four main women along the way, who he will try to win over by purchasing gifts that can be bought from money won at a casino.

The game was not initially advertised by Sierra, but word-of-mouth led to it becoming a sleeper hit, selling an estimated 250,000 copies. While some retailers refused to carry the game, reception of the title was favorable. Perhaps because it was not overly graphic (sex scenes were covered with a "censored" bar), the game did not lead to any major public controversies.

FIGURE 7.2 Box art to (a) *Softporn Adventure* (1981) and (b) *Custer's Revenge* (1982) and screenshot of (c) of *Custer's Revenge*.

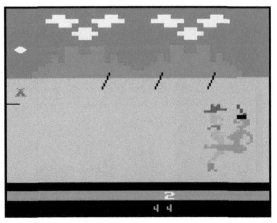

(a)　　　　　　　　　　(b)　　　　　　　　　　(c)

FIGURE 7.3 Screenshots and box art to the Amiga version of *Leisure Suit Larry in the Land of the Lounge Lizards* (1987).

(a)   (b)   (c)

In fact, it spawned several sequels and remakes on various platforms—including a home console version called *Leisure Suit Larry: Magna Cum Laude* in 2004. In 2012, *Time* magazine listed it as one of the 100 greatest video games of all time, calling it "a humor-filled adventure game that wasn't bashful about showing some skin [and that] the world hadn't seen anything like it" (Aamoth, 2012, p. 34).

∎ *NIGHT TRAP* AND FMV GAMES

CD-ROM games allowed for more memory, which meant the ability for **full motion video (FMV)**, more animation, and more realistic graphics featuring live actors. One of the first CD games to garner public attention for its mature content was *Night Trap* (1992) developed by **Digital Pictures** for Sega CD (Figure 7.4). The game plays like an interactive

B-movie about a group of females having a slumber party, who also happen to be under attack by vampire-like beings called "Augers." The player's job is to monitor a video surveillance camera system and activate traps at the right moment to catch the Augers before they attack the women.

While the game did not contain any nudity or sex scenes, its mature content was enough to catch the attention of Congressional leaders. In the eyes of certain politicians, "*Night Trap* was believed to be a simulator for would-be stalkers, murderers, and rapists. This stemmed from the misconception that the object was to trap and kill the girls—the exact opposite of what [the player] actually did" (Robertson, 2013, para. 10). This perception led to the game being removed from the store shelves by Toys "R" Us and Kay•Bee Toys just 2 weeks before Christmas of 1993 (GamePro, 1994, p. 184). The game's spotlight in the

FIGURE 7.4 Screenshots (a and c) and box art (b) to the original Sega CD version of *Night Trap* (1992).

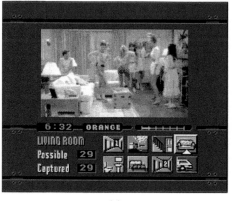

(a)   (b)   (c)

media may have aided in the title's popularity, as *Night Trap* was ported with better graphics to the Sega 32X, 3DO, MS-DOS, and Macintosh the following year.

Another controversial title on CD-ROM was *Phantasmagoria* (1995) by **Roberta Williams** and **Sierra On-Line** (formerly Online Systems). Like *Night Trap*, it contained live-action footage but was more explicit in its sexual and violent content—which included a rape scene. As a PC-only title in the United States, the game received less public attention—however, **CompUSA** (the largest U.S. PC retailer at the time) refused to stock the game.

Electronic Arts founder Trip Hawkins's **3DO Interactive Multiplayer** was released a year after *Night Trap* on October 4, 1993. By the following year, adult entertainment company **Vivid Interactive** began publishing "Adult Only" **video compact discs (VCDs)** for the system. These were not games, but rather edited adult films compressed into MPEG-1 video data similar to the resolution of VHS. While less explicit than the films they were adapted from, the presence of such adult content on a home video game console was a new concept and may have helped push mature video games forward.

▪ THE GUY GAME

One more controversial FMV game is *The Guy Game* (Figure 7.5), developed for PC, PS2, and Xbox by **Topheavy Studios** and published by **Gathering** in 2004. The game plays like a trivia game show on spring break, with every question followed by live-action video footage of host **Matt Sadler** giving the same question to different young women in bikinis. If the women get the question wrong, they flash their breasts toward the screen. Initially, these scenes appear with censored graphics, but successfully guessing the girls' answers eventually leads to full frontal nudity. The game's biggest controversy, however, came from a lawsuit from one of the contestants—claiming she was not informed the footage would be used for a video game and that she was only 17 years old when the footage was recorded (*Topheavy Studios, Inc. v. Jane Doe*, 2005, pp. 2–3).

Full motion video may have advanced sexual and mature themes in video games using live actors and anime—however 3D **polygon graphics** truly enabled developers to create sexy *video game* characters as seen during the original PlayStation era. As Eurogamer's Dave McCarthy (2007) pointed out,

> *Duke Nukem* achieved a certain amount of infamy thanks to its scantily clad strippers and hookers; *Fear Effect*'s promotion push made no bones about its lesbian protagonists; and the *Dead or Alive* series, and its adjustable boob bounce, took its titillatory tendencies to their logical conclusion with the [*Dead or Alive Xtreme*] *Beach Volleyball* series.
>
> (p. 2)

See Table 7.1 for popular video game series known for nudity and sexuality.

FIGURE 7.5 Screenshots (a and c) and box art (b) to the PS2 version of *The Guy Game*.

(a)

(b)

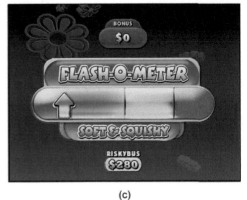
(c)

TABLE 7.1 Five Video Game Series Known for Nudity and/or Explicit Sexuality

Series	Debuted	Developer	Publisher(s)
Dead or Alive	1996	Team Ninja	Tecmo
God of War	2005	SCE Santa Monica	Sony Computer Entertainment
Grand Theft Auto	1997	Rockstar Games	Rockstar Games
Mass Effect	2007	BioWare	Microsoft/Electronic Arts
The Witcher	2007	CD Projekt RED	CD Projekt and Atari

▪ *GRAND THEFT AUTO* AND MODS

One of the most notorious polygonal games to bring sex and violence in gaming to the mainstream audience was the **Grand Theft Auto** series. The series became fully realized when Rockstar Games transformed it from a top-down perspective to a more realistic, third-person "**sandbox**" (open world) game in 2001 with *Grand Theft Auto III*. *GTA III* became instantly controversial by placing the player in the role of a criminal—introducing the ability to pay prostitutes for "services" to recover the player's health, in addition to killing civilians, police officers, and military personnel leading to the player becoming "Wanted."

Grand Theft Auto: Vice City (2002) received criticism for ethnic discrimination, where a scenario in the game put the player in a gang war between gangs referred to as the "Haitians" and "Cubans." It was *Grand Theft Auto: San Andreas* (2004) that drew global attention when a group of professional coders modified the game to unveil a disabled, partially complete, interactive sex **minigame** that was left in the game's code. Players could access the minigame by altering the game's code or by using a third-party device such as the **Action Replay**. Triggered by accepting a female character's invitation for coffee—the scene became known as the infamous "**Hot Coffee**" minigame (Figure 7.6).

When news of the minigame broke, the ESRB (Entertainment Software Rating Board) retroactively rerated the game with an "AO" (Adults Only) sticker until the publisher could release an updated version with the minigame removed. Despite the ESRB's confirmation that no violation had occurred, this led to a class action lawsuit against distributor **Take-Two Interactive**. Under the terms of the settlement, Take-Two provided a replacement disc with the sex scenes removed or a $5–$35 refund to qualifying consumers (Hatfield, 2007, p. 1). Consumers only claimed $27,000 in settlements, compared to more than $1 million in attorney fees absorbed by Take-Two.

Modifications to a game's code like in the *Grand Theft Auto: San Andreas* Hot Coffee minigame are known as "**mods.**" Mods were first made popular by techies in the PC world. They can come in the form of a

FIGURE 7.6 Screenshots before a Hot Coffee minigame in *Grand Theft Auto: San Andreas*.

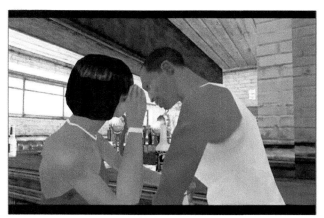

patch (code from the developer to fix or add content to a game)—or a **hack** (unauthorized and/or illegal code by a skilled programmer, which can alter certain graphics or other features of a game). "Art mods" alter a game's graphics and have been used to add sexual themes to games, such as nude or sexier "skins" (texture maps) to characters such as Laura Croft from *Tomb Raider*. These types of skin mod hacks have become a common part of gaming culture and eventually turn up in just about every major PC release today.

■ GENDER, IDENTITY, AND RACE

Historically, video games have been presented through the Caucasian, male perspective, with most game protagonists being white, male characters. Games have often depicted female characters as damsels in distress (*Super Mario Bros., Zelda*), **oversexualized** (early *Tomb Raider* games, *Dead or Alive* series), or as sex objects (*Grand Theft Auto, Duke Nukem*). A 1998 study by Tracy Dietz found the portrayal of female characters in video games to be "overwhelmingly stereotypical" and that "females portrayed in these games, even when they occupy the role of a hero, are often depicted as subordinate to male characters or are presented in terms of their sexuality" (p. 438). Stereotypical game characters are those with exaggerated features, which can be cultural, social, racial, religious, or gender-based.

While female game characters have often been oversexualized, games have commonly portrayed male characters as "**hypermasculine**" (Figure 7.7). A hypermasculine character is one who "has an extremely imposing physical body; someone who is very muscular; someone who is certainly very aggressive. An effect of this hypermasculine characterization can also be to link being male with being violent" (Scharrer, 2000). While modern games are making efforts to avoid these clichés, hypermasculine characters are still common in game series such as *Gears of War, God of War*, and fighting games such as *Street Fighter* and *Mortal Kombat*.

The lesbian, gay, bisexual, transgender, queer or questioning (**LGBTQ**) community has been commonly underrepresented in video games. Early games hinted at LGBTQ themes such as the **Birdo** character from the U.S. version of *Super Mario Bros. 2* (1988) on the NES. The first-edition manual for the game refers to Birdo as a "male who believes that he is a female" who would rather be called "Birdetta" (Loguidice, 2009, p. 280). Capcom's *Final Fight* (1989) featured a character named **Poison** who was rumored to be a trans woman. Non-straight characters were more common in Japanese titles during the 1990s and often modified or omitted for Western releases such as Ash in *Streets of Rage 3* (1994) and Flea's dialog in *Chrono Trigger* (1995).

Characters of color have also been presented in stereotypical ways or in subordinate roles over generations of video games. In the 1980s, games with leading Black characters were mostly celebrities in sports games like *One on One: Dr. J vs. Larry Bird* (1983) and *Mike Tyson's Punch-Out!!* (1987). This trend continued into the 1990s with games such as *Michael Jackson's Moonwalker* (1990), *Barkley Shut Up and Jam!* (1993), and *Shaq Fu* (1994). Most fighting and beat 'em up games at this time at least had selectable characters of color, as well as female heroines to choose from such

FIGURE 7.7 Images of an oversexualized woman (Ivy from *Soul Calibur IV*) (a) and a hypermasculine man (Marcus from *Gears of War*) (b).

(a)

(b)

as *Streets of Rage* (1991), *Street Fighter II* (1991), and *Mortal Kombat II* (1993).

Racial **stereotypes** became more prevalent when games became 3D, with more character-driven stories. A 2011 study by Burgess et al. reviewed 149 games across Xbox, GameCube, and PlayStation platforms and found that "100% of all Black males were portrayed as either athletic or violent or both" and that "minority characters were underrepresented as compared to U.S. Census statistics" (p. 296). Likewise, a 2009 survey by Williams, Martins, Consalvo, and Ivory found that in more than 150 games across nine platforms, white characters accounted "for 84.95 percent of all primary characters, black 9.67 percent, biracial 3.69 percent and Asian 1.69 percent. Hispanics and Native Americans did not appear as a primary character in any game; they existed solely as secondary characters" (p. 825). So how do these numbers line up with player ethnicity today? According to the ESA (2021), approximately 71% U.S. gamers identified as being white, 9% Hispanic, 8% Black/African American, 6% Asian/Pacific Islander, and 2% other (p. 5).

Modern games have done a better job with ethnic diversity, avoiding hypermasculine stereotypes, and depicting female characters in a less sexualized manner. Blockbuster titles such as *Grand Theft Auto, Prototype, The Walking Dead,* and *Marvel's Spider-Man: Miles Morales* feature Black characters as lead protagonists. Games *Shadows of the Damned, Guacamelee,* and the *Just Cause* series feature Hispanic lead characters. Female characters such as Laura Croft in *Tomb Raider* were redesigned to be less sexualized and more proportionally realistic. Games that allow the player to customize their character's appearance, gender, and ethnicity have added to this diversity—and many of those series (such as *Fable, Mass Effect* [Figure 7.8], and *Dragon Age*) allow the player to engage in same-sex relationships with other characters.

Gay and lesbian characters began seeing more prominent roles during the seventh and eighth generations of video games like in the *GTA IV* expansion, *The Ballad of Gay Tony* (2009), and *Borderlands: The Pre-Sequel!* (2014). While LGBTQ characters have become more popular in modern games, they are often designated to **non-player character (NPC)** roles such as Krem in *Dragon Age: Inquisition* (2014) and Parvati Holcomb in *The Outer Worlds* (2019). Progress has been made, however, with significant playable LGBTQ characters including Ciri from *The Witcher III: Wild Hunt* (2015), Max from *Life Is Strange* (2015), Tracer from *Overwatch* (2016), as well as Ellie and Dina from *The Last of Us Part II* (2020).

While developers have made efforts to include a more diverse pool of characters and protagonists in

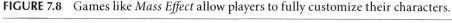

FIGURE 7.8 Games like *Mass Effect* allow players to fully customize their characters.

video games, there continues to be a lean toward the Caucasian, male perspective. A 2013 study by Stein, Mitgush, and Consalvo revealed that "sports video games are one of the few places that racial minorities are present as primary characters, in contrast with most other genres of video games" (pp. 346–347). More male video game protagonists are avoiding the hypermasculine stereotype, but white male characters continue to be the usual heroes—and female game characters still commonly find themselves in at least one sexual situation before the end of the game. The oversexualization of female heroines may have declined in the West (see Figure 7.9); however, these over-exaggerations continue to be prevalent in Japanese-developed games such as in *Dragon's Crown*, the *Dead or Alive* and *Soul Calibur* series, among other more fantasy-themed titles.

Reasons for gender and **racial inequity** in video games have included consumer demand, the idea that games are mere reflections of real inequalities in society, and the fact that most game developers have been white males. In a game developer survey by Adam Gourdin (2005), 88.5% of game respondents identified as male and only 11.5% of respondents identified as female (p. 11). Of the respondents, 92% of the game developers identified their sexual orientation as heterosexual (p. 15). Data from Williams, Martins, Consalvo, and Ivory (2009) suggests that "ethnically, [developers] are 83.3 percent white, 7.5 percent Asian,

2.5 percent Hispanic and 2.0 percent Black" (p. 830). Creating characters and scenarios outside of their own paradigms adds an additional layer of research and effort for developers but the effort must be made to accommodate a growing diverse pool of gamers.

Modern games have turned their attention toward creating greater gender equality in games; however, gender parity in the *workforce* has had its share of challenges. According to Boston Globe correspondent Leah Burrows, "women video game programmers earn an average of $10,000 a year less than their male counterparts … and women designers make $12,000 less. Such attitudes are beginning to change the atmosphere at video game companies," with the overall percentage of females employed by video game companies increasing from 12% to 20% between 2005 and 2013 (Burrows, 2013).

On the other hand, many of these female employees are not working directly on the games, and women today represent less than a quarter of workers in the video game business. The **Entertainment Software Association of Canada (ESAC)** reported in 2021 the Canadian video game "workforce is largely composed of men, with women constituting only 23% of the total workforce. This figure is, however, higher than in 2019 when women constituted 19% of the Canadian video game workforce" (ESA Canada, 2021, p. 25). Figure 7.10 illustrates female employee percentage by region and the percentage of those women working on games.

FIGURE 7.9 The average sexualization of female characters by year of release shows an overall decline in recent years.

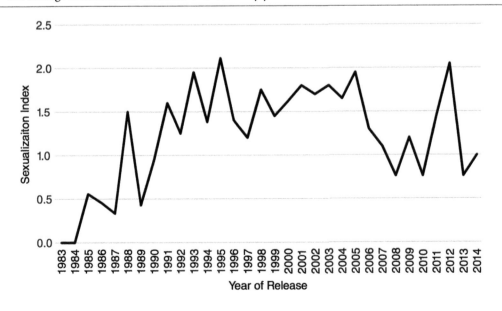

FIGURE 7.10 Share of employment of women at video game companies in Canada, by region.

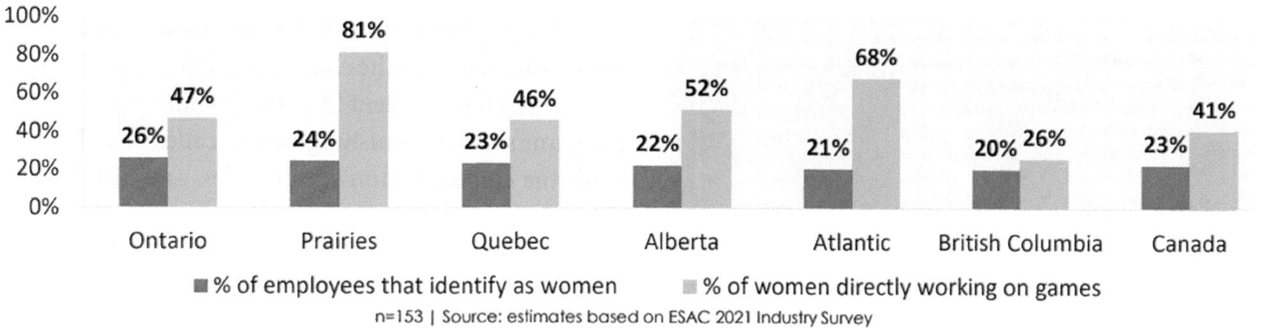

▪ % of employees that identify as women   ▪ % of women directly working on games

n=153 | Source: estimates based on ESAC 2021 Industry Survey

Women have also faced adversity in the video game business in part from the frat boy culture that has been prevalent in game companies for decades. Sexist behavior in the video game industry dates all the way back to the 1970s at Atari. The company "had hot tub parties where executives held meetings with women in bikinis" (Takahashi, 2018, para. 6). Executives have swept this culture under the rug for years, until a 2014 report by the **International Game Developers Association (IGDA)** helped break the silence.

According to the report that surveyed 2,202 workers, open-ended responses pertained to **gender discrimination** such as "females experiencing insubordination from subordinate male colleagues, lack of respect or consideration of opinions or suggestions, especially concerning inclusion or representation of female characters in games, and an overwhelming preference for white males in management positions" (IGDA, 2014, p. 13). The report also included testimonies of inappropriate sexual or discriminatory jokes, derogatory female imagery posted in office settings, belittlement of female gaming skills or work roles, and explicit cases of sexual harassment.

The **#MeToo movement** (a social campaign against sexual abuse, harassment, and rape culture) began spotlighting leaders in the entertainment industry in 2017. A year later, Los Angeles developer **Riot Games** came under fire for allegations of sexism in the company. Riot "agreed to pay out at least $10 million to women who worked at the company in the last five years as part of a settlement in a class action lawsuit over alleged gender discrimination" (Dean, 2019, para. 1). Next, employees of French game publisher **Ubisoft Entertainment SA** filed a wave of sexual misconduct allegations against company executives in 2020. This led to firings, resignations, and restructuring efforts within the company. Then, a 2-year investigation led the California Department of Fair Employment and Housing (DFEH) to file a suit alleging sexual harassment, employment discrimination, and retaliation on the part of **Activision Blizzard** on July 20, 2021. These cases may be negative, but they are slowly leading to positive change.

▪ **EARLY VIDEO GAME VIOLENCE**

Partly due to their primitive graphics and sound, most early video games did not create controversy for their violence. In 1984, J. R. Dominick reported that "videogame violence is abstract and generally consists of blasting spaceships or stylized aliens into smithereens. Rarely does it involve one human being doing violence to another" (p. 138). One early arcade game that did attract the attention of the media was **Death Race** (1976) by **Exidy** (Figure 7.11). Inspired by the 1975 cult film *Death Race 2000*, the object of the game is to run over stick figure beings called "gremlins" from an aerial perspective using a steering wheel and acceleration pedal.

Despite the primitive graphics, these "gremlins" looked just like being humans. This got the attention of national news programs such as *60 Minutes*, leading to negative press. Only around 500 units were manufactured before the game was banned and pulled from the arcades (Gonzalez, 2007, para. 11). Game violence was not a hot topic after this for about a decade, until Exidy released its next violent arcade game **Chiller** in 1986. *Chiller* was a light gun game featuring stages that included shooting and mutilating human characters bound in torture chambers. While much more graphic than *Death Race, Chiller* did not receive as

FIGURE 7.11 Screenshot of *Death Race* (1976).

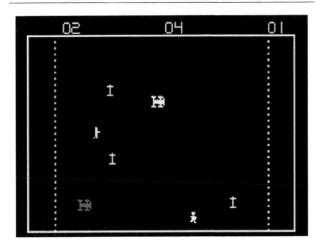

much media attention because of poor sales—since most arcades refused to carry it.

■ *MORTAL KOMBAT*

Midway Games released *Mortal Kombat* (Figure 7.12) to the arcades on October 7, 1992—exactly 1 week before *Night Trap* hit store shelves. Produced to compete with Capcom's popular *Street Fighter II* fighting game, developers **Ed Boon** and **John Tobias** chose to use **digitized graphics** of real actors to help their game stand out from the crowd. They initially approached famous martial arts actors Steven Segal and Jean Claude van Damme to appear in the game; however, each of them was busy with other projects (Kent, 2001, p. 462). Without a famous name attached to the game, Boon and Tobias turned to excessive violence to capture the attention of gamers.

They programmed blood to fly from most hits to a character's face—and being hit with an uppercut and certain special moves results in ridiculous amounts of blood spurting from the character and hitting the pavement. Even more violent than the in-game fighting are the game's unique finishing moves called "**fatalities.**" With the correct button combination and distance to the losing character, the winner of each match has a brief amount of time to assassinate the other character. Like the game's blood, these fatalities are not very realistic, but extremely violent. For example, the fatality for character Sub-Zero sees him tear his opponent's head off with one punch, surgically ripping out the opponent's still-attached spine in the process.

It was not long before *Mortal Kombat*'s violence and *Night Trap*'s mature themes caught the attention of Senator **Joseph Lieberman** (Democrat, CT). Lieberman, along with Senator **Herb Kohl** (Democrat, WI), who held Senate hearings with video game companies (particularly Nintendo and Sega) on the marketing of such video games.

☼ DID YOU KNOW?

When *Mortal Kombat* was released on home consoles (Sega Genesis and Super Nintendo), Nintendo insisted that publisher **Acclaim** release a less-violent version for the SNES. As such, developer **Sculptured Software** made numerous modifications to the game—changing the blood to sweat and toning down most of the fatalities.

FIGURE 7.12 Screenshots depicting the violence and gore from *Mortal Kombat* (1992).

▪ REGULATION AND THE ESRB

The hearings led by Lieberman and Kohl resulted in the formation of two organizations in 1994. The first organization they formed was the **Interactive Digital Software Association (IDSA)** in April to represent the video game industry in areas such as "a global content protection program, business and consumer research, government relations and intellectual property protection efforts" (ESA, 2015). **Douglas Lowenstein** was elected as the founding president and the IDSA became the Entertainment Software Association (ESA) in 2003.

The second group they formed in September 1994 was the **Entertainment Software Rating Board (ESRB)** with Dr. **Arthur Pober**. The ESRB became the industry standard for enforcing video game ratings, advertising guidelines, and privacy principles. Although Sega had developed and offered a rating system of its own years prior, the industry settled on the ESRB as the industry's self-regulatory body for interactive software. See Table 7.2 for ratings and descriptions.

To streamline the rating process, publishers submit a detailed questionnaire and footage of the game's most graphic and mature content, in addition to its proposed packaging. Everything from its context, storyline, reward system, unlockable content, and other elements are factored into the game's final rating. The ratings are then developed to include an icon on the front of the game's box art (depicting the suggested age group), followed by more detailed information on the backside of the packaging.

▪ PEGI, CERO, AND IARC

Similar rating systems created in other countries during 1994 included Unterhaltungssoftware Selbstkontrolle (USK) in Germany and the Video Standards Council (VSC) in the United Kingdom. VSC is an administrator of the **Pan-European Game Information (PEGI)** rating system, which was developed by the **Interactive Software Federation of Europe (ISFE)** headquartered in Belgium. PEGI "was launched in the spring of 2003 and replaced a number of national age rating systems with a single system now used throughout most of Europe, in more than 35 countries" (PEGI, 2022). Due to the many different languages spoken throughout Europe, visually descriptive symbols (rather than words) accompany the ratings to communicate whether a game contains bad language, discrimination, drugs, fear, horror, gambling, sex, violence, ingame purchases, or online requirements.

One year before the launch of PEGI, Tokyo's Computer Entertainment Supplier's Association developed a rating system branch of their own called the **Computer Entertainment Rating Organization (CERO)** in June 2002. CERO's mission is "to provide people in general and game consumers with information necessary for them to select computer and video games, help young people grow in a healthy and sound environment and maintain society's ethical standards at a proper level by implementing age-appropriateness ratings for computer and video games" (CERO, 2022). CERO's ratings match up closely to the ESRB as shown in Figure 7.13. Like PEGI, Japan's rating system also includes visual icons to identify the game's content. CERO's symbols represent love, sexual content, violence, horror, drinking/smoking, gambling, crime, drugs, and language.

Other countries have adopted ratings systems of their own. See Table 7.3 for a look at ratings systems across the globe. For mobile, Apple's App Store, Google Play, and

TABLE 7.2   Modern ESRB Video Game Ratings and Their Meanings

Icon	Stands For	Description
RP	Rating Pending	Game has not been assigned a final rating by the ESRB
EC	Early Childhood	Suitable for children ages three and older
E	Everyone	Originally known as Kids to Adults (K-A); for all ages
E10+	Everyone 10+	Suitable for everyone 10 years of age and older
T	Teen	Generally suitable for those aged 13 years and older
M	Mature	Ages 17+ for violence, blood/gore, sexual content, or language
AO	Adults Only	18+ for stronger sexual content, nudity, violence, language, etc.

FIGURE 7.13 Different symbols, similar meanings: A look at ESRB, CERO, and PEGI labels.

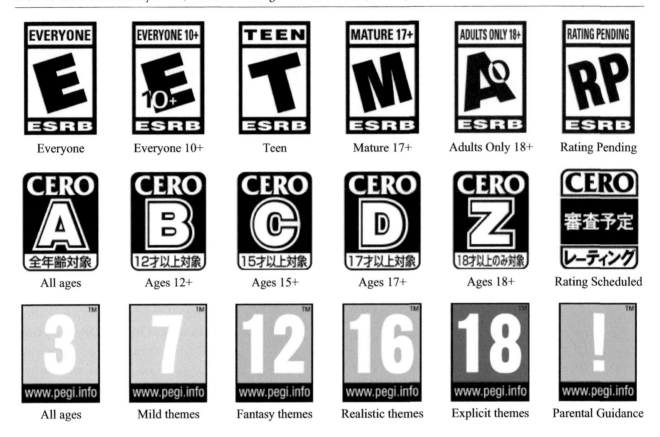

other mobile platforms have also developed rating systems. With so many systems in place, rating authorities from around the world, including ESRB, PEGI, USK, ClassInd, and the Australian Government Classification Board have come together to form a simplified, automated process of obtaining ratings from developers. The result was the **International Age Rating Coalition (IARC)** formed in 2013. The IARC rating process includes a questionnaire based on factors "weighed by each rating authority so that once a developer completes the questionnaire, the unique algorithms that have been programmed for each region instantly produce the appropriate age ratings" (IARC, 2022). Participating storefronts include Google Play, Microsoft Store for Windows and Xbox, Nintendo eShop, Oculus Store, Pico Store, PlayStation Store, and Stadia.

■ *DOOM* AND FIRST-PERSON SHOOTERS

About a year before the ESRB rating system was formed, another controversial game emerged on the PC landscape in December of 1993 with **Doom** by **id**

Software (Figure 7.14). *Doom* was primarily the product of programmers **John Carmack** and **John Romero**, who quickly became rock stars of the computer gaming community. It was the company's second major **first-person shooter (FPS)**, following *Wolfenstein 3D* (1992). A first-person shooter adds an additional layer of immersion because it is played through the eyes of the shooter. In *Wolfenstein 3D* the player assumes the role of a commando shooting Nazi soldiers. In *Doom,* the player is a space marine battling demons from hell. It was even bloodier, with carnage and gore filling the screen from blasting monsters in satanic environments.

Unlike *Night Trap* and *Mortal Kombat, Doom* did not receive much attention from lawmakers until years later, when school shootings began to arise starting in 1997. The incident that put *Doom* in the spotlight was the massacre at **Columbine High School** in Littleton, Colorado on April 20, 1999. After smuggling weapons into the school, 18-year-old Eric Harris and 17-year-old Dylan Klebold went on to kill 12 students and a teacher, injuring 23 others. The investigation on the

PRO FILE

DOUG LOWENSTEIN

KEY FACTS:

Founding president of the Entertainment Software Association (formerly IDSA)

Helped form the ESRB, E3 Tradeshow, and fought video game piracy and censorship

PRO FILE

HISTORY:
• Born: April 22, 1951 in New York City

EDUCATION:
• B.A. in Political Science, Washington University in 1973

CAREER HIGHLIGHTS:
• Legislative Director for U.S. Senator Howard M. Metzenbaum (Democrat, OH) 1982 to 1986
• Senior VP at National Strategies, Inc. 1986 to 1992
• Senior VP at Robinson Lake Sawyer Miller 1992 to 1994
• President of the ESA (Interactive Digital Software Association) June 1994 to February 2007
• Formed Entertainment Software Rating Board (ESRB) 1994
• Defeated hundreds of anti-video game legislation bills across the United States with the VSDA and IEMA

RECOGNITION:
Recipient of the Interactive Achievement Awards Lifetime Achievement Award, February 18, 2010

TABLE 7.3   Video Game Rating Systems by Country and First Year Utilized for Games

Country	Rating System	Year
Australia	Australian Government Classification Board	2005
Belgium	Pan-European Game Information (PEGI)	2003
Brazil	Classificação Indicativa (ClassInd)	2001
Chile	Calificación de Videojuegos	2018
Germany	Unterhaltungssoftware Selbstkontrolle (USK)	1994
Indonesia	Indonesian Game Rating System (IGRS)	2016
Iran	Entertainment Software Rating Association (ESRA)	2007
Japan	Computer Entertainment Rating Organization (CERO)	2002
Russia	Russian Age Rating System (RARS)	2012
Saudi Arabia	General Commission for Audiovisual Media (GCAM)	2012
South Africa	Film and Publication Board (FPB)	1996
South Korea	Game Rating and Administration Committee (GRAC)	2006
China	Game Software Rating Regulations	2006
United Kingdom	Video Standards Council (VSC)	1994
United States	Entertainment Software Rating Board (ESRB)	1994

boys revealed that they were obsessed with *Doom,* and they often referenced the game when planning their massacre (Kent, 2001, p. 545).

This led to congressional hearings led by Senator **Sam Brownback** (Republican, KS) as early as May 4, 1999. Discussions covered the interactive component of violent video games versus the more passive consumption of other violent media. Particularly harsh on the video game industry was retired Lieutenant Colonel **Dave Grossman**, psychology and military science professor (West Point and Arkansas State University). Grossman claimed that *Doom* was used by the military as a training simulator and that the home version was no different in training kids to kill. He often referred to the game as a "mass murder simulator" (Chalmers, 2009, p. 75).

Representing the video games industry was Interactive Digital Software Association president

FIGURE 7.14   Screenshots from *Doom* (1993).

TABLE 7.4 Five Video Game Series Known for Their Explicit Violence and Gore

Series	Debuted	Developer(s)	Publisher(s)
Dead Space	2008	Visceral Games	Electronic Arts
Manhunt	2003	Rockstar North	Rockstar Games
Mortal Kombat	1992	Midway Games (and more)	Midway, Williams, Warner Bros. Interactive
Postal	1997	Running With Scissors	Ripcord, Loki Ent., Whiptail Interactive, Akella, RWS
Soldier of Fortune	2000	Raven, Cauldron, Activision	Activision and Activision Value

Douglas Lowenstein. Lowenstein presented IDSA data, which showed that "70 percent of people playing PC games and 60 percent of people playing video games were over 18 years of age" (Kent, 2001, p. 553). He also referenced ESRB data showing that most published video games were not extremely violent and that there was a lack of research linking violent video games to violent behavior. Director of the Comparative Media Studies program at the Massachusetts Institute of Technology Dr. **Henry Jenkins** supported the gaming industry, claiming that "abolishing violent video games doesn't get us anywhere. These are the symbols of youth alienation and rage—not the causes" (Jenkins, 1999).

Another shooter used as an example on multiple occasions during the hearings was *Postal*, developed by **Running With Scissors** and published by **Ripcord Games** in 1997. The game is an isometric shooter (viewed from an overhead perspective) and while not as immersive as a first-person shooter, the main plot of the game is to kill everyone—from helpless pedestrians to law enforcement officials. The game's title led to the slang term "going postal," which became a phrase following a string of incidents between 1986 and 1997 where United States Postal Service (USPS) workers engaged in acts of mass murder against their superiors and others. While extremely violent, *Postal* was a poorly reviewed title that did not have strong sales—and Lowenstein pointed this out in his discussion.

Nothing really came about from Senator Brownback's 1999 hearings, and then in 2000 one of the most violent FPS games hit store shelves with *Soldier of Fortune*, developed by **Raven Software** and published by **Activision**. *Rolling Stone* magazine ranked the game as the number one most violent video game in 2013. As Donald Deane (2013) described, "this stunningly violent first-person shooter uses an aptly-named proprietary damage engine called GHOUL, which breaks character models down into 26 discrete 'gore zones.'

In other words, enemies can literally be shot to pieces" (para. 13). Table 7.4 summarizes *Soldier of Fortune* and other video games known for explicit violence and gore.

■ ROCKSTAR GAMES AND LEGISLATION

Other violent titles that reached the market in the following years included Rockstar Games' **Manhunt** in 2003 (Figure 7.15). *Manhunt* puts the player in the shoes of a death row prisoner saved from lethal injection and ordered to execute gang members on closed-circuit television (CCTV) to save his family. The game awards players with stars for the speed and brutality of the executions. The game caught the attention of U.S. Representative **Joe Baca** (Democrat, CA), who claimed "it's telling kids how to kill someone, and it uses vicious, sadistic and cruel methods to kill" (Gwinn, 2003, para. 8).

A year later, Rockstar Games released *Grand Theft Auto: San Andreas*, based on South Central L.A. in the 1990s. Along with its hackable "Hot Coffee" sex scenes, the game contained realistic violence in an open world setting. Examples of violence in *GTA: San Andreas* include shooting police officers, running over pedestrians with vehicles, as well as hijacking a train, among other acts. By March 2005, the game had sold more than 12 million copies, making it the highest selling title for the PlayStation 2.

The popularity of violent, M-rated games motivated Senator **Hillary Clinton** (Democrat, NY) to introduce a bill called the **Family Entertainment Protection Act (FEPA)** on December 16, 2005, which called for a federal mandate to enforce the ESRB rating system for video games. Major proposals of the bill included the prohibition on selling mature and adult-only video games to minors, an annual analysis of the ESRB rating system, the authority for the **Federal Trade Commission (FTC)** to investigate misleading ratings,

FIGURE 7.15 Screenshots of (a) *Manhunt* (2003) and (b) *Grand Theft Auto: San Andreas* (2004).

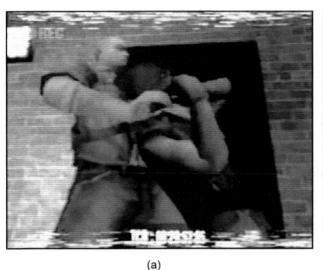

(a)

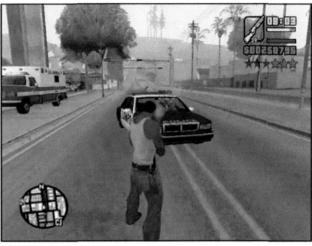

(b)

the authority to register complaints, and annual retailer audits. This and similar bills never became laws and eventually expired with no further action.

> ### 💡 DID YOU KNOW?
>
> In addition to its resume of "best-selling" records, Guinness World Records (2009) lists *Grand Theft Auto* as the most controversial video game series in history, where more than 4,000 articles have been published on the series (pp. 108–109).

Another attempt to enforce the ESRB ratings and prevent the sale of violent videogames to children was **California bill AB 1179**. Introduced by Senator **Leland Yee** (Democrat, CA) and approved by Governor **Arnold Schwarzenegger** (Republican, CA) in October 2005, the bill banned the sale of violent video games to children under 18 and asked for clearer labeling of ratings than what was currently being used by the ESRB. It imposed a maximum $1,000 fine on retailers for each infraction. The bill passed as **CA Law AB 1793** in January 2006, but only resulted in requiring stores to display the ESRB rating system and to provide parents with information on the ratings.

The Entertainment Software Association (ESA) challenged the law in the United States District Court for the Northern District of California. U.S. District Judge **Ronald M. Whyte** ruled that the law was a violation of the First Amendment. Insufficient evidence that video games were different from other media or caused violent behavior was also part of the decision (*Video Software Dealers Ass'n et al. v. Schwarzenegger et al.*, 2007). Schwarzenegger appealed, but the Ninth Circuit Court of Appeals affirmed Whyte's decision in 2009. Finally, Schwarzenegger appealed to the Supreme Court, followed by hearings on November 2, 2010.

Jerry Brown (Democrat, CA) succeeded Schwarzenegger as California governor in 2010 and attorneys renamed the case as "**Brown v. Entertainment Merchants Ass'n**" after the hearings (Clements, 2012, p. 680). Once again, the ESA was there to defend its case, along with the support of industry giants such as Microsoft, Activision Blizzard, the National Association of Broadcasters, Motion Picture Association of America, and Recording Industry Association of America, among others. Following the deliberations, the Supreme Court struck down the California law as unconstitutional with a 7–2 decision on June 27, 2011. The ruling claimed that video games were protected under the First and Fourteenth Amendments.

Video games have a solid record of protection by the U.S. Constitution. On the other hand, video games that saw Western releases have been banned by governing bodies in countries such as Germany, Australia, China, Saudi Arabia, and the United Arab Emirates. And while there is no federal law prohibiting the sale of M-rated video games to minors in the United States, most retailers strictly adhere to the ratings set forth by the ESRB. At **GameStop**, "if an hourly employee sells an M-rated game to a minor, not only will he or she lose their job, but the salaried store manager will be terminated as well" (Chester, 2007, para. 2).

■ EFFECTS OF VIDEO GAME VIOLENCE

Scientific studies on the effects of video games have focused particularly on the effects of young people who play violent video games. A 2015 policy statement by the **American Psychological Association** claimed that "scientific research has demonstrated an association between violent video game use and both increases in aggressive behavior, aggressive affect, aggressive cognitions and decreases in prosocial behavior, empathy, and moral engagement" (p. 3). Former attorney **Jack Thompson** and studies by Barbara J. Wilson of University of Illinois at Urbana-Champagne (2008) and psychologist Craig A. Anderson (2010) support the assertion that exposure to violent video games can contribute to aggressive behavior. Most of these studies revealed **short-term aggression** during or immediately after playing a violent game—similar to a moviegoer feeling sad or depressed during and/or after viewing an emotionally heartbreaking film.

Other social scientists argue that there is no significant **correlation** (relationship), such as Associate Professor of Sociology at Western Michigan University, **Whitney DeCamp**. DeCamp acknowledges that some studies have shown a connection between children playing violent video games and violent behavior but argues that the two variables have been observed "in a vacuum" and that children who are attracted to violent video games likely have a predisposition toward aggression. DeCamp claims, "the evidence points to either no relationship between playing video games and violent behavior or an 'insignificant' link between the two" (Scutti, 2016, p. 2). His study showed that playing violent video games was not a predictor of violent behavior among 6,567 eighth-graders.

Associate Professor and Co-Chairman of the Department of Psychology at Stetson University **Christopher Ferguson** claims that "data in studies linking video games and violence have been improperly analyzed ... that this research ignores important social factors—such as mental health status and family environment—that can trigger violence, while

pinning all the blame on gaming" (Pellissier, 2016, p. 2). Ferguson suggests that rather than video games, factors such as antisocial personality traits, depression, family, and peer influence are more likely to trigger aggressive behavior.

A 2014 study from Ferguson examined the best-selling games from 1996 to 2011 and ranked each game for violent content based on ESRB ratings. For the study,

> youth violence was charted over the same time period using a government database of per capita youth violence in ages 12–17. With these two data sets in hand, Ferguson correlated the numbers to see if any trend would emerge. It did. It was *negative*.
>
> (Hill, 2014, para. 5)

In other words, youth violence rates dropped while the consumption of violent video games increased over the 15 years observed in the study (Figure 7.16).

Ferguson's findings were consistent with data assembled by **Nicholas Lovell** of *GAMESbrief* in 2010. Lovell plotted North American software sales figures between 1990 and 2008 and then compared them to the FBI's official violent crime statistics for the United States during that same period. His data showed that during this time software sales grew by 461%, while violent crime in the United States had fallen by 25% (Lovell, 2010, p. 1). These correlational studies do not prove that playing violent video games decreases violence in society, although they may provide an argument against the claim that violent video game consumption increases youth violence. Ferguson does suggest that "violent video games may help reduce societal violence rather than increase it" (Scutti, 2016, p. 2). The idea is that by occupying young people with activities they enjoy—including video games—they will stay off the streets and potentially away from trouble.

☼ DID YOU KNOW?

Studies by Gitter et al. (2013) found a significant decrease in aggression of participants who played violent video games with an explicit **prosocial motive** (pp. 346–354).

FIGURE 7.16 Data from Ferguson (2015) showing a decline in youth violence and increase in video game violence consumption from 1996 to 2011.

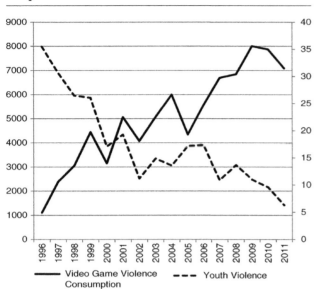

There is a hypothesis known as **catharsis theory**, which is the belief that "playing violent video games or watching violent TV/movies allows people to 'vent' their aggressive inclinations and therefore behave less aggressively after playing/watching" (Gentile, 2013, p. 492). Rather than becoming more violent, it is possible that individuals seek violent video games as a form of stress release. Researchers who support this theory include Dr. **Henry Jenkins** (MIT/USC) and Nottingham Trent University's Professor **Mark D. Griffiths.** Professor Griffiths (1999) explains that "it might be precisely the fantasy aggression that releases the energy that would otherwise be expressed as aggressive behavior" (p. 206).

Another concern about video game violence—like other media violence—is **desensitization**, where gamers develop a diminished emotional response to video game violence after repeated exposure to it. A longitudinal study by University of Buffalo's Dr. **Andrew Grizzard** et al. found that repeatedly playing the same violent game reduces emotional responses (such as guilt) both in the original game and in other violent video games as well (2016). The study did not identify how or why the phenomenon occurred, or whether such desensitization could be transferred into real-life violent situations.

■ OTHER EFFECTS OF VIDEO GAMES

Like other forms of media, the oversexualization of women, hypermasculinization of men, or underrepresentation of minority groups in video games can influence a gamer's perception of people and society. For instance, several studies on gender stereotyping propose that "negative representations of female characters in many video games can lead players to learn, emulate, and internalize the values and norms associated with stereotypes of women as sexual objects and victims of violence, who are vulnerable and ineffective" (Yang, 2012, p. 72; Brenick, Henning, Killen, O'Connor, & Collins, 2007; Dietz, 1998; Harrison & Cantor, 1997). Likewise, stereotypical representations of male or minority characters in games may also influence players' perceptions regarding masculinity, race, and ethnicity, or aspects of sexuality.

The added interactive component of video games may give this form of media even more influential power on consumers. While there is still debate over how video games may influence players, a vulnerable audience certainly exist—particularly children. The gaming industry and retailers have raised the bar in adopting rating systems and regulating the sale of video games to minors. Moreover, it is parents who must play a pivotal role in mentoring and monitoring children's consumption of video games—as well as any other form of media.

■ ACTIVITY: VIDEO GAMES DEBATE

Working in groups of two, choose one of the following topics to debate for and against:

1. Modern video games contain too much violence and gore [or] too much sex and nudity.
2. Today's video games still tend to oversexualize women [or] hypermasculinize men.
3. U.S.-developed characters in modern video games have lost their sex appeal.
4. Most (choose one race) people remain underrepresented in today's video games.
5. LGBTQ characters are well-represented in modern games with sexual themes.

6. (One ethnic or gender group) is presented as a stereotype in most video games.
7. Violent video games lead to long-term aggressive behavior in players.
8. Violent video games lead to real-life desensitization in younger players.
9. Explicit violence and gore make M-rated games more [or less] enjoyable.
10. Playing violent video games can relax or help people vent their aggression.

STRUCTURE

The introduction should (1) gain attention through shock, question, humor, example, or anecdote, (2) preview the main points of the speech, and (3) cite the hypothesis of the speech. The body of the debate should contain three main points and two quotes of supporting research from peer-reviewed journals that can be paraphrased or cited verbally in the presentation. Sources should be cited in APA format, mentioning both the author(s) and the year of their studies. The conclusion should close with a memorable summary of your main points. The total length of each debate should be 3–4 minutes, not to exceed 5 minutes total.

GUIDELINES

- A typed outline should accompany the debate and is due on the first day of the debates.
- The outline must include a references page of all cited sources from the presentation.
- The presentation must include a visual aid (such as PowerPoint) that enhances the debate.
- Video clips should not exceed more than 20% of the total length of the presentation.

■ CHAPTER 7 QUIZ

1. Which of the following was *not* a reason that sexual themes in video games became more popular during the 1990s?
   a. Improved graphics
   b. CD-ROM technology
   c. Revocation of the IDSA
   d. Advancements in FMV

2. One of the first titles known for strong sexual content was this text-only adventure in 1981 by On-Line Systems where the player is out to win the affections of three women:
   a. *Custer's Revenge*
   b. *The Guy Game*
   c. *Leisure Suit Larry*
   d. *Softporn Adventure*

3. This company created three adult video games for the Atari 2600, including *Custer's Revenge*, *Beat 'Em & Eat 'Em*, and *Bachelor Party*:
   a. On-Line Systems
   b. Mystique
   c. Martech
   d. Vivid Interactive

4. Companies such as Kōei, Enix, Square, and Nihon Falcom helped create the early demand for Japanese erotic games known as _____ games:
   a. eroge
   b. mahjong
   c. pachinko
   d. none of the above

5. This graphical adventure series was first released in 1987 and follows a story of a 38-year-old virgin on a quest to get lucky in the fictional city of Lost Wages:
   a. *Custer's Revenge*
   b. *The Guy Game*
   c. *Leisure Suit Larry*
   d. *Softporn Adventure*

6. One of the first CD-ROM games to garner public attention in the United States; about a group of females having a slumber party who are under attack by vampire-like beings:
   a. *Duke Nukem*
   b. *Fear Effect*
   c. *Night Trap*
   d. *Phantasmagoria*

7. This 2004 trivia game hosted by Matt Sadler was controversial for nudity and a lawsuit from one of the contestants who was only 17 years old when the footage was recorded:
   a. *Dead or Alive*
   b. *The Guy Game*
   c. *Softporn Adventure*
   d. *You Don't Know Jack*

8. This "sandbox"-style series game became instantly controversial by placing the player in the role of a criminal—with the ability to pay prostitutes for "services" to recover health, in addition to killing innocent civilians, police officers, and military personnel:
   a. *Dead or Alive*
   b. *Duke Nukem*
   c. *Fear Effect*
   d. *Grand Theft Auto*

9. Female video game characters have been commonly depicted as:
   a. Damsels in distress
   b. Oversexualized
   c. Sex objects
   d. All of the above

10. Characters of color and LGBTQ identity have often been _____ in video games.
    a. excluded
    b. underrepresented
    c. limited to non-playable characters
    d. all of the above

11. The vast numbers of video games on the market tend to be presented through the:
    a. Asian, male perspective
    b. Black, male perspective
    c. Caucasian, female perspective
    d. Caucasian, male perspective

12. An early arcade game that attracted the attention of the media where the object of game is to run over stick figure beings called "gremlins" using a steering wheel and gas pedal:
    a. *Death Race*
    b. *Outrun*
    c. *Nitro*
    d. *X-terminator*

13. Midway's *Mortal Kombat* was developed by:
    a. John Carmack and John Romero
    b. Ed Boon and John Tobias
    c. Doug Lowenstein and Arthur Pober
    d. Joseph Lieberman and Herb Kohl

14. *Mortal Kombat* and *Night Trap* led to hearings on video game marketing by Senators:
    a. John Carmack and John Romero
    b. Ed Boon and John Tobias
    c. Doug Lowenstein and Arthur Pober
    d. Joseph Lieberman and Herb Kohl

15. ESRB stands for the:
    a. Entertainment Software Rating Board
    b. Entertainment Software Reconciliation Board
    c. Electronic Software Reconciliation Bureau
    d. Electronic Software Ruling Bureau

16. These id Software developers made the first-person shooter genre popular with *Wolfenstein 3D* and *Doom*:
    a. John Carmack and John Romero
    b. Ed Boon and John Tobias
    c. Doug Lowenstein and Arthur Pober
    d. Joseph Lieberman and Herb Kohl

17. Of the following, who has *not* blamed violent video games for influencing real acts of violence in society?
    a. American Psychological Association
    b. Dave Grossman
    c. Henry Jenkins
    d. Jack Thompson

18. Introduced a bill called the Family Entertainment Protection Act (FEPA) in 2005, which called for a federal mandate to enforce the ESRB ratings system for video games:
    a. Arnold Schwarzenegger
    b. Hillary Clinton
    c. Joe Baca
    d. Leland Yee

19. California bill AB 1179 was introduced by Senator _____ and approved by Governor _____ in October of 2005.
    a. Leland Yee and Arnold Schwarzenegger
    b. Hillary Clinton and Arnold Schwarzenegger
    c. Joe Baca and Arnold Schwarzenegger
    d. None of the above

20. The hypothesis known as _____ is the belief that playing violent video games is a form of stress release that allows people to vent their aggression.
    a. catharsis theory
    b. desensitization
    c. prosocial motive
    d. short-term aggression theory

True or False

21. According to the ESA, the age of the average U.S. video game player is 33 years old.

22. Females now represent approximately half of all Western video game players.

23. In the video game business, FMV stands for "Frequently Modded Video Game."

24. *Grand Theft Auto: San Andreas* (2004) was relabeled with an AO (Adults Only) until its "Hot Coffee" minigame mod could be removed from the game's code.

25. While the oversexualization of female heroines may have declined in the United States, these over-exaggerations continue to be prevalent in Japanese-developed games.

■ **FIGURES**

Figure 7.1 Distribution of U.S. gamers by age in 2022. (Data from Entertainment Software Association. (2022). Entertainment Software Association. (2022). *2022 essential facts about the video game industry.* Retrieved from https://www.theesa.com/wp-content/uploads/2022/06/2022-Essential-Facts-About-the-Video-Game-Industry.pdf. Chart by Wardyga.)

Figure 7.2 Box art to (a) *Softporn Adventure* (1981), (b) *Custer's Revenge* (1982), and (c) screenshot of *Custer's Revenge.* (a) *Softporn Adventure* (On-line Systems, 1981), (b) *Custer's Revenge* (Mystique, 1982), and (c) screenshot of *Custer's Revenge* (Mystique, 1982).

Figure 7.3 Screenshots and box art to the Amiga version of *Leisure Suit Larry in the Land of the Lounge Lizards* (1987). (On-line Systems, 1987. Courtesy of Wardyga.) (Part of this image was used on the introductory page of this chapter.)

Figure 7.4 Screenshots and box art to the original Sega CD version of *Night Trap* (1992). (Digital Pictures/Sega, 1992). (Courtesy of Wardyga. Part of this image was used on the introductory page of this chapter.)

Figure 7.5 Screenshots and box art box art to the PS2 version of *The Guy Game.* (Courtesy of Topheavy Studios/Gathering, 2004.)

Figure 7.6 Screenshots before a Hot Coffee minigame in *Grand Theft Auto: San Andreas.* (Rockstar North/Rockstar Games, 2004. Courtesy of Wardyga.)

Figure 7.7 Images of an oversexualized woman (Ivy from *Soul Calibur IV*) (a) and a hypermasculine man (Marcus from *Gears of War*) (b). (Ivy from *Soul Calibur IV,* courtesy of Project Soul/Namco Bandai, 2008; and Marcus from *Gears of War,* courtesy of Epic Games/Microsoft Studios, 2006.)

Figure 7.8 Games like *Mass Effect* allow players to fully customize their characters. (Courtesy of BioWare/Electronic Arts, 2012.)

Figure 7.9 The average sexualization of female characters by year of release shows an overall decline in recent years. (From Lynch et al., 2016, p. 574.)

Figure 7.10 Share of employment of women at video game companies in Canada, by region. (Entertainment Software Association of Canada. (2021, October). The Canadian video game industry 2021. Retrieved from https://theesa.

ca/wp-content/uploads/2021/11/esac-2021-final-report. pdf.)

Figure 7.11 Screenshot of *Death Race* (1976). (Exidy, 1976. Courtesy of Wardyga.)

Figure 7.12 Screenshots depicting the violence and gore from *Mortal Kombat* (1992). (Midway Games, 1992. Courtesy of Wardyga. Part of this image was used on the introductory page of this chapter.)

Figure 7.13 Different symbols, similar meanings: A look at ESRB, CERO, and PEGI labels. (By Entertainment Software Association—ESRB Ratings Brochure, Public Domain, https://commons.wikimedia.org/w/index. php?curid=28407765. Symbol for ESRB rating category "Everyone 10+." By Entertainment Software Association—ESRB Ratings Brochure, Public Domain, https://commons. wikimedia.org/w/index.php?curid=28407766. Symbol for ESRB rating category "Teen." By Entertainment Software Association—ESRB Ratings Brochure, Public Domain, https://commons.wikimedia.org/w/index.php? curid=28407671. Symbol for ESRB rating category "Mature." By Entertainment Software Association— ESRB Ratings Brochure, Public Domain, https://commons.wikimedia.org/w/index.php?curid=28407772. Symbol for ESRB rating category "Adults Only." By Entertainment Software Association—Personal correspondence, Public Domain, https://commons.wikimedia. org/w/index.php?curid=50309477. Symbol for ESRB rating category "Rating Pending." By Entertainment Software Association—Nintendo 2DS Operations Manual, Public Domain, https://commons.wikimedia.org/w/index. php?curid=50321311. "A" label for all ages. By CERO, vector by GANO–CERO official site, Public Domain, https:// commons.wikimedia.org/w/index.php?curid=10290132. "B" label for ages 12 and up. By CERO, vector by GANO– CERO official site, Public Domain, https://commons. wikimedia.org/w/index.php?curid=10290140. "C" label for ages 15 and up. By CERO, vector by GANO–CERO official site, Public Domain, https://commons.wikimedia.org/w/index.php?curid=10290177. "D" label for ages 17 and up. By CERO, vector by GANO–CERO official site, Public Domain, https://commons.wikimedia.org/w/index.php?curid=10290211. "Z" label for ages 18 and up only. By CERO, vector by GANO–CERO official site, Public Domain, https://commons.wikimedia.org/w/index. php?curid=10290244. "Shin Sa Yo Tei" (審査予定) label. Scheduled examination (before the software and pre-screening). By CERO, vector by GANO–CERO official site, Public Domain, https://commons.wikimedia.org/w/index.php?curid=10290409. PEGI-Logo für ab 3 Jahren freigebene Spiele. By PEGI, extrahiert von StG1990, http://www.pegi.info/de/index/id/1071/nid/media/pdf/345.pdf. Public Domain, https://commons.wikimedia.org/w/index. php?curid=11261667. PEGI-Logo für ab 7 Jahren freigebene Spiele. By PEGI, extrahiert von StG1990, http://www.pegi. info/de/index/id/1071/nid/media/pdf/345.pdf. Public Domain, https://commons.wikimedia.org/w/index. php?curid=11239536. PEGI-Logo für ab 12 Jahren freigebene Spiele. By PEGI, extrahiert von StG1990, http:// www.pegi.info/de/index/id/1071/nid/media/pdf/345. pdf. Public Domain, https://commons.wikimedia.org/w/ index.php?curid=11239595. PEGI-Logo für ab 16 Jahren freigebene Spiele. By PEGI, extrahiert von StG1990. Own work using: http://www.pegi.info/de/index/id/1071/nid/ media/pdf/345.pdf. Public Domain, https://commons. wikimedia.org/w/index.php?curid=11261662. PEGI-Logo für ab 18 Jahren freigebene Spiele. By PEGI, extrahiert von StG1990, http://www.pegi.info/de/index/id/1071/nid/ media/pdf/345.pdf. Public Domain, https://commons. wikimedia.org/w/index.php?curid=11261669. PEGI-Logo Parental Control Recommended. By PEGI—https://play. google.com. Public Domain, https://commons.wikimedia. org/w/index.php?curid=100267393.)

Figure 7.14 Screenshots from *Doom* (1993). (id Software, 1993. Courtesy of Wardyga.) (Part of this image was used on the introductory page of this chapter.)

Figure 7.15 Screenshots of (a) *Manhunt* (2003) and (b) *Grand Theft Auto: San Andreas* (2004). (*Manhunt,* courtesy of Rockstar North/Rockstar Games, 2003; and *Grand Theft Auto: San Andreas,* courtesy of Rockstar North/Rockstar Games, 2004.)

Figure 7.16 Data from Ferguson (2015) showing a decline in youth violence and increase in video game violence consumption from 1996 to 2011. (From Ferguson, C., 2015, *Journal of Communication*, 65, E1–E22.)

PRO FILE: Doug Lowenstein. Photo courtesy of Doug Lowenstein, 2017. Retrieved from https://convergencyus. com/who-we-are/douglas-lowenstein/.

■ REFERENCES

Aamoth, D. (2012, November 15). *All-TIME 100 video games.* Time Magazine, p. 34. Retrieved from http://techland. time.com/2012/11/15/all-time-100-video-games/ slide/leisure-suit-larry-1987/.

American Psychological Association. (2015, August). *Resolution on violent video games.* Retrieved from http://www.apa.org/news/press/releases/2015/08/violent-video-games.pdf.

Brenick, A., Henning, A., Killen, M., O'Connor, A., & Collins M. (2007). Social reasoning about stereotypic images in video games: Unfair, legitimate, or "just entertainment"? *Youth and Society*, 38, pp. 395–419.

Burgess, M. C. R., Dill, K. E., Stermer, S. P., Burgess, S. R., & Brown, B. P. (2011). Playing with prejudice: The prevalence and consequences of racial stereotypes in video games. *Media Psychology*, 14(3), pp. 289–311.

Burrows, L. (2013, January 27). *Women remain outsiders in video game industry: Female characters are hypersexualized and workers discomforted in an industry known for its frat boy culture.* Boston Globe. Retrieved from https://www.bostonglobe.com/business/2013/01/27/women-remain-outsiders-video-game-industry/275JKqy3rFylT7TxgPmO3K/story.html.

CERO (Computer Entertainment Rating Organization). (2022). *About CERO.* Retrieved from https://www.cero.gr.jp/en/publics/index/3/.

Chalmers, P. (2009). *Inside the mind of a teen killer.* Nashville, TN: Thomas Nelson Inc., p. 75.

Chester, N. (2007, February 2). *GameStop: Sell an M-rated game to a minor, enjoy unemployment.* Retrieved from https://www.destructoid.com/gamestop-sell-an-m-rated-game-to-a-minor-enjoy-unemployment-29690.phtml.

Clements, C. (2012, March 1). Protecting protected speech: Violent video game legislation post-Brown v. Entertainment Merchants Ass'n. *Boston College Law Review*, 53(2), pp. 661–692. Retrieved from http://lawdigitalcommons.bc.edu/cgi/viewcontent.cgi?article=3217&context=bclr.

Dean, S. (2019, December 2). Riot Games will pay $10 million to settle gender discrimination suit. *Los Angeles Times.* Retrieved from https://www.latimes.com/business/technology/story/2019-12-02/riot-games-gender-discrimination-settlement.

Deane, D. (2013, October 11). *12 Horrifyingly violent video games: History's most blood-soaked and gore-spattered releases.* Retrieved from http://www.rollingstone.com/culture/pictures/12-horrifyingly-violent-video-games-20131011.

Dietz, T. (1998). An examination of violence and gender role portrayals in video games: Implications for gender socialization and aggressive behavior. *Sex Roles*, 38, 425–442.

Dominick, J. R. (1984). Videogames, television violence, and aggression in teenagers. *Journal of Communication*, 34, 136–147.

Editorial: Major stores pull Night Trap. (1994, March). *GamePro*, 56, p. 184.

Editorial: Top ten shameful games. (2011, April 26). *GameSpy.com.* Retrieved from https://web.archive.org/web/20110426012823/http://archive.gamespy.com/top10/december02/shame/index4.shtml.

Ellison, C. (2014, August 27). *A gloriously stupid history of sex in video games.* Retrieved from http://www.vice.com/read/a-completely-incomplete-history-of-sex-in-video-games-876.

Entertainment Software Association. (2015). *Overview.* Retrieved from http://www.theesa.com/about-esa/overview/.

Entertainment Software Association. (2016). *2016 Sales, demographic and usage data: Essential facts about the computer and video game industry.* Retrieved from http://essentialfacts.theesa.com/Essential-Facts-2016.pdf.

Entertainment Software Association. (2021). *2021 Essential facts about the video game industry.* Retrieved from https://www.theesa.com/wp-content/uploads/2021/08/2021-Essential-Facts-About-the-Video-Game-Industry-1.pdf.

Entertainment Software Association. (2022). *2022 Essential facts about the video game industry.* Retrieved from https://www.theesa.com/wp-content/uploads/2022/06/2022-Essential-Facts-About-the-Video-Game-Industry.pdf.

Entertainment Software Association of Canada. (2021, October). *The Canadian video game industry 2021.* Retrieved from https://theesa.ca/wp-content/uploads/2021/11/esac-2021-final-report.pdf.

Ferguson, C. J. (2015). Does media violence predict societal violence? It depends on what you look at and when. *Journal of Communication*, 65, pp. E1–E22.

Gentile, D. A. (2013). Catharsis and media violence: A conceptual analysis. *Societies*, 3(4), pp. 491–510.

Gitter, S. A., Ewell, P. J., Guadagno, R. E., Stillman, T. F., & Baumeister, R. F. (2013). Virtually justifiable homicide: The effects of prosocial contexts on the link between violent video games, aggression, and prosocial and hostile cognition. *Aggressive Behavior*, 39, pp. 346–354.

Gonzalez, L. (2007, January 10). *When two tribes go to war: A history of video game controversy.* Retrieved from http://www.gamespot.com/articles/when-two-tribes-go-to-war-a-history-of-video-game-controversy/1100-6090892/.

Gourdin, A. (2005). *Game developer demographics: An exploration of workforce diversity.* Mt Royal, NJ: International Game Developers Association. Retrieved from http://c.ymcdn.com/sites/www.igda.org/resource/collection/9215B88F-2AA3-4471-B44D-B5D58FF25DC7/IGDA_DeveloperDemographics_Oct05.pdf.

Griffiths, M. (1999). Violent video games and aggression: A review of the literature. *Aggression and Violent Behavior*, 4(2), pp. 203–212. Retrieved from http://dx.doi.org/10.1016/S1359-1789(97)00055-4.

Grizzard, A., Tamborini, R., Sherry, J. L., & Weber, R. (2016, March 30). Repeated play reduces video games' ability to elicit guilt: Evidence from a longitudinal experiment. *Media Psychology*, 1, pp. 1–24.

Guinness World Records (ed.). (2009). *Guinness World Records 2009 gamer's edition*. London, UK: Hit Entertainment, pp. 108–109.

Gwinn, D. (2003, November 23). Manhunt the next step in video game violence. *Chicago Tribune*. Retrieved from http://articles.chicagotribune.com/2003-11-24/features/0311240176_1_gaming-scene-optional-headset-manhunt.

Harrison, K., & Cantor J. (1997). The relationship between media consumption and eating disorders. *Journal of Communication*, 47, pp. 40–67.

Hatfield, D. (2007, November 9). *Hot coffee lawsuit finally mopped up*. IGN. Retrieved from http://www.ign.com/articles/2007/11/09/hot-coffee-lawsuit-finally-mopped-up.

Hill, K. (2014, November 8). *The most objective study yet finds no link between video games and violence*. Retrieved from http://nerdist.com/the-most-objective-study-yet-finds-no-link-between-video-games-and-violence/.

IARC (International Age Rating Coalition). (2022). *About IARC*. Retrieved from https://www.globalratings.com/about.aspx.

Interactive Software Federation of Europe. (2020). *Europe's video game industry key facts 2020*. Retrieved from https://www.isfe.eu/wp-content/uploads/2021/10/2021-ISFE-EGDF-Key-Facts-European-video-games-sector-FINAL.pdf.

International Game Developers Association. (2014, June 25). *Developer satisfaction survey 2014 summary report*. Retrieved from https://igda-website.s3.us-east-2.amazonaws.com/wp-content/uploads/2019/04/21173808/IGDA_DSS_2014-Summary_Report1.pdf.

Jenkins, H. (1999). *Professor Jenkins goes to Washington*. Retrieved from http://web.mit.edu/21fms/People/henry3/profjenkins.html.

Kent, S. (2001). *The ultimate history of video games: The story behind the craze that touched our lives and changed the world*. Roseville, CA: Three Rivers Press.

Loguidice, B. & Barton, M. (2009). *Vintage games: An insider look at the history of Grand Theft Auto, Super Mario, and the most influential games of all time*. Waltham, MA: Focal Press, p. 280.

Lovell, N. (2010, August 6). *If video games cause violence, there should be a correlation between game sales and violent crime, right?* Retrieved from http://www.gamesbrief.com/2010/08/if-video-games-cause-violence-there-should-be-a-correlation-between-game-sales-and-violent-crime-right/.

Lynch, T., Tompkins, J. E., van Driel, I. I., & Fritz, N. (2016). Sexy, strong, and secondary: A content analysis of female characters in videogames across 31 years. *Journal of Communication*, 66, pp. 564–584.

Maher, J. (2012, February 29). *Softporn*. Retrieved from http://www.filfre.net/2012/02/softporn/.

McCarthy, D. (2007, November 28). *Sex: A concise history*. Retrieved from http://www.eurogamer.net/articles/sex-article.

PEGI (Pan-European Game Information). (2022). *The PEGI organisation*. Retrieved from https://pegi.info/page/pegi-organisation.

Pellissier, H. (2016, February 26). *Your child's brain on technology: Video games – Our kids are awash in technology 24/7—Should we worry about the effects on their developing brains?* Retrieved from http://www.greatschools.org/gk/articles/child-brain-development-and-video-games/.

Robertson, L. (2013, July 9). *The most controversial moments in video games: Part 1*. Gaming Lore. Retrieved from http://www.retrocollect.com/Articles/the-most-controversial-moments-in-video-games-part-1.html.

Savanta. (2019, November). *Game on: A study of UK gaming attitudes and behaviours*. Retrieved from https://cdn2.hubspot.net/hubfs/5043860/Game_on_%20a_study_of_UK_attitudes_and_behaviours_November_2019.pdf.

Scharrer, E. (2000). *Interview by Sut Jhally in Game over: Gender, race & violence in video games*. Media Education Foundation.

Scutti, S. (2016, July 26). *Do video games lead to violence?* CNN. Retrieved from http://www.cnn.com/2016/07/25/health/video-games-and-violence/.

Stein, A., Mitgush, K., & Consalvo M. (2013). Who are sports gamers? A large-scale study of sports video game players. *Journal of Research into New Media Technologies*, 19, pp. 345–363.

Takahashi, D. (2018, February 2). *The DeanBeat: With Bushnell award, history became herstory*. Retrieved from https://venturebeat.com/2018/02/02/the-deanbeat-with-bushnell-award-history-became-herstory/.

Topheavy Studios, Inc. v. Jane Doe. (2005). *WL 1940159 Tex. App. Austin, 2005*. Retrieved from http://www.kentlaw.edu/faculty/rwarner/classes/privacy/materials_2008/cases/Topheavy%20Studios.doc.

Video Software Dealers Ass'n et al. v. Schwarzenegger et al., (2007). *U.S. Dist. LEXIS 57472 (N.D. Cal. 2007)*.

Williams, D., Martins, N., Consalvo, M., & Ivory J. D. (2009). The virtual census: Representations of gender, race and age in video games. *New Media & Society*, 11(5), pp. 815–834. Retrieved from http://dmitriwilliams.com/virtualcensusfinal.pdf.

Yang, G. S. (2012). *Do the gender and race of video game characters matter? The effects of violent game playing on implicit stereotyping and aggressive behavior* (Doctoral dissertation). The University of Michigan. Retrieved from https://deepblue.lib.umich.edu/bitstream/handle/2027.42/93881/gyang_1.pdf?sequence=1&isAllowed=y.

The 3D Era

■ OBJECTIVES

After reading this chapter, you should be able to:

- Describe the industry's move to 3D and its influence on arcades and home video games.

- Discuss why the first wave of fifth-generation consoles (3DO and Jaguar) failed.

- Provide a brief overview of the history of Panasonic and Sony.

- Review key people behind the video games and consoles.

- Explain why the Sega Saturn was less successful in North America and Europe.

- Illustrate how Sony dominated the fifth-generation market.

- Discuss why Nintendo stayed with cartridge format for the N64.

- Identify graphics and other capabilities of fifth-generation consoles.

- Compare technological differences among 3DO, Jaguar, Saturn, PlayStation, and Nintendo 64.

- List key video game titles and peripherals for each fifth-generation console.

- Describe important innovations brought to gaming during this period.

- Summarize fifth-generation market sales, breakthroughs, and trends.

DOI: 10.1201/9781003315759-8

■ KEY TERMS AND PEOPLE

3D Pad
3D polygon graphics
3DO
Acclaim
Action Replay
American Laser Games
Anti-Aliasing
Arcade Racer
Atari Jaguar
Atari Panther
Martin Brennan
Capcom CPS2
Compact Disc (CD)
Control Stick
Controller Pak
Copy protection
Daisy chain
Demo disc
Draw distance
DualShock controller
E3
Electronic Arts
Expansion Pak
Extended RAM Cartridge
Flare Technology
Martz Franz
Game Boy Color
Gamegun

GameWorks
Glove controller
Goldstar
Gouraud shading
Guncon
Phil Harrison
Hitachi SH2 CPU
Home Arcade Systems
Masaru Ibuka
Interpolation
Jaglink
Jaguar CD
Tom Kalinske
Konami
Ken Kutaragi
Licensed soundtrack
Local area network
Logitech
Peter Main
John Mathieson
Konosuke Matsushita
Memory card
Memory Track
R. J. Mical
Midway
Joe Miller
Jay Miner
MK-80100

Akio Morita
Motorola MC68000
Multiplayer Adaptor
Multitap
Yuji Naka
Hayao Nakayama
NEC VR4300
Dave Needle
Nintendo 64 (N64)
Nintendo 64DD
Norio Ohga
Panasonic
Pirated games
Play Cable
PlayStation Underground
ProController
PSone
Psygnosis
Rareware/Rare
Real-time lighting
Reality coprocessor
Redbook audio
Region-free
Regional lockout
David Rosen
Rumble Pak
Sanyo
Hideki Sato

Sega 32X
Sega Netlink
Sega Saturn
Sega ST-V
Silicon Graphics, Inc.
Sonic Team
Sony Computer
  Entertainment.
Sony Corporation
Sony PlayStation
Sony Walkman
Steven Spielberg
Sprite-generated polygons
SquareSoft
Bernie Stolar
Stunner light gun
Taito
Team Tap
Transfer Pak
Transparency
Treasure
Video compact disc (VCD)
Video display processor
  (VPD)
Virtual Boy
Voice recognition unit
Andrew Whitaker
Gunpei Yokoi

■ CONSOLE TIMELINE

Panasonic 3DO	Atari Jaguar	Sega Saturn	Sony PlayStation	Nintendo 64	Game Boy Color
1993	**1993**	**1995**	**1995**	**1996**	**1998**

▪ ARCADES IN FLUX

The arcade scene in the mid-1990s was where consumers saw a surge of games utilizing **3D polygon graphics**. **Sega** pioneered the genre with *Virtua Racing* (1992) (shown in Figure 8.1), *Virtua Fighter* (1993), and *Virtua Cop* (1994). Their most prolific hardware of this generation was the Saturn-based **ST-V** (Sega Titan Video) system board, which powered more than 60 games. **Namco** went head-to-head with Sega by releasing competing racing, fighting, and shooting games: *Ridge Racer* (1993), *Tekken* (1994), and *Time Crisis* (1995). These titles appeared on Namco's "System 11" and "System 22" arcade hardware. Racing, fighting, and light gun shooting games were the main draw during this period and it was common for these games to cost 50 cents or more to play. According to *Businessweek*, by 1994 Americans were pouring $7 billion into arcade games each year—approximately $1 billion more than they were spending on the home console market at that time (Armstrong, 1994, p. 58).

Capcom introduced its (Capcom Power) CP System II (or **CPS2**) in 1993 for *Super Street Fighter II*. The company would produce more than 40 titles on the hardware, including *1944: The Loop Master, Alien Vs. Predator, Armored Warriors* (aka *Powered Gear*), two *Dungeons & Dragons* beat-em ups, *Super Puzzle Fighter 2 Turbo*, five *Marvel Super Heroes/X-Men* fighting games, another five *Darkstalkers/Vampire* fighting games, and the entire *Street Fighter Alpha* trilogy. **Konami** continued pumping out double-digit titles on its GX and GV hardware (called "Baby Phoenix" in the United States). Aside from a few shoot 'em ups such as Japan-only *Salamander 2* and fighter *Dragoon Might*, most releases on Konami's boards were sports or puzzle games like *Crazy Cross* (aka *Taisen Puzzle-Dama*).

The renaissance period would only last for so long. Despite producing more than 30 titles on its F3 arcade hardware, **Taito** closed its U.S. offices in 1995 (Kent, 2001, p. 500). In addition to arcade games becoming more expensive, home video game rentals became more popular and 32-bit home consoles were right around the corner. Game companies built their new home systems around 3D polygonal technology that would be able to match the graphics and sound of the arcades more closely than ever before. Sega's **Model 3** arcade hardware (*Virtua Fighter 3*, 1996, *Sega Rally 2*, 1997, and *Daytona USA 2: Battle on the Edge*, 1998) continued to be one step ahead and more advanced than home consoles. However, the gap was beginning to narrow. The average consumer could no longer notice a significant difference between home ports and the original arcade games.

With revenues on the decline again, the arcade industry would see another small resurgence in 1996 when motion picture companies DreamWorks (Steven Spielberg) and Universal Studios teamed up with Sega to form the arcade mega complex **GameWorks**. The first location had over "35,000 square feet of floor space [and] opened in downtown Seattle in March of 1997. The opening was treated more like a movie premier, with stars such as Will Smith, Gillian Anderson, and Weird Al Yankovic in attendance" (Kent, 2001, pp. 528–529). Openings of GameWorks in other major U.S. cities soon followed. Japanese arcades remained strong with more than 50,000 arcade venues in Japan in the mid-1990s (McKirdy, 2019).

FIGURE 8.1 Screenshots of defining arcade games from the mid-1990s: (a) *Virtua Racing* (Sega, 1992), (b) *Tekken* (Namco, 1994), and (c) *Area 51* (Mesa Logic/Atari 1995).

(a)　　　　　　　　(b)　　　　　　　　(c)

■ THE 3D ERA

Following in the footsteps of the arcades, the fifth generation was driven by 32- and 64-bit technology, with an emphasis on 3D polygonal graphics. Every console could now display millions of colors on screen, shifting players' "tech specs" focus from on-screen colors to polygon counts. Not since the second generation were so many home consoles available to the public, with certain systems only being released in Japan with a limited library of games. There were close to a dozen consoles released during the fifth generation, with five key systems that would define the 3D era. This generation also saw the largest release of handheld systems, most of which were complete market failures. This chapter will focus primarily on the major five home consoles that publishers released and marketed in the United States, Europe, and Japan.

■ 3DO INTERACTIVE MULTIPLAYER

The first major system in the fifth generation of game consoles was the **3DO Interactive Multiplayer** (Figure 8.2), developed by Amiga computer and Atari Lynx designers **Dave Needle** and **R. J. Mical**. **Electronic Arts** founder **Trip Hawkins** devised the concept of the 3DO and provided ample support for the system. The name "3DO" had really no significance. Hawkins told *Retro Gamer Magazine* that he simply wanted the name of the system to end with an "o" like "radio" or "video" and that someone had suggested adding "3D" to the title (Retro Gamer, 2009,

p. 189). Hawkins added the subtitle "Multiplayer" because the system could play video games, music CDs, photo discs, and **video compact discs** (or VCDs).

The business model for the system was unlike any other console. Hawkins derived a plan for his new **3DO Company** to profit by licensing the hardware to multiple electronics manufacturers, starting with **Panasonic**. Another part of Hawkins's business plan was to attract software developers by only collecting a small, $3 royalty for every game sold. This was significantly lower than the royalty fees collected by Nintendo and Sega. Thanks to Hawkins's wide network of industry contacts, the system received strong media coverage initially, including articles in *The Wall Street Journal, New York Times, Los Angeles Times, San Francisco Chronicle, Chicago Tribune*, and *Businessweek*, among others (Matthews, 2013, p. 21). *Time* magazine even awarded the 3DO as the "1993 Product of the Year."

Panasonic was the first manufacturer to release the system on October 4, 1993, followed by a 1994 release in Japan and Europe. Founded in 1918 by **Konosuke Matsushita**, Panasonic became one of Japan's largest electronics producers. Before the 3DO, the company manufactured versions of the MSX computer system in Japan. The initial challenge for the 3DO was cost. The technology at that time was expensive, and for it to be profitable, the 3DO launched at the suggested retail price of $699.99. Games were also sparse. When the 3DO first hit store shelves, the only game available was the pack-in title *Crash 'N Burn*. However, as Table 8.1 illustrates, 13 more titles were released by the end of the year. Panasonic eventually lowered the

FIGURE 8.2 The Panasonic R•E•A•L 3DO Interactive Multiplayer with standard controller (Model FZ-1).

TABLE 8.1 3DO Interactive Multiplayer 1993 U.S. Titles

• *20th Century Video Almanac*	• *The Life Stage: Virtual House*
• *The Animals!*	• *Star Control II*
• *Battle Chess*	• *Stellar 7: Draxon's Revenge*
• *Crash 'N Burn* (Figure 8.3a)	• *Total Eclipse* (Figures 8.3b and 8.4)
• *Crime Patrol*	• *Twisted: The Game Show*
• *Escape from Monster Manor*	• *Fatty Bear's Birthday Surprise*
• *Lemmings*	• *Guardian War*

price of the system to $399.95 in 1994, but the excitement for the 3DO had worn off and sales remained low (Kent, 2001, p. 487).

Despite its slow sales, the 3DO introduced unique innovations to the home video game market. While its controller design was just a mix between the Genesis and Super Nintendo game pads, it had a unique **daisy chain** feature where players could plug one controller into another. This daisy chain concept allowed players to link up to eight controllers together and eliminated the need for more than one controller port on the system—or the need for an extra multiport peripheral. The original "FZ-1" controller even included a 3.5 mm **headphones jack** and volume control dial at the bottom of the game pad.

Another innovative feature of the 3DO was that it was one of the first **region-free** systems. In other words, the console did not contain any **regional lockout** components, allowing most international games to work on domestic systems and vice versa. Unfortunately, 3DO software lacked any **copy protection**, leaving the door wide open for **pirated games** (i.e., illegal copies). The system could display 16 million colors on screen for photorealistic image quality as boasted in its advertisements (Figure 8.4). Because of its technical capabilities, the 3DO also became a popular platform for adult film companies such as Vivid Interactive to release abridged, erotic VCDs (Video Compact Discs) on.

Third-party developer **American Laser Games** designed the "**Gamegun**" light gun for the system to play its ports of popular arcade shooters including *Mad Dog McCree*. Panasonic and **Logitech** also released a mouse to make it easier to play games such as *Myst* and *Lemmings*. The last key peripheral was a steering wheel developed by **Home Arcade Systems** for racing games such as *Crash 'N Burn* and *The Need for Speed*. Consumers often referred to the original home console as the "Panasonic 3DO" when the system debuted, however, because of Trip Hawkins's licensing structure, two other companies would go on to manufacture versions of the 3DO, including **GoldStar** and **Sanyo** (see Figure 8.5). Panasonic also released an updated, flip-top unit dubbed the "FZ-10," with better memory management and a smaller controller featuring round Stop and Start buttons but no headphones jack.

FIGURE 8.3 Screenshots from early 3DO titles: (a) *Crash 'N Burn* and (b) *Total Eclipse*.

(a)

(b)

FIGURE 8.4 Two-page magazine advertisement for the Panasonic 3DO in 1993.

■ CONSOLE COMPARISON: 3DO VS. 16-BIT SYSTEMS

Compared to its 16-bit predecessors, the 3DO was unlike any other home console on the market at the time of its release. While the older, 16-bit consoles mostly relied on passwords and cartridge batteries to save game data, the 3DO was more like a computer in that it had **32 kB** of **internal memory** to save games and other data. Its **12.5 MHz, 32-bit ARM60 RISC** processor (Table 8.2) was both faster and much more

capable—delivering tens of thousands of polygons per second.

Its native resolution was 320×240 but the 3DO used **interpolation**, a computer algorithm that upscaled its graphics to 640×480 resolution. The 3DO's two accelerated video co-processors could produce 9–16 million "REAL" pixels per second. The co-processors could also distort, scale, rotate, texture map, as well as support transparency, translucency, and color-shading effects for the system. Add textured polygons into the equation and the console's 3D games looked light

FIGURE 8.5 Other 3DO Interactive Multiplayer systems, including the redesigned (a) Panasonic FZ-10, (b) GoldStar (LG) model, and (c) the Japan-exclusive Sanyo 3DO TRY.

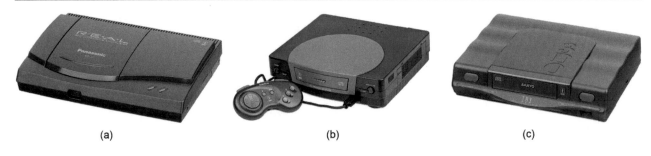

(a)   (b)   (c)

TABLE 8.2 3DO Interactive Multiplayer Tech Specs

Manufacturer:	Panasonic (then GoldStar and Sanyo)
Launch price:	$699.99
Release date:	10/04/93 (US), 3/20/94 (JP), 1994 (EU)
Format:	CD-ROM
Processor:	32-bit ARM 60 RISC CPU (12.5 MHz and 32 kB SRAM)
Performance:	20,000 polygons per second (15,000 textured)
Memory:	2 MB DRAM and 1 MB VRAM
Resolution:	640 × 480 (interpolated), 320 × 240 (actual)
Sound:	17-channel, 16-bit stereo (44.1 kHz)

years ahead of anything the Super NES could render with its Super FX chip.

The 3DO "multiplayer" was a stand-alone, CD-ROM system capable of playing more than just video games. DVD technology was still years away, and so VCDs were quite popular on the system—especially in Japan. A single 3DO CD-ROM could contain up to 650–**700 MB of data**, compared to just 4–8 MB of the average Genesis or Super Nintendo cartridge. Its **CD-quality sound** and higher storage capacity allowed for **licensed soundtracks**, as heard with music from White Zombie in *Way of the Warrior* and Soundgarden in *Road Rash*.

Of course, three of the four main consoles from the 16-bit era included CD-ROM add-on units (TurboGrafx-16 and Sega Genesis) or optical disc

versions of the hardware (Neo•Geo), so the concept of optical media was not entirely new. However, the 3DO was much more capable with a separate bus for video refresh updates. Games such as *Sewer Shark* and *Night Trap* displayed on 3DO with fuller FMV and featured better color compared to those same games on Sega CD.

HEAD-TO-HEAD

Compare the 3DO to its 16-bit predecessors. Try *Starfox* (SNES) versus *Total Eclipse* (3DO), *Super Street Fighter II* (SNES/Genesis) against *Super Street Fighter II Turbo* (3DO), *Road Rash* (Genesis vs. 3DO version), and *FIFA International Soccer* (SNES/Genesis vs. 3DO).

■ KEY 3DO TITLES

The 3DO Interactive Multiplayer benefited from an impressive lineup of games published by Electronic Arts, such as *Immercenary, John Madden Football, FIFA International Soccer, Road Rash, The Need for Speed*, and well over a dozen others. **Crystal Dynamics** made a name for itself on 3DO with *Total Eclipse, Star Control II*, and *Gex* (seen in Figure 8.6). Gex was the closest video game character the system got to having a mascot, but Crystal Dynamics later ported the game to other consoles.

FIGURE 8.6 Box art to five defining 3DO titles including (a) *Star Control II*, (b) *Road Rash*, (c) *Gex*, (d) *The Need for Speed*, and (e) *Super Street Fighter II Turbo*.

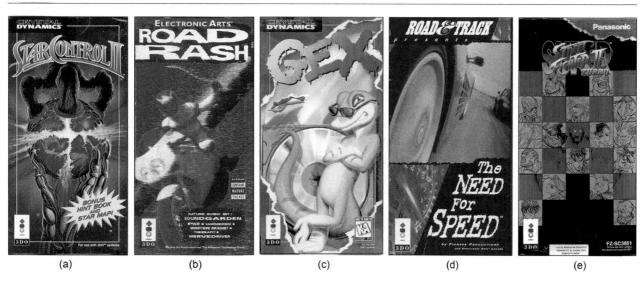

| (a) | (b) | (c) | (d) | (e) |

PRO FILE

Trip Hawkins

KEY FACTS:

Left Apple Computer in 1982 to form Electronic Arts

EA has become one of the largest video game publishers in the world

PRO FILE

HISTORY:
- Born: December 28, 1953 in Pasadena, CA

EDUCATION:
- Designed his own major at Harvard University in Strategy and Applied Game Theory, B.A. in 1976
- MBA from Stanford University in 1978

CAREER HIGHLIGHTS:
- Director of Strategy and Marketing at Apple
- Founded Electronic Arts in 1982, which promoted its game developers, packaged titles like album covers, and was first to license athletes for video games
- Formed 3DO in 1991, which released the most powerful video game console of its time in 1993
- Co-Founder/CEO of mobile game developer Digital Chocolate in 2003 and If You Can Company in 2012

RECOGNITION:
Eighth person inducted into the Academy of Interactive Arts and Sciences' Hall of Fame (2005), Board member/Advisor to more than a dozen organizations

Interplay published important titles on the system including survival horror pioneer *Alone in the Dark, Battle Chess, Wolfenstein 3D,* and *Out of This World*. American Laser Games released around 10 FMV shooters to support its light gun peripheral, while Digital Pictures ported its popular Sega CD games to 3DO, including *Sewer Shark* and *Night Trap*. Ports of popular arcade fighting games including Capcom's *Super Street Fighter II Turbo* and SNK's *Samurai Shodown* were also well-made titles on the system.

More than 150 games were released for the 3DO in North America, with just under 100 reaching PAL territories. More consoles were sold in Asia than in the United States (Kent, 2001, p. 487), with well over 100 additional games released exclusively in Japan. Notable Japanese exclusives included *Doctor Hauzer, Yu Yu Hakusho*, and Hideo Kojima's *Policenauts* (Retro Gamer, 2009, p. 192). North America saw about three dozen exclusive 3DO titles such as *Casper* by Logicware, IntelliPlay's *ESPN* series, ReadySoft's *Brain Dead 13* and *Space Ace*, and every title released by American Laser Games.

> ### ⚲ DID YOU KNOW?
>
> Developer **Naughty Dog** produced its first 32-bit home console game on 3DO with the fighting game *Way of the Warrior* (1994). The game featured fatalities similar to *Mortal Kombat* and music from the White Zombie album *La Sexorcisto: Devil Music, Vol. 1*.

■ ATARI JAGUAR

Atari began work with U.K. computer hardware company **Flare Technology** on its next system around 1989. Flare would go into development on two consoles: a 32-bit system known as the **Atari Panther** to compete in what would become the fourth generation of video games, in addition to its successor—a 64-bit system called **Atari Jaguar** (Figure 8.7). Rapid progress on the Jaguar by Flare engineers **Martin Brennan** and **John Mathieson** resulted in the Panther system's cancelation. After completely missing the last home console market, Atari launched the Jaguar on November 23, 1993, for $249.99. It was released in Japan and Europe the following year.

The engineers built the Jaguar with a total of five main processors contained within three chips. Similar to how the TurboGrafx-16 was marketed as a 16-bit system (even though it only contained an 8-bit CPU), the Jaguar (which contained two 32-bit processors nicknamed "Tom" and "Jerry") was promoted by Atari as a 64-bit system. This created controversy in the gaming world on whether the Jaguar was a true 64-bit system. Atari contributed to this ongoing debate with their advertising, which included the slogan "Do The Math." The system's multiple processors, incomplete developer instructions, and architectural issues made it difficult to program games for the Jaguar, resulting in sparse third-party support.

Atari bundled the system with one controller and a mediocre 3D shooter called *Cybermorph* (Figure 8.8a), which felt like an incomplete prototype. The game

FIGURE 8.7 Atari Jaguar and a standard controller with its numeric keypad.

FIGURE 8.8 Screenshots from Jaguar U.S. launch titles: (a) *Cybermorph* and (b) *Trevor McFur in the Crescent Galaxy*.

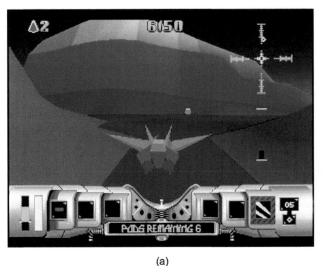

(a)

(b)

contained no in-game music, its polygons lacked detail, and it had a noticeably short **draw distance** where polygonal structures (like mountains) would abruptly pop up in front of the player's spaceship. Other than *Cybermorph*, the only other title available at launch was the side-scrolling shooter *Trevor McFur in the Crescent Galaxy* (Figure 8.8b). *Trevor McFur* also lacked in-game background music and featured no parallax scrolling (common in older, 16-bit shooters). Atari did not release any other titles for the system until after the holidays, when a handful of decent games finally arrived on the market in 1994.

The Jaguar controller contained three main action buttons and two shoulder buttons like the 3DO pad; however, it was quite wide, with curved edges and rounded rolls along the bottom to create an ergonomic feel (Kent, 2001, p. 489). The bottom half of the controller contained a numeric keypad not seen on a game controller since the Atari 5200. This gave the gamepad a unique function that—just like the older consoles—allowed players to clip game-specific overlays onto the keypads. While interesting in theory, most gamers found the controllers to be cumbersome and argued they were inferior to the older, Super NES pads (Szczepaniak, 2009, p. 198). Atari later released the "**ProController**," which added three more action buttons but was just as bulky.

After teasing it for close to 2 years, Atari released a CD-ROM add-on unit called the **Jaguar** CD (pictured in Figure 8.9) on September 21, 1995. Priced $149.95, the Jaguar CD came with two games (*Blue Lightning* and *Vid Grid*), as well as a demo of the game *Myst* and a

CD soundtrack for *Tempest 2000*. The unit sold poorly and only a dozen games officially released for it. Beyond the CD unit, key peripherals for the Jaguar included a **Memory Track** cartridge for saving CD game data, **Team Tap** adapter for players to connect up to four controllers, and a link cable called the **JagLink** for **local area network (LAN)** gaming between two consoles. Only two licensed games utilized the JagLink, including *Doom* and the lesser-known *Aircars*.

☼ **DID YOU KNOW?**

Atari unveiled a "Jaguar VR" virtual reality headset at the 1995 Winter Consumer Electronics Show. An image of the prototype was even pictured in Jaguar advertising, but the peripheral was never released for the console.

■ **CONSOLE COMPARISON:
ATARI JAGUAR VS. 3DO**

While the Atari Jaguar did contain some 64-bit components, it was difficult to justify the system as a completely 64-bit console. Comparing specs on paper, the Jaguar might initially appear to be more powerful than 3DO (Table 8.3). The Jaguar's maximum **720×576** resolution (720×480 on NTSC displays) produced a sharper picture next to the 3DO's 640×480 interpolated display. Atari's **two 32-bit processors** each ran at more than double the speed of the 3DO's single RISC processor and had double the bus bandwidth.

FIGURE 8.9 Part of a 1994 foldout brochure for Atari Jaguar showing the Jaguar CD unit.

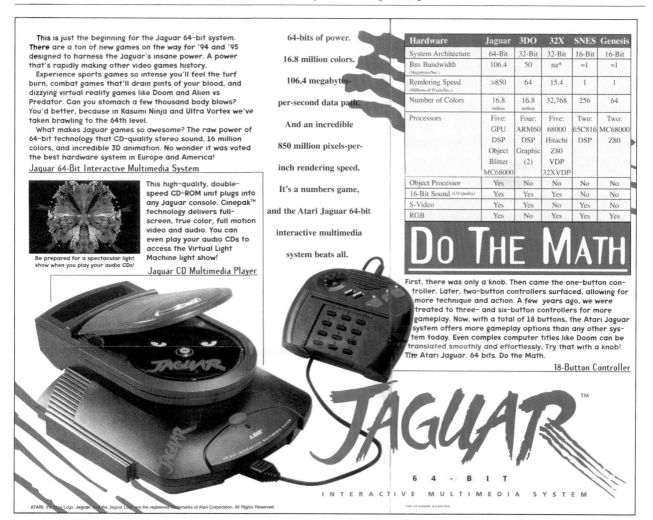

Hardware	Jaguar	3DO	32X	SNES	Genesis
System Architecture	64-Bit	32-Bit	32-Bit	16-Bit	16-Bit
Bus Bandwidth (Megabytes/Sec.)	106.4	50	na*	≈1	≈1
Rendering Speed (Millions of Pixels/Sec.)	>850	64	15.4	1	1
Number of Colors	16.8 million	16.8 million	32,768	256	64
Processors	Five: GPU DSP Object Blitter MC68000	Four: ARM60 DSP Graphic (2)	Five: 68000 Hitachi Z80 VDP 32XVDP	Two: 65C816 DSP	Two: MC68000 Z80
Object Processor	Yes	No	No	No	No
16-Bit Sound (CD Quality)	Yes	Yes	Yes	No	No
S-Video	Yes	Yes	No	Yes	No
RGB	Yes	No	Yes	Yes	Yes

This is just the beginning for the Jaguar 64-bit system. There are a ton of new games on the way for '94 and '95 designed to harness the Jaguar's insane power. A power that's rapidly making other video games history.

Experience sports games so intense you'll feel the turf burn, combat games that'll drain pints of your blood, and dizzying virtual reality games like Doom and Alien vs Predator. Can you stomach a few thousand body blows? You'd better, because in Kasumi Ninja and Ultra Vortex we've taken brawling to the 64th level.

What makes Jaguar games so awesome? The raw power of 64-bit technology that CD-quality stereo sound, 16 million colors, and incredible 3D animation. No wonder it was voted the best hardware system in Europe and America!

Jaguar 64-Bit Interactive Multimedia System

This high-quality, double-speed CD-ROM unit plugs into any Jaguar console. Cinepak™ technology delivers full-screen, true color, full motion video and audio. You can even play your audio CDs to access the Virtual Light Machine light show!

Be prepared for a spectacular light show when you play your audio CDs!

Jaguar CD Multimedia Player

64-bits of power.

16.8 million colors.

106.4 megabytes-per-second data path.

And an incredible 850 million pixels-per-inch rendering speed.

It's a numbers game, and the Atari Jaguar 64-bit interactive multimedia system beats all.

DO THE MATH

First, there was only a knob. Then came the one-button controller. Later, two-button controllers surfaced, allowing for more technique and action. A few years ago, we were treated to three- and six-button controllers for more gameplay. Now, with a total of 18 buttons, the Atari Jaguar system offers more gameplay options than any other system today. Even complex computer titles like Doom can be translated smoothly and effortlessly. Try that with a knob! The Atari Jaguar. 64 bits. Do the Math.

18-Button Controller

ATARI, the Atari Logo, Jaguar, and the Jaguar Logo are the registered trademarks of Atari Corporation. All Rights Reserved.   *data not available at press time.

JAGUAR™

6 4 - B I T
INTERACTIVE MULTIMEDIA SYSTEM

TABLE 8.3 Atari Jaguar Tech Specs

Manufacturer:	Atari
Launch price:	$249.99
Release date:	11/23/93 (US), 6/27/94 (EU), 11/21/94 (JP)
Format:	Cartridge (w/CD add-on)
Processors:	32-bit Custom RISC ("Tom") (26.59 MHz) 32-bit GPU ("Jerry") (26.59 MHz) Motorola MC68000 RISC (13.295 MHz)
Performance:	10,000 polygons per second
Memory:	2 MB main RAM
Resolution:	720 × 576
Sound:	16-bit stereo

On the other hand, the Jaguar was difficult to program for and so programmers were not able to take full advantage of the system's capabilities. Furthermore, its **Motorola MC68000** RISC chip (which functioned as a coprocessor) was "barely superior to past consoles" (Szczepaniak, 2009, p. 197), while the 3DO's CPU was complimented by two accelerated video co-processors that could produce a wide array of effects. Each system tried to be innovative with its controllers. While neither game pad was great, 3DO had a more comfortable controller with the addition of two shoulder buttons and a headphones jack on the original model.

This was the dawn of the 3D generation. Even though both systems were capable of more than 16 million colors, the 3DO could push **twice** the number of **polygons** on screen. Comparing 3D games on both consoles showed a significant difference in performance, with 3DO games pushing more polygons on the screen with more detailed texture mapping. Then there was the obvious difference in the original media format. The 3DO's CD-ROM drive may have added additional loading times to its games but 3DO discs could hold over 100 times more data compared to a **6 MB** Jaguar cartridge. Furthermore, the 3DO's CD-quality soundtracks gave it a major edge in the sound department. Atari would release a CD add-on for the Jaguar nearly two years into its lifecycle, but poor sales, reliability issues, and only about a dozen games meant there was little left to compare.

■ KEY ATARI JAGUAR TITLES

Less than 70 licensed games were released during the initial lifespan of the Jaguar (and that figure includes its CD titles). Among those games were an even smaller number of standout hits. One of its first key titles was an update to arcade classic *Tempest*. *Tempest 2000* was the product of Atari veteran **Jay Miner** and was released on April 1, 1994. October 20th of that year saw the release of *Alien vs. Predator* by **Andrew Whitaker**. This first-person shooter was unique because it "could be played from the perspective of the space parasites from the movie *Alien*, the intergalactic hunter from the movie *Predator*, or a space marine" (Kent, 2001, p. 489).

The system also received excellent ports of id Software's *Wolfenstein 3D* and *Doom*, however, like a handful of other Jaguar titles, *Doom* lacked

background music. Ubisoft's *Rayman* began as a Jaguar exclusive (Retro Gamer Team, 2014, para. 10) and is one of the best side-scrolling titles on the system. It would later be ported to Atari's competition with better CD audio. In addition to the titles depicted in Figure 8.10, Eclipse Software's *Iron Soldier* games were notable first-person mech shooters.

HEAD-TO-HEAD

To compare the graphics and sound between the Jaguar and 3DO, check out *Total Eclipse* (3DO) versus *Cybermorph* (Jaguar), *Killing Time* (3DO) versus *Alien vs. Predator* (Jaguar), plus *Flashback, Soccer Kid*, and *Wolfenstein 3D*, which released on both systems.

■ SEGA 32X

Sega's first entry into the 32-bit arena was the cartridge-based **Sega 32X** (Figure 8.11) by **Joe Miller** and **Martz Franz** from Sega of America. Originally codenamed "Project Mars," the 32X was an add-on unit for the Sega Genesis released toward the end of 1994 in the United States for $159 and in Europe for £169. The add-on unit was also released in Japan. Its two launch titles included *Doom* and *Star Wars Arcade*. Like the Power Base Converter, the 32X plugged into the cartridge slot of the Genesis and had its own slot to insert 32X games. The unit contained two **Hitachi SH2** 32-bit RISC CPUs and a 3D graphics processor that allowed up to 32,768 on-screen colors and could render 50,000 mapped polygons per second.

FIGURE 8.10 Box art to five defining Jaguar titles including (a) *Alien vs. Predator*, (b) *Wolfenstein 3D*, (c) *Rayman*, (d) *Doom*, and (e) *Tempest 2000*.

(a) (b) (c) (d) (e)

FIGURE 8.11 The Sega 32X on the top of a Model II Sega Genesis, on top of a Sega CD II.

The main purpose of the 32X was to give American consumers a low cost, 32-bit experience until the launch of its next stand-alone console. The unit sold out of the nearly 500,000 units shipped during the 1994 holiday season (Business Wire, 1995). Then sales plummeted once consumers learned that 32X games would not be compatible with Sega's next console—which was right around the corner. During the time of its production, American developers were unaware that the 32X would release in the United States just one day before Sega's 32-bit stand-alone system launched in Japan. Only 40 games were officially released for the 32X, and retailers sold off the remaining stock at clearance prices in 1995.

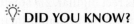 **DID YOU KNOW?**

Sega's decision to use the same Hitachi SH2 CPU chips for both the 32X and Saturn resulted in a chip shortage for Sega of America's 32X development because Sega of Japan prioritized the chips for the Saturn (McFerran, 2018).

■ SEGA SATURN

Sega's 32-bit stand-alone **Sega Saturn** system (Figure 8.12) was launched in Japan on November 22, 1994. Developed by a team supervised by **Hideki Sato** and debuting at 44,800 yen (approximately $469), Sega sold its entire first shipment of 200,000 units thanks to the popularity of launch title *Virtua Fighter* (Kent, 2001, p. 201). A lot of the decisions Sega made for the 32X and Saturn were influenced by news from their competitors, such as the marketing of Atari Jaguar's capabilities and the announcement of an upcoming game console by Sony. Sega initially designed the Saturn to be a powerful 2D console with secondary 3D abilities, capable of emulating their top arcade games of that time. However, news of Sony's 3D architecture sent the company back to the drawing board and Sega completely redesigned the Saturn with "two RISC processors [the same Hitachi SH2 32-bit RISC CPUs as the 32X], along with dual **VPDs [video display processors]**" (McFerran, 2009, pp. 204–206). Like the Jaguar before it, its complex architecture of so

FIGURE 8.12 Sega Saturn with the original U.S./European MK-80100 controller.

many processors (including its rectangular, 2D **sprite-generated polygons**) would make the system difficult to program for.

The Saturn contained 32 kB of internal memory for saving games. It also featured a cartridge slot located just above the CD lid. This was an expansion slot for additional storage. The Japanese market would receive a 1 MB and 4 MB **Extended RAM Cartridge** that enhanced the performance of games such as *Marvel Super Heroes*. Certain titles (mostly fighting games) required a RAM cartridge to play and thus never officially released outside of Japan. Western gamers would eventually be able to purchase an **Action Replay** cartridge, which provided the additional RAM, storage to save games, plus the ability to play import titles.

While the 32X failed to make an impression on Western consumers, the Saturn launch was an enormous success in Japan. Even though the Genesis was still selling well in North America, Sega wanted to carry its momentum with the Saturn to the United States as soon as possible. Saturn had planned a "Saturnday" launch in the United States for Saturday, September 2, 1995. However, about 4 months earlier on May 11th at the **Electronic Entertainment Expo (E3)** video games conference in Los Angeles, Sega president **Tom Kalinske** revealed that the console had secretly been released that very same day (Buchanan, 2008, para. 2).

The surprise announcement caught everyone off guard, including third-party publishers who were still developing games for a September launch—as well as retailers who Sega did not include in the advance release. Sega shipped 30,000 systems to four major retailers comprising Toys "R" Us, Electronics Boutique, Software Etc., and Babbage's. This resulted in Sega losing Kay•Bee Toys, who responded to the exclusion by dropping the Saturn from its catalog all together (Kent, 2001, pp. 516–157). No third-party developed games were available for the launch, resulting in just five launch titles developed and published by Sega (Table 8.4).

The launch price was set to $399, which was lower than its initial cost in Japan, but still considered a high price tag for a video game system in the United States during that time. Sega's early U.S. advertisements for the console had an eccentric, sci-fi theme to them.

TABLE 8.4   Sega Saturn U.S. Launch Titles

- *Clockwork Knight*
- *Daytona USA*
- *Panzer Dragoon* (Figure 8.13a)
- *Virtua Fighter* (Figure 8.13b)
- *Worldwide Soccer: Sega International Victory Goal Edition*

One series of ads featured a bald woman with rings around her head like the planet Saturn. Sega even featured rapper Ice Cube in a Saturn print ad with rings around his head, along with the words "Head For Saturn." This campaign only lasted about a year before Sega shifted to a more traditional marketing approach.

For the Western version of Saturn, Sega changed the color of the system from gray (with blue and dark gray highlights) to all black. The controller looked like the six-button Genesis game pad, with the inclusion of two shoulder buttons. Sega redesigned the pad for North America and Europe to accommodate the larger hands of Western consumers. Known only by its model number, the **MK-80100** controller had the same functionally as the Japanese controller but was slightly larger with a concave D-Pad. Critics often regarded the Western controller to be less comfortable than the Japanese version and Sega began phasing out the MK-80100 in the summer of 1996. The new controller was a black version of the original Japanese Saturn controller, with a traditional D-Pad and a smaller casing. Also like in Japan, the controller came in multiple colors, including black, gray, white, and clear.

For peripherals, Sega released the **Stunner** light gun (known as the "Virtua Gun" in Japan). Its round **3D pad** (designed to work with *NiGHTS into Dreams*) featured an analog control stick. Sega also manufactured a stylish, dual-handle **Arcade Racer** steering wheel. Like Jaguar's Jag Link, Sega introduced a **Play Cable** that could connect two Saturn consoles for multiplayer LAN gaming. Its **Multiplayer Adaptor** allowed players to plug up to six controllers into each main controller port, while the **Sega NetLink** 28.8k modem featured online capabilities such as email and early online gaming with five compatible titles. Other accessories available for the system included a joystick, memory cartridges, plus a keyboard and a mouse.

FIGURE 8.13   Sega Saturn launch titles: (a) *Panzer Dragoon* and (b) *Virtua Fighter.*

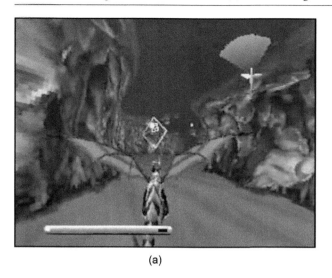

(a)

(b)

■ CONSOLE COMPARISON: SEGA SATURN VS. 3DO AND JAGUAR

Compared to the first wave of fifth-generation consoles, the Saturn had the potential to be a faster system for developers who learned how to take advantage of its **dual 28.63 MHz Hitachi processors** and two video display processors (Table 8.5). The **VDP1** handled sprites, polygons, and geometry, while the **VDP2** managed games' backgrounds (Base Media, 2016, p. 2). Its games often displayed higher frames per second (fps) compared to 3DO and Jaguar games. With dismal sales of the Atari Jaguar, Saturn's main "next-gen" competitor at the time of its release was the 3DO.

When compared to the 3DO, Saturn games typically looked sharper, with displays up to **704×480**

pixels, compared to the 640×480 (interpolated) resolution on the 3DO. The Saturn could display 13–25 times more polygons per second. Combine this power with its smoother framerate, and games released on both systems often looked and played significantly better on Saturn. *Super Street Fighter II* for example, not only contained more frames of animation on the Saturn but also included parallax scrolling missing in the 3DO version of the game. Both 3DO and Saturn had CD-quality sound, but the Saturn had nearly twice the number of sound channels, with **32 channels** of sound for programmers to work with.

HEAD-TO-HEAD

To compare the graphics and sound between the Saturn and 3DO, try (or watch video clips of) *Road Rash, The Need for Speed, Primal Rage*, and *Gex*. Compare Saturn to Jaguar with each console's version of *Rayman, NBA Jam, Worms*, and *Tempest 2000*.

■ KEY SATURN TITLES

According to NPD analyst Mat Piscatella, *Madden NFL 97* was the best-selling Saturn game in the United States, followed by *NiGHTS into Dreams* and *Virtua Fighter 2* (Kohler, 2018). Saturn was also known for exclusive titles such as its *Panzer Dragoon* series (Figure 8.14), as well as strong RPGs *Shining the Holy*

TABLE 8.5   Sega Saturn Tech Specs

Manufacturer:	Sega Electronics
Launch price:	$399.99
Release date:	11/22/94 (JP), 5/10/95 (US), 7/08/95 (EU)
Form at:	CD-ROM (2× speed)
Processors:	2 Hitachi SH2 32-bit CPUs (28.63 MHz)+2 VPDs
Performance:	500,000 polygons per second (200,000 textured)
Memory:	5 MB total RAM
Resolution:	320 × 224, 640 × 224, and 704 × 480 pixels
Sound:	Motorola 68EC000-32-channel, 16-bit stereo at 44.1 kHz

FIGURE 8.14 Magazine advertisement for the Sega Saturn in 1996.

FIGURE 8.15 Box art to five popular Saturn titles including (a) *Shining Force III*, (b) *NiGHTS into Dreams*, (c) *Virtua Fighter 2*, (d) *Panzer Dragoon Saga*, and (e) *Guardian Heroes*.

(a)   (b)   (c)   (d)   (e)

Ark and *Shining Force III* (Figure 8.15), *Magic Knight RayEarth,* and *Dragon Force*. It was the strongest console for 2D platformers such as *Astal* and numerous 2D shoot 'em ups, along with being the best platform to play 2D fighters such as *Marvel Super Heroes* and *Street Fighter Alpha 3*. Furthermore, Saturn was the only system in which gamers could play *NiGHTS into Dreams*, the new title by *Sonic the Hedgehog* creator **Yuji Naka** and **Sonic Team**.

Unfortunately, the Saturn also became known for the games it did not receive. After many development struggles, Sega ended up canceling *Sonic X-treme*, leaving the Saturn without an exclusive *Sonic the Hedgehog* platformer. The console only received a graphically enhanced port of the Genesis game *Sonic 3D Blast*, a compilation game called *Sonic Jam*, and the racing title *Sonic R* (McFerran, 2009, p. 208). Because the system was not as popular in the West, excellent Saturn titles such as *Radiant Silvergun, Keio Flying Squadron 2, Princess Crown*, and *X-Men vs. Street Fighter* remained Japanese exclusives. Even Saturn's *Akumajou Dracula X: Gekka no Yasoukyoku* (*Castlevania: Symphony of the Night*) did not release outside of Japan. More than 1,000 games were released for Sega Saturn and 75% of them never reached Western shores.

■ CHANGES AT SEGA

While Saturn sales remained strong in Japan, the system struggled in the United States and Sega of Japan officials blamed Sega of America for its problems. In America, Sega sold over 2 million Genesis systems in 1995 and did not have enough units to meet the holiday demand. According to Sega of America president and CEO Tom Kalinske, Sega could have sold an additional 300,000 Genesis systems between November and December of that year if the company had not been so focused on the Saturn (Business Wire, 1996, p. 1). Kalinske reportedly began to feel powerless after long-standing disagreements like this with Sega of Japan and announced his resignation on July 15, 1996 (Kent, 2001, p. 535). Soon after that, Sega co-founder **David Rosen** would resign that same year.

■ SONY PLAYSTATION

Sony Corporation was founded in 1946 by **Akio Morita** and **Masaru Ibuka**. Similar to Sega ("Service Games") and Famicom ("Family Computer"), the name "Sony" comes from a combination of two words: "**so**nus," which is Latin for sonic and sound, and "son**ny**," which was a slang word for "boy" in the United States (Sony Japan, 2011, p. 1). Sony became a leading electronics manufacturer from its electronic innovations and diversified business ventures. After its success with manufacturing transistor radios, Sony invented the world's first portable music player with the **Sony Walkman** in 1979. The company went on to pioneer video formats **Betamax** and **Video8**, its own line of computers, **3.5-inch floppy disks**, as well as **Digital Audio Tape (DAT)** in the 1980s. Sony was also one of the leading developers of **Compact Disc (CD)** and later **Blu-ray Disc** optical disc formats. The company had a foot in just about all consumer

FIGURE 8.16 The Sony PlayStation video game console with original D-pad controller.

electronics by the late 1980s and the home video game market would be next.

The **Sony PlayStation** (Figure 8.16) was designed by engineer **Ken Kutaragi** (who also developed the SNES sound chip). It originally began as a CD-ROM expansion unit for the Super Famicom in 1988, where "Sony made sure that it held the sole international licensing rights—in other words, it would profit handsomely from every single SNES CD-ROM title that was sold" (McFerran, 2010, p. 47). Nintendo had second thoughts about the deal but still "allowed Sony to announce plans for the drive at the [1991] Consumer Electronics Show, then appeared the next day to say that they had struck up a deal with Philips" (Kent, 2001, p. 452). The embarrassment from Nintendo's announcement, coupled with the time and money Sony had invested in the PlayStation provoked Sony president **Norio Ohga** and Kutaragi to continue developing the project as a stand-alone system.

After years of development and the newly formed **Sony Computer Entertainment (SCE)** division, the Sony released the PlayStation on December 3, 1994, in Japan and in the United States on September 9, 1995, for $299. The console reached Europe later that month. The system did not initially include a launch title but did come packed with a **demo disc** containing samples of several games. Due to the low cost of CD-ROMs, these demo discs became a popular medium for advertising, leading to Sony's **PlayStation Underground** disc series featuring demos, articles, interviews, game trailers, and more. Other publications on CDs soon followed.

While its 10 launch titles included a handful of 2D games (see Table 8.6), Sony built the PlayStation to be a 3D powerhouse. Its single processing chip contained a 3D geometry engine in its CPU, which made PlayStation an easy system to program games for, and a liberal $10 per game licensing fee helped Sony attract nearly 100 game companies by the time the system launched in the United States (Kent, 2001, p. 504). Sony aggressively pursued third-party developers, obtaining the support of Sega rival Namco (*Tekken, Ridge Racer*) and acquiring the Liverpool-based developer **Psygnosis** (*Destruction Derby, WipEout*). Executive Vice President of Sony Computer Entertainment of America **Bernie Stolar** also helped secure key third-party deals.

Another part of Sony's marketing strategy was to appeal to the specific age of 19. Executive Vice President of SCE Europe **Phil Harrison** (2005) explained that the idea behind the strategy was that younger teenagers wished they were 19, while older adults often wished they were 19 (again) as well. Early marketing slogans were clever secret messages created to get gamers talking about the system. For example, "ENOS Lives" was basically SONY written backward. A second interpretation was "Ready Ninth of September," with the red E meaning 'ready' and 'NOS'

TABLE 8.6 Sony PlayStation U.S. Launch Titles

- *Battle Arena Toshinden* (Figure 8.17a)
- *ESPN Extreme Games*
- *Kileak: The DNA Imperative*
- *NBA Jam Tournament Edition*
- *Power Serve 3D Tennis*
- *Raiden Project*
- *Rayman*
- *Ridge Racer* (Figure 8.17b)
- *Street Fighter: The Movie*
- *Total Eclipse Turbo*

FIGURE 8.17 Screenshots from PS launch titles: (a) *Battle Arena Toshinden* and (b) *Ridge Racer*.

(a)

(b)

standing for 'Ninth of September' (Oravasaari, 2012, para. 2). A third slogan "U R NOT **E**" was easier for consumers to decode.

Aesthetically, the system was sleek and simplistic with circular buttons and a circular disc lid (Figure 8.18). Its light gray color was reminiscent of previous Nintendo consoles and helped it stand out where all the other new systems were shades of black (save for the Japanese version of Saturn). Even its controller looked like an enhanced SNES controller with its face buttons layout and shoulder triggers—adding two additional shoulder buttons, comfortable handles, and a unique D-Pad, which was comprised of four separate directional buttons. Above the controller ports on the system were two **memory card** slots where players could insert separate memory cards for saving game data. Like its CD-based predecessors, the PlayStation could also play music CDs in addition to games.

The PlayStation received the standard array of peripherals, including memory cards, light guns such as Namco's **GunCon**, joysticks, steering wheels, and other third-party controllers. There were also dance pads available for games like *Dance Dance Revolution*, **Multitap** adaptors, link cables, and more. Eventually, Sony unveiled its **DualShock controller** in 1997, which added touch-sensitive control and a vibration feature made popular by Nintendo's fifth-generation system discussed later in this chapter. In 2000, Sony released a more compact version of the console branded the

PSone (Figure 8.19). There was also a "Combo" version of the PSone featuring its own LCD screen.

🔅 DID YOU KNOW?

Many PlayStation and Saturn games (plus other CD-ROM systems) used standard **redbook audio** tracks for sound. Specifically, consumers could listen to audio tracks (often an entire game's soundtrack) by inserting the game disc into a standard CD player.

■ CONSOLE COMPARISON: SONY PLAYSTATION VS. SEGA SATURN

Table 8.7 summarizes the major technical specifications of the Sony PlayStation. Unlike the Sega Saturn (and even 3DO), the PlayStation did not contain any internal storage, making the purchase of a memory card mandatory for players to save game data. True to the nature of how the manufacturers conceived the machines, Saturn was the more powerful system for 2D games (such as *Marvel vs. Capcom*), while the PlayStation typically delivered better 3D games (as seen in *WipEout*). One reason Sega's machine fared better in Japan was its Extended RAM Cartridges, which enhanced dozens of games, particularly fighting games by Capcom and SNK.

Technically, Saturn was the more powerful system with more total RAM, higher screen resolution, greater polygon counts, and 25% more sound channels to work with. However, its complex, dual-processor

FIGURE 8.18 1995 PlayStation magazine ad featuring Sofia from *Battle Arena Toshinden*.

architecture made the Saturn difficult to program for and much of its power often went underutilized. Sony's single processor ran at **33.8688 MHz**—slightly faster than either of Saturn's Hitachi processors but when effectively used in tandem with its dual VDPs, Saturn was a faster machine.

What really gave the PlayStation the edge was that it contained a built-in special effects processor. For instance, the PlayStation could generate effects including **transparency** and **Gouraud shading** (which gave graphics a smoother, more detailed look) with minimal impact on the system's performance. For Saturn

FIGURE 8.19 The smaller "PSone" with matching DualShock controller and memory card.

TABLE 8.7 Sony PlayStation Tech Specs

Manufacturer:	Sony Computer Entertainment
Launch price:	$299.99
Release date:	12/03/94 (JP), 9/09/95 (US), 9/29/95 (EU)
Format:	CD-ROM (2× speed)
Processor:	32-bit MIPS R3000A RISC CPU (33.8688 MHz)
Performance:	360,000 polygons per second (180,000 textured)
Memory:	2 MB main RAM, 1 MB video RAM, 512 kB sound RAM
Resolution:	256 × 224 to 640 × 480
Sound:	24-channel, 16-bit stereo at 44.1 kHz

HEAD-TO-HEAD

To compare the graphics and sound between PlayStation and Saturn, check out (or watch video clips of) *Marvel vs. Capcom*, *WipEout*, *Tomb Raider*, and *Dead or Alive*.

■ KEY PLAYSTATION TITLES

Ease of programming and aggressive marketing helped Sony lock down a parade of quality titles. Thousands of games released for the PlayStation worldwide. Key series were born on and/or exclusive to the system and spawned two or more sequels, such as *Tekken*, *Crash Bandicoot*, *Spyro the Dragon*, and *Twisted Metal*. *Tomb Raider* helped revolutionize 3D platformers and Laura Croft (shown in Figure 8.20) became synonymous with the system, with certain *Tomb Raider* sequels exclusive to PlayStation on the home console market.

One of the most pivotal acquisitions for Sony was when RPG developer **SquareSoft** abandoned Nintendo, selecting the PlayStation as the sole console for its epic *Final Fantasy* series. *Final Fantasy VII* was so massive that it required the use of three CDs. SquareSoft followed *FFVII* with other exclusive titles including *Final Fantasy VIII* and *IX*, *Xenogears*, *Chrono Cross*, *Einhänder*, *Parasite Eve*, and more. To top it off, **Konami** chose the system for hits *Metal Gear Solid* and *Silent Hill*, while Sony Computer Entertainment's *Gran Turismo* racing games became the company's best-selling series of all time, shipping more than 20 million units combined.

to emulate similar effects, the system had to pull extra processing power, which often meant programmers had to lower their games' resolution to 320×224 or abandon such effects altogether. The PlayStation also used triangular polygons, which were more efficient compared to the Saturn's quadrilaterals.

FIGURE 8.20 Box art to five defining PlayStation titles including (a) *Resident Evil*, (b) *Final Fantasy VII*, (c) *Tomb Raider*, (d) *Metal Gear Solid*, and (e) *Tekken 3*.

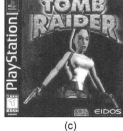

(a)　　　(b)　　　(c)　　　(d)　　　(e)

FIGURE 8.21 Nintendo Virtual Boy.

■ VIRTUAL BOY

A year before Nintendo's next home console launch, the company released its **Virtual Boy** (Figure 8.21), a portable, 32-bit tabletop console capable of displaying monochrome 3D graphics using red LED technology. The system was developed by **Gunpei Yokoi** (Game & Watch, Game Boy) who "looked into making a color version of the technology but found that it would have to retail for over $500, far too expensive" (Kent, 2001, p. 514). The resulting red and black head-mounted display became notorious for causing dizziness, nausea, and headaches. The system was a commercial failure and discontinued in less than a year.

■ NINTENDO 64

Nintendo's next home console would go through a couple of name changes over the course of its development. Originally called "Project Reality" (based on the name of its coprocessor), the system became known as "Ultra 64" for quite some time before Nintendo changed the name to **Nintendo 64 (N64)** before its launch in Japan on June 23, 1996. Despite the Virtual Boy's failure, the N64 (Figure 8.22) sold its entire launch inventory of 300,000 units in Japan, and all 500,000 launch units in the United States the following fall.

Originally scheduled to release in North America on September 30, 1996, for $249.99, the system was released 1–3 days earlier for just $199.99. The price drop followed Sony, who had recently dropped the price of

FIGURE 8.22 The Nintendo 64 with its unique, three-handle controller.

FIGURE 8.23   Screenshots from N64 U.S. launch titles: (a) *Super Mario 64* and (b) *Pilotwings 64.*

(a)   (b)

the PlayStation to $199. Only two titles were available for the U.S. release, including *Super Mario 64* and *Pilotwings 64* (Figure 8.23). Despite having only two games at launch, both were strong titles. Marketing slogans used for the console included "Change the System" and "Get N, or get Out!" Nintendo released the console in Europe and Australia on March 1, 1997. See Figure 8.24 for a magazine advertisement announcing Nintendo's original North American launch date.

TurboGrafx-16 and PC manufacturer **NEC** developed the system's 64-bit CPU, along with its "**Reality**" **coprocessor** (RCP) by **Silicon Graphics, Inc.** (SGI). Its 93.75 MHz main processor was the fastest on the home console market. The Reality coprocessor consisted of a Reality Signal Processor (RSP) and Reality Display Processor (RDP) providing enhancements not seen on other consoles such as **real-time lighting** effects and **anti-aliasing** (edge smoothening). The system also included four controller ports—something not seen on a home console since the Atari 5200. Like Sega Saturn, Nintendo included a memory expansion slot between the power and reset buttons, where players could insert an **Expansion Pak** to increase the console's RAM from 4 to 8 MB—which enhanced certain games.

With Sega and Sony adopting CD format for their consoles, Nintendo built the N64 to play cartridge games. As Nintendo's vice president of marketing **Peter Main** explained, "The choice we made is not cartridge versus CD, it's silicon over optical. When it comes to speed, no other format approaches the silicon-based cartridge" (GamePro, 1994, p. 170). In addition to speed, it was an ideal format for younger gamers who were more prone to scratching CDs. Cartridges could also save data internally with a battery, without the need for an external memory card. While more expensive to manufacture, "Nintendo still controlled their production, [and] profited directly from every one made. Cartridges were also harder to pirate, which is likely to be another reason for sticking with that format" (Retro Gamer, 2009, p. 221).

While it may have made sense at the time, the N64 would become the last major home console to use cartridges as its primary media format until the Nintendo Switch was released two decades later. Nintendo's decision to stay with the cartridge format for the N64 was not without its controversy. It was the main reason SquareSoft moved to the PlayStation for *Final Fantasy VII* and other titles. Gamers saw CD-ROM technology as the future, with its 700 MB storage capacity, superb audio, and full motion video capabilities. The average N64 cartridge was only 8–24 MB, with its largest game pack being Capcom's *Resident Evil 2,* which was 64 MB.

One of the most distinguishing features of the N64 was its three-pronged, M-shaped controller designed by Nintendo's R&D3 team. The left handle housed a traditional D-Pad and left shoulder trigger, the center handle provided access to the digital "**control stick**" and center "Z" trigger, and the right handle housed

FIGURE 8.24 Magazine advertisement for the Nintendo 64 gaming console from 1996.

ON SEPTEMBER 30th, DINOSAURS WILL FLY!

Because on that day, the home entertainment world starts spinning at 64 bits —
faster than any video game system or personal computer ever made. Live your dream:
Nintendo 64 and its revolutionary 3-D controller will send you as far into the game as you dare to go.
Over the top. Out on the edge. Choose your hero: *James Bond, Ken Griffey, Jr.,*
Super Mario. Or even *Darth Vader.* You'll find them on games
exclusive to Nintendo 64. Players will rock. Competitors will weep.

Is it worth the wait?

Only if you want the best!

♪♫ NINTENDO.⁶⁴   (Nintendo)

the "A" and "B" buttons, four smaller "C" buttons, and a right shoulder trigger. The underside of the controller included an expansion slot where players could insert accessories such as the **Controller Pak** for saving data, the **Rumble Pak,** which provided force feedback, as well as the **Transfer Pak** for moving game data between Game Boy and N64. Nintendo designed the controller for gamers to hold in multiple ways and its complexity may have been intimidating for casual players. Complexity aside, its touch-sensitive (analog-style) control stick and force feedback revolutionized the future of video game controllers.

Aside from the numerous "Pak" add-ons, the N64 did not have a wide variety of peripherals. Key accessories included a cleaning kit, **Glove Controller** (like the NES Power Glove), **Voice Recognition Unit (VRU),** which was only compatible with two games, a mouse (available as a pack-in with *Mario Artist*), and the **Nintendo 64 Disk Drive (64DD)** add-on unit. The 64DD used 64 MB magnetic disks and featured rewritable data storage, a real-time clock (RTC), and Internet connection but only received 10 software titles and was never released outside of Japan.

☼ DID YOU KNOW?

While the Nintendo 64's digital control stick revolutionized video game controllers and developed the standard for playing 3D games, it was not the first console with a touch-sensitive control stick. That credit goes to the Atari 5200.

▪ CONSOLE COMPARISON: NINTENDO 64 VS. SONY PLAYSTATION

The Nintendo 64 controller was innovative for its time with its M-shaped configuration and its touch-sensitive digital control stick. However, the control stick tended to loosen over time—something that was not much of a problem with the PlayStation's Dual Shock controller sticks. Furthermore, the N64 controller required players to insert the separate Rumble Pak accessory into the controller's memory cartridge slot for vibration feedback, whereas the PlayStation's Dual Shock had the force feedback feature built in. On the contrary, the N64 had four controller ports, whereas Sony's system only contained two.

TABLE 8.8	Nintendo 64 Tech Specs
Manufacturer:	Nintendo
Launch price:	$199.99
Release date:	6/23/96 (JP), 9/29/96 (US), 3/01/97 (EU & AU), 12/10/97 (BR)
Format:	Cartridge
Processors:	64-bit NEC VR4300 CPU (93.75 MHz) Reality coprocessor (RCP) for GFX and sound (62.5 MHz)
Performance:	100,000 polygons per second in Fast3D (up to 160,000 PPS)
Memory:	4 MB RDRAM (expandable to 8 MB with Expansion Pak)
Resolution:	256×224, 320×240, and 640×480 pixels
Sound:	100-channel, 16-bit stereo at 44.1 kHz (up to 48 kHz)

On the inside, Nintendo 64's **NEC VR4300** processor (Table 8.8) made it the fastest system on the market at **93.75 MHz**—2.77 times the clock rate of the PlayStation. Both consoles could run games at low and high resolutions (up to 640×480). The N64 had more random access memory, with **4 MB** versus Sony's 2 MB. Like Saturn, players could increase the N64's RAM with an external Expansion Pak. Nintendo's system ran at 4.26 times the bus speed and its 64-bit **graphics processing unit (GPU)** was also more powerful. Sticking with cartridge format meant that N64 games benefited from next to no loading times versus CD-ROM games; however, their smaller storage space meant less quality sound and inferior full motion video. Titles that appeared on both systems often had lower quality music, less dialog, and sometimes omitted FMV altogether on the N64 version.

For other memory, the N64 only had **4 kB** of **texture memory**, compared to 512 kB for textures on Saturn and PlayStation's 1 MB of dedicated video memory. "This meant that developers had to make serious concessions in texture design. Two common solutions were to either tile small textures across a surface or resort to Gouraud shading of polygons instead of proper textures" (White, 2014, para. 10). By comparison, the Saturn and PlayStation could push far more textured polygons.

The N64 contained better texture filters such as anti-aliasing, which smoothened the edges of otherwise jagged graphics. Nintendo's advantages led to better-looking fantasy-themed games while Sony's strengths led to better realistic-looking games. Comparing similar titles on each system, Saturn and PlayStation games often ran at smoother frame rates and looked sharper but more pixilated, while N64 games had a smoother (occasionally blurry) look to them and sometimes sacrificed frame rate for better graphics. For gamers, the debate on which system had better graphics was a matter of personal preference.

HEAD-TO-HEAD

Compare the graphics and sound between the N64 and PlayStation by playing (or watching video clips of) *A Bug's Life, Mortal Kombat 4, Quake II, Rayman 2, Resident Evil 2, Spider-Man, Tony Hawk's Pro Skater 2,* and *Toy Story 2.*

■ KEY NINTENDO 64 TITLES

Just under 400 games were released for the N64, with the majority of titles reaching Western shores. British developer of *Battletoads* and *Donkey Kong Country,* **Rareware** (Rare) created many of the best games on the system. "From the regal beauty and genius of the *Banjo-Kazooie* games, the addictiveness of *Diddy Kong Racing,* to the offbeat destructive nature of *Blast Corps,* and the frantic bug blast of *Jet Force Gemini,* Rare games were held in high esteem and rivaled the releases of Nintendo itself" (Retro Gamer, 2009, p. 222). The company was responsible for the hit fighting game *Killer Instinct Gold,* the hilariously mature 3D platformer *Conker's Bad Fur Day,* in addition to two of the best first-person shooters on the system with *Goldeneye 007* and *Perfect Dark* (Figure 8.25).

Other major third-party support came from companies including **Acclaim** (*Turok, Extreme-G*), Electronic Arts (*Madden, FIFA*), Konami (*International Superstar Soccer, Castlevania*), and **Midway** (*Mortal Kombat, NFL Blitz*). **Treasure** only produced a few titles for the system but each one was superb, such as *Mischief Makers* and *Sin and Punishment* (Japan).

Nintendo developed many first-party classics for the console, with *Super Mario 64* and *The Legend of Zelda: Ocarina of Time* quickly becoming two of the highest rated video games of all time. Other first-party hits included *The Legend of Zelda: Majora's Mask, Wave Race 64, 1080° Snowboarding, Star Fox 64, F-Zero X, Pilotwings 64,* and *Mario Kart 64.* Nintendo also published *Excitebike 64* by Left Field Productions, Hudson's *Mario Party* series, in addition to *Super Smash Bros.* and several *Pokémon* games by HAL Laboratory.

FIGURE 8.25 Box art to five defining Nintendo 64 titles: (a) *The Legend of Zelda: Ocarina of Time,* (b) *Perfect Dark,* (c) *Super Mario 64,* (d) *Goldeneye 007,* and (e) *Banjo-Kazooie.*

(a)　　　　　(b)　　　　　(c)

(d)　　　　　(e)

■ HANDHELD SNAPSHOT: GAME BOY COLOR

The **Game Boy Color** (GBC) (Figure 8.26) was released in Japan on October 21, 1998, and in other countries the following month. It retailed in the United States for just $79.99. This was the first **backward-compatible** handheld system, able to play all the original Game Boy games. The system even included a feature that allowed players to add colors to the four shades of gray when playing monochrome Game Boy titles.

The GBC launched in the West with four titles: *Centipede, Game & Watch Gallery 2, Pocket Bomberman,* and *Tetris DX.* While the system did not contain a backlit screen or enhanced resolution, it could display up to 56 colors on screen from a palette of 32,768 colors. Its CPU could run twice as fast and contained three times more RAM than the original Game Boy (Table 8.9).

The GBC was compatible with the original Game Link Cable for linking two systems together. It also included an **infrared (IR) communications port** for wireless linking but only around 17 games supported this feature. More than 900 games were officially released for the GBC in what would prove to be a very divided market between the East and the West.

More than 350 GBC titles released exclusively in Japan, with an even greater number of games that only released in the West. Examples of GBC series that stayed in Japan included *Beatmania, Dance Dance Revolution, Doraemon,* the *Hamster* games, *Nakayoshi Cooking* and *Pet* series, and the *Wizardry* RPGs. Games series that were exclusive to Western markets included *Barbie, Disney, Lego,* and various sports titles.

FIGURE 8.26   Game Boy Color featuring *Pokémon Crystal.*

Nintendo included the GBC sales figures within the 18 million units sold with the original Game Boy. It was the best-selling handheld system of its time as the GBC's strong library of games (Figure 8.27) totally eclipsed the rest of the portable market. Competitors included Sega's Genesis-based **Nomad,** Tiger's **R-Zone** and **Game.com** handhelds, as well as the **Neo•Geo Pocket,** and Bandai's Japan-only **WonderSwan.**

TABLE 8.9   Game Boy Color Tech Specs

Format:	Cartridge/2 AA batteries (20 hours)
Processor:	8-bit Sharp LR35902 CPU (4.194 or 8.338 MHz)
Memory:	32 kB RAM, 16 kB Video RAM
Resolution:	160 × 144 pixels/3.5″ diagonal LCD screen
Colors:	10, 32, or 56 from a palette of 32,768 colors
Sound:	4-channel stereo/3.5 mm headphones jack

FIGURE 8.27   Five defining Game Boy Color titles: (a) *Legend of Zelda: Oracle of Seasons,* (b) *Bionic Commando: Elite Forces,* (c) *Pokémon Crystal Version,* (d) *Metal Gear Solid,* and (e) *Wario Land 3.*

(a)　　　　　(b)　　　　　(c)　　　　　(d)　　　　　(e)

■ FIFTH-GENERATION MARKET SUMMARY

Not since the second generation of video games has the market seen so many console releases—many of which never reached American shores (see Figure 8.28). Among those examined in this chapter, 3DO's unique business model may have been its biggest downfall. While the $3 royalty fee for each game sold benefited software manufacturers, it was not high enough to compensate for the high price of the console's manufacturing costs. The small royalties collected also did not provide enough funding for strong marketing (Retro Gamer, 2009, p. 190). Furthermore, having three manufacturers producing the same console put them in competition with each other for the same product, which did not make sense to either consumers or retailers.

The Atari Jaguar outsold the 3DO initially, but ended up being a complete market failure, selling only around 250,000 units worldwide. Beyond its architectural complexity, which made it difficult to program games for, everything from the Tramiel family's business choices to Atari just not being a large enough force anymore to compete have been blamed for the console's demise (Szczepaniak, 2009, p. 200). In its 1995 fiscal year-end report, Atari (1995) attributed the poor performance of Jaguar to extensive delays in game development, consumer concern as to when Atari would make titles available, and "the introduction of competing products by Sega and Sony in May 1995 and September 1995, respectively" (p. 3). Market success in the video game industry comes down to great games, and the Jaguar had very few.

In retrospect,

> concentrating on Saturn proved to be a tactical mistake that cost Sega millions, if not billions, of dollars at the end of 1995. According to TRST data released in 1997, 32-bit products made up less than 20 percent of 1995 video game sales, while 16-bit sales accounted for approximately 64 percent of the market.
>
> *(Kent, 2001, p. 531)*

Following the departure of Kalinske and Rosen, Sega reached out to executive vice president of Sony Computer Entertainment of America, Bernie Stolar, who would become Sega of America's next president and chief operating officer. Stolar did not hesitate to point out "major mistakes [that] had been made by Sega with the Saturn's design and the subsequently

---

FIGURE 8.28 A look at less-popular fifth-generation consoles released outside of the United States.

Fujitsu FM Towns Marty
February 1993 (Japan)

Commodore Amiga CD32
September 1993 (Europe+)

Bandai Playdia
September 1994 (Japan)

NEC PC-FX
December 1994 (Japan)

Casio Loopy
October 1995 (Japan)

Apple Bandai Pippin
March 1996 (Japan)

FIGURE 8.29 Fifth-generation console sales graph.

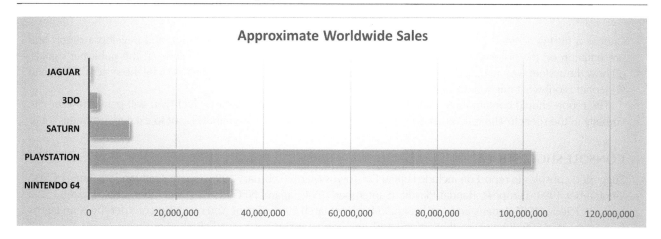

fragmented marketing of platforms and sub-plat-forms" (Fahs, 2009, p. 8). His mission was to discontinue the Saturn system as smoothly as possible. In 1998 Sega of America laid off 30% of its U.S. workforce.

The millions of dollars Sony spent on acquiring developers and on marketing paid off. Within just 2 days of its launch in North America, the PlayStation sold more units than the Saturn had in the 5 months following its surprise launch, completely selling out its initial shipment of 100,000 units (Kent, 2001, pp. 519–520). Within its first year, the PlayStation secured over 20% of the entire U.S. video game market (Finn, 2002, p. 50). For its first system, Sony's PlayStation dominated the industry, eventually making Sony the new leader of the home console market (see Figure 8.29).

The Nintendo 64 was "the top-selling system in America for each of the eight months since its introduction" (Business Wire, 1997). It was most popular in North America, selling more than 20 million of 30+ million units sold in the United States. Still, Nintendo found itself in a distant second place under Sony after being a market leader in the previous two generations. Much of Nintendo's struggle was due to its cartridge format, which led to the loss of SquareSoft and sparse support from Capcom and Namco. The system did not cater to adult consumers as well as Sony's console, and featured a lower number of quality role-playing games. N64 cartridges also typically cost around $10 more than CD games. "By August 1997, Nintendo controlled 40 percent of the next-generation console market and Sony controlled 47 percent, leaving Sega with a mere 12 percent" (Kent, 2001, p. 558).

■ FIFTH-GENERATION BREAKTHROUGHS AND TRENDS

There were unique breakthroughs and trends that defined the fifth generation of video games. Here is a list of the top 10 features that defined the generation:

1. 32-bit and 64-bit microprocessors

2. Higher display resolution (typically 640 × 480 pixels, i.e., 480i)

3. 3D polygon graphics with texture mapping

4. Optical disc (CD-ROM) game media (leading to "demo disc" marketing)

5. Full motion video (FMV) animation and live action footage

6. CD-quality audio (16-bit, 44.1 kHz)

7. Color depth up to 16,777,216 colors (24-bit true color)

8. Texture lighting and Gouraud (continuous, interpolated) shading

9. Graphics smoothening such as anti-aliasing and texture filtering

10. Analog stick (touch-sensitive) controllers

■ ACTIVITY: FAILED CONSOLES REPORT AND PRESENTATION II

Choose a fifth-generation home console or handheld system that was a market failure and develop a report and presentation on the history, business, and technology of that system. Be sure to include (1) the publisher's goals, (2) how the system was marketed, (3) technical specifications and notable game titles, (4) why the system failed, and (5) [conclusion] what might have saved the console from its demise.

The report should contain three main points and a minimum of *two* quotes which you will paraphrase or cite verbally in the speech. The recommended total presentation length is 4:30 minutes, not to exceed 5 minutes total.

CONSOLE SUGGESTIONS

Suggested consoles to report on include Fujitsu FM Towns Marty (February 1993, Japan), Commodore Amiga CD32 (September 1993, Europe+), Bandai Playdia (September 1994, Japan), NEC PC-FX (December 1994, Japan), Casio Loopy (October 1995, Japan), and Apple Bandai Pippin (March 1996, Japan). You may also consider the Atari Jaguar CD (September 1995); however, that was an add-on peripheral and not a stand-alone console.

HANDHELD SUGGESTIONS

Suggested handheld systems to report on include Genesis Nomad (October 1995), R-Zone (1995), Virtual Boy (August 1995), Game.com (September 1997), NeoGeo Pocket (October 1998, Japan), and WonderSwan (March 1999, Japan).

■ CHAPTER 8 QUIZ

1. Sega's first polygonal racing and fighting arcade games that helped pioneer the genre:
   a. *Hard Drivin'* and *Pit Fighter*
   b. *Ridge Racer* and *Tekken*
   c. *Virtua Racing* and *Virtua Fighter*
   d. *Mario Kart* and *Smash Bros.*

2. The arcade mega complex GameWorks was formed by three companies, except:
   a. Steven Spielberg's Dreamworks
   b. Sega Enterprises
   c. Sony Pictures
   d. Universal Studios

3. Who was *not* directly responsible for creating the 3DO Interactive Multiplayer?
   a. Atari Lynx designer Dave Needle
   b. Atari Lynx designer R. J. Mical
   c. Electronic Arts founder Trip Hawkins.
   d. Panasonic founder Konosuke Matsushita

4. Which of the following was *not* a trait of the 3DO Interactive Multiplayer system?
   a. The first fifth-generation, 32-bit console
   b. Original launch price of $299.99
   c. 3DO did not manufacture its own hardware
   d. No regional copy protection on its games

5. In addition to the 64-bit Jaguar, Atari was initially planning a 32-bit console called:
   a. Leopard
   b. Lynx
   c. Panther
   d. Tiger

6. Which of these reasons has been blamed for Jaguar's sparse third-party support?
   a. Complex, multiple processor architecture
   b. Incomplete developer instructions
   c. Both a and b
   d. None of the above

7. To give North American gamers a 32-bit experience before the U.S. launch of Saturn, Sega introduced an add-on to the Sega Genesis called the:
   a. 32X
   b. Nomad
   c. Power Base Converter
   d. None of the above

8. Due to Saturn's early launch in the United States, which store did not carry the system?
   a. Toys "R" Us
   b. Kay•Bee Toys
   c. Electronics Boutique
   d. Software Etc.

9. Who was the main designer of the Sony PlayStation?
   a. Konosuke Matsushita
   b. Akio Morita
   c. Masaru Ibuka
   d. Ken Kutaragi

10. Which game publisher produced *Final Fantasy VII* as a PlayStation exclusive?
    a. Namco
    b. SquareSoft
    c. Psygnosis
    d. Rareware

11. Prior to launching the N64, Nintendo released a portable, 32-bit tabletop console capable of displaying monochrome 3D graphics using red LED technology called:
    a. Game Boy Color
    b. Project Reality
    c. Ultra 32
    d. Virtual Boy

12. Why did Nintendo stay with a cartridge format for the N64?
    a. Cartridges were harder to copy/pirate
    b. Faster to boot up/with little to no load times
    c. Production control/profit
    d. All of the above

13. Had exclusive titles NiGHTS into Dreams, Panzer Dragoon Saga, and Guardian Heroes:
    a. 3DO
    b. Saturn
    c. PlayStation
    d. Nintendo 64

14. Which two consoles included internal storage memory for saving game data?
    a. 3DO and Jaguar
    b. Jaguar and Saturn
    c. Saturn and 3DO
    d. PlayStation and Nintendo 64

15. Based its marketing campaign on targeting gamers around the age of 19:
    a. Panasonic REAL 3DO
    b. Sega Saturn
    c. Sony PlayStation
    d. Nintendo 64

16. This console's controllers included 3.5 mm headphones jacks and could also be "daisychained" for multiplayer gaming:
    a. Sega Saturn
    b. Nintendo 64
    c. Sony PlayStation
    d. Panasonic REAL 3DO

17. The only fifth-generation system to only use cartridges as the sole format for its games:
    a. Sega Saturn
    b. Nintendo 64
    c. Sony PlayStation
    d. Panasonic REAL 3DO

18. This system dominated the fifth generation in worldwide console sales:
    a. Panasonic REAL 3DO
    b. Nintendo 64
    c. Sony PlayStation
    d. Atari Jaguar

19. Sega Saturn's demise in the United States was primarily because of:
    a. Entering the fifth-generation market too late
    b. Fragmented marketing of platforms and sub-platforms like 32X
    c. Too many product recalls due to bad chip sets
    d. Direct competition from the N64 at its launch

20. This console's "control stick" and force feedback (rumble) pioneered the way future video game controllers would be made:
    a. Panasonic REAL 3DO
    b. Sega Saturn
    c. Sony PlayStation
    d. Nintendo 64

True or False

21. The 3DO used interpolation, a computer algorithm that upscaled its graphics to 640×480 resolution.

22. Around 200 games were released for the Atari Jaguar in the United States, with more than 100 additional games that were released exclusively in Japan.

23. With its two Hitachi SH2 32-bit RISC CPUs, the Sega Saturn was the first self-proclaimed 64-bit home console.

24. The PlayStation initially began as a Super Nintendo CD add-on unit that was under development by Sony.

25. Compared to game cartridges, CD-ROMs are cheaper to manufacture.

■ FIGURES

Figure 8.1 Screenshots of defining arcade games from the mid-1990s: (a) *Virtua Racing* (Sega, 1992), (b) *Tekken* (Namco, 1994), and (c) *Area 51* (Mesa Logic/Atari 1995). (*Virtua Racing,* courtesy of Sega, 1993; *Tekken,* courtesy of Namco, 1994; and *Area 51,* courtesy of Mesa Logic/Atari 1995.)

Figure 8.2 The Panasonic R•E•A•L 3DO Interactive Multiplayer with standard controller (Model FZ-1).

("The Panasonic 3DO FZ-1, a video game console released in 1993" by Evan Amos—own work, CC BY-SA 3.0. Available at https://commons.wikimedia.org/w/index.php?curid=18370417. Retrieved from https://en.wikipedia.org/wiki/3DO_Interactive_Multiplayer#/media/File:3DO-FZ1-Console-Set.jpg.) (Part of this image was used on the introductory page of this chapter.)

Figure 8.3 Screenshots from early 3DO titles: (a) *Crash 'N Burn* and (b) *Total Eclipse.* (*Crash 'N Burn,* courtesy of Crystal Dynamics, 1993; and *Total Eclipse,* courtesy of Crystal Dynamics, 1993.)

Figure 8.4 Two-page magazine advertisement for the Panasonic 3DO in 1993. (Retrieved from *Electronic Gaming Monthly* Issue 53, December 1993, pp. 70–71.)

Figure 8.5 Other 3DO Interactive Multiplayer systems, including the redesigned (a) Panasonic FZ-10, (b) GoldStar (LG) model, and (c) the Japan-exclusive Sanyo 3DO TRY. (Left: "*Panasonic FZ-10* R•E•A•L 3DO Interactive Multiplayer" by Evan Amos—own work, public domain. Available at https://commons.wikimedia.org/w/index.php?curid=36701232. Retrieved from https://en.wikipedia.org/wiki/3DO_Interactive_Multiplayer#/media/File:3DO-FZ-10-Console-FL.jpg. Center: "GoldStar (LG) 3DO Interactive Multiplayer" by Evan Amos—own work, CC BY-SA 3.0. Available at https://commons.wikimedia.org/w/index.php?curid=19709831. Retrieved from https://en.wikipedia.org/wiki/3DO_Interactive_Multiplayer#/media/File:3DO-GDO-101M-Console-Set.jpg. Right: "The Sanyo 3DO TRY (Japan only)" by Evan Amos—own work, public domain. Available at https://commons.wikimedia.org/w/index.php?curid=36699908. Retrieved from https://en.wikipedia.org/wiki/3DO_Interactive_Multiplayer#/media/File:3DO-TRY-Console-FL.jpg.)

Figure 8.6 Box art to five defining 3DO titles including (a) *Star Control II,* (b) *Road Rash,* (c) *Gex,* (d) *The Need for Speed,* and (e) *Super Street Fighter II Turbo.* (*Star Control II,* courtesy of Toys for Bob/Crystal Dynamics, 1993; *Road Rash* courtesy, of Monkey Do Productions/Electronic Arts, 1994; *Gex,* courtesy of Crystal Dynamics/BMG Interactive Entertainment, 1994; *Road & Track Presents: The Need for Speed,* courtesy of Pioneer Productions/Electronic Arts Victor, 1994; and *Super Street Fighter II Turbo,* courtesy of Capcom, 1994.)

Figure 8.7 Atari Jaguar and a standard controller with its numeric keypad. ("The Atari Jaguar console shown with the standard controller" by Evan Amos—own work, CC BY-SA 3.0. Available at https://commons.wikimedia.org/w/index.

php?curid=18269034. Retrieved from https://en.wikipedia. org/wiki/Atari_Jaguar#/media/File:Atari-Jaguar-Console-Set.jpg. Part of this image was used on the introductory page of this chapter.)

Figure 8.8 Screenshots from Jaguar U.S. launch titles: (a) *Cybermorph* and (b) *Trevor McFur in the Crescent Galaxy.* (*Cybermorph,* courtesy of Attention to Detail/ Atari Corporation, 1993; and *Trevor McFur in the Crescent Galaxy,* courtesy of Atari Corporation, 1993.)

Figure 8.9 Part of a 1994 foldout brochure for Atari Jaguar showing the Jaguar CD unit. Featured in *Electronic Gaming Monthly* magazine in 1994.

Figure 8.10 Box art to five defining Jaguar titles including (a) *Alien vs. Predator,* (b) *Wolfenstein 3D,* (c) *Rayman,* (d) *Doom,* and (e) *Tempest 2000.* (*Alien vs. Predator,* courtesy of Rebellion/Atari Corporation, 1994; *Wolfenstein 3D,* courtesy of id Software/Atari Corporation, 1994; *Rayman,* courtesy of Ubisoft, 1995; *Doom,* courtesy of id Software/ Atari Corporation, 1994; and *Tempest 2000,* courtesy of Llamasoft/Atari Corporation, 1994.)

Figure 8.11 The Sega 32X on the top of a Model II Sega Genesis, on top of a Sega CD II. ("Sega-CD II with a Genesis II and a 32X attached. Each device requires its own power supply." by Evan Amos—own work, public domain. Available at https://commons.wikimedia.org/w/index. php?curid=14303771. Retrieved from https://en.wikipedia. org/wiki/Sega_CD#/media/File:Sega-Genesis-Model-2-Monster-Bare.jpg.)

Figure 8.12 Sega Saturn with the original U.S./European MK-80100 controller. ("The original NA Sega Saturn" by Evan Amos—own work, public domain. Available at https:// commons.wikimedia.org/w/index.php?curid=17351615. Retrieved from https://en.wikipedia.org/wiki/Sega_ Saturn#/media/File:Sega-Saturn-Console-Set-Mk1.png. Part of this image was used on the introductory page of this chapter.)

Figure 8.13 Sega Saturn launch titles: (a) *Panzer Dragoon* and (b) *Virtua Fighter.* (*Panzer Dragoon,* courtesy of Team Andromeda/Sega, 1995; and *Virtua Fighter,* courtesy of Sega AM2/Sega, 1995.)

Figure 8.14 Magazine advertisement for the Sega Saturn in 1996. (From *GamePro*: The Cutting Edge, Spring 1996, p. 47.)

Figure 8.15 Box art to five popular Saturn titles including (a) *Shining Force III,* (b) *NiGHTS into Dreams,* (c) *Virtua Fighter 2,* (d) *Panzer Dragoon Saga,* and (e) *Guardian Heroes.* (*Shining Force III,* courtesy of Camelot Software Planning/Sega, 1998; *NiGHTS into Dreams,* courtesy of Sonic Team/Sega, 1996; *Virtua Fighter 2,* courtesy of Sega AM2/Sega, 1996; *Panzer Dragoon Saga,* courtesy of Team Andromeda/Sega, 1998; and *Guardian Heroes,* courtesy of Treasure/Sega, 1996.)

Figure 8.16 The Sony PlayStation video game console with original D-pad controller. ("The very first PlayStation model, the Japanese SCPH-1000, shown with original controller and memory card" by Evan Amos—own work, public domain. Available at https://commons.wikimedia.org/w/index.php? curid=31719221. Retrieved from https://en.wikipedia.org/ wiki/PlayStation_models#/media/File:PlayStation-SCPH-1000-with-Controller.jpg. Part of this image was used on the introductory page of this chapter.)

Figure 8.17 Screenshots from PS launch titles: (a) *Battle Arena Toshinden* and (b) *Ridge Racer.* (*Ridge Racer,* courtesy of Namco/SCEA, 1995; and *Battle Arena Toshinden,* courtesy of Tamsoft/SCEA, 1995.)

Figure 8.18 1995 PlayStation magazine ad featuring Sofia from *Battle Arena Toshinden.* (From *GamePro* 74, September 1995, p. 101. IDG Publishing.)

Figure 8.19 The smaller "PSone" with matching DualShock controller and memory card. ("A PSone game console shown with matching controller and memory card" by Evan Amos—own work, CC BY-SA 3.0. Available at https:// commons.wikimedia.org/w/index.php?curid=17670847. Retrieved from https://en.wikipedia.org/wiki/PlayStation_ (console)#/media/File:PSone-Console-Set-NoLCD.jpg.)

Figure 8.20 Box art to five defining PlayStation titles including (a) *Resident Evil,* (b) *Final Fantasy VII,* (c) *Tomb Raider,* (d) *Metal Gear Solid,* and (e) *Tekken 3.* (*Resident Evil,* courtesy of Capcom, 1996; *Final Fantasy VII,* courtesy of SquareSoft/SCEA, 1997; *Tomb Raider,* courtesy of Core Design Ltd./Eidos Interactive, 1996; *Metal Gear Solid,* courtesy of KCEJ/Konami, 1998; and *Tekken 3,* courtesy of Namco, 1998.)

Figure 8.21 Nintendo Virtual Boy. ("A North American Virtual Boy game console, made by Nintendo" by Evan Amos—own work, CC BY-SA 3.0. Available at https:// commons.wikimedia.org/w/index.php?curid=19135757. Retrieved from https://en.wikipedia.org/wiki/Virtual_ Boy#/media/File:Virtual-Boy-Set.jpg.)

Figure 8.22 The Nintendo 64 with its unique, three-handle controller. ("The Nintendo 64, a fifth generation gaming console released by Nintendo in 1996, over a year later than its rivals the Sega Saturn and Sony PlayStation" by Evan Amos—own work, public domain. Available at https://commons.wikimedia.org/w/index.php?curid=36531250. Retrieved from https://en.wikipedia.org/wiki/Nintendo_64#/media/File:Nintendo-64-wController-L.jpg. Part of this image was used on the introductory page of this chapter.)

Figure 8.23 Screenshots from N64 U.S. launch titles: (a) *Super Mario 64* and (b) *Pilotwings 64*. (Courtesy of Nintendo, 1996.)

Figure 8.24 Magazine advertisement for the Nintendo 64 gaming console from 1996. (From *GamePro* 91 April, 1996, p. 15. IDG Publishing.)

Figure 8.25 Box art to five defining Nintendo 64 titles: (a) *The Legend of Zelda: Ocarina of Time*, (b) *Perfect Dark*, (c) *Super Mario 64*, (d) *Goldeneye 007*, and (e) *Banjo-Kazooie*. (The *Legend of Zelda*: *Ocarina of Time*, courtesy of Nintendo, 1998; *Perfect Dark*, courtesy of Rare Ltd./Nintendo, 2000; *Super Mario 64*, courtesy of Nintendo, 1996; *Goldeneye 007*, courtesy of Rare Ltd./Nintendo, 1997; and *Banjo-Kazooie*, courtesy of Rare Ltd./Nintendo, 1998.)

Figure 8.26 Game Boy Color featuring *Pokémon Crystal*. ("The Game Boy Color, a handheld gaming console released by Nintendo in 1998" by Evan Amos—own work, public domain. Available at https://commons.wikimedia.org/w/index.php?curid=38957124. Retrieved from https://en.wikipedia.org/wiki/Game_Boy_Color#/media/File:Nintendo-Game-Boy-Color-FL.jpg. Screenshot of *Pokémon* Crystal Version, courtesy of Game Freak/Nintendo, 2001.)

Figure 8.27 Five defining Game Boy Color titles: (a) *Legend of Zelda: Oracle of Seasons*, (b) *Bionic Commando: Elite Forces*, (c) *Pokémon Crystal Version*, (d) *Metal Gear Solid*, and (e) *Wario Land 3*. (*Legend of Zelda*: Oracle of Seasons, courtesy of Flagship/Nintendo, 2001; *Bionic Commando*: Elite Forces, courtesy of Nintendo Software Technology/Nintendo, 2000; *Pokémon* Crystal Version, courtesy of Game Freak/Nintendo, 2001; *Metal Gear Solid*, courtesy of TOSE/Konami, 2000; and *Wario Land 3*, courtesy of Nintendo, 2000.)

Figure 8.28 A look at less-popular fifth-generation consoles released outside of the United States. ("An FM Towns Marty video game console, released only in Japan by Fujitsu" by Evan Amos—own work, public domain. Available at https://commons.wikimedia.org/w/index.php?curid=17385778.

Retrieved from https://en.wikipedia.org/wiki/FM_Towns_Marty#/media/File:FM-Towns-Marty-Console-Set.png. "The Amiga CD32, a 32-bit, CD-ROM based video game console from Commodore, with one controller" by Evan Amos—own work, public domain. Available at https://commons.wikimedia.org/w/index.php?curid=33879250. Retrieved from https://en.wikipedia.org/wiki/Amiga_CD32#/media/File:Amiga-CD32-wController-L.jpg. "The PC-FX, a fifth-generation gaming console by NEC" by Evan Amos—own work, public domain. Available at https://commons.wikimedia.org/w/index.php?curid=34653886. Retrieved from https://en.wikipedia.org/wiki/PC-FX#/media/File:NEC-PC-FX-wController-R.jpg. "The Japanese Bandai Pippin (Atmark Player) and wireless controller" by Evan Amos—own work, public domain. Available at https://commons.wikimedia.org/w/index.php?curid=18341966. Retrieved from https://en.wikipedia.org/wiki/Apple_Bandai_Pippin#/media/File:Pippin-Atmark-Console-Set.jpg. "The Bandai Playdia, a video game console that was only released in Japan" by Evan Amos—own work, public domain. Available at https://commons.wikimedia.org/w/index.php?curid=34696628. Retrieved from https://en.wikipedia.org/wiki/Playdia#/media/File:Bandai-Playdia-Set-R.jpg. "The Casio Loopy, a 1995 video game console only released in Japan that was marketed to girls and could print stickers" by Evan Amos—own work, public domain. Available at https://commons.wikimedia.org/w/index.php?curid=18341210. Retrieved from https://en.wikipedia.org/wiki/Casio_Loopy#/media/File:Casio-Loopy-Console-Set.png.)

Figure 8.29 Fifth-generation console sales graph. (Designed by Wardyga using data from Resource Site for Video Game Research, "Console Wars through the Generations." http://dh101.humanities.ucla.edu/DH101Fall12Lab4/graph—console-wars and GamePro. "The 10 Worst-Selling Consoles of All Time." Retrieved from http://www.gamepro.com/gamepro/domestic/games/features/111822.shtml and Consoles +, issue 73. Retrieved from http://i.imgur.com/wQPBhdL.jpg.)

PRO FILE: Trip Hawkins. Photo by Christopher Michel. https://www.flickr.com/photos/cmichel67/18972740201/, CC BY 2.0, https://commons.wikimedia.org/w/index.php?curid=41635723. Retrieved from https://commons.wikimedia.org/wiki/File:Trip_Hawkins_(18972740201).jpg#/media/File:Trip_Hawkins_(18972740201).jpg.

■ REFERENCES

Armstrong, L. (1994, October 17). Raiders of the video arcade. *Businessweek*, 3394, p. 58.

Atari. (1995, December 31). *Annual report pursuant to section 13 or 15(d) of the securities exchange act of 1934 for the fiscal year ended*. Retrieved from https://www.sec.gov/Archives/edgar/data/802019/0000891618-96-000213.txt.

Base Media (2016). *Sega Saturn console information*. Consoles Database. Retrieved from http://www.consoledatabase.com/consoleinfo/segasaturn/.

Buchanan, L. (2008, May 2). *The sad legacy of the Saturn launch*. IGN. Retrieved from http://www.ign.com/articles/2008/05/02/the-sad-legacy-of-the-saturn-lau.

Business Wire (Atlanta, GA). (1997, June 18). *1997: So far, the year of Nintendo; company sales up 156 percent; driven by Nintendo 64 success*. Retrieved from https://www.thefreelibrary.com/1997%3a+So+far%2c+the+year+of+Nintendo%3b+company+sales+up+156+per cent%3b…-a019518838.

Business Wire (Las Vegas, NV). (1995, January 6). *Sega threepeat as video game leader for Christmas sales; second annual victory; Sega takes No. 1 position for entire digital interactive entertainment industry*. Las Vegas, NV: Sega of America.

Business Wire (Redwood City, CA). (1996, January 10). *Sega captures dollar share of video game market - again; diverse product strategy yields market growth; Sega charts path for 1996*. Retrieved from https://www.thefreelibrary.com/Sega+captures+dollar+share+of+videogame+market+again%3B+diverse…-a018001580.

Editorial. ProNews: Project reality. (1994, May). *GamePro*, 58, p. 170.

Fahs, T. (2009, April 21). *IGN presents the history of Sega*. IGN, p. 8. Retrieved from http://www.ign.com/articles/2009/04/21/ign-presents-the-history-of-sega?page=8.

Finn, M. (2002). Console games in the age of convergence. *Computer Games and Digital Cultures: Proceedings of the Computer Games and Digital Cultures Conference, June 6–8, 2002*. Tampere, Finland, Tampere University Press, pp. 45–58. Retrieved from http://www.digra.org/wp-content/uploads/digital-library/05164.16278.pdf.

Harrison, P. (2005, September 8). *Interview from PlayStation Icons*, episode 5007.

Kent, S. (2001). *The ultimate history of video games: The story behind the craze that touched our lives and changed the world*. Roseville, CA: Three Rivers Press.

Kohler, C. (2018, November 11). *The best-selling games for PS1, N64, Saturn, and Dreamcast*. Retrieved from https://kotaku.com/the-best-selling-games-for-ps1-n64-saturn-and-dreamc-1830239627.

Matthews, W. (2013, December). Ahead of its time: A 3DO retrospective. *Retro Gamer*, 122, pp. 18–29. London, UK: Imagine Publishing, Ltd.

McFerran, D. (2009). Retroinspection: Sega Saturn. In: Damien McFerran (Ed.), *Videogames Hardware Handbook: 1977 to 1999*. London, UK: Imagine Publishing, Ltd, pp. 204–206, 208.

McFerran, D. (2010). Retroinspection: PlayStation. In Damien McFerran (Ed.), *Videogames Hardware Handbook: 1977 to 2001*. London, UK: Imagine Publishing, Ltd., p. 47.

McFerran, D. (2018, April 11). *Hardware classics: Unpacking the 32X, Sega's most catastrophic console failure*. Retrieved from https://www.nintendolife.com/news/2018/04/hardware_classics_unpacking_the_32x_segas_most_catastrophic_console_failure.

McKirdy, A. (2019, August 17). Game not over: Japan's amusement arcades tap community spirit to stay relevant. *Japan Times*. Retrieved from https://www.japantimes.co.jp/culture/2019/08/17/general/japan-video-game-arcades-relevant/.

Oravasaari, D. (2012, March 1). *The history of PlayStation ads: PSone*. Retrieved from http://www.playstation-lifestyle.net/2012/03/01/the-history-of-playstation-ads-psone/.

Retro Gamer Team. (2014, November 4). *The making of Rayman*. Retrieved from http://www.retrogamer.net/retro_games90/the-making-of-rayman/.

Sony Japan. (2011). *Sony corporate history*. Retrieved from http://www.sony.co.jp/SonyInfo/CorporateInfo/History/.

Szczepaniak, J. (2009). Retroinspection: Atari Jaguar. In J. Szczepaniak (Ed.), *Videogames Hardware Handbook: 1977 to 1999*. London, UK: Imagine Publishing, Ltd., 197–198, 200.

White, M. (2014, July 18). *PlayStation versus N64: A hardware analysis*. Retrieved from https://thesolidstategamer.wordpress.com/2014/07/18/playstation-versus-n64-a-hardware-analysis/.

Video Games Become Big Business

■ OBJECTIVES

After reading this chapter, you should be able to:

- Review the process and traditional value chain of producing a video game.
- Describe the common milestones in a video game development cycle.
- Define the major roles and job positions in a game development studio.
- Provide the basic steps for how a video game is made.
- Recap well-known market rush problems with both consoles and software.
- Explain video game bugs and patches and why they have become more common.
- List types of intellectual properties and licensed video games.
- Compare physical versus digital distribution methods and sales curves.
- Summarize the top publishers and best-selling video game franchises.
- Illustrate market trends using data from the NPD Group and other services.
- Discuss major video game conventions such as CES, E3, and PAX.
- Describe the business of eSports and its rapid growth in recent years.

DOI: 10.1201/9781003315759-9

◼ KEY TERMS AND PEOPLE

Alpha stage
Analytics
Artificial intelligence
Artist
Beta stage
Big data
BlizzCon
Bug
Capital and publishing layer
Chip shortage
Cloud gaming
Code freeze stage
Code release
Community management
Consumer Electronics Show (CES)
Crowdfunding
Crunch time
Cyberathlete
Designer
Developer
Digital distribution
Distribution layer
Distributor
Downloadable content (DLC)
DreamHack
Eco-Box
EEDAR
Electronic Arts (EA)

Electronic Entertainment Expo (E3)
Electronic Sports League (ESL)
End User
Enterbrain
Entertainment Software Association (ESA)
ESL Pro Tour
eSports
Evolution Championship Series (EVO)
Expansion pack
First-party developer
First playable stage
Flurry
Franchise
Free-To-Play (F2P)
Freemium
GAME (retailer)
Game Developers Conference (GDC)
Game engine
Gamescom
GameStop
Gartner
The Gathering
Gold Master stage
Hardware layer
In-House developer
Indie fund
Intel Extreme Masters

Intellectual property
Interactive Software Federation of Europe
The International
Jewel case
Keep case
Kickstarter
Korean e-Sports Association (KeSPA)
LAN party
Level designer
Licenses/licensing
Live service game
Localization
Longbox
Loot box
Major League Gaming Inc. (MLG)
Manufacturer
Massively Multiplayer Online (MMO)
Microtransactions
Milestones
MineCon
Monetization
Multiplayer Online Battle Arena (MOBA)
Gabe Newell
Newzoo
Nielsen Media Research
NPD Group, Inc.
Open-world game

Packaging line
Patch
Pay-To-Win (P2W)
Penny Arcade Expo (PAX)
PlayStation Store
Poly-box
Pro gaming
Product and talent layer
Production and tools layer
Programmer
Publisher
QuakeCon
Quality assurance
Red Ring of Death
Retailer
Royalty fees
Second-party developer
Sound engineer
Statista
Steam
Studio
Summer Game Fest
SuperData Research
Tester
Third-party developer
Twitch
User Interface (UI)
Value chain
VGChartz
World Cyber Games (WCG)
Xbox Games Store

◼ CHAPTER OUTLINE

 Develop/Publish **p. 245**

 Manufacturing **p. 249**

 Distribution/Retail **p. 250**

 End Users/Data **p. 253**

 Big Business **p. 255**

 Conventions/eSports **p. 258**

▪ INTRODUCTION

The video games industry, also known as the "interactive entertainment industry," is now worth more than $300 billion. As the economic sector responsible for the development, marketing, and sales of video games, it encompasses a plethora of job disciplines and employs thousands of professionals from across the globe (Zackariasson & Wilson, 2012). This chapter elaborates on the people and process of making a video game, including the hurdles and considerations the industry must tackle along the way. The chapter will also cover top developers and publishers, gamer demographics, and other data research. This includes information on best-selling video game franchises, in addition to major events including video game conventions and eSports.

▪ GAME INDUSTRY VALUE CHAIN

A **value chain** is a set of processes or operations that add value to the conception and completion of a service or product. Ben Sawyer of Digitalmill described the value chain of the video game industry as consisting of six connected layers. These six layers include (1) Capital and Publishing, (2) Product and Talent, (3) Production and Tools, (4) Distribution, (5) Hardware, and (6) End users (Sawyer, 2009). Each of these layers is found within the "value chain" sections presented in this chapter. For instance, the capital and publishing layer is located in the section about development funding and publishing priorities. The product and talent layer, as well as the production and tools layer are covered in the section on development—and so on.

The process begins with the **developer**, who conceives an idea to create a game. The developer often seeks out a **publisher** to fund the game. Sometimes, the publisher approaches a developer first, to create a game the publisher is interested in funding. Traditionally, once the developer completes the game, the **manufacturer** produces mass quantities of physical cartridges or discs (along with cases and paperwork). The **distributor** then delivers the game to **retailers**, who stock their store shelves to sell the game to consumers—referred to as **end users**. Mobile games, online titles, and games from smaller companies may only receive a digital release and will bypass some of these steps as seen on the right side of Figure 9.1. The following sections will examine each of these steps in detail.

FIGURE 9.1 Traditional value chain of the video game industry (left); digital distribution chain (right).

▪ FUNDING

Video game publishers are responsible for the capital, marketing, legal, and licensing aspects of a video game production. A major part of this **capital and publishing layer** includes the process of funding of the game—which today can cost tens of millions of dollars for a single big-budget title. Traditional ways publishers fund the development of a game is through **milestones** (development stages). The publisher funding a game draws up a milestone schedule during the negotiation phase of a publishing agreement, which outlines the milestones the developer must meet to continue receiving revenue advances from the publisher (Victory Media, 2014b, p. 16). Since milestones vary depending on the publisher and project, there is no industry standard for defining them. There are, however, common milestones for video game development as illustrated in Table 9.1.

While not exactly a milestone, **crunch time** is the name of the overtime phase that can happen during any of the above milestones when development is behind schedule. During crunch time, workers put in many extra (often unpaid) hours to bring the project up to speed. Sixty- to eighty-hour work weeks are

TABLE 9.1 Common Milestones in a Video Game Development Cycle

First playable	The first functional version of the game. First playable and Alpha can refer to a single milestone in smaller projects (Bethke, 2003, p. 293).
Alpha	By this phase, all fundamental gameplay is functioning, and the developer has finalized all major game features.
Code freeze	At the code freeze stage, no new code is added. Here developers largely work on debugging the game.
Beta	The game appears complete and should contain no evident bugs. No changes are made to the game features, assets, or code (Chandler, 2009, p. 245).
Code release	Final bugs are fixed, and game is ready to be shipped or reviewed by the manufacturer and tested for quality assurance.
Gold master	The final game's build that is used as the master version for production of the game (Bethke, 2003, p. 295).

common during these times. Publishers can and often do reimburse these extra hours with additional (sometimes paid) time-off, which they may grant when the milestone is reached or after the game is completed.

A less traditional but growing means of financing the development of a video game is through **crowdfunding** (fundraising through Internet donations on websites such as **Kickstarter** and other collection methods). This method of raising money for game development is one way developers can sidestep a publisher who may be unwilling to invest in a game they see as too niche or risky for traditional funding. Developer "Double Fine's Tim Schafer shattered Kickstarter records when his campaign for *Broken Age*—previously known as *Double Fine Adventure*—raised $3.3 million. Like *Broken Sword*, *Broken Age* is a point-and-click adventure game, a niche genre not typically backed by major publishers" (Hiscott, 2014, para. 10). Today's most popular funded gaming projects on Kickstarter easily double that figure.

💡 DID YOU KNOW?

"Frosthaven was the highest funded gaming project on Kickstarter, as of April 2022, raising nearly 13 million U.S. dollars. The game is a board game and players can purchase expansion packs and upgrades to improve their performance" (Statista Research Department, 2022).

▪ PUBLISHING

Beyond financing development, other publisher functions include paying for **localization** (adapting the game's text, symbols, and language for other cultures), as well as covering design, layout, and printing costs

(of box art, inserts, and/or instruction manuals) for physical releases. It is also customary practice for publishers to pay **royalty fees** for physically manufactured games. Unlike most industries where companies pay royalties on actual sales of a product, video game publishers typically pay royalty fees upfront at the time of manufacturing. This adds an obvious risk, where the publisher (not the manufacturer) absorbs the loss for any games that are unsold.

Another consideration of publishing includes whether any party will be seeking returns through **licensing** the title—granting permission to use certain logos, characters, and/or other **intellectual properties** (IPs). Intellectual property rights are the legally recognized exclusive rights to intangible assets, such as musical scores, video game characters, words, phrases, symbols, and other game design attributes. Often, a game series or character is part of a *franchised* IP. "A **franchise** is the licensing of intellectual property from an original work, to other parties or partners for commercial exploitation" (Victory Media, 2014a, p. 20). Once the publisher has attained all legal rights and copyrights, their next step is to market the game. Today, publishers can spend more on marketing than on the actual development of a big-budget title. The returns on such investments can be significant, with the highest-grossing video game companies earning billions of dollars as illustrated in Figure 9.2.

▪ DEVELOPMENT

The **developer** includes the **product and talent layer** of writers, producers, designers, programmers, artists, animators, and other talent responsible for the design phase of the game. These professionals work under individual contracts or as part of in-house

FIGURE 9.2 Top 10 highest-grossing video game companies by game revenue.

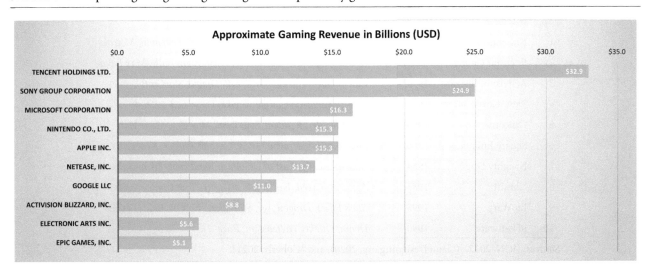

development teams, and often under one roof called a **studio.** "Studios are mostly local companies with staffs from a handful of persons up to several hundred, depending on the types of games developed and progress of the company" (Zackariasson & Wilson, 2012, p. 3). Development studios are located all over the world, with some of the largest development markets coming from Asia, North America, and Europe.

There are three main types of developers: third-party, in-house, and independent. **Third-party developers** are external teams who provide outsourced work for publishers. **In-house developers** (also called **first-party developers**) are owned by the publisher and commonly share a building or campus with them. **Independent developers** are the smallest—usually consisting of one person to a small group of people. Like third-party developers, they are independent of major publisher ownership and usually publish their games themselves. Because they do not operate under the constraints of publisher demands, independent developers typically have the most creative freedom of the three. See Table 9.2 for ten of the most influential video game developers of all time.

> ⚲ **DID YOU KNOW?**
>
> The term **second-party developer** can represent an independent studio or subsidiary developer who accepts a development contract from a publisher or platform holder like Sony, Nintendo, or Microsoft.

Typically, a company must obtain three **licenses** before the developer begins work on a game: (1) a license to *develop* the game for a specific console, (2) a license to *publish* the game for the console (obtained by the publisher), and (3) a license for the specific *game/IP* to be developed. This falls under Sawyer's **hardware (or virtual machine/software platform) layer.** Will the game be PC, console-based, or multiplatform—and on which console(s)? Will content for the game be accessible online, or available on mobile devices? This layer now includes network infrastructure and non-hardware platforms including online and mobile web browsers, plus social media platforms such as Facebook (Sawyer, 2009). Sometimes a developer designs a game for a specific platform and later **ports** (reprograms) the title to another system. There are even development companies whose specific function is porting games to different platforms.

This leads to the **production and tools layer,** which involves the programming phase of the game. This layer involves the creation of content production tools, as well as customizable game engines and production management tools for developers to work with. A **game engine** (such as RenderWare, Unity, and Unreal) provides prebuilt, reusable game components that the developer can use to build a game more efficiently. The components may include "loading, displaying, and animating models, collision detection between objects, physics, input, graphical **user interfaces [UI]**, and even portions of a game's **artificial intelligence [AI]**" (Ward, 2008, para. 4). Testing,

TABLE 9.2 Ten of the Most Influential Video Game Developers

No.	Developer	Founded	Key Game Series
1	Nintendo	1889	*Super Mario Bros., The Legend of Zelda, Pokémon, Metroid*
2	Rockstar Games	2002	*Grand Theft Auto, Red Dead Redemption, Bully, Max Payne*
3	Activision Blizzard	1979/1991	*Call of Duty, World of Warcraft, Diablo, StarCraft*
4	Valve Corporation	1996	*Half-Life, Portal, Counter-Strike, Dota, Left 4 Dead*
5	Capcom	1983	*Street Fighter, Resident Evil, Devil May Cry, Mega Man*
6	Square Enix	1986/1975	*Final Fantasy, Dragon Quest, Chrono Trigger, Xenogears*
7	Naughty Dog	1984	*Uncharted, The Last of Us, Crash Bandicoot, Jak and Daxter*
8	Ubisoft	1986	*Assassin's Creed, Far Cry, Just Dance, Tom Clancy series*
9	BioWare	1995	*Mass Effect, Dragon Age, Star Wars: KotOR, Baldur's Gate*
10	id Software	1990	*Doom, Quake, Wolfenstein, Rage*

Sources: (IGN, 2012), (GameDesigning.org, 2020), and (Coberly, 2021).

debugging, and localization may also fall under this layer of development.

One feature that has unfortunately become more commonplace in video games is the presence of **bugs** (glitches and other problems). Ever since consoles have been able to connect to the Internet, the market has seen a dramatic increase in the number of games released with bugs, which often require a download-able **patch** (software update). Bugs have turned up in a variety of games but are most common in large open-world games, where there is more room for game testers to miss something. Bugs can be game-breaking, requiring the user to restart from a recent checkpoint and so testing and debugging are an important part of the development process.

The roles of a developer continue to expand as the video game market changes and becomes more of an online medium. Table 9.3 lists six common roles of a video game development team. New roles of the developer in the digital age now include analytics, monetization, and community management (Llamas, 2014, p. 23). With **analytics**, developers collect and analyze data about players to create a more custom-tailored experience for them. **Monetization** includes the various methods of collecting returns on a game, which includes but is not limited to: (1) retail sales of physical copies, (2) digital downloads, and (3) in-game **microtransactions** (additional game content that can be bought after the initial purchase of the game—such as new costumes, weapons, characters, maps, etc.). **Community management** includes maintaining relations with a game's community of players, strategic planning, customer service, and execution and reporting of all community activity.

A shared portion of these roles can also exist under the publisher—further blurring the lines of responsibility as the market evolves. As the traditional value chain dissolves, developers may find themselves with more leverage than ever before. For example, "developers who self-fund a game, either through investors,

TABLE 9.3 Common Roles of a Video Game Development Team

Designer	Designs the gameplay, rules, and structure of a game; may also work on the game's narrative (Moore & Novak, 2010, pp. 74, 94).
Artist	Often overseen by an **art director** or **art lead**, responsible for conceptual designs and/or the actual game graphics.
Programmer	The **software engineer** who works on the game's codebase, including but not limited to physics, AI, graphics, sound, gameplay, scripting, UI, input processing, network communications, and other game tools.
Level Designer	The level designer creates the game's stages, maps, and environments.
Sound Engineer	Responsible for sound effects and sound positioning; may oversee voice acting and other sound asset creation (Moore & Novak, 2010, p. 91).
Tester	Extensively analyzes the game for bugs; provides quality assurance that the game both works and is entertaining (Bates, 2004, p. 177).

crowdfunding or partnerships like **Indie Fund**, can publish their games on [a console or other device] without having to fork over their IP or sign an exclusivity agreement" (Hiscott, 2014, para. 18). Because of the massive amount of work that goes into games today, development studios may consist of hundreds of employees.

■ MANUFACTURING

Console **manufacturers** consist of the platform holders such as Sony, Nintendo, and Microsoft and the production of their consoles and video games takes place in manufacturing plants. Physical games require raw materials such as polycarbonate plastics and aluminum to create today's optical discs. Manufacturers require even more materials to produce the intricate circuits of a cartridge or game card. There is also the plastic, paper, and ink needed to produce the **keep case** (also called a poly-box) and paper inlays. Once manufactured, the company sends the game's components to a **packaging line** where the game is placed in its protective case, conveyored to a shrink-wrap machine, and boxed for shipment (Romanowski, 2006, para. 18).

Because of the cost and resources required to produce a game, manufacturers have been working toward reducing the amount of materials needed to make them. Early cost-saving changes in the game industry included the shift from cartridge-based games to optical disc games. Keep cases have also gotten smaller and lighter over the years. A prime example of this is when Sony changed its initial "**longbox**" keep case to the CD-style **jewel case** for all of its PlayStation games in 1996 (Figure 9.3).

In 2009, Hong Kong-based case manufacturer Viva Group introduced a more economically and environmentally friendly keep case called the "**Eco-Box**." Microsoft and Nintendo were first to adopt these lighter, hollow keep cases for Xbox 360 and Nintendo Wii games. The cases used around 20% less plastic compared to traditional keep cases and significantly reduced CO_2 production emissions. Publishers have seen small savings from these changes, however even more efficient are digital titles, which require no physical materials at all.

FIGURE 9.3 *Twisted Metal* (1995) original "longbox" (a) versus the smaller jewel case packaging (b).

Original "longbox" version
(a)

Jewel case version
(b)

⋇ DID YOU KNOW?

In 2010, Ubisoft declared they would no longer be including a physical instruction manual with their games. Sony and Electronic Arts, among others, followed suit and this trend became the norm during the eighth generation.

Hardware manufacturing has not been without its flaws. Over the years there have been well-documented instances of video game products being pushed to manufacturing before they met acceptable **quality assurance (QA)** standards. Nintendo had to recall its initial shipment of Famicom systems due to a bad chipset (Kent, 2001, p. 279). Years later, consumers complained about the original Sony PlayStation overheating, which would often lead to video and sound skipping during full motion video sequences. A 2009 *Game Informer* survey estimated that more than 54% of every Microsoft Xbox 360 suffered from hardware failure (p. 12). Commonly referred to as the "**Red Ring of Death,**" systems that encountered internal problems would display flashing red lights around the console's power button, indicating the console would need servicing.

Another manufacturing challenge that has plagued the Xbox Series X|S and PlayStation 5 generation has been **chip shortages**. Major semiconductor companies including Nvidia and AMD (Advanced Micro Devices) suffered manufacturing delays and shortages from the COVID-19 pandemic. This problem was compounded by the fact that both the PS5 and Xbox Series consoles ran on similar chips by AMD. To remain cutting-edge, game companies will always be under the pressure of constantly evolving technology and shifting consumer habits.

■ DISTRIBUTION

The **distribution layer** is the true "publishing" part of the process, which involves generating and marketing catalogs of games for retail and online distribution (Sawyer, 2009). Large video game publishers typically distribute the games themselves, while smaller publishers often hire an independent distribution company to deliver the games to retailers. Such external distributors serve as the intermediary between the publisher and the retailer, adding yet another cost onto the publishing layer. Companies have cut this cost in recent generations with a reduction in physical distribution from the steady growth of instant, online delivery—aka **digital distribution**.

While commonplace in the PC and mobile markets, **digital downloads** did not gain momentum on home consoles until the mid-2000s after the release of Xbox 360, PlayStation 3, and Nintendo Wii. With faster broadband connections and greater hard drive space, digital, downloadable versions of once physical-only games started to appear. After 2009, physical-only releases began a steady decline, while digital-only titles trended upward as shown in Figure 9.4. Following a similar path as mobile game stores and Valve's **Steam** platform on PC, Sony's **PlayStation Store** and Microsoft's **Xbox Games Store** (formerly Xbox Live Marketplace) have set new standards for online distribution, making it easier than ever for users to purchase and instantly download digital versions of games without ever leaving home.

This process has made it easier for smaller, independent companies to sell their titles with little to no overhead, while larger publishers continue to release games in both physical and digital formats. Digital titles can also help publishers pass cost savings onto consumers, as discounting digital games does not equivocate to the same losses as discounting a physical title.

FIGURE 9.4 Digital and retail console game trends, seventh and eighth generation.

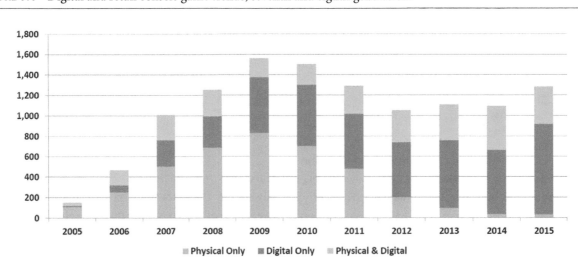

KEY FACTS:

Co-founder and Managing Director of Valve Corp.

Nicknamed "Gaben," his Steam platform exceeded 120 million players per month

GABE NEWELL

PRO FILE

HISTORY:
- Born: November 3, 1962 in Seattle, WA

EDUCATION:
- Studied computer science at Harvard University (1980-1983)

CAREER HIGHLIGHTS:
- Became a millionaire working on early versions of Windows for Microsoft from 1983-1996
- Co-founded Valve Corporation with former Microsoft colleague Mike Harrington on August 24, 1996
- Developed the Steam digital distribution service in 2003
- Series by Valve include *Half-Life, Counter-Strike, Portal, Team Fortress, Dota, Left 4 Dead*, and *Day of Defeat*
- Game engines include GoldSrc and Source engines

RECOGNITION:
Game Developers Choice Awards Best Game Award for *Half-Life 2* (2005), BAFTA Best Multiplayer Award for *Left 4 Dead* (2009), BAFTA Best Multiplayer Award for *Left 4 Dead 2* (2010), Game Developers Choice Awards Pioneer Award (2010), BAFTA Games Academy Fellowship (2013), Academy of Interactive Arts & Sciences Hall of Fame (2013)

With connection speeds continuing to expand, so will on-demand **cloud gaming** where game companies distribute titles via streaming over remote servers. Today, "distribution has become more of a portfolio management function than a single decision: pricing control, level of customer interaction, and ownership of gamer-related data are important variables in determining channel strategy" (González-Piñero, 2017, p. 43).

■ RETAIL

Along with distributors, another member of the value chain who may not be as enthusiastic about video games shifting to the digital download market is the brick-and-mortar **retailer**. Traditional retailer roles have included providing shelf space for games, initiating customer loyalty programs, and offerings such as preorder bonuses for customers who put a deposit down to reserve a game before its release. As Figure 9.5 shows, digital-only sales continue to rise even with major publishers. Smaller and independent companies paint an even broader picture, with the majority of those titles releasing as digital only.

Digital downloads are inevitably the future of video games since they save tremendous publishing costs. With digital downloads, there is no go-between distributor, no physical game, box, or paperwork to manufacture, and no retail shelves to stock. This becomes important as manufacturing costs continue to rise. The average cost of a new video game in the 1990s was $50. That price rose to $60 during the seventh generation of gaming in the 2000s. Of course, it takes far more people and money to make a blockbuster title

today compared to earlier generations, and inflation contributes to this equation.

The $60 earned from a video game goes to multiple recipients. For a traditional (physical) game purchase, the retailer might earn $12–$15, while the developer could earn anywhere from $4–$10. The manufacturer and distributor will also take a small portion of this amount, leaving the publisher with $24–$27. Remember, the publisher has to pay a platform license fee and/or royalty fee and also cover costs for marketing, rebates, and returns. After these expenses, the publisher might earn a 20% bottom line. Figure 9.6 illustrates how all parties can take a cut of the earnings from a video game.

With all of these costs associated with producing a video game, what is the value of a physical title? One advantage of a physical game is that it presents itself as a tangible item for gift giving. Data from retail outlets show the largest spikes in physical game sales are typically between the third and fourth quarters when a large portion of video games are released for

FIGURE 9.6 Estimated dollar distribution of a $60 retail video game purchase.

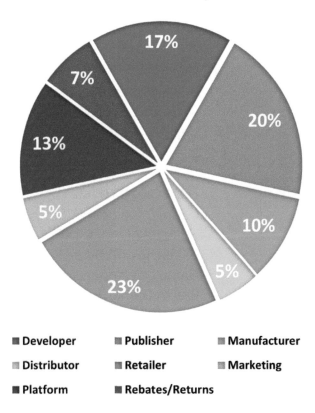

Cost Division of a $60 Game

- ■ Developer
- ■ Publisher
- ■ Manufacturer
- ▨ Distributor
- ■ Retailer
- ▨ Marketing
- ■ Platform
- ■ Rebates/Returns

FIGURE 9.5 Digital and retail console game trends of major publishers by percentage (NPD, 2022).

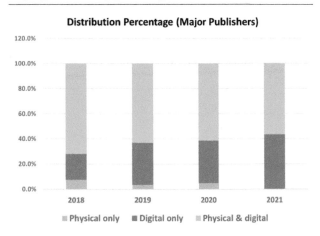

Distribution Percentage (Major Publishers)

■ Physical only   ■ Digital only   ▨ Physical & digital

the holiday season. Retailers might also argue that a packaged game holds more value with its cover artwork and supplementary paperwork. The physical product is what meets the customer's eye at a retailer. The importance of shelf space is relevant because this visibility provides attraction power to the consumer (Zackariasson & Wilson, 2012, p. 4). To maintain this retail visibility as video games make a shift to digital, retailers like **GameStop** began selling digital download codes for games since signing a deal with Blizzard back in 2012. *Diablo III* was the first game sold through download codes in the stores (Crecente, 2012).

Lastly, unlike typical digital titles that game companies link to a person's user account, physical games can be anonymously shared, sold, and traded among players. As GameStop's slogan states, this is "Power to The Players." Time will tell if these and other strategies like selling ancillary merchandise are enough for brick-and-mortar retailers such as GameStop and British retailer **GAME** to survive the trend toward digital distribution. Whatever the format, retailers have a fairly short window to sell new releases. As Figure 9.7 indicates, most new video game sales occur within the first 2 ½ months of a game's retail debut, leveling off after about 5 months on the market. Since the highest volume of sales happens within the first month, it is no wonder publishers and developers work so hard to meet each game's publicized release date.

■ END USERS

"**End user**" is the industry term for the consumer who plays video games. End users make up the final layer of the video game value chain and are the lifeblood of the industry. Newzoo reports that there are more than **3 billion gamers** in the world today (Newzoo, 2021, p. 8). "China is, undoubtedly, the biggest market in the world when it comes to video games, having doubled in size between 2010 and 2020. Online gaming is massive in this country, with 532 million people saying that they play online games or engage in online multiplayer gaming in some way" (Jovanovic, 2022, para. 6).

According to Statista, Europe contains the second-largest number of gamers with an audience of 715 million (Clement, 2022b). The Entertainment Software Association (ESA) reported more than 215 million active video game players across all ages in the United States and "66% of Americans play video games at least weekly" (ESA 2022, p. 4). Gamers span the globe in all age ranges, with more than one-third of all gamers ranging between 18 and 34 years old. These figures indicate that children continue with their hobby well into their adult years, and longitudinal data shows that the average age of gamers is on the rise. See Chapter 7 for even more demographic data.

FIGURE 9.7   PlayStation and Xbox 12-month game sales curve (EEDAR and NPD, 2015).

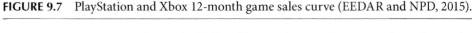

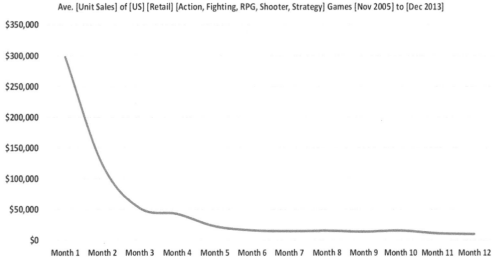

Whether players purchase the games themselves or receive their games as gifts, the desire to play the latest, cutting-edge games is a key factor in keeping the industry moving forward. The most popular game genres among consumers include shooter and action-adventure games. These have led the way in nearly every age group as the top two video game genres across the globe. A 2021 study by Statista ranked shooter games as the most-played gaming genre for all age groups except for online users aged 55–64 years, where they ranked third. Action-adventure titles were the second-most popular gaming genre, with only puzzle platform games ranking slightly higher among gamers over age 55. "Online users aged 16 to 24 years were the only age group to have battle royale games in their top gaming genres, whereas older age groups also played MMO or online board games" (Clement, 2022a). See Table 9.4 for a breakdown of player percentages per age group for the top 10 genres.

The types of games people play are becoming more congruent between home console and PC gamers. NPD data from 2016 suggested that console gamers favored action games, shooters, and sports games,

while PC gamers were mostly interested in strategy games, casual, and role-playing games. The latter made up more than 82% of the best-selling games on personal computers during that time. These findings are only partly the case today, with traditional sports games still selling best on home consoles. Otherwise, action-adventure and shooter games are becoming more popular with PC gamers, and more console gamers are playing casual titles and role-playing games.

Another trend has been that the majority of top-grossing PC games, like mobile, are not entirely new games. A 2021 year-end report by Valve showed that two-thirds of the best-selling games that year originally released *2–9 years* prior. The ability to expand a game's lifespan for this long can be attributed to consistent publisher and developer support with new online modes, subscriptions, social features, **expansion packs** (add-on levels, quests, storylines, etc.), and the game's inclusion in eSports (discussed later in this chapter). Take a look at the initial release dates of the top 12 best-selling PC games on Steam in Table 9.5.

Comparing this list to the top console game releases of that year reveals that every one of the top 12 console games were released between November 2020 and 2021 except for *Mario Kart 8*, which debuted on Nintendo

TABLE 9.4 Most Popular Video Game Genres by Age

Genre/Age	16–24	25–34	35–44	45–54	55–64
Action-adventure	56%	54%	46%	35%	21%
Action platform	31%	33%	28%	20%	13%
Fighting	-	34%	28%	19%	-
MOBA	36%	36%	28%	20%	-
Puzzle platform	33%	36%	34%	27%	23%
Racing	38%	40%	35%	26%	15%
Shooter	60%	57%	48%	35%	21%
Simulation	39%	38%	32%	24%	15%
Sports	34%	38%	33%	23%	15%
Strategy	34%	36%	31%	22%	15%

Source: (Clement, 2022a).

TABLE 9.5 Top 12 Best-selling PC Games on Steam in 2021

Game Title	Developer	First Release
Apex Legends	Respawn Entertainment	2019
PUBG: Battlegrounds	PUBG Corporation	2016
Counter-Strike: Global Offensive	Valve Software	2012
Battlefield 2042	EA DICE	2021
Naraka: Bladepoint	24 Entertainment	2021
Dead by Daylight	Behavior Interactive	2016
Destiny 2	Bungie	2017
New World	Amazon Game Studios	2021
Tom Clancy's Rainbow Six Siege	Ubisoft Montreal	2015
Valheim	Iron Gate AB	2021
Dota 2	Valve Software	2013
Grand Theft Auto V	Rockstar North	2013

Source: (Valve, 2022).

Switch in 2017. According to the NPD (2022), the top 12 console games that year included *Call of Duty: Vanguard* (Activision Blizzard), *Call of Duty: Black Ops: Cold War* (Activision Blizzard), *Madden NFL 22* (Electronic Arts), *Pokémon: Brilliant Diamond/ Shining Pearl* (Nintendo), *Battlefield 2042* (Electronic Arts), *Marvel's Spider-Man: Miles Morales* (Sony Corp), *Mario Kart 8* (Nintendo), *Resident Evil: Village* (Capcom USA), *MLB: The Show 21* (Sony Corp), *Super Mario 3D World* (Nintendo), *Far Cry 6* (Ubisoft), and *FIFA 22* (Electronic Arts) (Grubb, 2022).

■ DATA RESEARCH

All of this information on end users and the gaming market is serious business for research organizations focused on tracking the sales and trends of video games. Among the early companies specializing in technological research is **Gartner, Inc.** from Stamford, Connecticut. Gideon Gartner founded the firm in 1979. Today, Gartner, Inc. conducts technological research and consulting in over 100 offices worldwide. The **NPD Group, Inc.** (formerly National Purchase Diary) began its retail tracking service for toys in 1984. It is now a global company that monitors consumer purchase data from over 300,000 stores.

Doug Lowenstein founded the **Entertainment Software Association (ESA)**, formerly the Interactive Digital Software Association, in 1994. The ESA "conducts business and consumer research and provides analysis and advocacy on issues like global content protection, intellectual property, technology, e-commerce and the First Amendment in support of interactive software publishers" (ESA, 2015, p. 16). Like the NPD Group, the ESA produces annual reports on video game market trends. **VGChartz** is a video game sales tracking website launched in 2005 by Brett Walton. The website provides weekly sales figures of both console software and hardware by region (North America, Europe, Japan, and globally). See Table 9.6 for the company's top 25 console sales figures.

Another company founded in 2005 is the American mobile analytics firm **Flurry**. Flurry specializes in analyzing consumer interactions with mobile applications, as well as monetization and advertising strategies. In 2006, a team of interactive software veterans founded **Electronic Entertainment Design and Research (EEDAR)**. Their focus was specifically on video game industry market research, such as sales data, industry trends, market predictions, and review score forecasts, among other services. EEDAR partnered with the NPD Group for video game market research in 2011, which led to the NPD Group acquiring the firm in 2016.

Peter Warman and Thijs Hagoort founded **Newzoo** in 2007 and "officially started researching, modeling, and reporting on the games market in 2008" (Newzoo, 2018). The company is now a global leader in video games, eSports, and mobile intelligence, as well as a consultant to entertainment, technology, and media companies. Another key research firm founded in 2007 is **Statista** from Hamburg, Germany. Statista specializes in market and consumer data across nearly two dozen industries—from consumer goods to Internet and multiple areas of technology.

Finally, veteran game industry researchers founded **SuperData Research, Inc.** in 2009. The group provided market intelligence on free-to-play and digital games, as well as key trends, revenue estimates, and market change analysis for all major types of video game platforms. **Nielsen Media Research (NMR)** acquired SuperData in September 2018, where it became part of the Nielsen Sports network of analysts. Much of the data in this chapter came from the aforementioned research companies.

■ BIG BUSINESS

The biggest change in gaming occurred when game consoles and mobile phones joined personal computers with the ability to connect to the Internet. This led to rapid growth in the business of patching/updating games, online multiplayer, digital downloads, microtransactions, social gaming, live service games, and most importantly, **big data**. Before the Internet, companies had to conduct research with surveys and test groups to collect data beyond sales figures. With online connectivity, game companies can monitor exactly how many people are playing their devices, what games they are playing, when, and for how long—among other data.

It is no wonder that since 2007 the video game industry has been outperforming box office and music sales in overall returns. Video games have become big business in the entertainment industry with total worldwide hardware and software sales exceeding $91

TABLE 9.6 Total Worldwide Sales (in millions of Units) per Platform

Pos	Platform	North America	Europe	Japan	Rest of World	Total
1	PlayStation 2 (PS2)	53.65	55.28	23.18	26.59	158.7
2	Nintendo DS (DS)	57.92	51.84	32.99	11.28	154.02
3	Nintendo Switch (NS)	42.95	30.15	27.44	18.45	118.99
4	Game Boy (GB)	43.18	40.05	32.47	2.99	118.69
5	PlayStation 4 (PS4)	38.2	45.92	9.59	23.33	117.04
6	PlayStation (PS)	40.78	31.09	21.59	9.04	102.49
7	Nintendo Wii (Wii)	45.51	33.12	12.77	10.23	101.63
8	PlayStation 3 (PS3)	29.92	30.87	10.47	16.14	87.4
9	Xbox 360 (X360)	47.09	25.08	1.66	11.9	85.73
10	Game Boy Advance (GBA)	40.39	21.31	16.96	2.85	81.51
11	PlayStation Portable (PSP)	21.41	24.39	20.01	14.98	80.79
12	Nintendo 3DS (3DS)	25.47	20.45	24.67	5.35	75.94
13	Nintendo Entertainment System (NES)	33.49	8.3	19.35	0.77	61.91
14	Xbox One (XOne)	31.6	13.04	0.12	6.53	51.28
15	Super Nintendo Entertainment System (SNES)	22.88	8.15	17.17	0.9	49.1
16	Sega Genesis (GEN)	18.5	8.39	3.58	3.59	34.06
17	Nintendo 64 (N64)	20.11	6.35	5.54	0.93	32.93
18	Atari 2600 (2600)	23.54	3.35	2.36	0.75	30
19	Xbox (XB)	15.77	7.17	0.47	1.24	24.65
20	PlayStation 5 (PS5)	8.69	7.84	1.81	3.48	21.82
21	GameCube (GC)	12.55	4.44	4.04	0.71	21.74
22	Sega Master System (MS)	2	6.95	2.52	9.37	20.84
23	Xbox Series X/S (XS)	8.27	4.71	0.29	2.86	16.12
24	PlayStation Vita (PSV)	2.7	3.94	5.73	3.44	15.82
25	Nintendo Wii U (WiiU)	6.15	3.27	3.33	0.82	13.56

Source: Platform totals. Retrieved from https://www.vgchartz.com/charts/platform_totals/Hardware.php/.

billion in 2015 (Sinclair, 2015) and forecasted to reach $256 billion by 2025 (Dobrilova, 2022). Researchers predict growth in just about every video game market in the world over the near future. Mobile has been the fastest growing platform for gaming in the 2020s, leading to rapid market growth in regions such as China, MENA (Middle East and North Africa), and South America.

The industry has grown particularly fast in the Asia-Pacific region, which now makes up nearly half of the world's gamers. A 2021 Newzoo report valued the global video game market at $175.8 billion. The report estimated Asia-Pacific video game revenue at $88.2 billion, North America at $42.6 billion, Europe at $31.5 billion, Latin America at $7.2 billion, along with the Middle East and Africa reaching $6.3 billion. See Figure 9.8 for a breakdown of video game revenue share among markets.

One feature that separates the gaming landscape of today from the early days of video games is the process of how publishers and developers can earn money on a title after its initial sale. Publishers may even make the title available for free and acquire revenue by other methods after a player has been hooked. Of course, traditional-style games still exist where a consumer buys the game for its campaign and the title does not receive any additional content other than patches or QA updates. However, since technology has advanced with online and mobile gaming, consumers have witnessed a shift in what a video game can be.

FIGURE 9.8   Global game revenuesshare in 2021.

REVENUE IN BILLIONS (USD)

■ Asia-Pacific   ■ North America

■ Europe   ■ Latin America

■ Middle East & Africa

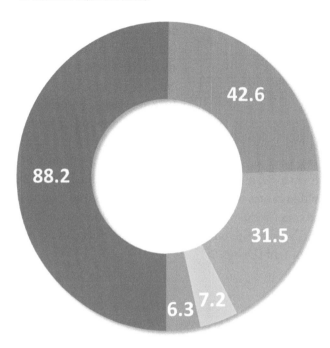

One of the first trends for publishers to earn revenue from a game beyond the initial purchase price was **downloadable content** (**DLC**). The concept of selling new campaigns with expansion packs (a long-time PC practice) began making its way onto consoles through online gaming. Once gamers became wired to the Internet, a whole new form of revenue was born through digital downloads. These "extra" purchases in games are known as **microtransactions**. Microtransactions are virtual goods that players can purchase to enhance their gaming experience. They can be simple aesthetic items, such as retro uniforms for a sports team, to game-changing items like powerful armor and weaponry.

Controversy has developed in gaming communities from games in which players can purchase virtual goods to level up their character and gain an advantage over other players—especially if players cannot acquire the purchased items by non-monetary means. Gamers have commonly used the derogatory phrase "**pay-to-win**" (**P2W**) to describe these types of microtransactions. One controversial microtransaction that began in the mid-2000s was the **loot box.** Loot boxes are similar to "gacha games" in Japan, which game developers derived from Gashapon vending machines where users exchange a token for a capsule with a random toy inside.

Loot boxes can contain anything from virtual playing cards to in-game currency and other game-changing items. In addition to leading to "pay-to-win" scenarios, the concept of paying for a chance to win something is similar to gambling, which is unfit for children and even addictive to certain players. Examples of games that received negative press for their loot box systems include Blizzard's *Overwatch* (2016), EA's *Star Wars Battlefront II* (2017) and *FIFA 18,* as well as Valve's *Counter-Strike: Global Offensive* (*CS:GO*).

The business of microtransactions has led to another video game business model where games are marketed as "**free-to-play**" (**F2P**) but can actually end up costing gamers quite a bit of money. The strategy involves offering a game free to play, only to charge players for certain features or functionality to progress after investing a reasonable amount of time in the game. This concept was coined the "**freemium**" model by Jarid Lukin in 2006 (Schenck, 2011, para. 2) and has become the key source of revenue in mobile and online games as Table 9.7 illustrates. It has been the primary model for successful mobile titles *Clash of Clans, Game of War,* and *Candy Crush Saga.* Other successful free-to-play models have been with **massively multiplayer online** (**MMO**) games such as *World of Warcraft,* **multiplayer online battle arena** (**MOBA**) games *League of Legends, Dota 2,* and *Honor of Kings,* plus **battle royale** games *Apex Legends, PUBG Battlegrounds,* and *Fortnite.* Then there are sandbox titles such as *Roblox,* whose publisher sells gift cards for the game's "Robux" currency at most major retailers.

The free-to-play or freemium model may be most popular in mobile and PC gaming; however, the amount of dollars spent on microtransactions by console owners continues to rise. Stephanie Llamas of SuperData Research, Inc. provided information on the types of microtransactions that console gamers have been spending their money on. According to Llamas, 55% of spenders purchase weapons or weapon upgrades, 36% spend money on vanity items, 33% on vehicles or upgrades, 32% on expansion packs, 26% on map packs, 26% on songs, 19% on class unlocks, and

TABLE 9.7 Top 10 Grossing "Free-to-Play" Games by Revenue

Rank	Game Title	Publisher	Released	Earnings
1	*Honor of Kings*[a]	Tencent	2015	$2.45 bil.
2	*Peacekeeper Elite (PUBG Mobile)*[a]	Tencent	2018	$2.32 bil.
3	*Roblox*[a]	Roblox Corporation	2006	$2.29 bil.
4	*Garena Free Fire*	111dots Studio	2017	$2.13 bil.
5	*Pokémon GO*[a]	Niantic	2016	$1.92 bil.
6	*League of Legends*	Riot Games	2009	$1.75 bil.
7	*Candy Crush Saga*[a]	King	2012	$1.66 bil.
8	*AFK Arena*	Lilith Games	2018	$1.45 bil.
9	*Gardenscapes: New Acres*	Playrix	2016	$1.43 bil.
10	*Dungeon Fighter Online*	Neople/Nexon	2005	$1.41 bil.

[a] Also a Top 10 Grossing Mobile Game in 2022.
Source: (Valentine, 2021).

10% on side stories (2014, p. 68). These titles that continue adding content to keep gamers playing them as long as possible are known as **live service games**. They appear on all major platforms today and many require a monthly subscription fee to play—adding to a consistent revenue stream that the modern video games can provide.

■ VIDEO GAME CONVENTIONS

Conventions where game publishers can display their latest titles and technology have always been an important part of the video game business. The first major convention to display the latest in gaming technology was the **Consumer Electronics Show (CES)** (shown in Figure 9.9a). Debuting in New York City in 1967 by the Consumer Technology Association (formerly Consumer Electronics Association [CEA]), CES was a showcase of all the latest electronic technology—TVs, sound systems, appliances, and eventually video games. From 1978 to 1994, CES held both a winter (January) show in Las Vegas and a summer (June) show in Chicago. While CES brought positive exposure to the video game business, veterans like former Sega of America CEO Tom Kalinske felt that video games were not always given the same treatment as other industries—often delegated floor space in the far back of the building or in some cases, in an outdoor tent (Dring, 2013).

☼ DID YOU KNOW?

The **Game Developers Conference (GDC)** began as a meeting of around 27 developers in game designer Chris Crawford's San Jose, California living room in April 1988. It has since grown from hundreds to thousands of attendants.

FIGURE 9.9 A spectacle of lights, displays, and people: (a) CES 2012 and (b) E3 2011.

(a)

(b)

Tired of competing for CES floor space with other electronics industries and "with the creation of the Interactive Digital Software Association (IDSA) [now the ESA], the video game industry had its own trade organization and was large enough and prosperous enough to run its own show" (Kent, 2001, p. 503). This led to the **Electronic Entertainment Expo (E3)**, which held its first video game industry-only convention during May 11–13 in 1995 at the Los Angeles Convention Center (GamePro, 1995, p. 211). Rumored to have attracted over 50,000 attendees, E3 (seen in Figure 9.9b) quickly became one of the largest conferences in the world for video game publishers and manufacturers to market upcoming games and video game-related merchandise.

E3 garnered tremendous press with its size and scope for years. The electrified atmosphere of E3 remained closed to the public until 2017. As exciting as it was for the public to attend the event, the change sent the conference into an identity crisis of trying to cater to two vastly different audiences and a series of hardships followed. Sony withdrew from the event in 2019. Then The ESA canceled E3 due to the pandemic in 2020. The company hosted an online-only version of the event in 2021, and then canceled E3 again in 2022. With the 2020 cancelation of E3 and **Gamescom** (Germany), journalist and Game Awards host Geoff Keighley gathered developers from across the industry to host a 4-month series called **Summer Game Fest** between May and August of 2020. Other developers and publishers followed suit and began hosting their own exclusive online presentations.

Since the ESA originally limited E3 access to individuals with a professional connection to the video game industry, another game convention formed to service the general public. The **Penny Arcade Expo (PAX)** launched in 2004 in Bellevue, Washington and became the largest public video game convention in North America. The main conference quickly grew to two events per year with "PAX West" held annually in Seattle and "PAX East" in Boston since 2010. Other PAX conferences include "PAX Australia" in Melbourne, Australia from 2013 and "PAX South" in San Antonio, Texas since 2015. Similar to E3, PAX offers attendants hands-on exhibits of upcoming titles, video game presentations, and other game-related entertainment. For other notable video game conventions, see Table 9.8.

In addition to the industry-wide conventions, publishers, developers, and gamers have created their own regular gaming events. Popular conventions from publishers and developers include **BlizzCon**, for Blizzard Entertainment to promote their major franchises, **QuakeCon** by ZeniMax Media, which celebrates and promotes the games of developer id Software, and **MineCon** for the video game *Minecraft*—hosted by developer Mojang. Gamers across the world have come together to create **LAN parties** where they link their systems together over a local area network for a

TABLE 9.8 Notable Video Game Conventions Around the World

Convention	Recent Location	Inaugurated
Consumer Electronics Show (CES)	Las Vegas, NV	1967
Game Developers Conference (GDC)	Various	1988
Electronic Entertainment Expo (E3)	Los Angeles, CA	1995
Tokyo Game Show (TGS)	Chiba, Japan	1996
Asia Game Show (AGS)	Hong Kong, China	2002
Penny Arcade Expo (PAX Prime)	Various	2004
ChinaJoy	Shanghai, China	2004
IgroMir	Moscow, Russia	2006
Dubai World Game Expo (DWGE)	Dubai, UAE	2007
Eurogamer Expo (EGX)	United Kingdom, Germany	2008
Brasil Game Show (BGS)	São Paulo, Brazil	2009
Gamescom	Cologne, Germany	2009
EB Games Expo	Sydney, Australia	2011

FIGURE 9.10 Winter 2004 DreamHack LAN party (a) and eSports at The International 2014 (b).

(a)

(b)

shared gaming experience. Norway's **The Gathering** and Sweden's **DreamHack** (shown in Figure 9.10) are among the largest festivals of this type—many of which have been paving the way for major video game tournaments, now commonly referred to as **eSports**.

■ eSPORTS

eSports (electronic sports) is the term used for professional competitive video gaming, also known as "**pro gaming**." Unlike most other sports, which are athletic-based, eSports are facilitated by electronic means—screens and monitors, consoles and computers, controllers, mice, and keyboards. "eSports commonly refer to competitive (pro and amateur) video gaming that is often coordinated by different leagues, ladders and tournaments, and where players customarily belong to teams or other 'sporting' organizations who are sponsored by various business organizations" (Hamari & Sjöblom, 2017, p. 1).

Among the first popular eSports games were real-time strategy titles including *StarCraft*, first-person shooters (FPSs) such as *Quake* and *Call of Duty*, multiplayer online battle arena (MOBA) games such as *League of Legends*, and fighting games including the *Street Fighter* series.

Video game tournaments have existed since the earliest days of gaming; however, top gamers did not see it as a lucrative profession until the early 2000s with the help of **World Cyber Games (WCG)** and the **Korean e-Sports Association (KeSPA)** in South Korea.

South Korea's Ministry of Culture, Sports and Tourism founded KeSPA in 2000 to promote and regulate eSports as a big-ticket industry for their country. From the beginning, teams wore uniforms similar to NASCAR racers, bearing the logos of South Korean sponsors such as CJ Entus, KT Rolster, Samsung Galaxy, and SK Telecom T1. As the leagues gained popularity, the top players have gained celebrity status, selling out large arenas and stadiums. The eSports industry has grown rapidly across the globe, with prize pools doubling from 2013 to 2014 and again from 2014 to 2015. Recent global prize pools have exceeded $200 million per year.

One of the first major tournaments focused exclusively on fighting games was the **Evolution Championship Series (EVO)**. Tom Cannon started EVO (formerly Battle by the Bay) in 1996 as a *Super Street Fighter II Turbo* and *Street Fighter Alpha 2* tournament. In 1997, Turtle Entertainment established the **Electronic Sports League (ESL**, formerly ESPL) in Cologne, Germany. The ESL has held **Intel Extreme Masters (IEM)** tournaments around the world for games such as *StarCraft II, Counter-Strike: Global Offensive, Quake Live, League of Legends*, and *Hearthstone: Heroes of Warcraft*. By 2016, the event had grown to more than 6 million registered members and over a million teams—which had played in over 12.1 million games (ESL Play, 2016).

Other eSports organizations include Sundance DiGiovanni and Mike Sepso's **Major League Gaming Inc. (MLG)** from 2002, which was acquired by Activision Blizzard in 2016. Notable eSports organizations headed by major publishers and developers include **The International** (hosted by Valve since 2011), the **League of Legends World Championship** (held by Riot Games), and the Battle. net World Championship Series (hosted by Blizzard Entertainment), now the **ESL Pro Tour**. Like eSports in South Korea, these organizations provide live broadcasts of the competition, in addition to the large pools of prize money and salaries for its competitors.

The explosive growth of eSports can be credited to the developers behind the games, the organizations supporting the business, the players (or **cyberathletes**), and of course the fans. The emergence of live streaming webcasts has contributed to the growth of eSports and is the most common method of watching tournaments. In 2014, SuperData Research estimated that the average eSports fan spent an average of 2.2 hours viewing an eSports session 19 times per month (Llamas, 2014, p. 55). Recent Nielsen reports show those viewing hours to have grown to around 4 hours a week for eSports fans today. Online streaming platform **Twitch** (launched in 2011) routinely streams popular eSports competitions. In 2013, "45 million users watched 12 billion minutes of video on Twitch from six million total videos broadcast. That's over a 100 percent increase in each of those metrics from 2012, when 20 million users watched six billion minutes from three million broadcasts" (O'Neill, 2014, para. 3).

The eSports industry saw steady growth for more than a decade, reaching "a combined global audience of 495 million people in 2020" (WePC, 2022, para. 1). The global coronavirus pandemic hampered this growth in 2020 when it halted most major live events around the world (see Figure 9.11). Still, global eSports market revenue surpassed 1 billion dollars that year, with *Fortnite* offering the largest prize pool—a combined total of $10.3 million (WePC, 2022, para. 2). The majority of this revenue comes from sponsorships, with $641 million in revenue from sponsorships alone in 2021. Compare this to media rights, which brought in $192.6 million, followed by publisher fees of $126.6 million, merchandise and tickets sales of $66.6 million, and both digital and streaming revenue combining for $57.4 million (Wise, 2022).

The top eSports players can earn millions of dollars, including members of teams. A sizable portion of the top eSports organizations come from Los Angeles, California, including Team SoloMid (TSM), Cloud9, 100 Thieves, and NRG eSports. Other teams that have roots in Los Angeles include FeZe Clan (Los Angeles, New York) and Gen.G (South Korea, Los Angeles, China). Other key eSports teams include Team Liquid (Utrecht, Netherlands), Enthusiast Gaming (Toronto, Canada), G2 eSports (Berlin, Germany), and T1 (formerly SK Telecom T1, South Korea). "In 2020, *Forbes* revealed that TSM is the most valuable eSports company with a market value

FIGURE 9.11 Worldwide eSports prize pool and tournament 10-year growth.

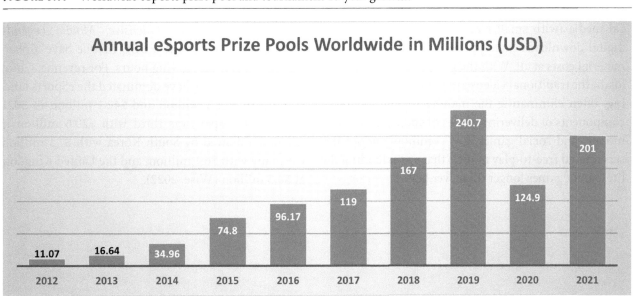

of $410 million. Cloud9 is second with $350 million" (Wise, 2022).

> ### ☼ DID YOU KNOW?
>
> According to eSports.com (2022), *League of Legends* is the most-watched eSports title in the world with more than 664 million hours watched and 4.1 million peak viewers. "The popular MOBA continued to grow even in 2021, increasing viewership by up to 13%" (para. 5).

■ MARKET SUMMARY

The video game business is worth more than the movie and music industries combined. Its substantial worth can be attributed to technological growth that has led to significant changes in the video game industry over the years. Video games were once designed and programmed by one to a small handful of people on a modest budget. Today's blockbuster titles are built by teams of hundreds of people, costing tens of millions of dollars. Funding for video game development once dominated by wealthy publishers is now being challenged with crowdfunding initiatives including Kickstarter and partnerships such as Indie Fund. The role of video game developers is expanding from just creating a game, to being responsible for data analytics, monetization, as well as community management.

The format of games has changed from cartridges and floppy disks to CD, DVD, Blu-ray, and other optical media (with smaller and lighter keep cases)—to digital downloads that require no manufacturing or material costs at all. With the growth of digital downloads, the traditional video game value chain is shrinking, often eliminating the manufacturing and retail components of delivering games to end users. Online, mobile, and social games now commonly adopt live service and free-to-play models that are extending the lifespan of games longer than ever before.

Players have proven they will pay to unlock levels, power up their characters, and buy into such monetization strategies.

> As monetization now takes place within the game at a moment the consumer chooses, publishers and developers are even more incentivized to keep their gamer engaged as long as possible. Video content and eSports are increasingly becoming part of this strategy. Running games as a service requires a different organizational structure than selling (boxed) products.
>
> *González-Piñero (2017, p. 43)*

Video game conferences were once only for professionals in the business. Today, conventions such as PAX offer consumers access to the latest news and exhibits of upcoming video game releases. Video game tournaments have been around since the beginning of gaming; however, today's skilled players can now earn a healthy salary in eSports. Research by SkyQuest Technology valued the global eSports market at $1.08 billion in 2021, and it is expected to exceed $2 billion by 2028. "The future of the global eSports industry will likely be fueled by mobile phones, which will further reduce obstacles to entry and allow even more gamers and fans to get in" (SkyQuest Technology, 2022, para. 3).

Millions of fans follow eSports across the globe. The ease of being able to follow the sport via streaming has contributed to its growth. Combined viewing hours for the top eSports franchises *League of Legends, Counter-Strike: Global Offensive, Mobile Legends: Bang Bang, Dota 2,* and *PUBG Mobile* have already exceeded 2 billion viewing hours. For revenue, China and North America have dominated the eSports landscape with $44.2 million and $42.1 million in 2021, respectively. Japan was third with $20.6 million in revenue, followed by South Korea with $7.3 million, Germany with $6.1 million, and the United Kingdom at $4.5 million (Wise, 2022).

▪ ACTIVITY: INTO THE FUTURE

The video game industry is constantly evolving. Here is an opportunity to share your predictions on where the business is headed in the next 10–20 years.

GUIDELINES

Write a 1,000- to 1,500-word essay on the future of the video game industry. Be sure to cover each area of the traditional video game value chain including publishing, development, manufacturing, distribution, retail, and the end users that play the games.

QUESTIONS TO CONSIDER

1. Will publishers continue to dish out tens of millions of dollars on triple A titles?
2. Will "indie" evolve into mainstream? What about indie eSports?
3. Do you foresee any new methods of video game funding taking off?
4. Will brick-and-mortar retailers still exist or will gaming be "all digital?"
5. What about used games? Will digital rights management end used game sales altogether?
6. Will end users even still be playing games on consoles and/or computers?
7. Will video games eventually just become subscription-based services like Netflix?
8. What about virtual reality? Where will it go? Will multiplayer VR gain popularity?
9. What other predictions do you have on how video games will change?
10. What about the metaverse? What do you see that being like?

▪ CHAPTER 9 QUIZ

1. Which of the following was *not* part of the video game industry value chain?
   a. Capital and Publishing
   b. Product and Talent
   c. Brainstorming and Negotiation
   d. Production and Tools

2. The traditional value chain of the video game industry begins with the:
   a. Publisher or Developer
   b. Manufacturer
   c. Distributor
   d. Retailer

3. Traditional ways publishers fund the development of a game are through:
   a. Keystones
   b. Coldstones
   c. Milestones
   d. Publishers never fund the development of a game

4. By this development phase, the game appears complete and should contain no evident bugs. No changes are made to the game features, assets, or code.
   a. First Playable
   b. Alpha
   c. Code Freeze
   d. Beta

5. During this development phase, no new code is added. Here developers are largely debugging the game.
   a. First Playable
   b. Alpha
   c. Code Freeze
   d. Beta

6. The licensing of an IP from an original work to other parties for commercial exploitation:
   a. Crowdfunding
   b. Royalty fee
   c. Localization
   d. Franchise

7. In-house developers that are owned by the publisher and commonly share a building or campus are also known as:
   a. First-party developers
   b. Second-party developers
   c. Third-party developers
   d. Independent developers

8. The highest-grossing video game company by game revenue, with more than $32 billion in estimated game revenue:
   a. Microsoft
   b. Nintendo
   c. Sony
   d. Tencent

9. Which of the following licenses is *not* commonly obtained before a developer begins work on a game?
   a. A license to *develop* the game for a specific console
   b. A license to *develop* a game for a specific language
   c. A license to *publish* the game for the console
   d. A license for the specific *game/IP* to be developed

10. This video game development team member plans the gameplay, rules, and structure of a game; may also work on the game's narrative:
    a. Designer
    b. Artist
    c. Programmer
    d. Level Designer

11. Monetization includes the following methods of collecting returns on a game, *except*:
    a. New retail sales of physical copies
    b. Used (pre-owned) game sales data
    c. Digital downloads
    d. In-game microtransactions

12. The rush to release games to the market sometimes results in games with bugs. Once a bug is found, developers often release a software update called a _____ to alleviate the problem.
    a. band-aid
    b. repair kit
    c. gold master
    d. patch

13. Traditional roles of a brick-and-mortar retailer include:
    a. Providing shelf space for games
    b. Customer loyalty programs
    c. Product offerings such as preorder bonuses
    d. All of the above

14. Estimated dollar distribution of a $60 retail video game purchase shows the largest percentage of revenue goes to the:
    a. Developer
    b. Publisher
    c. Manufacturer
    d. Retailer

15. Which of the following companies tracks retail video game sales figures and other industry trends in the video game business?
    a. NPD Group
    b. Newzoo
    c. Statista
    d. All of the above

16. The video game industry has grown particularly fast in the _____ region, which now makes up nearly half of the world's gaming population:
    a. Asia-Pacific
    b. Europe
    c. Middle East & North Africa
    d. North America

17. These types of games can actually end up costing gamers who are willing to pay money to progress after investing a reasonable amount of time in a game:
    a. Pay-to-win (P2W)
    b. Free-to-play (F2P)
    c. Freemium
    d. All of the above

18. This video game console holds the #1 spot for highest total worldwide sales according to VGChartz.com:
    a. PlayStation 2 (PS2)
    b. PlayStation (PS)
    c. Wii (Wii)
    d. Xbox 360 (X360)

19. The first major convention to display the latest in gaming technology was the:
    a. Consumer Electronics Show (CES)
    b. Electronic Entertainment Expo (E3)
    c. Penny Arcade Expo (PAX Prime)
    d. Tokyo Game Show (TGS)

20. The first-year eSports prize pools and revenue took a dip, after a decade of consistent growth:
    a. 2016
    b. 2018
    c. 2020
    d. 2022

True or False

21. Publishers are reducing manufacturing costs by less physical distribution from the steady growth of instant online delivery known as *digital distribution*.

22. Founded by Doug Lowenstein, the ESA stands for "Electronics Sales Assessment."

23. "Front users" is the industry term for the consumers who play video games.

24. eSports (electronic sports) is the term used for professional competitive video gaming, also known as "pro gaming."

25. The video games industry in now worth more than $700 billion.

■ FIGURES

Figure 9.1 Traditional value chain of the video game industry (left); digital distribution chain (right). (Courtesy of Wardyga.)

Figure 9.2 Top 10 highest-grossing video game companies by game revenue. (Figure by Wardyga with combined data from industry reports; Rousseau, J. (2022, May 12). *Report: Top 10 companies made 65% of global games market in 2021.* Retrieved from https://www.gamesindustry.biz/report-top-10-companies-made-65-percent-of-global-games-market-in-2021.)

Figure 9.3 *Twisted Metal* (1995) original "longbox" versus the smaller jewel case packaging. (Courtesy of SingleTrac/Sony Computer Entertainment of America, 1995.)

Figure 9.4 Digital and retail console game trends, seventh and eighth generation. (Nelva, G. (2016). *PS4 and Xbox One's combined sales in North America will be 23.5 million by November according to EEDAR.* Retrieved from https://www.dualshockers.com/ps4-and-xbox-ones-combined-sales-in-the-u-s-will-be-23-5-million-by-november-according-to-eedar/.)

Figure 9.5 Digital and retail console game trends of major publishers by percentage (NPD, 2022). (Figure by Wardyga with data from Orland, K. (2022, February 17). *Physical console games are quickly becoming a relatively niche market: Ars-exclusive analysis shows discs and cartridges becoming rarer and rarer.* Retrieved from https://arstechnica.com/gaming/2022/02/fewer-and-fewer-console-games-are-seeing-a-physical-release/.)

Figure 9.6 Estimated dollar distribution of a $60 retail video game purchase. (Figure by Wardyga with data from Edwards, R. (2012, June 16). *The economics of game publishing: A look at the costs that go into making videogames.* Retrieved from https://www.ign.com/articles/2006/05/06/the-economics-of-game-publishing and *Unreality Magazine*, 2011. How your $60 video game is chopped up. Editorial. Retrieved from http://unrealitymag.com/video-games/how-your-60-video-game-is-chopped-up/ and FeedVibe http://feedvibe.com/2011/videogame-revenue-split/ and Pham, A. (2010, February 19). Anatomy of a $60 video game. Retrieved from http://latimesblogs.latimes.com/entertainmentnewsbuzz/2010/02/anatomy-of-a-60-dollar-video-game.html and GR Staff. (2015, July 20). *Video game prices: Why games are $60, where your money goes, & who benefits most.* Retrieved from https://gamerant.com/video-game-prices-breakdown-514/.)

Figure 9.7 PlayStation and Xbox 12-month game sales curve (EEDAR and NPD, 2015). (Published on Jun 7, 2015, from the Game Developers Conference. PowerPoint slides by Geoffrey Zatkin. EEDAR PC F2P Report. "Sales Curve: All PlayStation and Xbox Games." p. 52. Retrieved from http://www.slideshare.net/AleixRisco/gdc2015-awesome-video-game-data.)

Figure 9.8 Global game revenuesshare in 2021. (Figure by Wardyga with data from Editorial. Next-gen mobile games: The arrival of cross-platform and evolution of high-fidelity. (2021). *Newzoo 2021 Global Games Market Report*. p. 7. Retrieved from https://armkeil.blob.core.windows.net/developer/Files/pdf/report/arm-next-gen-mobile-games.pdf.)

Figure 9.9 A spectacle of lights, displays, and people: (a) CES 2012 and (b) E3 2011. (CES 2012 central hall floor photo 2012 Pop Culture Geek taken by Doug Kline. January 10, 2012. CC BY 2.0. Available at http://creativecommons.org/licenses/by/2.0, via Wikimedia Commons https://commons.wikimedia.org/wiki/File%3ACES_2012_central_hall_floor_(6764012529).jpg. The Community—Pop Culture Geek from Los Angeles, CA, USA. E3 2011—the South Hall floor photo 2011 PopCultureGeek.com taken by Doug Kline. June 8, 2011. E3 2011—the South Hall floor https://commons.wikimedia.org/wiki/File:E3_2011_-_the_South_Hall_floor_(5831111978).jpg. The Community—Pop Culture Geek from Los Angeles, CA, USA.)

Figure 9.10 Winter 2004 DreamHack LAN party and eSports at The International 2014. ("Winter 2004 DreamHack LAN Party," July 24, 2009, by en:User:Toffelginkgo. CC BY-SA 3.0, Retrieved from https://commons.wikimedia.org/w/index.php?curid=7380926. "The stage and crowd at KeyArena for The International," July 18, 2014, 72157645379601078 by Jakob Wells. Retrieved from https://www.flickr.com/photos/jakobwells/14516251507/in/set.)

Figure 9.11 Worldwide eSports prize pool and tournament 10-year growth. (Figure by Wardyga with data 2010–2017 data by EEDAR. (2018). Published by Nate Nead of Investment Bank. *eSports & Gaming Video Content (GVC)—Industry Overview*. Retrieved from https://investmentbank.com/esports-gaming-video-content/. 2017–2021 data by Gambling Insider. (2022, January 13). *Esports prize money increased by 60% to $201m in 2021*. Retrieved from https://www.gamblinginsider.com/news/14591/esports-prize-money-increased-by-60-to-201m-in-2021.)

Title page image: Tokyo_Game_Show_2004_2 by No machine-readable author provided. Calton assumed (based on copyright claims). No machine-readable source provided. Own work assumed (based on copyright claims), CC BY-SA 3.0, https://commons.wikimedia.org/w/index.php?curid=311928.

PRO FILE: Gabe Newell. Photo credit: By steamXO-Follow Valve 稱在做遊戲 外媒打臉：這都是那些年 G胖畫下的餅　在日前的《石器牌（Artifact）》媒體發佈會上，Valve 首席執行官 Gabe Newell 親口表示，除了《石器牌》，他們還會推出幾款遊戲（新聞回顧）。此消息一出，立馬有許多玩家欣喜. March 11, 2018. Public Domain Mark 1.0. This work has been identified as being free of known restrictions under copyright law, including all related and neighboring rights.

■ REFERENCES

Bates, B. (2004). *Game design* (2nd ed). Boston, MA: Thomson Course Technology.

Bethke, E. (2003). *Game development and production*. Texas: Wordware Publishing, Inc.

Chandler, H. (2009). *The game production handbook* (2nd ed). Hingham, MA: Infinity Science Press.

Clement, J. (2022a, March 9). *Most popular video game genres among internet users worldwide as of 3rd quarter 2021, by age group*. Retrieved from https://www.statista.com/statistics/1263585/top-video-game-genres-worldwide-by-age/.

Clement, J. (2022b, July 27). *Number of video gamers worldwide 2021, by region*. Retrieved from https://www.statista.com/statistics/293304/number-video-gamers/.

Coberly, C. (2021, December 20). *Top 10 game developers of all time*. Retrieved from https://www.techspot.com/article/2367-top-10-gamedevelopers-all-time/.

Crecente, B. (2012, March 22). *GameStop signs deal with Blizzard, looks to digital sales for its future: Would you like to pre-order a virtual pet?* Retrieved from http://www.polygon.com/gaming/2012/3/22/2893912/gamestop-blizzard-digital-sales.

Dobrilova, T. (2022, July 5). *How much is the gaming industry worth in 2022? [+25 powerful stats]*. Retrieved from https://techjury.net/blog/gaming-industry-worth/#gref.

Dring, C. (2013, July 11). *A tale of two E3s – Xbox vs. Sony vs. Sega*. MCV. Retrieved from http://www.mcvuk.com/news/read/tale-of-two-e3s-xbox-vs-sony-vs-sega/0118482.

Editorial: E3 replaces summer CES. (1995, January). *GamePro*, 66, p. 211, IDG [International Data Group].

Editorial: Epic fail. (2009, September). *Game Informer*, 197, p. 12.

Editorial: ESports gaming statistics 2022. (2022, June 10). *WePC*. Retrieved from https://www.wepc.com/statistics/esports-gaming/.

Editorial: Newzoo's history: From startup to world leader. (2018, November 14). *Newzoo*. Retrieved from https://newzoo.com/news/newzoos-history-from-startup-to-world-leader.

Editorial. Next-gen mobile games: The arrival of cross-platform and evolution of high-fidelity. (2021). *Newzoo 2021 global games market report*. Retrieved from https://armkeil.blob.core.windows.net/developer/Files/pdf/report/arm-next-gen-mobile-games.pdf.

Editorial: The biggest video game design studios and game publishers of all time. (2020). *GameDesigning.org*. Retrieved from https://www.gamedesigning.org/game-development-studios/.

Editorial. The global eSports market is expected to reach a value of USD 2.8 billion by 2028, at a CAGR of 14.50% (2022–2028). (2022, June 6). *SkyQuest Technology*. Retrieved from https://www.globenewswire.com/en/news-release/2022/06/06/2456862/0/en/The-Global-Esports-Market-is-expected-to-reach-a-value-of-USD-2-8-Billion-by-2028-at-a-CAGR-of-14-50-2022-2028-SkyQuest-Technology.html.

Editorial: Top 50 video game makers. (2012, July). IGN. Retrieved from http://www.ign.com/top/video-game-makers.

Editorial: Platform totals. (2022). *VGChartz* Retrieved from https://www.vgchartz.com/charts/platform_totals/Hardware.php/.

Entertainment Software Association. (2015). *Essential facts about the computer and video game industry: 2015 sales, demographic and usage data*. Retrieved from http://www.theesa.com/wp-content/uploads/2015/04/ESA-Essential-Facts-2015.pdf.

Entertainment Software Association. (2022). *2022 Essential facts about the video game industry*. Retrieved from https://www.theesa.com/wp-content/uploads/2022/06/2022-Essential-Facts-About-the-Video-Game-Industry.pdf.

ESL Play. (2016, March 4). *Homepage*. Retrieved from http://play.eslgaming.com/global.

González-Piñero, M. (2017, January). *Redefining the value chain of the video games industry 2017*. Retrieved from Retrieved from https://www.kulturradet.no/documents/10157/3bc79547-fbec-4aa3-976c-9f985c4757f1.

Grubb, J. (2022, January 18). *NPD: The top 20 best-selling games of 2021 in the U.S.* Retrieved from https://venturebeat.com/games/npd-the-top-20-best-selling-games-of-2021-in-the-u-s/.

Hamari, J. & Sjöblom, M. (2017). What is eSports and why do people watch it? *Internet Research, 27*(2), 211–232.Hiscott, R. (2014, March 08). *Why indie game devs thrive without big publishers*. Retrieved from http://mashable.com/2014/03/08/indie-developers-self-publishing/#pRjx5jNqCPqE.

Jovanovic, B. (2022, August 02). *Gamer demographics: Facts and stats about the most popular hobby in the world*. Retrieved from https://dataprot.net/statistics/gamer-demographics/.

Kent, S. (2001). *The ultimate history of video games: The story behind the craze that touched our lives and changed the world*. Roseville, CA: Three Rivers Press.

Llamas, S. (2014, August 18). *Digital vs. retail revenues from quarterly filings and estimates for: Activision, EA, Ubisoft, Take-Two, Square Enix, Konami, Capcom, Disney, THQ*. Super Data for Digital Games. Retrieved from http://www.slideshare.net/StephanieLlamas/gdc-europe-super-data-for-digital-games.

Moore, M. & Novak J. (2010). *Game industry career guide*. New York, NY: Delmar/Cengage Learning.

O'Neill, P. (2014, January 16). Twitch dominated streaming in 2013, and here are the numbers to prove it. *The Daily Dot*. Retrieved from http://www.dailydot.com/esports/twitch-growth-esports-streaming-mlg-youtube-2013/.

Romanowski, P. (2006). *How products are made: Video game*. Retrieved from http://www.madehow.com/Volume-5/Video-Game.html.

Sawyer, B. (2009, May 12). *Ben Sawyer to speak at FuturePlay 2009. FuturePlay Game Developers Conference [Conference]*. Vancouver, Canada.

Schenck, B. (2011, February 7). Freemium: Is the price right for your company? *Entrepreneur*. Retrieved from http://www.entrepreneur.com/article/218107.

Sinclair, B. (2015, April). Gaming will hit $91.5 billion this year. *Newzoo*. Retrieved from http://www.games-industry.biz/articles/2015-04-22-gaming-will-hit-usd91-5-billion-this-year-newzoo.

Statista Research Department. (2022, May 25). *Most popular funded gaming projects on Kickstarter as of April 2022*. Retrieved from https://www.statista.com/statistics/283843/crowdfunding-most-funded-gaming-projects/.

Valentine, R. (2021, January 6). *Digital games spending reached $127 billion in 2020*. Retrieved from https://www.gamesindustry.biz/digital-games-spending-reached-usd127-billion-in-2020.

Valve. (2022). Best of 2021: *The year's top 100 games as measured by gross revenue*. Retrieved from https://store.steampowered.com/sale/ BestOf2021?tab=1.

Victory Media. (2014a, September 21). *Game industry: Trends*. Retrieved from http://www.slideshare.net/jcolebrook/game-industry-trends.

Victory Media. (2014b, October 8). *The game industry: Financial aspects*. Retrieved from http://www.slideshare.net/jcolebrook/4-game-industry-financial?next_slideshow=1.

Ward, J. (2008, April 29). *What is a game engine?* Retrieved from http://www.gamecareerguide.com/features/529/what_is_a_game_.php.

Wise, J. (2022, August 3). *Esports statistics 2022: Market size, revenue & viewership*. Retrieved from https://earthweb.com/esports-statistics/.

Zackariasson, P. and Wilson, T. (eds.) (2012). *The video game industry: Formation, present state, and future*. New York, NY: Routledge.

The Sixth Generation

■ OBJECTIVES

After reading this chapter, you should be able to:

- Discuss the decline and restructuring of arcade industry during this time.
- Provide a brief overview of Microsoft and its development of the Xbox console.
- Review key people behind the video games and consoles.
- Illustrate the reasons why Sega withdrew from the home console market.
- Identify graphics and capabilities of sixth-generation consoles.
- Compare technological differences among Dreamcast, PlayStation 2, GameCube, and Xbox.
- Discuss the strengths and features of the Nintendo Game Boy Color.
- List key video game titles and peripherals for each console.
- Explain why Sony dominated the sixth-generation market.
- Describe important innovations introduced to gaming during this period.
- Recognize the importance the technology had on the video game industry.
- Summarize sixth-generation market sales, breakthroughs, and trends.

DOI: 10.1201/9781003315759-10

■ KEY TERMS AND PEOPLE

3dfx, Acclaim, J Allard, Paul Allen, AMD, ArtX, ASCII keyboard controller, Kenichiro Ashida, Atari, ATI, Kevin Bachus, BASIC, Otto Berkes, BioWare, Seamus Blackley, Broadband, Bungie Studios, Chuck E. Cheese's, Cordless Action Controller, Dave & Buster's, DirectX, DK Bongos, Dream Blaster, Dreamcast, Dreameye, Driving Force GT, DualShock 2, Duke controller

DVD format, Electronic Arts, Emotion Engine, Ethernet, EyeToy, Factor 5, Cameron Ferroni, Firmware, Flipper GPU, Floating-point unit, Ed Fries, Game Boy Advance, Game Boy Player, GameCube, Bill Gates, GCN-GBA cable, GD-ROM, Gekko CPU, Gigaflops, GunCon 2, Harmonix, Ted Hase, Hitachi SH4, IBM, IEEE 1394, Intel, Satoru Iwata, Jump Pak

Hideo Kojima, Konami, Ken Kutaragi, Ken Lobb, Logitech, Horace Luke, Richard Marks, Matsushita EI, Microsoft Corporation, Microsoft Office, Shigeru Miyamoto, Modem, Peter Moore, MS-DOS, Multitap, Namco, NAOMI, Neo•Geo Pocket Color, Network Adapter, Network Play, Leonard Nimoy, Nokia N-Gage, Nvidia, Isao Okawa, Pentium III, PlayStation 2, Polygons per second (PPS), Progressive scan

Rare, Redemption game, Retro Studios, Inc., Rhythm game, Rockstar Games, Sammy, Sandbox game, Hideki Sato, Brian Schmidt, Second-level cache, Sega, Silicon Knights, Bernie Stolar, System Link, Tecmo, Toshiba, VGA Box, VideoLogic PowerVR2, Visual Concepts, VMU, Voodoo 3, VPU0 and VPU1, WaveBird, Windows/95, Xbox, Xbox Live, Tatsuo Yamamoto, Hiroshi Yamauchi

■ CONSOLE TIMELINE

Dreamcast 1998 — PlayStation 2 2000 — Game Boy Advance 2001 — GameCube 2001 — Xbox 2001

■ ARCADE DECLINE AND RESTRUCTURING

With the rising cost of arcade games and near-identical graphics and sound on home consoles, Western gamers began to choose the convenience of playing games at home. Video game rentals became increasingly more popular and retail sales continued to rise. This shift boosted the home console market but resulted in a sharp decline in arcade gaming revenue throughout the end of the decade. *The Wall Street Journal* reported that arcade revenues in the United States dropped all the way down to $1.33 billion in 1999 (Henry, 2001, p. 3). Consequently, many small arcade venues (such as those found in malls) began to gradually disappear.

With better graphics and sound no longer being motives for gamers to go to the arcades, reasons people traveled to the arcades included the social experience, cooperative gaming, or head-to-head competition of fighting and other competitive games. Eventually, **broadband** (high-speed) Internet and online gaming would allow gamers to play cooperatively or competitively online, further reducing people's desires to leave their homes and TVs. The industry had to evolve to stay relevant. Revenue from arcade machines was no longer enough to support most venues, so a greater emphasis on food and beverage service became necessary.

Venues such as **Chuck E. Cheese's** and **Dave & Buster's** were prime examples of this strategy. They provided experiences that consumers could not typically duplicate in the home—such as giant screens, unique game controllers, and motion-controlled, hydraulic cabinets. Shooting and racing games remained popular for these reasons. **Sega** and **Namco** would produce the most arcade games during this generation with well over 100 titles combined. However, it was **Konami** who would pioneer the next big genre.

FIGURE 10.1 *Dance Dance Revolution* (Konami, 1999).

Konami's success in Japan with *Beatmania* in 1997 led the company to further develop the **rhythm game** genre with *Pop'n Music, GuitarFreaks,* and *DrumMania.* It was the company's breakthrough *Dance Dance Revolution* (Figure 10.1) that popularized music games on a global scale. *DDR* became a hit for its unique competitive play, as well as being a platform for skilled gamers to show off their dance moves in public. Physical-style games such as *Skee-Ball* and *Whack-A-Mole* continued to be popular, in addition to a plethora of other **redemption games** where players could accumulate tickets or points for prizes. See Figure 10.2 for other key arcade games during this era.

FIGURE 10.2 Screenshots of popular arcade games from 2000: (a) *Silent Scope 2: Dark Silhouette* (Konami), (b) *Marvel vs. Capcom 2* (Capcom), and (c) *18 Wheeler: American Pro Trucker* (Sega).

(a) (b) (c)

■ THE SIXTH GENERATION

The sixth generation was the era of the 128-bit systems and would be the last time most journalists discussed "bits" when comparing consoles. From this generation forward, the focal point changed from bits to CPU or GPU power and RAM. Konami's success with *Dance Dance Revolution* would lead to a rhythm game boom followed by **Harmonix** producing *Frequency, Amplitude, Guitar Hero,* and the *Rock Band* series. Eventually **progressive scan** output and the ability to play titles online became priorities for serious gamers. The generation kicked off with a new console from Sega, in an attempt to reestablish retailer and consumer confidence in the company and to reach a broader audience.

■ SEGA DREAMCAST

Sega's new system began as two separate projects, the U.S.-based project "Blackbelt" led by IBM veteran **Tatsuo Yamamoto** followed by internal development from longtime Sega console designer **Hideki Sato.** Sato's project, which would become codenamed "Katana" after the Japanese sword, proceeded unbeknownst to the U.S. development team. Both designs used "off-the-shelf" (commercially produced) parts, including the **Hitachi SH4** processor; however, they differed in their choice of graphics cards (GPUs). Yamamoto's team went with U.S. company **3dfx** for a custom version of its **Voodoo 3** card, while Sato's team chose the **VideoLogic PowerVR2** card by Japanese manufacturer **NEC.** In

1997, 3dfx went public and "revealed Sega's blueprint for a new, unannounced console, and angered executives at Sega Japan" (Perry, 2009, p. 2). Even though the 3dfx chip was more powerful, Sega chose Sato's design with the NEC graphics card.

The **Dreamcast** (Figure 10.3) debuted in Japan on November 27, 1998, for ¥329,800 (approximately $260). Sega sold out of its initial shipment of 150,000 units but may have been able to sell up to twice as many units had it not been (ironically) for manufacturing problems, which prevented NEC from producing enough graphics cards (Kent, 2001, p. 563). Further challenge arose when on March 2, 1999, Sony announced the specs for its impressive new system that would be ready the following year—leading hopeful consumers to hold onto their wallets.

It was up to Sega of America president **Bernie Stolar** and his team to ensure a more successful U.S. launch. Stolar's team was successful in repairing relationships with American retailers and securing a better lineup of games. While the Japanese debut only had four launch titles, a record 19 titles were available for the U.S. release (Table 10.1)—including a long-awaited *Sonic* game. The American console maintained the look of the Japanese system, focusing more on the name "Dreamcast" than "Sega." Other clever marketing included the memorable Western launch date "9.9.99" (see Figure 10.5) and lower retail price of $199. However, with all the cards lined up, Sega had to push the European launch to October. Then an argument with Sega chairman **Isao Okawa** led to Stolar's termination from the company

FIGURE 10.3 Sega Dreamcast console and controller with LCD screen memory card.

TABLE 10.1 Sega Dreamcast U.S. Launch Titles

- *AeroWings*
- *AirForce Delta*
- *Blue Stinger*
- *Expendable*
- *Flag to Flag*
- *The House of the Dead 2*
- *Hydro Thunder*
- *Monaco Grand Prix*
- *Mortal Kombat Gold*
- *NFL 2K*
- *NFL Blitz 2000*
- *Pen Pen TriIcelon*
- *Power Stone*
- *Ready 2 Rumble Boxing*
- *Sonic Adventure* (Figure 10.4a)
- *SoulCalibur* (Figure 10.4b)
- *TNN Motorsports Hardcore Heat*
- *Tokyo Xtreme Racer*
- *TrickStyle*

just a month before the system's launch. Despite the abrupt loss of its president, Sega's U.S. Dreamcast debut was a success, with more presales than Sony had with the PlayStation during its entry into the market.

The Dreamcast (Figure 10.5) had a lot going for it when it was released. It was the most powerful home console at the time. It used its own **GD-ROM** (Gigabyte Disc) format for its media, which cost about the same as a CD-ROM to manufacture but could hold up to **1.2 GB** of data. While CD-ROMs were easy to copy, the higher capacity of GD-ROMs made Dreamcast games more difficult to pirate. The console also included four controller ports. The Dreamcast controller featured an analog stick, D-Pad, and four action buttons, in addition to two touch-sensitive shoulder triggers. The center of the controller housed a slot for the innovative 128 kB **VMU** (Visual Memory Unit) memory card. Each VMU contained a small LCD screen and a single channel of audio output. Since Sega did not build the console with a reset button, players needed to reset games with the controller by pressing the Start button and the four face buttons (A+B+X+Y) simultaneously.

Another unique feature of the Dreamcast was that it included a built-in **modem** for connecting to the Internet for online play. However, it was not until a full year after its North American release when the Dreamcast's Internet gaming service **SegaNet** became available on September 7, 2000 under new Sega of America president **Peter Moore**. Most consumers at this time connected to the Internet with a slow 56K modem and a subscription to SegaNet cost $21.95 per month. Still, Sega was able to obtain more than a million subscribers within its first month of service (Sega Enterprises, Ltd., 2000, p. 2). Soon, Sega offered free one-year subscriptions with the purchase of every new Dreamcast. Following a price drop to $149, Sega even offered a rebate for the full price of the system, where consumers could receive a "free" Dreamcast with the purchase of an 18-month SegaNet subscription.

☼ DID YOU KNOW?

Sega considered over 5,000 names for the Dreamcast. As for its logo, "in Japan and the U.S. the Dreamcast swirl is orange, but it had to be changed to blue in Europe due to a German company using the exact same logo" (McFerran, 209, pp. 239–240).

FIGURE 10.4 Screenshots of Dreamcast launch titles: (a) *Sonic Adventure* and (b) *SoulCalibur*.

(a)

(b)

FIGURE 10.5 Magazine advertisement for the Dreamcast in 1999.

For peripherals, the Dreamcast received the typical arcade joystick variants, steering wheel, fishing controller for games like *Sega Bass Fishing*, and a keyboard and mouse for games such as *The Typing of the Dead*. Sega's VMU was much more than just a memory card. Its interactive LCD display allowed for each player to have their own private screen, which they could use for calling plays in *NFL 2K*. Players could also use controller slot for the VMU to insert a **Jump Pak** for force feedback. The slot was also a port to plug in a microphone. A microphone

was required for Sega's *Seaman* title, narrated by **Leonard Nimoy** in the English-language version. This unusual game involved caring for and "talking to" virtual, fish-like creatures with human faces— who also spoke back!

Possibly due to the then-recent Columbine High School massacre, Sega never released a light gun in the United States. However, third-party manufacturer Mad Catz did release a **Dream Blaster** light gun for the system. Sega's **Dreameye** was a digital camera accessory that players could connect to the system for exchanging pictures or use like a webcam for video chat. Among the most unique accessories for the system were a pair of **maracas** that gamers would shake to the music of *Samba de Amigo*. Finally, the **VGA Box** adapter allowed the Dreamcast to output progressive scan (480p) on capable displays.

■ CONSOLE COMPARISON: DREAMCAST VS. FIFTH-GENERATION CONSOLES

Unlike the Saturn, Sega built the Dreamcast to be easy to program for. *Retro Gamer's* Damien McFerran praised the system's motherboard as being "a masterpiece of clean, uncluttered design and compatibility," which included development tools for Microsoft Windows CE, in addition to Sega's own development kits (McFerran, 2009, p. 240). The fastest processor in the previous generation was the N64's NEC VR4300 processor, which ran at 93.75 MHz. By contrast, the Dreamcast's Hitachi SH-4 32-bit RISC clocked at **200 MHz** with additional bells and whistles outlined in Table 10.2.

The Dreamcast was theoretically capable of rendering 7 million raw polygons per second, but a more realistic figure is about **3 million PPS** since "game logic and physics reduce peak graphic performance" (Hagiwara, 1999). Still, this was nearly 10 times the polygon count of the Sony PlayStation and 30 times that of Nintendo 64. Sega's GD-ROM format could hold nearly twice the amount of game data as a CD-ROM and the Dreamcast's **16 MB of RAM** was eight times the memory of PlayStation and four times the N64 without an Expansion Pak. By now, all new game systems used optical media and had comparable stereo sound. Surround sound would be the next feature for home consoles but its quality and usage varied by developer.

TABLE 10.2	Sega Dreamcast Tech Specs
Manufacturer:	Sega Electronics
Launch price:	$199.99
Release date:	11/27/98 (JP), 9/09/99 (US), 10/14/99 (EU), 11/30/99 (AU)
Format:	12× speed GD-ROM "Giga Disc" (1.2 GB)
Processors:	128-bit HitachiSH-4 CPU (200 MHz), PowerVR2 CLX2 GPU
Performance:	100 MHz GPU/3+ million PPS (2+ million w/effects)
Memory:	16 MB RAM, 8 MB video RAM, 2 MB audio RAM
Resolution:	640 × 480 pixels
Sound:	Yamaha AICA—64-channel, 32-bit stereo, at 48 kHz

■ KEY DREAMCAST TITLES

More than 600 titles released for the Dreamcast, of which about 250 reached the United States and PAL territories. Sega's $10 million purchase of *NFL 2K* developers **Visual Concepts** led to *Madden* developer **Electronic Arts** abandoning support of the Dreamcast altogether (Fahs, 2009, p. 9). While not having any EA titles on Dreamcast may have hurt the system, the *2K* series matured into a notable sports franchise and became the biggest competitor to EA Sports Capcom; on the other hand, attracted the attention of action/adventure enthusiasts when *Resident Evil—Code: Veronica* (shown in Figure 10.6) debuted on the system. Because Sega built the Dreamcast from the same technology as its popular **NAOMI** (New Arcade Operation Machine Idea) arcade hardware, "home conversions were more often than not exact replicas of what was seen in the arcade" (McFerran, 2009, p. 241).

FIGURE 10.6 Box art to five popular Dreamcast titles including (a) to *Resident Evil—Code: Veronica*, (b) *NFL 2K1*, (c) *SoulCalibur*, (d) *Jet Grind Radio*, and (e) *Sonic Adventure*..

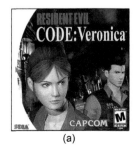

(a)　　　　(b)　　　　(c)　　　　(d)　　　　(e)

Consequently, the system received ports of just about every NAOMI-based arcade game at that time, including fighting games *Dead or Alive 2* and *Marvel vs. Capcom 2* and driving games *18 Wheeler* and *Crazy Taxi*. Arcade guru Yu Suzuki's "interactive novel"-style game *Shenmue* cost upward of $50 million to make, but was a commercial failure (Kent, 2001, p. 578) despite positive reviews. Notwithstanding its losses, Sega released a sequel the following year—although *Shenmue II* never released on the U.S. Dreamcast.

HEAD-TO-HEAD

To compare the graphics and sound between the Dreamcast and PlayStation or N64, check out each system's version of *Gauntlet Legends*, *Hydro Thunder*, *NFL Blitz*, *Rayman 2: The Great Escape*, and *Ready 2 Rumble Boxing*.

■ SONY PLAYSTATION 2

After a year of being the promise that kept many gamers from buying a Dreamcast, Sony released the **PlayStation 2** (**PS2**) (Figure 10.7) in Japan on March 4, 2000, for ¥39,800 yen ($364). All 600,000 units available at launch sold out in just 3 hours (Kent, 2001, p. 570). The PS2's unique design abandoned the circle-heavy look of the original PlayStation in favor of a simpler, more sophisticated look. The console could rest either flat or vertically, which was more similar to a small PC than a traditional video game console. One of its major assets was the ability to play **DVDs** (Digital Versatile Discs) and a PS2 cost about the same or less than a regular DVD player at the time.

In addition to playing CDs and DVDs, the PS2 was backward compatible with almost all original PlayStation games. Its memory card slots and controller ports supported PS1 peripherals, although the 1 MB PS1 memory cards could only be used for PS1 games and PS1 controllers were not always fully compatible with PS2 games. Technological advances allowed PS2 memory cards to hold 8 MB or more data and the new **DualShock 2** controller included pressure-sensitive buttons. The PS2 also added **USB** (Universal Serial Bus) and **IEEE 1394** (Firewire) expansion ports for peripherals.

The American version (with upgraded **firmware**) made its U.S. debut on October 26, 2000, for $299.99. A parts shortage resulted in only 500,000 units being

FIGURE 10.7 PlayStation 2 with DualShock 2 controller.

available on launch day, "with an additional 100,000 consoles being shipped into the United States every week for the remainder of the year" (Kent, 2001, pp. 585–586). Just like Sega with Dreamcast, Sony had intended on a simultaneous European launch, but Europe did not receive the system until November 24. Even with its delays, the PS2 continued to outsell the Dreamcast, in part due to its own record-breaking 28 titles available at launch, DVD player capability, and sheer processing power.

The PS2 was powered by a custom 128-bit CPU developed by Sony and **Toshiba**. Dubbed the "**Emotion Engine**" by **Ken Kutaragi**, the processor was publicized for being capable of producing graphics realistic enough to both convey and provoke human emotion. According to Steve Kent (2001), "its graphics processor had 1,000 times more bandwidth than current PC graphics processors at the time and its floating-point calculation performance was rated at 6.2 **gigaflops** (billion) per second, making it as fast as most super computers" (p. 561).

Since the system doubled as a CD and DVD player, marketing and discussion around the PS2 focused on its value as a home entertainment machine. Its main slogan (which began on the PS1) was "Live in Your World, Play in Ours." It was difficult for Sony to target a specific audience for the PS2. Much of the gaming world had grown up, and "players who became captivated as children [were] now buying more advanced hardware and more sophisticated software" (Marketing Papers, 2017, p. 3). This led to a target market age range as wide as 16–26 years old. Casual consumers may have initially purchased the system because it was an affordable DVD player and only later decided to purchase games for it.

Early PS2 games were manufactured either on CD-ROM or on DVD-ROM format. Consumers could identify CD-ROM games by their blue bottom side, while DVD-ROMs were silver on the bottom. Among the system's 28 launch titles were a handful of standout games to help the system compete with the Dreamcast's well-established library. Key introductory titles on the PS2 included *DOA2: Hardcore, SSX, Tekken Tag Tournament, TimeSplitters*, and *Unreal Tournament* (Table 10.3).

☼ DID YOU KNOW?

With the Dreamcast failing to reach its sales goals to keep the company afloat, Sega discontinued production of the system on March 31, 2001, opening up the field for Sony's PlayStation 2 to become the only active piece of hardware in the sixth generation for a period of 6 months (Briers, 2016, para. 6).

TABLE 10.3 Sony PlayStation 2 U.S. Launch Titles
• *Armored Core 2*
• *DOA2: Hardcore*
• *Dynasty Warriors 2*
• *ESPN International Track & Field*
• *ESPN Winter X Games Snowboarding*
• *Eternal Ring*
• *Evergrace*
• *FantaVision*
• *Gungriffon Blaze*
• *Madden NFL 2001*
• *Midnight Club: Street Racing*
• *NHL 2001*
• *Orphen: Scion of Sorcery*
• *Q-Ball: Billiards Master*
• *Ready 2 Rumble Boxing: Round 2*
• *Ridge Racer V*
• *Silent Scope*
• *Smuggler's Run*
• *SSX* (Figure 10.8a)
• *Street Fighter EX3*
• *Summoner*
• *Surfing H3O*
• *Swing Away Golf*
• *Tekken Tag Tournament* (Figure 10.8b)
• *TimeSplitters*
• *Unreal Tournament*
• *Wild Wild Racing*
• *X-Squad*

Sony released an optional infrared **DVD remote control** to accompany its DVD playback functionality. Other common accessories included the **Multitap** adapter (for connecting four controllers and memory cards), component cables, **GunCon 2** (light gun), guitars and dance pads for rhythm games, a USB keyboard and mouse, and a headset for communicating

FIGURE 10.8 Screenshots from PS2 launch titles: (a) *SSX* and (b) *Tekken Tag Tournament*.

(a)

(b)

PRO FILE

KEY FACTS:

Developed the first three PlayStation consoles and PlayStation Portable

Known as "The Father of the PlayStation"

KEN KUTARAGI

PRO FILE

HISTORY:
- Born: August 2, 1950 in Tokyo, Japan

EDUCATION:
- Degree from DenkiTsūshin University of Electro-Communications, Chōfu, Tokyo, Japan in 1975

CAREER HIGHLIGHTS:
- Joined Sony Corporation in 1975
- Designed the S-SMP audio chip for the SNES
- Developed the SNES CD-ROM adapter that became the widely successful PlayStation console
- Named Chairman and CEO of Sony Computer Entertainment of America in April of 1997
- Became President and CEO for Sony Computer Entertainment, Inc. from 1999 -2006
- His PS2 is the best-selling game console of all time

RECOGNITION:
Interactive Achievement Awards Lifetime Achievement Award in 2008, Game Developers Choice Awards Lifetime Achievement Award in March of 2014

in multiplayer games or for voice commands in certain titles. A hard disk drive (HDD) also released for the original PS2. The HDD was popular in Japan but was only supported by about three dozen titles in the West.

The PlayStation **Network Adapter** (Figure 10.9) landed on store shelves in late 2002, allowing gamers to play online via the PS2 **Network Play** service. In October 2003 Sony released its **EyeToy** color digital camera, conceived by **Richard Marks** and manufactured by **Logitech**. The webcam-like device would become a major influence on the next generation of consoles with its focus on controlling games with motion. Other peripherals by Logitech included the **Driving Force GT** steering wheel kit and the **Cordless Action Controller**. A smaller, quieter PS2 called the **PlayStation 2 Slim** launched on November 1, 2004. The new model included a top-loading disc tray (like PS1) and a built-in network adapter.

■ CONSOLE COMPARISON: PLAYSTATION 2 VS. DREAMCAST

In contrast to Dreamcast's 1.2 GB Giga Discs, PS2's DVD-5 (single layer) discs could hold up to 4.7 GB of data, while DVD-9 (dual layer) games featured a capacity of 8.5 GB (Table 10.4). At a glance, the PS2 appears leagues ahead of the competition, with a claim of 75 million raw polygons per second versus around 3 million PPS on the Dreamcast. However, when using textures, lighting, and other effects, the PS2's true polygon count "could be as low as three million polygons, as seen in games like *Ridge Racer V* and as high as 20 million" (IGN, 2000a, para. 6). Still, the PS2 was the most powerful system on the market at the time of its release.

The PS2's CPU took time for programmers to grasp. The system operated best in tandem with its **vector processing units** (**VPU0** and **VPU1**), its graphics synthesizer GPU, and its **floating-point unit (FPU)** math co-processor to render 3D graphics. While first-generation PS2 software certainly held up to Dreamcast games, it was not until developers mastered the use of the CPU's vector units that consumers could notice a substantial difference in graphics between the consoles. Like the late Dreamcast Broadband Adapter, the PS2's network adapter was capable of connecting via **Ethernet** for high-speed Internet gaming.

HEAD-TO-HEAD

To compare gameplay between early PS2 and Dreamcast games, check out these titles released on both systems: *4×4 Evolution, Dead or Alive 2 (DOA2), MDK2, Ready 2 Rumble Boxing: Round 2, Resident Evil—Code: Veronica,* and *Unreal Tournament.*

■ KEY PLAYSTATION 2 TITLES

More than 4,000 titles released for the PlayStation 2. A big part of the PS2's success was its plethora of high-profile, often exclusive titles (Figure 10.10). Sony's system was the first to receive the groundbreaking "**sandbox**" (open-world) games *Grand Theft Auto III, Grand Theft Auto: Vice City*, and *Bully* by **Rockstar Games**. The PS2 was also first to receive **Hideo Kojima**'s story-driven, motion picture-like *Metal Gear Solid 2: Sons of Liberty* and was the

TABLE 10.4 PlayStation 2 Tech Specs	
Manufacturer:	Sony Computer Entertainment
Launch price:	$299.99
Release date:	3/04/00 (JP), 10/26/00 (US), 11/24/00 (EU), 11/30/00 (AU)
Format:	CD-ROM and DVD-ROM (up to 8.5GB)
Processors:	128-bit "Emotion" RISCCPU (295–299 MHz), GFX Synthesizer
Performance:	"GS" GPU (147 MHz) 75 million PPS (20 million with effects)
Memory:	32 MB main RAM, 4 MB video RAM
Resolution:	720 × 480i, 720 × 480p, 1920 × 1080i (upscaled)
Sound:	48-channel, Dolby Digital Surround, at 44.1 or 48 kHz

FIGURE 10.9 Magazine advertisement for the Sony PlayStation 2 Network Adapter in 2002.

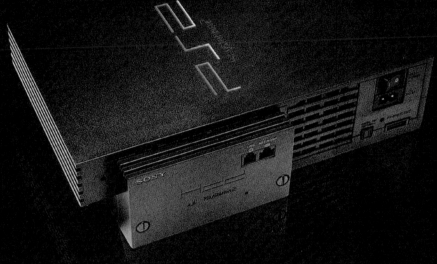

FIGURE 10.10 Five defining PS2 titles: (a) *Metal Gear Solid 2: Sons of Liberty*, (b) *Ratchet & Clank: Going Commando*, (c) *Grand Theft Auto III*, (d) *God of War*, and (e) *Shadow of the Colossus*.

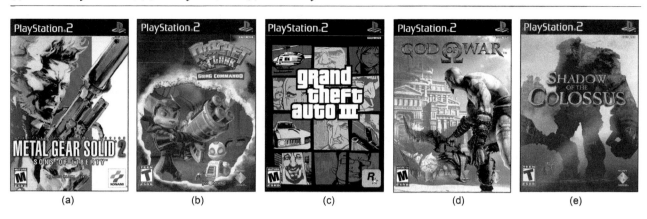

| (a) | (b) | (c) | (d) | (e) |

exclusive console for its follow-up, *Metal Gear Solid 3: Snake Eater*.

Lucrative Sony-published titles included two epic *God of War* action/adventure games, as well as dual entries from the *Gran Turismo* racing series and *Dark Cloud* RPG franchises. Other games released by Sony included *Twisted Metal Black*, the emotional *Ico* and *Shadow of the Colossus* titles, as well as the *Sly Cooper* trilogy. Speaking of trilogies, the system received numerous trifectas from a variety of game publishers, with no less than three titles from the *Jak* series by *Crash Bandicoot* developers **Naughty Dog**, the *Devil May Cry* and *Onimusha* games by Capcom, survival horror hits *Fatal Frame* (*Project Zero* in Europe) by Tecmo and *Silent Hill* (Konami), along with role-playing trilogies from *Final Fantasy* (SquareSoft/Square Enix), *Shadow Hearts* (Midway/Xseed), and *Xenosaga* (Namco).

Even Sega published exclusive titles on the system, such as *Virtua Fighter 4, Shinobi, Nightshade,* and the first two games in the *Yakuza* series. The PS2 attracted more third-party support than any other system that generation, reinforcing the golden rule that outstanding and exclusive software drives console sales.

■ NINTENDO GAMECUBE

Nintendo's next home console was known internally as "Project Dolphin." Electronics company **ArtX** developed its "**Flipper**" graphics processor. ArtX was comprised of former Silicon Graphics, Inc. engineers who worked on the graphics chip for the Nintendo 64. **ATI** (Array Technology Inc.) acquired ArtX in April 2000 after most of the work on the chip was complete (Parker, 2001, para. 4). Because of this, GameCube consoles came with a sticker on the front that read "Graphics By ATI." Computer giant **IBM** (International Business Machines) developed the console's CPU, codenamed "**Gekko**." Before the system's release, longtime Nintendo of America Chairman **Howard Lincoln** retired from the video game business to become owner of the Seattle Mariners baseball team.

Nintendo officially named the system **GameCube** (Figure 10.13) due to its box-like shape. **Kenichiro Ashida** and his team designed the casing to be a compact, portable, friendly looking system (Rogers, 2014, pp. 13–14). It even had a curved handle attached to the rear of the unit for easy carrying. The system was first available in two colors (indigo and jet black), followed by a platinum color "limited edition" GameCube released a year later. Other design considerations for the system included four controller ports, two memory card slots, as well as being the first Nintendo console to use optical media.

⠀☼ DID YOU KNOW?

Only the original indigo and jet black GameCube consoles included an output for component (progressive scan) display. Nintendo removed the output on the platinum model and eventually discontinued it on later models (presumably to save money).

Designed by **Matsushita Electric Industrial** (Panasonic), the company made its MiniDVD-based

◾ HANDHELD SNAPSHOT: GAME BOY ADVANCE

Designed by **Gwénaël Nicolas** and **Curiosity Inc.**, Nintendo's 32-bit **Game Boy Advance (GBA)** (Figure 10.11) was released in Japan on March 21, 2001. It arrived in the United States on June 11, 2001, for $99.99 and in Europe and Australia 11 days later. The system had an impressive number of launch titles with two dozen games in Japan and more than a dozen in the West. Key launch titles included *Castlevania: Circle of the Moon, F-Zero: Maximum Velocity,* and *Tony Hawk's Pro Skater 2.*

The system was like a portable SNES and Nintendo ported countless SNES games to the handheld, including *Super Mario World, The Legend of Zelda: A Link to the Past,* and *Donkey Kong Country.* Like the SNES, the GBA had two shoulder buttons and was **backward compatible** with Game Boy and Game Boy Color titles. Like those handhelds, however, the original GBA lacked a backlit screen. Because of the smaller, non-lit screen, games ported to the system typically had brighter color palettes and a more zoomed-in perspective compared to their SNES originals. See Table 10.5 for specs.

The GBA was a 32-bit system and it was even more capable than the SNES in ways, such as having the ability to render

FIGURE 10.11 Game Boy Advance featuring *Metroid Zero Mission.*

3D textured polygons. Games that utilized this power looked similar to PS1 titles on the handheld, such as *007 Nightfire, Iridion 3D, Top Gear Rally,* and *Driv3r.* Like its predecessors, the GBA operated on just two AA batteries.

In 2003, Nintendo released an updated GBA with a backlit screen called **Game Boy Advance SP.** That same year, Nintendo's **Game Boy Player** accessory became available. This was a dock that plugged into the bottom of a GameCube and allowed users to play GBA (as well as Game Boy and Game Boy Color) games on a TV. Nintendo released a third, smaller and lighter GBA handheld called **Game Boy Micro** in 2005.

Over 1,500 games were released for the GBA, and more than 81 million systems sold (Nintendo, 2010). See Figure 10.12 for five of the system's key titles. As in previous generations, Nintendo continued its dominance over the handheld market to such an extent, that the average consumer may not have even been aware of its two main competitors at the time—the **Neo•Geo Pocket Color** and **Nokia N-Gage** (which doubled as a cell phone).

TABLE 10.5 Game Boy Advance Tech Specs

Format:	Cartridge/2 AA batteries (approximately 15 hours)
Processor:	32-bit ARM7TDMI (16.8 MHz) with 8-bit Z80 co-processor
Memory:	32 kB RAM, 96 kB VRAM + 256 kB DRAM (outside CPU)
Resolution:	240 × 160 pixels/2.9″ diagonal LCD screen
Colors:	512 from a palette of 32,768
Sound:	6-channel (two 8-bit) with 3.5 mm stereo headphones jack

FIGURE 10.12 Box art to key GBA titles: (a) *Castlevania: Aria of Sorrow,* (b) *Metroid: Zero Mission,* (c) *WarioWare: Twisted!,* (d) *Pokémon Emerald* Version, and (e) *The Legend of Zelda: The Minish Cap.*

(a)   (b)   (c)   (d)   (e)

FIGURE 10.13 Nintendo GameCube console, controller, and one black memory card.

discs with enhanced copy protection as a top priority (Hara, 1999, para. 7). The smaller (8 cm) GameCube game discs could only hold up to **1.5 GB** of data and, as such, larger titles required two discs. The system was not capable of playing standard DVDs or audio CDs. On the other hand, Nintendo created the system "to attract third-party developers by offering more power at a cheaper price" (IGN Staff, 1999, para. 17). See Table 10.6 for a list of launch titles.

The GameCube debuted in Japan on September 14, 2001, shipping approximately 500,000 units—followed by another 700,000 units launched in the United States on November 18th. The company would have 500,000 units available in Europe the following May. It was another launch record for Nintendo and the company reportedly spent an estimated

TABLE 10.6 Nintendo GameCube U.S. Launch Titles

- *All-Star Baseball 2002*
- *Batman: Vengeance*
- *Crazy Taxi*
- *Dave Mirra Freestyle BMX 2*
- *Disney's Tarzan Untamed*
- *Luigi's Mansion* (Figure 10.14a)
- *Madden NFL 2002*
- *NHL Hitz 20-02*
- *Star Wars Rogue Squadron II: Rogue Leader* (Figure 10.14b)
- *Super Monkey Ball*
- *Tony Hawk's Pro Skater 3*
- *Wave Race: Blue Storm*

$75 million dollars on its launch campaign, including "a celebrity-studded Hollywood party featuring celebrities such as Ryan Reynolds, Paris Hilton, Tara Reid, Christina Aguilera, Michelle Rodriguez, and Lil' Kim" (Rogers, 2014, p. 40). Priced at just $199, it was the most affordable new console (not counting the discontinued Dreamcast) going into the holiday season. Advertisements soon included the slogan "Born to Play," along with television commercials ending with a voice whispering "GameCube."

As with previous Nintendo consoles, **Shigeru Miyamoto** had a hand in designing its unique controller. Miyamoto set out to create a more optimal game pad after mixed reactions to the N64 controller. He designed four to five versions before settling on the final product. The controller put an emphasis on the main "A" button, being surrounded by smaller buttons—all with varying shapes and sizes. Miyamoto felt this would "help players identify each button's level of importance on the controller's layout" (Rogers, 2014, p. 21).

The GameCube controller also included built-in vibration feedback, along with two analog sticks. The right stick (labeled the "C-stick") was predominantly used for camera control similar to the four yellow "C" buttons on the N64 controller. The top of the game pad housed two pressure-sensitive (clickable) "L" and "R" trigger buttons, along with a smaller, purple "Z" shoulder button on the right side. The only part of the controller that seemed like an afterthought was the

FIGURE 10.14 Screenshots of (a) *Luigi's Mansion* and (b) *Star Wars Rogue Leader: Rogue Squadron II.*

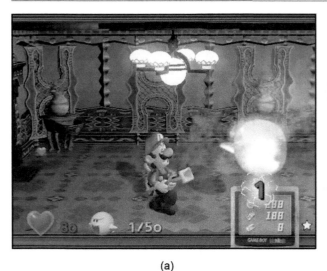

(a)

(b)

D-Pad, which was smaller and less responsive than D-Pads from previous Nintendo controllers.

In 2002, Nintendo introduced the earliest first-party wireless controller with the **WaveBird**. The WaveBird ran on just two AA batteries but lacked the vibration feature of the standard controller. Other peripherals included memory cards that could hold between 4 and 64 MB of game data, **DK Bongos** for rhythm games such as *Donkey Konga*, a microphone, racing wheel, and an **ASCII keyboard controller** (which looked like a standard GameCube controller with a full-size computer keyboard in the middle). The GameCube also featured accessories for interacting with the GBA handheld. The **GameCube-Game Boy Advance (GCN-GBA) cable** was a link cable developed for players to access exclusive content in certain GC games (such as *The Legend of Zelda: Four Swords Adventures* and *Final Fantasy Crystal Chronicles*). For instance, players could use a GBA as a second screen and controller. Finally, the **Game Boy Player** dock allowed gamers to play Game Boy, Game Boy Color, and GBA games on their TV.

■ CONSOLE COMPARISON:
  GAMECUBE VS. PLAYSTATION 2

The GameCube and PlayStation 2 were vastly different types of hardware. Nintendo designed the GameCube to be easier to program for, avoiding the more complex architecture of the PS2 (which divided tasks between its CPU and two vector units). "Whereas PlayStation

2's CPU and two Vector Units split up the tasks of various graphic procedures, like transformation and lighting, for example, all of this is handled singularly by Gamecube's Flipper chip, which also decompresses textures at a 6:1 ratio" (IGN Staff, 2000a, para. 17).

By itself, the GameCube's **485 MHz** Gekko CPU (Table 10.7) was much faster than PS2's 299 MHz processor. And while its floating-point calculation performance clocked at just **1.9 gigaflops** compared to 6.2 GFLOPS on the PS2, the GC's 162 MHz Flipper graphics processor was rated at **9.4 GFLOPS**. Furthermore, the GameCube CPU's 256 kB of **second-level cache** (which determines the speed of general game code) was leagues ahead of the 16 kB of second-level cache used by the PS2.

Looking beyond the inflated raw polygon counts to polygons per second with effects, the systems' polygon counts were about equal. On the other hand, the GameCube was capable of rendering "up to eight effects layers to a polygon in a single pass, whereas the PS2 features a multi-pass rendering system … so essentially PS2 [had] to render 1,000 polygons eight times over whereas GameCube only [had] to render 1,000 polygons once for the same effect" (IGN Staff, 2000a, para. 19). While GameCube had its advantages, experienced programmers were eventually able to develop techniques to conquer the PS2's shortcomings. Beyond pure performance, it was GameCube's small disc capacity, lack of DVD playback, and next to no online gaming that gave PS2 a market edge.

TABLE 10.7	Nintendo GameCube Tech Specs
Manufacturer:	Nintendo
Launch price:	$199.99
Release date:	9/14/01 (JP), 11/18/01 (US), 5/03/02 (EU), 5/17/02 (AU)
Format:	8 cm optical disc (1.5 GB)
Processors:	IBM Power PC "Gekko" processor (485 MHz) ATI "Flipper" GPU (162 MHz)
Performance:	90 million polygons per second (6–20 PPS with effects)
Memory:	24 MB main RAM, 3 MB video RAM, 16 MB audio RAM
Resolution:	640 × 480i, 640 × 480p
Sound:	64-channel, Pro Logic Surround Stereo at 48 kHz

■ KEY GAMECUBE TITLES

Just over 650 games were released for the GameCube. Returning first-party favorites included *Super Mario Sunshine* (Figure 10.15), *The Legend of Zelda: The Wind Waker* and *Twilight Princess, Mario Kart: Double Dash!!*, and the console's best-selling game, *Super Smash Bros. Melee* (shown in Figure 10.16). Nintendo also introduced new franchises on the system such as *Pikmin* and *Animal Crossing*, while in-house **Retro Studios, Inc.** brought the *Metroid* franchise to 3D with two *Metroid Prime* releases. Initially criticized for attempting to evolve the series from 2D to 3D, the *Metroid Prime* games exceeded all expectations and became two of the best titles on the system. Key N64 developer **Rare** released its last Nintendo exclusive with *Starfox Adventures* before being acquired by Microsoft in 2002 (McFerran, 2016, p. 171).

> ### ☼ DID YOU KNOW?
>
> "Out of the top 25 best-selling games for the GameCube, 19 of them were published by Nintendo" (Coulter, 2011, para. 16). The company's last official title for the system was its swan song, *The Legend of Zelda: Twilight Princess.*

Third-party support included **Factor 5**'s *Star Wars Rogue Squadron II: Rogue Leader* and its sequel *Rebel Strike.* Canadian developer **Silicon Knights** worked on just two GameCube games but both *Metal Gear Solid: Twin Snakes* (published by Konami) and *Eternal Darkness* (published by Nintendo) were Triple-A titles.

Atari ported the Japanese Dreamcast exclusive shoot 'em up *Ikaruga* to the system as a U.S. exclusive and Sega even ported its own Dreamcast hits including *Crazy Taxi, Skies of Arcadia Legends, Phantasy Star Online*, and the *Sonic Adventure* games. Sega's *Super Monkey Ball* franchise began as GameCube exclusives but would later appear on competing consoles.

What the GameCube severely lacked was online gaming support. While Nintendo did release a broadband and modem adapter for the system, just a handful of games utilized a LAN connection and only Sega's *Phantasy Star Online* games (and a game called *Homeland* in Japan) were playable online. Speaking of Sega, in early 2003 Sega announced that it would be discontinuing all of its sports titles on the GameCube in favor of other platforms (Berghammer, 2003, p. 1). That same year, longtime developer **Acclaim** dropped support for GameCube altogether.

Similar third-party issues came from Capcom, who also started off as a firm supporter for GameCube. Capcom initially announced five exclusive titles for the system, including survival horror shooters *Resident Evil 4* and *Killer7*, sci-fi shooter *P.N.03*, side-scrolling action-platformer *Viewtiful Joe*, and a shoot 'em up called *Dead Phoenix*. "In the end, the only title out of the fabled 'Capcom Five' to remain GameCube exclusive was *P.N.03*—the fifth game, *Dead Phoenix* was canceled in 2003 and Suda51's *Killer7* launched on the GameCube and PlayStation 2 at the same time" (McFerran, 2016, p. 172). To its credit, Capcom did maintain other amazing exclusives for the system, including the remake of the original *Resident Evil* and its prequel, *Resident Evil Zero.*

FIGURE 10.15 Magazine advertisement for GameCube title Super Mario Sunshine in 2002.

POLLUTION AND PARADISE DON'T MIX.

It's up to Mario, his water pack and you to make things less toxic and more tropic in Super Mario Sunshine.™ only for Nintendo GameCube.™

 Visit www.esrb.org or call 1-800-771-3772 for more info.

© 2002 Nintendo. ™, ® and the Nintendo GameCube logo are trademarks of Nintendo. © 2002 Nintendo. Game and Nintendo GameCube sold separately. www.nintendogamecube.com

FIGURE 10.16 Box art to five defining GameCube titles including (a) *Super Smash Bros. Melee*, (b) *Metroid Prime*, (c) *The Legend of Zelda: The Wind Waker*, (d) *Eternal Darkness*, and (e) *Resident Evil 4*.

| (a) | (b) | (c) | (d) | (e) |

HEAD-TO-HEAD

Dozens of games were released on both the GameCube and PS2. Compare the gameplay and graphics to each system's version of *Extreme-G 3, Killer7, Resident Evil 4, Sonic Heroes, TimeSplitters 2*, and *Viewtiful Joe 1 & 2*.

■ CHANGES AT NINTENDO

Similar to how the previous generation saw a multitude of personnel changes at Sega, 2002 would become a major turning point for the leadership at Nintendo. It began in January when Nintendo of America president **Minoru Arakawa** retired from the company. Two months later, Nintendo of America's **Ken Lobb** (producer/supervisor on projects such as *Star Wars Rogue Squadron II: Rogue Leader* and *Metroid Prime*) left the company to join Microsoft in March. Then, after more than five decades of running the company, Nintendo president **Hiroshi Yamauchi** decided it was time to retire from the company he inherited from his great grandfather. Yamauchi would remain a board member for the 3 years following his retirement. Head of Nintendo's Corporate Planning Division, **Satoru Iwata,** replaced Yamauchi as the new president of Nintendo Co., Ltd. that summer. Finally, on September 24, 2002, Nintendo sold Rareware to Microsoft "for 100% ownership for $375 million" (Rogers, 2014, p. 56).

■ MICROSOFT XBOX

Paul Allen and **Bill Gates** founded **Microsoft Corporation** on April 4, 1975. Headquartered in Redmond, Washington, the company quickly developed a reputation for its computer software and operating systems (OS). Starting with **BASIC** (Beginner's All-purpose Symbolic Instruction Code) interpreters for the Altair 8800, the company would begin to revolutionize personal computers with its **MS-DOS** operating system for IBM in the mid-1980s. The company developed a graphical extension for MS-DOS in 1985 called **Windows,** followed by its **Microsoft Office** suite in 1990. It was on August 24, 1995, when Microsoft released its **Windows 95** OS, solidifying its dominance in the personal computer world and skyrocketing past Apple in annual revenue.

Being the leader of the PC OS, Bill Gates naturally felt threatened when early announcements of the PS2 positioned the system as a competitor to both the home entertainment and personal computer industries. His strategy was to build a better game console and compete directly with Sony. Development for Microsoft's first home console began with four engineers from Microsoft's **DirectX** (multimedia programming interfaces) team including **Kevin Bachus, Seamus Blackley, Otto Berkes,** and **Ted Hase** (Takahashi, 2011, p. 2). Shortly thereafter, head of Microsoft's game publishing division **Ed Fries** joined the team and the group set out to construct a home console based on Microsoft's DirectX technology that

FIGURE 10.17 Microsoft Xbox console with a "Controller S" model controller.

was initially known as the "DirectX Box." Despite its unpopularity with Microsoft's marketing team, the name "**Xbox**" (Figure 10.17) outscored all other titles in focus tests and become the official name of the system (Alexander, 2009, para. 16).

J. Allard and **Cameron Ferroni** were in charge of creating the Xbox's operating system, which they had originally planned to run the Windows OS. After removing everything it did not need, it became apparent that the system would not run Windows and it more or less became a DirectX OS (Takahashi, 2011, p. 3). Still, the system's inner components more closely resembled a PC than any video game system before it. Similar to Sony's surprise when Nintendo announced that Philips would be manufacturing a CD drive for the SNES, "the Xbox was originally built using **AMD** [Advanced Micro Devices] hardware. At the last second, right before a major conference, the technology stack shifted to **Intel**" (White, 2015, para. 2).

In addition to using the PC-popular Intel **Pentium III** processor and an **Nvidia** graphics chip, the console also contained an **8 GB internal hard drive** and a **broadband Ethernet port**. Although it was not the first home console to include internal storage, its 8 GB hard drive was much larger and more capable than the internal storage of the 3DO or Sega Saturn. In addition to game data storage, users could download game patches and even rip entire music CDs to the hard drive. The decision to make the system broadband-only (with no dial-up modem) seemed controversial at first; however, it raised the bar for online gaming and the absence of a dial-up modem saved Microsoft

around $5.18 per unit sold (Takahashi, 2011, p. 3). That added up to an overall savings of $100 million.

> ### 💡 DID YOU KNOW?
>
> Seamus Blackley explained that the system's trademark green color was a product of the console's designer **Horace Luke**. Luke had a fancy set of paint markers that everyone in the office would take, except for the green ones—so he would draw all his artist renderings with green markers and the color stuck (McCaffrey, 2015).

The Xbox was the first home game console made by an American company since the Atari Jaguar. It was released first in North America on November 15, 2001, for $299.99—just two months after the 9/11 terrorist attacks on U.S. soil. Microsoft chose Toys "R" Us in the heart of Times Square for its launch party. Thousands of New Yorkers came out for the event, which was "bathed in acid green search lights. Microsoft gave them Krispy Kreme donuts with green sprinkles. Bill Gates walked up and down the line and shook hands with all of the fans" (Takahashi, 2011, p. 6). Compared to Nintendo's $75 million launch campaign for GameCube, Microsoft spent $500 million on the launch campaign for Xbox, including television and print ads, as well as "national promotions with companies such as Taco Bell, SoBe and Vans" (Rogers, 2014, p. 41).

Its U.S. launch was a success with more than a million Xbox consoles sold in its first three weeks

TABLE 10.8   Microsoft Xbox U.S. Launch Titles

- *4×4 EVO2*
- *AirForce Delta Storm*
- *Arctic Thunder*
- *Cel Damage*
- *Dark Summit*
- *Dead or Alive 3*
- *Fuzion Frenzy*
- *Halo: Combat Evolved* (Figure 10.18a)
- *Mad Dash Racing*
- *Madden NFL 2002* (Figure 10.18b)
- *NASCAR Heat 2002*
- *NASCAR Thunder 2002*
- *NFL Fever 2002*
- *NHL Hitz 20-02*
- *Oddworld: Munch's Oddysee*
- *Project Gotham Racing*
- *Shrek*
- *Test Drive Off-Road Wide Open*
- *Tony Hawk's Pro Skater 2X*
- *TransWorld Surf*

on the market. The popular first-person shooter (FPS) *Halo: Combat Evolved* would see similar success in its first few months on store shelves. *Halo* was the definitive system-seller for the Xbox, thanks to Microsoft acquiring the game's developer **Bungie Studios** in June 2000. "Xbox release dates in Japan (February 22, 2002) and Europe (March 14, 2002) soon followed, though the system failed to catch fire in either of the two regions with the same energy that fueled its arrival in North America" (Marshall, 2013, para. 10). Its launch titles (Table 10.8) consisted primarily of sports and action games, which were not the style of games that attracted Japanese gamers.

The Xbox controller featured a similar button layout to its competition. It only had two shoulder triggers but included two additional "black-and-white" face buttons. The original controller (nicknamed the "**Duke**") was so large that Microsoft designed a smaller "Controller S" model for the Japanese market. The "Duke" (shown in Figure 10.19) received frequent criticism in the West for its cumbersome shape and oval face buttons. Within a year, Microsoft discontinued it in favor of the Controller S, which became the standard Xbox gamepad in all regions. In addition to its more comfortable design, Microsoft completely relocated the black-and-white buttons to be more accessible.

The system's online network "**Xbox Live** arrived in November 2002 with a starter kit to get users into multiplayer games. More than 150,000 people signed up in the first week" (Griffith, 2013, para. 7). Like the PS2, the Xbox offered DVD playback but required a separate remote control with an adapter that plugged into a controller port. In addition to its external hard drive, users could store data on memory cards, which plugged into the back of the controllers like Nintendo 64 gamepads.

The system received the standard line of peripherals including light guns, steering wheels, **System Link** cables (for LAN gaming), headsets, component cables, microphones, third-party wireless controllers, rhythm game accessories, along with a keyboard and mouse. Its most unique accessory was a gigantic controller from Capcom that came bundled with its *Steel Battalion* mech game. The $200 multi-section

FIGURE 10.18   Screenshots of Xbox launch titles: (a) *Halo: Combat Evolved* and (b) *Madden NFL 2002*.

(a)

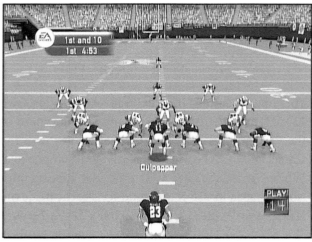

(b)

FIGURE 10.19 2001 Xbox ad featuring characters from *Tony Hawk's Pro Skater 2, Abe from Oddworld: Munch's Oddysee,* and the original "Duke" controller.

unit measured nearly three feet wide and contained approximately 40 different buttons, multiple control sticks, and three different foot petals.

▪ CONSOLE COMPARISON: XBOX VS. PLAYSTATION 2 AND GAMECUBE

The Intel Pentium III CPU ran at an impressive **733 MHz** (Table 10.9)—more than twice the speed of the PS2 Emotion Engine, but about on par with the GameCube's Gekko when considering all components. While GameCube's 485 MHz processor appears inferior on paper, its 256 K of second-level cache made the Gekko and Pentium III comparable. This is because "the size of a CPU's second-level cache determines how fast general game-code runs" (IGN, 2010a, para.

22). The PS2 included only 16 K of second-level cache, while the Xbox had **128 K**. The Xbox's Nvidia **NV2A GPU** ran at 233 MHz—a faster clock speed than the GameCube's Flipper, but at a lower floating-point performance of **7.3 GFLOPS**.

Processing speed aside, the Xbox could push more polygons than either the GameCube or PS2, both raw or with various effects. On the other hand, its GPU could only run half of the number of effects layers to a polygon compared to GameCube, with **four effects layers** in a single pass. Overall, however, Xbox games typically looked the best when comparing the same titles on each console. In almost every case, the Xbox version of cross-platform games looked sharper—often containing extra details such as lighting and bump mapping effects missing on the other consoles.

TABLE 10.9   Microsoft Xbox Tech Specs

Manufacturer:	Microsoft
Launch price:	$299.99
Release date:	11/15/01 (US), 2/22/02 (JP), 3/14/02 (EU & AU)
Format:	CD-ROM & DVD-ROM (up to 8.5 GB)
Processors:	Intel Pentium III CPU (733 MHz) Nvidia NV2A GPU (233 MHz)
Performance:	125 million polygons per second (29 million PPS w/effects)
Memory:	64 MB RAM with 8 GB hard drive
Resolution:	720 × 480i plus 480p, 576i, 576p, 720p, & 1080i
Sound:	64-channel, Dolby Digital 5.1 (plus DTS for movies)

The *Tom Clancy's Splinter Cell* series was a prime example of this—especially on a progressive scan setup with component video cables.

Xbox also had an advantage in sound for gamers with the proper setup. Audio expert **Brian Schmidt** was able to integrate Dolby Digital 5.1 surround sound into the system—a first for home video game consoles. Other firsts included the ability for Xbox gamers to mod their system and download game patches via its built-in hard drive. Online gaming became a major feature of the Xbox and PS2. The original PS2 required an external network adaptor but accommodated both dial-up and broadband users. Xbox only supported broadband, but Microsoft built the modem into the system from the beginning. Gaming online with Xbox required a paid monthly subscription to Xbox Live, whereas online gaming with PS2 was managed by each game publisher and on their own servers. Overall, it was Xbox that set the standard for online gaming on home consoles.

HEAD-TO-HEAD

Many Xbox games were also released on both GameCube and PS2. Compare all three systems by checking out each console's version of *007: Nightfire, Beyond Good and Evil, BloodRayne, Metal Arms: Glitch in the System*, and any of the *Prince of Persia* titles.

■ KEY XBOX TITLES

Close to one thousand games released for the Xbox. *Halo: Combat Evolved* quickly took the crown for best-selling launch title and its sequel *Halo 2* became the best-selling Xbox game of all time. For shooter fans, the *Halo* franchise was reason enough to buy the system. Other home console exclusives published by Microsoft Game Studios included Peter Molyneux's action-RPG *Fable*, two *MechAssault* games, and key racing series including *Project Gotham Racing, RalliSport Challenge*, and *Forza Motorsport*.

The system received exclusive support from **Tecmo** with its *Dead or Alive* and *Ninja Gaiden* franchises, including exclusive Sega titles such as *Panzer Dragoon Orta, The House of the Dead III*, and *Jet Set Radio Future*. Developer **BioWare** made a name for itself on the console with its renowned *Jade Empire* and *Star Wars: Knights of the Old Republic* (in Figure 10.20) RPGs. The acquisition of Rare on the other hand, only led to the mediocre *Grabbed by the Ghoulies* and an updated version of the N64 game *Conker: Live & Reloaded*.

Sony's PS2 was the debut console for the first two *Grand Theft Auto* games, but the games looked far superior when Rockstar Games later released them on the Xbox. Sports games (especially the *2K* series) also looked the best on Xbox—often containing scenes and features not seen on competing consoles. Such was the case with most cross-platform games, with the Xbox version of titles often featuring additional special effects and progressive scan support. While only around a quarter of all PS2 games featured progressive scan support, 480p was a standard option in most Xbox games. Unfortunately, most consumers did not have enhanced or high-definition TVs during this time to take full advantage of these features.

FIGURE 10.20 Xbox hits: (a) *Star Wars: Knights of the Old Republic*, (b) *Burnout 3: Takedown*, (c) *Halo: Combat Evolved*, (d) *Tom Clancy's Splinter Cell: Chaos Theory*, and (e) *Ninja Gaiden Black*.

(a)   (b)   (c)   (d)   (e)

■ SIXTH-GENERATION MARKET SUMMARY

Despite a successful launch, the Dreamcast's 3 million units sold in America fell far short of Sega's goals and the company was incurring major financial losses. Several price cuts later (including the rebate offer where consumers could obtain a free Dreamcast with an 18-month SegaNet subscription) were simply not enough to keep the company afloat. On January 24, 2001, Sega announced it would be discontinuing the Dreamcast. Less than 3 months later, the company would lose cofounder and chairman Isao Okawa to congestive heart failure after a battle with cancer—but not before he gifted his entire $695 million worth of Sega and CSK stock to help the company survive its third-party transition (Kent, 2001, pp. 588–589). The Dreamcast would become Sega's last home video game system, ending its 18-year run as a console manufacturer.

The company repositioned itself as a sole software publisher and continued to manufacture Dreamcast games for about a year, in addition to releasing third-party (often exclusive) titles for PlayStation 2, GameCube, and Xbox. In 2004, pachinko manufacturer **Sammy** acquired Sega for $1.4 billion, becoming **Sega Sammy Holdings Inc**. The restructuring would result in Sega laying off nearly one-third of its Tokyo workforce. This was followed by the departure of Sonic Team leader Yuji Naka who left in 2006, and significantly reduced contributions by Sega's arcade pioneer Yu Suzuki in subsequent years (Fahs, 2009,

p. 11). Despite its losses, Sega maintained its status as a leading manufacturer of arcade games and would continue to be a reputable name on arcade cabinets for years to come.

Sony sold more than half a million PS2 consoles on the day of its Japanese launch, exceeding $250 million in sales when combined with software and peripherals. This was "more than double that of the Dreamcast's first-day total of $97 million" (IGN Staff, 2000b, p. 1). By 2005, Sony solidified its market dominance when the PS2 became the fastest game system to ship 100 million units worldwide. To date, the PlayStation 2 is the best-selling video game console of all time, with more than 155 million units sold (Figure 10.21).

By June 2003, both the GameCube and Xbox had a 13% market share—far behind the 60% market share of the PlayStation 2 (Frederick & Sekiguchi, 2003, para. 4). Even after a price drop to $99 that September, Nintendo would land in a close third place in global console sales, just behind Xbox. Beyond its lack of DVD playback, smaller game disc size, and next to no online gaming, other reasons for the GameCube's lower sales included less third-party support from certain developers and its image of being a system for younger gamers. That image was difficult for Nintendo to shake—even with its exclusive lineup of *Resident Evil* games. Furthermore, "CNN reported that Nintendo was charging a much higher licensing fee for GameCube ($11) while Microsoft and Sony charged ($7–$9)" (Rogers, 2014, p. 33).

FIGURE 10.21 Sixth-generation console sales graph.

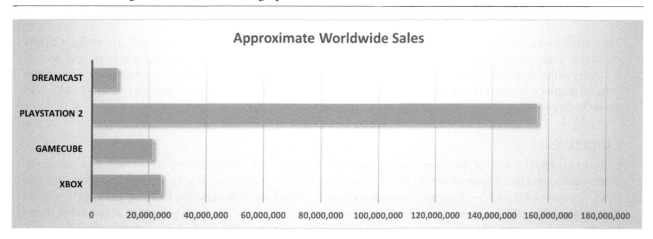

The Xbox broke launch records in the United States when it sold 1.53 million units just three months after its North American debut (Orland, 2013, para. 9). By May 2006, the console had sold approximately 2 million more units than GameCube but was a distant second place to the record-breaking PlayStation 2. While Microsoft may have sold more game consoles than Nintendo, it did so at a hefty cost. While it is not unusual for console manufacturers to sell their game systems at a loss (to recuperate later in software sales), "for every machine that Microsoft sold at $299 at the outset, it was losing about $126, thanks to the $425 cost of the machine" (Takahashi, 2011, p. 6). The Xbox may have been a huge economic loss for Microsoft—about $4 billion—however, it would prove to be a valuable investment in the generations to come.

▪ SIXTH-GENERATION BREAKTHROUGHS AND TRENDS

There were unique breakthroughs and trends that defined the sixth generation of video games. Here is a list of the top 10 features that defined the generation:

1. 128-bit microprocessors

2. Faster, more powerful CPUs (up to 733 MHz) and GPUs (up to 233 MHz)

3. Progressive scan and higher display resolutions (up to 720p and 1080i)

4. Greater RAM (up to 64 MB) and tens of millions of polygons per second

5. Digital versatile disc (DVD) format with DVD movie playback

6. Surround sound with higher audio sampling frequency (48 kHz)

7. Broadband Internet speed and online, multiplayer gaming on home consoles

8. Open-world "sandbox"-style games and first-person shooters break new ground

9. Cross-platform releases on both home console and PC

10. Game publisher mergers (such as Square Enix, Sega Sammy, and Bandai Namco)

◼ ACTIVITY: PERFORMANCE OPTIONS

There were multiple options available for gamers during the sixth generation of home video game consoles. Gamers could play their consoles via LAN (local area network), online, or two-player and even four-player via split screen. For users with ED or HDTVs, key titles could be played in progressive scan mode, which resulted in crisper, more colorful graphics, and less screen blurring. This activity will allow modern gamers a chance to compare older with newer technologies.

GUIDELINES

Obtain two HDTVs, two of the same sixth-generation consoles, system link cables, component and composite video cables, and two copies of two to three games that include (1) progressive scan support and (2) multiplayer modes both via LAN and (3) split-screen multiplayer modes. Since the online networks for these consoles have been discontinued, the LAN-supported games will offer a similar experience. Compare progressive scan vs. interlaced scan by playing a game on one screen with component cables and the other screen with a composite video cable. Then play a multiplayer game in split screen mode, followed by full screen, LAN multiplayer mode.

QUESTIONS

1. How do the games' graphics compare playing them in progressive (component) versus interlaced scan (composite)?
2. Describe the experience of playing multiplayer games via split screen mode on one television versus playing on a LAN where each player has his or her own screen.

◼ CHAPTER 10 QUIZ

1. Arcades declined in the United States for all of the following reasons, except:
   a. Arcade games became more expensive
   b. Console games became nearly equal in quality
   c. Not enough arcade games were being made
   d. Game rentals became more popular

2. This arcade manufacturer moved the rhythm game genre forward with games like *Beatmania* and *Dance Dance Revolution*:
   a. Sega
   b. Harmonix
   c. Namco
   d. Konami

3. Venues like Chuck E. Cheese's and Dave & Buster's have been successful from their:
   a. emphasis on food and beverage service
   b. inclusion of various redemption games
   c. large screens, unique game controllers, and motion-controlled hydraulic cabinets
   d. all of the above

4. Sega's Dreamcast began as two separate projects. In the end, the company went with:
   a. U.S.-based project "Blackbelt" led by IBM veteran Tatsuo Yamamoto
   b. the internal "Katana" project by longtime Sega console designer Hideki Sato
   c. the "Emotion Engine" by Ken Kutaragi
   d. the "Gekko" CPU developed by computer giant IBM

5. Which format did Dreamcast use for its game media?
   a. CD-ROM (700 MB)
   b. GD-ROM (Gigabyte Disc, 1.2 GB)
   c. MiniDVD (1.5 GB)
   d. DVD (up to 8.5 GB)

6. This third-party developer decided not to develop games for the Dreamcast:
   a. Electronic Arts
   b. Capcom
   c. Namco
   d. Visual Concepts

7. The central processing unit for the PlayStation 2:
   a. 128-bit Hitachi SH-4 processor
   b. Intel Pentium III processor
   c. 128-bit "Emotion" RISC processor
   d. IBM Power PC "Gekko" processor

8. The PS2's CPU took time for programmers to grasp, since it operated best in tandem with the console's:
   a. Nvidia NV2A GPU
   b. Flipper GPU
   c. Vector processing units (VPU0 and VPU1)
   d. None of the above

9. This compact, portable, friendly looking system included a curved handle for easy carrying:
   a. Xbox
   b. GameCube
   c. PlayStation 2 Slim
   d. Dreamcast

10. Nintendo GameCube's "Gekko" CPU was developed by:
   a. IBM
   b. AMD
   c. NEC
   d. Motorola

11. Introduced the earliest first-party wireless controller with the WaveBird:
   a. Xbox
   b. GameCube
   c. PlayStation 2 Slim
   d. Dreamcast

12. This 32-bit handheld dominated the sixth generation of video games with more than 81 million systems sold:
   a. Neo•Geo Pocket Color
   b. Nintendo Game Boy Advance
   c. Nokia N-Gage
   d. None of the above

13. The publisher who chose Toys "R" Us in the heart of Times Square for its launch party, handing out Krispy Kreme donuts as customers waited in line:
   a. Sega
   b. Sony
   c. Microsoft
   d. Nintendo

14. This console's version of cross-platform games typically looked sharper—often containing extra details such as lighting and bump mapping effects not included on the other systems:
   a. Sega Dreamcast
   b. Sony PlayStation 2
   c. Nintendo GameCube
   d. Microsoft Xbox

15. Which of the following features was *not* a characteristic of the Microsoft Xbox?
   a. Most powerful sixth-generation console powered by an Intel Pentium III processor
   b. Its GPU could run eight simultaneous effects layers to a polygon
   c. Built-in broadband port; set the standard for online gaming on home consoles
   d. Could download game patches and rip music CDs to its built-in hard drive

16. This console never fully realized the importance of online gaming, with only two games playable online:
   a. Nintendo GameCube
   b. Sega Dreamcast
   c. Sony PlayStation 2
   d. Microsoft Xbox

17. Which systems were incapable of DVD playback?
   a. PlayStation 2 and GameCube
   b. GameCube and Dreamcast
   c. Xbox and GameCube
   d. Dreamcast and PlayStation 2

18. This company acquired game developer Bungie Studios in June 2000.
    a. Sega
    b. Sony
    c. Microsoft
    d. Nintendo

19. This company was acquired by Sammy for $1.4 billion, resulting in a layoff of nearly one-third of its Tokyo workforce:
    a. Sega
    b. Capcom
    c. Namco
    d. Konami

20. Which game console totally dominated the generation in total number of units sold?
    a. Sega Dreamcast
    b. Microsoft Xbox
    c. Sony PlayStation 2
    d. Nintendo GameCube

True or False

21. An argument with Sega chairman Isao Okawa led to Sega of America president Bernie Stolar's termination from the company just a month before the Dreamcast's launch.

22. The Dreamcast included a built-in modem for connecting to the Internet.

23. One of the drawbacks of the PlayStation 2 was its inability to play DVD movies without an adapter.

24. The GameCube was capable of playing Game Boy Advance games with the "Game Boy Player" dock accessory.

25. The original Xbox suffered from poor initial sales because its original, first-party controller was far too small for the average gamer's hands.

■ FIGURES

Figure 10.1 *Dance Dance Revolution* (Konami, 1999). ("Dance Dance Revolution." Vintage Arcade Superstore, 2017. Retrieved from https://www.vintagearcade.net/shop/arcade-games/dance-dance-revolution-arcade-game/.)

Figure 10.2 Screenshots of popular arcade games from 2000: (a) *Silent Scope 2: Dark Silhouette* (Konami), (b) *Marvel vs. Capcom 2* (Capcom), and (c) *18 Wheeler: American Pro Trucker* (Sega). (*Silent Scope 2: Dark Silhouette*, courtesy of KCET/Konami, 2000; *Marvel vs. Capcom 2*, courtesy of Capcom, 2000; and *18 Wheeler: American Pro Trucker*, courtesy of Sega, 2000.)

Figure 10.3 Sega Dreamcast console and controller with LCD screen memory card. ("A North American Sega Dreamcast video game console," by Evan Amos—own work, CC BY-SA 3.0. Available at https://commons.wikimedia.org/w/index.php?curid=20590083. Retrieved from https://en.wikipedia.org/wiki/Dreamcast#/media/File:Dreamcast-Console-Set.png.) (Part of this image was used on the introductory page of this chapter.)

Figure 10.4 Screenshots of Dreamcast launch titles: (a) *Sonic Adventure* and (b) *SoulCalibur*. (*Sonic Adventure*, courtesy of Sonic Team/Sega, 1999; and *SoulCalibur*, courtesy of Namco, 1999.)

Figure 10.5 Magazine advertisement for the Dreamcast in 1999. (From "Sega Dreamcast (9.9.99)" GamePro 120, July 1999, p. 95. IDG Publishing.)

Figure 10.6 Box art to five popular Dreamcast titles including (a) to *Resident Evil—Code: Veronica*, (b) *NFL 2K1*, (b) *SoulCalibur*, (d) *Jet Grind Radio*, and (e) *Sonic Adventure*. (*Resident Evil—Code: Veronica*, courtesy of NexTech/Capcom, 2000; *NFL 2K1*, courtesy of Visual Concepts/Sega, 2000; *SoulCalibur*, courtesy of Namco, 1999; *Jet Grind Radio*, courtesy of Smilebit/Sega, 2000; and *Sonic Adventure*, courtesy of Sonic Team/Sega, 1999.)

Figure 10.7 Sony PlayStation 2 with DualShock 2 controller. ("An SCPH-30000 model with DualShock 2" by Evan Amos—own work, public domain. Available at https://commons.wikimedia.org/w/index.php?curid=12826957. Retrieved from https://en.wikipedia.org/wiki/PlayStation_2_models#/media/File:PS2-Fat-Console-Set.jpg.) (Part of this image was used on the introductory page of this chapter.)

Figure 10.8 Screenshots from PS2 launch titles: (a) *SSX* and *Tekken Tag Tournament*. (*SSX*, courtesy of EA Sports Big, 2000; and *Tekken Tag Tournament*, courtesy of Namco, 2000.)

Figure 10.9 Magazine advertisement for the Sony PlayStation 2 Network Adapter in 2002. (From GamePro, Issue 171, December 2002, p. 1.)

Figure 10.10 Five defining PS2 titles: (a) *Metal Gear Solid 2: Sons of Liberty*, (b) *Ratchet & Clank: Going Commando*, (c) *Grand Theft Auto III*, (d) *God of War*, and (e) *Shadow of the Colossus*. (a) *Metal Gear Solid 2: Sons of Liberty* (courtesy of KCEJ/Konami, 2001), (b) *Ratchet & Clank: Going Commando* (courtesy of Insomniac Games/SCEA, 2003), (c) *Grand Theft Auto III* (courtesy of DMA Design/Rockstar Games, 2001), (d) *God of War* (courtesy of SCE Santa Monica/SCEA, 2005), and (e) *Shadow of the Colossus* (courtesy of SCE Japan Studio/SCEA, 2005).

Figure 10.11 Game Boy Advance featuring *Metroid Zero Mission*. ("The Game Boy Advance (GBA), a 32-bit handheld gaming system made by Nintendo and released in 2001." By Evan Amos—own work, public domain. Available at https://commons.wikimedia.org/w/index.php?curid=18970777. Retrieved from https://en.wikipedia.org/wiki/Game_Boy_Advance#/media/File:Nintendo-Game-Boy-Advance-Purple-FL.jpg.) Screenshot of *Metroid: Zero Mission* by Wardyga Courtesy of Nintendo, 2004.

Figure 10.12 Box art to key GBA titles: (a) *Castlevania: Aria of Sorrow*, (b) *Metroid: Zero Mission*, (c) *WarioWare: Twisted!*, (d) *Pokémon Emerald* Version, and (e) *The Legend of Zelda: The Minish Cap*. (*Castlevania: Aria of Sorrow*, courtesy of KCET/Konami, 2003; *Metroid: Zero Mission*, courtesy of Nintendo, 2004; *WarioWare: Twisted!*, courtesy of Nintendo, 2005; *Pokémon Emerald* Version, courtesy of Game Fream/Nintendo, 2005; and *The Legend of Zelda: The Minish Cap*, courtesy of Flagship/Nintendo, 2005.)

Figure 10.13 Nintendo GameCube console, controller, and one black memory card. ("A Nintendo GameCube console shown with memory card and a standard controller." By Evan Amos—own work, public domain. Available at https://commons.wikimedia.org/w/index.php?curid=12836518. Retrieved from https://en.wikipedia.org/wiki/GameCube#/media/File:GameCube-Console-Set.png.) (Part of this image was used on the introductory page of this chapter.)

Figure 10.14 Screenshots of (a) *Luigi's Mansion* and (b) *Star Wars Rogue Leader: Rogue Squadron II*. (*Luigi's Mansion*, courtesy of Nintendo, 2001; and *Star Wars Rogue Leader: Rogue Squadron II*, courtesy of Factor 5/LucasArts, 2001.)

Figure 10.15 Magazine advertisement for GameCube title Super Mario Sunshine in 2002. ("Super Mario Sunshine PRINT AD video game Nintendo GameCube advertisement 2002" posted by Rick Obee on November 22, 2016. Retrieved from http://addio.ecrater.com/p/13765408/super-mario-sunshine-print-ad.)

Figure 10.16 Box art to five defining GameCube titles including (a) *Super Smash Bros. Melee*, (b) *Metroid Prime*, (c) *The Legend of Zelda: The Wind Waker*, (d) *Eternal Darkness*, and (e) *Resident Evil 4*. (*Super Smash Bros. Melee*, courtesy of HAL Labs/Nintendo, 2001; *Metroid Prime*, courtesy of Retro Studios/Nintendo, 2002; *The Legend of Zelda: The Wind Waker*, courtesy of Nintendo, 2003; *Eternal Darkness*, courtesy of Silicon Knights/Nintendo, 2002; and *Resident Evil 4*, courtesy of Capcom, 2005.)

Figure 10.17 Microsoft Xbox console with a "Controller S" model controller. ("Xbox console with 'Controller S'" by Evan Amos—own work, public domain. Available at https://commons.wikimedia.org/w/index.php?curid=11333075. Retrieved from https://en.wikipedia.org/wiki/Xbox_(console)#/media/File:Xbox-console.jpg.) (Part of this image was used on the introductory page of this chapter.)

Figure 10.18 Screenshots of Xbox launch titles: (a) *Halo: Combat Evolved* and (b) *Madden NFL 2002*. (*Halo: Combat Evolved*, courtesy of Bungie/Microsoft Game Studios, 2001; *Madden NFL 2002*, courtesy of EA Sports, 2001.)

Figure 10.19 2001 Xbox ad featuring characters from *Tony Hawk's Pro Skater 2*, Abe from *Oddworld: Munch's Oddysee*, and the original "Duke" controller. ("Early Xbox Marketing—2" posted November 15, 2001, by Microsoft. Retrieved from https://news.microsoft.com/early-xbox-marketing-2/#d7wgjIlOSVSctmmQ.99.)

Figure 10.20 Xbox hits: (a) *Star Wars: Knights of the Old Republic*, (b) *Burnout 3: Takedown*, (c) *Halo: Combat Evolved*, (d) *Tom Clancy's Splinter Cell: Chaos Theory*, and (e) *Ninja Gaiden Black*. (*Star Wars: Knights of the Old Republic*, courtesy of BioWare/LucasArts, 2003; *Burnout 3: Takedown*, courtesy of Criterion Games/Electronic Arts, 2004; *Halo: Combat Evolved*, courtesy of Bungie/Microsoft Game Studios, 2001; *Tom Clancy's Splinter Cell: Chaos Theory*, courtesy of Ubisoft Montreal/Ubisoft, 2005; and *Ninja Gaiden Black*, courtesy of Team Ninja/Tecmo, 2005.)

Figure 10.21 Sixth-generation console sales graph. (Designed by Wardyga using data from Resource Site for Video Game Research, "Console Wars through the Generations." Available at http://dh101.humanities.ucla.edu/DH101Fall12Lab4/graph—console-wars and GamePro. "The 10 Worst-Selling Consoles of All Time." Retrieved from http://www.gamepro.com/gamepro/domestic/games/features/111822.shtml.)

PRO FILE: Ken Kutaragi. Photo credit: Ken Kutaragi receiving a Lifetime Achievement Award at the Game Developers Choice Awards 2014. Retrieved from https://en.wikipedia.

org/wiki/Ken_Kutaragi#/media/File:Ken_Kutaragi_-_ Game_Developers_Choice_Awards_2014_(cropped).jpg.

■ REFERENCES

Alexander, L. (2009, August 14). *Interview: Former Microsoft exec Fries talks Xbox's genesis*. Retrieved from http://www.webcitation.org/5yxGkLXlW.

Berghammer, B. (2003, February 7). *Sega officially kills GameCube sports development*. Retrieved from http://www.nintendoworldreport.com/news/8261/ sega-officially-kills-gamecube-sports-development.

Briers, M. (2016, October 26). *This day in PlayStation history: PS2 launch*. Retrieved from http://www. playstationlifestyle.net/2016/10/26/this-day-in- playstation-history-ps2-retrospective-launch/# MO7X8HPODdApUQGE.99.

Coulter, S. (2011, November 18). *GameCube 10th anniversary: Fun facts*. Retrieved from https://nintendo-okie. com/2011/11/18/gamecube-10th-anniversary-fun-facts/.

Editorial: GameCube versus PlayStation 2. (2000a, November 3). *IGN*. Retrieved from http://www.ign. com/articles/2000/11/04/gamecube-versus-play- station-2.

Editorial: It's alive! IGN64 brings you the scoop on Nintendo's ArtX-designed 128-bit console. (1999, March 12). *IGN*. Retrieved from http://www.ign.com/ articles/1999/03/13/its-alive-3.

Editorial: Sony pulls in over $250 million at launch. (2000b, November 6). *IGN*. Retrieved from http://www. ign.com/articles/2000/11/07/sony-pulls-in-over- 250-million-at-launch.

Fahs, T. (2009, April 21). *IGN presents the history of Sega*. IGN. Retrieved from http://www.ign.com/ articles/2009/04/21/ign-presents-the-history-of-sega.

Frederick, J. & Sekiguchi T. (2003). The console wars: Game on. *Time International South Pacific Edition*, 49, pp. 56–59. Business Source Complete. Retrieved from http://eds.a.ebscohost.com.lasproxy.minlib.net/ eds/detail/detail?sid=9ab10a5c-9a29-408c-8eb4- 6e0656b35cb8@sessionmgr 4009&vid=4&hid= 4208&bdata=JnNpdGU9ZWRzLWxp dmU=#AN= 23510940&db=buh.

Griffith, E. (2013, November 21). *The story behind the Xbox*. Retrieved from http://www.pcmag.com/arti- cle2/0,2817,2427358,00.aspa.

Hagiwara, S. & Oliver, I. (1999, November–December). Sega Dreamcast: Creating a unified entertainment world. *IEEE Micro: Institute of Electrical and Electronics Engineers*, 19(6), pp. 29–355.

Hara, H. (1999, May 12). Matsushita allies with Nintendo on next-generation game console. *EE Times*. Retrieved from http://www.eetimes.com/document. asp?doc_id=1139403.

Henry, L. (2001, April 26). Skee-ball mania. *Reading Eagle*, p. 36.

Kent, S. (2001). *The ultimate history of video games: The story behind the craze that touched our lives and changed the world*. Roseville, CA: Three Rivers Press.

Marketing Papers. (2017). *Marketing the PlayStation 2*. Retrieved from http://www.marketing-papers.com/ marketing-the-playstation-2.html.

Marshall, R. (2013, May 12). *The history of the Xbox*. Retrieved from http://www.digitaltrends.com/ gaming/the-history-of-the-xbox/.

McCaffrey, R. (2015, July 1). *Podcast unlocked 201: Xbox bosses past and present share stories, secrets*. Retrieved from http://www.ign.com/articles/2015/07/02/pod- cast-unlocked-201-xbox-bosses-past-and-present- share-stories-secrets.

McFerran, D. (2016). *Nintendo Archives*. Bournemouth, UK: Future Publishing Ltd. pp. 166–171.

McFerran, D. (2009). Retroinspection: Dreamcast. *Videogames hardware handbook: 1977–1999*. UK: Imagine Publishing, Ltd., p. 239.

Nintendo Co., Ltd. (2016, April 27). *Consolidated sales transition by region*. Retrieved from https://www.nin- tendo.co.jp/ir/library/historical_data/pdf/consoli- dated_sales_e1603.pdf.

Orland, K. (2013, February 15). *Wii U has historically bad January, sells about 50,000 units in US*. Retrieved from http://arstechnica.com/gaming/2013/02/wii-u-has- historically-bad-january-sells-about-50000-units-in- us/.

Parker, S. (2001, June 6). *Nintendo tweaks GameCube's specs*. Retrieved from http://www.zdnet.com/article/ nintendo-tweaks-gamecubes-specs/.

Perry, D. (2009, September 9). Features – The rise and fall of the Dreamcast. *Gamasutra*. Retrieved from http:// www.gamasutra.com/view/feature/4128/the_rise_ and_fall_of_the_dreamcast.php?print=1.

Rogers, E. (2014, January 7). *A dolphin's tale: The story of GameCube*. Retrieved from https://dromble.wordpress. com/2014/01/07/dolphin-tale-story-of-gamecube/.

Sega Enterprises, Ltd. (2000, October 27). *Sega announces new corporate focus on networked entertainment: Leading gaming content provider leverages Internet to disseminate content on multiple appliances*. Retrieved from https://www.segasammy.co.jp/english/ir/ release/pdf/past/sega/2001/20001027e.pdf.

Takahashi, D. (2011, November 14). *The making of the Xbox: How Microsoft unleashed a video game revo- lution (part 1)*. Retrieved from http://venturebeat. com/2011/11/14/making-of-the-xbox-1/.

White, C. (2015, July 3). *The history of Xbox as told by the leaders of the company*. Retrieved from https://www. neowin.net/news/the-history-of-xbox-as-told-by-the- leaders-of-the-company.

The Rise of PC Gaming and VR

■ OBJECTIVES

After reading this chapter, you should be able to:

- Explain how IBM and its clones revolutionized the personal computer business.

- Provide an overview of Microsoft and the contribution Windows made to gaming.

- Review key people behind the video games and computer technology.

- Identify the graphics and capabilities of PC games as they evolved.

- Discuss online gaming and its influence on the video game market.

- Recap the history of Steam and its developments leading up to today, including Steam Deck.

- Compare how PC gaming is different from home console gaming.

- Name key video game titles by genre made popular on personal computers.

- Explain how and when indie games became popular again.

- Describe the developments of virtual online worlds and virtual reality games.

- Discuss historical and recent technological breakthroughs in personal computers.

- Summarize key PC gaming market sales and trends.

DOI: 10.1201/9781003315759-11

■ KEY TERMS AND PEOPLE

3D graphics accelerator
3dfx
Achievements
Adobe Flash
Daisuke Amaya
Amazon Luna
Amiga series
API
Apple
Apple Arcade
Arc Graphics
Atari ST series
ATI Technologies
Avatar
Ayaneo Next
Battle royale
Bethesda
BioWare
Blizzard
    Entertainment
Blockchain
Bugs
CAD
Anshe Chung
Jess Cliffe
Cloud gaming
Commodore
Compaq
CPU
Cross-play
Deathmatch
Digital distribution
Direct3D
DirectX
Discord
DOS

EA Play
EGA (display)
Craig Eisler
Eric Engstrom
Epic Games
Epic Games Store
Episodic gaming
eSports
Farming
First-person shooter (FPS)
Charles R. Flint
Free-to-Play (F2P)
Freemium
Full-motion video (FMV)
Game subscription
Richard Garriott
Garry's Mod
GeForce 256/NOW/ RTX
Google Stadia
GPU
Ailin Graef
Graphics Core Next (GCN)
Morton Heilig
Hewlett-Packard (HP)
HTC
HTC Vive VR series
Humble Bundle
IBM
IBM clones
IBM PC 5150
id Software
iMac
Indie games
Infogrames Entertainment
    SA
Internet

Jonathan Ive
Jon Jacobs
Java
Steve Jobs
JTS company
Jaron Lanier
Minh Le
Linden Lab
Linux
Lotus 1-2-3
Palmer Luckey
Macintosh series
Matchmaking
Metaverse
Microtransactions
MIDI
MMORPG
MMOW
Modding
Mojang
MS-DOS
Multiplayer
NCsoft
Neverdie
Nvidia
Nvidia Turing
Oculus VR
OpenGL
OS X & OS/2
Patches
PC/AT
PC-compatible
PCjr
Personal Computer
    (PC)
PlayStation PC

Power Glove
Quest VR series
Radeon series
Ray tracing
Real-time strategy (RTS)
Roblox
Ryzen series
Samsung Gear VR
Shareware
Sony Online
    Entertainment
Sound Card
SoundBlaster
Alex St. John
Steam
Steam Deck
SteamVR
Ivan Sutherland
Telltale Games
Twitch
Ubisoft+
Unreal Engine series
Valve
Valve Index
VGA (display)
Virtual item
Virtual reality
Virtual worlds
Virtuality
Viverse
Voodoo (card)
Windows OS
Will Wright
Xbox Cloud Gaming
Yamaha YM3812
YouTube

■ COMPUTER MILESTONES TIMELINE

IBM & VGA	Windows 95	Steam	World of Warcraft	Virtual Reality	Cloud Gaming
1987	1995	2003	2004	2016	2019

▪ INTRODUCTION

Since the beginning of video games, **personal computer (PC)** gaming has typically stayed one step ahead of console gaming. This is because of the nature of a computer's ability for users to customize game performance settings such as resolution, frame rate, and texture quality—as well as upgrade a PC's memory, graphics card, and other features to the absolute latest technology. PC gamers may also contend that a computer keyboard and mouse provide added functionality and more precise controls than a console's gamepad, while players can still opt to play most PC games with a standard controller if that is their preference.

This chapter reviews the rise of PC gaming from the late 1980s to today and the technological developments that helped shape the computer gaming landscape. It will discuss breakthroughs in hardware such as graphics chips, sound cards, and game engines, as well as the people behind the scenes and the innovative game titles synonymous with each era. The chapter will also review the rise of indie games and digital distribution platforms including Steam. Coverage extends from the rise of the PC compatibles, to the explosive growth of Windows 95 and online gaming, to virtual online worlds, virtual reality, and cloud gaming.

▪ IBM AND THE RISE OF THE CLONES

In 1985, Bill Gates predicted

> the advent of inexpensive, 100%-compatible clone computers that was propelling the PC ahead, and that any defects in the design of the computer would eventually be remedied by the combined force of the many companies selling PCs and PC add-on products, such as new graphics cards.
>
> *Reimer (2005, p. 6)*

As an early supporter of the **Macintosh** computer, Gates even reached out to Apple with a plan to license their technology to other companies—a proposal that Apple would reject. Gates' prediction came true, and a different company would lead the evolution of PCs into the next decade.

IBM (International Business Machines) Corporation began operation in Endicott, NY as the Computing-Tabulating-Recording Company (CTR) when **Charles Ranlett Flint** led the consolidation of four major companies in 1911. The merger included companies by

Alexander Dey (inventor of the dial recorder), **Herman Hollerith** (who patented the Electric Tabulating Machine), **Julius E. Pitrat** (who patented the computing scale in 1885), and Bundy Manufacturing Company whose co-founder **Willard Bundy** invented the employee time clock. IBM began as a machinery manufacturer and in 1937 the U.S. government hired the company for its tabulating equipment to maintain 26 million employment records in accordance with the Social Security Act. Nicknamed "Big Blue," the company continued to grow and soon IBM's support extended from mainframe computers to space exploration and even nanotechnology.

The company entered the PC market with the **IBM PC 5150** (Figure 11.1) in 1981 and became popular in the home market with **PCjr** in 1984. IBMs did not become a viable gaming platform until the 16-bit **PC/AT** ("Advanced Technology") computers in 1984. Advancements such as **EGA** (**Enhanced Graphics Adapter**) display allowed for more on-screen colors (16 from a palette of 64) and higher graphics resolution (up to 640×350 pixels). However, early IBM PCs lacked the graphics and sound power of the **Atari ST** and Commodore's **Amiga** computer systems. Additionally, the high cost of IBM and **PC-compatible** systems (known as **IBM clones**) deterred gamers through a significant part of the 1980s. It was IBM's spreadsheet application **Lotus 1-2-3** that helped drive initial sales of the computers in the business sector.

☀ DID YOU KNOW?

Compaq (**Comp**atibility **a**nd **Q**uality) was first to legally reverse engineer the IBM PC and "by the late 1990s and early 2000s, Compaq was the largest PC manufacturer in the world, before it was absorbed by **Hewlett-Packard**" (**HP**) (McCullough, 2014).

A 1985 survey by *Fortune Magazine* indicated that 56% of American businesses were using IBM PCs, compared to 16% using Apple computers (Kennedy, 1985, p. 42). As its market share increased and IBM became the dominant name in personal computers, the price of IBM PCs and clones became more affordable. The immense market share of the PC attracted game developers in 1987, which was the year that much-improved **VGA** (**Video Graphics Array**) displays on the new **IBM PS/2** and FM synthesis **sound cards** (such as Ad Lib's **Yamaha YM3812**) became widely available. See Table 11.1 for a look at the 10-year progression of graphics display cards.

FIGURE 11.1 IBM PC 5150 magazine advertisement from 1982.

"My own IBM computer.
Imagine that."

One nice thing about having your own IBM Personal Computer is that it's *yours*. For your business, your project, your department, your class, your family and, indeed, for yourself.

Of course, you might have thought owning a computer was too expensive. But now you can relax.

The IBM Personal Computer starts at less than $1,600[†] for a system that, with the addition of one simple device, hooks up to your home TV and uses your audio cassette recorder.

You might also have thought running a computer was too difficult. But you can relax again.

Getting started is easier than you might think, because IBM has structured the learning process for you. Our literature is in *your* language, not in "computerese." Our software *involves* you, the system *interacts* with you as if it was made to—and it was.

That's why you can be running programs in just one day. Maybe even writing your *own* programs in a matter of weeks.

For ease of use, flexibility and performance, no other personal computer offers as many advanced capabilities. (See the box.)

But what makes the IBM Personal Computer a truly useful tool are software programs selected by IBM's Personal Computer Software Publishing Department. You can have programs in business, professional, word processing, computer language, personal and entertainment categories.

You can see the system and the software in action at any ComputerLand® store or Sears Business Systems Center. Or try it out at one of our IBM Product Centers. The IBM Data Processing Division will serve those customers who want to purchase in quantity.

Your IBM Personal Computer. Once you start working with it, you'll discover more than the answers and solutions you seek: you'll discover that getting there is half the fun. Imagine that.

IBM PERSONAL COMPUTER SPECIFICATIONS
*ADVANCED FEATURES FOR PERSONAL COMPUTERS

User Memory	Display Screen	Color/Graphics
16K - 256K bytes[*]	High-resolution	*Text mode:*
Permanent Memory	(720h x 350v)[*]	16 colors[*]
(ROM) 40K bytes[*]	80 characters x 25 lines	256 characters and
Microprocessor	Upper and lower case	symbols in ROM[*]
High speed, 8088[*]	Green phosphor	*Graphics mode:*
Auxiliary Memory	screen[*]	4-color resolution:
2 optional internal	**Diagnostics**	320h x 200v[*]
diskette drives,	Power-on self testing[*]	Black & white resolution:
5¼", 160K bytes	Parity checking[*]	640h x 200v[*]
per diskette	**Languages**	Simultaneous graphics &
Keyboard	BASIC, Pascal	text capability[*]
83 keys, 6 ft. cord	**Printer**	**Communications**
attaches to	Bidirectional[*]	RS-232-C interface
system unit[*]	80 characters/second	Asynchronous (start/stop)
10 function keys[*]	12 character styles, up to	protocol
10-key numeric pad	132 characters/line[*]	Up to 9600 bits
Tactile feedback[*]	9 x 9 character matrix[*]	per second

The IBM Personal Computer and me.

[†] This price applies to IBM Product Centers. Prices may vary at other stores.

For the IBM Personal Computer dealer nearest you, call (800) 447-4700. In Illinois, (800) 322-4400. In Alaska or Hawaii, (800) 447-0890.

TABLE 11.1 Common Early PC Graphics Display Cards

Year	Abbr.	Name	Colors via Resolution	Notes
1981	MDA	Monochrome Display Adapter	Mono at 80 columns×25 lines	Only displayed monochrome text
1981	CGA	Color Graphics Adapter	16 colors at 320×200	First IBM color graphics card
1982	HGC	Hercules Graphics Card	Mono at 720×348	Enabled graphics on MDA
1984	EGA	Enhanced Graphics Adapter	16 colors at 640×350	Backward comp. games often 320×200
1984	PGC	Professional Graphics Controller	256 colors at 640×480	Also called Professional Graphics Array
1987	VGA	Video Graphics Array	256 colors at 320×200	Became the base standard for PCs
1989	SVGA	Super Video Graphics Array	256 colors to millions at 800×600	Maximum colors depend on memory
1990	XGA	Extended Graphics Array	256 at 1024×768 | 65,536 at 640×480	Was actually a subset of SVGA

▪ GAMING IN DOS

PC games at this time ran on **DOS** (**disk operating system**). There were several types of DOS, but it was Microsoft's **MS-DOS** (Figure 11.2) that dominated IBM and PC-compatible systems. After booting up the computer, a DOS command prompt would appear on the screen. The user then had to enter a series of commands to launch a program and only one program could be launched at a time. For example, C:\>**a:** [**Enter**] would access the floppy disk drive, while A:\>**game_title.bat** [**Enter**] would launch the game from that drive. If the game utilized a sound card, the user would also have to enter a command for that specific card to activate sound. Once the user launched the game, the program would occupy the entire screen.

Users typically had to configure games for resolution, sound, and other settings prior to playing, to allow DOS programs direct access to the computer's hardware. For a DOS game to use Creative Technology's (1989) **SoundBlaster** card to output sound, the game had to support that hardware directly. In other words, the game developer would need to program support for every major sound card so the user could select their card on the configuration screen (Hoffman, 2014, para. 14). This same scenario applied to peripheral devices including game controllers. Microsoft's popular **Windows 3.0** (1990) made playing games such as *Solitaire* easier to open; however, more complex games still required the user to launch MS-DOS.

▪ GENRE PIONEERS OF THE EARLY 1990s

The early 1990s brought about a series of revolutionary games that began on the PC. *The Secret of Monkey Island* (1990) set the standard for graphical adventure games. Sid Meier's *Civilization* (1991) became one of the most influential turn-based strategy games. Then *Dune II* revolutionized **real-time strategy** (**RTS**) games in 1992, while *Ultima Underworld: The Stygian Abyss* (1992) was regarded for its 3D world and sloped surfaces. *Ultima Underworld*'s "complex levels and the immersion of its dungeon environment were both unparalleled in any game" (PC Gamer, 2016, p. 4). Also that year, *Alone in the Dark*'s puzzles and changing camera views would influence the yet unnamed "survival horror" genre.

id Software's *Wolfenstein 3D* (1992) advanced **first-person shooter** (**FPS**) games with its super smooth movement, paving the way for the genre-defining

FIGURE 11.2 A look at the MS-DOS prompt screen.

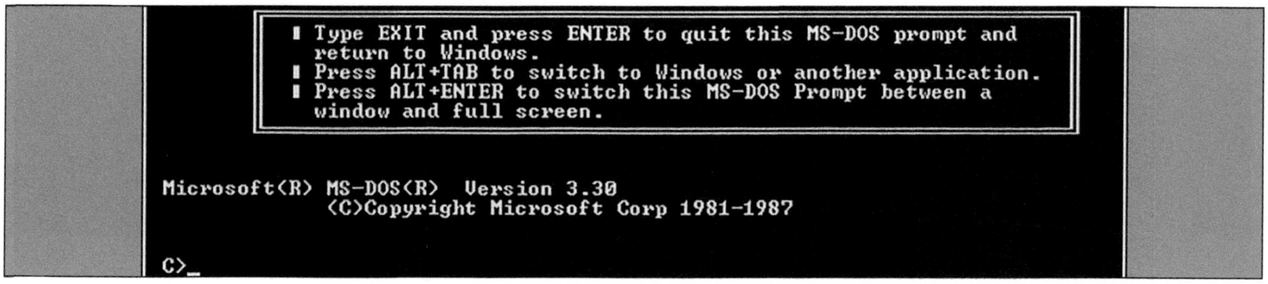

```
▪ Type EXIT and press ENTER to quit this MS-DOS prompt and
  return to Windows.
▪ Press ALT+TAB to switch to Windows or another application.
▪ Press ALT+ENTER to switch this MS-DOS Prompt between a
  window and full screen.

Microsoft(R) MS-DOS(R)  Version 3.30
          (C)Copyright Microsoft Corp 1981-1987

C>_
```

Doom in 1993. In addition to promoting networked **multiplayer** gaming, *Doom* introduced the concept of the "**deathmatch**" where the object is to kill or "frag" as many other players as possible until a time limit or other condition is met. id Software also popularized the **shareware** distribution method (i.e., giving away the first level[s] of a game to entice gamers into purchasing the full release), as well as **modding** (slang for "modifying") where users could change entire attributes of the game such as textures and character graphics.

That same year *Frontier: Elite 2* provided an entire universe to explore, while the gorgeous environments and sounds of best-sellers *Myst* and *The 7th Guest* (Figure 11.3) displayed the photorealism that newer **CD-ROM** media was capable of delivering in 1993. Notable titles from 1994 included *X-COM: UFO Defense* (Mythos Games/MicroProse), which transformed the strategy genre with its turn-based tactical action. Blizzard Entertainment released the first *Warcraft* title—an overhead RTS called *Warcraft: Orcs & Humans*. First-person, action-RPG *System Shock* broke new ground with its 3D engine, physics simulation, and multifaceted gameplay; while *Wing Commander III: Heart of the Tiger* brought cinematic gaming to the forefront with its lengthy narrative and **full-motion video** (**FMV**) featuring Hollywood actors like Mark Hamill.

Even with these revolutionary titles appearing on the PC platform, the enormous success of the home console market (particularly the Nintendo Entertainment System) took a toll on the PC gaming industry by the early 1990s. In 1993, ASCII Entertainment Software's Alan Chaplin reported that the market for home console games had reached $5.9 billion in revenue—12 times that of the computer gaming market's $430 million (Wilson, 1993, p. 98). The computer gaming industry needed a boost, and it would find it with the next operating system (OS) from Microsoft.

■ WINDOWS 95 AND 3D GRAPHICS

Two major PC OSs introduced to compete with MS-DOS included the free and open-source **Linux** in 1991 and IBM's **OS/2 2.0** released in 1992. While millions of users adopted these platforms, it was Microsoft's **Windows 95** that would become the mainstream OS that both the general public and game developers would crown king. The launch of Windows 95 on August 24, 1995, was a huge media event where people lined up in droves to be among the first to receive the new software at midnight. "*Tonight Show* host Jay Leno emceed [hosted] the launch party, with 'Start Me Up' by The Rolling Stones playing as the official theme song of the event" (Reimer, 2005, p. 8).

Where DOS allowed direct access to hardware and system components, Windows 95 used a more protected memory model that restricted user access to these areas. To provide a solution for programmers to develop great games and other multimedia on the OS, Microsoft included a set of application programming interfaces (**APIs**) known as **DirectX**. DirectX was created by development lead **Craig Eisler, Alex St.**

FIGURE 11.3 Screenshots from popular early 1990s PC titles: (a) *Myst* and (b) *The 7th Guest*.

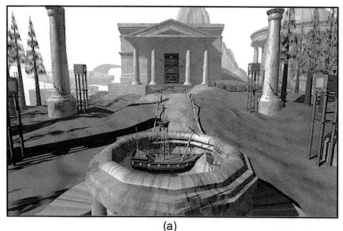

(a)

(b)

FIGURE 11.4   Two-page magazine advertisement for *Tomb Raider* in 1996.

John, and program manager **Eric Engstrom**. Unlike in DOS, gamers could play high-quality Windows 95 games "without leaving the Windows environment, making computer game installation suddenly easier" (Kent, 2001, p. 519).

IBM-compatible **3D graphics accelerator** cards soon followed with the **Nvidia** NV1 (aka "Diamond Edge 3D"), the **ATI** Rage 3D, **VideoLogic** PowerVR, and **Rendition** Verite 1000. These chips cost hundreds of dollars, and the price and performance of 3D accelerator cards did not satisfy consumers until **3dfx Interactive** released its **Voodoo** chipset in 1996. The Voodoo chip produced some of the most detailed 3D graphics of its time and quickly became the most popular PC graphics card. Use of the **Internet** also became increasingly popular with consumers during this time and the popularity of online gaming would quickly follow.

That year *Tomb Raider* (Figure 11.4) revolutionized third-person 3D exploration and introduced the world to the iconic **Laura Croft**. Then id Software's

Quake (Figure 11.5a) pioneered online FPS multiplayer with its "Quakeworld" update and Blizzard's *Diablo* took action-role-playing games to new heights with its randomly generated dungeons, fast action, item variety, and immersive atmosphere. The first *Fallout* title debuted in 1997. That year, Origin Systems released *Ultima Online* (Figure 11.5b), which provided an entire virtual world to explore for a monthly fee. Series creator **Richard Garriott** coined the term **"Massively Multiplayer Online Role-Playing Game"** (**MMORPG**), and a new genre of online gaming was born.

■ THE GOLDEN AGE OF PC GAMING

By the late 1990s, APIs such as DirectX, **OpenGL** by **Silicon Graphics**, and later Microsoft's **Direct3D**, would mature and eliminate the need for proprietary interfaces. This, in turn, led to the rapid development of 3D gaming technology over the next few years. Microsoft discontinued MS-DOS after the

FIGURE 11.5 Screenshots from popular mid-1990s PC titles: (a) *Quake* and (b) *Ultima Online*.

(a)

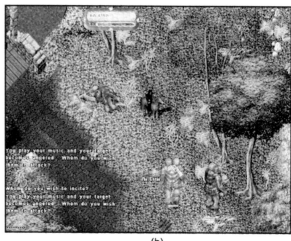

(b)

decade ended and online gaming became increasingly popular for PC gamers. Other developments like web browser plug-ins such as **Sun Microsystems' Java** and **Adobe Flash** became common platforms for simple browser-based games. The period would see the release of countless classic franchises that set new standards for PC gaming, many of which still remain popular today.

One genre that saw explosive growth in the late 1990s was real-time strategy (see Table 11.2). Unlike early turn-based strategy games, RTS games take place in real time, requiring the player to perform numerous, often complex functions where speed is a major factor. The frantic gameplay in titles such as *Age of Empires* (1997) and *StarCraft* (1998) made these games especially fun to watch, with the latter helping establish the **eSports** industry beginning in South Korea. The genre became synonymous with PC gaming due to its multitude of commands requiring a keyboard and the precision needed from a mouse.

Another pivotal PC title was *Half-Life* (1998) with its "then-revolutionary use of scripted events that propelled the action forward without ever removing [the player] from the game (Figure 11.6a). It was the first shooter with a completely seamless presentation from beginning to end: No levels, no loading screens, no cutscenes—just one long take from beginning to end" (PC Gamer, 2016, p. 7). Also, that year *Starsiege: Tribes* was among the first multiplayer-only games, while *Thief: The Dark Project* advanced the "stealth game" genre on PC. The role-playing game *Baldur's Gate* put Canadian developer **BioWare** on the map—who would become one of the most renowned action-RPG developers in the industry.

Breakthrough 3D MMORPGs soon followed, and 1999 was an exceptional year with **Sony Online Entertainment**'s *EverQuest* (Figure 11.6b) in March and Turbine's *Asheron's Call* in November. Both games offered 3D worlds, which were even more immersive than the isometric view in *Ultima Online*. Like *Ultima Online*, these games were "pay-to-play"

TABLE 11.2 Real-Time Strategy Pioneers

Developer	Origin	Game Series	Debuted
Blizzard Entertainment	United States (CA)	*Warcraft, StarCraft*	1994, 1998
The Creative Assembly	United Kingdom	*Total War*	2000
Ensemble Studios	United States (TX)	*Age of Empires*	1997
Relic Entertainment	Canada (Vancouver)	*Homeworld, Company of Heroes*	1999, 2006
Westwood Studios	United States (NV)	*Command and Conquer*	1995

FIGURE 11.6   Screenshots of late hit 1990s titles: (a) *Half-Life* and (b) *EverQuest*.

(a)   (b)

although *EverQuest* also used the "**freemium**" strategy of offering the game **free-to-play** (**F2P**) but charging players for particular features or functionality (Schenck, 2011, para. 2). *Ultima Online, EverQuest,* and *Asheron's Call* became collectively known as the "Big Three" MMORPGs of the early era due to their influence on popularizing the genre in the West (Ivory, 2015, p. 15).

Before the decade ended, the *Unreal* first-person shooter franchise would make a name for itself with *Unreal* in 1998 and *Unreal Tournament* in 1999. The game's **Unreal Engine** gained prominence when U.S. developer **Epic Games** began licensing it to other companies to build games on. Then **Minh Le** and **Jess Cliffe** released a first-person multiplayer mod for *Half-Life* called *Counter-Strike*. *Half-Life* developer **Valve** hired the two men and acquired the game's intellectual property, resulting in sequels and spinoffs. The decade ended with FPS hits *System Shock 2* and *Quake III Arena*, along with the first game in the *RollerCoaster Tycoon* simulation series.

PC technology took a step further when **Nvidia** released the **GeForce 256** near the turn of the century. Called the world's first **GPU** or graphics processing unit, this 256-bit 3D processor offered innovations in geometric polygons, dynamic lighting effects, as well as advanced textures and blending abilities (Nvidia, 1999, p. 1). The integrated features of the GeForce 256 distinguished it from older 3D

accelerators that took power from the main processor, freeing up the computer's **CPU** (central processing unit) and making 3D development easier than older **computer-aided design** (**CAD**). GPUs also helped make PC hardware more affordable. A new rivalry would ensue between Nvidia with its GeForce product line and **ATI Technologies** with its **Radeon** graphics chips.

Apple was on a steady decline into the mid-1990s and in December 1996 Steve Jobs reacquired the company for $400 million. The company's financial losses allowed Jobs to regain control of the company as CEO where he would achieve some of his greatest goals. In addition to saving the company, the stylish and colorful line of all-in-one **iMac** computers (monitors with built-in hard drives and such) in 1998 "revived Apple's fortunes, and with Mac OS X [Operating System X] on the horizon, the Macintosh enjoyed a bump in sales to 3.8 million units in both 1999 and 2000" (Reimer, 2005, p. 8). Apple's Industrial Design Group conceived the original iMac G3 (Figure 11.7) under the leadership of **Jonathan Ive** and tight supervision of Steve Jobs.

☼ DID YOU KNOW?

Apple coined the original color of the iMac "Bondi blue" like the water of Bondi Beach in Sydney, Australia. The word "Bondi" also means "surf," as the iMac was well-equipped for "surfing" the Internet.

FIGURE 11.7 The original "Bondi blue" iMac G3.

▪ A NEW MILLENNIUM OF MMOs

The graphics card market saw a string of acquisitions at the beginning of the new millennium. "ATI announced the acquisition of ArtX Inc. in February 2000, for around $400 million in stock. ArtX was developing the GPU codenamed Project Dolphin [eventually named 'Flipper'] for the Nintendo GameCube, which added significantly to ATI's bottom line" (Singer, 2020, para. 2). Before the end of the year, Nvidia acquired most of Voodoo graphics chip manufacturer 3dfx for $70 million and 1 million shares of common stock. 3dfx filed for bankruptcy less than 2 years later and would cease support of all products. Nvidia's GeForce series and ATI's Radeon line became the next exciting battle between graphics card manufacturers.

Microsoft released **Windows XP** in 2001, which combined the solid performance of its corporate Windows NT with the user-friendliness of Microsoft's home versions. Apple released its tenth operating system that year with **OS X**. Sales remained flat for Macintosh computers, until "the release and overwhelming sales success of the **iPod** in 2001, [when] positive buzz began surrounding Apple again and Macintosh sales started to creep up again in late 2004 … despite the PC and Windows gaining a completely dominant 97% market share" (Reimer, 2005, p. 9).

The popularity of PC gaming continued into the new millennium, although developers continued shifting their focus to home consoles, which had a larger user base and were easier to develop for. One of the factors that makes PC game development more complex is that a PC game's performance depends on the graphic capabilities of a player's hardware. To make a computer game that is compatible with as many systems as possible, developers have to program computer games to run at different resolutions and qualities. By contrast, home consoles have traditionally provided a level of standardization where developers only have to program one version of the game per platform.

Furthermore, it is highly impracticable to test a PC game on every combination of hardware and configuration, meaning that game **bugs** (glitches) are inevitable. This leads to further work of developing downloadable **patches** (fixes) for PC games. On the plus side, playing a PC game 3 feet away from a computer monitor (often with a keyboard and mouse) provides a different, somewhat more intimate experience than playing on a home console. The PC has remained the central platform for strategy, simulation, and online role-playing games for this reason.

Important games in the early part of the twenty-first century included *Deus Ex* (2000) for combining action role-playing with an emphasis on the freedom of choice, along with first-person shooting and elements of stealth. *The Elder Scrolls III: Morrowind* (2002) also provided the player with an unprecedented amount of choice in its open world and established Rockville, Maryland's **Bethesda** as a leader in these types of games. The year 2003 saw the release of *DotA (Defense of the Ancients)*, which began as a mod for *Warcraft III* and pioneered what would become known as the **Multiplayer Online Battle Arena** (MOBA) genre years later. That same year saw the release of Icelandic developer CCP Games' *EVE Online*, an unscripted MMORPG universe with 7,800 star systems for players to visit as they created their own experience.

One publisher/developer who would become legendary in the PC community throughout the 2000s was the California-based **Blizzard Entertainment**. In addition to successful sequels to its classic *Diablo* and *Star Craft* franchises, the company broke new records with the release of *World of Warcraft (WoW)* in 2004. *WoW* grew to become the world's most-subscribed-to MMORPG of all time, obtaining more than 12 million subscriptions by 2010 (McDougall, 2010, para. 1). See Table 11.3 for other popular MMORPGs released before and after *WoW*.

TABLE 11.3 Popular MMORPGs in the New Millennium by Year

Year	Game Title	Developer	Origin	Model
2001	*RuneScape*	Jagex	England	Free-to-Play; Freemium
2002	*Ragnarok Online*	Gravity	South Korea	Freemium; and Pay-to-play
2003	*EVE Online*	CCP Games	Iceland	Freemium
2004	*World of Warcraft*	Blizzard	California	Pay-to-play; Free to level 20
2005	*Guild Wars*	ArenaNet	Washington	Free-to-play with purchase
2006	*Dungeons & Dragons Online*	Turbine	Massachusetts	Freemium
2007	*Lord of the Rings Online*	Turbine	Massachusetts	Freemium
2008	*Warhammer Online: Age of Reckoning*	Electronic Arts	California	Freemium
2009	*Champions Online*	Cryptic Studios	California	Free-to-play; Freemium
2010	*Final Fantasy XIV*	Square Enix	Japan	Pay-to-play; 30-day trial

▪ INDIE AND SOCIAL GAMES GATHER [ON] STEAM

On September 12, 2003, *Half-Life* developer Valve released a new **digital distribution** platform called **Steam**. Steam was unique in that it provided both large and small game companies with a central platform to sell games and for users to download updates and patches. To this day, the platform has offered developers free access to the "Steamworks" API, which can be used to integrate a variety of features—from networking and **matchmaking** (pairing gamers with similar skill sets to play together)—to **microtransactions** (collecting additional money for game features or items) and parameters for in-game **achievements** (trophies, awards).

Another key feature of Steam has been its **digital rights management** (DRM), which "is access-control technology used by manufacturers, publishers, and copyright holders to limit the usage of digital devices or information" (EC-Council, 2010, pp. 9–26). In other words, DRM prevents the unauthorized use or distribution of video games with a **payment gateway** used for collecting user fees and/or verifying user credentials before players can access all or parts of a game.

Along with Xbox Live and the PlayStation Network on home consoles, Steam has become an important contributor to the rise of independent video game development, which began to take off in the late 2000s. Known as "**indie games**," independent video games are developed by individuals or small teams who are free from the influence of big publisher budgets and time constraints. Countless creative games have come

from the indie scene, beginning with the NES-style 2D platformer *Cave Story* in 2004 by Japan's **Daisuke Amaya**. The game was "developed in his free time over the course of five years. Amaya wrote, developed, designed, composed, and everything else imaginable in this game himself" (Watlington, 2015, para. 5).

It would be years before the indie gaming scene would really gain momentum with 2D platformers *Braid* (Figure 11.8a) by Jonathan Blow (2008) and *Spelunky* by Derek Yu (2009). The indie game movement continued into 2010 with *Limbo* by Danish developer Playdead and *Super Meat Boy* by American designers Edmund McMillen and Tommy Refenes. These and other indie games homed in on the 2D platformer style of gaming that was both easier to program for and a style of game that most large publishers had long since abandoned in favor of 3D games. The year 2011 was particularly big for indie games with *Terraria* by Re-Logic (Floyds Knobs, IN) and *Minecraft* (Figure 11.8b) by **Mojang** (Stockholm, Sweden). Both games emphasized exploration, crafting, and construction. Successful indie role-playing titles that year included *Bastion* by Supergiant Games (San Jose, CA) and *To the Moon* by Canadian developer Freebird Games. The indie market would see more success in 2012 with games such as *Fez, FTL: Faster than Light*, and *Journey*.

In addition to the indie scene, Steam has been a big supporter of mods, such as **Garry's Mod** (or **GMod**). In 2006, **Garry Newman** created the sandbox physics game as a mod for Valve's *Half-Life 2*, and like *Counter-Strike*, it later became a stand-alone release. Another feature of Steam is the "Steam Workshop," an account-based hosting service that encourages the

FIGURE 11.8 Screenshots of popular indie titles: (a) *Braid* and (b) *Minecraft*.

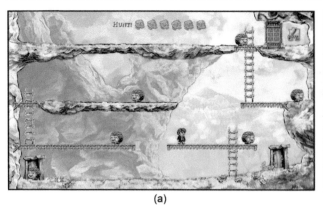

(a)

(b)

development of user-created content or mods. While once a niche concept in games such as *Doom*, game mods are now a popular part of PC gaming culture and commonly developed for popular titles. Mods can also help extend the life of a game or make an older title popular again.

A common PC trend that began in the mid-2000s became known as **episodic gaming**, where companies began releasing games in smaller segments over a period of time and players would pay a small price for each new chapter of the game. This modern take on the concept of expansion packs included **NCsoft**'s *Guild Wars* (2005) and in Valve's own *Half-Life* series with *Half-Life 2: Episode One* (2006) and *Half-Life 2: Episode Two* (2007). Companies such as **Telltale Games** (California) have built their entire development cycle around this structure. This can lead to extra publicity when the publisher releases each new chapter of a game, versus the shorter-lived publicity of a single release, stand-alone title.

With mobile gaming and social media on the rise, Steam quickly became a huge **social network** for gamers. The platform provided each gamer with their own page (public or private) to list the player's achievements, game wish lists, and other information. It also included community features such as friend lists and groups, as well as in-game voice and chat functionality for users to communicate freely. Gamers could now see when their friends were online and what games they were playing and could invite friends to their groups or join other groups for multiplayer interactions.

☀️ **DID YOU KNOW?**

Valve released the **Steam app** for iOS and Android in 2012, and Windows Phone in 2016. The app allows users to manage games, browse the storefront, and chat with friends.

The year 2009 saw an emergence of online **social games** that encouraged or required social interaction between players. Some of the most popular social games were actually "social network games" played through social networks such as **Facebook**. It was farming games including **Zynga**'s *Farmville* (2009) [influenced by *Happy Farm* in China (2008)] that helped the genre gain mainstream popularity (Kohler, 2009, para. 6). Other Zynga titles that helped lead the social gaming revolution included *Mafia Wars* (2008) and the top-ranking *Words with Friends* (2009). Social gaming would continue to grow over the next couple of years and many of these titles landed on mobile gaming platforms.

The popularity of social gaming peeked in 2012 and then saw a steady decline as "revenue from social gaming apps fell 10 percent year over year" through 2015 (DiChristopher, 2015, para. 2). Zynga's stock price plummeted from $14.69 to less than $3 per share and Electronic Arts shut down its Facebook-based social games *SimCity Social*, *The Sims Social*, and *Pet Society* in June 2013. While fewer consumers were playing these games on social networks, social gaming remained popular on mobile devices. Developers continue to integrate social capabilities in games today, where hits such as *WoW* and *GTA V* allow players to interact in a personal capacity. Other social platforms are not games at all but exist as **virtual online worlds**.

■ VIRTUAL ONLINE WORLDS

Beyond Steam and MMORPGs, virtual online worlds (sometimes referred to as **massively multiplayer online worlds** or **MMOWs**) have become a common form of social interaction in the twenty-first century. Dr. Carina Girvan (2013) defined such a world as "a persistent, simulated and immersive environment, facilitated by networked computers, providing multiple users with **avatars** and communication tools with which to act and interact in-world and in real-time" (p. 4). An avatar is the user's virtual representation of themselves, also regarded as the user's "alter ego" or their "character."

Interacting in massively multiplayer online games and virtual worlds can be a great escape from reality, as well as a safe environment for players to let go of inhibitions and release a side of their personality they may otherwise have suppressed. These worlds may also be beneficial to the disabled or chronically ill, where users can create an avatar free of disabilities or illnesses—and temporarily engage in activities, which they may not be capable of in real life. Virtual worlds can also provide people with social disorders a more comfortable environment to socialize and form friendships. It is common to hear stories of cyber-dating and even virtual marriages that have occurred in these worlds, including people who have taken such relationships into the real world. Such interactions can also lead to criminal activity, so participants should always take the utmost precautions with such interactions.

☀ DID YOU KNOW?

Researchers at Syracuse University studied 375 people playing *World of Warcraft* and found that 23% of male players chose female avatars, while 7% of female participants played as male characters (Duntley, 2014, p. 1).

The game that popularized the genre was "life simulation" game *The Sims* (2000) by **Will Wright**. According to John Seabrook from *The New Yorker* (2006), "while he was at home with his daughter, Wright began to turn over the idea for a new game, a kind of interactive doll house that adults would like as much as children" (pp. 15–16). The avatars players create in *The Sims* are called "sims" and the gameplay revolves around the sandbox-style game where players are free to roam about and interact with objects and characters.

Each sim also has six learnable skills (cooking, mechanical, charisma, body, logic, and creativity), which not only affect the way a sim interacts with his fellow sims but also how well he can make use of the objects in his house and how well he can perform his job.

Park (2000, para. 4)

The Sims went on to sell more than 16 million copies and earned world records, including "Best-Selling PC Game" in the *Guinness World Records: Gamer's Edition 2016* (Guinness World Records, 2015, p. 185). The series went massively multiplayer online with *The Sims Online* (Figure 11.9a) in 2002.

The following year, a new virtual online world emerged from **Linden Lab** with *Second Life* in 2003 (Figure 11.9b). "*Second Life* pioneered the idea of a virtual world built by its users, and the freedom to build anything from a fully interactive Neverland to a functional virtual university" (PC Gamer, 2016, p. 4). The use of real currency exchange in virtual worlds such as *Second Life* (called "Linden Dollars") has led many of its million or so users to focus on using the platform to design and sell **virtual items**, from virtual clothing and accessories to the construction and sales of virtual real estate. Users like **Anshe Chung** (*Second Life* avatar of real-life **Ailin Graef**) have made a living "**farming**" such virtual goods and selling them in the virtual community. Graef became the first virtual millionaire in 2006 from buying and developing virtual land and then renting or reselling the plots to other users (Parloff, 2005, para. 3). Chung is rumored to have earned $2 million over a period of just 30 months.

A similar success story includes the real-life, British actor and entrepreneur **Jon Jacobs** and his avatar **Neverdie** in the virtual world *Project Entropia* (now *Entropia Universe*) (Figure 11.9c). Jacobs mortgaged his home in 2005 to buy a virtual asteroid for $100,000. He then constructed a virtual space resort called "Club Neverdie," which attracted players with "more than a dozen biodomes, a night club, stadium and a mall, where other players flocked to spend real cash on virtual goods and services" (Chiang, 2010).

FIGURE 11.9 Screenshots of (a) *The Sims Online*, (b) *Second Life*, and (c) *Entropia Universe*.

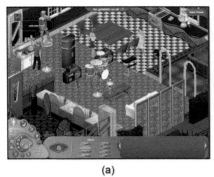  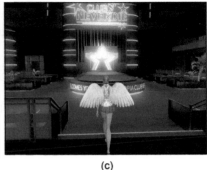

(a) (b) (c)

Jacobs sold Club Neverdie in 2010 for $635,000. See Table 11.4 for a list of other popular virtual online worlds, most of which debuted in the 2000s.

More recently, the industry has adopted the term "**Metaverse**" to describe the concept of these virtual online worlds. The term dates back to Neal Stephenson's 1992 science fiction novel *Snow Crash*. In the novel, the author described the Metaverse as "a virtual world in the imagined future where **virtual reality (VR)** goggle-wearing users inhabit three-dimensional (3D) avatars and buy and sell virtual real estate on a planet-encircling market" (Shilina, 2022, para. 1). Ernest Cline explored the concept further and coined it "The OASIS" in his 2011 science fiction novel *Ready Player One*—which was adapted into a feature film directed by Steven Spielberg in 2018.

In today's world, "the Metaverse concept refers to a persistent simulated online digital universe that combines multiple elements of technology, such as VR, augmented reality (AR), mixed reality (MR) and **blockchain** (digital ledger technology [DLT] like bitcoin cryptocurrency), along with social media concepts" (Shilina, 2022, para. 2). Examples of platforms pushing the Metaverse moniker include *Bloktopia, Decentraland, HyperVerse, Matrix World, Metahero,* and *Somnium Space.* These and similar platforms are the next wave of virtual online worlds, which can offer an experience even closer to Stephenson's Metaverse concept when players can experience all of these worlds in virtual reality.

TABLE 11.4 Classic Virtual Worlds (Listed Alphabetically)

Title	Developer	Origin	Notes	Years Active
Active Worlds	ActiveWorlds Inc.	Massachusetts	Research "Hitomi Fujiko"	1995–
Blue Mars	Avatar Reality	Hawaii	Similar to Second Life	2009–
Entropia Universe	MindArk	Sweden	Became a MMORPG	2003–
Habbo	Sulake	Finland	Teens to young adults	2000–
IMVU	IMVU Creators	California	3D social network	2004–
Onverse	Onverse, LLC.	Arizona	Aka "Online Universe"	2009–2018
PlayStation Home	London Studio	England	Made for PlayStation 3	2008–2015
Second Life	Linden Lab	California	For ages 16 and older	2003–
SmallWorlds	Outsmart Games	New Zealand	Browser-based Flash world	2008–2018
There	Makena Technologies	California	Shut down 3/2/10–5/2/12	2003–
Twinity	Metaversum GmbH	Germany	Now hosted by ExitReality	2008–
Utherverse	Utherverse Digital	British Columbia	Social and business network	2006–

PRO FILE

WILL WRIGHT

KEY FACTS:

Popularized virtual life simulation games

Created the best-selling PC game of its time with *The Sims* in 2000

PRO FILE

HISTORY:
- Born: January 20, 1960 in Atlanta, GA

EDUCATION:
- Louisiana State University (2 yrs), Louisiana Tech University (2 yrs) and The New School in Manhattan (1 yr)

CAREER HIGHLIGHTS:
- First game: *Raid on Bungeling Bay* (1984) for C64
- Formed Maxis with Jeff Braun in 1987 and made *SimCity* (1989), *SimEarth* (1990), *SimAnt* (1991), and co-designed *SimCity 2000* (1993) with Fred Haslam
- Designed *The Sims* (2000), *The Sims Online* (2002), *The Sims 2* (2004), and *Spore* (2008)

RECOGNITION:
Game Developers Choice Awards Lifetime Achievement Award (2001), Academy of Interactive Arts and Sciences' Hall of Fame (2002), *PC Magazine* Lifetime Achievement Award (2005), BAFTA Awards Academy Fellowship (2007), Albert R. Broccoli Britannia Award for Worldwide Contribution to Entertainment (2012), Called one of the most important people in gaming, technology, and entertainment by *Entertainment Weekly*, *Time Magazine*, *PC Gamer*, and others

▪ VIRTUAL REALITY

The concept of **Virtual reality** (**VR**) spans decades into the twentieth century. In the 1950s, American filmmaker **Morton Heilig** penned the idea of an "experience theatre" that could incorporate the human senses. He patented the concept of what he coined the "Telesphere Mask" in 1960 and built a mechanical device called "Sensorama" in 1962. Heilig also produced five short films to communicate his ideas. Subsequent inventions in the late 1960s by computer scientist **Ivan Sutherland** advanced the inclusion of computer graphics and head-mounted display systems.

Jaron Lanier made the term "virtual reality" popular in the mid- to late 1980s. Lanier founded VPL Research in 1985 to develop VR devices such as the DataGlove, which VPL licensed to Mattel for the Nintendo **Power Glove**. The 1992 film *The Lawnmower Man* further explored the concept of VR. Leading VR technology at that time like **Virtuality** consisted of primitive graphics and cost tens of thousands of dollars. The technology began to make strides after the turn of the century and virtual reality made its mainstream debut with a series of VR headsets released for Windows and PlayStation 4 in 2016.

☀ DID YOU KNOW?

The military uses virtual reality to train soldiers in simulated environments and scenarios before deployment. They also use VR during post combat to help soldiers with conditions such as PTSD. See Chapter 13 for more details.

Virtual reality places the gamer inside the video game world for the ultimate sense of immersion by eliminating the TV screen or computer monitor that would otherwise serve as a buffer between the player and the game. VR headsets include one screen for each eye that completely occupy the player's field of view in true 3D. VR also presents game sound in **3D audio**, whether through built-in speakers or external headphones. With 3D audio, the player can hear directional sounds in front, behind, to the sides, and even from above or below. In addition to 3D visuals and sound, VR systems further enhance the experience with motion tracking technology.

Early VR technology required the user to set up external sensor cameras or "base stations" around the playfield for the systems to track player movement.

Newer systems include "inside-out" tracking inside the headset. The player's movement in VR is known as **degrees of freedom** (**DoF**). Mobile VR headsets such as Google Cardboard feature 3 degrees of freedom (**3DoF**). In 3DoF, the user has the ability to (1) look left or right (yaw), (2) rotate their head up or down (pitch), and (3) pivot side to side (roll). More advanced VR systems including those on PC offer 6 degrees of freedom (**6DoF**), adding the ability to move (4) forward or backward (surge), (5) laterally (strafe or sway), and (6) up or down (elevate or heave). In other words, in a 6DoF playfield, players can lean forward (surge) for a closer look at something, move sideways (strafe) for a different view, or squat down (heave) to duck. These movements have no effect in a 3DoF environment.

Locomotion is the term for moving through a physical or virtual space with 6DoF. Since movement is limited in 3DoF, physically moving in ways the 3DoF environment cannot replicate in the virtual space can lead people to feel off balance. Users can also experience motion sickness from too much movement in a 6DoF playfield. With the space limitations in a person's home, along with the dizziness gamers can experience from VR, it has been common for early VR games to feature fixed camera positions, "**snap turning**," and "**teleportation**" to reduce locomotion.

With snap turning (also called "click turning"), the player can surge forward and backward, or strafe left and right, but cannot smoothly rotate the field of view independently of head turning. Instead, snap turning limits such movement to changing the field of view in increments, where the environment jumps or skips ahead several degrees at a time. With teleportation, a game may limit players to a fixed camera position where they must point and click where they want to "teleport" to in the virtual space. Players who can handle the excessive movement can often switch these features off and opt for "smooth scrolling" on the options menu of certain games.

▪ MODERN VR PIONEERS

Among the pioneer companies of modern VR game systems was **Oculus VR**, whose prototype headset was designed by **Palmer Luckey** in 2010. Oculus VR generated positive media attention and Facebook purchased the company in 2014. After collaborating with Samsung Electronics on the $99 **Samsung Gear VR** headset in 2015, Oculus VR released the $599 **Oculus**

FIGURE 11.10   Virtual Reality headsets: (a) Oculus Rift CV1 and (b) HTC Vive.

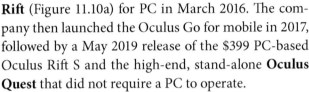

(a)   (b)

Rift (Figure 11.10a) for PC in March 2016. The company then launched the Oculus Go for mobile in 2017, followed by a May 2019 release of the $399 PC-based Oculus Rift S and the high-end, stand-alone **Oculus Quest** that did not require a PC to operate.

The Rift S and Quest featured "inside-out" tracking inside the headsets, which eliminated the need for external sensor cameras. The Quest came in two options: a 64 GB version for $399 and a 128 GB option for $499. It was a bit front-heavy, and the company quickly replaced it with the lighter, more affordable Oculus Quest 2 in October 2020. The Oculus Quest 2 was then rebranded as **Meta Quest 2** in November 2021 after Facebook changed its corporate name to Meta. Like its predecessor, this stand-alone unit sold with two available options, including a 64 GB version for $299 and a 256 GB version for $399.

If all of these name changes and different models were not enough to grasp, another leading VR series had a similarly complex history. A week after the release of the Oculus Rift, **HTC** and Valve Corporation debuted the **HTC Vive** VR headset (Figure 11.10b) on April 5, 2016, for $799. Like the Rift, the Vive was not a stand-alone unit and required a powerful PC to operate, making the total cost of a VR setup at that time around $2,000. Sony, meanwhile, became the leader of the console VR market when it released its own **PlayStation VR** (**PSVR**) for the PS4 for just $399 in October 2016. HTC followed up the Vive with the higher resolution and more affordable $599 **Vive Pro** in April 2018, followed by the $599 **Vive Focus** in April 2019. Like the Oculus Quest, the Vive Focus was a stand-alone headset that did not require a computer to operate.

Then came the PC-powered **Vive Pro Eye** in June 2019 and the $699 **Vive Cosmos** in October 2019. The Vive Pro Eye added built-in eye tracking but cost $799 for just the headset or $1,599 for the headset with controllers and base stations. The Vive Cosmos was similar to the Oculus Quest with its "inside-out" tracking inside the headset, which eliminated the need for external base stations. HTC released three models of the Cosmos with different faceplates, including the Vive Cosmos Elite, Vive Cosmos XR, and Vive Cosmos Play. The company then released the $1,300 **Vive Pro 2** and **Vive Focus 3** in June 2021 with even higher resolution and refresh rates, which basically eliminated the "screen-door effect" of seeing empty spaces between screen pixels.

If anything, the brief history of modern VR headsets shows its rapid progression over just a handful of years. Valve has supported the medium from the beginning with its **SteamVR** platform, and in June 2019 the company released its own consumer VR headset with the **Valve Index**. The Index debuted at $999 with controllers, base stations, and came bundled with the hit game, *Half-Life: Alyx*. It also supported HTC Vive and Vive Pro controllers and base stations. Countless other manufacturers have released VR headsets in recent years such as 3Glasses, Acer, DPVR, HP, Huawei, Pimax, and Varjo. Table 11.5 compares five leading VR headsets by the top manufacturers.

Modern VR titles have excited those who experienced their head-tracking and hand/controller-tracking immersion; however, a lot of early games felt more like tech demos rather than fully realized video games. That trend has been changing in recent years

TABLE 11.5 VR Headset Tech Specs Comparison

	PlayStation VR	Valve Index	Meta Quest 2	HP Reverb G2	HTC Vive Pro 2
Launch date:	10/13/2016	6/28/2019	10/13/2020	10/31/2020	6/4/2021
Base price:	$399	$999	$299-$399	$599	$799
Display type:	OLED	LCD	LCD	LCD	LCD
Resolution per eye:	960×1080	1440×1600	1832×1920	2160×2160	2448×2448
Refresh rate:	up to 120 Hz	up to 144 Hz	up to 120 Hz	up to 90 Hz	up to 120 Hz
Field of view:	100°	130°	100°	114°	120°
Tracking type:	Outside in	Markers	Inside out	Inside out	Markers
Wireless:	No	No	Yes	No	Optional adapter
Speakers:	Integrated	Off ear	Integrated	Off ear	Headphones
Controllers:	PS Move or DualShock 4	Index	Oculus touch	Windows mixed reality	Vive Pro
Required system:	PS4 or PS5	PC	None/PC-optional	PC	PC

with VR games matching traditional game lengths of 15–45 hours. The technology is evolving quickly with higher resolutions, faster refresh rates, plus better tracking and haptic capabilities. Pistol grips and peripherals such as the PlayStation VR Aim Controller have taken shooting games to the next level, while the technology already exists for finger tracking, haptic vests, tactile body suits, and omnidirectional treadmills. Much of this will reach the consumer market as the VR userbase expands and prices become more affordable.

Now is an exciting time for able individuals who have yet to experience VR to give it a try. Just a sample of VR titles worth checking out include rhythm games such as *Beat Saber* and *Thumper*, sci-fi adventure games such as the *Lone Echo* series and Steam-exclusive *Half-Life Alyx,* as well as horror titles such as *The Walking Dead: Saints and Sinners* and *The Exorcist: Legion VR.* Traditional games that have made the successful transition to VR include *Hellblade: Senua's Sacrifice VR Edition, L.A. Noire: The VR Case Files, Rez Infinite, Resident Evil 4 VR,* and *Skyrim VR.* For more kid-friendly games to explore, try *Fujii, Rec Room,* and the *Moss* series.

■ TRENDS OF THE 2010s

Stepping out of the "virtual" space to review other trends of the 2010s—strategy, RPG, and casual games remained the dominant platforms on PC. Other genres that remained strong on PC included simulation, adventure, first-person shooters, and MOBAs. MOBAs such as Riot Games' *League of Legends*

(2009), Valve's *DotA 2* (2013), Hi-Rez Studios' *Smite* (2014), and Blizzard Entertainment's *Heroes of the Storm* (2015) continued to be popular among gamers and eSports fans into the 2020s. Before the end of the decade, most publishers were selling PC games exclusively via digital distribution. Games that received physical versions were often just redeemable gift cards or a download code packaged in a clamshell case.

Streaming, recording, and viewing video games online became a prevalent trend, not only for eSports but also for the average gamer thanks to modern technology that allows players to record and/or stream their gameplay live. **YouTube** remains the world's largest video streaming website, while Amazon subsidiary **Twitch** (twitch.tv) has become a phenomenon in the gaming world. In 2015, Twitch was host to over 1.5 million broadcasters and a place for 100 million fans to watch and chat about their favorite video games every month (Needleman, 2015). By the 2020s, that number had risen to an average of 100,000 daily streams and 2.5 million daily viewers.

Watching video games has become so popular that according to the *Guinness World Records* (2015), "more than 27 million unique viewers tuned in to the Season 4 *League of Legends* World Championship finals [on October 19, 2014] with a peak audience figure of 11.2 million" (p. 29). Compare that to the 10.3 million viewers for the season finale of the hit TV show *Breaking Bad* in 2013. TwitchMetrics (2022) reported *Just Chatting* to be the most-viewed title with more than 249 million viewer hours, while *League of Legends* (Figure 11.11a) remained a hit in the #2 spot with more than 126 million viewer hours. Speaking of chatting, Discord Inc. launched its **Discord** instant messaging platform on May 13, 2015. Discord quickly became one of the most-used platforms by PC gamers for organizing groups via "servers" and communicating outside of in-game chat. The platform also became popular for voice and video calls.

Indie games began garnering more attention than ever during the 2010s. *Minecraft* (2011) became the best-selling indie game of all time with 60 million copies sold before Microsoft acquired the Swedish developer Mojang in 2014 (Guinness World Records, 2015, p. 103). The indie scene continued to deliver consistent hit titles including *Guacamelee!* by DrinkBox Studios and *Gone Home* by Fullbright in 2013, as well as *Monument Valley* by Ustwo Games and *Shovel Knight* by Yacht Club Games in 2014. The following year saw the indie scene grow even more prominent with games such as *Axiom Verge* by Thomas Happ and *Undertale* by Toby Fox.

Notable titles from 2016 included *Owlboy* by D-Pad Studio, *Hyper Light Drifter* by Heart Machine and *Inside* by Playdead. Indie games made 2017 an especially memorable year with hits such as *Night in the Woods* by Infinite Fall, *Cuphead* by Studio MDHR, *Pyre* by Supergiant Games, *Hollow Knight* by Team Cherry, and *What Remains of Edith Finch* by Giant Sparrow. The year 2018 kept the momentum going with *Celeste* by Matt Makes Games Inc., *Dead Cells* by Motion Twin, *Return of the Obra Dinn* by Lucas Pope, and *Subnautica* by Unknown Worlds Entertainment. The decade ended with creative indie hits *Disco Elysium* by ZA/UM, *Katana ZERO* by Askiisoft, *Outer Wilds* by Mobius Digital, LLC, and *Untitled Goose Game* by House House.

The end of the 2010s saw a surge of popularity in **battle royale** games. These last-person-standing competitions got their name from the 2,000 Japanese film *Battle Royale*, which was based on the novel of the same name. Games that defined the genre included *PlayerUnknown's (PUBG) Battlegrounds* and *Fortnite Battle Royale* in 2017 (Figure 11.11b), *Apex Legends* in 2019, and *Call of Duty: Warzone* in 2020. These titles garnered a following in the tens of millions of players within months of reaching the market.

Along with the games, the technology behind them continued to make impressive strides. At Gamescom 2018 Nvidia introduced its **Turing** architecture, which combined with its **GeForce RTX** platform, "fuses together real-time **ray tracing** (advanced lighting effects), artificial intelligence, and programmable shading to give [players] a whole new way to experience games" (Nvidia, 2018). AMD followed with its 2019 announcement of a successor to their **Graphics Core Next (GCN)** architecture called **Radeon DNA (RDNA)**. The company also introduced its third-generation **Ryzen** processor based on its "Zen 2" core architecture. AMD called it "the most advanced desktop processor in the world with ground-breaking performance across gaming, productivity, and content creation applications" (AMD, 2019). Intel continued producing its Core processors and began moving into the GPU market with its **Arc Graphics** cards.

Epic Games launched its **Epic Games Store** for Windows and macOS in December 2018. To help the platform compete with Steam, the company offered publisher and developer incentives such as higher revenue cuts for games published through their store, as well as lower licensing fees for titles built on their Unreal Engine. Epic enticed gamers to sign up with a plethora of free games as well. The following year, Epic unveiled its **Unreal Engine 5**, featuring

FIGURE 11.11 PC MOBA hit *League of Legends* (a) and the successful *Fortnite Battle Royale* (b).

(a)   (b)

its "Nanite" virtualized geometry system for high-detailed rendering at pixel scale. Other highlights of the engine included its "Virtual Shadow Maps" system for high-resolution shadowing, "Lumen" for fully dynamic global illumination and reflections, and "World Partition" system for large world management.

■ SUBSCRIPTION AND CLOUD GAMING

Game subscription services and cloud gaming are major trends in PC gaming business models today. Subscription-based games are part of the live service games model, where players pay a monthly subscription fee to play games. With a game subscription, subscribers can download and play rotations of hundreds, if not thousands of games. It is a terrific way for players to preview blockbuster and indie titles without the risk of paying full price for a game and then not liking it. Subscriptions also provide a consistent income stream for publishers and developers which makes it easier for game companies to predict earnings versus the traditional method of releasing games and hoping they sell.

Examples of subscription gaming platforms on PC include **Humble Bundle**, Inc., which launched its "Humble Monthly" subscription service in October 2015. This provided subscribers with a new set of games at the start of each month. The company launched its "Humble Trove" library of DRM-free games in June 2017 and the "Humble Choice" monthly subscription service in December 2019. Other subscription services to launch around this time included **Ubisoft+** (formerly Uplay+) on September 3, 2019, for $14.99 per

month, **Apple Arcade**, which debuted on September 19, 2019, for $4.99 per month, and **EA Play**, which launched for PC on Steam August 31, 2020 for $4.99 per month.

Subscription platforms typically require players to download part or all of a game to a PC before playing. They contain online features such as online gameplay, live chat, microtransactions, and cloud storage with "cloud save" capability—but are not necessarily cloud games. With true **cloud gaming** (also called "gaming on demand"), the rendering of the games takes place on an external "cloud" server, which streams the games to the players. Since cloud games run on cloud-based servers rather than the device the gamer is playing on, the user is able to play high-end games without the need for high-end hardware. Cloud gaming also benefits publishers and developers because its streaming format eliminates video game piracy.

Early cloud gaming pioneers included **OnLive** in 2010 (acquired by Sony Computer Entertainment in 2015) and Nvidia's **GeForce NOW** which released a 2015 beta On October 1 and full public release on February 4, 2020. Google made headlines when it launched its **Google Stadia** cloud gaming service on November 19, 2019. Since then, other major companies have followed suit such as Microsoft's **Xbox Cloud Gaming** service (formerly Project xCloud), which launched on September 15, 2020, and **Amazon Luna** from March 1, 2021. A key point to remember is that cloud gaming is often a subscription service, however not all game subscription services feature cloud gaming. See Table 11.6 for look at 10 leading subscription and/or cloud gaming platforms.

TABLE 11.6 Ten Leading Subscription and/or Cloud Gaming Platforms

Service	Publisher	Launch Date	Cost
Amazon Luna[a]	Amazon	3/1/2021	Free to $10 per month
Apple Arcade	Apple	9/19/2019	$5 per month
GeForce NOW[a]	Nvidia	2/4/2020	Free to $20 per month
Google Stadia[a]	Google	11/19/2019	Free to $10 per month
Humble Choice	Humble Bundle	12/6/2019	$12 per month
Nintendo Switch Online	Nintendo	9/18/2018	$4 per month–$50 per year
PlayStation Plus (formerly Now)	Sony	1/28/2014	$10–$18 per month
Roblox Premium	Roblox Corporation	9/23/2019	Free to $20 per month
Xbox Cloud Gaming[a]	Microsoft	9/15/2020	Free for Game Pass members
Xbox PC Game Pass	Microsoft	6/1/2017	$10–$15 per month

[a] Launched as a cloud gaming service.

■ HANDHELD SNAPSHOT: VALVE STEAM DECK

Valve's **Steam Deck** (Figure 11.12) aimed to move traditional portable PC gaming from laptops to a more portable console approach. The company debuted its handheld on February 25, 2022. Three options were available at launch, including $399 for 64 GB of internal storage, $529 for 256 GB and $649 for a 512 GB SSD. All models include a high-speed microSD card slot for additional storage on microSD, SDXC, or SDHC cards. Other than the storage differences, the three units are identical with an AMD Zen 2 CPU and RDNA 2 GPU (Table 11.7). The handheld runs on the Linux-based SteamOS out of the box; however, Valve offers official Windows drivers for users looking for more of a portable PC experience.

The Steam Deck is a large piece of hardware, measuring $11.7 \times 4.6 \times 1.9$ inches ($298 \times 117 \times 49$ mm) and weighing 1.475 pounds (669 g). While too big to fit in most pockets, its 7-inch LCD touchscreen provides a clear image at 1280×800 and 60 Hz. The stereo speakers also deliver an equally crisp sound.

> While heavy, the unit feels good in the hand, with a pleasing round curve beneath the palms that is more like a PlayStation controller than the flat Switch handholds against which it's most likely to be compared. The thumbsticks are snappy and textured, though even larger hands will feel their placement is a bit too high for a completely relaxing at-rest position.
>
> *Miller (2022, para. 4)*

Below the thumbsticks are two pressure-sensitive touchpads (aka trackpads) with haptic feedback. In addition to the four standard shoulder triggers and four face buttons, the back of the unit features four additional grip buttons (two on each side).

Unlike games optimized for the Nintendo 3DS or PlayStation Vita, Valve does not guarantee the performance of every Steam title, although the company continues to release firmware updates to improve compatibility. In addition to using more processing power, high-end games can drain the rechargeable battery faster, leading to playtimes as low as 2–3 hours before the user needs to find an outlet or USB port to recharge. Like a PC, however, the Steam Deck is fully customizable, and users can adjust framerate limits, brightness, volume, and other settings to adjust performance and increase battery life. The Steam Deck was not the first nor the last handheld PC on the market. Three of its competitors worth considering include the Anbernic Win 600, Ayaneo Next, and One-Netbook's ONEXPLAYER series.

TABLE 11.7   Steam Deck Tech Specs

Format:	64 GB eMMC, 256 GB or 512 GB NVMe SSD/40 Wh Li-ion battery (2–6 hours)
Processors:	AMD Zen 2 CPU and AMD RDNA 2 GPU
Performance:	4-core and 8-thread CPU (2.4–3.5 GHz), GPU with 8 CUs (1.0–1.6 GHz)
Memory:	16 GB LPDDR5 SDRAM (5500 MT/s)
Resolution:	1280×800 7-inch LCD touchscreen (60 Hz)
Sound:	Stereo speakers, Dual microphone array, 3.5 mm stereo headphone jack

FIGURE 11.12   Steam Deck by Valve featuring *Dead Cells, Deathloop, Ghostrunner, Hollow Knight, Portal 2, Psychonauts 2, Stardew Valley, Tales of Arise, Tetris Effect Connected,* and *The Witcher 3: Wild Hunt.*

■ MARKET SUMMARY

Reviewing the numbers behind the early events in this chapter, PCs and clones "went from a 55[%] market share in 1986 to an 84% share in 1990. The Macintosh stabilized at about 6% market share and the Amiga and Atari ST at around 3% each" (Reimer, 2005, p. 6). By December of 1992, *Computer Gaming World* (1992) reported that MS-DOS software accounted for 82% of computer game sales, while Macintosh held an 8% share, leaving Amiga with 5% (p. 156). Apple would reach an average 9% market share for a couple of years before dropping down to around 3% toward the end of the decade.

Commodore could not keep up with the explosive sales of IBM and PC compatibles. "Stuck with tons of old machines that couldn't sell and unable to build enough new machines for the Christmas '93 season, the company fell into a downward financial spiral which led inevitably to its bankruptcy in April 1994" (Reimer, 2005, p. 7) (Figure 11.13). Atari merged with hard drive manufacturer **JTS** in 1996, was sold to Hasbro in 1998, and then purchased by **Infogrames Entertainment SA** (IESA) in 2001 where Atari, Inc. remained a subsidiary. In 2009 the company was rebranded "Atari SA."

PC-compatible sales continued to rise while Apple's "Macintosh sales slumped. By 1998, PCs were closing in on sales rates of 100 million units per year, while Macintosh sales fell from 4.5 million in 1995 to just 2.7 million in 1998" (Reimer, 2005, p. 8). Windows 95 was a major contributor to the PC industry boom and Microsoft continued to release prominent successors such as Windows XP in 2001, Windows 7 in 2009, and Windows 10 in 2015. To maintain its dominance, Microsoft even offered free upgrades to compatible PCs, including upgrades from Windows 10 to 11.

Traditional, retail packaged software sales declined while digital distribution and free-to-play revenues continued to grow. A key pioneer of this shift from PC retail to digital retail and F2P was Steam. Steam grew rapidly, with the quantity of games released per year rising from just over 500 new games in 2013, to over 1,500 titles in 2014, and nearly 3,500 new titles in 2015. The platform exceeded 50,000 total games by 2021 (Bailey, 2021, para. 1). Active Steam users nearly doubled from around 60 million in October 2013 to 120 million users today. Accordingly, Steam revenues more than doubled from $1.5 billion in 2014 to $3.5 billion in 2015 (Clayton, 2016, p. 1). Video Game Insights (2022) reported that Steam's game market reached a peak of $6.6 billion in gross revenue in 2021.

Super Data Research reported that "interactive entertainment generated $91 billion in revenues in 2016" with $40.6 billion spent on mobile gaming (up 18%) and $35.8 billion on PC gaming (up 6.7%).

FIGURE 11.13 Computer sales in thousands of units in the early 1990s.

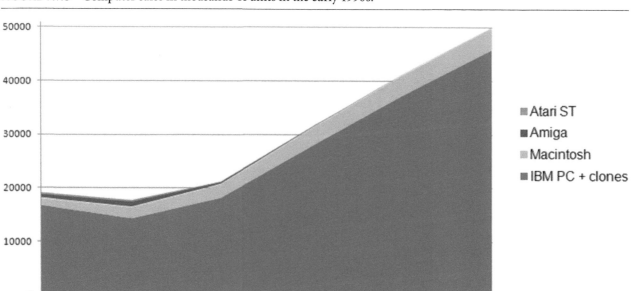

FIGURE 11.14   10-year PC gaming revenue market percentage.

10-Year PC Games Revenue Market Percentage

Year	Percentage
2012	37%
2013	38%
2014	36%
2015	34%
2016	30%
2017	27%
2018	24%
2019	22%
2020	21%
2021	19%

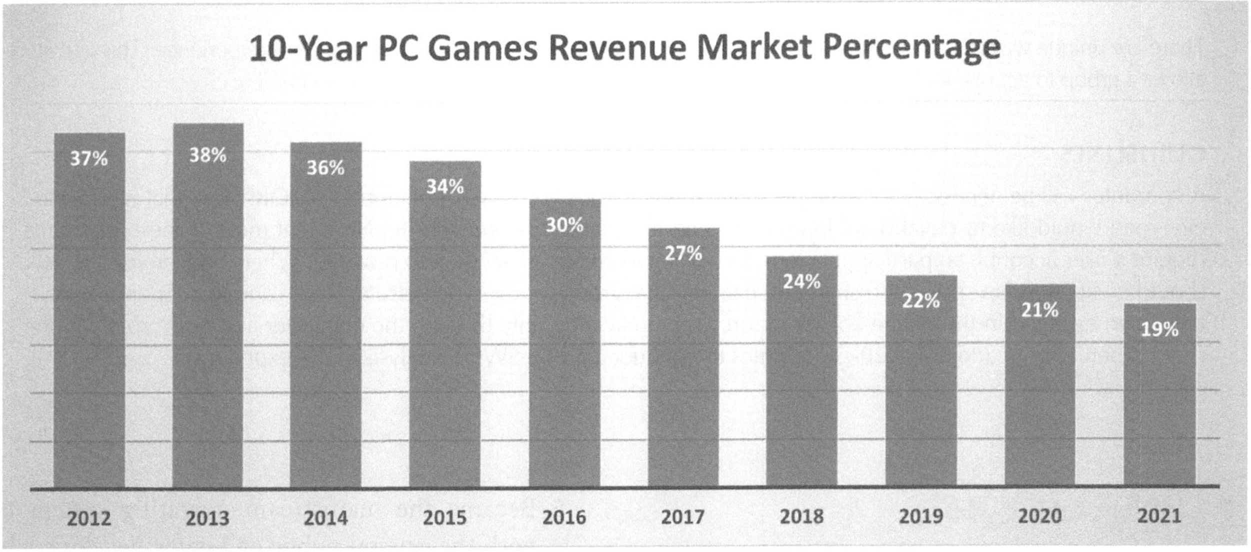

Retail games generated $6.6 billion on digital downloads and another $2.7 billion on VR. By 2021, global market revenue from mobile games more than doubled in 5 years to $90.7 billion, while PC gaming remained flat but profitable at $35.9 billion (Newzoo, 2021, p. 5). By comparison, console gaming took in $49.2 billion in 2021. See Figure 11.14 for PC revenue percentage changes from 2012 to 2021.

One reason these numbers show a decline is because of the convergence of gaming platforms.

> Ten years ago, each respective gaming ecosystem—console, PC, and mobile—was essentially siloed from one another. Thanks to continual innovations in cross-platform play (aka **cross-play**), cross-progression, subscriptions, and franchises intersecting all platforms, the lines between these platforms are obscuring .
>
> *Newzoo (2021, p 27)*

Even Sony has been moving into PC territory, releasing previous console exclusives *Death Stranding* on PC in July 2020 and *Horizon Zero Dawn* less than a month later. Sony launched its own **PlayStation PC** label in 2021, followed by PC releases of *Days Gone, God of War,* and *Uncharted: Legacy of Thieves Collection.*

The coronavirus pandemic also played a role in the video game business. While live events such as video game conventions and eSports saw a decline, gaming at home increased significantly. For example, the online gaming platform **Roblox** became so popular during the pandemic (especially for younger gamers) that from February 2020 to January 2021, Roblox experienced an increase in valuation from $4 billion to $29.5 billion (Jacobs, 2021, para. 3). These online platforms and the concept of the Metaverse hold exciting possibilities for the future of PC gaming. The same holds true for VR. VR company HTC unveiled **Viverse** in February 2022, a Metaverse ecosystem of content for entertainment, education, creation, and social interactivity. The video games industry is expanding rapidly, with more platforms available than ever before. With so many options, the main question for gamers might not be "What game to play?" but "Where?"

■ ACTIVITY: LET'S NETWORK

There are unique ways PC gamers and game fans can get together and share an online gaming experience. This activity allows a group to get together in one of these capacities and experience online gaming firsthand.

GUIDELINES

A computer will be necessary for each person in this activity. Discuss what platform (MMORPG, virtual world, etc.) everyone would like to collaborate in and proceed to the appropriate website. Note that most of these platforms require a user account, so participants must be willing to create an account to proceed. When applicable, one user should create a group server and share the name of that group for everyone else to locate and join. Spend 30 minutes or so engaged in the online collaboration, communicating only through the computer and not verbally in the room. Then take an additional 20–30 minutes to conduct a group SWOT analysis of the experience.

■ CHAPTER 11 QUIZ

1. Who was *not* affiliated with Charles Ranlett Flint's consolidation to form IBM?
   a. Willard Bundy
   b. Alexander Dey
   c. Bill Gates
   d. Julius E. Pitrat

2. All of these were common early PC graphics display cards, except:
   a. CGA
   b. EGA
   c. VGA
   d. ZGA

3. Many early PC games ran on _____ in which a command prompt would appear on the screen requiring the user to enter a series of commands to launch the program:
   a. DOS
   b. Linux
   c. OS X
   d. Windows

4. Developer of *Wolfenstein 3D* and *Doom* known for promoting networked multiplayer gaming, the concept of the "deathmatch," the shareware distribution method, and game modding:
   a. Ad Lib
   b. BioWare
   c. Creative Technology
   d. id Software

5. Became the mainstream operating system of both the general public and game developers in 1995:
   a. Linux
   b. OS/2
   c. OS X
   d. Windows 95

6. Which of the following is an application programming interface (API)?
   a. DirectX
   b. OpenGL
   c. Direct3D
   d. All of the above

7. Which game title was *not* one of the "big three" Massively Multiplayer Online Role-Playing Game (MMORPG) pioneers of the late 1990s?
   a. *Asheron's Call*
   b. *EverQuest*
   c. *Ultima Online*
   d. *World of Warcraft*

8. Which of the following titles is not a real-time strategy (RTS) game?
   a. *Age of Empires*
   b. *Command & Conquer*
   c. *Guild Wars*
   d. *StarCraft*

9. 3D accelerator cards like 3dfx Voodoo were out-muscled by GPUs such as:
   a. Microsoft's Direct3D
   b. Nvidia's GeForce 256
   c. Silicon Graphics' OpenGL
   d. None of the above

10. A new digital distribution platform called Steam released in September 2003 by:
    a. Apple
    b. Bethesda
    c. Microsoft
    d. Valve

11. Games that are developed by individuals or small teams who are free from the influence of big publisher budgets and time constraints:
    a. Freemium
    b. Indie games
    c. MMORPGs
    d. None of the above

12. A virtual representation of a user, also called the user's "alter ego" or "character":
    a. Alias
    b. Avatar
    c. Bug
    d. Mod

13. Popularized virtual life simulation games with the best-selling game *The Sims* in 2000:
    a. Gary Newman
    b. Daisuke Amaya
    c. Jon Jacobs
    d. Will Wright

14. Researchers at Syracuse University studied 375 people playing *World of Warcraft* and found that _____ % of male players chose female avatars, while _____ % of female participants played as male characters:
    a. 23% of males and 7% of females
    b. 53% of males and 27% of females
    c. 17% of males and 23% of females
    d. None of the above

15. Became wealthy by selling virtual real estate as alter egos Anshe Chung and Neverdie:
    a. Ailin Graef and Jon Jacobs
    b. Daisuke Amaya and Jon Jacobs
    c. Ailin Graef and Daisuke Amaya
    d. Minh Le and Jess Cliffe

16. In VR, 6 degrees of freedom (6DoF) adds the ability to _____, which is not possible with 3 degrees of freedom (3Dof):
    a. look left or right (yaw)
    b. rotate one's head up or down (pitch)
    c. pivot side to side (roll)
    d. move forward or backward (surge)

17. Which of these VR headsets was a stand-alone unit that did not require a PC to operate?
    a. HTC Vive
    b. Meta Quest 2
    c. Oculus Rift
    d. Valve Index

18. Which of the following features was NOT part of Epic Games' Unreal Engine 5?
    a. "Nanite" virtualized geometry system
    b. "Virtual Shadow Maps" high-resolution shadowing
    c. "Lumen" fully dynamic global illumination and reflections
    d. "Shaman" 3D phantom surround sound

19. Each of the following subscription services launched as a cloud gaming service, except:
    a. Amazon Luna
    b. Apple Arcade
    c. GeForce NOW
    d. Google Stadia

20. This game platform experienced an increase in valuation from $4 billion to $29.5 billion from February 2020 to January 2021:
    a. *Google Stadia*
    b. *Minecraft*
    c. *Roblox*
    d. *Second Life*

True or False

21. PC-compatible systems were IBM-style computers built by other companies and also referred to as "IBM clones."

22. The abbreviation MMORPG stands for "Mass Multimedia Role-Playing Game."

23. Purchasable downloads such as extra maps (stages), costumes, sports teams, and other bonus content are known as "macro-transactions."

24. Microsoft released the Steam Deck handheld computer system in December 2020.

25. Overall, the revenue market percentage for PC gaming has been on the decline from 2012 to 2021.

■ FIGURES

Figure 11.1 IBM PC 5150 magazine advertisement from 1982. (My Own IBM Computer Ad for the IBM PC 5150 from 1982. *Byte Magazine*, January 1982, p.61. UBM.)

Figure 11.2 A look at the MS-DOS prompt screen. (Screenshot by Wardyga.)

Figure 11.3 Screenshots from popular early 1990s PC titles: (a) *Myst* and (b) *The 7th Guest* . (*Myst,* courtesy of Cyan Worlds/Broderbund, 1995; and *The 7th Guest,* courtesy of Trilobyte/Virgin Interactive, 1993.)

Figure 11.4 Two-page magazine advertisement for *Tomb Raider* in 1996. (From *GamePro* 88, November 1996, pp. 152–153.)

Figure 11.5 Screenshots from popular mid-1990s PC titles: (a) *Quake* and (b) *Ultima Online*. (*Quake,* courtesy of id Software, 1996; and *Ultima Online,* courtesy of Origin/Electronic Arts, 1997.)

Figure 11.6 Screenshots of late hit 1990s titles: (a) *Half-Life* and (b) *EverQuest* . (*Half-Life,* courtesy of Valve Software/Sierra Entertainment, 1998; and *EverQuest,* courtesy of Sony Online Entertainment, 1999.)

Figure 11.7 The original "Bondi blue" iMac G3. Attribution 2.0 Generic (CC BY 2.0) by Brett Jordan. June 28, 2010. "10 years." Retrieved from https://www.flickr.com/photos/x1brett/4742540168.

Figure 11.8 Screenshots of popular indie titles: (a) *Braid* and (b) *Minecraft*. (*Braid,* courtesy of Number None Inc., 2009; and *Minecraft,* courtesy of Mojang AB, 2011.)

Figure 11.9 Screenshots of (a) *The Sims Online*, (b) *Second Life*, and (c) *Entropia Universe*. (*The Sims Online,* courtesy of Maxis/EA Games, 2002; *Second Life,* courtesy of Linden Lab, 2003; and *Entropia Universe,* courtesy of MindArk, 2003.)

Figure 11.10 Virtual Reality headsets: (a) Oculus Rift CV1 and (b) HTC Vive. Oculus Rift CV1: "The Oculus Rift CV1 (Consumer Version 1), a virtual reality headset made by Oculus VR and released in 2016." July 14, 2017. By Evan Amos—Own work, Public Domain, https://commons.wikimedia.org/w/index.php?curid=64845104. Retrieved from https://en.wikipedia.org/wiki/Oculus_Rift#/media/File:Oculus-Rift-CV1-Headset-Front_with_transparent_background.png and HTC Vive: "htc-vive-large-1" by Okefenokee Regional Library System. 2022. Retrieved from https://okrls.org/makerspace/htc-vive-large-1/.

Figure 11.11 PC MOBA hit *League of Legends* (a) and the successful *Fortnite Battle Royale* (b). (*League of Legends* courtesy of Riot Games, 2009; and *Fortnite Battle Royale* (courtesy of Epic Games/People Can Fly, 2017.)

Figure 11.12 Steam Deck by Valve featuring *Dead Cells, Deathloop, Ghostrunner, Hollow Knight, Portal 2, Psychonauts 2, Stardew Valley, Tales of Arise, Tetris Effect Connected,* and *The Witcher 3: Wild Hunt. Dead Cells* (Motion Twin, 2018), *Deathloop* (Arkane Studios/Bethesda Softworks, 2021), *Ghostrunner* (ONE MORE LEVEL/All in! Games, 2020), *Hollow Knight* (Team Cherry, 2017), *Portal 2* (Valve Software, 2011), *Psychonauts 2* (Double Fine Productions/Xbox Game Studios, 2021), *Stardew Valley* (ConcernedApe/Chucklefish, 2016), *Tales of Arise* (Bandai Namco Games, 2021), *Tetris Effect Connected* (Monstars Inc./Enhance Games, 2020), and *The Witcher 3: Wild Hunt* (CD Projekt Red Studio/Warner Bros. Interactive Entertainment, 2015). "JOSM on the Steam Deck.jpg" By https://wiki.openstreetmap.org/wiki/User:Riiga, March 22, 2022; https://wiki.openstreetmap.org/wiki/File:JOSM_on_the_Steam_Deck.jpg, CC BY-SA 4.0, https://commons.wikimedia.org/w/index.php?curid=116757742. Retrieved from https://commons.wikimedia.org/wiki/File:JOSM_on_the_Steam_Deck.jpg and Valve Steam Deck Press Photo edited by Wardyga with UI from "The library page for the Steam client used on the Steam Deck. The additional icons on the top left game image indicate the game is Steam Deck verified." By Valve Corporation February 26, 2022—https://www.steamdeck.com/en/software, Fair use, https://

en.wikipedia.org/w/index.php?curid=68273459. Retrieved from https://en.wikipedia.org/wiki/Steam_Deck#/media/File:Steam_Deck_Steam_UI.jpg.

Figure 11.13 Computer sales in thousands of units in the early 1990s. (Adapted from data by Reimer, J. (2012). *Personal computer market share: 1975-2004.* Retrieved from http://www.jeremyreimer.com/m-item.lsp?i=137.)

Figure 11.14 10-year PC gaming revenue market percentage. Graph by Wardyga. (Adapted from data by Newzoo reported by Takahashi, D. (2018, April 30). *Newzoo: Games market expected to hit $180.1 billion in revenues in 2021.* Retrieved from https://venturebeat.com/games/newzoo-global-games-expected-to-hit-180-1-billion-in-revenues-2021/.)

Title page image: *Myst* (Cyan Worlds/Broderbund, 1995), *The Sims Online* (Maxis/EA Games, 2002), *World of Warcraft* (Blizzard Entertainment, 2004), and *League of Legends* (Riot Games, 2009).

PRO FILE: Will Wright. Photo credit: By Official GDC—Game Developers Choice Awards @ GDC 2010, CC BY 2.0, https://commons.wikimedia.org/w/index.php?curid=9783149 March 12, 2010. Retrieved from https://en.wikipedia.org/wiki/Will_Wright_(game_designer)#/media/File:Will_Wright_-_Game_Developers_Conference_2010_(2).jpg.

▪ REFERENCES

Bailey, D. (2021, February 12). *Steam just reached 50,000 total games listed.* Retrieved from https://www.pcgamesn.com/steam/total-games.

Carina, G. (2013). *What is a virtual world? Definition and classification.* Dublin, Ireland: School of Computer Science and Statistics (SCSS) at Trinity College Dublin. Retrieved from https://www.scss.tcd.ie/publications/tech-reports/reports.13/TCD-CS-2013-10.pdf.

Chiang, O. (2010, November 13). Meet the man who just made a half million from the sale of virtual property. *Forbes.* Retrieved from http://www.forbes.com/sites/oliverchiang/2010/11/13/meet-the-man-who-just-made-a-cool-half-million-from-the-sale-of-virtual-property/.

Clayton, D. (2016, January 26). *The history of PC gaming.* Retrieved from http://www.geeksquad.co.uk/articles/gaming/2012/07/the_history_of_pc_gaming.

DiChristopher, T. (2015, April 15). *Zynga and Mark Pincus face declining social games sales.* Retrieved from https://www.cnbc.com/2015/04/16/zynga-and-mark-pincus-face-declining-social-games-sales.html.

Duntley, S. M. (2014, May 12). *Syracuse University researchers help figure out whether that female avatar player is really a woman.* Retrieved from http://www.syracuse.com/news/index.ssf/2014/05/how_to_tell_if_that_female_avatar_player_is_really_a_woman.html.

EC-Council (International Council of E-Commerce Consultants). (2010). *Computer forensics: Investigating network intrusions and cybercrime.* Clifton Park, NY: Cengage Learning. pp. 9–26.

Editorial: AMD Announces Next-Generation Leadership Products at Computex 2019 Keynote. (2019). *AMD.* Retrieved from https://www.amd.com/en/press-releases/2019-05-26-amd-announces-next-generation-leadership-products-computex-2019-keynote.

Editorial: Game history. (2017). *Computer Hope.* Retrieved from http://www.computerhope.com/history/game.htm.

Editorial: Gartner says worldwide tablet sales grew 68 percent in 2013, with Android capturing 62 percent of the market. (2014, March 3). *Gartner.* Retrieved from http://www.gartner.com/newsroom/id/2674215.

Editorial: Global games market report: The VR & Metaverse edition. (2021). *Newzoo,* pp. 5, 25. Retrieved from https://newzoo.com/insights/trend-reports/newzoo-global-games-market-report-2021-free-version.

Editorial: Industry news: Reaching a broader market. (1992, December). *Computer Gaming World,* 101, p. 156. Retrieved from http://www.cgwmuseum.org/galleries/issues/cgw_101.pdf.

Editorial: Nvidia launches the world's first graphics processing unit: GeForce 256. (1999, August 31). *Nvidia.* Retrieved from http://www.nvidia.com/object/IO_20020111_5424.html.

Editorial: Report: Steam games market size will decline in 2022 after reaching $6.6bn in 2021. (2022, July 10). *Video game insights.* Retrieved from https://vginsights.com/insights/article/report-steam-games-market-size-likely-to-decline-in-2022-after-reaching-6-6bn-in-2021.

Editorial: RTX. It's on: NVIDIA Turing. (2018). *Nvidia.* Retrieved from https://www.nvidia.com/en-us/geforce/turing/.

Editorial: The 50 most important PC games of all time. (2016, January 18). *PCGamer.* Retrieved from http://www.pcgamer.com/most-important-pc-games/4/.

Guinness World Records. (2015). *Guinness World Records: Gamer's Edition 2016. Guinness World Records,* New York, NY: Jim Pattison Group.

Hoffman, C. (2014, May 11). *PCs before windows: What using MS-DOS was actually like.* Retrieved from http://www.howtogeek.com/188980/pcs-before-windows-what-using-ms-dos-was-actually-like/.

Jacobs, P. (2021, January 28). *Roblox converts 'robux' to big bucks.* Retrieved from https://www.palisadeshudson.com/2021/01/roblox-converts-robux-to-big-bucks/.

Kennedy, D. (1985, April 16). PCs rated number one. *PC Magazine.* p. 42.

Kent, S. (2001). *The ultimate history of video games: The story behind the craze that touched our lives and changed the world*. Roseville, CA: Three Rivers Press.

Kohler, C. (2009, December 4). The 15 most influential games of the decade. *Wired*. Retrieved from https://www.wired.com/2009/12/the-15-most-influential-games-of-the-decade/2/.

Ivory, J. D. (2015, September). History of video games. In Kowert, R. & Quandt, T. (Eds.), *The video game debate: Unravelling the physical, social, and psychological effects of video games*. New York and London: Routledge, pp. 1–15.

McCullough, B. (2014, May 29). *Behind 'halt and catch fire': Compaq's rise to pc domination*. Retrieved from http://mashable.com/2014/05/29/halt-and-catch-fire-amc-compaq/#faDEVcxERsqy.

McDougall, J. (2010, October 7). *World of Warcraft has 12 million active subscribers*. Retrieved from http://www.pcgamer.com/world-of-warcraft-has-12-million-active-subscribers/.

Miller, M. (2022, February 25). The Steam Deck review. *Game Informer*. Retrieved from https://www.gameinformer.com/hardware/2022/02/25/the-steam-deck-review.

Needleman, S. E. (2015, January 29). Twitch's viewers reach 100 million a month. *The Wall Street Journal*. Retrieved from http://blogs.wsj.com/digits/2015/01/29/twitchs-viewers-reach-100-million-a-month/.

Park, A. (2000, February 11). The sims review. *Gamespot*. Retrieved from http://www.gamespot.com/reviews/the-sims-review/1900-2533406/.

Parloff, R. (2005, November 28). From megs to riches. *Fortune Magazine*. Retrieved from http://archive.fortune.com/magazines/fortune/fortune_archive/2005/11/28/8361953/index.htm.

Reimer, J. (2005, December 15). Total share: 30 years of personal computer market share figures. *Ars Technica*. Retrieved from http://arstechnica.com/features/2005/12/total-share/.

Seabrook, J. (2006, November 6). Game master: Will Wright changed the concept of video games with The Sims. Can he do it again with Spore? *The New Yorker*. Retrieved from http://www.newyorker.com/magazine/2006/11/06/game-master.

Schenck, B. (2011, February 7). Freemium: Is the price right for your company? *Entrepreneur*. Retrieved from http://www.entrepreneur.com/article/218107.

Singer, G. (2020, December 6). *History of the modern graphics processor, part 3: Market consolidation, the Nvidia vs. ATI era begins*. Retrieved from https://www.techspot.com/article/657-history-of-the-gpu-part-3/.

TwitchMetrics. (2022, August 30). *The most watched games on Twitch, August 2022*. Retrieved from https://www.twitchmetrics.net/games/viewership.

Super Data Research. (2016). *Market brief: Year in review 2016*. Retrieved from https://www.superdataresearch.com/market-data/market-brief-year-in-review/.

Watlington, W. (2015, March 17). *A short history of indie games, and a look into the future*. Retrieved from https://updownright.com/2015/03/07/a-short-history-of-indie-games-and-a-look-into-the-future/.

Wilson, J. L. (1993, June). The Software Publishing Association Spring Symposium 1993. *Computer Gaming World*, p. 98. Retrieved from http://www.cgwmuseum.org/galleries/issues/cgw_107.pdf.

The Seventh Generation

■ OBJECTIVES

After reading this chapter, you should be able to:

- Discuss the developments of the arcade and console industries during this time.
- Review key people behind the video games and consoles.
- Identify graphics and capabilities of seventh-generation consoles.
- Compare technological differences among the Xbox 360, PlayStation 3, and Nintendo Wii.
- Recap the strengths and features of the Sony PlayStation Portable and Nintendo DS.
- List key video game titles and peripherals for each console.
- Explain why Nintendo dominated the seventh-generation market.
- Describe important innovations introduced to gaming during this period.
- Recognize the importance the technology had on the video game industry.
- Summarize seventh-generation market sales, breakthroughs, and trends.

DOI: 10.1201/9781003315759-12

■ KEY TERMS AND PEOPLE

Accelerometer
Achievements
J Allard
Amazon Prime
Analog Devices
Apple
Kenichiro Ashida
ATI Technologies
BD-ROM
BioWare
Blu-ray
Bluetooth
Kevin Butler
Cell Processor
Mark Cerny
Classic Controller
CompactFlash
Component cable
Dashboard
Dolby Digital 7.1
Dual screen
DualShock 3
Gamer card
Gamer tag Teiyu Goto
GUI
Guide button
Gyroscope
HDMI

Hers Experimental Design
   Laboratory
Hulu
IBM
Insomniac
Eugene Jarvis
Kinect
Hideo Kojima
Ken Kutaragi
Jerry Lambert
Leap year bug
Life with PlayStation
Lindbergh Yellow
Linux
LPCM
Memory Card Adaptor
Memory Stick
Memory Unit
Messenger Kit
Microtransactions
Mii
Shigeru Miyamoto
Motion controller
Multicore
Naughty Dog
Navigation controller
Netflix
Nintendo DS

NIS America
Nunchuk
Nvidia
Operation Rainfall
Optical audio output
Pack-in title
Pipelines
Pixel shaders
Play Mechanix
PlayStation 3
PlayStation Home
PlayStation Move
PlayStation Network
PlayStation Plus
PlayStation Portable (PSP)
PlayStation Store
Pro Controller
PSP Go
Raw Thrills
Red Ring of Death
Ring of light
Hironobu Sakaguchi
SD/Mini SD
Sensor Bar
Shader architecture
Sixaxis
Skins
Stylus

Toshiba
Touchscreen
Trophy system
Ubisoft
Universal Media Disc
Vertex shaders
Virtual Console
WebTV team
Wi-Fi
Wii
Wii Balance Board
Wii Menu
Wii MotionPlus
Wii Speak
Wii Wheel
Wii Zapper
Wiimote
Wireless Gaming Receiver
Wireless Keypad
Wireless Network Adapter
Xbox 360
Xbox 360 GUIs
Xbox Live
Xenon
Xenos
XrossMediaBar
Xseed Games
YouTube

■ CONSOLE TIMELINE

Nintendo DS	Sony PSP	Xbox 360	PlayStation3	Nintendo Wii
2004	**2005**	**2005**	**2006**	**2006**

▪ ARCADE APOCALYPSE?

NPD figures showed that the decline of the U.S. arcade industry in the late 1990s continued into the early to mid-2000s (Ivanovs, 2016, p. 12). The number of traditional arcade venues plummeted from 10,000 to fewer than 3,000. "According to Vending Times' latest Census of the Industry, the number of arcade game units nationwide—at locations ranging from mini golf spots to movie theaters—sank from 860,000 in 1994 to 333,000 in 2004. Revenue from the games dropped from $2.3 billion to $866 million in that period" (East Valley Tribune, 2006, p. 1). Many consumers considered the arcades to be dead.

By maintaining a focus on experiences unique from gaming at home and repositioning themselves as "family entertainment centers," North American arcades rebounded from a 2003 low of 2,500 game venues to 3,500 in 2008 (Hurley, 2008, para. 13). This resurgence of arcades in the United States occurred in part by venues' focus on food and drink service, party catering, and a variety of niche games and prizes. While still nowhere near the magnitude of the "Golden Age," arcades proved that they still had a place in America as a social activity for both younger and older gamers. By this time, most video arcade game hardware was based on the exact same technology as home consoles, such as the Dreamcast-compatible **NAOMI** and **Atomiswave**, along with the PlayStation 2-compatible **System 246**. Using the same technology greatly reduced development costs, making it easy for developers to port arcade games to home systems and vice versa.

Sega led the way with an accumulated 60% share of the arcade market in 2006 (Kikizo, 2006, p. 2).

The company's **Lindbergh Yellow** hardware powered the return of key franchises with *The House of the Dead 4* (Figure 12.1) in 2005, as well as *After Burner Climax* and *Virtua Fighter 5* in 2006. Despite leading the arcade market, Sega Sammy Holdings (2008) "recorded a substantial decline in net sales, an operating loss, and a net loss" (p. 4). This led the company to close and/or sell 110 arcade centers with low profitability, in addition to "offering voluntary early retirement to about 400 employees at Sega" (p. 5).

From the consumer perspective, new games continued to appear on the market each year. Rail shooters and racing games were most popular in the West, followed by rhythm games including **Konami**'s *Dance Dance Revolution SuperNova* and later *Guitar Hero Arcade*. Drum rhythm games such as *Taiko: Drum Master* remained more popular in Japan, as well as "bullet hell" shooters (where the screen is frequently flooded with bullets). Japanese publishers Konami, Namco, and Taito continued releasing arcade games but a fair share of those titles never reached the West.

In their place arrived cabinets by Illinois-based development studio **Raw Thrills**. Raw Thrills was founded by *Defender* and *Robotron: 2084* creator **Eugene Jarvis** and other arcade veterans, including former employees from Midway Games. The company produced *The Fast and the Furious* game in 2004 and partnered with **Play Mechanix** to release the popular *Big Buck Hunter* series. Other than the Raw Thrills logo appearing on more cabinets, a handful of pinball tables, fighting games, and shoot 'em ups could still be found—along with retro cabinets such as *Galaga* and *Ms. Pac-Man*.

FIGURE 12.1 Screenshots of top arcade rail shooters from 2006: (a) *Aliens: Extermination* (Global VR), (b) *Big Buck Hunter: Call of the Wild* (Raw Thrills), and (c) *House of the Dead 4* (Sega).

(a)   (b)   (c)

▪ THE SEVENTH GENERATION

The seventh generation of video games began with the North American release of the **Nintendo DS** hand-held on November 21, 2004. Sony was right behind the DS with its launch of **PlayStation Portable (PSP)** a month later. It would be another year until Microsoft released the earliest seventh-generation home console, followed by offerings by Sony and Nintendo in late 2006. Home video games would see key breakthroughs and changes during this era, with influences from consumers' mass adoption of HDTVs and smart phones. Wireless game controllers became standard. Other trends included larger internal storage, a rise in online, indie, and casual gaming, as well as new ways of playing games using motion technology. The first of these game changers came from Microsoft in 2005.

▪ XBOX 360

The first console of the seventh generation was Microsoft's **Xbox 360** (Figure 12.2), which released on November 22, 2005, in the United States and the following month in Japan and Europe. The extravagant launch party involved a competition for tickets to an undisclosed location in the Mojave Desert, which turned out to be "a retired military hangar in Palmdale, Calif., that once housed the Space Shuttle. The massive set-up treated gamers to the first available consoles, as well as demo stations and cryptic viral marketing set-ups" (Huffman, 2013, para. 3). Two console options were available, including the core system for $299 and the 20 GB hard drive version for $399. The system shipped 1.5 million units by year's end, selling out of 900,000 systems in North America and 500,000 consoles in Europe. The Xbox 360 struggled with its Japanese launch, with just 100,000 units sold (Microsoft, 2006, p. 14). Microsoft bundled the original "Pro/Premium" package with one wireless controller, a component (HD-capable) AV cable, Ethernet cable, headset, and a removable 20 GB hard drive. Early versions also included a DVD remote control (Valdes, 2006, p. 2). See Table 12.1 for launch titles.

Where Microsoft sold the original Xbox at a loss, they designed the Xbox 360 to be more cost-effective and easier to program—even though developers would have to learn how to program for a more complex **multicore** chip. The company originally called

FIGURE 12.2 Xbox 360 with controller. "The Xbox 360, a video game console released by Microsoft in 2005.

the console "Project Xenon" after its main CPU by **IBM**. Microsoft's **WebTV team** worked closely with major chip vendor **ATI Technologies** on the development of its **Xenos** graphics chip. Beyond its faster processors, the Xbox 360 made advancements on features from the previous generation, such as improving its **Xbox Live** online gaming service. Xbox Live provided two membership options. The free "Xbox Live Silver" option allowed for the creation of a **gamer tag** (username) and a new ID type called a **gamer card**. "The gamer card is a profile that displays a gamer's interests, skill level, competitiveness and gaming accomplishments" (Valdes, 2006, p. 7). Silver plans also included system and game updates, chat functionality, and other downloadable content. For $59.99 per year, "Xbox Live Gold" added the ability to participate in multiplayer games online.

The original model required a separate **Wireless Network Adapter** to connect to the Internet via **Wi-Fi**; however, later models featured built-in Wi-Fi capability. Microsoft continuously updated Xbox Live with new looks and features. "It was a live service that changed with a simple update of its software. By 2007, Microsoft had more than 8 million subscribers to Xbox Live. By 2011, that number had climbed past 35 million (Takahashi, 2011, p. 3).

☀ DID YOU KNOW?

According to Microsoft Corporate Vice President and Chief XNA Architect **J. Allard**, rather than naming the console "Xbox 2," Microsoft chose "Xbox 360" to represent a focus on "putting the gamer at the center of the experience" (Torres & Thorsen, 2005, para. 21).

The Xbox 360 received a more comfortable standard controller that featured a 2.5 mm headset jack. The wireless version operated on either two AA batteries or a rechargeable battery pack. It also included backward compatibility with many original Xbox titles such as *Halo 2*. Its emphasis on digital media distribution and social networking helped promote the indie game revolution and console games became more like PC games. It was now commonplace for consoles to feature regular firmware updates, game updates such as bug patches, new content, and in-game **microtransactions**. Furthermore, it was Microsoft and the Xbox 360 that introduced the world to the concept of **achievements**—digital rewards unlocked by completing various milestones in a game.

TABLE 12.1 Xbox 360 U.S. Launch Titles
• *Amped 3*
• *Call of Duty 2* (Figure 12.3a)
• *Condemned: Criminal Origins*
• *FIFA '06: Road to FIFA World Cup*
• *GUN*
• *Kameo: Elements of Power*
• *Madden NFL 06*
• *NBA 2K6*
• *NBA Live 06*
• *Need for Speed: Most Wanted*
• *NHL 2K6*
• *Perfect Dark Zero*
• *Peter Jackson's King Kong*
• *Project Gotham Racing 3* (Figure 12.3b)
• *Quake 4*
• *Ridge Racer 6*
• *Tiger Woods PGA Tour 2006*
• *Tony Hawk's American Wasteland*

The 360 established a greater focus on the home console's **GUI (graphical user interface)**, which like the original Xbox, Microsoft called the **Dashboard**. Players could quickly access the Xbox 360 Dashboard by pressing the **Guide button** in the center of the controller. The Guide button was surrounded by four quadrants that light up in different ways to provide information to the player. "For instance, during a split screen multiplayer match, a particular quadrant will light up to indicate to a player which part of the screen he or she is playing on at that time" (Valdes, 2006, p. 5). The console also featured a ring indicator around the power button called the "**ring of light**."

FIGURE 12.3 Xbox 360 launch titles: (a) *Call of Duty 2* and (b) *Project Gotham Racing 3*.

(a)   (b)

TABLE 12.2 Seven Versions of the Xbox 360 (Not Including Special Editions)

Model	Debut	Internal Storage	Notes
Core	2005	None	Bundled with a standard-definition composite video cable and a wired controller
Original	2005	20 and 60 GB	Called "Pro" or "Premium," with a component cable, optional **optical audio output**, and hard drive; 2007 version had HDMI output
Arcade	2007	265 and 512 MB	Replaced core system with a small amount of internal memory and a wireless controller
Elite	2007	120 GB	Matte black finish and redesigned power connector with a 175 Watt power supply
Super Elite	2009	250 GB	More than double the hard drive space and bundled with two wireless controllers
S (Slim)	2010	4, 250, & 320 GB	Slim design, built-in Wi-Fi, no **Memory Unit** slots, 2 extra rear USB ports, proprietary port for Kinect sensor; new, quieter "Valhalla" motherboard; 50% less power consumption
E	2013	4, 250, & 500 GB	Xbox One-inspired design, one less USB port and no optical audio or S/PDIF connections

The original Xbox 360 design was created by **Astro Studios** in San Francisco and manufactured by **Hers Experimental Design Laboratory** in Japan. "While the original Xbox looked like it was about to explode, the Xbox 360 looked like it was inhaling" (Takahashi, 2011, p. 4). Like the lights around the controller's Guide button, the ring of light around the console's power button had four glowing green lights that provided information such as which wireless controllers were active. Other messages the ring could display included the overheating code where the left half of the ring would flash red—and the dreaded "General Hardware Failure" error indicated by three flashing red quadrants around the power button. Known as the "**Red Ring of Death**," such hardware failures required users to ship their consoles to Microsoft for repairs.

The Red Ring of Death was a major problem and a 2009 reader poll by *Game Informer* showed a console failure rate of 54.2% from nearly 5,000 respondents (p. 12). Microsoft addressed the issue in an open letter from then Vice President of Microsoft's Interactive Entertainment Business division **Peter Moore**. Moore addressed the letter to the Xbox Community and stated,

"if a customer has an issue indicated by the three flashing red lights, Microsoft will repair the console free of charge—including shipping—for three years from the console's purchase date" (Moore, 2007). The decision to repair every console with the Red Ring of Death cost Microsoft an estimated 1.1 billion dollars (Crossley, 2016, p. 9). The company fixed the problem for subsequent versions of the system, including the **Xbox 360 S** (Slim) released in 2010 and the **Xbox 360 E** (not to be confused by the older Elite model) in 2013. Table 12.2 summarizes the different versions of the console.

Along with new shapes and sizes of its console, Microsoft also reinvented the **Xbox 360 Dashboard (GUI)** two times (Figure 12.4). The original Dashboard (known as "Blades") was the standard interface between 2005 and 2008. The second version was "NXE (New Xbox Experience)" in 2008, which could install full games onto the hard drive. The final Dashboard was the multimedia-rich, Windows Phone-inspired "Metro" design in 2011.

Accessories released for the Xbox 360 included various headsets, remote controls, removable hard drives, force-feedback steering wheels, keyboard and mouse,

FIGURE 12.4 Evolution of Xbox 360 Dashboard: (a) Blades, (b) NXE, and (c) Metro.

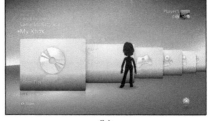

(a) (b) (c)

FIGURE 12.5   2010 Ingram Micro ad featuring Xbox 360S, Kinect and *Kinect Adventures!*.

rhythm game controllers, microphones, console **skins** (stickers), cooling systems, and rechargeable batteries. One unique peripheral was the **Messenger Kit**, which featured a miniature keyboard called the "Chatpad" that attached to a standard controller. Gamers could even play compatible Xbox 360 games on a Windows computer with the **Wireless Gaming Receiver** for Windows. Its **Live Vision Camera** was like Sony's EyeToy, allowing "players to create an in-game version of themselves in select games" (Valdes, 2006, p. 5).

The console's best-selling peripheral was the **Kinect**, shown in Figure 12.5. Formerly known as "Project Natal," the Kinect debuted on November 4, 2010, at Toys "R" Us in Times Square. Microsoft built the unique sensor device with the ability of detecting full-body 3D motion, facial recognition, as well as recognizing user voice commands. The "controller-free" experience offered by Kinect was much more advanced than the EyeToy and quickly earned the Guinness World Record for "fastest selling consumer electronics device" with 8 million units sold in its first 60 days on the market—an average of 133,333 units per day between November 4 and January 3 (Guinness World Records, 2010).

■ CONSOLE COMPARISON: XBOX 360 VS. SIXTH-GENERATION CONSOLES

The casual consumer might assume that the Xbox 360's **3.2 GHz PC Tri-Core Xenon** CPU (Table 12.3) is a little more than 10 times faster than the 295 MHz "Emotion" CPU of the PS2. However, with a tri-core processor, each core functions as a separate processor, resulting in faster computing and more efficient energy consumption. And "because the Xbox 360 cores can each handle two threads at a time, the 360 CPU is the equivalent of having six conventional processors in one machine" (Valdes, 2006, p. 3). Likewise, its **500 MHz** GPU may appear just over twice the speed of the original Xbox and GameCube GPUs, but its dedicated **10 MB of eDRAM** makes the Xbox 360 chip much faster than the raw numbers suggest.

ATI built the Xbox 360 GPU on unified **shader architecture**, utilizing **pixel shaders** that alter the lighting, color, and surface of each pixel to help smoothen out 3D objects, giving them a more organic texture—as well as **vertex shaders** that manipulate an object's position in 3D space, resulting in more realistic animation and special effects such as "morphing"

TABLE 12.3 Xbox 360 Tech Specs

Manufacturer:	Microsoft
Launch price:	$299.99 (Core) and $399.99
Release date:	11/22/05 (US), 12/02/05 (EU), 12/10/05 (JP), 3/23/06 (AU)
Format:	12× speed DVD, CD, and HD-DVD with add-on
Processors:	Power PC Tri-Core Xenon CPU (3.2 GHz) ATI Xenos GPU (500 MHz) with 10 MB of eDRAM
Performance:	Up to 1080p HD/500 million raw PPS/240 GFLOPS
Memory:	512 MB GDDR RAM (700 MHz)
Sound:	256-channel, 48 kHz 16-bit audio with Dolby 5.1 support

(Valdes, 2006, p. 4). These computations must be processed through the **pipelines** of the chip. However, unlike last-generation consoles that required *several* pipelines for multiple effects, the ATI card in the Xbox 360 could process both types of shaders over just *one* pipeline, making it much more efficient. Other advantages included more RAM, polygon count, and its selection of multimedia features.

HEAD-TO-HEAD

To compare the graphics and sound between the Xbox 360 and sixth-generation systems, check out each console's version of *Peter Jackson's King Kong, Tomb Raider: Legend, Hitman: Blood Money, Burnout: Revenge, Madden NFL 07,* and *NBA 2K7.*

▪ KEY XBOX 360 TITLES

Close to 1,400 games released for the Xbox 360, not including more than 750 downloadable titles. Because it beat the competition to the market by a full year, multiplatform games commonly released on the 360 first. Being the lead platform (particularly in the first few years) meant that the Xbox 360 versions of games were often superior. Such was the case with games like *Assassin's Creed, Bayonetta, BioShock, F.E.A.R.,* and *Fallout 3.*

It was the earliest console to receive **BioWare**'s *Mass Effect* game. Aside from developing the superior console version of *The Orange Box,* **Valve** would produce two *Left 4 Dead* shooters for the system. Action/horror that did not appear on other home consoles at the time included *Alan Wake, Dead Rising,* and *Metro 2033.* Xbox 360 was also the only home console to receive *The Witcher 2: Assassins of Kings.* The system had a variety of RPG exclusives including multiple *Fable* games, *Blue Dragon, Tales of Vesperia,* and *Lost Odyssey* (co-written by **Hironobu Sakaguchi** (creator of *Final Fantasy*). Among its most successful titles were war games such as *Call of Duty* and *Battlefield,* as well as its best-selling *Halo, Forza,* and *Gears of War* franchises. See Figure 12.6 for top picks.

FIGURE 12.6 Box art to five popular 360 titles including (a) *Halo 3,* (b) *The Orange Box,* (c) *Mass Effect 3,* (d) *Grand Theft Auto IV,* and (e) *Gears of War 2.*

| (a) | (b) | (c) | (d) | (e) |

▪ HANDHELD SNAPSHOT: NINTENDO DS

The **Nintendo DS** (Figure 12.7) was the first seventh-generation handheld, releasing first in the United States on November 21, 2004, for $149. It landed on store shelves in Japan about a week later, followed by PAL territories in early 2005. While the public commonly interpreted "DS" to stand for the system's **dual screen** display, Nintendo (2017) claimed it also stands for "Developers' System" since "it gives game creators brand new tools which will lead to more innovative games for the world's players" (p. 1).

Among those tools are two backlit screens with the lower screen featuring touchscreen capability players can interact with using a finger or a **stylus**. Nintendo also constructed the system with an internal microphone, built-in Wi-Fi support, and a rechargeable lithium-ion battery. The DS offered even greater power than the Game Boy Advance and was perfectly capable of handling 3D games. Nintendo produced an updated version of the N64 classic *Super Mario 64 DS* for the system's launch. See Table 12.4 for specs.

If there was one weakness to the NDS, it was Nintendo's push to make use of the lower touch screen. There were countless games (including the DS *Zelda* games) that required players to use the touch screen to control the on-screen action. Many of these titles could have offered players the option to control the gameplay with either the touch screen or D-Pad—but were not.

The original DS and the slimmer **DS Lite** (introduced in 2006) contained a second cartridge slot for backward compatibility with GBA games. Nintendo released a third version of the system in 2008 called the **DSi**. The DSi model was unable to play GBA games but added two digital cameras, internal and external storage, and online access to the Nintendo DSi Shop. A year later, Nintendo produced a fourth, larger model to the series with the **DSi XL**.

Over 3,300 games released for the DS (see Figure 12.8 for top picks) and all but Chinese-version games are region free. Altogether, Nintendo sold more than 154 million DS systems, making it the best-selling handheld video game system of all time (Nintendo, 2016).

FIGURE 12.7 Nintendo DS featuring *Mario Kart DS*.

TABLE 12.4 Nintendo DS Tech Specs

Format:	Mask ROM card/3.7 V lithium-ion battery (10 hours)
Processors:	32-bit ARM946E-S CPU (67 MHz)/33 MHz co-processor
Performance:	262,144 colors/120,000 polygons per second
Memory:	4 MB (expandable via the Game Boy Advance slot)
Resolution:	256 × 192 pixels/dual backlit LCD screens (3″ diagonal)
Sound:	16-channel, 8 and 16-bit PCM virtual surround/3.5 mm jack

FIGURE 12.8 Box art to DS hits: (a) *New Super Mario Bros.*, (b) *Castlevania: Dawn of Sorrow*, (c) *The Legend of Zelda: Phantom Hourglass*, (d) *GTA: Chinatown Wars*, and (e) *Mario Kart DS*.

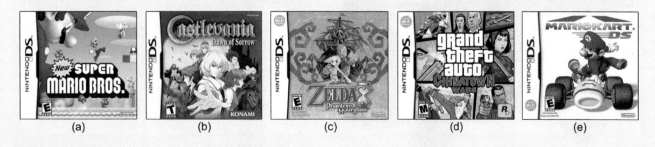

(a) (b) (c) (d) (e)

■ SONY PLAYSTATION 3

The **PlayStation 3 (PS3)** (Figure 12.9) was the most powerful seventh-generation system. It was the first **Blu-ray** console, and its multicore **Cell Processor** (by IBM, **Toshiba**, and Sony) was "essentially seven microprocessors on one chip, allowing it to perform several operations at once. In order to provide the sharpest graphics of any game system, Sony turned to **Nvidia** to build its graphics card" (Altizer, 2016, para. 8). The Nvidia GPU was called the "Reality Synthesizer" and handled most but not all of the console's graphics processing.

The PS3 released in Japan on November 11 and in the United States on November 17, 2006. Europe and other areas would not see the console until March 23, 2007, due to "problems in mass producing elements of the high-definition Blu-ray disc drives in

FIGURE 12.9 PlayStation 3 with DualShock 3 controller.

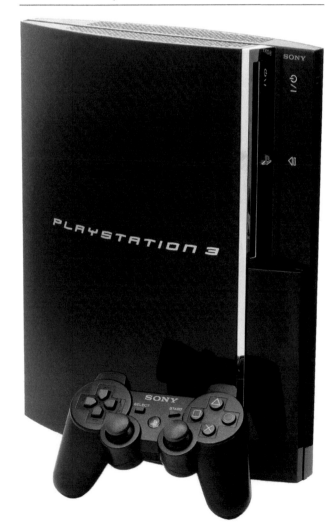

the machines" (BBC News, 2006, para. 3). Sony had initially planned to have 400,000 PS3 units ready for launch day, however research analyst Paul-Jon McNealy estimated that less than 200,000 were available for its North American debut (Baertlein, 2006, para. 3–4). Despite a successful, star-studded launch party (see Table 12.5 for launch titles), the shortage led to empty-handed consumers and resellers making a hefty profit on eBay, with consoles selling for upward of $2,000.

The suggested retail price for the system was still a whopping $599 for the 60 GB hard drive unit with built-in Wi-Fi capability, and a flash card reader beneath a compartment next to the disc slot (for **CompactFlash (CF)**, **SD/Mini SD**, and **Memory Stick** formats). A stripped-down, 20 GB version was available for $499, but that model lacked all the aforementioned features.

> Sony had essentially painted itself into a corner with the PS3's design. Between the system's highly touted Cell processor and its inclusion of a Blu-ray drive before that standard had established itself as the future ahead of HD-DVD … as high as the U.S. retail price of the PS3 was, Sony was still losing up to $300 on every system.
>
> *Sinclair (2016, para. 5)*

Fortunately, Blu-ray won the battle over HD-DVD as the next generation optical disc and the PlayStation 3 was one of the most affordable Blu-ray players at the time of its release—similar to the PS2 as a DVD player 6 years earlier.

TABLE 12.5 Sony PlayStation 3 U.S. Launch Titles

- *Call of Duty 3*
- *Genji: Days of the Blade*
- *Madden NFL 07*
- *Marvel: Ultimate Alliance*
- *Mobile Suit Gundam: CF*
- *Need for Speed: Carbon*
- *NBA 07*
- *NBA 2K7* (Figure 12.10a)
- *NHL 2K7*
- *Resistance: Fall of Man* (Figure 12.10b)
- *Ridge Racer 7*
- *Tiger Woods PGA Tour 07*
- *Tony Hawk's Project 8*
- *Untold Legends: Dark Kingdom*

For its logo, PS3 console designer **Teiyu Goto** followed SCEI president **Ken Kutaragi**'s wishes of using the text font from the then-current Spider-Man movies which Sony had the rights to (Ogden, 2007, p. 1). Sony replaced its original boomerang-shaped prototype controller with a new **Sixaxis** controller than looked nearly identical to the PS2's DualShock 2. The Sixaxis pad contained a built-in, rechargeable lithium-ion battery, as well as motion sensing ability along the X, Y, and Z axes for "six degrees of freedom." The original Sixaxis did not feature force-feedback vibration until Sony upgraded and replaced the controller with the **DualShock 3** in 2008.

The PS3 contained innovative features, such as remote connectivity with PlayStation Portable and **Bluetooth** 2.0 connectivity with other devices. Its Cell processor contained eight cores (six accessible to developers, one for the operating system and one for backup purposes). The CPU was so powerful that the U.S. military purchased a couple thousand PS3 consoles and clustered them together to form a giant PS3-based supercomputer (Stokes, 2009, p. 1). The original console even included the ability to install operating systems such as **Linux**, although Sony would remove that feature with firmware update 3.21 in April 2010 due to security concerns. For game creation, the Core was such new and complex technology that developers struggled with the chip early on.

In addition to longer development cycles, the new **PlayStation Network (PSN)** experienced growing pains before it reached a comparable level with Xbox Live. Players could access PSN through the PS3 GUI called the **XrossMediaBar** (XMB)—pronounced "Cross Media Bar"—along with other services such as *Photo, Music, Video, TV/Video Services,* and *Friends*. It would not be until 2008 when Sony introduced its **trophy system**, PS3's answer to Xbox 360's achievements. "Trophy support became mandatory for all new games in January 2009" (Hutchings, 2013, para. 5). The year 2009 would be a pivotal one for the console, with the release of the smaller, lighter, and more efficient **PS3 Slim**, coupled with a brand new logo and complete redesign of its games' packaging (see Figure 12.11).

The PS3 did not experience a failure rate epidemic like Xbox 360's Red Ring of Death; however, a 2009 study by warranty provider SquareTrade showed a 2-year failure rate for the original PlayStation 3 to be around 10%. Called the "yellow light of death" (YLOD) by the BBC's *Watchdog* program, Sony refuted the figure to be "less than half a percent of the 2.5 million consoles it has sold" (BBC News, 2009, para. 14). Other challenges the system faced included a **leap year bug** on March 1, 2010, when original PS3 systems experienced problems with their internal system clock, followed by a complete shutdown of the PlayStation Network due to a massive external **intrusion** (hack) on April 20, 2011. While Sony solved the leap year bug in about a day, the PSN **outage** lasted over 3 weeks. CBS News reported that the security breach affected more than 100 million online accounts and cost Sony roughly $171 million in damages (Martinez, 2011). Sony restored the network on May 15 with no sign of credit card fraud and offered users a section of free digital perks as an apology.

Like the system's inclusion and then removal of features like Linux support and backward compatibility with PS2 games, the PSN saw other features come

FIGURE 12.10 Screenshots from PS3 launch titles: (a) *NBA 2K7* and (b) *Resistance: Fall of Man.*

(a)   (b)

FIGURE 12.11 Old cover art and spine (a) and new style (b) for *LittleBigPlanet: GOTY edition.*

(a)

(b)

and go. **Folding@home** (March 2007–November 2012) was an initiative with Stanford University where PS3 users could share part of their console's computing power for disease research when the console was idle. **Life with PlayStation** (September 2008–November 2012) provided users with weather forecasts and other news headlines. Then there was *PlayStation Home* (December 2008–March 2015) which was a beta virtual 3D social networking service similar to *Second Life*, where users created an avatar to communicate, shop, and engage in other virtual activities.

Advantages to PSN included free multiplayer gaming for all users and access to the **PlayStation Store**, among other services. For an annual cost of $49.99, users could subscribe to **PlayStation Plus**—a premium PSN membership that provided users with early or exclusive access to betas, game demos, and even complete games with its "**Instant Game Collection**." On par with Xbox 360, the PS3 was also a popular platform for watching movies and TV shows with apps like **Netflix**, **Hulu**, and **Amazon Prime**. Also, like the 360, the PlayStation 3 saw different models over the years with varying hard drive capacities and console designs. Three years after the remodeled PS3 Slim, Sony released an even smaller PS3 system called the **Super Slim** in late 2012. Table 12.6 summarizes the different versions of the system.

TABLE 12.6 Five Versions of the PS3 (Not Including Special Editions)

Model	Debut	Internal Storage	Notes
CECHAxx CECHBxx	2006	40 or 60 GB	Also called "Fat," had HDMI output, Sixaxis controller, 4 USB 2.0 ports, PS2 backward compatible, Linux support until update 3.21
CECHCxx CECHExx	2007	60 and 80 GB	60 GB was PAL only; 80 GB was NTSC only, Wi-Fi and flash card readers now standard; no Emotion chip and so less backward compatible
CECHGxx through CECHQxx	2007–2008	40, 80, and 160 GB	Reduced to two USB 2.0 ports; no longer PS2 backward compatible; added DualShock3 controller in 2008; more efficient Cell chip
CECH-20 through CECH-30	2009–2010	120 and 250, then 160 and 320 GB	Slim model: 33% smaller, 36% lighter and consumes 34%–45% less power (Miller, 2009); cooler and quieter; remote control with HDMI
CECH-40 through CECH-43	2012	12, 250, and 500 GB	Super Slim model; approximately 25% smaller and 20% lighter than PS3 Slim; replaced motorized disc-loading slot with a manual sliding cover

For better or for worse, the PlayStation 3 had some unforgettable television ads. The first series of ads took place in a white room, featuring all kinds of paranormal activity and ending with the caption "PLAY B3YOND." One ad featured a floating Rubik's Cube that explodes in the middle of the room, painting the walls blue, red, and green, and the floor yellow. Another showed a floating Sixaxis controller possessing a dozen eggs, which roll toward it before flying backward and crashing into the wall—turning into a horde of crows. Among the creepiest ads was a commercial involving a deranged crying baby doll, whose tears suddenly retract before saying "ma ma" to a PS3 console on the floor (Figure 12.12a).

For the 2008 holidays, Sony released a series of "Entertainment Unleashed" spots "that focused on creating a portrait of the PSN's unrivaled ability to download movies to the PSP, and the PS3's ability to create unique experiences" (Oravasaari, 2012, para. 8). The next 3 years featured the fictional PlayStation rep **Kevin Butler** portrayed by actor **Jerry Lambert** (Figure 12.12b). The character had a different (humorous) subtitle for each commercial such as "Chief Weaponologist" and "VP of Fanboy Relations." Sony produced dozens of these commercials featuring the popular "It Only Does [fill in blank]" slogans.

Accessories released over the PS3's lifespan included charging stands, Blu-ray disc remotes, and rhythm game peripherals like mics, guitars, and drum kits. There was also **Buzz**—a "buzzer" controller for game show titles featuring extra-large buttons in the same vein as Xbox 360's **Big Button Pad** controller. The **Wireless Keypad** featured a miniature keyboard that clipped onto the standard controller just like Xbox

360's Messenger Kit. Logitech produced key accessories such as the Driving Force GT steering wheel/pedal combo and the Cordless Precision. Other peripherals included headsets, a **Memory Card Adaptor** for previous generation game saves, an updated version of the EyeToy called **PlayStation Eye**, and the **PlayTV** digital video broadcasting (**DVB-T**) tuner peripheral with digital video recorder (DVR) functionality.

Sony added further development in motion game controller technology with the **PlayStation Move** in response to Microsoft's Kinect and Nintendo's seventh-generation controllers. The Move consisted of two different controllers: the **motion controller** was a wand that contained an orb at the end that glowed in an assortment of colors. It housed internal sensors in which the player's movements could be tracked by PlayStation Eye or **PlayStation Camera**. The handle featured a large "Move" button in the center, surrounded by the four action buttons, with the start and select buttons positioned on the sides. The underside of the controller included one analog trigger, while the base of the unit contained a USB port, extension port, and a wrist strap. The second controller was the **navigation controller** which contained the left analog control stick, D-Pad, and two trigger buttons (L1 and L2). Each controller contained the PS button on the topside.

■ CONSOLE COMPARISON: PLAYSTATION 3 VS. XBOX 360

Both the Xbox 360 Xenon and PS3 Cell Processor ran at 3.2 GHz and each system performed at a comparable number of **Gflops** at 240 and 230, respectively (see Table 12.7). The Cell was a complex powerhouse

FIGURE 12.12 Screenshots from PS3 (a) "baby" commercial and (b) a "Kevin Butler" spot.

(a)

(b)

TABLE 12.7 PlayStation 3 Tech Specs

Manufacturer:	Sony Computer Entertainment
Launch price:	$499.99 & $599.99
Released date:	11/11/06 (JP), 11/17/06 (US), 3/23/07 (EU)
Format:	2× Blu-Ray, 8x DVD, CD, and Super Audio CD
Processors:	Cell Broadband Engine CPU (3.2 GHz) Nvidia-based SCEI RSX "Reality Synthesizer" (550 MHz)
Performance:	Up to 1080p HD/275 million PPS/228.8 GFLOPS
Memory:	256 MB XDR DRAM (system) and 256 MB GDDR3 (video)
Sound:	320-channel, Dolby 5.1 & DTS Surround

that contained more than twice as many cores versus Xbox 360's CPU. Despite its core size advantage, "the Cell Processor, for all its sophistication, had its plusses and minuses. It was designed to support complex programming—and, at the same time, to resist hacking. Unfortunately, the complexity of the system made it so different from typical CPUs that developers became frustrated" (Altizer, 2016, para. 9).

Early cross-platform games on PS3 were commonly inferior to Xbox 360 versions, featuring lower framerates and/or resolutions, as well as longer load times. PS4 system architect **Mark Cerny** "admitted that PlayStation 3 had a 'weak lineup' of titles available at launch … describing Cell as a 'Rubik's cube' which made it difficult for developers to perform 'the most basic tasks'" (Scammell, 2013, para. 1–2). It took most developers years to master the Cell to finally get the most out of the chip, resulting in many of the best PS3 titles not releasing until the latter half of the console's lifespan.

As for their GPUs, the Xbox **Xenos** shared its 512 MB with its system RAM, while the PS3 had **256 MB** of dedicated video RAM and could share another **224 MB** from the system RAM. "The Xbox had an advantage with its 10 MB of eDRAM, however, the PS3's **3.2 GHz** XDR RAM was much faster and more efficient than the Xbox 360's 700 MHz GDDR3 RAM, giving the PS3 the performance edge" (Schedeen, 2010). Originally both systems were backward compatible with last-generation software (albeit far from perfect), however, Sony removed its Emotion Engine (PS2) chip in later models and discontinued

backward compatibility with PS2 discs altogether by 2008. All PS3 models retained the ability to play PS1 CD-ROMs.

While each system supported full high-definition and stereoscopic 3D games, being a Blu-ray drive allowed PS3 owners to also watch 3D Blu-ray movies on compatible displays. Compared to Xbox 360's dual layer (DVD-9) discs that had an 8.5 GB capacity, PS3's Blu-ray Disc ROM (**BD-ROM**) format could hold between 25 and **33.4 GB** of data. Games such as *Final Fantasy XIII, L.A. Noire,* and *Rage* required three discs for the Xbox 360 but only one disc for the PS3. The Xbox 360 had stronger analog sound with Dolby Pro Logic II support, while the PS3 was the obvious choice for players with digital setups—offering Dolby Digital 5.1 (like Xbox 360), in addition to supporting **Dolby Digital 7.1** and **LPCM** (linear pulse code modulation) output.

Wi-Fi speeds were the same for both consoles, but the PS3 could connect to the Internet via Ethernet at **1 GB per second**, 10 times faster than the 360's 100 Mbps Ethernet speed. Furthermore, the PS3 supported Bluetooth 2.0 for connecting to various devices. Comparing online networks, Xbox Live pioneered features that Sony often replicated afterward. Microsoft typically led in this area, although the PSN was available for free and PlayStation Plus offered exclusive content for paying members. By the end of the generation, both platforms' online networks were fairly comparable. Likewise, neither the Kinect nor Move peripherals advanced the consoles as much as initially expected, with libraries consisting mostly of casual games.

HEAD-TO-HEAD

To compare gameplay and graphics between the PS3 and Xbox 360, check out games released on both systems. For games superior on PS3, compare *Darksiders, Grand Theft Auto V, L.A. Noire, Tomb Raider,* and *Vanquish.* For games superior on Xbox 360, compare *BioShock, DmC: Devil May Cry, Ghostbusters, GTA IV,* and *The Elder Scrolls V: Skyrim.*

■ KEY PLAYSTATION 3 TITLES

Not counting its library of digital downloads, more than 1,400 titles released for the PS3 on disc. Early blockbuster titles included **Insomniac**'s *Resistance: Fall of Man* and *Ratchet & Clank Future: Tools of Destruction.* A handful of other *Ratchet & Clank* games would follow. **Naughty Dog** pioneered a new hit franchise with *Uncharted: Drake's Fortune,* and **Hideo Kojima** produced another PlayStation exclusive with *Metal Gear Solid 4: Guns of the Patriots.*

A steady release of games followed with exclusive hits like *LittleBigPlanet, Resistance 2, Valkyria Chronicles,* and *Uncharted 2: Among Thieves* (shown in Figure 12.13). Key cross-platform games included *Batman: Arkham Asylum and Arkham City, BioShock,* and sequels to *Assassin's Creed* and *Call of Duty: Modern Warfare.* Popular fighting games during this time included *Street Fighter IV,* a *Mortal Kombat* reboot, *Injustice,* and a string of titles by *Guilty Gear* developer **Arc System Works.**

Starting with *God of War: Collection* in 2009, each year the PS3 would receive more **"HD Collection"** bundles of popular PS2 series on one Blu-ray disc such as *The Sly Collection* in 2010. Must-have titles really picked up after 2010 with *Heavy Rain* and *God of War III,* and by 2011 most cross-platform games were equal to or better than their Xbox 360 counterparts. Sony's last hurrah with the PS3 was in 2013 with a slew of exclusives including *Ni no Kuni: Wrath of the White Witch, The Last of Us, Beyond: Two Souls,* and *Dragon's Crown.*

DID YOU KNOW?

Up to this point, with each new generation, blockbuster titles have required more money and labor to produce and develop. "One Electronic Arts executive estimated that it took 20 employees to make a PlayStation game, 80 to make a PS2 game, and 150 to make a PS3 game" (Takahashi, 2011, p. 1).

FIGURE 12.13 Five defining PS3 titles including (a) *Batman: Arkham City,* (b) *Uncharted 2: Among Thieves,* (c) *Grand Theft Auto V,* (d) *The Last of Us,* and (e) *BioShock Infinite.*

(a) (b) (c) (d) (e)

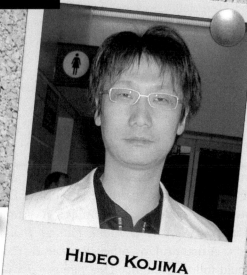

HIDEO KOJIMA

PRO FILE

KEY FACTS:

Pioneer of cinematic storytelling in video games

Called "The Father of the Stealth Genre"

PRO FILE

HISTORY:
- Born: August 24, 1963 in Setagaya, Tokyo, Japan

EDUCATION:
- Degree in Economics, Japan, 1986

CAREER HIGHLIGHTS:
- Writer, Director, & Designer for *Metal Gear* (1987)
- Writer & Director for graphic adventure games *Snatcher* (1988) and *Policenauts* (1994)
- Planner, Producer, & Director for *Tokimeki Memorial Drama* series (1997-98), Producer for *Beatmania* ports (1998–2002)
- Writer, Producer, Director, & Designer for all major entries in the *Metal Gear Solid* series (1998-2015)
- Producer & Designer for *Zone of the Enders* and *Boktai* series (2001-2006), and Producer, Director, Writer, & Designer for *Death Stranding* (2019)

RECOGNITION:
GDCA Lifetime Achievement Award (2009), Golden Joystick Lifetime Achievement Award (2014), Academy of Interactive Arts and Sciences' Hall of Fame (2015), The Game Awards Industry Icon Award (2016), NAVGTR Award for *MGSV: TPP* (2016), BAFTA Awards Academy Fellowship (2020)

▪ HANDHELD SNAPSHOT: SONY PSP

Sony released the **PlayStation Portable** (PSP) (Figure 12.14) in Japan on December 12, 2004. It launched in North America on March 24, 2005, for $249 and the rest of the world on September 1. Each release date had twice the amount of launch titles, beginning with six games in Japan, more than a dozen in North America, and 24 titles available for its September 1 release.

The PSP was the most powerful handheld for its time (see Table 12.8). Its large, bright 4.3″ diagonal backlit LCD featured widescreen support and offered between 4.5 and 7 hours of use with its rechargeable lithium-ion battery. The left side of the unit included both a directional pad and a small analog stick. The system's action buttons consisted of the standard four face buttons and two shoulder buttons. Like the Nintendo DS, the PSP featured built-in Wi-Fi capability. There was no web browser installed at launch, but the PSP would eventually receive a NetFront web browser with its system 2.0 update. In addition to connecting to the Internet, players could connect the handheld to a PlayStation 2 console, as well as a PC.

For media, the PSP used proprietary optical **UMD (Universal Media Disc)** format for both games and movies. Each **1.8 GB** UMD featured a plastic casing around the optical disc called a "protective shutter," similar to a MiniDisc. This made inserting the discs feel more like inserting a cartridge than a standard optical disc. The stylish system felt like an expensive, luxury device compared to the Nintendo DS and Sony priced the PSP accordingly. For consumers however, the $100 price difference made the PSP a tougher sell. The Nintendo DS outsold the PSP nearly 2:–1, however Sony would go on to sell more than 80 million total systems.

There were five different PSP models in all, which consumers could identify by their series codes. The original PSP was known as the PSP-1000. Sony followed this up with the slimmer and lighter PSP-2000 in 2007 (called "Slim" and "Lite" in Europe). Third was the PSP-3000 in 2008, which added a built-in microphone. The PSP-2000 and 3000 models could output

FIGURE 12.14 PlayStation Portable featuring *WipEout Pure*.

TABLE 12.8 PlayStation Portable Tech Specs

Format:	UMD/3.7 V lithium-ion battery (4.5–7 hours)
Processors:	32-bit Sony CPU (333 MHz)/166 MHz 512-bit GFX core
Performance:	16.77 mil. 16 or 24-bit colors/33 mil. PPS
Memory:	32 MB RAM+4 MB combined eDRAM
Resolution:	480 × 272 pixels/4.3″ diagonal backlit LCD
Sound:	Multichannel 3D sound, stereo speakers with 3.5 mm jack

video and stereo audio to a television via **component cable**. Next came the **PSP Go** (PSP-N1000) in 2009. The PSP Go featured a sliding screen and replaced the UMD drive with 16 GB of internal flash memory for digital-only games. Lastly, Sony released a stripped-down version called the PSP-E1000 that omitted stereo sound, Wi-Fi, and microphone functionality. More than 1,900 titles released for the PSP. See Figure 12.15 for recommended games.

FIGURE 12.15 Five defining PSP titles: (a) *Metal Gear Solid: Peace Walker*, (b) *Grand Theft Auto: Vice City Stories*, (c) *Lumines: Puzzle Fusion*, (d) *WipEout Pure*, and (e) *God of War: Ghost of Sparta*.

(a) (b) (c) (d) (e)

▪ NINTENDO WII

Originally known as the "Revolution" for its promise to revolutionize video games, Nintendo's **Wii** (Figure 12.16) became the company's first home console to release in the United States before Japan. The system launched in New York's Times Square on November 19, 2006, for $249—less than half the cost of a PS3 at the time. The Wii reached other countries in the following weeks and would sell more than 1 million units during its launch, with more than 600,000 of those systems sold in the United States (Goldstein, 2006, para. 1).

In addition to being the most affordable new console on the market, its **Wii Remote** (also called a "**Wiimote**") set it apart from the competition from the very beginning. Its simplistic design reduced the complex amount of action buttons that had become mainstream on other consoles, making it

more accessible to non-gamers. Its resemblance to a remote control gave it a familiar appearance, but it also contained a built-in speaker and an **accelerometer** (by **Analog Devices**) that could sense motion (Takahashi, 2011, p. 6). Arriving roughly four full years before Microsoft Kinect and PlayStation Move, the motion controls offered by the Wii were one of a kind for home consoles and attracted gamers and non-gamers of all ages.

Nintendo took the complete opposite approach to the competition, using less advanced but more established technology that was much more affordable (rendering profits from day one). The system even featured full backward compatibility with all 8 cm **GameCube** games and included four GameCube controller ports and two memory card slots beneath its top panel. Like with GameCube, Nintendo commissioned IBM for its main CPU and ATI for its graphics processor—each of which were only a third faster than the chips in the GameCube. Other than added Wi-Fi capability and the capacity for full-size 12 cm optical discs, the Wii's RAM and polygon performance were also not huge leaps forward from the previous system. This led to arguments by journalists and gamers that the Wii was just an upgraded GameCube with motion controls. Further rumors indicated Nintendo had originally developed the motion controls for the struggling GameCube but then shelved the technology until its next system.

Regardless of its processing power or history, the Wii's extensive launch lineup had something for everyone (Table 12.9). And just when the concept of a **pack-in title** with a launch edition console seemed like a concept of the past, Nintendo went against the grain even further by bundling *Wii Sports* with every console. The decision to bundle such an accessible "killer app" game with the Wii was a remarkable strategy by Nintendo and most certainly played a key role in the console's instant success.

GameCube designer **Kenichiro Ashida** created the Wii console along with **Shigeru Miyamoto**. Its disc slot produced a stylish blue glow, and its simplistic design complimented the easy-to-grasp controls, resembling the elegance of **Apple** products during that time. Similar to how Sega removed their name

FIGURE 12.16 Nintendo Wii with Wiimote.

TABLE 12.9   Nintendo Wii Launch Titles

- *Avatar: The Last Airbender*
- *Call of Duty 3*
- *Cars*
- *Dragon Ball Z: Budokai Tenkaichi 2*
- *Excite Truck*
- *Grim Adventures of Billy & Mandy*
- *GT Pro Series*
- *Happy Feet*
- *Legend of Zelda: Twilight Princess* (Figure 12.17a)
- *Madden NFL 07*
- *Marvel: Ultimate Alliance*
- *Monster 4×4: World Circuit*
- *Need for Speed: Carbon*
- *Rampage: Total Destruction*
- *Rayman*
- *Red Steel*
- *SpongeBob SquarePants: Creature from the Krusty Krab*
- *Super Monkey Ball: Banana Blitz*
- *Tony Hawk's Downhill Jam*
- *Trauma Center: Second Opinion*
- *Wii Sports* (Figure 12.17b)

from the forefront when marketing the **Dreamcast**, Nintendo's name and logo took a backseat in the marketing of the Wii. The company simply referred to the console as "Wii," which was always written larger and more pronounced than "Nintendo" in its marketing and packaging.

Its advertising featured players of all ages engaging in a shared Wii experience, as seen in Figures 12.18 and 12.19. Early advertising slogans included "Experience a new way to play" and "Wii would like to play." Like avatars on Xbox 360, users could create a "**Mii**" character of themselves (as shown in Figure 12.18). As simplistic as the Mii characters looked, their style gave the console a unique personality of its own. Taking the concept one step further, gamers could use each Mii as a playable character in games such as *Wii Sports* and over 60 other titles. Along with the console, the original Wii package included *Wii Sports*, a system manual, an external power adapter, composite AV cable, a plastic gray stand with a clear round base (for positioning the system vertically), **Sensor Bar**, one Wii Remote with batteries, and one **Nunchuk** attachment used for controlling certain games with an analog stick and its two action buttons labeled "C" and "Z."

The main graphical interface for the Wii was the **Wii Menu**, which included various "channels" such as the *Disc Channel* (which was where users opened disc-based Wii or GameCube games), the *Mii Channel* (for Mii creation), the *Photo Channel* (for loading picture slideshows from an SD card), as well as weather forecast and news channels. The *Wii Shop Channel* provided online access to other Wii channels, including *WiiWare* and **Virtual Console** where users could purchase downloadable versions of popular titles from previous Nintendo consoles, as well as games from the Sega Master System and Genesis, TurboGrafx-16, Neo•Geo, and new, exclusive Wii titles. Like the other seventh-generation consoles, the Wii featured a web browser and downloadable apps such as **YouTube**, Netflix, Hulu Plus, and Amazon Video.

FIGURE 12.17   Screenshots of (a) *The Legend of Zelda: Twilight Princess* and (b) *Wii Sports*

(a)

(b)

FIGURE 12.18 Early Wii ad featuring *Wii Sports* and testimonial by Tracey Clark.

FIGURE 12.19 Nintendo Wii ad for *Complex* (2006) featuring Tim Leong and Jared Ryder.

Nintendo released countless accessories for the Wii, along with borderline gimmicks such as hollow plastic golf clubs and tennis rackets built to hold the Wiimote. While typically inexpensive, these often did little to enhance a person's performance in the games—but were fun and new peripherals, nonetheless. The **Wii Wheel** and **Wii Zapper** certainly made driving and shooting games more entertaining. Nintendo released a **Classic Controller** to accommodate its retro and non-motion games. The Classic Controller resembled the Super Nintendo controller with an additional two shoulder buttons and twin analog sticks. Nintendo later released a **Pro** version which featured more comfortable handles, similar to the PlayStation controller.

The **Wii MotionPlus** adapter used **gyroscope** technology to enhance the Wiimote's accuracy in games such as *Wii Sports Resort, Red Steel 2*, and *The Legend of Zelda: Skyward Sword*. Nintendo later built the feature into a **Wii Remote Plus** controller. Other accessories included a **Wii Speak** microphone, headsets, sensor bars, and popular rhythm game products (including microphones, guitars, and drums). One of the most popular products was the **Wii Balance Board** for games such as *Wii Fit* and *We Ski*. The Balance Board earned a Guinness World Record for the "Best-selling Personal Weighing Device" in November 2010 when it sold over 32 million units (Whitehead, 2012, para. 1).

Nintendo produced two variations of the Wii late in the console's lifespan that did not release outside of Japan. Both were inferior to the original model. The first was the **Wii Family Edition** in 2011, which removed backward compatibility GameCube games and accessories. Its casing was identical to the original Wii; however, Nintendo haphazardly left empty holes under the top cover where the GameCube controller ports and memory card slots used to be. The **Wii Mini** was released a little over a year later. It was Nintendo's first major redesign of a console since the Super Nintendo **SNS-101** in 1997. Beyond its stylish, smaller size, the Mini also removed GameCube compatibility. Furthermore, this model omitted all networking abilities and was only capable of composite video output.

■ CONSOLE COMPARISON: WII VS. PLAYSTATION 3 AND XBOX 360

It was never Nintendo's intention to go head-to-head with Microsoft and Sony, and unlike those giants, the Wii was the only major seventh-generation console that did not feature high-definition resolution or HDMI support. Nintendo passionately believed that an affordable system with unique, motion control gameplay would help it stand on its own among its competitors. As Shigeru Miyamoto explained, "power isn't everything for a console. Too many powerful consoles can't coexist. It's like having only ferocious dinosaurs. They might fight and hasten their own extinction" (Cios, 2015, para. 9).

Comparing the Wii to the technical specs of the PS3 or Xbox 360 shows the Wii was inferior in almost every category (Table 12.10). Its network offerings were not as robust as Xbox Live or PlayStation Network, but it was a step in the right direction for Nintendo after the network-lacking GameCube. While Microsoft and Sony's machines contained internal hard drives up to hundreds of gigabytes in size, the Wii only contained 12 MB of internal flash memory and an SD card slot for external storage. It shared certain features such as wireless controllers, Wi-Fi connectivity, and the ability to stream Netflix—however, it lacked high-definition resolution.

Besides HDMI, the Wii also lacked optical audio output and was "physically unable to output audio in Dolby Digital surround sound" (Casamassina, 2006, para. 1). While it could accept full-size 12 cm optical discs, Nintendo did not program the console for DVD movie playback. It did feature Bluetooth capability, including wireless connectivity with the Nintendo DS—something that was sorely lacking on Microsoft's system.

Like the Xbox 360 controller, the Wiimote required two AA batteries or a lithium-ion battery pack but lacked a built-in rechargeable battery like the PS3 controller. On the other hand, the Wiimote was the only seventh-generation controller to feature a built-in speaker, which made for unique gameplay experiences. For example, when shooting an arrow in *The Legend of Zelda: Twilight Princess*, the sound of the released arrow travels from the Wiimote to the television speaker, creating a sense of depth. Moreover, for its first 4 years on the market, the Wii was the only console to feature such unique motion controls.

HEAD-TO-HEAD

There were plenty of games that were released on all three seventh-generation consoles. Compare the gameplay and graphics to each system's version of *Call of Duty: Black Ops, Rock Band 2, Sonic & Sega All-Stars Racing*, and *Tomb Raider: Underworld*.

TABLE 12.10	Nintendo Wii Tech Specs
Manufacturer:	Nintendo
Launch price:	$249.99
Release date:	11/19/06 (US), 12/02/06 (JP), 12/07/06 (AU), 12/08/06 (EU)
Format:	6 × speed 8 cm and 12 cm Optical Discs
Processors:	IBM Power PC "Broadway" CPU (729 MHz) ATI "Hollywood" GPU (243 MHz)/12 GFLOPS
Performance:	720×480p, 16:9/49.5 million PPS (up to 30 million with effects)
Memory:	88 MB (24 int.+64 ext.), 3 MB texture
Sound:	64-channel, Dolby Pro Logic II

■ KEY WII TITLES

More than 1,500 games officially released for the Wii, not including download-only titles. More than 80% of these games reached U.S. retail shelves and, like GameCube, the top 10 best-selling games on the Wii were all from Nintendo (Hill, 2012, para. 9). Nintendo produced a steady stream of key Mario titles for the console, including the four-player *New Super Mario Bros. Wii*, *Super Paper Mario*, and two *Super Mario Galaxy* games. Other key titles published by Nintendo included two new *Zelda* and *Kirby* games, *Super Smash Bros. Brawl*, *Metroid Prime 3: Corruption* (and *Trilogy*), *Donkey Kong Country Returns*, *Punch-Out!!*, *WarioWare: Smooth Moves*, and *Mario Kart Wii*.

The system received decent third-party support from companies such as **Capcom** who published exclusives such as *Zack & Wiki: Quest for Barbaros*, *Tatsunoko vs. Capcom: Ultimate All-Stars*, *Monster Hunter Tri*, and two *Resident Evil* rail shooters. Sega also published exclusive hits for the system such as *Super Monkey Ball: Banana Blitz*, *The House of the Dead: Overkill*, *MadWorld*, and *Sonic Colors*. While a handful of these games would eventually release on other consoles, Wii owners got to enjoy them first. More notable titles included the *Red Steel, Rayman, Rabbids*, and *Just Dance* games published by **Ubisoft**, along with Grasshopper Manufacture's *No More Heroes 1* and *2*.

Lesser-known titles that deserve mention include Treasure's *Sin and Punishment: Star Successor*, Vanillaware's *Muramasa: The Demon Blade*, WayForward's *A Boy and His Blob*, and Hudson

Entertainment's *Marble Saga: Kororinpa*. In addition to third-party support from Activision Blizzard, Electronic Arts, and Square Enix, the Wii was a popular platform for Japanese role-playing games during this generation. Companies such as **Xseed Games** and **NIS America** released a fair amount of JRPGs for the system. The most cherished titles were among the fan-supported **Operation Rainfall** campaign, which led to the Western localization of three key titles including *Xenoblade Chronicles* (2011) (shown in Figure 12.20), *The Last Story* (2012), and *Pandora's Tower* (2013).

■ SEVENTH-GENERATION MARKET SUMMARY

Microsoft got off to an early lead by releasing the Xbox 360 a full year before Nintendo and Sony's new consoles. For the first few years, cross-platform games typically looked and/or ran better on Xbox 360 because developers were more familiar with the hardware, which was much easier to program for than the PS3. It was also the leading system for online gaming through much of the generation thanks to the company's commitment to Xbox Live. The console was less expensive to produce than the PS3 although not as lucrative as Nintendo's Wii, taking around a year before the units began to turn a profit.

While Microsoft was able to survive the Red Ring of Death epidemic with its first model systems, it struggled to make a dent in the Japanese market, selling even fewer units than the original Xbox with only 1.5 million sold after nearly 6 years on the market (Phillips, 2011, para. 1). In comparison,

FIGURE 12.20 Five Wii hits: (a) *Super Mario Galaxy*, (b) *Metroid Prime 3: Corruption*, (c) *Xenoblade Chronicles*, (d) *Super Smash Bros. Brawl*, and (e) *The Legend of Zelda: Twilight Princess*.

(a) (b) (c) (d) (e)

Microsoft Corporation (2008) reported that Xbox 360 had "sold over ten million units in the United States, making it the first [seventh] generation gaming console to break the ten million mark in the U.S., and contributing to global sales of over 19 million" (para. 1). In the end, the 360 sold more than three times as many units as the original Xbox, breaking 85 million units sold.

Sony had a rough start with the PS3, with its high price tag that lost the company approximately $300 per unit, along with negative press to go with it. "Sony's Game division recorded a JPY 232.3 billion [$1.97 billion USD] loss, primarily due to selling the PS3 lower than the manufacturing price, as well as the associated costs of the worldwide launch" (Martin, 2007, para. 5). The following month, President of Sony Computer Entertainment Ken Kutaragi announced his plans to retire.

It took most developers a couple of years to gain a solid grasp on the Cell Processor and begin producing games that utilized more of the chip's potential. During that learning curve, the console suffered from subpar ports compared to Xbox 360 versions of the same games. Furthermore, games that used to be exclusives (or timed exclusives) on Sony consoles (such as *Final Fantasy, Grand Theft Auto,* and *Resident Evil*) began appearing on Microsoft's system simultaneously.

Falling manufacturing costs and the omission of the Emotion Engine helped Sony become profitable; however, the company continued to lose money on each console sold until around a year after the release of the PS3 Slim in 2010 (Reilly, 2010, para. 2). After dominating the previous two generations with the PlayStation and PlayStation 2, Sony found itself in unfamiliar territory. For the larger part of the console's lifespan, Sony was playing catch-up in North America where the "Xbox 360 outsold the PS3 in the U.S. for 32 consecutive months" (Metz, 2013, para. 1).

It took Sony 6 years to catch up to Microsoft, tying the number of units sold with Xbox 360 in November 2012 at approximately 70 million sales (Gera, 2012, p. 1). Like Microsoft's console, the PlayStation 3 would go on to sell over 85 million systems—an exceptional comeback, but still not as significant as the 155 million PS2 consoles it was able to move in the prior generation. The missteps of the PS3 taught Sony serious lessons and it would be careful not to repeat those mistakes with its next console.

Nintendo struck gold with the Wii, outselling both Sony and Microsoft for years after its release. After just 20 months on the market, the Wii surpassed the Xbox 360 in number of console sales with 10.9 million units sold (Keiser, 2008). It was the first time Nintendo led the home console market in overall units sold since the Super NES three generations prior. The company sold more than 57 million Wii systems by December 2010, which at the time was nearly equivalent to the total sales of Xbox 360 and PS3 consoles combined (VGChartz, 2010, p. 1).

On top of becoming the generation leader in consoles sold, Nintendo was also enjoying a greater profit margin since the Wii cost much less to manufacture. The company attained its goal of reaching a broader audience with the system, capturing the interest of gamers and non-gamers, young and old. It was common at that time to hear stories of the Wii being played by residents in nursing homes, retirement communities, and other medical centers as a form of rehabilitation.

The Wii maintained the largest market share throughout the generation and by the end of 2011 Nintendo had sold 89.5 million Wii consoles for a 44% market share. The Wii would go on to sell more than 100 million units (Figure 12.21)—more than four times

FIGURE 12.21 Seventh-generation console sales graph.

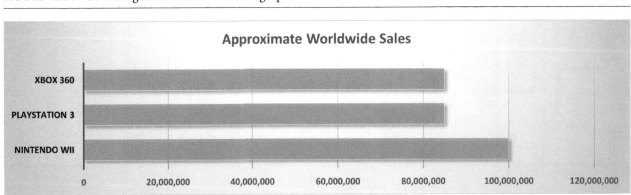

the number of GameCube consoles sold in the previous generation. On top of that, Nintendo's portable DS system went on to sell over 154 million units—the best-selling handheld system of all time and second overall only to the PS2, which holds the record for best-selling home video game console of all time.

▪ SEVENTH-GENERATION BREAKTHROUGHS AND TRENDS

There were unique breakthroughs and trends that defined the seventh generation of video games. Here is a list of the top 10 features that defined the generation:

1. Higher definition display resolutions via HDMI (up to 1080p)

2. Blu-ray capability (PS3) and HD-DVD add-on (Xbox 360)

3. More advanced online capabilities (microtransactions, games, movies, social)

4. Standard wireless controllers and rechargeable lithium-ion battery packs

5. Motion controls with Wiimote, PS3 Move, and Xbox Kinect

6. Console games became more like PC games with patches and updates

7. Rise of casual, indie, and episodic games

8. Powerful multicore processors and more RAM to work with

9. Higher efficiency GPUs and hundreds of millions of polygons per second

10. Multitude of console versions with various hard drive capacities and features

▪ ACTIVITY: A VIRTUAL WORKOUT

In addition to entertainment-based games, fitness titles such as *Wii Fit* and *Zumba* released during the seventh generation to take advantage of each console's motion control abilities.

GUIDELINES

Obtain a seventh-generation console and one or two compatible fitness titles, comfortable clothing, and a pair of sneakers. Be sure the console has its motion controllers and any required fitness accessories. Then obtain one or two regular fitness DVDs that do not contain any video game interactivity. Spend 10–15 minutes following the exercise routine from one of the regular fitness DVDs, followed by 10–15 minutes of a similar exercise routine from one of the fitness video game titles. Note that you may require additional time to enter personal information into the video game title before proceeding to the workout.

QUESTIONS

1. How do the experiences compare exercising to a regular DVD versus a fitness game?
2. What are the advantages and disadvantages to working out with each medium?
3. Do you think video game fitness titles will become more popular? Explain.

■ CHAPTER 12 QUIZ

1. This arcade company recorded substantial losses by 2008 that led them to close or sell 110 arcade centers and offer voluntary early retirement to about 400 employees:
   a. Capcom
   b. Konami
   c. Namco
   d. Sega

2. This seventh-generation home console released approximately 1 year before the rest:
   a. PlayStation 3
   b. Xbox 360
   c. Wii
   d. None of the above

3. Introduced world to the concept of "achievements"—digital rewards unlocked by completing various milestones in a game:
   a. PlayStation 3
   b. Xbox 360
   c. Wii
   d. None of the above

4. Earned the Guinness World Record for "fastest selling consumer electronics device" with 8 million units sold in its first 60 days on the market:
   a. Microsoft Kinect
   b. Nintendo Wii
   c. PlayStation Move
   d. Wii Fit

5. One trait that sets the Sony PS3 apart from the Xbox 360 and Wii is its ability to play:
   a. Sega Dreamcast discs
   b. PSP discs
   c. Blu-ray discs
   d. All of the above

6. The Xbox 360's Dashboard, PlayStation 3's XrossMediaBar, and the Wii Menu are all examples of a:
   a. CPU
   b. GPU
   c. GUI
   d. HUD

7. Its Xenon CPU was built by IBM and its Xenos graphics chip made with ATI Technologies:
   a. PlayStation 3
   b. Xbox 360
   c. Wii
   d. None of the above

8. This system featured an optical UMD (Universal Media Disc) drive for both games and movies and an optional TV tuner:
   a. PlayStation 3
   b. Xbox 360
   c. Wii
   d. None of the above

9. A "General Hardware Failure" on Xbox 360 indicated by three flashing red quadrants around the power button:
   a. Ring of Light
   b. Red Ring of Death
   c. Overheating Warning
   d. None of the above

10. Which of the following was NOT a model of the Xbox 360 console released by Microsoft?
    a. Arcade
    b. Compact
    c. Elite
    d. Slim (S)

11. This console's Balance Board peripheral earned a Guinness World Record for the "Best-selling Personal Weighing Device":
    a. Xbox 360
    b. PlayStation 3
    c. Nintendo DS
    d. Nintendo Wii

12. The initial cost to manufacture the PS3 was so high that Sony lost approximately _____ on each system sold:
    a. $100
    b. $200
    c. $300
    d. $400

13. Which motion control device allowed for a "controller-free" experience?
    a. Wiimote
    b. Sixaxis
    c. Move
    d. Kinect

14. This system's multicore Cell Processor was essentially seven microprocessors on one chip, allowing it to perform several operations at once:
    a. PlayStation 3
    b. Xbox 360
    c. Wii
    d. None of the above

15. Writer, director, and designer for all major *Metal Gear Solid* entries (1998–2015):
    a. Ken Kutaragi
    b. Shigeru Miyamoto
    c. Hideo Kojima
    d. Eugene Jarvis

16. Which of the following features was *not* a characteristic of the Nintendo Wii?
    a. Wiimote required two AA batteries or a lithium-ion battery pack
    b. Was the only seventh-generation controller to feature a built-in speaker
    c. Supported Dolby Digital 7.1 and LPCM (linear pulse code modulation) output
    d. It could accept full-size 12 cm optical discs, but Nintendo did not program it for DVD movie playback

17. In shader architecture, _____ shaders alter the lighting, color, and surface of each pixel to help smoothen out 3D objects, while _____ shaders manipulate an object's position in 3D space, resulting in more realistic animation and special effects such as morphing.
    a. pixel (shaders) and vertex (shaders)
    b. pixel (shaders) and axis (shaders)
    c. spectra (shaders) and axis (shaders)
    d. spectra (shaders) and vertex (shaders)

18. Each of these systems saw multiple models, including three different console shape designs:
    a. PlayStation 3 and Wii
    b. Wii and Xbox 360
    c. Xbox 360 and PlayStation 3
    d. All of the above

19. This network suffered a complete shutdown for 3 weeks due to a massive external intrusion (hack) on April 20, 2011, which affected more than 100 million online accounts and cost roughly $171 million in damages:
    a. Virtual Console
    b. PlayStation Network
    c. WiiWare
    d. Xbox Live

20. Which game console dominated the seventh generation in terms of overall units sold?
    a. Sega Dreamcast
    b. Microsoft Xbox 360
    c. Sony PlayStation 3
    d. Nintendo Wii

True or False

21. North American arcades rebounded from a 2003 low of 2,500 game venues to an increase of 3,500 in 2008.

22. The original Xbox 360 model required a separate Wireless Network Adapter to connect to the Internet via Ethernet.

23. Sony released two subsequent models of the PS3 with different form factors, dubbed "Slim" and "Elite," respectively.

24. The Nintendo Wii launched at a lower price than both the Xbox 360 and PS3.

25. In almost every generation of video game consoles, the most powerful console had the highest sales figures and won the console war for that time period.

◼ FIGURES

Figure 12.1 Screenshots of top arcade rail shooters from 2006: (a) *Aliens: Extermination* (Global VR), (b) *Big Buck Hunter: Call of the Wild* (Raw Thrills), and (c) *House of the Dead 4* (Sega). (*Aliens: Extermination*, courtesy of Play Mechanix/Global VR, 2006; *Big Buck Hunter: Call of the Wild*, courtesy of Incredible Technologies/Raw Thrills, 2006; and *House of the Dead 4*, courtesy of Sega, 2006.)

Figure 12.2 Xbox 360 with controller. "The Xbox 360, a video game console released by Microsoft in 2005. This is the 'Pro' model from the launch line-up, which featured a 20 GB hard drive, wireless controller and a silver DVD bezel." By Evan Amos. Own work, Public Domain, https://commons.wikimedia.org/w/index.php?curid=33220305. Retrieved from https://en.wikipedia.org/wiki/Xbox_360#/media/File:Xbox-360-Pro-wController.jpg. (Part of this image was used on the introductory page of this chapter.)

Figure 12.3 Xbox 360 launch titles: (a) *Call of Duty 2* and (b) *Project Gotham Racing 3*. (*Call of Duty 2*, courtesy of Infinity Ward/Activision, 2005; and *Project Gotham Racing 3*, courtesy of Bizarre Creations/Microsoft Game Studios, 2005.)

Figure 12.4 Evolution of Xbox 360 Dashboard: (a) Blades, (b) NXE, and (c) Metro. ("The new Xbox dashboard arrives tomorrow—Let's look at how it's evolved" by Joey Davidson, November 11, 2015. Retrieved from https://www.technobuffalo.com/2015/11/11/xbox-dashboard-history/.)

Figure 12.5 2010 Ingram Micro ad featuring Xbox 360S, Kinect and *Kinect Adventures!* ("*Xbox Kinect Adventures*," Posted March 22, 2011. Available at http://rwee406rib.blogspot.com/2011/05/xbox-kinect-adventures.html.)

Figure 12.6 Box art to five popular 360 titles including (a) *Halo 3*, (b) *The Orange Box*, (c) *Mass Effect 3*, (d) *Grand Theft Auto IV*, and (e) *Gears of War 2*. (*Halo 3*, courtesy of Bungie/Microsoft Game Studios, 2007; *The Orange Box*, courtesy of Valve Software/EA Games, 2007; *Mass Effect 3*, courtesy of BioWare/Electronic Arts, 2012; *Grand Theft Auto IV*, courtesy of Rockstar North/Rockstar Games, 2008; and *Gears of War 2*, courtesy of Epic Games/Microsoft Game Studios, 2008.)

Figure 12.7 Nintendo DS featuring *Mario Kart DS*. ("An original Nintendo DS 'Fat' in blue" by Evan Amos—own work, public domain. Available at https://commons.wikimedia.org/w/index.php?curid=14501145. Retrieved from https://en.wikipedia.org/wiki/Nintendo_DS#/media/File:Nintendo-DS-Fat-Blue.png.) Screenshot of *Mario Kart DS* courtesy of Nintendo 2005.

Figure 12.8 Box art to DS hits: (a) *New Super Mario Bros.*, (b) *Castlevania: Dawn of Sorrow*, (c) *The Legend of Zelda: Phantom Hourglass*, (d) *GTA: Chinatown Wars*, and (e) *Mario Kart DS*. (*New Super Mario Bros.*, courtesy of Nintendo, 2006; *Castlevania: Dawn of Sorrow*, courtesy of Konami, 2005; *The Legend of Zelda: Phantom Hourglass*, courtesy of Nintendo, 2007; *GTA: Chinatown Wars*, courtesy of Rockstar Leeds/Rockstar Games, 2009; and *Mario Kart DS*, courtesy of Nintendo 2005.)

Figure 12.9 PlayStation 3 with DualShock 3 controller. ("Original PlayStation 3 model" by Evan Amos—own work, public domain. Available at https://commons.wikimedia.org/w/index.php?curid=11346934. Retrieved from https://en.wikipedia.org/wiki/2011_PlayStation_Network_outage#/media/File:Ps3-fat-console.png.) (Part of this image was used on the introductory page of this chapter.)

Figure 12.10 Screenshots from PS3 launch titles: (a) *NBA 2K7* and (b) *Resistance: Fall of Man*. (*NBA 2K7*, courtesy of Visual Concepts and Kush Games/2K Sports, 2006; and *Resistance: Fall of Man*, courtesy of Insomniac Games/SCEA, 2006.)

Figure 12.11 Old cover art and spine (a) and new style (b) for *LittleBigPlanet: GOTY edition*. (Courtesy of Media Molecule/SCEA, 2009.)

Figure 12.12 Screenshots from PS3 (a) "baby" commercial and (b) a "Kevin Butler" spot. (Courtesy of TBWA\Chiat\Day Los Angeles.)

Figure 12.13 Five defining PS3 titles including (a) *Batman: Arkham City*, (b) *Uncharted 2: Among Thieves*, (c) *Grand Theft Auto V*, (d) *The Last of Us*, and (e) *BioShock Infinite*. (*Batman: Arkham City*, courtesy of Rocksteady Studios/Warner Bros. Interactive Entertainment, 2011; *Uncharted 2: Among Thieves*, courtesy of Naughty Dog/SCEA, 2009; *Grand Theft Auto V*, courtesy of Rockstar North/Rockstar Games, 2013; *The Last of Us*, courtesy of Naughty Dog/SCEA, 2013; and *BioShock Infinite*, courtesy of Irrational Games/2K Games, 2013.)

Figure 12.14 PlayStation Portable featuring *WipEout Pure*. ("Original Model PSP (PSP-1000)" by Evan Amos—own work, public domain. Available at https://commons.wikimedia.org/w/index.php?curid=11337256. Retrieved from https://en.wikipedia.org/wiki/PlayStation_Portable#/media/File:Psp-1000.jpg. Screenshot of *Wipeout Pure* courtesy of Studio Liverpool/SCEA, 2005.)

Figure 12.15 Five defining PSP titles: (a) *Metal Gear Solid: Peace Walker*, (b) *Grand Theft Auto: Vice City Stories*, (c) *Lumines*, (d) *WipEout Pure*, and (e) *God of War: Ghost* of Sparta. (*Metal Gear Solid: Peace Walker,* courtesy of Kojima Productions/Konami, 2010; *Grand Theft Auto: Vice City Stories,* courtesy of Rockstar Leeds/Rockstar Games, 2006; *Lumines,* courtesy of Q Entertainment/Ubisoft, 2005; *Wipeout Pure,* courtesy of Studio Liverpool/SCEA, 2005; and *God of War: Ghost of Sparta,* courtesy of Ready at Dawn/SCEA, 2010.)

Figure 12.16 Nintendo Wii with Wiimote. ("Wii with Wii Remote" by Evan Amos—own work, public domain. Available at https://commons.wikimedia.org/w/index. php?curid=11477211. Retrieved from https://en.wikipedia. org/wiki/Wii#/media/File:Wii-Console.png. Wrist strap graphics modified by Wardyga.) (Part of this image was used on the introductory page of this chapter.)

Figure 12.17 Screenshots of (a) *The Legend of Zelda: Twilight Princess* and (b) *Wii Sports* (Courtesy of Nintendo, 2006.)

Figure 12.18 Early Wii ad featuring *Wii Sports* and testimonial by Tracey Clark. (Courtesy of Tracey Clark. (2020, November 8). *14 Nov Wii made it to Oprah.* Retrieved from https://traceyclark.com/wii-made-it-to-oprah/.)

Figure 12.19 Nintendo Wii ad for *Complex* (2006) featuring Tim Leong and Jared Ryder. ("Nintendo Wii Gives Back to Africa" photo by Jared Ryder, September 3, 2009. Retrieved from https://djtreats.com/2009/09/03/ nintendo-wii-gives-back-to-africa/.)

Figure 12.20 Five Wii hits: (a) *Super Mario Galaxy,* (b) *Metroid Prime 3: Corruption,* (c) *Xenoblade Chronicles,* (d) *Super Smash Bros. Brawl,* and (e) *The Legend of Zelda: Twilight Princess.* (*Super Mario Galaxy,* courtesy of Nintendo, 2007; *Metroid Prime 3: Corruption,* courtesy of Retro Studios/Nintendo, 2007; *Xenoblade Chronicles,* courtesy of Monolith Soft/Nintendo, 2012; *Super Smash Bros. Brawl,* courtesy of Game Arts/Nintendo, 2008; and *The Legend of Zelda: Twilight Princess,* courtesy of Nintendo, 2006.)

Figure 12.21 Seventh-generation console sales graph. (Designed by Wardyga using data from VGChartz. (2017). Global Hardware Totals. Retrieved from http://www. vgchartz.com/.)

PRO FILE: Hideo Kojima. Hideo Kojima at E3 2006 with Gameplay (magazine) award for Best story of the year 2005. Posted June 28, 2007. By Sergey Galyonkin from Kyiv, Ukraine—Hideo Kojima Uploaded by Yakiv Gluck, CC BY-SA 2.0, https://commons.wikimedia.org/w/index. php?curid=27482064. Retrieved from https://commons. wikimedia.org/wiki/File:Hideo_Kojima_at_E3_2006.jpg.

■ REFERENCES

Altizer, R. (2016, October 19). *History of the PlayStation 3: From its release date to PS3 specs.* Retrieved from https://www.lifewire.com/playstation-3-ps3-revealed-before-e3-2717709.

Baertlein, L. (2006, November 30). *Analyst: PlayStation 3 shipments below forecast: Researcher says initial U.S. units fell far short of 400,000 Sony promised.* NBC News. Retrieved from http://www.nbcnews.com/ id/15854413/ns/technology_and_science-games/t/ analyst-playstation-shipments-below-forecast/.

BBC News. (2006, September 6). *PlayStation 3 Euro launch delayed.* Retrieved from http://news.bbc.co.uk/2/hi/ technology/5319190.stm.

BBC News. (2009, September 18). *Sony rebuts BBC PlayStation claim.* Retrieved from http://news.bbc. co.uk/2/hi/8263063.stm.

Carless, S. (2006, April 27). *Breaking: Nintendo announces new Revolution name – 'Wii.'* Retrieved from http:// www.gamasutra.com/php-bin/news_index.php? story=9075.

Casamassina, M. (2006, May 23). *No Dolby Digital for Wii: Official Wii developer documentation backs up what Wii games at E3 suggested.* Retrieved from http:// www.ign.com/articles/2006/05/23/no-dolby-digital-for-wii.

Cios, A. (2015, July 14). *How Nintendo CEO Satoru Iwata changed video games forever.* Retrieved from http:// www.konbini.com/us/entertainment/nintendo-ceo-satoru-iwata-changed-video-games-forever/.

Crossley, R. (2016, April 20). *How Xbox 360 dominated a decade.* Retrieved from http://www. gamespot.com/articles/how-xbox-360-dominated-a-decade/1100-6432469/.

Dave & Buster's Entertainment, Inc. (2016, March 19). *Form 10-K (Annual Report): Filed 03/29/16 for the Period Ending 01/31/16.* Powered by Edgar Online. Retrieved from http://files.shareholder.com/down-loads/AMDA-16L7N9/3876164492x0xS1193125-16-521591/1525769/filing.pdf.

East Valley Tribune. (2006, April 20). *Video killed the arcade star.* Retrieved from http://www.eastvalley-tribune.com/article_9b22d9ea-1810-5465-8bd9-a4e3204de569.html?mode=story.

Editorial: Yu Suzuki: The Kikizo Interview. (2006, February 15). *Kikizo Staff at Video Games Daily.* Retrieved from http://archive.videogamesdaily.com/features/sega_ yu_suzuki_iv_feb06_p2.asp.

Editorial: Epic Fail. (2009, September). *Game Informer,* p. 12.

Gera, E. (2012, November 16). *PlayStation 3 sales reach 70 million worldwide, tie with Xbox 360: PlayStation Move sales hit over 15 million.* Retrieved from http:// www.polygon.com/2012/11/16/3653206/playstation-3-sales-reaches-70-million-worldwide-ties-with-xbox-360.

Goldstein, H. (2006, November 27). *Wii Sells Through 600K: Nintendo's new system goes off with a bang—and so does Zelda.* Retrieved from http://www.ign.com/articles/2006/11/28/wii-sells-through-600k.

Guinness World Records. (2010). Fastest-selling gaming peripheral. *Guinness World Records 2011 Gamer's Edition.* Retrieved from http://www.guinnessworldrecords.com/world-records/fastest-selling-gaming-peripheral/.

Guinness World Records. (2015). *Guinness World Records: Gamer's Edition 2016. Guinness World Records,* New York: Jim Pattison Group.

Hill, S. (2012, April 17). *The truth about the Nintendo Wii.* Hartman, M. (Ed.) Retrieved from http://www.alter-edgamer.com/wii-gaming/51452-the-truth-about-the-nintendo-wii/.

Huffman, S. (2013, November 15). *PS4 and the history of lavish gaming system parties.* Retrieved from https://www.marketplace.org/2013/11/15/tech/numbers/ps4-and-history-lavish-gaming-system-parties.

Hurley, O. (2008, February 6). Game on again for coin-operated arcade titles. *The Guardian.* Retrieved from https://www.theguardian.com/technology/2008/feb/07/games.it.

Hutchings, S. (2013, November 14). *A brief history of the PlayStation 3.* Retrieved from http://ps4attitude.com/opinion/2013/11/brief-history-playstation-3.

Ivanovs, G. (2016, April). *Consumer behavior in games preorder.* Retrieved from http://pure.au.dk/portal-asb-student/files/99706817/Georgijs_Ivanovs_Thesis_201305929.pdf.

Keiser, J. (2008, July 17). *NPD: Wii Overtakes 360 in US.* Retrieved from http://www.next-gen.biz/news/npd-wii-overtakes-360-us.

Martin, M. (2007, May 16). *PS3 launch damages Sony profits: 'Strategic price' contributes to a 68 per cent drop in operating profits as worldwide shipments of next gen console reach 5.5 million.* Retrieved from http://www.gamesindustry.biz/articles/ps3-launch-damages-sony-profits.

Martinez, E. (2011, May 24). *PlayStation Network breach has cost Sony $171 million.* CBS News. Retrieved from http://www.cbsnews.com/news/playstation-network-breach-has-cost-sony-171-million/.

Metz, C. (2013, November 7). Exclusive: The American who designed the PlayStation 4 and remade Sony. *Wired.* Retrieved from https://www.wired.com/2013/11/playstation-4/.

Miller, R. (2009, August 27). *PlayStation 3 Slim review.* Retrieved from https://www.engadget.com/2009/08/27/playstation-3-slim-review/.

Moore, P. (2007). *Open letter from Peter Moore.* Retrieved from https://web.archive.org/web/20071023004948/http://xbox.com/en-ca/support/petermooreletter.htm.

Nintendo Co., Ltd. (2016, April 27). *Consolidated sales transition by region.* Retrieved from https://www.nintendo.co.jp/ir/library/historical_data/pdf/consolidated_sales_e1603.pdf.

Nintendo Co., Ltd. (2017). *What does "DS" stand for?* Retrieved from http://en-americas-support.nintendo.com/app/answers/detail/a_id/3904/p/606.

Oravasaari, D. (2012, March 4). *The history of PlayStation ads: PS3.* Retrieved from http://www.playstationlifestyle.net/2012/03/04/the-history-of-playstation-ads-ps3/#ZRx9ZHrMFS73ceV4.99.

Ogden, G. (2007, March 31). *Kutaragi "insisted" on Spider-Man font for PS3.* Retrieved from http://www.gamesradar.com/kutaragi-insisted-on-spider-man-font-for-ps3/.

Phillips, T. (2011, June 17). *Xbox 360 sells 1.5 million in Japan: It's only taken six years.* Retrieved from http://www.eurogamer.net/articles/2011-06-17-xbox-360-sells-1-5-million-in-japan.

Reilly, J. (2010, June 28). *PS3 profitable, price cut unlikely: Sony looking at new console bundles rather than price drop.* Retrieved from http://www.ign.com/articles/2010/06/28/ps3-profitable-price-cut-unlikely.

Sega Sammy Holdings Inc. (2008, March 31). *Back on the right track: Annual Report 2008.* Retrieved from https://www.segasammy.co.jp/english/ir/library/pdf/printing_annual/2008/e_2008_annual.pdf.

Sinclair, B. (2016, November). *Wii and PS3 launches a study in contrasts.* Retrieved from http://www.gamesindustry.biz/articles/2016-11-01-wii-and-ps3-launches-a-study-in-contrasts.

Schedeen, J. (2010, August 26). *Xbox 360 vs. PlayStation 3: The hardware throwdown.* Retrieved from http://www.ign.com/articles/2010/08/26/xbox-360-vs-playstation-3-the-hardware-throwdown.

Stokes, J. (2009, November 27). *Sony still subsidizing US military supercomputer efforts: The PlayStation 3's price drop was a boon for more than just consumers.* Retrieved from https://arstechnica.com/security/2009/11/sony-still-subsidizing-us-supercomputer-efforts/.

Takahashi, D. (2011, November 15). *The making of the Xbox: Microsoft's journey to the next generation (part 2).* Retrieved from http://venturebeat.com/2011/11/15/the-making-of-the-xbox-part-2/.

Torres, R. & Thorsen, T. (2005, May 13). *Spot On: The road to the 360.* Retrieved from http://www.gamespot.com/articles/spot-on-the-road-to-the-360/1100-6124287/.

Valdes, R. (2006, November 29). *How Xbox 360 works.* Retrieved from http://electronics.howstuffworks.com/xbox-three-sixty.htm.

VGChartz. (2010). *Global Hardware Totals.* Retrieved from http://www.vgchartz.com/.

Whitehead, T. (2012, January 10). *Wii balance board enters record books: Wii European sales also announced.* Retrieved from http://www.nintendolife.com/news/2012/01/wii_balance_board_enters_record_books.

Military, Science, and Education Get into the Game

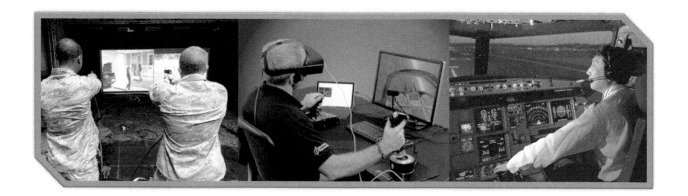

■ OBJECTIVES

After reading this chapter, you should be able to:

- Name classic military-themed board games used for war preparation.

- List Tactical Engagement Simulations used by police and the military.

- Discuss the DARWARS project, including *DARWARS Ambush!* and *TLCTS*.

- Illustrate the features of the *Virtual Battlespace* series and how it progressed.

- Describe how simulation software can help with PTSD and other disorders.

- Provide ways computer technology can help train students in the medical field.

- Explain the Serious Games Showcase and Challenge and recent winners.

- Discuss the significance of "games with a purpose" and how they help scientists.

- List commercially available medical simulation titles and GWAPs.

- Reflect on potential positive and negative effects of video games on people.

- Explain how educators are using video games in the classroom today.

- Provide examples of educational game titles and video game websites.

- Be familiar with Quest schools and The Princeton Review's Top Game Design Schools.

DOI: 10.1201/9781003315759-13

■ KEY TERMS AND PEOPLE

After Action Review
America's Army
Mark Appelbaum
Avalon Hill
Avatar
Scott Barnett
Battlezone
Daphne Bavelier
Vikranth Bejjanki
Ben's Game
Bohemia Interactive
Bradley Trainer
CICS ChicagoQuest
Citizen science
Clinical Skills and
    Simulation Centers
Close Combat
Crowd-sourced science
DARPA
DARWARS
DAUNTLESS
Desensitization
Disney Interactive
Edutainment
EndeavorRx
ESP Game
EST (simulator)
EteRNA

Exposure therapy
F.A.T.S (simulator)
Field exercises
First-person shooter
Flight simulator
Foldit
Full Spectrum Warrior
Game After Ambush
Game with a purpose
Game-based learning
Gamification
Adam Gazzaley
GCompris
Glorious Mission
Berni Good
Google Image Labeler
Hexgrids
Hi-Fi patient simulations
Human dimension
modeling
Institute of Play
Kahoot!
Knowledge Adventure
Königsspiel
Kriegsspiel
Simone Kühn
David Lagettie
LeapPad

Leapster
Learning Company
Life & Death
Life simulation app
M2 Bradley
Marine Doom
Military exercises
MILO
Minecraft
*Multipurpose Arcade
    Combat Simulator*
NeuroRacer
Maressa Hecht Orzack
Pandemic Studios
PBS Kids
Princeton Review
PTSD
Quest to Learn
Tom Quinn
Real Virtuality 2
Real-time tactics
Chen Rong-Yu
James Rosser Jr.
SAFE
Second Life
SECTER
Self Determination
    Theory
Serious games

SG Showcase and
    Challenge
David Sheff
SIMNET
Smart Board
Dan Snyder
Society for Simulation in
    Healthcare
Steam (platform)
Stroop Effect test
The Surgeon
Tactical Engagement
    Simulation
Tactical Iraqi
*Tactical Language &
    Culture Training
    System (TLCTS)*
TitanIM
TRADOC
Video game addiction
VirTra
VIRTSIM
Virtual battlefield
*Virtual Battlespace
    (VBS)*
Virtual reality therapy
Luis von Ahn
War games
Casey Wardynski

■ CHAPTER OUTLINE

Military Sims	DARWARS to VBS	Serious Games	Games w/Purpose	Research/Science	Educational Use
p. 359	**p. 364**	**p. 367**	**p. 371**	**p. 372**	**p. 374**

▪ INTRODUCTION

As the technology matured, interactive media began to receive more attention and usage by military, science, education, as well as other fields. Today, companies are turning to games as ways of assessing skills to screen and also to train employees. For example, "banking and asset-management companies are leaning more heavily into … stock-picking 'contests' and other games that act as tests in disguise. To date, no industry has embraced games as warmly as the military, though" (Morris, 2022, para. 9–10).

Military and law enforcement officials are now utilizing computer programs in capacities from training simulators for combat and rescue operations. Scientists are using the technology for studies on motor skills, stress relief, and social development. Educators are now exploring virtual learning as a safe place for students to develop perceptual, attentional, and cognitive abilities—and the number of colleges and universities offering degrees in and related to game development continues to grow. This chapter will review how the military, scientific, and educational communities have used the technology—from training and simulation programs to advancements in science and education.

▪ EARLY WAR GAMES

The U.S. military has a long history of using games as a part of combat training. Even "before video games, troops were encouraged to play military-themed board games" (Romaniuk and Burgers, 2017, para. 3). One of the earliest games used for war preparation was *Königsspiel*, or "The King's Game" developed in 1664 by Germany's Christopher Weikmann. This extension of the classic game of *chess* was a breakthrough in that it provided a visualization of the player's movements and actions on a game board where the behavior of forces could be analyzed.

More than a century would pass until Baron Georg Leopold von Reiswitz produced the next significant, German-developed war game *Kriegsspiel* in 1811. *Kriegsspiel* was "a more detailed board game using contoured terrain and porcelain soldiers, which introduced the concept of a starting scenario with a stated military objective" (McLeroy, 2008, para. 5). **War games** of the 1950s added hexagonal overlays (**hexgrids**) for tracking movement and engagement, later used in strategy video games such as *Nobunaga's Ambition* (1983) and *Military Madness* (1989).

Major developments came from board game publisher **Avalon Hill** by entrepreneur Charles Roberts and Douglas Aircraft Company's RAND Corporation (Research and Development). Soon, theater-level warfare games such as *SAFE (Strategy and Force Evaluation)* introduced combat-results tables and the use of dice to randomize the events and outcomes of each battle, allowing for "more mathematically accurate actions than those found on sand tables and board games of earlier centuries" (McLeroy, 2008, para. 7). In addition to planning and training tools for the military, war games eventually became popular forms of entertainment for the general public. When video games took off in the late 1970s, the popularity of electronic war games and simulations followed.

▪ MILITARY SIMULATION

The military commonly refers to the war games they use as **military exercises**. These exercises provide insightful training for military operations, such as testing various strategies without actual combat, in addition to the assessment of warfare effects. These simulations can range from the full-scale rehearsal of military maneuvers known as **field exercises**, to more virtual-based simulations like computer simulations and analytical models (see Figure 13.1). While full-scale field exercises more closely replicate the

FIGURE 13.1 The simulation spectrum.

FIGURE 13.2 (a) *Firearms Training Simulator (F.A.T.S)* and (b) *Engagement Skills Trainer (EST)*.

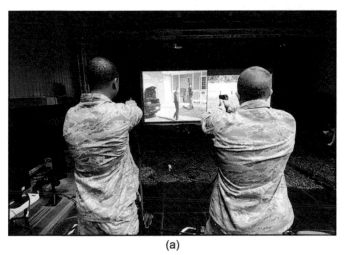

(a)

(b)

real-life battlefield, they are also costlier and so a combination of field exercises and virtual training is often necessary.

A **Tactical Engagement Simulation (TES)** is a training system involving the use of weapons. Two examples of TES systems include the *F.A.T.S (Firearms Training Simulator)* used by the police and military and the *EST (Engagement Skills Trainer)* used by the U.S. Army (Figure 13.2). These simulations involve the use of various weapons and interactive screens displaying multiple scenarios in various environments. The systems provide marksmanship training, the simulation of police calls and stops, de-escalation and judgmental force continuum scenarios, rehearsal in calibrating weapons, and weapons qualification. Two major providers of interactive simulation trainers include **VirTra** and **MILO** (Multiple Interactive Learning Objectives).

▪ THE BRADLEY TRAINER

One of the earliest attempts to create a military training simulator based on a popular video game was derived from Atari's first-person tank combat arcade hit *Battlezone* in 1980. The U.S. **Army Training Doctrine and Command (TRADOC)** approached Atari "to turn its sci-fi shooter into a training simulator for the Army's latest infantry fighting vehicle, the **M2 Bradley**. Two *Army Battlezone* prototypes [also known as *Military Battlezone*] were produced, but no Bradley crewman ever trained on the system" (Beekman, 2014, para. 3). Nothing became of the *Bradley Trainer* (Figure 13.3) prototypes, but the effort showed the military's interest in using video games for training. They would later use a WAN (wide area network) simulator called *SIMNET* for training from 1987 into the 1990s.

FIGURE 13.3 Screenshot of (a) *Bradley Trainer* (1980) and (b) an M2 Bradley Fighting Vehicle.

(a)

(b)

FIGURE 13.4   A close-up look at the (a) *MACS* rifle and (b) *MACS* Super Nintendo cartridge.

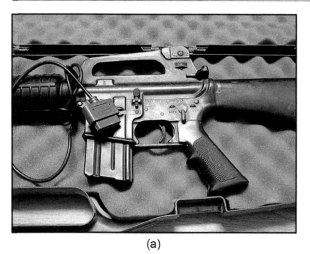

(a)

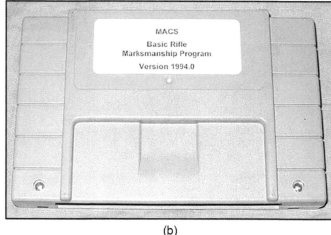

(b)

■ MULTIPURPOSE ARCADE COMBAT SIMULATOR

Another military training device that used video game hardware and software was the ***Multipurpose Arcade Combat Simulator (MACS)***. Patented in 1986, Sculptured Software developed a version of the MACS for Super Nintendo around 1993. It remained a secret from the general public for over a decade until units began appearing for sale on the Internet. A complete set included a replica Jäger AP 74 rifle and a cartridge (Figure 13.4). The rifle (which plugged into the SNES) included a scope and had the look and feel of a real weapon. "While interest was primarily focused on its use as a rifle marksmanship trainer, **MACS** was designed so that the basic hardware could be used to provide training on a variety of weapons systems" (AusRetroGamer, 2016, para. 3). Three cartridge versions are thought to exist, and game/rifle bundles have sold online for upwards of $3,000.

■ *MARINE DOOM*

With the growing popularity of **first-person shooter (FPS)** games, the Marine Corps assigned Lieutenant **Scott Barnett** (of its Modeling and Simulation Management Office) the project of researching various PC games that could be modified for Marine training purposes. Barnett settled on id Software's *Doom II* (1994) and "enlisted the help of Sgt. **Dan Snyder** to modify the game from its sci-fi Mars terrain to [a] small desert village and replace the game's demon enemies with more real-world adversaries" (Beekman, 2014, para. 4). The game, which became *Marine Doom*, focused on aggressive combat and cooperative teamwork. In 1996, the team authorized the installation of *Marine Doom* (Figure 13.5) on government PCs. While officers encouraged Marines to play it, the game never became an official military training instrument.

Following the *Marine Doom* initiative, Marine Corps General Charles C. Krulak issued a directive in 1997 supporting the use of computer games for "Military Thinking and Decision-Making Exercises" and "the stage was set for the Marine Corps and other branches of the military to work hand in hand with game developers" (Beekman, 2014, para. 5). The rationale for simulated training included availability of resources, financing, convenience, and accessibility. Beyond supplementary training, the purpose behind using video games has extended to include the recruitment of soldiers, and even "to treat their psychological disorders, such as **PTSD [post-traumatic stress disorder]**" (Shaban, 2013, para. 5).

PRO FILE

JOHN CARMACK

KEY FACTS:

Revolutionized first-person shooter games like *Doom* with John Romero

Built key graphics engines and advocated for open-source software & mods

PRO FILE

HISTORY:
- Born: August 20, 1970 in Shawnee Mission, KS

EDUCATION:
- University of Missouri–Kansas City (1 year); Received Doctor of Engineering Honoris Causa in 2017

CAREER HIGHLIGHTS:
- Formed id Software with Softdisk colleagues John Romero, Tom Hall, and Adrian Carmack on February 1, 1991
- Led the First-Person Shooter genre and 3D gaming with *Wolfenstein 3D* (1992), *Doom* (1993), and *Quake* (1996)
- Programmer for more than 40 games
- Pioneered techniques such as adaptive tile refresh, binary space partitioning, ray casting, surface caching, z-fail stencil shadows (aka Carmack's Reverse) and other algorithms
- Chief Technology Officer for Oculus VR (2013-2019)

RECOGNITION:
IGDA Award for Community Contribution (2000), Academy of Interactive Arts & Sciences' Hall of Fame (2001), Walk of Game (2006), Emmy Award (2007), GDCA Lifetime Achievement Award (2010), BAFTA Fellowship Award (2016), and more

FIGURE 13.5   Screenshots from *Marine Doom* (1996).

■ *AMERICA'S ARMY*

The principal title for recruiting soldiers was the online multiplayer, FPS game ***America's Army*** (Figure 13.6). U.S. Army Chief Economist and Professor, Colonel **Casey Wardynski** conceived the idea for the title in 1999. The U.S. Army financed and developed the game using the **Unreal Engine** from Epic Games. The first iteration, subtitled *Recon*, released for PC on July 4, 2002. Since its inception, players could download the game for free or install it on their computers from a free CD-ROM. *America's Army* would later become available on the **Steam** online video game platform.

Following a virtual boot camp and marksmanship test, the game allowed players to assume the role of various infantry-related jobs in the U.S. Army. Players could unlock roles such as medic or sniper through multiple tiers of training. The title garnered "criticism for targeting teenagers in its recruiting strategy; the game aimed to get high schoolers thinking about a career in the Army long before they turned 18. This controversy did not impact the game's massive popularity" (Beekman, 2014, para. 7).

"*America's Army* was only supposed to be a seven-year project, but its success encouraged the Defense Department to stay with the game, with the Pentagon spending more than $3 million a year to evolve and promote it" (Morris, 2022, para. 10). Its userbase reached 20 million players and lasted for 20 years until the U.S. Army shut down its official servers on May 5, 2022. While the Army shifted its attention to new innovations in recruiting, private servers for *America's Army: Proving Grounds* have remained available on Steam. The Army's latest use of video games as a part of its modern outreach efforts includes its eSports team that launched in November 2018.

FIGURE 13.6   Screenshots from the original *America's Army* (2002).

■ *FULL SPECTRUM WARRIOR*

Another title commissioned by the U.S. military for training troops in four-person, squad-based fireteam scenarios was **Full Spectrum Warrior (FSW)** (Figure 13.7). The U.S. Army-funded Institute for Creative Technologies (ICT) began working on the title in 2000 in collaboration with game developer **Pandemic Studios**, under the direction of William Henry Stahl. THQ (Toy Headquarters) published the title on June 1, 2004, and the title would become known as a **real-time tactics (RTT)** game. Gameplay in *Full Spectrum Warrior* revolved around the player issuing commands to Alpha and Bravo fireteams consisting of a team leader, rifleman, automatic rifleman, and grenadier. Because the game was not a FPS, the player could not directly control the fireteam members. Rather, the game limited first-person view to issuing orders to squad members.

The publisher produced both a commercial and an Army version of the game, however, the Army only needed around 2,000 copies when the minimum order for an Xbox game at that time was around 50,000 (Smith, 2016, para. 25). The solution was to bundle the initial Army version with the commercial version of the game, which players could access by inputting a code on the Extras menu. The U.S. Army used a heavily modified version of the game "as a tool to help determine, in troops returning from war, the presence and severity of post-traumatic stress disorder" (Smith, 2016, para. 31).

Another real-time tactics game made specifically for military training purposes was **Close Combat: Marines** by Atomic Games in 2004. This computer game was based on the much-admired Avalon Hill board game *Advanced Squad Leader (ASL)*. Like *Full Spectrum Warrior*, the publisher would also release a commercial version of the game *(The Road to Baghdad)*, in addition to multiple commercial releases over the years such as *Close Combat: Gateway to Caen* (2014) and *Close Combat: The Bloody First* (2019).

■ *DARWARS*

Long after *SIMNET*, another project sponsored by the U.S. Defense Advanced Research Projects Agency **(DARPA)** was **DARWARS**. The project started in 2003 as a low-cost, mobile research program to aid in the advancement and usage of military training systems. *DARWARS* itself was not a game, but a scalable (adjustable) architectural framework for military instructors,

FIGURE 13.7   Screenshots from *Full Spectrum Warrior* (2004).

FIGURE 13.8 Screenshots of *DARWARS Ambush!* (2004).

which supported individual and team training on a **virtual battlefield**. This included tools, web services, and system interface definitions that allowed for customized network training systems. These training systems tracked user progress and provided both individual and group feedback on performance.

Two widely used PC-based trainers of the *DARWARS* project included *DARWARS Ambush!* and the *Tactical Language & Culture Training System (TLCTS)*. **DARWARS Ambush!** (2004) (Figure 13.8) was a convoy simulator based on the commercial FPS game *Operation Flashpoint* (2001). Total Immersion Software and Savage Entertainment developed the title under BBN Technologies. The fully networked, multiplayer training simulator provided military training that officers could customize to accommodate various experience levels. Lessons ranged from road-convoy-operations training, platoon-level mounted and dismounted infantry tactics, rules of engagement (ROE) training, and cross-cultural communications training. For example, one lesson demonstrated how to anticipate and react to an ambush, while another activity explored how to handle an IED (improvised explosive device), i.e., bomb.

The key feature of *DARWARS Ambush!* was its user-authorability. Soldiers stationed around the world have learned how to customize and add modifications to the game to simulate various scenarios that best fit their current location and mission. These modifications could include situations beyond combat, such as medical scenarios and cultural interaction (Crawford, 2009, p. 3). The game "continued to be enhanced, deployed, and utilized until a successor Army program, known as **Game After Ambush (GAA)**, was deployed in 2009. Between 2004 and 2009, more than four thousand copies of the game were distributed, with Army, Air Force, and Marine units using the system at hundreds of installations" (Hussain and Coleman, 2014, p. 465).

Another program sponsored by DARPA was the **Tactical Language & Culture Training System (TLCTS)** to teach both foreign languages and cultural knowledge to soldiers for effective and safe conduct operations abroad. These self-paced courses included fully interactive 3D environments not unlike those in a video game. Students not only learned what to say, but also how and when such words and phrases were appropriate. An example of a *TLCTS* was **Tactical Iraqi** by Alelo Inc. (Figure 13.9), which "brought scenario-based PC gameplay to the third Battalion, seventh Marines before their Surge deployment to Iraq in 2007. The game was developed to teach Iraqi situational language and gestures as well as cultural nuances in a virtual world" (Stilwell, 2016, para. 5).

These simulated *TLCTS* missions often ran from 80 to 100 hours, reducing what could normally amount to months of real-life cultural training. A variety of language and cultural programs have been available free of charge to any member of the U.S. Armed Forces, including *Pashto, French*, and *Dari*. Both *DARWARS Ambush!* and the *Tactical Language & Culture* tutors have dramatically decreased the need for human trainers. However, to be completely effective, this training software must be properly administered by

FIGURE 13.9 Screenshots of *Tactical Iraqi* (2007).

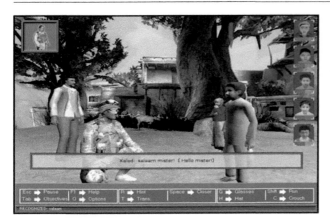

a trained instructor, in the appropriate setting, with both training goals and **AARs (After Action Reviews)** (Chatham, 2006, p. 7).

■ VIRTUAL BATTLEFIELDS

The term "virtual battlefield" represents the digital simulation of a war environment, which is typically accomplished by combining several unique features (such as weapons, screens, and vehicles) into the training area. One of the most prevalent virtual battlefield systems developed has been the *Virtual Battlespace* (*VBS*) series created by **David Lagettie** and *Operation Flashpoint* developer **Bohemia Interactive**. The original *VBS1 (Virtual Battlespace 1)* released to the United States Marine Corps (USMC) in 2001, followed by usage from the Australian Defence Force (ADF) in 2003 and a public release in 2004.

The system offered training for land, sea, and air vehicles and users could even customize it to include the simulation of weather effects such as wind, rain, and fog. Instructors could create both lethal and non-lethal scenarios from multiple viewpoints, including the time of day, with sunrise, midday, or sunset lighting, and even customize high or low tides for ocean settings. *VBS1* even included data collection systems such as After Action Review and Observer, as well as mission playback capability.

Bohemia Interactive Simulations (BISim) released *VBS2* in 2007 following close collaboration with the USMC, ADF, and other military users. It was this simulator that became the foundation for the *DARWARS Ambush!* successor *Game After Ambush*

in 2009 (Shephard Press, 2013, p. 1). Based on the company's **Real Virtuality 2** engine, *VBS2* instructors could construct virtual battlefields over 10,000 square kilometers ($km^{2)}$ (3,900 $mile^2$) in size (Robson, 2008, para. 22) and then populate the terrain area with millions of texture-mapped objects built from real satellite imagery and/or aerial photography. The developer improved view distances to produce draw distances up to five times greater than *VBS1*.

Another prominent virtual battlefield system was the **VIRTSIM** system (Figure 13.10a) by Raytheon Company and Motion Reality Inc. (MRI) in 2012. The program used virtual immersion simulation technology with reflective markers for full-motion body capture, including **virtual reality** (**VR**) headsets, weapon props, and even shock-feedback when a soldier was hit (Lang, 2012, para. 1). Virtual engagement utilized large areas, such as a basketball court-sized game space with up to 13 participants. Motion Reality developed a follow-up program to *VIRTSIM* called **DAUNTLESS** at the end of 2019 with an even more immersive virtual reality training, "including ascending and descending stairs" (Motion Reality, 2021).

The third iteration of *Virtual Battlespace*, *VBS3*, released to the U.S. Army in 2014. Terrain size increased to up to 4,000,000 km^2 and the program used a "**human dimension modeling**" system to create an **avatar** based on the soldier's actual appearance and abilities. In other words, the user's avatar looked, shot, traversed terrain, and became fatigued—just like its operating soldier. It mirrored not only height and weight, but also the user's marksmanship and PT scores. The system even took a soldier's fitness rating

FIGURE 13.10 Soldiers using (a) *VIRTSIM* and (b) BISim Co-CEO Pete Morrison on *VBS Blue*.

(a)

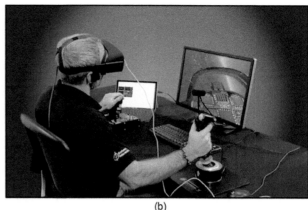

(b)

and factored it into the system to affect the avatar's performance (Barrie, 2014, para. 2).

Another simulator was ***TitanIM*** by Outerra (December 2014), which was "capable of recreating planet-wide environments from ocean floors to Earth's orbit at equally high fidelity for any point between" (TitanIM Pty Ltd., 2017). Unlike older platforms with limited map space, *TitanIM* integrated air, land, sea, and space into one seamless, uninterrupted experience. Likewise, BISim's ***VBS Blue*** (2015) (Figure 13.10b) featured whole-earth rendering technology representing the entire planet and a VR-based F/A-18 Hornet flight simulator created under contract for the U.S. Navy. In 2021, ***VBS4*** version 20.2 introduced extended features such as cloud-enabled scaling and additional Call For Fire (CFF) and Close Air Support (CAS) capabilities.

■ AT EASE

Thanks in part to the popularity of video games, computer technology has become an integral part of military training and operations today. As defense budgets tighten, virtual simulation technology will progressively allow military units to train at a significantly reduced cost, along with a reduction in the physical exhaustion of its real-life equipment and vehicles, including the soldiers themselves. After the battle, officials can use the simulation software for After Action Review (AAR), as well as to help soldiers with post-traumatic stress disorder (PTSD).

By immersing soldiers in a controlled, interactive virtual environment "soldiers are able to confront traumatic memories in a process called **exposure therapy**. By recalling distressing episodes from their past, soldiers learn to habituate themselves to those fearful experiences. Games help them manage their negative emotions and troubled thoughts" (Shaban. 2013, para. 15). Such therapy can help soldiers with self-reflection and the development of a more positive outlook on life. Recent studies have also shown positive results using virtual reality technology in the treatment of mental illness.

■ VIDEO GAMES IN SCIENCE

Like the military, more scientists and doctors are using interactive technology each day for training and research initiatives. With motion technology, many games are now being used as physical fitness applications, such as with rehabilitation programs in hospitals and nursing homes. Researchers are also conducting studies on the physical and psychological effects of video games on the brain. This section focuses on ways the scientific and medical communities have used video games and computer technology. It will also look at recent studies on the behavioral effects of playing video games.

■ SERIOUS GAMES

Coined by Clark C. Abt in the 1970s, **serious games** are games designed with a purpose other than to simply entertain. They are also known as "applied games." These are typically simulation-style games like those

FIGURE 13.11 Screenshots of (a) *The Surgeon* and (b) *Life & Death.*

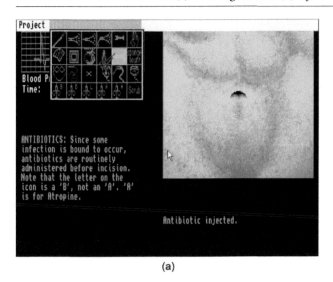
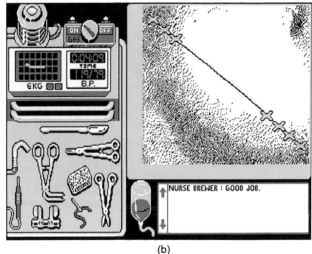

(a)   (b)

used by the military, which officials can use for training individuals in the medical and science professions. Medically oriented simulation software began to appear with the improved graphics and functionality of computers during the 1980s.

Information Systems for Medicine published a game in 1985 called *The Surgeon* (Figure 13.11a) for Macintosh and Amiga, which accurately simulated procedures such as operating on an aortic aneurysm (Boosman, 1986, p. 42). Another commercial release on multiple computer platforms was *Life & Death* published by The Software Toolworks in 1988 (Figure 13.11b). Players assumed the role of a resident abdominal surgeon at the fictional "Toolworks General Hospital" and gameplay involved diagnosing and treating everything from kidney stones to arthritis and appendicitis, in addition to performing virtual surgery. Players assumed the role of a neurosurgeon in its sequel, *Life & Death II: The Brain* (1990).

More recent medical-related games on popular platforms have included the *Emergency Room* series on PC (1995–2009), *Trauma Center* series on Nintendo Wii and DS (2005–2010), *LifeSigns: Surgical Unit* (DS, 2007), *Amateur Surgeon* series on iOS (2008–2016), and the *Surgeon Simulator* series (2013–2020), which has appeared on PC, mobile, PS4, Switch, Xbox One, and Xbox Series X.

High-fidelity programs emerged in the 1990s and by the end of the century, companies were developing simulation products for the medical community.

In 2004, medical professionals created the **Society for Simulation in Healthcare** (**SSH**) (formerly known as the Society for Medical Simulation) to advance medical simulation technology in healthcare. Today both medical schools and teaching hospitals are using medical simulation for training healthcare professionals. Known as **Clinical Skills and Simulation Centers** (**CSSCs**), "their simulation training is an essential link between medical student training and clinical experience and has proven to be an effective tool for assessing technical skills, critical thinking, and team-orientated behavior throughout medical training" (Tufts University School of Medicine, 2016, para. 1). Figure 13.12 shows the high use of simulation in medical schools and teaching hospitals after the turn of the century, often matching or exceeding student training with standardized patients.

Similar to how the military combines modified artillery and vehicular components with computer software in the creation of their simulation products, medical simulation typically employs a combination of computer applications with full-scale computerized mannequins and smaller partial task trainers called **high-fidelity patient simulations** (**HPS**). As early as 2011, 95% of medical schools and 87% of teaching hospitals were using full-scale mannequins, and more than half contained screen-based simulation as part of their training operations. Examples of screen-based medical simulations (SBSs) include *ACLS Simulator, Anatomy Module, Anesthesia SimSTAT, CardioSim, DrSim, MicroEKG,*

FIGURE 13.12   Types of simulation used in medical education (AAMC, 2011, p. 28).

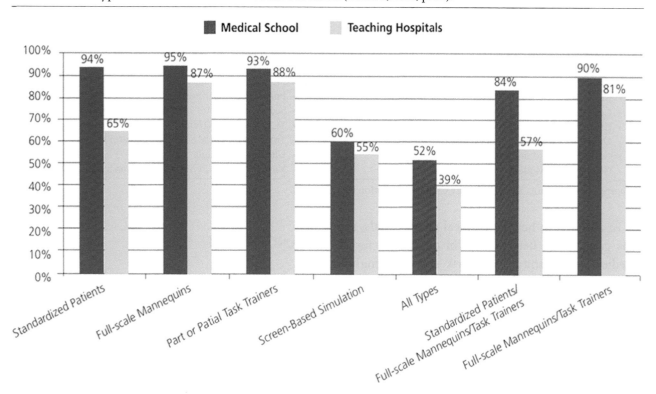

Neonatal Simulator, Ultrasound Simulator, and *Virtual Dental Implant Trainer (V-DIT)* (Figure 13.13).

There is also evidence that suggests gamers may make better surgeons. A study in 2007 by Dr. **James Rosser Jr.** and colleagues showed a positive correlation between surgical residents and medical students who played video games and their laparoscopic surgery skills. In fact,

> Dr. Rosser's study found that surgeons who had played video games in the past for more than three hours per week made 37 percent fewer errors, were 27 percent faster, and scored 42 percent better on laparoscopic surgery and suturing drills than surgeons who never played video games.
>
> *Hampton (2013, para. 5)*

See Table 13.1 for a sample list of commercially available computer simulation titles for the medical community.

FIGURE 13.13   (a) *Ultrasound Simulator* and (b) screenshot of *Virtual Dental Implant Trainer.*

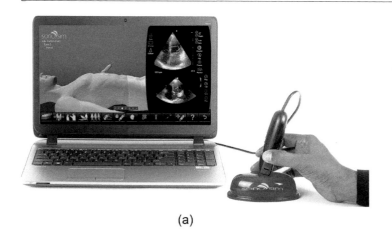

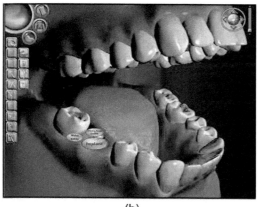

(a)   (b)

TABLE 13.1 Flat Screen Computer Medical Simulators

• A-Ware (NEC SIM-series)	• Hemodynamics Simulator (AneSoft)
• Anatomy Module (HeartWorks)	• MicroEKG (Mad Scientist Software)
• Anesthesia Simulator (AneSoft)	• PAC Simulator (Manbit Technologies)
• Body Simulation (Advanced Simulation Corp.)	• Pediatric Simulator (AneSoft)
• CardioSim (Cardionics)	• PhysioLogical (Mark Colson)
• Clinical Simulator (TheraSim)	• PneumoSim (Cardionics)
• Code Team (Mad Scientist Software)	• Sedation Simulator (AneSoft)
• CritiControl (NEC SIM-series)	• TCD Simulator (Hemodynamic.com)
• Dynamics Pipeline (MusculoGraphics)	• Trauma One (Mad Scientist Software)
• GasMan (Med Man Simulations)	• Ultrasound Module (HeartWorks)
• Generic Knee Model (MusculoGraphics)	• Virtual Anesthesia Machine (University of Florida)

Source: (Pennsylvania State University Clinical Simulation Center, 2022).

In addition to helping medical professionals, serious games have become a form of therapy for the medical community. LucasArts software engineer Eric Johnston designed ***Ben's Game*** in collaboration with Ben Duskin, an 8-year-old boy who was in remission from leukemia. The game helped child patients understand the process of fighting cancer in a comic-style environment where players battled cancer cells on a hoverboard. Make-A-Wish Foundation published *Ben's Game* in 2004.

Doctors have also used serious games in treating patients with conditions such as attention deficit hyperactivity disorder (ADHD). On June 15, 2020, the U.S. Food and Drug Administration (FDA) approved the first prescribable video game, ***EndeavorRx*** by Akili. Doctors can prescribe the game to children between ages 8 and 12 with particular types of ADHD. The title looks like a cartoon racing game and involves piloting a craft through tracks while avoiding obstacles and collecting items for rewards. The dosage: "25 minutes [per day], 5 days a week, for at least 4 consecutive weeks, or as prescribed" (Akili, 2022).

▪ SERIOUS GAMES SHOWCASE AND CHALLENGE

The **Serious Games Showcase and Challenge** is a competition and event created to display and encourage the development of serious games. The organization was formed in 2005 when military coalition Team Orlando formed a partnership with the National Training Simulation and Association (NTSA) and the Interservice/Industry Training, Simulation and Education Conference (I/ITSEC). Their goal was "to stimulate industry creativity and generate institutional interest toward the use of digital game technology and approaches for training and education" (Serious Games Showcase & Challenge, 2012, para. 1). The event made its debut in 2006 and each year the group awards the best serious games in the categories such as business, government, student, mobile, and social media. Visit the SGS&C website at www.sgschallenge.com for current and previous winners and to explore a plethora of serious games from around the world. See Table 13.2 for 2021 winners.

TABLE 13.2 Serious Games Showcase and Challenge 2021 Award Winners

Game Title	Category	Developer
Street Smarts VR	Business	Street Smarts VR (New York)
CoronaQuest	Government	Etat de Vaud - Ed., Youth & Culture Dept. (Switzerland)
Basic Vectoring powered by StrataGem	Business	Rigil (USA)
Vector Unknown: Echelon Seas	Student	Arizona State University (USA)
Legends of Europe	Government	Regional Council of Brittany (France)
Tactical Combat Casualty Care Simulation	Business	Engineering & Computer Simulations, Inc. (Orlando)
CodAR	Student	Indian Institute of Technology (Kharagpur, India)

Source: (Serious Games Showcase & Challenge, 2022).

■ GAMES WITH A PURPOSE

Another genre of video games used in the scientific community is known as the human-based computation game or "**game with a purpose**" (**GWAP**). Based on the "human computation" concept of Dr. **Luis von Ahn**, the idea behind these games is to harness human brainpower with computer programs to find solutions that neither may have been able to discover separately. The concept of amateur scientists working on such solutions is known as **citizen science** or **crowdsourced science**. His first game to utilize this idea was the *ESP Game* (short for Extra Sensory Perception) (Figure 13.14a).

Dr. von Ahn created the *ESP Game* to improve image tagging on the World Wide Web. Gameplay involved showing the same picture to two different players and asking them to guess what the other person wrote to describe it. If the players agreed, the game would use that word or phrase to annotate the picture. By repeating the same picture with other pairs of players, the program would eventually build up a detailed label for the image (Saini, 2008, para. 5). Dr. von Ahn licensed the *ESP Game* to Google, which developed its own version of the program called **Google Image Labeler** in 2006.

A second example of how GWAPs can lead to scientific discovery was the 2011 breakthrough on the Mason-Pfizer AIDS-causing monkey virus (M-PMV). An unsolved problem for approximately 15 years was solved after just 10 days of concentrated effort by a group of gamers playing the title ***Foldit*** (2008) (Figure 13.14b). In the game, "players have to manipulate 3D shapes to create a solution to a pre-identified problem. The 3D shapes are in fact proteins and the potential solutions are ones that science is seeking in real life" (Rawlings, 2016, para. 1). *Foldit* reached over a quarter million players by 2013 and continues to be an important contributor in protein folding research for the treatment of AIDS, cancer, and Alzheimer's disease.

In ***EteRNA*** (2011), players

> are given a real-world RNA [ribonucleic acid] shape and asked to manipulate a chain of nucleotides to fit that shape, by observing how different patterns of nucleotides form certain structures, like loops or tails. Then, every week, a few molecules are selected for synthesis in a lab at Stanford to see how closely they match the desired shape.
>
> *Dunning (2012, para. 2)*

In just 3 years and with the help of more than 37,000 citizen scientists, *EteRNA* has already helped generate a more accurate algorithm for predicting RNA folding (Olena, 2014, para. 1).

Other popular GWAP titles include *Eyewire*, which combines coloring and treasure hunting to assist scientists in deciphering how the brain is wired; *Phylo*, where arranging colored blocks to swinging jazz music can help with genetic disease research in animals; and NASA's *Be a Martian*, where players participate as

FIGURE 13.14 Screenshots of (a) *ESP Game* and (b) *Foldit*.

(a)

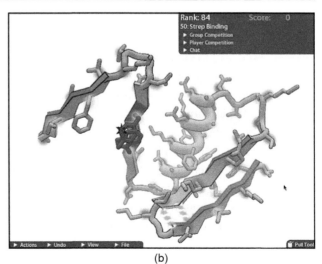

(b)

TABLE 13.3 List of Influential Games with a Purpose

• Apetopia	• Happy Match	• Quantum Moves
• Artigo	• JeuxDeMots	• Reverse The Odds
• Be a Martian	• MajorMiner	• Robot Trainer
• Cropland Capture	• MalariaSpot	• Sea Hero Quest
• ESP game	• Mark With Friends	• Smorball
• EteRNA	• Nanocrafter	• TagATune
• Eyewire	• Nanodoc	• Train Robots
• Foldit	• OnToGalaxy	• Verbosity
• Forgotten Island	• PeekaBoom	• Whale FM
• Fraxinus	• Phrase Detectives	• Wikispeedia
• Galaxy Zoo	• Phylo	• Worm Watch Lab
• Guess the Correlation	• Play to Cure: Genes in Space	• ZombiLingo

citizen scientists to assist real science teams in studying data about planet Mars. See Table 13.3 for even more influential "games with a purpose."

■ VIDEO GAME RESEARCH

Beyond using video game technology for medical training and scientific research, scientists and researchers have been studying the effects and benefits of video games on its players. This section will review research that has looked at video game effects on the human brain, in addition to ways professionals can use this interactive medium for physical, social, and mental development. See Chapter 7 for additional coverage on video game effects, stereotypes, and video game violence

■ NEGATIVE SIDE EFFECTS

For the first couple of decades since the early 1990s, the majority of studies conducted on the effects of video games focused on their possible negative side effects. Researchers have sought to discover whether video games could lead to violent or antisocial behavior, and whether extensive game playing could lead to other negative effects on one's health or psyche. In 2015, Dr. **Mark Appelbaum** of the American Psychological Association (APA) concluded that data from over 300 studies between 2005 and 2013 showed a consistent relationship between playing violent video games and an increase in aggressive behavior, "but insufficient evidence exists about whether the link extends to criminal violence or delinquency" (APA, 2015).

In contrast, Dr. Cheryl Olson and her team at Harvard and Mass General Hospital have found

violent games to be an outlet for stress and aggression. Another possible negative side effect of video games is **desensitization**. A study by Dr. Alessandro Gabbiadini from the University of Milano Bicocca with The Ohio State University professor Dr. Brad Bushman and others suggested that "young male gamers who strongly identify with male characters in sexist, violent video games show less empathy than others toward female violence victims" (Grabmeier, 2016, para. 1). Other studies, such as the 2016–2017 research by Dr. Gregor R Szycik et al. did not find a strong association between long-term exposure to violent video games (VVGs) and desensitization to violence or a lack of pain empathy toward others.

Video game addiction has also become a reality for certain individuals, particularly for players of games that never end, such as in massively multiplayer online (MMO) titles. Researchers at Stanford University School of Medicine have found evidence that video games possess addictive characteristics. Clinical psychologist and founder of Computer Addiction Service Dr. **Maressa Hecht Orzack** has claimed that as many as 40% of gamers playing *World of Warcraft* have been addicted to the game (Dale & Lewis, 2016, p. 495). Countries such as South Korea, China, the Netherlands, Canada, Australia, and the United States have established addiction centers specializing in video game addiction. The American Psychiatric Association (APA) added "Internet gaming disorder" under "Conditions for Further Study" in the Diagnostic and Statistical Manual of Mental Disorders (DSM-5) in 2013. Five years later, the World Health Organization added "gaming disorder" as a mental health condition in its 11th edition of the International Classification of Diseases (ICD).

While further research is necessary to determine all the risk factors for video games to cause aggressive behavior or addiction, excessive video game playing (like any other activity) can disrupt a person's social life, school and/or work priorities, along with one's physical health. Too many hours in front of any screen without enough physical activity can result in serious health problems, such as obesity and even death in certain instances. While small in number, there have been reports of gamers such as **Chen Rong-Yu** of New Taipei (2012) who were found dead after playing video games for more than 20 consecutive hours. The cause of death on these occasions has often been cardiac arrest.

■ POSITIVE IMPACT

Aside from the possible negative side effects of violent games or simply playing too much, recent studies have uncovered hidden benefits to playing video games. From improved reaction times and better hand–eye coordination, motor skill development with motion games, to critical thinking skills and emotional fulfillment—playing video games might be more beneficial than people once realized. One study in Proceedings of the National Academy of Sciences (PNAS) by research associate at Princeton University Dr. **Vikranth Bejjanki** et al. (2014) found that "action video game play results in enhanced perceptual templates and does so by facilitating the rapid learning of task relevant statistics" (p. 16964). In other words, playing fast-paced, action-oriented games may improve gamers' performance in real-world perception, attention, and cognition.

Another study involved University of Geneva professor Dr. **Daphne Bavelier** comparing the visual tracking abilities between gamers and non-gamers. One of the tests challenged subjects to keep track of the positions of multiple moving objects. The results found that individuals who played action video games performed markedly better than those participants who did not (BBC News, 2015, p. 2). Bavelier's work has also shown gamers to be much more proficient than non-gamers at the **Stroop Effect test** where subjects were shown colors written as words such as RED, BLUE, **YELLOW**, and asked to quickly identify the color of each word without confusing the color with the written word.

A review of research in *American Psychologist* suggested that playing video games may help children develop critical thinking skills, with reports of adolescents playing strategic video games (like role-playing games) correlating to improved problem solving and school grades the following year (Bowen, 2014, para. 7). Cyberpsychologist **Berni Good** synthesized research from across the globe in studying video games' effects on personal well-being. Good's research has shown a positive correlation with gaming and **Self Determination Theory** (**SDT**) whereby players can address three psychological needs through playing games: the need to feel competent, the need to relate to others in a meaningful way, and the need for autonomy—being in control of one's destiny (Wells, 2016, para. 15–20).

Doctors are using **virtual reality therapy** (**VRT**) like the customizable *SECTER* (Simulated Environment for Counseling, Training, Evaluation and Rehabilitation) to treat everything from anxiety, to eating disorders and Asperger's syndrome (Frenkel, 2009, p. 1). In place of traditional therapy, patients log into these programs to communicate with therapists in a 3D virtual space using avatars. SECTER avatars can assume various human postures and facial expressions, and sessions often involve role-playing as part of therapy. Such programs have proved successful for patients who would otherwise have difficulty collaborating with a counselor in a face-to-face environment.

■ BRAIN DEVELOPMENT

"People who play video games are quicker at processing information," said Dr. Ray Perez, a program officer in [the Office of Naval Research] ONR's Warfighter Performance Department. "Ten hours of video games can change the structure and organization of a person's brain" (Cummings, 2022, para. 6). Max-Planck Institute of Human Development instructor **Simone Kühn** has researched the effects of video games on the human brain using "fMRI (functional MRI) technology to study the brains of subjects as they played *Super Mario 64 DS*, over a period of two months. Remarkably, she found that three areas of the brain had grown—the prefrontal cortex, right hippocampus, and cerebellum—all involved in navigation and fine motor control" (BBC News, 2015). The combination

FIGURE 13.15 (a) Dr. Gazzaley with Ann Stewart (67) playing *NeuroRacer* and (b) *NeuroRacer* screenshot.

(a)

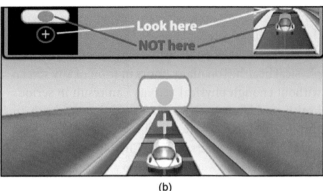

(b)

of navigating the 3D world on the top screen with a 2D map on the lower screen may be a key facilitator of stimulated brain growth.

University of California, San Francisco, professor Dr. **Adam Gazzaley** and a team of video game designers developed a game called *NeuroRacer* (Figure 13.15) that has been shown to be able to improve older players' ability to multitask. The game "requires individuals to steer a car while at the same time performing other tasks. After playing the game for 12 hours, Prof. Gazzaley found pensioners had improved their performance so much they were beating 20-year-olds playing it for the first time. He also measured improvements in their working memory and attention span" (BBC News, 2015). Even more importantly, there is evidence that skills developed from the game can be utilized by players in the real world. Georgia State University researchers supported this concept in a 2022 study that found "frequent players of video games show superior sensorimotor decision-making skills and enhanced activity in key regions of the brain as compared to non-players" (Georgia State University, 2022).

■ FROM SCIENCE TO EDUCATION

The educational possibilities of computer technology are endless—from flat computer screens to virtual reality. As far back as 1994, *New York Times* best-selling author **David Sheff** claimed that "by playing video games children gain problem-solving abilities, perseverance, pattern recognition, hypothesis testing, estimating skills, inductive skills, resources management, logistics mapping, memory, quick thinking and

reasonable judgments" (Sheff, 1994, p. 33). With many positive studies showing the potential of interactive media for improving mental tasks and brain development, educators are using video games and computer simulations in a variety of ways today to teach both children and adults.

Educational games can be an effective motivational tool in the classroom. Interactive media provides the experience of novelty, curiosity, and challenge that can stimulate learning. As Michigan State University professor Dr. **John L. Sherry** explains,

> the right video games help children master everything from basic grammar to complex math without the drudgery of old-school flash cards. Many games require kids to anticipate movements and, in the case of three-dimensional video games, require players to manipulate objects through a three-dimensional place.
>
> *Weber (2017, para. 4)*

These 3D environments more closely replicate real-world scenarios and can improve spatial-relationship skills.

Instructors are now using simulation games in economics courses to provide an assortment of chance, skill, and strategy that replicates real-world scenarios like the New York stock exchange and other forms of competition. Like the military and medical community, industries from ground transportation to aviation training are also using interactive technology for training employees. There is "the opportunity to develop transferable skills, or practice challenging or

FIGURE 13.16 (a) Strategix bus simulator for pre-employment driving assessment and (b) CAE full-flight simulator of an Airbus A320 cockpit.

(a)

(b)

extraordinary activities, such as **flight simulators**, or [other] simulated operations" (Griffiths, 2014, para. 9). These virtual environments can provide a safe place to make mistakes and learn from failure and can often be more engaging or entertaining than traditional training methods. Figure 13.16 illustrates examples of how the transportation industry is using interactive technology for educational training by combining physical hardware with simulation software programs.

·ᩫ· DID YOU KNOW?

Gyration company founder **Tom Quinn** had originally developed the motion controls used on Nintendo Wii for controlling aircraft (Hart, 2022, p. 209).

Teachers and scientists have also used **life simulation** applications or virtual worlds such as *Second Life* for educational purposes. Examples range from the University of San Martin de Porres of Peru's prototypes of Peruvian archeological buildings to American Chemical Society's *ACS (American Cancer Society) Island*. Nature Publishing Group's *Elucian Islands Village* contained virtual laboratories for scientists and educators to conduct their own work free of charge. Professionals have used other spaces for virtual classrooms and museums, as well as interactive maps as shown in Table 13.4.

Gameplay that has defined learning outcomes is known as **game-based learning (GBL)**. Game-based learning is generally "designed to balance subject matter with gameplay and the ability of the player

TABLE 13.4 Five Science Education Areas in *Second Life*

Area	Description
Weather Map at the Science School	An interactive weather map from National Oceanic and Atmospheric Administration at the University of Denver
The 'splo	A virtual extension of San Francisco's *Exploratorium* science museum with displays and exhibits on observing the world
Genome Island	Texas Wesleyan University's exhibits on genetics, inheritance, and molecular and cell biology
The International Spaceflight Museum	Scale models of rockets from countries around the world, such as the Apollo lunar command and lander modules
History of Earth Walking Exhibit	A walking tour through 4.6 billion years of Earth's history, designed by students from the University of Arizona

Source: Knop, (2008).

FIGURE 13.17 Notable educational titles on the Nintendo DS: (a) *Art Academy*, (b) *Big Brain Academy*, (c) *Brain Age²: More Training in Minutes a Day*, and (d) *My Word Coach*.

(a)   (b)   (c)   (d)

to retain and apply said subject matter to the real world" (EdTechReview, 2013, para. 1). A teacher typically facilitates this form of learning to add depth and perspective to the experience. This is different from **gamification**, which borrows incentives from video games (like points, achievements, and other rewards) and uses them in a non-game setting like a classroom. People have also used gamification for research and crowdsourcing purposes like how the science community gamified *Foldit*. For educational video games, most teachers use **commercial off-the-shelf (COTS)** titles.

■ POPULAR COTS EDUCATIONAL GAMES

Educational video games have been around since video games became popular in the late 1970s and early 1980s—from managing inventory in *Lemonade Stand* (1979), to practicing computer keyboard skills in *MasterType* (1981). **The Learning Company** became known for its *Reader Rabbit* series from 1984, in addition to its *Zoombinis* (1996) franchise and *The ClueFinders* series, which launched in 1998. **Knowledge Adventure** was a popular company for its *JumpStart* franchise and *Blaster Learning System* (originally by Davidson) series, which both debuted in 1994. Other big names in educational software from the 1990s included **GCompris**, **Disney Interactive**, and **PBS Kids** which launched in 1999.

The new millennium saw a flood of educational games such as LeapFrog Enterprises' **LeapPad**, which released in 1999. This children's tablet contained an electrographic sensor for interactive, touch-sensitive books. Following the success of its LeapPad, LeapFrog Enterprises produced a cartridge-based handheld

game system called **Leapster** in 2003. Then Nintendo released its DS handheld in 2004 and the Apple iPad released 6 years later in 2010. These handheld and mobile devices quickly became popular platforms for COTS educational titles. Often referred to as "**edutainment**" games, titles such as *Brain Age* (2006) and *Art Academy* (2011) (shown in Figure 13.17) have sold particularly well, attracting both young and older gamers alike.

More schools are replacing traditional blackboards for **Smart Boards** and almost all schools provide some kind of curriculum on computer literacy. A nationwide study from NYU and University of Michigan researchers found that over half of 488 K-12 teachers in the United States were using digital games in class on a weekly basis (The A-Games Project, 2016). Most of these teachers were from grades K through five, with 79% or more of teachers in grades 3–5 reporting video game usage in the classroom. Use of video games declined in subsequent grade groups but was still 40% or greater as shown in Figure 13.18.

Educational video games provide more immediate feedback to both the student and the teacher. They demonstrate a systematic way of thinking, as well as an understanding for how different variables affect each other (Tannahill, Tissington, & Senior, 2012, pp. 1–2). These types of games are available for free via online platforms such as Norway's **Kahoot!**, which launched in 2013 and reached over 50 million users. *Kahoot!* "enables anyone to create their own game-based educational content, and helps to found new types of classrooms in which to best exploit it" (Collins, 2015, para. 1–2). Disney Junior and Nick Jr. also contain educational games on their websites featuring popular cartoon characters. See Table 13.5 for more.

FIGURE 13.18 Percentage of digital game use by grade.

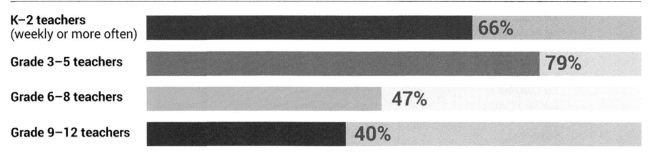

One of the most commercially successful COTS titles that teachers have applied in classrooms across the globe is Mojang's **Minecraft**, which debuted in 2011. The sandbox title involves constructing virtually anything out of textured cubes in a 3D world. Players mine resources and then use them to build anything from cabins to castles—and from islands to entire continents. An estimated 7,000+ classrooms around the world have used *Minecraft* during its first 5 years on the market, from courses on the arts to STEM (Science, Technology, Engineering, and Mathematics) programs. *Minecraft: Education Edition* (formerly *MinecraftEdu*) released in 2016, adding a camera and portfolio for students to take screenshots and document their work, in addition to allowing them to download the software outside of school to continue their class work free of charge.

While the current research on video games and learning has been generally positive, there have not been enough studies to conclusively determine whether educational video games (like those in Table 13.6) actually improve academic performance. Video games have however, proven to be an effective motivational tool to stimulate learning. They appear to aid in cognitive function and students can develop game-specific skills such as hand–eye coordination, decision-making skills, reflexes, and spatial awareness. How much these abilities transfer into the classroom or real-world remains in the hands of future studies.

∎ SCHOOLS SPECIALIZING IN GAMING

Designed by **Institute of Play,** the New York-based **Quest to Learn** is a middle school and high school launched in 2009 that bases its curriculum on game theory and game mechanics. Quest to Learn "students create virtual worlds in the online game *Minecraft*, communicate over an in-house social network, and learn about Pi by stepping into an immersive digital environment [with] infrared cameras that are tacked to the classroom walls" (Sutter, 2012, p. 2). The curriculum is so immersed in gaming that the school replaced letter grades with ranking terms such as "novice" and "expert" and final exams are referred to as "boss levels." A second "Quest" high school, **CICS ChicagoQuest**, opened in Chicago in 2011.

TABLE 13.5 Popular Educational Video Game Websites

Resource	Description	Website
ABCya	Pre-K to grade 5	www.abcya.com
BBC Schools Games	History, science, and more!	www.bbc.co.uk/bitesize/collections/primary-games/
Disney Junior	Dozens of games	www.disneynow.com/all-games
Education.com	Over 300 games	www.education.com/games
FunBrain	K through grade 8	www.funbrain.com
Kahoot!	Requires membership	www.kahoot.com
Learning Games for Kids	Games by subject	www.learninggamesforkids.com
National Geographic Kids	For children 6 and up	www.kids.nationalgeographic.com/games
Nick Jr.	Featuring Paw Patrol	www.nickjr.com/games
PBS Kids	Cartoon-based games	www.pbskids.org/games

TABLE 13.6 Top Educational Video Games over the Decades from A to Z

Art Academy	*History of Biology game*	*The Oregon Trail*
Big Brain Academy (series)	*I.M. Meen*	*PlaceSpotting*
Bot Colony	*Immune Attack*	*Quest Atlantis*
Brain Age (series)	*InLiving*	*Reader Rabbit*
Carmen Sandiego (series)	*JumpStart (series)*	*Reading Blaster*
The ClueFinders	*Ko's Journey*	*Storybook Weaver*
EcoQuest (series)	*Magic School Bus (series)*	*Swamp Gas Visits the USA*
Food Force	*Math Blaster (series)*	*Tuxmath*
GCompris	*Meister Cody*	*The Typing of the Dead*
Genomics Digital Lab	*Minecraft*	*Urban Jungle*
Get Water!	*My Word Coach*	*WolfQuest*
Gizmos & Gadgets	*NoteBlaster*	*Word Munchers*
Gus Goes to Cybertown	*Number Munchers*	*Zoombinis*

TABLE 13.7 The Princeton Review's Top 25 Schools to Study Game Design (2022)

Rank	Undergraduate Programs	Graduate Programs
1	University of Southern California (Los Angeles)	University of Central Florida (Orlando)
2	New York University (Brooklyn, NY)	New York University (Brooklyn, NY)
3	Clark University (Worcester, MA)	Southern Methodist University (Dallas, TX)
4	Rochester Institute of Technology (Rochester, NY)	University of Southern California (Los Angeles)
5	DigiPen Institute of Technology (Redmond, WA)	University of Utah (Salt Lake City)
6	Michigan State University (East Lansing)	Rochester Institute of Technology (Rochester, NY)
7	University of Utah (Salt Lake City)	Abertay University (Dundee, Scotland)
8	Drexel University (Philadelphia, PA))	DigiPen Institute of Technology (Redmond, WA)
9	Shawnee State University (Portsmouth, OH)	Clark University (Worcester, MA)
10	Champlain College (Burlington, VT)	Drexel University (Philadelphia, PA)
11	Worcester Polytechnic Institute (Worcester, MA)	Breda University of Applied Sciences (Breda, Noord Brabant)
12	Breda University of Applied Sciences (Breda, Noord Brabant)	Michigan State University (East Lansing, MI)
13	University of Central Florida (Orlando, FL)	The University of Texas at Dallas (Richardson, TX)
14	Vancouver Film School (Vancouver, BC)	Worcester Polytechnic Institute (Worcester, MA)
15	University of Silicon Valley (San Jose, CA)	University of California Santa Cruz (Santa Clara, CA)
16	LaSalle College Vancouver (Vancouver, BC)	Savannah College of Art and Design (Savannah, GA)
17	Abertay University (Dundee, Scotland)	Northeastern University (Boston, MA)
18	Laguna College of Art and Design (Laguna Beach, CA)	Rensselaer Polytechnic Institute (Troy, NY)
19	Bradley University (Peoria, IL)	American University (Washington, DC)
20	Savannah College of Art and Design (Savannah, GA)	Laguna College of Art+Design (Laguna Beach, CA)
21	The University of Texas at Dallas (Richardson, TX)	University of Wisconsin–Stout (Menomonie, WI)
22	Quinnipiac University (Hamden, CT)	University of Malta (Msida, Malta)
23	Rensselaer Polytechnic Institute (Troy, NY)	New York Film Academy (Burbank, CA)
24	Miami University (Oxford, OH)	Bradley University (Peoria, IL)
25	Howest University of Applied Sciences (Belgium)	DePaul University (Chicago, IL)

Source: (The Princeton Review, 2022).

As for video game-specific curriculums, the ESA reported that during the 2015–2016 academic year, a record 406 American colleges, universities, and technical schools offered "programs in video game-related topics" (Entertainment Software Association, 2017). Furthermore, **The Princeton Review** (also known for its test preparation programs for the SAT and other exams) compiles annual rankings of colleges, business, and law schools in dozens of categories that it reports on its website and in print publications. Since 2010, the company has published ranking lists for the top schools for studying game design. See Table 13.7 for schools with top honors.

■ FINAL EXAMINATION

Interactive technology has come a long way in a short amount of time. From their earliest years, computer games have been examined and eventually utilized by the military, science, and medical communities, as well as educational institutions across the globe. New research is being conducted all the time to better comprehend the effects and benefits of this technology. More industries continue to find new and exciting ways to use video game and computer technology today and this trend shows no signs of slowing down.

■ ACTIVITY: FURTHER RESEARCH

Option 1: Research and conduct a SWOT analysis on one of the following military simulation programs that this chapter did not cover in detail:
- Cubic I-MILES—https://www.cubic.com/solutions/training
- JANUS—http://www.janusresearch.com/Virtual-Environment-Training
- Laser Shot—https://www.lasershot.com/
- MILO (Multiple Interactive Learning Objectives)—https://www.faac.com/milo/
- VirTra: Firearms Training Simulator—http://www.virtra.com/

Option 2: Play and conduct a SWOT analysis on one of the medical simulation games or educational titles listed in Tables 13.1–13.6:
- Table 13.1 Flat Screen Medical Simulation Titles
- Table 13.2 Serious Games Showcase and Challenge Award Winners
- Table 13.3 List of Influential Games with a Purpose
- Table 13.4 Five Science Education Areas in *Second Life*
- Table 13.5 Popular Educational Video Game Websites
- Table 13.6 Top Educational Video Games Over the Decades from A to Z

■ CHAPTER 13 QUIZ

1. Which of the following military simulations is more on the end of operational realism (rather than increased abstraction)?
   a. Field exercises
   b. Map exercises
   c. Computer simulations
   d. Analytical models

2. Two military training simulators that never became official military training instruments:
   a. *Battlezone* and SIMNET
   b. SIMNET and *Military Doom*
   c. *Military Doom* and *Battlezone*
   d. None of the above

3. The principal title that the U.S. Army has used for recruiting soldiers is the online multiplayer, first-person shooter game:
   a. Multipurpose Arcade Combat Simulator
   b. *Marine Doom*
   c. *America's Army*
   d. *Full Spectrum Warrior*

4. This four-person, squad-based real-time tactics (RTT) game is used by troops returning from war to help determine the presence and severity of PTSD:
   a. Multipurpose Arcade Combat Simulator
   b. *Marine Doom*
   c. *America's Army*
   d. *Full Spectrum Warrior*

5. Two widely used PC-based trainers of the *DARWARS* project included:
   a. *DARWARS Ambush!* and Tactical Language & Culture Training System
   b. SIMNET and *DARWARS Ambush!*
   c. Tactical Language & Culture Training System and SIMNET
   d. *DARWARS Ambush!* and Multipurpose Arcade Combat Simulator

6. *Virtual Battlespace (VBS1)* offered training for land, sea, and air vehicles and users could customize to include the simulation of:
   a. Weather effects such as wind, rain, and fog
   b. Lethal and non-lethal scenarios
   c. Time of day, with sunrise, midday, or sunset lighting
   d. All of the above

7. This program uses virtual immersion simulation technology that uses reflective markers for full-motion body capture, including virtual reality (VR) headsets, weapon props, and even shock-feedback when a soldier gets hit:
   a. *DARWARS Ambush!*
   b. *Real Virtuality 2*
   c. *VIRTSIM*
   d. *Virtual Battlespace 3 (VBS3)*

8. Immersion in an interactive virtual environment where soldiers can confront traumatic memories with the help of clinicians in controlled settings is called:
   a. High-fidelity patient simulation
   b. Exposure therapy
   c. Desensitization
   d. Stroop effect

9. Programmers design these games with a purpose other than to simply entertain:
   a. Serious games
   b. Human-based computation games
   c. Games with a purpose (GWAP)
   d. All of the above

10. High-fidelity patient simulations (HPS):
    a. employ a combination of computer applications with high tech mannequins
    b. use full-scale computerized mannequins but not screen-based simulation
    c. are solely screen-based computer simulation programs
    d. do not include smaller partial task trainers such as specific body parts

11. Video games used in the scientific community known as "human-based computation" games or "_____" harness human brainpower with computer programs to find solutions to scientific problems:
    a. Games for Life
    b. Games with Goals
    c. Games with a Mission
    d. Games with a Purpose

12. The concept of amateur scientists working on solutions to scientific problems is known as "citizen science" or "crowd-sourced science." Which of the following games does *not* fit into this category?
    a. *ESP Game*
    b. *EteRNA*
    c. *Foldit*
    d. *The Surgeon*

13. Dr. von Ahn licensed this game to Google, which developed its own version of the program called *Google Image Labeler* in 2006:
    a. *ESP Game*
    b. *EteRNA*
    c. *Foldit*
    d. *The Surgeon*

14. This title led to a scientific breakthrough on the Mason-Pfizer AIDS-causing monkey virus (M-PMV) in 2011:
    a. *ESP Game*
    b. *EteRNA*
    c. *Foldit*
    d. *The Surgeon*

15. Negative side effect(s) linked to violent or excessive gaming:
    a. Desensitization
    b. Video game addiction
    c. Death
    d. All of the above

16. Princeton University's Dr. Vikranth Bejjanki found that playing fast-paced, action-oriented games may improve gamers' performance in the real world:
    a. Perception
    b. Attention
    c. Cognition
    d. All of the above

17. Gamers were much more proficient than non-gamers at this test where subjects were shown written as words such as RED, BLUE, YELLOW in various colors and asked to quickly identify the color of each word without confusing the color with the written word:
    a. NeuroRacer
    b. SECTER test
    c. Stroop effect test
    d. Color autonomy test

18. Gameplay that has defined learning outcomes is known as:
    a. Curricular off-the-shelf (COTS)
    b. Edutainment
    c. Game-based learning (GBL)
    d. Gamification

19. Which of the following games does *not* fit into the educational video game category?
    a. Art Academy
    b. Frequency
    c. Minecraft
    d. Reader Rabbit

20. Designed by Institute of Play, this New York-based middle school and high school launched in 2009 and bases its curriculum on game theory and game mechanics:
    a. House of Pi
    b. Minecraft Technical Institute
    c. Outerra
    d. Quest to Learn

True or False

21. *Königsspiel* and *Kriegsspiel* were war games designed by Douglas Aircraft Company's RAND Corporation in the 1950s.

22. *F.A.T.S (FireArms Training Simulator)* and the *EST (Engagement Skills Trainer)* are examples of Tactical Engagement Simulation (TES) training systems.

23. An example of a *TLCTS* was *Tactical Iraqi* by Alelo Inc., which brought scenario-based PC gameplay to the Marines before their Surge deployment to Iraq in 2007.

24. Today both medical schools and teaching hospitals are using medical simulation in facilities known as Clinical Skills and Simulation Centers (CSSCs).

25. Dr. Mark Appelbaum of the American Psychological Association concluded that data from over 300 studies between 2005 and 2013 showed no consistent relationship between playing violent video games and an increase in aggressive behavior.

■ FIGURES

Figure 13.1 The simulation spectrum. ("Military Simulations range from field exercises through computer simulations to analytical models; the realism of live manoeuvres is countered by the economy of abstract simulations." By Ordoon—own work, public domain. Available at https://commons.wikimedia.org/w/index.php?curid=3401402. Retrieved from https://en.wikipedia.org/wiki/Military_simulation#/media/File:MilSim_Spectrum.svg.)

Figure 13.2 (a) *Firearms Training Simulator (F.A.T.S)* and (b) *Engagement Skills Trainer (EST)*. ("FATS: English: 8th SFS hosts Korean National Police." August 10, 2012. From The Official Web Site of Kunsan Air Base (direct link). United States Air Force Senior Airman Jessica Hines. Media Gallery, page 1, The Official Web Site of Kunsan Air Base (direct link). Public domain. Available at https://commons.wikimedia.org/w/index.php?curid=23854217. Retrieved from https://commons.wikimedia.org/wiki/File:Airmen_from_the_8th_Security_Forces_Squadron_complete_a_training_scenario_using_a_firearms_training_simulator_on_Kunsan_Air_Base.jpg. "Engagement Skills Trainer." Public domain.

Available at https://en.wikipedia.org/w/index.php?curid= 19243134. Retrieved from https://en.wikipedia.org/wiki/ Engagement_Skills_Trainer#/media/File:Engagement_ skills_trainer.jpg.)

Figure 13.3 Screenshot of (a) *Bradley Trainer* (1980) and (b) an M2 Bradley Fighting Vehicle. ("A standard enemy tank in the player's sights in the military training version The Bradley Trainer." By U.S. Army, http://www.atariage. com/news/Bradley/, public domain. Available at https:// commons.wikimedia.org/w/index.php?curid=29061823. Retrieved from https://en.wikipedia.org/wiki/Battlezone_ (1980_video_game)#/media/File:Bradley_Trainer_screen-shot.png. "An M2A2 Bradley Fighting Vehicle kicks up plumes of dust as it leaves Forward Operating Base MacKenzie in Iraq for a mission on Oct. 30, 2004." By Shane A. Cuomo, U.S. Air Force http://www.defenselink.mil/pho-tos/newsphoto.aspx?newsphotoid=5657. Public domain. Available at https://commons.wikimedia.org/w/index. php?curid=224. Retrieved from https://en.wikipedia.org/ wiki/M2_Bradley#/media/File:M2a3-bradley07.jpg4980.)

Figure 13.4 A close-up look at the (a) *MACS* rifle and (b) *MACS* Super Nintendo cartridge. (MACS rifle image from Amazon.com. Retrieved from https://www.amazon. com/gp/product/B00UYCF2W0/ref=as_li_qf_sp_asin_il_ tl?ie=UTF8&camp=1789&creative=9325&creativeASIN= B00UYCF2W0&linkCode=as2&tag=austretrgame-20&li nkId=STDYSVM2MXFM7XWF. Cartridge image posted by GAMESOGRE on October 7, 2010 in "Rare Game Showcase: Atari Jaguar Developer's Cart, 3 SNES M.A.C.S., and a Mario Pipe Phone." Retrieved from http://www. videogamemuseum.com/2010/10/07/rare-game-show-case-atari-jaguar-developers-cart-3-snes-m-a-c-s-and-a-mario-pipe-phone/.)

Figure 13.5 Screenshots from *Marine Doom* (1996). (Courtesy of United States Marine Corps, 1996.)

Figure 13.6 Screenshots from the original *America's Army* (2002). (Courtesy of United States Army, 2002.)

Figure 13.7 Screenshots from *Full Spectrum Warrior* (2004). (Courtesy of Pandemic Studios/THQ, 2004.)

Figure 13.8 Screenshots of *DARWARS Ambush!* (2004). ("DARWARS Ambush." By soldiersmediacente—Flickr, CC BY 2.0. Available at https://commons.wikime-dia.org/w/index.php?curid=3729705. Retrieved from https://en.wikipedia.org/wiki/DARWARS#/media/ File:ArmyDARWARS.jpg.)

Figure 13.9 Screenshots of *Tactical Iraqi* (2007). (Courtesy of Alelo, Inc./DARPA, 2007.)

Figure 13.10 Soldiers using (a) *VIRTSIM* and (b) BISim Co-CEO Pete Morrison on *VBS Blue*. ("VIRTSIM is the Virtual Reality Platform That Gamers Crave but Can't Have." By Ben Lang—November 4, 2012. Retrieved from http://www.roadtovr.com/virtsim-virtual-reality-plat-form/. Photograph VBS3 © 2007–2017 Bohemia Interactive Simulations, k.s. All rights reserved.)

Figure 13.11 Screenshots of (a) *The Surgeon* and (b) *Life & Death*. (*The Surgeon*, courtesy of Winchell Chung/ Information Systems for Medicine, 1985; *Life & Death*, courtesy of The Software Toolworks, 1988.)

Figure 13.12 Types of simulation used in medical educa-tion (AAMC, 2011, p. 28). ("Medical Simulation in Medical Education: Results of an AAMC Survey." By Association of American Medical Colleges, September 2011. Retrieved from https://www.aamc.org/download/259760/data.)

Figure 13.13 (a) *Ultrasound Simulator* and (b) screen-shot of *Virtual Dental Implant Trainer*. (Screenshot from promotional video, "SonoSim transforms medical educa-tion by placing virtual ultrasound devices, patients, and teachers into lab coat pockets." By SonoSim, Inc. April 18, 2013. Retrieved from http://www.prnewswire.com/ news-releases/sonosim-transforms-medical-education-by-placing-virtual-ultrasound-devices-patients-and-teach-ers-into-lab-coat-pockets-203540851.html.) Screenshot of *Virtual Dental Implant Trainer* courtesy of BreakAway Games. (2015). *Virtual Dental Implant Trainer* (V-DIT) [Video]. YouTube. https://youtu.be/0wgEW012-4U.

Figure 13.14 Screenshots of (a) *ESP Game* and (b) *Foldit*. (*ESP Game*, courtesy of Luis von Ahn, 2006; *Foldit*, cour-tesy of University of Washington Center for Game Science & Department of Biochemistry, 2008.)

Figure 13.15 (a) Dr. Gazzaley with Ann Stewart (67) playing *NeuroRacer* and (b) *NeuroRacer* screenshot. ("Dr. Adam Gazzaley looks on as Ann Stewart plays his NeuroRacer game." from "Can brain games keep aging minds young? There's an app for that, says scientists." By Cynthia McFadden, Jake Whitman, and Tracy Connor for NBC News. February 17, 2016. Retrieved from http://www. today.com/health/can-brain-games-keep-aging-minds-young-there-s-app-t73811.)

Figure 13.16 (a) Strategix bus simulator for pre-employ-ment driving assessment and (b) CAE full-flight simulator of an Airbus A320 cockpit. ((a) "Strategix Bus Simulator."

By Strategix, 2014. Retrieved from http://www.strategix.com.au/news/strategix-bus-simulator.php. (b) "CAE Expands Its Training Footprint in Asia Pacific." By Nigel Moll. February 13, 2012. Retrieved from http://www.ainonline.com/aviation-news/singapore-air-show/2012-02-13/cae-expands-its-training-footprint-asia-pacific.)

Figure 13.17 Notable educational titles on the Nintendo DS: (a) *Art Academy*, (b) *Big Brain Academy*, (c) *Brain Age²: More Training in Minutes a Day*, and (d) *My Word Coach*. (*Art Academy*, courtesy of Headstrong Games/Nintendo, 2010; *Big Brain Academy*, courtesy of Nintendo, 2006; *Brain Age²: More Training in Minutes a Day*, courtesy of Nintendo, 2007; and *My Word Coach*, courtesy of Ubisoft, 2007.)

Figure 13.18 Percentage of digital game use by grade. (From Fishman, B., Riconscente, M., Snider, R., Tsai, T., & Plass, J., 2014. Empowering Educators: Supporting Student Progress in the Classroom with Digital Games (Part 1: A National Survey Examining Teachers' Digital Game Use and Formative Assessment Practices). Ann Arbor: University of Michigan. http://gamesandlearning.umich.edu/agames.)

Title page image: "Marksmanship simulator trains soldiers without spending ammunition." By Airman first Class R. Alex Durbin | 633rd Air Base Wing Public Affairs. March 25, 2013. Retrieved from http://www.jble.af.mil/News/Features/Display/Article/260507/marksman ship-simulator-trains-soldiers-without-spending-ammunition. Image 2: "EA Sports Active More Workouts video game review: EA's new fitness game builds on the solid foundations of its predecessor to offer a more well-rounded home exercise experience." By Nick Cowen for *The Telegraph*. December 2, 2009. Retrieved from http://www.telegraph.co.uk/technology/video-games/6702486/EA-Sports-Active-More-Workouts-video-game-review.html. Image 3: "Strategix Bus Simulator." By Strategix, 2014. Retrieved from http://www.strategix.com.au/news/strategix-bus-simulator.php.

PRO FILE: John Carmack. Photo credit: By Official GDC—Flickr: Game Developers Choice Awards @ GDC 2010, CC BY 2.0, https://commons.wikimedia.org/w/index.php?curid=9758546 March 12, 2010. Retrieved from https://en.wikipedia.org/wiki/John_Carmack#/media/File:John_Carmack_GDC_2010.jpg.

■ REFERENCES

Akili. (2022). *Improving attention function in children with ADHD*. Retrieved from https://www.endeavorrx.com/about-endeavorrx/.

American Psychological Association. (2015, August 13). *APA review confirms link between playing violent video games and aggression: Finds insufficient research to link violent video game play to criminal violence*. Retrieved from http://www.apa.org/news/press/releases/2015/08/violent-video-games.aspx.

AusRetroGamer: The Australian retro gamer e-zine. (2016, April 1). *SNES M16 multipurpose arcade combat simulator*. Retrieved from http://www.ausretrogamer.com/snes-m16-multipurpose-arcade-combat-simulator/.

Barrie, A. (2014, May 22). *Army battles with brawn and beer bellies*. FoxNews.com. http://www.foxnews.com/tech/2014/05/22/army-battles-with-brawn-and-beer-bellies.html.

BBC News. (2015, September 16). *Horizon: How video games can change your brain*. Retrieved from http://www.bbc.com/news/technology-34255492.

Beekman, C. (2014, November 17). *The history of video games and the military*. Retrieved from http://taskandpurpose.com/us-militarys-close-history-video-games/.

Bejjanki, V. R., Zhanga, R., Lia, R., Pougeta, A., Greend, S., Lue, Z., & Bavelier, D. (2014, November 25). Action video game play facilitates the development of better perceptual templates. *Proceedings of the National Academy of Sciences of the United States of America (PNAS)*, 111(47). Retrieved from http://www.pnas.org/content/111/47/16961.full.pdf.

Boosman, F. (1986, November). Macintosh windows. *Computer Gaming World*, 6(8), p. 42.

Bowen, L. (2014, February). Video game play may provide learning, health, social benefits, review finds. *American Psychological Association*, 45(2). Retrieved from https://www.apa.org/monitor/2014/02/video-game.

Chatham, R. E. (2006). *Games for training: The good, the bad, and the ugly*. Retrieved from http://www.cl.cam.ac.uk/~rja14/shb08/chatham2.pdf.

Collins, K. (2015, June 22). Kahoot! Is gamifying the classroom. *Wired*. Retrieved from http://www.wired.co.uk/article/kahoot-gaming-education-platform-norway.

Crawford, S. (2009). *Do gamers make good soldiers?* Retrieved from http://science.howstuffworks.com/gamer-soldier.htm.

Cummings, B. (2022, February 17). *Video games can enhance warrior cognitive performance*. Retrieved from https://www.navy.mil/Press-Office/News-Stories/Article/2938975/video-games-can-enhance-warrior-cognitive-performance/.

Dale, N. & Lewis J. (2016). *Computer science illuminated* (6th ed). Burlington, MA: Jones & Bartlett Learning, LLC.

Dunning, H. (2012, June 26). *Toying with RNA: A new online game challenges users to design RNA sequences with the opportunity to have them brought to life.* Retrieved from http://www.the-scientist.com/?articles.view/articleNo/32270/title/Toying-with-RNA/.

Editorial: US Army selects new 'Game for Training' solution. (2013, July 16). *Shephard Press Limited.* Retrieved from https://www.shephardmedia.com/news/landwarfareintl/us-army-selects-new-game-training-solution/.

Editorial: What is GBL (Game-Based Learning)? (2013, April). *EdTechReview.* p. 1. Retrieved from http://edtechreview.in/dictionary/298-what-is-game-based-learning.

Entertainment Software Association. (2017). *ESA newsletters: U.S. colleges and universities offering video game courses & degrees.* Retrieved from http://www.theesa.com/article/u-s-colleges-and-universities-offering-video-game-courses-degrees/.

Frenkel, K. A. (2009, April 3). Therapists use virtual worlds to address real problems: An emerging technique to help troubled teens combines role-play in computer-generated environments with talk therapy. *Scientific American.* Retrieved from http://www.scientificamerican.com/article/therapists-use-virtual-worlds/.

Georgia State University. (2022, July 11). Video game players show enhanced brain activity, decision-making skill study: The findings suggest that video games could be a useful tool for training in perceptual decision-making. *ScienceDaily.* Retrieved from www.sciencedaily.com/releases/2022/07/220711135321.htm.

Grabmeier, J. (2016, April 13). *Sexist video games decrease empathy for female violence victims: Danger comes when males strongly identify with game character.* Retrieved from https://news.osu.edu/news/2016/04/13/sexist-games/.

Griffiths, M. (2014, November 11). *Playing video games is good for your brain – here's how.* Retrieved from http://theconversation.com/playing-video-games-is-good-for-your-brain-heres-how-34034.

Hampton, T. (2013, March). *Can video games help train surgeons?* Retrieved from http://www.bidmc.org/Your Health/Health-Notes/SurgicalInnovations/Advances/VideoGames.aspx.

Hart, M. (2022, October 31). *Secrets of video game consoles.* England: White Owl.

Hussain, T. S. & Coleman, S. L. (2014, November 10). *Design and development of training games: Practical guidelines from a multidisciplinary perspective.* New York, NY: Cambridge Press University.

Knop, R. (2008, March 17). *Five great science education places in Second Life.* Retrieved from http://www.sonic.net/~rknop/blog/?p=34.

Lang, B. (2012, November 4). *VIRTSIM is the virtual reality platform that gamers crave but can't have.* Retrieved from http://www.roadtovr.com/virtsim-virtual-reality-platform/.

McLeroy, C. (2008, August 27). History of military gaming. *Soldiers Magazine.* Retrieved from https://www.army.mil/article/11936/History_of_Military_gaming.

Morris, C. (2022, February 11). *After 20 years, the U.S. Army is shutting down its recruitment video game, 'America's Army'.* Retrieved from https://www.fastcompany.com/90720653/after-20-years-the-u-s-army-is-shutting-down-its-recruitment-video-game-americas-army.

Motion Reality, Inc. (2021). *Dauntless.* Retrieved from https://www.motionreality.com/dauntless.

Olena, A. (2014, January 28). Gamers solve RNA structures: An online competition gives citizen scientists a chance to design RNA molecules to generate a target structure. *The Scientist.* Retrieved from http://www.the-scientist.com/?articles.view/articleNo/39020/title/Gamers-Solve-RNA-Structures/.

Pennsylvania State University Clinical Simulation Center. (2022). *Computer (flat screen) simulators.* Retrieved from https://sites.psu.edu/hersheysimulation/computer-flat-screen-simulators/.

Rawlings, T. (2016, January 26). *Playing at science: How video games and science can work together.* Retrieved from https://longitudeprize.org/blog-post/playing-science-how-video-games-and-science-can-work-together.

Robson, S. (2008, November 23). *Not playing around: Army to invest $50M in combat training games.* Stars and Stripes. Retrieved from https://www.stripes.com/news/not-playing-around-army-to-invest-50m-in-combat-training-games-1.85595#.WMqlrm_ysdU.

Romaniuk, S. N. & Burgers, T. (2017, March 7). *How the US military is using 'violent, chaotic, beautiful' video games to train soldiers.* Retrieved from http://theconversation.com/how-the-us-military-is-using-violent-chaotic-beautiful-video-games-to-train-soldiers-73826.

Saini, A. (2008, May 14). *Solving the web's image problem.* BBC News. Retrieved from http://news.bbc.co.uk/2/hi/technology/7395751.stm.

Serious Games Showcase & Challenge. (2022). *2021 SGS&C Winners.* Retrieved from http://sgschallenge.com/2021-sgsc-winners/.

Shaban, H. (2013, October 10). Playing war: How the military uses video games. *The Atlantic.* Retrieved from https://www.theatlantic.com/technology/archive/2013/10/playing-war-how-the-military-uses-video-games/280486/.

Sheff, D. (1994). *Video games: A guide for savvy parents.* New York, NY: Random House, p. 33.

Smith, E. (2016, August 24). *In the army now: The making of 'Full Spectrum Warrior.'* Retrieved from https://www.vice.com/en_us/article/in-the-army-now-the-making-of-full-spectrum-warrior-140.

Stilwell, B. (2016, May 13). *Six military video games used to train troops on the battlefield.* Retrieved from https://undertheradar.military.com/2016/05/6-military-video-games-used-to-train-troops-on-the-battle-field/.

Sutter, J. D. (2012, August). The school where learning is a game. *CNN.* Retrieved from http://www.cnn.com/interactive/2012/08/tech/gaming.series/teachers.html.

Tannahill, N. Tissington, P. & Senior, C. (2012, June). Video games and higher education: What can "Call of Duty" teach our students? *Frontiers in Psychology*, 3(210), pp. 1–3. Retrieved from https://www.ncbi.nlm.nih.gov/pmc/articles/PMC3382412/pdf/fpsyg-03-00210.pdf.

The A-Games Project. (2016). *Digital game use: Teachers in the classroom.* University of Michigan. Retrieved from http://gamesandlearning.umich.edu/a-games/key-findings/survey-report/digital-game-use/.

The Princeton Review. (2022). *Top game design schools 2022.* Retrieved from https://www.princetonreview.com/collegerankings?rankings=top-50-game-design-ugrad and https://www.princetonreview.com/college-rankings/game-design/top-25-game-design-grad.

TitanIM Pty Ltd. (2017). *What is TitanIM?* Retrieved from http://titanim.net/www/.

Tufts University School of Medicine. (2016). *Clinical skills & simulation center.* Retrieved from http://medicine.tufts.edu/Education/Clinical-Skills-and-Simulation-Center.

Weber, L. (2017). *Positive effects of video games on children.* Retrieved from http://oureverydaylife.com/positive-effects-video-games-children-16317.html.

Wells, J. (2016, June 9). Is video gaming bad for you? The science for and against. *The Telegraph.* Retrieved from http://www.telegraph.co.uk/men/thinking-man/is-video-gaming-bad-for-you-the-science-for-and-against/.

Mobile and Indie Change the Game

■ OBJECTIVES

After reading this chapter, you should be able to:

- Provide an overview of early smart devices released in the 1980s and 1990s.

- Recap the early days of indie and casual mobile games, from *Snake* to modern games.

- Discuss the contributions and failures of devices like N-Gage and Gizmondo.

- Explain how Apple revolutionized the mobile and indie gaming business.

- Illustrate how touchscreens and accelerometers influenced casual games.

- Review key people behind the video games and technology.

- Identify the graphics and capabilities of mobile games as they evolved.

- Distinguish how mobile gaming is different from PC and home console gaming.

- Explain how mobile games make money through advertisements and freemium.

- List key indie and big budget game titles, and genres made popular on mobile devices.

- Describe the influence of mobile and indie gaming on the video game market.

- Recognize key breakthroughs and milestones in mobile technology.

- Summarize key mobile gaming market trends and financial developments.

DOI: 10.1201/9781003315759-14

■ KEY TERMS AND PEOPLE

3G
4G/LTE
5G
4K Resolution
Accelerometer
Activision Blizzard
Activity feeds
Ancillary products
Android
Android Market
App Store
Apple/Apple A5
Arm
ASA
AT&T
Augmented reality (AR)
Sam Barlow
Big Fish Games
BlackBerry/850
Bluetooth
BREW
Casual game
Terry Cavanagh
Scott Cawthon
Convergence
Cross-play
Dell Streak
Digital Bridges
Digital Chocolate
EA Mobile
EEDAR
Endless runner
Stefan Eriksson
eSports

Feature phone
Firemint
Flurry (analytics)
Fragmentation
Freemium
Carl Freer
Game Developers
    Choice Awards
Gameloft
Gamevil
Gartner
Giant Interactive
Gizmondo
Glu Mobile
Google Play
GPRS
GSM
Hagenuk MT-2000
HandCircus
Trip Hawkins
High-fidelity game
HTC Dream
i-mode
IBM Simon
Ideaworks3D
Fredrik Idestam
Indie game
Iomo
iOS
iPad
iPhone
iPod Touch
Satoru Iwata
J2ME

Jackbox Games
JAMDAT Mobile
Steve Jobs
King (company)
Leaderboards
Mali-400
Match three game
Joel McDonald
Barry Meade
MMS
Mobile game
Mobile Games Awards
MOGA controller
Moppin
Motorola RAZR
Multi-touch
MultiMediaCard
N-Gage
Shane Neville
Newzoo
Nintendo
Nokia 6110
Nokia Corporation
Nokia N-Gage
NTT DoCoMo
Nvidia GoForce
OpenGL ES
Palm/PalmPilot
PDA
pdQ smartphone
Playdead
PlayLink
Playtika
PopCap Games

Psion Organiser
Push notification
Quad HD
Qualcomm
RedLynx
Rovio Ent.
Samsung
Samsung Galaxy Tab
Samsung Gear VR
Eric Schmidt
Sidetalking
Simogo
Smartphone
Social features
Social gaming
Sony Ericsson
Spectator mode
Steam app
Supercell
Supermassive Games
Symbian/OS 6.1
T-Mobile
Take-Two Interactive
Tencent
THQ Wireless
Tiger Telematics
Touchscreen
Unwired Planet
WAP
Windows 10 Mobile
Windows Phone
X-Forge 3D
Xperia Z5 Premium
Zynga

■ MOBILE PLATFORMS TIMELINE

Smart Phones	Nokia N-Gage	Motorola RAZR	Apple iPhone	Google Android	iPad/Tablets
1997	**2003**	**2004**	**2007**	**2008**	**2010**

■ INTRODUCTION

This chapter reviews the history and technological developments of mobile gaming, which has played a significant role in shaping the video game market of today. Coverage includes the companies and technologies that have fostered these platforms to the major breakthroughs over the evolution of mobile gaming. The chapter covers key **indie** (independent) and major publisher game titles from each decade, from mobile gaming's casual beginnings to the high-fidelity games of today. The chapter also highlights the key individuals who have helped shape today's mobile landscape, in addition to the organizations who celebrate the platform with annual awards.

■ MOBILE AND CASUAL GAMES DEFINED

A **mobile game** is a video game that runs on an older **feature phone** (multifunction cell phone), **smartphone**, or tablet—however, users can also play such games on **personal digital assistants (PDAs)**, graphing calculators, smartwatches, and other portable media players. Video games are not necessarily the primary function of most mobile gaming devices, which is a key characteristic that separates this platform from "handheld systems" such as the Nintendo 3DS and PlayStation Vita.

Another feature that separates popular mobile games from traditional handheld games is gameplay. Since most smartphones and tablets do not have dedicated action buttons, D-Pads, or analog sticks built into them, mobile game controls are often limited to the use of the device's **touchscreen** (control by one or more fingers) and/or **accelerometer** (motion sensor that detects tilting). While this can be limiting in ways, such controls are also unique compared to conventional PC and console games, leading to new and innovative gaming experiences that have facilitated a market boom of **casual games**.

While too broad of a term for a single definition, casual games typically (1) can be designed around virtually any theme, (2) are easy to learn, with relatively few rules, (3) involve simple gameplay (often requiring just one finger), (4) can be played in short bursts of time, and (5) are targeted toward a wide audience, from children to adults. Casual video games have been around since the dawn of gaming but were gradually overshadowed as the industry matured and games became more complex or "hardcore." Before mobile, casual, and indie gaming took off, extra buttons and longer adventures became routine with each new generation of video game consoles.

Along with mobile games, former Nintendo president **Satoru Iwata** helped reverse this trend. Historians often credit Iwata for leading the casual games revival with Nintendo's DS touchscreen and Wii's motion control games (Takenaka, 2008). Mobile games have since cemented the casual genre as a staple of modern gaming and its mass appeal has attracted a whole new audience of gamers—many of whom do not even consider themselves gamers at all.

■ PHONES GET SMART

Smartphones evolved from PDAs by utilizing their computer-like, multimedia functionality. The first PDAs were the **Organiser** series released by the British company **Psion** in the mid-1980s. A breakthrough for its time, Psion unfortunately never released the Organiser outside of Europe. The **IBM Simon Personal Communicator** (1994) (Figure 14.1a) was the first smartphone (Connelly, 2014, p. 1). The Simon featured a monochrome touchscreen display, address book, appointment scheduler, calculator, calendar, notepad, and world time clock. Priced at $899, most consumers requiring this type of technology elected to purchase a PDA instead. PDAs gained popularity in the late 1990s with offerings from companies like Palm, Inc. (U.S.). The **PalmPilot** (Figure 14.1b) debuted on March 10, 1997, and was the first PDA to be successfully sold across the globe.

Canada's **BlackBerry** became an early leader of smartphones, with the BlackBerry OS debuting in January 1999 on the **BlackBerry 850** pager (Figure 14.1c). **Qualcomm's pdQ smartphone** released that June, which was the first "smartphone to offer the Palm Computing platform and support full-time access to the Internet based upon standard Internet protocols" (Qualcomm, 1999, para. 1). Palm and BlackBerry were early leaders in mobile technology and the most common operating system for smartphones during that time was Psion's **Symbian**. As the century ended, Japan achieved mass adoption of the first smartphones thanks to backing from the country's three major telecom companies **NTT**

FIGURE 14.1 "Smart" devices: (a) IBM Simon, (b) PalmPilot with stylus, and (c) BlackBerry 850 pager.

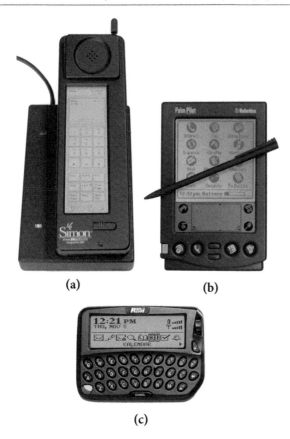

DoCoMo, KDDI, and Softbank (formerly Vodafone Japan) (Budmar, 2012, para. 3). While consumers praised PDAs and smart/feature phones for their multimedia capabilities, these devices in the 1990s lacked a reasonable selection of games.

◼ MOBILE GAMING ORIGINS

A major reason for the success of mobile and casual gaming was accessibility, as more consumers adopted feature phones, which included the ability to play video games. The first game to appear on a mobile phone was a preinstalled version of *Tetris* on the **Hagenuk MT-2000** cell phone by Danish manufacturer Hagenuk Corporation in 1994 (Microsoft Devices Team, 2013, para. 3). Three years would pass before the mainstream mobile market would receive its first big hit with *Snake* in 1997 (Figure 14.2).

Programmed by Finnish developer Taneli Armanto for the **Nokia 6110**, *Snake* was based on the 1976 arcade game *Blockade* by Gremlin. The object of the one-player game is to navigate a perpetually moving snake toward a dot (food), which increases the length of the snake. The goal is to grow as long as possible and the game ends when the snake crashes into a wall or itself when the snake is long enough. *Snake* was also the first multiplayer mobile game, where two people could play together via infrared ports on their Nokia phones.

> ### ☀ DID YOU KNOW?
>
> Since the debut of *Snake* in 1997, "it has been estimated that over 400 million copies have been shipped since and it's now in its eighth version" (Wright, 2016a, para. 4).

Aside from *Snake* in 1997, mobile games were not a major platform until the early 2000s when feature phones became more sophisticated and began offering greater multimedia functions. Games remained primitive during this time, using **Wireless Application Protocol (WAP)** as the standard technology for connecting to the Internet. One of the pioneers of WAP was **Unwired Planet** who developed a microbrowser for mobile phones—yet users most commonly used WAP for accessing email or text-based newsfeeds. It was most successful in Europe due to standardization across companies and was also popular in Japan, although market leader NTT DoCoMo used its own online system called **i-mode** (Wright, 2016a, para. 8). Adoption of WAP in the United States was slow, however, since each cell phone provider had its own data support and fee structures.

FIGURE 14.2 Snapshot of *Snake* (1997).

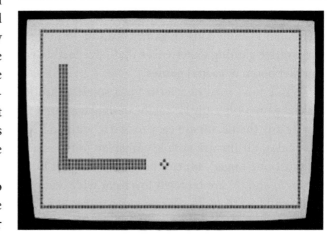

▪ THE NEW MILLENNIUM OF MOBILE

Subscription-based gaming began in Japan through NTT DoCoMo's i-mode in 1999. This was followed by an infrastructure for WAP users to purchase mobile games over the network. With the technology advancing, what the mobile industry needed was for innovative software companies to push the envelope with quality game titles. One of the first key publishers formed around this time was **JAMDAT Mobile**, founded by Activision game execs Scott Lahman, Zachary Norman, and Austin Murray. The other key company was French developer/publisher **Gameloft**, formed by a joint venture between Guillemot Corporation and Ubisoft (Wright, 2016b, para. 4 & 7). Other notable early mobile developers included **Digital Bridges** (U.K.), Hands-On Mobile (U.S.), Handy Games (Germany), IOMO (U.K.), Picofun (Sweden), and Riot-E (Finland). See Table 14.1 for key early WAP titles from these and other companies.

The early 2000s was a pivotal time for mobile gaming. Manufacturers would soon replace simple monochrome, dot matrix displays and single-channel tones with color screens, higher resolution graphics, and multichannel sound. Games became faster and more sophisticated with new mobile programming languages such as **Java 2 Micro Edition (J2ME)** and Qualcomm's **Binary Runtime Environment for Wireless (BREW)**. "J2ME proved to be a massive success in Europe, while BREW was more popular in North and South America and Asia" (Phone Arena, 2011, para. 4). Fathammer's **X-Forge 3D** game engine moved 3D gaming forward on the mobile platform in

2002. Sega and Sonic Team produced an impressive port of *Sonic the Hedgehog* on i-mode in Japan, and in 2003 Sega would release the game in other countries on a new platform by Nokia.

▪ NOKIA N-GAGE

Nokia Corporation is a Finnish company founded in 1865 by **Fredrik Idestam** as a wood pulp mill for manufacturing paper. The company expanded in the early 1900s to manufacturing cables and electronics, and eventually gas masks for the Finnish Defence Forces (Hahn, 2013, para. 2 & 8). After acquiring multiple telecommunications companies in the late 1980s, Nokia went on to become the world's largest mobile phone manufacturer in 1998 (Nokia, 1998, para. 2). The company also played a key role in the development of wireless communication standards including Global System for Mobile Communications (**GSM**), third generation (**3G**), and Long-Term Evolution (**LTE**).

With its formidable reputation in the mobile phone industry, Nokia announced in 2002 that it was working on a PDA that was both a phone and video game system, among other things. Codenamed "Starship," the completed device was officially titled "N-Gage" (Figure 14.3) and released on October 7, 2003, for $299. See Table 14.2 for launch titles. The unit ran on the then-popular **Symbian OS 6.1** (Series 60) operating system and used General Packet Radio Service (**GPRS**) for data transmission. "GRPS is considered a '2.5G' technology, meaning it is more advanced than standard 2G digital technology, but does not meet the requirements of a full-fledged 3G technology" (Phone Scoop, 2001, para. 8).

In addition to its access to WAP over GPRS, N-Gage featured full email support, an XHTML browser, **Bluetooth** connectivity for wireless multiplayer gaming, and a USB port for downloading data from a PC. For sound, the original model tripled as an MP3 music player, digital audio recorder, and an FM radio. Along with video playback and PDA features, Nokia bundled the system with just about everything except a digital camera. Of course, Nokia built the N-Gage to be a powerful mobile video game system that could handle complex 3D games that looked similar in quality to PS1 titles. Players controlled the games with the directional pad on the left of the unit and the main action buttons, which consisted of numbers five (5)

TABLE 14.1 Notable Early WAP Games from 2000 to 2001

Game	Developer	Country
Alien Fish Exchange	nGame	United Kingdom
DataClash	nGame	United Kingdom
Gladiator	JAMDAT Mobile	United States
Lifestylers	Picofun	Sweden
Picofun Football	Picofun	Sweden
Sorcery	Digital Bridges	United Kingdom
The Lord of the Rings	Riot-E	Finland
Void Raider	Unplugged Games	United States
WAP Tanks	Handy Games	Germany
Wireless Pets	The Games Kitchen	United Kingdom

FIGURE 14.3 Nokia N-Gage handheld game console and mobile phone featuring *Puyo Pop*.

TABLE 14.2 Nokia N-Gage Launch Titles

- *Pandemonium*
- *Puyo Pop* (Figure 14.4a)
- *Puzzle Bobble VS*
- *SonicN* (Figure 14.4b)
- *Super Monkey Ball*
- *Tomb Raider: Starring Laura Croft* (Figure 14.4c)

and seven (7) on its numerical keypad. Games came in the form of **MultiMediaCards** (**MMCs**), which looked just like SD cards. One design feature that frustrated gamers was how the game card slot was inconveniently located inside its battery compartment.

The original N-Gage came bundled with a cell phone battery and charger, hands-free headset, USB

FIGURE 14.4 Screenshots of N-Gage launch titles: (a) *Puyo Pop*, (b) *SonicN*, and (c) *Tomb Raider: Starring Laura Croft*.

(a)

(b)

(c)

cable, 3.5 mm adapter cables, music transfer software, and a 141-page user's guide. There was no memory card or physical pack-in game included. Speaking of games, the packaging for N-Gage games was quite unique. The small plastic cases are horizontally oriented and "included a mini game card case in which players can transport up to four games in. The plastic case is smaller in length and width than a standard business card and is roughly a quarter of an inch thick" (IGN Staff, 2003, para. 6–7).

Nokia's target market for N-Gage was consumers between the ages of 18 and 35 and the slogan for the device was "N-Gage—Anyone Anywhere." While its advertising for the system was relatively standard for the time, the **Advertising Standards Authority (ASA)** ended up banning one print and television campaign in the United Kingdom. The ads featured desolate environments with messages such as "This is where I made Kev look small" and "This is where I left Kate, Lucy and Michelle begging for more" (shown in Figure 14.5). Nokia claimed, "the ads were just promoting the wireless-gaming aspect of the phone … by showing unique environments where users wouldn't expect to play their games and highlighting the competitive nature of gaming" (Best, 2004, para. 3).

■ THE COMPETITION

The N-Gage's biggest competition at the time of its release was Nintendo's Game Boy Advance, which consumers could purchase for a third of the price at around $99 in 2003. Despite its more powerful processor (Table 14.3), N-Gage paled in comparison to the GBA's popularity, which eventually reached more than 81 million units sold. The real adversity came just over a year after reaching the market when the fate of N-Gage would be sealed with the release of even more powerful handhelds by Nintendo and Sony with the Nintendo DS and PlayStation Portable.

The N-Gage also faced competition among mobile phones such as the slim and stylish **Motorola RAZR** released during the third quarter of 2004. "Some classic RAZR games include *Spyro – Ripto Quest*, *Space Invaders*, and *Grid Runner++*" (Purewal, 2011, para. 8). The RAZR was an enormous success primarily due to its much-lauded, ultra-slim design, selling "over 50 million units by July 2006 and Motorola's top-shelf brand pushed 130 million units in four years" (Hachman, 2012, para. 3).

TABLE 14.3	Nokia N-Gage Tech Specs
Manufacturer:	Nokia | October 7, 2003
Format:	MultiMediaCard/850 mAh lithium-ion battery (3–4 hours)
Processor:	32-bit ARM920T CPU (104 MHz)
Memory:	3.4 MB internal storage (up to 64 MB with memory card)
Resolution:	176×208 pixels (2.1″ backlit display)
Colors:	4,096
Sound:	Built-in speaker with 2.5 mm stereo jack and Bluetooth 1.1

FIGURE 14.5   Screenshots from one of the banned Nokia commercials from 2003.

N-Gage's greatest competitor may have been itself. Along with some missteps in its advertising, the original system's high price, lack of original games, and design flaws (such as the cramped action buttons on the keypad and having to power off the system and remove the battery to change games) led to early criticism of the system among gamers and journalists (Snow, 2007a, para. 2).

One of the more unusual criticisms of the N-Gage was how it became infamously known for its "taco-like" shape. The speaker and microphone were located on the upper, flat side of the phone and it just looked plain silly when users held it up to their head to communicate with a caller—like a giant ear. This led to the Internet meme known as "**sidetalking**" (Giant Bomb, 2017, para. 2).

Nokia introduced a redesigned **N-Gage QD** (Figure 14.6) in May 2004, which improved upon many of the first model's shortcomings but removed features such as MP3 playback, FM radio reception, and USB connectivity to reduce costs. Sales remained slow and the company discontinued all N-Gage hardware in November 2005. Prior to its discontinuation, Nokia explained at their E3 presentation that the N-Gage name would survive as a gaming service platform that would be accessible to a variety of qualifying phone models. Nokia released the **N-Gage platform** (also called "N-Gage 2.0") on April 3, 2008, through the N-Gage official website. The service, however, was only compatible with five Nokia phones. With only 49 games released on the online platform, Nokia ceased production of new titles on October 30, 2009, and terminated all N-Gage services at the end of 2010 (Duncan, 2009, para. 2).

> ### ☼ DID YOU KNOW?
>
> Market analysts from Arcadia Research estimated that Nokia's U.S. launch for N-Gage "sold under 5000 units across both videogame and mobile phone retailers," placing it among the weakest console releases of all time (Fahey, 2003, para. 1 & 3).

▪ KEY N-GAGE TITLES

Only around 60 titles released for N-Gage. Its early lineup featured games that, while impressive to see on the small screen of a phone, were older titles that had been available on home consoles for years. Games from the PS1 era included *Tony Hawk's Pro Skater*, *Tomb Raider*, and *Pandemonium*, while *Puyo Pop*, *Puzzle Bobble*, and *Sonic* dated back to the 16-bit era. Stronger titles began to appear in 2004 including the turn-based strategy game *Pathway to Glory* by **RedLynx** and *The Sims Bustin' Out* (**Ideaworks3D**/EA Games) (shown in Figure 14.7). Other hits from 2004 included *Colin McRae Rally 2005* (Ideaworks3D), Sega's *Pocket Kingdom: Own the World*, *Tom Clancy's Ghost Recon: Jungle Storm* by Gameloft, a few soccer titles, and *Tiger Woods PGA Tour 2004* from Backbone Emeryville and EA Sports.

The year 2005 was the system's strongest, albeit last year for software releases. Top games from this year included another exclusive turn-based strategy game by RedLynx called *High Seize*, as well as two excellent 3D racing games with *Glimmerati* (Bugbear) and *System Rush* (Ideaworks3D). One of the best games of the year was **Iomo**'s free download of *Snakes*, which was a 3D reimagining of the classic *Snake*. Other notable titles from 2005 were *Mile High Pinball* by Bonus Mobile Entertainment, *Tom Clancy's Splinter Cell: Chaos Theory* by Gameloft, *Worms World Party* from Paragon 5, along with fighting games *King of Fighters Extreme* by Hudson and *ONE* from Digital Legends.

The majority of these and other games released for the N-Gage were intricate titles that provided console-like gaming experiences, requiring time and dedication to play. In an interview with Jonathan Keane (2015), Nokia producer and indie games developer **Shane Neville** explained, "If you look at mobile games now, it was never core gamers that made gaming work on mobile. It's casual gamers. Nokia wasn't going for that audience at all," he says. "I think that's the opportunity that Nokia missed" (para. 13). In the end, Nokia's N-Gage served as a prime example of a game system that was ahead of its time in many regards, but completely missed the mark in others.

▪ OTHER MOBILE DEVELOPMENTS

In addition to N-Gage, color displays on other mobile phones became more affordable in 2003 and casual puzzle games such as **PopCap**'s *Bejeweled* reached millions of users as a popular game bundled on phones. In May of that year, Electronic Arts and 3DO

FIGURE 14.6 Print advertisement for the N-Gage QD in 2005.

FIGURE 14.7 Five of the best N-Gage titles: (a) *Rayman 3*, (b) *Pathway to Glory*, (c) *The Sims Bustin' Out*, (d) *Glimmerati*, and (e) *Tom Clancy's Splinter Cell: Chaos Theory*.

 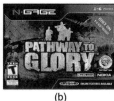   

(a)　　　　　(b)　　　　　(c)　　　　　(d)　　　　　(e)

founder **Trip Hawkins** "invested $405,000 of his own cash to buy back some of the company's patents and brands and set about launching **Digital Chocolate**," a mobile game publisher whose titles "would be based on original ideas, not expensive brands licensed from other media" (Wright, 2008, para. 6). It was also in 2003 that the first subset of **OpenGL ES** released, leading to a leap in mobile game graphics. Notable mobile titles from this period included *Space Invaders* (Distinctive Developments) and *Siberian Strike* (Gameloft), followed by *Ridge Racer 3D* (Namco) and *Nom* (**Gamevil**).

The year 2004 marked the year that large publishers including **EA Mobile** and JAMDAT Mobile dominated the cellular market and ports of popular console games became more commonplace. Popular mobile games at this time included Gameloft titles *Asphalt Urban GT, Might and Magic,* and *Prince of Persia: The Sands of Time* (Figure 14.8), plus sports titles *Tony Hawk's Pro Skater* (Ideaworks3D), *MotoGP*

2 (**THQ Wireless**), and *JAMDAT Bowling*. JAMDAT would have further success with *Neverwinter Nights* and *Bejeweled Multiplayer*, while Sony Online Entertainment developed the mobile RPG *EverQuest: Hero's Call* (Harz, 2004, para. 7). Scrolling shooter *Duke Nukem Mobile* (MachineWorks Northwest)was "designed for the Motorola T720, the LG VX4400, the LG VX4500, the LG VX6000, and the Samsung SCH-A530. The title proved to be popular enough that *Duke Nukem Mobile II: Bikini Project* was released a year later" (Purewal, 2011, para. 10).

■ GIZMONDO

The same year that software development ceased for the Nokia N-Gage, Europe's **Tiger Telematics** launched **Gizmondo** (Figure 14.9) in the United Kingdom on March 19, 2005, for £229. Tiger later released the device in mainland Europe and in the United States for $400. While it was not a mobile phone, "it did have a slot for

FIGURE 14.8 Early mid-2000s mobile hits: (a) *Prince of Persia: The Sands of Time*, (b) *The Fast and the Furious*, and (c) *Tower Bloxx*.

  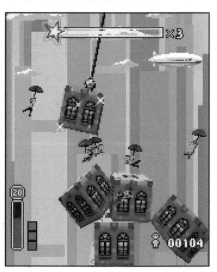

(a)　　　　　(b)　　　　　(c)

FIGURE 14.9 Gizmondo (2005) featuring *Richard Burns Rally*.

a SIM card and supported the likes of WAP, GPRS and SMS/MMS, so despite not having a number pad or voice capacity, it was near enough" (Wright, 2008, para. 3). Viewing text messages was the easy part. However, to compose messages users had to navigate through a menu of letters and numbers using the D-Pad and select one character at a time with the Play button.

Gizmondo was a technically superior game machine to N-Gage with a 400 MHz Samsung **ARM9** processor, **Nvidia GoForce** 3D 4500 GPU, and 320 × 240 resolution. However, critics panned the system for its high price tag and limited game library. Tiger quickly released an ad-enabled version of the system for £229 and $249; however, soon after its release, authorities linked Tiger CEO **Carl Freer** and Director of Gizmondo Europe **Stefan Eriksson** to criminal activity with Sweden's Uppsala Mafia. Records showed that Tiger "lost more than $300 million between January 2004 and July 2005" (Sullivan, 2006, para. 25 & 39) and the company ordered the system into liquidation. Fewer than 25,000 units sold and "only eight of the 14 planned games were ever released" in the United States (Snow, 2007b, para. 5).

■ STILL GROWING

Despite commercial failures such as N-Gage and Gizmondo, mobile gaming revenue continued to climb during 2005 and 2006. In June 2005, Sorrent (California) merged with Macrospace (London) to form **Glu Mobile**. Numerous other buyouts and mergers took place around this time, including EA Mobile's purchase of JAMDAT for $680 million in February

2006. The mobile gaming business was expanding, but **fragmentation** in the technology remained an issue.

While Nokia and Motorola supported Java for its devices, **Sony Ericsson** used **Mascot Capsule** for its phones. This fragmentation resulted in most game publishers focusing "on porting games to as many handsets as possible rather than making as many great games as possible" (Wright, 2009, para. 8). Furthermore, with the business structure of network operators and publisher portals distributing mobile games, small developers needed a more effective way of making money on their games.

■ APPLE IPHONE

The mobile world would change dramatically after **Apple** launched its **iPhone** (shown in Figure 14.10) on June 29, 2007. Mobile gaming, as well as Apple, would see a tremendous surge in popularity and revenue. Apple built the iPhone in collaboration with **AT&T** (then Cingular Wireless) for an estimated $150 million (Vogelstein, 2008). Essentially a handheld computer, the iPhone replaced the complex keypads and tiny buttons of older smartphone models with an easy-to-use touchscreen. It also included accelerometer support where developers could program games to react to tilting the phone in different directions, as well as "a proximity sensor that could automatically turn off the screen when close to the face, and an ambient light sensor that could automatically adjust brightness" (Ritchie, 2017, para. 8).

The original two iPhone models included 4 GB of memory for $499 and an 8 GB model for $599. See Table 14.4 for specs. Following the first-generation iPhones, Apple released the less expensive **iPod Touch** on September 5, 2007. The Touch included most of the iPhone's multimedia functionality such as a Safari browser, digital camera, music and video playback, typical PDA features, and the ability to play video games. The most noticeable difference was that the Touch lacked phone capabilities. It was not a smartphone and could not access cellular network data—however, users were able to connect to the Internet via Wi-Fi.

While it generated plenty of hype, the original iPhone did not take off right away and Apple dropped the price of the 8 GB model by $200 during the release of the Touch. The first model managed to sell more

FIGURE 14.10 Advertisement for the original Apple iPhone in 2007.

TABLE 14.4 Original iPhone Tech Specs

Manufacturer:	Apple, Inc. | June 29, 2007
Format:	4 GB or 8 GB flash memory Internal battery (3 gaming hours)
Processors:	Samsung 32-bit ARM 1176JZ (F)-S v1.0 CPU (412MHz) PowerVR MBX Lite 3D GPU
Memory:	128 MB eDRAM
Resolution:	320×480 pixels (3.5″ touchscreen display)
Colors:	262,144
Sound:	Stereo speaker with 3.5mm stereo jack and Bluetooth capability

than 6 million units "but it wasn't until 2008—when Apple unveiled the iPhone 3G with a new $200 price tag and access to the faster 3G network—that the smartphone exploded in popularity" with Apple selling more than 10 million iPhone 3G units worldwide in only 5 months (Chen, 2009, para. 4).

By cleverly using the first letters of "Apple" and "application," Apple coined the term "app" for all programs—including games that would run on its **iPhone operating system (iOS)**. Launched during the summer of 2008, the **App Store** digital storefront was a key factor behind the iPhone's success as a gaming

platform (Langshaw, 2011, para. 7–8). "Suddenly, here was a platform that enabled consumers to buy games as easily as they had bought MP3s via iTunes. It also enabled developers to sell their games directly to consumers without having to deal with publishers and operators" (Wright, 2009, para. 11).

This opened the door for the indie game scene to thrive and independent developers flocked to the platform. It was relatively easy for developers to upload games to the App Store. Software developers would "code an interesting app, submit it to the App Store for approval and market the app however they wished. Then, Apple [would] give developers 70 percent of each app sale, keeping 30 percent to cover credit-processing fees" (Chen, 2009, para. 16).

End users were provided with the ability to rate their apps in the App Store, helping quality games stand out over weaker titles. This user- and developer-friendly platform leveled the playing field between the large publishers and smaller developers, helping to facilitate an independent gaming boom that saw its principal audience on mobile devices. Consumers could purchase early iOS titles for $0.99–$9.99. Games also used monetization methods like those on PC, where players could download games for free using ad support as a means of revenue or played via **freemium** with limited free features such as restricted game time or lives.

■ EARLY iPHONE GAMES

With no App Store or 3G access in 2007, early iPhone adopters had to wait until 2008 to access a library of quality video games. Among the most memorable titles from 2008 was *Rolando* by **HandCircus** (Figure 14.11a), released on December 18. At $9.99, *Rolando* was one of the more expensive games but one of the first to utilize the iPhone's accelerometer, as well as its **multi-touch** technology. Multi-touch enabled the touchscreen's surface to sense the presence of more than one finger, providing functionality such as panning the screen. *Rolando's* interactive environments, intuitive controls, and catchy soundtrack made the game a hit for both critics and gamers alike.

While a handful of memorable game titles came out on iPhone during the first 2 years, it was in 2009 when the mobile gaming boom really took off. That year saw an explosion of highly rated titles including *Rolando 2: Quest for the Golden Orchid* (HandCircus) and *Zen Bound* (Secret Exit), along with best-selling titles *Doodle Jump* (Lima Sky) and *Angry Birds* by **Rovio Entertainment** (Figure 14.11b)—each game breaking 10 million units sold. Other notable titles included *Real Racing* and *Flight Control* by **Firemint** and Gameloft's *N.O.V.A.—Near Orbit Vanguard Alliance*. With the iPhone and App Store's success, it would only be a matter of time before other major companies would follow in Apple's footsteps with platform offerings from Google and Microsoft.

■ MORE PLATFORMS THAN EVER

Before the iPhone, Google acquired **Android, Inc.** in 2005 and the company was poised to compete with Windows Mobile and BlackBerry-style phones. This all changed after attending the iPhone launch event, when Google's then-CEO, **Eric Schmidt** refocused the company's **Android** technology to compete with the iPhone (Ritchie, 2017, para. 33). Google's Android OS was based on the Linux kernel and the first phone to use the operating system was the **HTC Dream** (also called the T-Mobile G1) on September 23, 2008. Manufacturers **Samsung**, LG, and Motorola quickly adopted the platform and became leading producers of Android smartphones. Like the App Store, Google launched its own **Android Market** (now **Google Play**) store on October 22, 2008. Behind the technology, **Arm** continued to advance its Mali GPU, and the 2008 **Mali-400** would become the first multi-core GPU for mobile devices.

FIGURE 14.11 Screenshots of early iOS games: (a) *Rolando* (2008) and (b) *Angry Birds* (2009).

(a)   (b)

PRO FILE

STEVE JOBS

KEY FACTS:

Co-founder, chairman, and CEO of Apple, Inc.

Pioneered the personal computer and modern smartphone revolution

PRO FILE

HISTORY:
- Born: February 24, 1955 in San Francisco, CA
- Deceased: October 5, 2011 in Palo Alto, CA

EDUCATION:
- Homestead High School (1972), Reed College (1 sem.)

CAREER HIGHLIGHTS:
- Joined Atari in 1973 and assisted Steve Wozniak with the arcade hit *Breakout* in 1976
- Co-founded Apple Computer Company with Wozniak on April 1, 1976 and founded NeXT Inc. in 1985
- Returned to Apple as CEO in 1997, launched iMac (1998), iTunes and iPod (2001), iPhone (2007), the App Store (2008) and iPad (2010)

RECOGNITION:
National Medal of Technology (1985), Jefferson Award for Public Service (1987), Entrepreneur of the Decade by *Inc.* (1989), Howard Vollum Award by Reed College (1991), California Hall of Fame (2007), Grammy Trustees Award (2012), Edison Achievement Award (2012), Disney Legend Award (2013), Presidential Medal of Freedom (2022)

Apple's next platform for the mobile gaming market was its **iPad** line of tablet computers released on April 3, 2010. Like the iPhone, the iPad ran on iOS and came bundled with multimedia capabilities. It was not a phone, but its larger, 9.7-inch screen size made it easier to play certain games. Android tablets emerged soon after in 2010, with releases such as the **Dell Streak** and **Samsung Galaxy Tab**. Like with smartphones, Android tablets eventually outsold the iPad due to the vast number of companies manufacturing them and their lower price tag. Microsoft followed with **Windows Phone** in 2010 followed by the **Windows Phone Store**. Amazon became a popular digital distribution platform for Android apps soon after.

These platforms offered "more flexibility than Apple's store since developers could distribute their games via any platform they desired" (Langshaw, 2011, para. 9). Multiple storefronts, smartphone platforms, and tablets made titles easier to obtain, leading to tremendous growth and greater competition. The year 2010 also saw the end of AT&T's exclusivity deal with iPhone. Soon, other service providers (beginning with Verizon) would obtain the rights to carry the phone. The iPhone continued to evolve and "the iPhone 4 was named the fastest-selling portable gaming system by Guinness after selling an estimated

1.5 million handsets on the first day it was released on June 24, 2010" (Los Angeles Times, 2011, para. 3).

While the technology had been in development for years, 2010 marked the year that 100 Mbps **4G LTE** wireless networks started gaining ground, making downloading apps and online gaming faster than ever. Popular multiplatform games that debuted on iOS in 2010 included casual hit *Fruit Ninja* by Halfbrick Studios (Figure 14.12a), *Cut the Rope* (ZeptoLab/Chillingo), *Real Racing 2* (Firemint), and *Plants vs. Zombies* by PopCap (Figure 14.12b). iOS also remained the exclusive platform for titles such as the graphically intensive *Infinity Blade, Helsing's Fire*, and *Space Miner: Space Ore Bust*.

It was 2011 when smartphones finally outsold standard feature phones and the growing popularity of Android led to the platform receiving more ports of games that were once exclusive to iOS. Android users even saw a handful of decent platform-exclusive titles of their own. iOS games received a major boost in performance with the release of the 32-bit **Apple A5** chip, which allowed the iPhone and iPad to "render graphics seven times faster, according to Apple. Titles like *Infinity Blade 2, Real Racing 2* and *The Dark Meadow* showed how the additional power could be used to change the conception of what a mobile game can look like" (Savitz, 2012, para. 4). One major acquisition that year included Electronic Arts buying PopCap Games for $750 million.

Three years after its launch on the Wii and Windows, developer 2D Boy finally ported *World of Goo* to iPhone and Android. Another late but important port was *Words with Friends* by **Zynga**, when it brought its **social gaming** hit to Android. The year

FIGURE 14.12 Screenshots of multiplatform hits: (a) *Fruit Ninja* and (b) *Plants vs. Zombies* (2010).

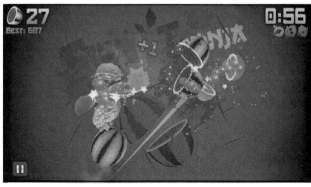
(a)

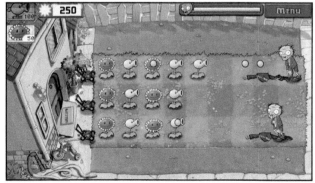
(b)

2011 also saw the release of "**endless runner**" (forced progression) games *Jetpack Joyride* (Halfbrick Studios) and *Tiny Wings* (Andreas Illiger). The adventure game *Superbrothers: Sword & Sworcery EP* (Capy Games/ Superbrothers) would follow *Cut the Rope* as the Game Developers Choice Awards winner for Best Mobile/ Handheld Game. On a more somber note, 2011 was also the year that the world said goodbye to Apple's visionary CEO **Steve Jobs** when he lost his battle with pancreatic cancer on October 5.

■ MOBILE MILESTONES

By 2012, there were more than 500 million mobile gamers across the globe and mobile game revenue surpassed $9 billion with an annual growth rate of 32% (Nouch, 2013, para. 1 & 3). While casual games continued to dominate the medium, hardcore-style games such as *Horn* (Phosphor Games Studio, LLC/ Zynga) and *The Walking Dead* (Telltale Games) showed that mobile was capable of delivering more console-like experiences. Bluetooth gamepads such as the **MOGA** (Mobile Gaming) controller by PowerA began to emerge, allowing users to play compatible mobile games with analog sticks, face buttons, and shoulder triggers.

Top games from 2012 included *Bastion* (Supergiant Games/Warner Bros. Interactive Entertainment), *The Room* (Fireproof Games), *Angry Birds Star Wars* (Rovio Entertainment), *Rayman Jungle Run* (Pasta Games/ Ubisoft), and *Super Hexagon* (**Terry Cavanagh**). Two of the highest grossing games included the freemium strategy game *Clash of Clans* by **Supercell**

(Figure 14.13a) and **King**'s free-to-play casual puzzler *Candy Crush Saga* (Figure 14.13b). Essentially a touchscreen reimagining of *Bejeweled*, *Candy Crush Saga* popularized the tile-matching genre on mobile, often referred to as "**match three**" games.

Technology research firm **Gartner** reported that 79% of all smartphones sold between April and June 2013 were running on Android—that is 177.9 million Android handsets compared to 31.9 million iPhones (Dredge, 2013, para. 1). Yet the trend of developing games for iOS before Android would continue. The main reason for this is that it is easier to program an app for a small pool of iOS platforms that use similar technology. Android, on the other hand, can take longer to develop for due to the vast number of devices on the market using different versions of the Android OS, at various resolutions, with an assortment of processors.

This mobile fragmentation is less of a problem for large developers. Furthermore, "improved development tools are making porting easier, and there's more data (including Google's own) to help developers decide which Android devices to focus their energies on first" (Dredge, 2013, para. 12). Also, by the time developers port games (that premiered on iOS) to Android, most of the bugs have been worked out. As Fireproof Games developer **Barry Meade** explained; "What Android users forget is that because their versions come later, they get the least buggy, higher performance version of the game because iOS users are, in an indirect way, guinea pigs for the other releases" (Kuchera, 2015, para. 10).

As Table 14.5 indicates, mobile port times are improving. For example, *The Room* (2012) took

FIGURE 14.13 Screenshots of (a) *Clash of Clans* and (b) *Candy Crush Saga* (2012).

(a)

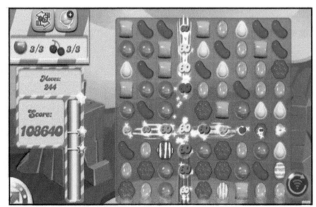

(b)

TABLE 14.5 iOS versus Android Release Dates for Popular Games by Year

Game Title	iOS Date	Android Date	Port Time
Real Racing 2	12/16/10	12/22/11	>1 year
Words With Friends	09/01/11	09/28/12	>1 year
Super Hexagon	08/31/12	01/19/13	>4 months
The Room Two	12/12/13	02/13/14	>2 months
Monument Valley	04/03/14	05/14/14	>1 month
Lara Croft GO	08/27/15	08/27/15	None
Clash Royale	03/02/16	03/02/16	None

Fireproof Games 6 months to port to Android, while *The Room Two* took just over 2 months. Along with *The Room Two*, other creepy, atmospheric titles to launch in 2013 included *Limbo* (**Playdead**), along with *Year Walk* and the modern-day, text-based adventure *DEVICE 6*, both by Swedish developer **Simogo**. Strategy games continued to be popular with chart toppers such as *XCOM: Enemy Unknown, Rymdkapsel,* and 17-Bit's *Skulls of the Shogun*. Frogmind's *Badland* and RobTop Games' *Geometry Dash* satisfied endless runner fans, while one of the best casual titles of the year was the hilariously fun *Ridiculous Fishing: A Tale of Redemption* by Dutch development studio Vlambeer (Figure 14.14a).

By 2014, the number of global Android users had reached double that of the total number of Apple's iOS users (Vining, 2014, p. 1). High-end smartphones began to release with 2560 × 1440 "**Quad HD**" resolutions and the following year Sony revealed the **Xperia Z5 Premium**, which featured 3840 × 2160 "**4K**" resolution. Before the end of 2015, Microsoft released its **Windows 10 Mobile** operating system, which like on Xbox One, helped to unify the Windows OS across multiple device platforms. Game developers moved the platform forward by accompanying these innovations with ground-breaking releases.

Popular platformers from 2014 included *Traps n' Gemstones, Leo's Fortune, Thomas Was Alone,* and Terry Cavanagh's *VVVVVV*. Strategy fans received titles from major publishers such as *Hitman GO* (Square Enix Montreal) and the card-based *Hearthstone: Heroes of Warcraft* (Blizzard Entertainment), while the puzzle game genre received the innovative *Monument Valley* by Ustwo Games (Figure 14.14b), *Framed* (Loveshack), and *Threes!* (Sirvo). Other notable titles from 2014 included the casual *Freeway/Frogger*-inspired *Crossy Road: Endless Arcade Hopper* (Hipster Whale), a unique visual novel adventure called *80 Days* by Inkle, and **Scott Cawthon**'s indie debut of what would become a major survival horror franchise—*Five Nights at Freddy's*.

The year 2014 saw the most mobile developer acquisitions to date, such as China's Zhongji Holding buying

FIGURE 14.14 Screenshots of mobile hits: (a) *Ridiculous Fishing: A Tale of Redemption* (2013), (b) *Monument Valley* (2014), and (c) *Prune* (2015).

(a)   (b)   (c)

DianDian Interactive for $960 million, Kentucky-based Churchill Downs Incorporated acquiring Seattle's **Big Fish Games** for $885 million, and social gaming guru Zynga purchasing NaturalMotion for $527 million. These major buyouts slowed down in 2015, but not before **Activision Blizzard** announced it would be purchasing *Candy Crush* developer King for a whopping $5.9 billion.

The year 2015 was another strong year, especially for independent developers with inventive titles such as *Prune* by **Joel McDonald** (Figure 14.14c), *Her Story* by **Sam Barlow**, and *Downwell* by **Moppin**. Square Enix continued its "GO" series with *Laura Croft GO* and *Bastion* developer Supergiant Games finally returned with action RPG *Transistor, Alto's Adventure*, and *Badlands 2* were solid endless runners, Fireproof Games completed a trilogy with *The Room Three*, and *Call of Champions* showed that gamers could play MOBAs in short bursts.

■ NINTENDO GOES MOBILE

Historians will remember 2016 as the year that **Nintendo** finally entered the mobile market with the *Miitomo* social app, the breakthrough success of the year, *Pokémon GO* (developed by Niantic Labs) (Figure 14.15), and the endless runner game, *Super Mario Run*. While *Super Mario Run* and *Miitomo* provided decent Nintendo experiences on mobile devices, it was *Pokémon GO* that took the world by storm.

> The game—in which players try to capture exotic monsters from *Pokémon*, the Japanese cartoon franchise—uses a combination of ordinary technologies built into smartphones, including location tracking and cameras, to encourage people to visit public landmarks, seeking virtual loot and collectible characters that they try to nab.
>
> *Wingfield & Isaac (2016, para. 2)*

The game brought **augmented reality (AR)** to mainstream audiences by superimposing the cartoon *Pokémon* monsters over real-life locations seen through the cameras of players' phones. The game's social element led to a phenomenon of gamers going on "*Pokémon* walks" together and/or meeting other players in the physical world.

FIGURE 14.15 Screenshot of *Pokémon GO* (2016).

☼ DID YOU KNOW?

Pokémon GO set five Guinness World Records for a mobile game in its first month, including "Most revenue grossed," "Most downloaded," "Most international charts topped simultaneously for a mobile game" (for both downloads and revenue), and "Fastest time to gross $100 million by a mobile game" (Swatman, 2016).

Pokémon GO grossed $270.2 million and was only second to Supercell's real-time strategy blockbuster, *Clash Royale* which topped the mobile charts in the United States in 2016, generating $277.1 million (Cowley, 2017, para. 5). In addition to other *Pokémon* titles, Nintendo continued to publish one to two new mobile games each year, including *Fire Emblem*

Heroes (2017), *Animal Crossing: Pocket Camp* (2017), *Dragalia Lost* (2018), *Dr. Mario World* (2019), *Mario Kart Tour* (2019), and *Pikmin Bloom* (2021).

▪ MOBILE MERITS

As the mobile games industry was still finding its place in the video games market, the French division of Discreet and mobile gaming partners Nokia, Orange, Intel, IBM, In-Fusio, Criterion, Fathammer, NVIDIA, Kaolink, and Ideaworks3D launched the first international 3D mobile gaming competition in 2004 under the leadership of Maarten Noyons (Ball, 2004, para. 1). The group renamed the event the **International Mobile Gaming Awards (IMGA)** and it has continued to grow in entries and award categories. Mobile award categories include Best AR Game, Best Game for 5G, Best Meaningful Play, Best Quickplay Game, Best Technical Achievement, and Best VR Game. The ceremony also has Excellence awards in Art, Audio, Design, Gameplay, Innovation, and Storytelling.

Shortly after the success of IMGA, the annual **Game Developers Choice Awards** (presented at the Game Developers Conference since 2001) added Mobile to its Handheld Game Award category. The first mobile game to win the Best Mobile/Handheld Game award was *Cut the Rope* in 2010. Mobile games have since earned all but one of the last 11 awards for this category—beating out handheld offerings from Nintendo and Sony as shown in Table 14.6.

TABLE 14.6 Game Developers Choice Awards: Best Mobile/Handheld Games

Year	Game Title	Original Platform(s)
2010	*Cut the Rope*	iOS
2011	*Superbrothers: Sword & Sworcery EP*	iOS
2012	*The Room*	iOS
2013	*The Legend of Zelda: A Link Between Worlds*	Nintendo 3DS
2014	*Monument Valley*	iOS, Android
2015	*Her Story*	iOS, OS X, Windows
2016	*Pokémon GO*	iOS, Android
2017	*Gorogoa*	iOS, Windows, Switch
2018	*Florence*	iOS, Android
2019	*What the Golf?*	iOS, MacOS, Windows
2020	*Genshin Impact*	iOS, Android, Windows, PS4

TABLE 14.7 Pocket Gamer Mobile Games Awards "Game of the Year" Winners

Year	Game Title	Developer
2018	*Golf Clash*	Playdemic Ltd.
2019	*Fortnite*	Epic Games
2020	*Call of Duty: Mobile*	TiMi Studio
2021	*Genshin Impact*	miHoYo
2022	*Beatstar—Touch Your Music*	Space Ape Games

Mobile games continued to receive new accolades from established video game affiliates in subsequent years. The **Steel Media** team (Pocket Gamer, PG.biz) formed "the first ever **Mobile Games Awards** presentation [which] took place on the second night of Pocket Gamer Connects London 2018 on Tuesday, January 23, 2018. It was hosted at the prestigious BAFTA" [British Academy of Film and Television Arts] in London (Steel Media Ltd., 2022). See Table 14.7 for the first five recipients of the Mobile Games Awards "Game of the Year."

▪ RECENT TRENDS

The early growth of mobile gaming came from casual and indie titles. Then mobile VR gaming came and faded away by the end of the decade. Thanks to more powerful processors, triple-A or and "**high-fidelity**" **games** began trending on mobile in the 2020s. British technology company **Arm** refers tomobile games as "high-fidelity" if they feature advanced graphics and/or complex mechanics and gameplay. Popular high-fidelity mobile gaming titles include *PUBG Mobile, Fortnite Mobile, Call of Duty Mobile* and *Honor of Kings*" (Winburn, 2021, para. 3). Each of these titles launched on PC and/or console before becoming successful mobile games.

The ability to play triple-A, high-fidelity titles on mobile has led to another trend, which is the convergence between mobile with console and PC gaming—called **cross-platform gaming** (or **cross-play**). Cross-play allows console, PC, and mobile gamers to play the same game together, typically in online multiplayer settings. Convergence with home consoles began to gain ground with the *Party Pack* series from **Jackbox Games** where participants could use their phones or tablets as controllers. In 2017, Sony introduced a series of **PlayLink** titles, which allowed players to use iOS or Android devices as controllers. **Supermassive Games'** crime thriller *Hidden Agenda* showed promise for the technology, however less than 20 games supported PlayLink, culminating with *Melbits World* and *Erica* in 2019. It was not until cross-play became possible that mobile, console, and PC games truly converged. "Now, it's far more common to see cross-platform development with mobile games built from the same code and using the same game engine as PC and console titles" (Winburn, 2021, para. 8).

Another trend in mobile gaming has been an increase in **social features** where players can interact with one another through mobile games. Features including cooperative multiplayer, guild formations, and in-game chat help users feel like they are part of a group. **Activity feeds** such as **leaderboards** bring news and updates into games and allow players to monitor each other's progress. **Push notifications** can alert players when their friends are playing online. Other ways mobile game publishers are incorporating social features in games include social media integration (the ability to connect games with social media accounts), social currency and in-game sharing of items, as well as **spectator modes** to watch friends play. Among the most popular social games on mobile have been *Minecraft, Clash of Clans, Roblox* (Figure 14.16a), *Among Us* (Figure 14.16b), and *Fortnite Mobile*.

Finally, faster mobile connection speeds on **5G** networks will lead to even further growth in mobile gaming technology. South Korea was the first country to introduce 5G networks with SK Telecom, KT Corporation, and LG U Plus, launching across major cities in April 2019. **T-Mobile** premiered the technology in the United States, becoming the first company in the world to launch a commercial nationwide **stand-alone architecture (SA)** 5G network on August 4, 2020 (T-Mobile, 2020). 5G networks can reach speeds up to 100 times faster than 4G, at a peak of 10 Gbps compared to 100 Mbps on 4G networks. Faster speeds will mean a growth in cloud gaming, subscription-based gaming, and mobile **eSports**, which have already seen tremendous growth with games such as *Hearthstone, Clash Royale, PUBG Mobile, Arena of Valor* (aka *King of Glory*), *Garena Free Fire*, and *Mobile Legends: Bang Bang*.

■ **MOBILE GAMER PROFILE**

As for *who* plays mobile games, casual puzzle and word games including *Candy Crush Saga* and *Words with Friends* skew toward females over the age of 45, while strategy games such as *Clash of Clans* attract a younger male audience with "a significant proportion (about 40%) of players over the age of 35" (Hwong, 2016, para. 3). A recent report from **Newzoo** (2021) showed that

> complex and competitive genres, such as MOBA, shooter, battle royale and racing, are much more popular in mobile-first countries (e.g., China, India and Saudi Arabia) than in the U.S. and the U.K., where mobile gamers tend to enjoy more casual genres like puzzle, match and arcade.
>
> *(p. 15)*

EEDAR head of consumer research Dr. Heather Nofziger dispelled the notion that mobile games were

FIGURE 14.16 Screenshots of popular cross-play and social mobile games: (a) *Roblox* and (b) *Among Us*.

(a)

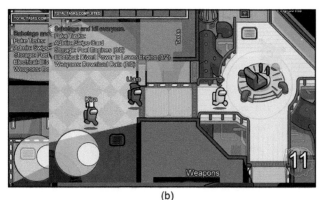

(b)

strictly a product for casual players in a 2018 survey of 5,000 U.S. gamers. The study found that 96% of what the survey identified as "Super Gamers" played mobile games and that they were just as likely to play on mobile as they were on PC. This Super Gamer segment played an average of 26 total hours a week and represented 13% of the U.S. gaming market. The group consisted of 64% male, 36% female, and skewed to the average age of 25.7, relative to the total market average of 32 (Nofziger, 2018, para. 2–4). As for *what* platform people use to play mobile games on, about two-thirds of mobile gamers use Android, with about one-third iOS. A report from **Flurry** indicated that larger screen size correlated with longer playing times, with game sessions on large tablets lasting roughly 61% longer than sessions on medium-sized phones (Perez, 2017).

Another report from EEDAR indicated *why, where,* and *how* mobile gamers typically play. Among the top five reasons adult mobile gamers play, 83% said it was an "easy way to pass the time," while 65% play because it is "cheap or free entertainment." About 63% enjoy mobile games because they are "playable anywhere," 53% reported they are "easy to pick up and put down," while 49% play mobile games because they are "playable on a convenient device."

As for where or how mobile gamers play, the top three responses included "relaxing at home (other than bathroom, bed, or watching TV)," "in bed, before sleep," and "while watching TV/movies" (EEDAR, 2016, pp. 25–26). Late night gaming was also the trend for *when* mobile gamers play, with a 2017 report by Flurry showing that smartphone and tablet gamers alike follow a similar gaming pattern of playing more often as the day goes on, with peak playtime between 6 pm and 9 pm (Figure 14.17).

FIGURE 14.17 Flurry Analytics mobile gaming usage trends.

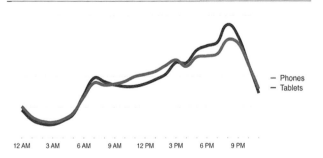

■ MARKET SUMMARY

Mobile and casual gaming have seen tremendous growth since the turn of the century. It was big news in 2002 for WAP gaming when "Digital Bridges announced it had clocked up its 10 millionth session, which accounted for over 70 million minutes of airtime" (Wright, 2016c, para. 12). Then 2003's N-Gage was a commercial failure but still sold 3 million units (Snow, 2007a, para. 2) and was profitable for Nokia. Microsoft's late entry with the Windows Phone resulted in sparse support by developers and it could never catch up to iPhone or Android. After 7 years on the market, the company announced it would discontinue development for Windows 10 Mobile in October 2017.

Apple, on the other hand, made tremendous strides with its iPhone and other iOS products. In January 2012, "Apple reported its best quarterly earnings ever, taking in more than $46 billion over three months. 53% of that revenue was from the sale of 37 million iPhones, at an average selling price of nearly $660" (Golson, 2012, para. 1). In addition to augmented reality making its way into mobile games, mobile VR (virtual reality) began trending in 2016.

Android tablet sales grew from a 45.8% worldwide market share in 2012 to a 61.9% share in 2013 (Gartner, 2014, p. 1). By 2016, Android commanded "over 80 percent of the mobile OS market share globally, and just under 60 percent in the U.S." (Heiman, 2016, para. 1). That market share began to decline when in July 2018 "Android controlled 77.32% of the global OS market [and] as of January 2022, four years later, that percentage had dropped to 69.74% [while] iOS adoption grew from 19.4% to 25.49%, a 6% increase" (Hardwick, 2022, para. 3).

Mobile VR headsets such as the **Samsung Gear VR** ($99.99) became popular during this time, with Samsung announcing that the company had sold 5 million Gear VR headsets by the 2017 Consumer Electronics Show (CES) (Takahashi, 2017, para. 1). A series of mobile VR games released over the next couple of years but then tapered off by 2019 when developers shifted their attention to more capable VR platforms on PC and PlayStation 4.

Similar to *Pac-Man* in the 1980s, the casual *Angry Birds* became a huge intellectual property, becoming the first mobile game to receive a full-length feature film when Columbia Pictures and Rovio Animation released *The Angry Birds Movie* in May 2016. Even before the movie, stores flooded the shelves with *Angry Birds* stuffed animals and other **ancillary products**—from toys and board games, to backpacks and other school supplies. *Five Nights at Freddy's* was another mobile franchise that saw dolls and other products based on its game characters. Soon after, *Fortnite, Roblox,* and *Among Us* saw an explosion in ancillary merchandise—from Nerf guns and action figures to board games and plush toys.

As the mobile industry grew, so did the number of significant developer acquisitions. 2016 set new financial records with mobile revenues matching global box office sales. That year China invested $1.9 billion in game technology and research, along with more than $20 billion spent in mobile game company mergers and acquisitions (Minotti, 2017, para. 2). Major acquisitions included China's **Tencent** purchasing Finnish developer Supercell for $8.6 billion, followed by China's **Giant Interactive** buying Israeli developer Playtika for $4.4 billion. The following year, American social gaming giant **Zynga** purchased the card games studio from Turkey's Peak Games (*Toon Blast, Toy Blast*) for $100 million in 2017. Three years later Zynga acquired the entire company for $1.8 billion in 2020 and then purchased 80% of another Turkish developer, Rollic Games, for $168 million.

Key acquisitions continued in 2021 when **Electronic Arts** moved deeper into mobile territory with the purchase Glu Mobile for $2.4 billion in February. Then Chinese social media company **ByteDance** bought out *Mobile Legends* developer/publisher Moonton Games in March, followed by Swedish media giant **Modern Times Group (MTG)** acquiring India's PlaySimple Games in July for $360 million. Another Swedish company, **Embracer Group**, acquired a total of eight studios in 2021 for a total of $313 million, including Crazy Labs (Israel), Ghost Ship Games (Denmark), Easy Trigger (Sweden), Force Field (The Netherlands), DigixArt (France), Slipgate Ironworks (Denmark), 3D Realms (Denmark), and Grimfrost (Sweden). Zynga would go on to acquire Echtra Games, Chartboost, and StarLark in 2021 before **Take-Two Interactive** purchased Zynga for $12.7 billion in May 2022.

In addition to being the fastest-growing gaming platform, mobile gaming became the dominant video game market by revenue in 2021—nearly doubling its earnings in just 5 years after generating $46.1 billion in 2017. More than half of all video games' global market revenue came from mobile gaming in 2021 with $90.7 billion in earnings. By comparison, console gaming took in $49.2 billion and PC gaming earned $35.9 billion (Newzoo, 2021, p. 5). Newzoo projected the mobile gaming industry to exceed $92 billion in 2022 and $116 billion by the end of 2024. See Figure 14.18 for a look at the mobile gaming industry's growth from 2017 to 2021.

FIGURE 14.18   Five-year mobile gaming revenue growth chart.

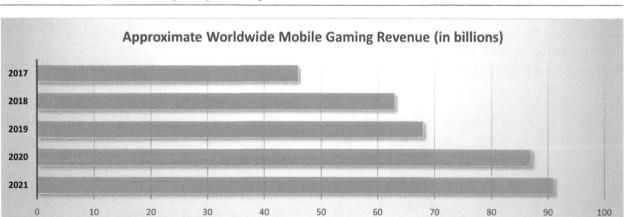

Approximate Worldwide Mobile Gaming Revenue (in billions)

■ ACTIVITY: MOBILE MULTIPLAYER

There are many ways gamers and game enthusiasts can get together and share a mobile gaming experience. Examples include social deduction titles such as *Among Us,* tower defense-shooters including *Fortnite Mobile,* and a wide variety of game types on *Roblox.* This activity will have a group of people play one of these games together and discuss the interactive experience.

GUIDELINES

A smartphone will be necessary for each person in the activity. Choose what game everyone would like to participate in and download the appropriate app. Note that most of these online platforms require a user account, so participants must be willing to create an account to proceed. Spend 30 minutes or so engaged in the mobile game, communicating only through mobile devices and not verbally in the room. Then take an additional 20–30 minutes to conduct a group SWOT analysis of the experience.

■ CHAPTER 14 QUIZ

1. Which of the following is not a common characteristic of a casual game?
   a. Easy to learn, with relatively few rules
   b. Simple gameplay (often requiring just one finger)
   c. Can be played in short bursts of time
   d. Targeted toward a narrow audience

2. Considered the first smartphone, with features such as an address book, appointment scheduler, calculator, calendar, notepad, and world time clock:
   a. Psion Organiser
   b. IBM Simon
   c. PalmPilot
   d. BlackBerry 850

3. Helped lead the mass adoption of the first smartphones in Japan with its subscription-based online gaming platform called i-mode in 1999:
   a. NTT DoCoMo
   b. KDDI
   c. Softbank
   d. Hagenuk Corporation

4. Aside from ports of *Tetris*, this game programmed by Finnish developer Taneli Armanto for the Nokia 6110 was one of the first mainstream mobile games:
   a. Bejeweled
   b. Sorcery
   c. Snake
   d. Void Raider

5. The original Nokia N-Gage featured a game card slot that was located:
   a. On the top of the device, near the speaker
   b. Inside of its pop-out video screen
   c. Inside its battery compartment
   d. None of the above

6. Which of the following was not true of the Tiger Telematics Gizmondo?
   a. Featured a slot for a SIM card
   b. Supported WAP, GPRS, and SMS/MMS
   c. Was a technically superior game machine to N-Gage
   d. Sold more than 50,000 units worldwide

7. Pioneered the smartphone revolution with its multimedia features and App Store:
   a. Apple iPhone
   b. Samsung Galaxy
   c. Windows Phone
   d. None of the above

8. The first mobile service provider used by Apple for the iPhone:
   a. AT&T (then Cingular Wireless)
   b. Sprint
   c. T-Mobile
   d. Verizon

9. A common monetization method used by modern mobile games:
   a. Pay once/non-freemium
   b. Free with ad support, a.k.a. Free-to-play (F2P)
   c. Freemium
   d. All of the above

10. The first generation of this device did not support Multimedia Messaging Service (MMS) for sending or receiving multimedia messages:
    a. Android
    b. Gizmondo
    c. iPhone
    d. None of the above

11. Popularized the tile-matching genre on mobile, often called "match three" games:
    a. Candy Crush Saga
    b. Clash of Clans
    c. Fruit Ninja
    d. Words with Friends

12. Which of the following titles is NOT an "endless runner" style of game?
    a. Alto's Adventure
    b. Jetpack Joyride
    c. Laura Croft GO
    d. Super Mario Run

13. By this year, high-end smartphones began to release with 2560 × 1440 "Quad HD" resolutions and there were more than double the number of Android users compared to iOS users:
    a. 2010
    b. 2012
    c. 2014
    d. None of the above

14. One of the biggest mobile releases of 2016, bringing augmented reality (AR) to mainstream audiences and its social element led to a phenomenon of players going for walks together and/or meeting other players in the physical world:
    a. Clash Royale
    b. Mini Metro
    c. Pokémon GO
    d. Super Mario Run

15. In 2017, Sony introduced a series of _____ titles (such as *Hidden Agenda* by Supermassive Games) allowing players to use iOS or Android devices as controllers.
    a. PlayLink
    b. PlayMobile
    c. Kickstarter
    d. RedTooth

16. Which of the following is NOT a current trend in mobile gaming?
    a. Convergence and cross-platform play
    b. More triple-A and "high-fidelity" games
    c. Mobile VR gaming
    d. Increased gaming social features

17. Which of the following is an example of mobile game social features?
    a. In-game chat and leaderboards
    b. Activity feeds and push notifications
    c. Social media integration and spectator modes
    d. All of the above

18. Flurry Analytics showed that smartphone and tablet gamers follow a similar gaming pattern of playing mobile games the most between the hours of:
    a. 12 pm and 3 pm
    b. 3 pm and 6 pm
    c. 6 pm and 9 pm
    d. 9 pm and midnight

19. As of 2022, Android commanded approximately _____ of the mobile OS market share across the globe.
    a. 40%
    b. 50%
    c. 70%
    d. 80%

20. This company purchased Zynga for $12.7 billion in May 2022:
    a. ByteDance
    b. Electronic Arts
    c. Take-Two Interactive
    d. Tencent

True or False

21. Early mobile games used the primitive Wireless Application Protocol (WAP) as the standard technology for connecting to the Internet.

22. The N-Gage Platform (also called "N-Gage 2.0") was a flip phone version of the original, dedicated N-Gage gaming phone.

23. In the mobile gaming world, "fragmentation" is the result of different platforms using different operating systems, which results in more work for developers to port games.

24. A common trend with early mobile games was to develop games first on Android and then port them over to iOS after the bugs were worked out.

25. Global mobile gaming market revenue reached $91.7 billion in 2021 and exceeded both console and PC gaming market revenue combined.

■ FIGURES

Figure 14.1 "Smart" devices: (a) IBM Simon, (b) PalmPilot with stylus, and (c) BlackBerry 850 pager. (Blackberry_850 1999年発売・初代モデル_2014-01-30_17-54.jpg, by Lutra98 railway [1], CC BY-SA 3.0. Available at https://commons.wikimedia.org/w/index.php?curid=30883500. Retrieved from https://commons.wikimedia.org/wiki/File:Blackberry_2014-01-30_17-54.jpg.)

Figure 14.2 Snapshot of *Snake* (1997). (Courtesy of Taneli Armanto/Nokia, 1997.)

Figure 14.3 Nokia N-Gage handheld game console and mobile phone featuring *Puyo Pop*. ("The Nokia N-Gage, a device that combined gaming, mobile phones and tacos. This mobile phone and handheld gaming hybrid came out in 2003 and was followed by the N-Gage QD a year later. It was not successful as a phone or a gaming platform." By Evan Amos—own work, public domain. Available at https://commons.wikimedia.org/w/index.php?curid=33692791. Retrieved from https://en.wikipedia.org/wiki/N-Gage_(device)#/media/File:Nokia-NGage-LL.jpg.) (Screenshot of *Puyo Pop* courtesy of Sega, 2003.)

Figure 14.4 Screenshots of N-Gage launch titles: (a) *Puyo Pop,* (b) *SonicN,* and (c) *Tomb Raider: Starring Laura Croft.* (*Puyo Pop,* courtesy of Sega, 2003; *SonicN,* courtesy of Sonic Team/Sega, 2003; and *Tomb Raider,* courtesy of Ideaworks3D/Nokia, 2003.) (Part of the *SonicN* image was used on the introductory page of this chapter.)

Figure 14.5 Screenshots from one of the banned Nokia commercials from 2003.

Figure 14.6 Print advertisement for the N-Gage QD in 2005. (Retrieved from *Maximum PC,* December 2005, p. 113.)

Figure 14.7 Five of the best N-Gage titles: (a) *Rayman 3,* (b) *Pathway to Glory,* (c) *The Sims Bustin' Out,* (d) *Glimmerati,* and (e) *Tom Clancy's Splinter Cell: Chaos Theory.* (*Rayman 3,* courtesy of Gameloft, 2003; *Pathway to Glory,* courtesy of RedLynx/Nokia, 2004; *The Sims Bustin' Out,* courtesy of Ideaworks3D/EA Games; *Glimmerati,* courtesy of Bugbear/Nokia, 2005; and *Tom Clancy's Splinter Cell: Chaos Theory,* courtesy of Gameloft/Nokia, 2005.)

Figure 14.8 Early mid-2000s mobile hits: (a) *Prince of Persia: The Sands of Time*, (b) *The Fast and the Furious*, and (c) *Tower Bloxx*. (*Prince of Persia: The Sands of Time*, courtesy of Gameloft, 2004; *The Fast and the Furious*, courtesy of Digital Bridges, 2004. "A Brief History of Mobile Games: 2005—Making a big splash" by Chris Wright December 31st, 2008. *The Fast and the Furious* (Digital Bridges). Retrieved from http://www.pocketgamer.biz/feature/10710/a-brief-history-of-mobile-games-2004-money-for-nothing/; and *Tower Bloxx*, courtesy of Sumea/Digital Chocolate, 2005. *Tower Bloxx* (Digital Chocolate). Retrieved from http://www.pocketgamer.biz/feature/10719/a-brief-history-of-mobile-games-2006-squaring-the-3d-circle/.)

Figure 14.1 Gizmondo (2005) featuring *Richard Burns Rally*. (Courtesy of Evan Amos—own work, public domain. Available at https://commons.wikimedia.org/w/index.php?curid=12391181. Retrieved from https://en.wikipedia.org/wiki/Gizmondo#/media/File:Gizmondo.jpg.) (Screenshot *Richard Burns Rally* courtesy of Warthog Games/Gizmondo Studios, 2005.)

Figure 14.10 Advertisement for the original Apple iPhone in 2007. ("Apple iPhone Turns 8: How Steve Jobs' smartphone changed the world in less than a decade" by Mike Brown June 29, 2015. International Business Times. Photo Credit: Apple.)

Figure 14.11 Screenshots of early iOS games: (a) *Rolando* (2008) and (b) *Angry Birds* (2009). (*Rolando*, courtesy of HandCircus/ngmoco, 2008; and *Angry Birds*, courtesy of Rovio Entertainment, 2009.) (Part of the *Angry Birds* image was used on the introductory page of this chapter.)

Figure 14.12 Screenshots of multiplatform hits: (a) *Fruit Ninja* and (b) *Plants vs. Zombies* (2010). (*Fruit Ninja*, courtesy of Halfbrick, 2010; and *Plants vs. Zombies*, courtesy of PopCap Games/Electronic Arts 2010.)

Figure 14.13 Screenshots of (a) *Clash of Clans* and (b) *Candy Crush Saga* (2012). (*Candy Crush Saga*, courtesy of King, 2012; and *Clash of Clans*, courtesy of Supercell, 2012.) (Part of these images were used on the introductory page of this chapter.)

Figure 14.14 Screenshots of mobile hits: (a) *Ridiculous Fishing: A Tale of Redemption* (2013), (b) *Monument Valley* (2014), and (c) *Prune* (2015). (*Ridiculous Fishing: A Tale of Redemption,* courtesy of Vlambeer, 2013; *Monument Valley,* courtesy of Ustwo Games, 2014; and *Prune,* courtesy of Joel McDonald, 2015.)

Figure 14.15 Screenshot of *Pokémon GO* (2016). (*Pokémon GO*, courtesy of Niantic/Nintendo, 2016.)

Figure 14.16 Screenshots of popular cross-play and social mobile games: (a) *Roblox* and (b) *Among Us*. (*Roblox,* courtesy of Roblox Corporation, 2008–2022; *Among Us,* courtesy of InnerSloth LLC, 2018–2022.)

Figure 14.17 Flurry Analytics mobile gaming usage trends. From "Mobile gaming sessions down 10 percent year-over-year, but revenue climbs." Posted June 21, 2017, by Sarah Perez. Retrieved from https://techcrunch.com/2017/06/21/mobile-gaming-sessions-down-10-percent-year-over-year-but-revenue-climbs/.

Figure 14.18 Five-year mobile gaming revenue growth chart. 2017 data from McDonald, E. (2017, April 20). The Global Games Market Will Reach $108.9 Billion in 2017 with Mobile Taking 42%. Retrieved from https://newzoo.com/insights/articles/the-global-games-market-will-reach-108-9-billion-in-2017-with-mobile-taking-42. Subsequent data from Editorial. Next-gen mobile games: The arrival of cross-platform and evolution of high-fidelity. *Newzoo 2021 Global Games Market Report*. Retrieved from https://armkeil.blob.core.windows.net/developer/Files/pdf/report/arm-next-gen-mobile-games.pdf.

PRO FILE: Steve Jobs. Photo credit: "Steve Jobs holding a MacBook Air (at MacWorld Conference & Expo 2008. Moscone Center, San Francisco, CA)" by Matthew Yohe. Own work (Original text: self-made), CC BY 3.0, https://commons.wikimedia.org/w/index.php?curid=6022486. Retrieved from https://en.wikipedia.org/wiki/Steve_Jobs#/media/File:Steve_Jobs.jpg.

■ REFERENCES

Ball, R. (2004, February 10). *Discreet hosts 3d mobile gaming competition*. Retrieved from https://www.animationmagazine.net/tv/discreet-hosts-3d-mobile-gaming-competition/.

Best, J. (2004, March 4). *Nokia ads are too "offensive and distressing."* Retrieved from http://www.zdnet.com/article/nokia-ads-are-too-offensive-and-distressing/.

Budmar, P. (2012, July 11). Why Japanese smartphones never went global: Despite being ahead of the technology curve, Japanese smart phones never saw a global release even in key markets such as the U.S. and Europe. *PC World*. Retrieved from https://www.pcworld.idg.com.au/article/430254/why_japanese_smartphones_never_went_global/.

Chen, B. (2009, June 29). iPhone, you phone, we all wanna iPhone. Wired Magazine. Retrieved from https://www.wired.com/2009/06/dayintech_0629/.

Connelly, C. (2014, August 16). World's first 'smartphone' celebrates 20 years. BBC News. Retrieved from http://www.bbc.com/news/technology-28802053.

Cowley, R. (2017, April 21). *2016's top five grossing mobile games in the US made up 28% of all revenues.* Retrieved from http://www.pocketgamer.biz/news/65580/sega-sensor-tower-mobile-market-report-2016/.

Dredge, S. (2013, August 15). *If Android is so popular, why are many apps still released for iOS first?* Retrieved from https://www.theguardian.com/technology/appsblog/2013/aug/15/android-v-ios-apps-apple-google.

Duncan, G. (2009, October 30). *Nokia to disengage N-Gage gaming in 2010.* Retrieved from https://www.digitaltrends.com/gaming/nokia-to-disengage-n-gage-gaming-in-2010/.

Editorial: 17th Annual Game Developers Choice Awards Finalists: Honoring the Best Games of 2016. (2016). *Game Developers Choice Awards.* Retrieved from http://www.gamechoiceawards.com/winners/.

Editorial: Apple App Store, iPhone 4, Angry Birds earn Guinness World Records. (2011, May 13). *Los Angeles Times.* Retrieved from http://latimesblogs.latimes.com/technology/2011/05/apple-app-store-iphone-4-angry-birds-tap-tap-revenge-plants-vs-zombies-earn-guin ness-world-records.html.

Editorial: Deconstructing mobile & tablet gaming 2016: EEDAR 2016 syndicated report - free version. (2016). *EEDAR.* Retrieved from http://www.eedar.com/sites/default/files/EEDAR%20-Mobile%20Report%202016%20-%20Whitepaper.pdf.

Editorial: GPRS. (2001). *Phone Scoop.* Retrieved from http://www.phonescoop.com/glossary/term.php?gid=106.

Editorial: Inside the N-Gage box: What comes with the N-Gage? (2003, October 24). *IGN.* Retrieved from http://www.ign.com/articles/2003/10/24/inside-the-n-gage-box.

Editorial: History of mobile gaming. (2011, April 7). *Phone Area.* Retrieved from https://www.phonearena.com/news/History-of-mobile-gaming_id17949.

Editorial: N-Gage (Platform). (2017). *Giant Bomb.* Retrieved from https://www.giantbomb.com/n-gage/3045-34/.

Editorial. Next-gen mobile games: The arrival of cross-platform and evolution of high-fidelity. (2021). *Newzoo 2021 global games market report.* Retrieved from https://armkeil.blob.core.windows.net/developer/Files/pdf/report/arm-next-gen-mobile-games.pdf.

Editorial: Nokia to invest about FIM 1 billion in mobile phone production in Bochum, Germany. (1998, December 21). *Nokia.* Retrieved from http://www.nokia.com/en_int/news/releases/1998/12/21/nokia-to-invest-about-fim-1-billion-in-mobile-phone-production-in-bochum-germany.

Editorial: Qualcomm's pdQ smartphone provides ideal platform for wireless business solutions. (1999, June 15). *Qualcomm press release.* https://www.qualcomm.com/news/releases/1999/06/15/qualcomm-s-pdq-smartphone-provides-ideal-platform-wireless-business.

Editorial: T-Mobile launches world's first nationwide standalone 5G network. (2020, August 4). *T-Mobile.* Retrieved from https://www.t-mobile.com/news/network/standalone-5g-launch.

Fahey, R. (2003, October 21). *N-Gage sells under 5,000 units at US launch.* Retrieved from http://www.gamesindustry.biz/articles/n-gage-sells-under-5000-units-at-us-launch.

Golson, J. (2012, January 26). *iPhone average selling price remains steady even with free 3GS offer.* Retrieved from https://www.macrumors.com/2012/01/26/iphone-average-selling-price-remains-steady-even-with-free-3gs-offer/.

Hachman, M. (2012, September 19). *The Motorola Razr through the years.* Retrieved from https://www.pcmag.com/feature/302824/the-motorola-razr-through-the-years.

Hahn, J. (2013, September 4). *#FactsOnly: The most interesting things you didn't know about Nokia.* Retrieved from http://www.complex.com/pop-culture/2013/09/most-interesting-things-about-nokia/.

Hardwick, T. (2022, April 22). *Android's vast global mobile market share shrinks while iOS continues to grow.* Retrieved from https://www.macrumors.com/2022/04/22/ios-grows-mobile-market-share/.

Harz, C. (2004, March 31). *Growing possibilities: Mobile gaming 2004.* Retrieved from http://www.awn.com/animationworld/growing-possibilities-mobile-gaming-2004.

Heiman, M. (2016, May 1). *How Android gets to 100% market share.* Retrieved from https://techcrunch.com/2016/05/01/how-android-gets-to-100-market-share/.

Hwong, C. (2016, July 28). *Chart of the week: Mobile gamer demographics.* Retrieved from http://www.vertoanalytics.com/chart-week-mobile-gamer-demographics/.

Keane, J. (2015, December 1). Before Mobile gaming exploded, there was the Nokia N-Gage. *Paste Magazine.* Retrieved from https://www.pastemagazine.com/articles/2015/12/before-the-mobile-gaming-explosion-there-was-the-n.html.

Kuchera, B. (2015, November 5). *I'm leaving Android for iOS, and I blame late games: Android gaming is all about waiting, and I'm fed up.* Retrieved from https://www.polygon.com/2015/11/5/9675740/apple-gaming-android-google-late-games.

Langshaw, M. (2011, April 10). *The history of mobile gaming: We chart the history of mobile phone gaming from pixelated snakes to angry birds.* Retrieved from http://www.digitalspy.com/gaming/news/a313439/feature-the-history-of-mobile-gaming/.

Microsoft Devices Team. (2013, January 16). *10 Things you didn't know about mobile gaming*. Retrieved from https://blogs.windows.com/devices/2013/01/16/10-things-you-didnt-know-about-mobile-gaming-2/.

Minotti, M. (2017, January 26). *2016 saw $30.3 billion in gaming mergers, acquisitions, and investments*. Retrieved from https://venturebeat.com/2017/01/26/2016-saw-30-3-billion-in-gaming-mergers-acquisitions-and-investments/.

Nofziger, H. (2018, August 7). *96% of heavily engaged US gamers play on mobile – EEDAR*. Retrieved from ttps://www.gamesindustry.biz/96-percent-of-heavily-engaged-us-gamers-play-on-mobile-eedar.

Purewal, S. (2011, February 23). Timeline: Cellphone games from snake to Angry Birds. *PC World*. Retrieved from https://www.pcworld.com/article/220374/Cellphone_Games_Through_the_Years.html#slide8.

Nouch, J. (2013, February 14). *Mobile games market grew 33 percent in 2012 to $9 billion*. Retrieved from http://www.pocketgamer.biz/news/48541/mobile-games-market-grew-33-percent-in-2012-to-9-billion/.

Perez, S. (2017, June 21). *Mobile gaming sessions down 10 percent year-over-year, but revenue climbs*. Retrieved from https://techcrunch.com/2017/06/21/mobile-gaming-ses sions-down-10-percent-year-over-year-but-revenue-climbs/.

Ritchie, R. (2017, June 29). *10 Years ago today, Apple and iPhone changed our world*. Retrieved from https://www.imore.com/history-iphone-original.

Savitz, E. (2012, January 5). The 10 most important events in mobile gaming in 2011. *Forbes*. Retrieved from https://www.forbes.com/sites/ciocentral/2012/01/05/the-10-most-important-events-in-mobile-gaming-in-2011/#2b6ffd5a7ab9.

Snow, B. (2007a, July 30). The 10 worst-selling handhelds of all time. *GamePro*. Retrieved from https://web.archive.org/web/20071012194600/http://gamepro.com/gamepro/domestic/games/features/125748.shtml.

Snow, B. (2007b, July 30). The 10 worst-selling handhelds of all time. *GamePro*. Retrieved from https://web.archive.org/web/20110607130452/http://www.gamepro.com/article/features/125749/the-10-worst-selling-handhelds-of-all-time/.

Steel Media Ltd. (2022). *The winners of 2018*. Retrieved from https://www.mobilegamesawards.com/winners-2018/.

Sullivan, R. (2006, October 1). Gizmondo's spectacular crackup. *Wired Magazine*. Retrieved from https://www.wired.com/2006/10/gizmondo/.

Swatman, R. (2016, August 10). *Pokémon Go catches five new world records*. http://www.guinnessworldrecords.com/news/2016/8/pokemon-go-catches-five-world-records-439327.

Takahashi, D. (2017, January 4). *Samsung confirms it sold 5 million Gear VR mobile headsets*. Retrieved from https://venturebeat.com/2017/01/04/samsung-confirms-it-sold-5-million-gear-vr-mobile-headsets/.

Takenaka, K. (2008, December 8). Nintendo chief: Man behind casual game boom. *Reuters*. Retrieved from http://www.reuters.com/article/us-nintendo-iwata/nintendo-chief-man-behind-casual-game-boom-idUSTRE4B73QI20081208.

Vining, S. (2014, February 4). *Infographic: Android pulls in twice as many users as Apple's iOS*. Retrieved from http://www.icrossing.com/uk/ideas/infographic-android-pulls-in-twice-as-many-users-as-apples-ios_11372.

Vogelstein, F. (2008, January 9). The untold story: How the iPhone blew up the wireless industry. *Wired Magazine*, 16(2). Retrieved from https://web.archive.org/web/20150213101032/http://archive.wired.com/gadgets/wireless/magazine/16-02/ff_iphone?currentPage=all.

Winburn, S. (2021, June 23). *What's driving high-fidelity mobile gaming?* Retrieved from https://www.arm.com/blogs/blueprint/high-fidelity-mobile-gaming#:~:text=We%20refer%20to%20mobile%20gamesMobile%20and%20Honor%20of%20Kings.

Wingfield, N. & Isaac, M. (2016, July 11). Pokémon Go brings augmented reality to a mass audience. *New York Times*. Retrieved from https://www.nytimes.com/2016/07/12/technology/pokemon-go-brings-augmented-reality-to-a-mass-audience.html?mcubz=0.

Wright, C. (2008, December 31). *A brief history of mobile games: 2005- making a big splash*. Retrieved from http://www.pocketgamer.biz/feature/10712/a-brief-history-of-mobile-games-2005-making-a-big-splash/.

Wright, C. (2009, January 1). *A brief history of mobile games: 2006- squaring the 3D circle*. Retrieved from http://www.pocketgamer.biz/feature/10719/a-brief-history-of-mobile-games-2006-squaring-the-3d-circle/.

Wright, C. (2016a, March 14). *A brief history of mobile games: In the beginning, there was Snake*. Retrieved from http://www.pocketgamer.biz/feature/10619/a-brief-history-of-mobile-games-in-the-beginning-there-was-snake/.

Wright, C. (2016b, March 15). *A brief history of mobile games: 2000- A brave new world*. Retrieved from http://www.pocketgamer.biz/feature/10626/a-brief-history-of-mobile-games-2000-a-brave-new-world/.

Wright, C. (2016c, March 17). *A brief history of mobile games: 2002- Wake up and smell the coffee*. Retrieved from http://www.pocketgamer.biz/feature/10705/a-brief-history-of-mobile-games-2002-wake-up-and-smell-the-coffee.

Modern Console Gaming

■ OBJECTIVES

After reading this chapter, you should be able to:

- Discuss the developments of the arcade and console industries.
- Review key people behind the video games and consoles.
- Identify graphics and capabilities of modern game consoles.
- Compare technological differences among game systems by Nintendo, Sony, and Microsoft.
- Discuss the strengths and features of the Nintendo 3DS and PlayStation Vita.
- List key video game titles and peripherals for each console.
- Describe important innovations introduced to gaming during this period.
- Account for fluctuations in market positions among leading manufacturers.
- Recognize the importance the recent technology had on the video game industry.
- Summarize recent sales figures, breakthroughs, and trends in gaming during this era.

DOI: 10.1201/9781003315759-15

■ KEY TERMS AND PEOPLE

343 Industries
4K
Amiibo
Attach rate
Augmented reality
Autostereoscopic
Bandai Namco
Bonaire GPU
Bungie
Capacitive touchpad
Casual games
Mark Cerny
Chat Headset
Chuck E. Cheese
Circle Pad Pro
Cloud gaming
Club Nintendo
Clubs (on XBL)
The Coalition
Compute unit (CU)
Cortana
Dashboard
Dave & Buster's
Day one patch
DeNA
DirectX
DLNA
Dolby Atmos
DRM
DTS:X

DualSense controller
DualShock 4
Dynamic Menu
E3
Elite controller
Espresso CPU
Reggie Fils-Aimé
FLOPS
Forward compatibility
Game cards
GameDVR
GameWorks
Genda, Inc.
Graphics Core Next
Impulse triggers
Intellectual property
Satoru Iwata
Jaguar CPU
Joy-Con
Tatsumi Kimishima
Kinect 2.0
Latte GPU
Carl Ledbetter
Mad Catz
MadLab
Don Mattrick
Medal games
Miiverse
Mojang
NetFront

New Xbox One
  Experience
NFC
Nintendo 3DS
Nintendo eShop
Nintendo Labo
Nintendo Network
Nintendo Switch
Nintendo World
Off-TV Play
OLED
OneGuide
OOE
Orbis
Picture-in picture
Play Anywhere
Play Mechanix
Playdead
PlayStation 4
PlayStation 5
PlayStation Camera
PlayStation Move
PlayStation Now
PlayStation Plus
PlayStation Vita
PlayStation VR
Raw Thrills
Ray tracing
Region-locked
Remedy Entertainment

Remote Play
Sega
Share Play
Smart Delivery
SpotPass
Stream processors
StreetPass
Tetsu Sumii
SuperData Research
Toy-Con
TV Control button
Twitch
Ultra HD Blu-ray
Videmption
Virtual Console
VR gaming
Wii U
Wii U GamePad
Wii U Pro Controller
Xbox App
Xbox Cloud Gaming
Xbox Game Pass
Xbox Live
Xbox One
Xbox Series X|S
Mike Ybarra
Shuhei Yoshida
Zynga

■ CONSOLE TIMELINE

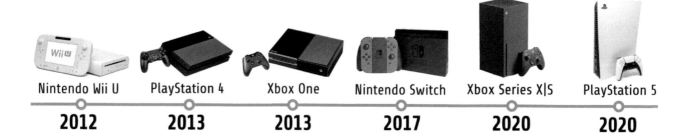

| Nintendo Wii U | PlayStation 4 | Xbox One | Nintendo Switch | Xbox Series X\|S | PlayStation 5 |
| 2012 | 2013 | 2013 | 2017 | 2020 | 2020 |

■ THE MODERN ARCADE

The Western arcade scene remained small but steady into the 2010s. **Raw Thrills** and **Play Mechanix** scored hits with arcade games such as *Big Buck Safari* (2008), *H2Overdrive* (2009), and *Terminator Salvation* (2010) (Figure 15.1a) among other movie-based titles. **Sega** continued to turn out machines on its "RingEdge" hardware and **Bandai Namco** saw the bulk of its earnings from arcade games such as *Deadstorm Pirates* (2010), *Tekken Tag Tournament 2* (2011), and *Dark Escape 4D* (2012). Subsequent arcade successes included *Mario Kart Arcade GP DX* (2013), *Star Wars: Battle Pod* (2014) (Figure 15.1b), and *Tekken 7* (2015).

Except for fighting games, the modern era of arcades implemented the business strategy of *not* porting arcade games to home consoles. Maintaining these games as exclusives in the arcades has given gamers a reason to return to them. Another trend that may have helped attract people back to the arcade scene was the rise of **casual games** made popular by online and mobile gaming. The style of these casual games was similar to the arcade hits of yesteryear, leading to retro game revivals such as the 108-inch *World's Largest Pac-Man* and *Galaga Assault* in 2016.

Most venues changed from coin slots to **card readers** and certain games began to combine video gaming with redemption (for tickets or points), creating hybrid machines known as video redemption or "**videmption**" games. Larger companies like **Dave & Buster's** grew from 80+ venues in North America in 2016, to 145 locations in 2022. Unlike other arcade restaurants or bar combos whose primary source of revenue is from food and drinks, dining and beverage income

for Dave & Buster's typically makes up around 46.8% of all revenues—with amusement and other revenues taking in 53.2% of its earnings. Upon further analysis, 78.3% of this "amusement and other revenues" is from redemption games, while only 18% of these earnings is from simulation and video games (Dave & Busters, 2016, p. 5). The arcade industry in the West was still viable but video games were no longer the primary source of revenue.

While the arcade market was always bigger in Japan, it was nowhere near as large as it used to be. "There were only 4,022 arcades across Japan in 2019, down from 26,573 in 1986" (Ashcroft, 2021, para. 2). Despite a lower number of game centers, the arcade market in Japan actually saw steady growth from 2015 to 2019—but not exactly from video games. Like in the West, games that offered points or prizes took in the highest earnings in Japanese arcades. "Prize games (which are 89.46% crane games) accounted for a whopping 55.3% of the arcade game market in 2019, with second place going to **medal games** [games that use tokens, like gambling] at 29%. Video games, trailing in third place, accounted for only 11.7% of the market in that year" (Johann, 2021, para. 4). Then came the pandemic.

The COVID-19 pandemic took a major toll on certain sectors of the arcade industry. **Chuck E. Cheese** owner CEC Entertainment filed for Chapter 11 bankruptcy on June 25, 2020. Among major Japanese closings including Shinjuku Playland Carnival and Adores Akihabara, the iconic Sega Akihabara Building 2 closed down on August 30, 2020, after a 17-year run. Sega Sammy would then sell off 85.1% of its stake in Sega Entertainment Co. to **Genda Inc.** that

FIGURE 15.1 Screenshots of arcade hits (a) *Terminator Salvation* and (b) *Star Wars: Battle Pod*.

(a)　　　　　　　　　　(b)

December. The following year, Sega announced the sale of its Western arcade branch, Sega Amusements International, on March 25, 2021. Then **GameWorks** reported the permanent closure of all its locations in late 2021. On January 28, 2022, Sega announced it would be selling its remaining shares to Genda—effectively ending its 56-year run in the arcades. Outside of arcades, console gaming was thriving.

🔆 DID YOU KNOW?

MadLab (Spain) took the Guinness World Record for "Largest Arcade Machine" on December 18, 2021. Its *Tetris* game measures 16 ft 1.15 in (4.90 m) tall and 6 ft 5.99 in (1.98 m) wide. Jason Camberis set the previous record in 2015 with his *Arcade Deluxe* that stood more than 14 feet tall and nearly 6.5 feet wide (Guinness World Records, 2015, p. 176).

■ MODERN CONSOLE GAMING

After a longer than usual life cycle for the seventh generation of video games, the modern gaming era began—like before—with the release of handheld systems by Nintendo and Sony. Due to greater competition by mobile devices, handheld sales were initially slow but eventually gained momentum. For home consoles, this era marked the first time that all major video game systems debuted in North America either before or simultaneous to their Japanese and European launches. As for tech specs, **FLOPS** (floating point operations per second) became the popular buzz word, dethroning polygon counts as indicators for processor speeds and console comparisons.

■ WII U

Codenamed "Project Café" and sometimes called "Wii HD" by journalists, Nintendo's **Wii U** (Figure 15.2) launched in the United States on November 18, 2012, at the **Nintendo World** store in Times Square. It was Nintendo's second console to debut in North America along with the original Wii and was the company's first high-definition system. Nintendo released the Wii U in PAL territories on November 30, followed by a Japanese launch on December 8. Two versions of the console were available. The $299 **Basic set** came bundled with a white controller and console with 8 GB of internal flash storage, along with a sensor bar, stylus, AC cables, and an HDMI cable. The $349 **Deluxe set** (Figure 15.3) (called "Premium" outside of the United States) featured a black controller and console, plus "32 GB of local storage, a Wii U controller charging cradle, Wii U console stand and a copy of *Nintendo Land*" (Burns, 2012, para. 4). Early press from sources such as *The Wall Street Journal* indicated that Nintendo aimed to attract both casual and hardcore gamers alike with its new system (Lejacq, 2012).

As for the name, Nintendo of America president **Reggie Fils-Aimé** announced, "It's a system we will all enjoy together but also one that's tailor-made for you … Is it unique, unifying, maybe even utopian? The answer is also yes to all of this" (Sutter and Gross, 2011, para. 8). Along with this perplexing description, naming it "Wii U" was somewhat of a paradox. It capitalized on the successful Wii brand but in doing so may have turned off hardcore gamers who were already disconnected from the original Wii. Its slogan

FIGURE 15.2 Nintendo's Wii U console with touchscreen-enabled Wii U GamePad.

FIGURE 15.3 Wii U print advertisement showing Deluxe set with black hardware (2012).

"How U will play next," was written as a question "How will U play next?" in PAL regions.

Early promotional videos showed gamers using the Wii U with the traditional Wiimote, leading many consumers to believe the Wii U was only an upgrade to the original Wii. This was further complicated by Nintendo's emphasis on its tablet-style **GamePad**, which was the focal point in most Wii U advertising. For consumers who understood the new concept, the Gamepad's 6.2-inch, 854×480 resolution touch screen was a unique innovation to gaming. Key features

included its ability to stream games and movies from the console without a TV (called **Off-TV Play**), easier web browsing, and serving as a second screen for asymmetrical, multiplayer gaming. Players could also use the GamePad as a secondary screen for maps, similar to the dual screens on the Nintendo DS.

Beyond the touchscreen and a camera, the GamePad featured motion controls and a familiar layout for the buttons and control sticks. New features included an **NFC (near-field communication)** reader/writer, which could interact with compatible cards and figurines, as well as a **TV Control** button, which allowed the GamePad to control most TVs and set-top boxes. On the downside, the GamePad only worked within about 15 feet of the console, reducing the portability potential that gamers had anticipated.

Nintendo built the Wii U to be fully backward compatible with all Wii software and accessories. And even without counting the five digital-only games, the system's 34 launch titles (Table 15.1) were the most ever for a home console. On the other hand, more than half of those games were on other consoles prior to or simultaneously with the Wii U's launch. While exclusives like *Nintendo Land* and *ZombiU* demonstrated the system's potential, other launch titles did not take full advantage of its unique features.

TABLE 15.1 Wii U U.S. Launch Titles

- *Assassin's Creed III*
- *Batman: Arkham City Armored Edition*
- *Ben 10: Omniverse*
- *Call of Duty: Black Ops II*
- *Chasing Aurora*[a]
- *Darksiders II*
- *Epic Mickey 2: The Power of Two*
- *ESPN Sports Connection*
- *FIFA Soccer 13*
- *Funky Barn*
- *Game Party Champions*
- *Just Dance 4*
- *Little Inferno*[a]
- *Madden NFL 13*
- *Mass Effect 3: Special Edition*
- *Mighty Switch Force! Hyper Drive Edition*[a]
- *Nano Assault Neo*[a]
- *NBA 2K13*
- *New Super Mario Bros. U* (Figure 15.4a)
- *Ninja Gaiden 3: Razor's Edge*
- *Nintendo Land* (Figure 15.4b)
- *Rabbids Land*
- *Scribblenauts Unlimited*
- *SING Party*
- *Skylanders: Giants*
- *Sonic & All-Stars Racing Transformed*
- *Tank! Tank! Tank!*
- *Tekken Tag Tournament 2: Wii U Edition*
- *Transformers Prime: The Game*
- *Trine 2: Director's Cut*[a]
- *Warriors Orochi 3 Hyper*
- *Wipeout 3*
- *Your Shape: Fitness Evolved 2013*
- *ZombiU*

[a] Digital-only.

More than 400,000 units were sold during the first week of the Wii U launch (Matthews, 2012). Like the original Wii, Nintendo's strategy with the Wii U focused on innovative gameplay rather than being a technological powerhouse. It was superior to preexisting hardware by Microsoft and Sony, but those companies would be releasing successors to the Xbox 360 and PS3 the following year. While its internal flash memory may have seemed small, Nintendo designed the Wii U with an SD card slot and four USB ports capable of expanding its capacity to 2 **terabytes (TB)**. For software, its slot-loading optical disc drive supported 25 GB proprietary Wii U discs, as well as original Wii discs.

> **DID YOU KNOW?**
>
> The Wii U was the first home console by Nintendo to be physically larger than its predecessor but used less energy than the Wii (at 37 kWh/year vs. Wii's 40 kWh/year).

Players could access the console's online features through the **Nintendo Network**, which did not charge players a monthly subscription fee. Key network apps included **Virtual Console** for downloading games; **Nintendo eShop** where players could utilize **Nintendo TVii** to search for programs on local TV, as well as video streaming services including Netflix and Amazon Video. There was also the social networking service **Miiverse**, where gamers could share content or use the GamePad's inner-facing camera to video chat with friends. The Nintendo Network also included access to the **Club Nintendo** loyalty program and an Internet browser, which was one of the best console web browsers of its time and extremely easy to use with the GamePad's tablet-style design.

The system featured backward compatibility with all original Wii accessories; however, the Wii U did not have as many original controllers and peripherals of its own. Aside from the GamePad, the **Wii U Pro Controller** was a more traditional game pad with a similar shape to the Xbox 360 controller. Other notable Wii U gamepads included the Nintendo GameCube *Super Smash Bros. Ultimate* edition controller and the *Tekken Tag Tournament 2* Arcade Fightstick by **Mad Catz**. Controller accessories included the Mad Catz Wii U GamePad Grip & Guard, NERF Armor for Wii

FIGURE 15.4 Screenshots of Wii U launch titles: (a) *New Super Mario Bros. U* and (b) *Nintendo Land*.

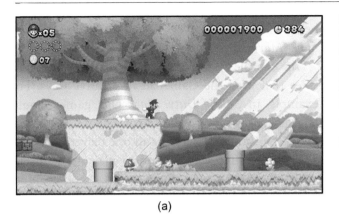

(a)

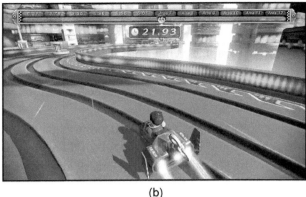

(b)

U GamePad, GameCube Controller Adapter, and Wii U GamePad Stand/Cradle Set.

Beyond controller-related peripherals, the Wii U had its share of headsets, battery packs, styluses, screen filter and protector sets, and **amiibo** figure carrying cases. Like Activision's *Skylanders* series, Nintendo developed its own series of figurines called "amiibo" to play with games such as *Super Smash Bros. for Wii U*. Once purchased, the player would scan the base of the figurine on the GamePad's NFC reader (marked with a rectangle below the D-Pad), register and name the amiibo—thus importing a virtual, playable version of that figurine into the game.

HEAD-TO-HEAD

In addition to the *Skylanders* games, there were many cross-platform titles released on the Wii U and its competitors. To compare the performance of the Wii U, Xbox 360, and PS3, check out each system's version of *Assassin's Creed IV, Batman: Arkham City, Call of Duty: Black Ops II, Darksiders II, Rayman Legends,* and *Watchdogs*.

■ **CONSOLE COMPARISON: WII U VS. XBOX 360 AND PS3**

The Wii U was the dominant machine compared to the PS3 and Xbox 360; however, these consoles were already 6 and 7 years old. Powering the Wii U was the coffee-themed IBM PowerPC Tri-Core "**Espresso**" CPU running at **1.24 GHz**, along with the **550 MHz** AMD Radeon "**Latte**" GPU capable of **320 shaders** (Table 15.2). While the CPU may seem slower compared to the 3.2 GHz processors found in the PS3 and Xbox 360, the Espresso was the first home console CPU to utilize **OOE (Out of Order Execution)** (Albert, 2013, para. 8). This process allowed it to carry out instructions in a nonlinear fashion (preloading data in the background), making it much more efficient than previous consoles. The CPU was also heavily supported by its Latte graphics processor, which carried the bulk of the load.

On paper, the Latte appeared to be barely superior to the 500 MHz ATI Xenos in the Xbox 360 and equal to the 550 MHz Nvidia-based SCEI RSX Reality Synthesizer in the PS3. However, with nearly double the amount of accessible RAM to work with, the Latte

TABLE 15.2 Wii U Tech Specs

Manufacturer:	Nintendo, Foxconn, & Mitsumi
Launch price:	$299.99 (8 GB) and $349.99 (32 GB Deluxe)
Release date:	11/18/12 (NA), 11/30/12 (EU), 12/08/12 (JP)
Format:	5× proprietary Wii U optical disc (25 GB) + Wii discs
Processors:	IBM PowerPC Tri-Core "Espresso" CPU (1.24 GHz) AMD Radeon "Latte" GPU (550 MHz with 320 shaders)
Performance:	Up to 1080p HD and 352 GFLOPS | GamePad = 3–5 hour battery
Memory:	2 GB DDR3 RAM + 8 or 32 GB internal flash storage
Sound:	5.1 Linear PCM surround or analog stereo via HDMI

could push approximately **352 GFLOPS**—compared to around 230 on PS3 and 240 on the Xbox 360. To look at it from another angle, the Wii U's GPU contained 320 shaders and **stream processors** (responsible for traditional graphics rendering tasks and general-purpose number crunching), giving it approximately 1.5 times the raw shader power compared to the Xbox 360 (Leadbetter, 2013, para. 5–6).

For software, the Wii U used proprietary optical discs that could store up to 25 GB of data—comparable to the Blu-ray discs of the PS3. Its faster optical drive could "read discs at a 22 MB/s compared to the 360's 15.85 MB/s (DVD) and the PS3's 9 MB/s (Blu-ray) speeds," which meant faster load times (Wong, 2012, para. 1). On the other hand, the Wii U lacked many of its competitor's standard features, including no trophy or achievement system, no optical audio output, and no DVD or Blu-ray support.

■ KEY WII U TITLES

The Wii U had hundreds of games available on its eShop but was severely lacking when it came to physical releases. By late 2016, Nintendo had released only 39 games in the United States, along with just 118 manufactured titles by third-party developers (Plunkett, 2016, para. 7). Among the first-party releases were the return of longtime franchises *Super Mario, Donkey Kong*, and *Zelda*—along with sequels to Wii games such as *Wii Fit*

U, Wii Party U, and *Wii Sports Club*. Mario remained the biggest star, with the console's best-selling titles being *Mario Kart 8, New Super Mario Bros. U*, and *Super Mario 3D World* (shown in Figure 15.5).

The console's more unique experiences came from titles that used the GamePad in creative ways. For example, in *Call of Duty: Black Ops*, gamers could engage in asymmetrical gameplay with one player using the GamePad screen and one player using the TV, which eliminated having to play the game in split-screen mode on a single screen. Another interesting feature of the GamePad was how players could use the tablet as a drawing pad in *Art Academy: SketchPad* or as a canvas for designing level layouts in *Super Mario Maker*. Similar to Sony's *LittleBigPlanet*, players could create their own levels in *Super Mario Maker* and then share them online with the rest of the world.

Lastly, the Wii U was home to a small library of exceptional then-exclusive titles including *Bayonetta 2, Super Smash Bros. for Wii U, Xenoblade Chronicles X, Pikmin 3, Donkey Kong Country: Tropic Freeze*, and *Splatoon*. It was the only home console at the time to feature downloadable/indie gems such as *Shantae: Risky's Revenge—Director's Cut, FAST Racing NEO, Runbow, Year Walk, Affordable Space Adventures*, and *Little Inferno*. The Wii U was also the exclusive console for *Shovel Knight* during the game's first 10 months on the market.

FIGURE 15.5 Box art to five Wii U hits including (a) *Super Mario 3D World*, (b) *Rayman Legends*, (c) *Super Smash Bros. for Wii U*, (d) *Bayonetta 2*, and (e) *Mario Kart 8*.

| (a) | (b) | (c) | (d) | (e) |

▪ HANDHELD SNAPSHOT: NINTENDO 3DS

Nintendo debuted the **3DS** (Figure 15.6) in Japan on February 26, 2011. It reached Europe on March 25 and North America on March 27 for $249. The new portable system retained the dual screen format of the original DS and had double-digit launch titles including *Nintendogs + Cats* and *Pilotwings Resort.* There were no Zelda or Mario games until *The Legend of Zelda: Ocarina of Time 3D* released in June and *Super Mario 3D Land* in November.

The 3DS was technically superior to the Nintendo DS (Table 15.3). Its key feature was an **autostereoscopic** upper screen that could display stereoscopic 3D effects without 3D glasses. Other new features included an analog circle pad or "C-Stick," **StreetPass** and **SpotPass** communication for Wi-Fi and data transfer, **augmented reality** (**AR**), plus apps such as Virtual Console, Nintendo eShop, YouTube, and Netflix. It was also backward compatible with DS video game cards. Like the DS, the 3DS included a lower touch screen that players could control with their fingers or a stylus.

Poor initial sales prompted Nintendo to drop the price to $169 in July 2011, in addition to offering 10 free NES and 10 free Game Boy Advance Virtual Console games. Sales picked up by the holidays with *Mario Kart 7* releasing in early December. A new **Circle Pad Pro** attachment added a second

FIGURE 15.6   Nintendo 3DS featuring *Super Mario 3D Land.*

C-stick, a substitute R button, and an extra set of triggers to the right side of the unit. It worked well for games such as *Resident Evil: Revelations,* which debuted as a 3DS exclusive. The system scored with franchise hits *Kid Icarus Uprising, Fire Emblem Awakening, The Legend of Zelda: A Link Between Worlds,* and a slew of *Pokémon* games. See Figure 15.7 for box art.

A **3DS XL** was released in July 2012 with a screen more than an inch larger than the original model. Nintendo introduced a non-folding **2DS** model in 2013, followed by the **New Nintendo 3DS** and **New Nintendo 3DS XL** in 2014. These were upgrades of the original 3DS and 3DS XL, with more powerful processors and twice the amount of memory. The newer handhelds also featured face tracking technology for improved 3D, plus a permanent right C-Stick and trigger buttons like those introduced on the Circle Pad Pro.

Nintendo went on to dominate the handheld market yet again with more than 75 million 3DS systems sold for an 80% handheld market share (VGChartz, 2022). While the 3DS sold less than half the number of units as the DS, it was vital to keeping Nintendo strong during the years the company struggled with the Wii U.

TABLE 15.3	Nintendo 3DS Tech Specs
Format:	Game Card (1–8 GB)/mAh lithium-ion battery (3–5 hours)
Processors:	Dual-Core ARM11 (268 MHz) + Single-Core ARM9 (134 MHz) Digital Media Professionals PICA200 GPU (268 MHz)
Performance:	16.77 million colors, 15.3 million PPS at 200 MHz, 4.8 GFLOPS
Memory:	128 MB FCRAM, 6 MB VRAM, and 1 GB internal flash memory
Resolution:	800×240 (3.53″ 3D LCD) and 320×240 (3.00″ touchscreen LCD)
Sound:	Stereo speakers (pseudo-surround)/3.5 mm mic/phones jacks

FIGURE 15.7   Five 3DS hits: (a) *Super Mario 3D Land,* (b) *Pokémon Sun,* (c) *The Legend of Zelda: A Link Between Worlds,* (d) *Fire Emblem: Awakening,* and (e) *Metroid: Samus Returns.*

(a) (b) (c) (d) (e)

■ PLAYSTATION 4

Codenamed **"Orbis"** after its operating system, the **PlayStation 4 (PS4)** (Figure 15.8) debuted on November 15, 2014, in North America for $399 and over the following weeks in other countries. For the launch party, "Sony's PR team rented out New York's Standard High Line Hotel, filling every room [including the showers] with PlayStation branded regalia. Around 500 gamers showed up to receive their preordered consoles and were given free food, T-shirts, and time with game demos while they waited" (Huffman, 2013, para. 3). The launch would earn Sony a new record for the fastest-selling game console with 1 million units sold in the United States in its first 24 hours, in addition to 250,000 systems sold within 48 hours in the United Kingdom (Guinness World Records, 2015, p. 178).

Bundled with the original console was a **DualShock 4** controller, power cable, HDMI cable (a first for Sony), micro-USB cable, savings voucher, and a small, mono earbud headset with a microphone and shirt clip. Fronted by lead architect and producer **Mark Cerny** (*Crash Bandicoot, Ratchet & Clank*), the technology in the PS4 was a refreshing change from the complex microarchitecture of PS3's Cell Processor. Behind its power was an AMD Accelerated Processing Unit (APU), which included an 8-Core **x86-64 "Jaguar"** CPU and Radeon **Graphics Core Next** GPU on a single chip. AMD's head of marketing John Taylor claimed the PS4's chip was the most powerful APU the company had built to date with its number of cores and teraflops (Moss, 2013, para. 3).

As for its initial games (Table 15.4), 10 of the console's 24 launch titles were digital-only, including *The Playroom*, which came preinstalled on every PS4 system to show off its optional **PlayStation Camera**

TABLE 15.4   Sony PlayStation 4 U.S. Launch Titles

- *Angry Birds Star Wars*
- *Assassin's Creed IV: Black Flag*
- *Battlefield 4*
- *Blacklight: Retribution*[a]
- *Call of Duty: Ghosts*
- *Contrast*[a]
- *DC Universe Online*[a]
- *FIFA 14* (Figure 15.9a)
- *Flower*[a]
- *Injustice: Gods Among Us Ultimate Ed.*
- *Just Dance 2014*
- *Killzone: Shadow Fall*
- *Knack*
- *Lego Marvel Super Heroes*
- *Madden NFL 25*
- *NBA 2K14*
- *Need for Speed: Rivals*
- *The Playroom*[a] (preinstalled)
- *Resogun*[a] (Figure 15.9b)
- *Skylanders: Swap Force*
- *Sound Shapes*[a]
- *Super Motherload*[a]
- *Trine 2: Complete Story*[a]
- *Warframe*[a]

[a] Digital-only.

FIGURE 15.8   Sony PlayStation 4 with DualShock 4 controller.

FIGURE 15.9 Screenshots from PlayStation 4 launch titles: (a) *FIFA 14* and (b) *Resogun*.

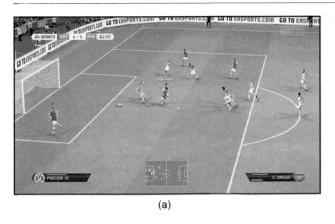

(a)

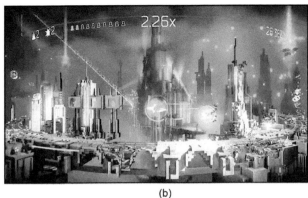

(b)

and DualShock 4 gamepad capabilities. The game included three augmented reality mini games, which projected the player onto the TV screen to interact with superimposed robots or engage in a game of virtual air hockey. *The Playroom* required the PlayStation Camera to interact with. Users without the accessory had the option to watch a 3-minute trailer demonstrating its features.

Sony added new features to the DualShock 4 controller with input from former *Halo* and *Destiny* developer **Bungie** (Rougeau, 2014, para. 7). The gamepad included a clickable, two-point **capacitive touchpad** for gameplay mechanics such as navigating the map on *Assassin's Creed IV: Black Flag* or calling "quick plays" in *NBA 2K14*. The top of the controller added a **light bar** (shown in Figure 15.10) with three LEDs to display assorted colors and provide the player with key information. For example, with four controllers active, player one's controller illuminated in blue, player two in red, player three in green, and player four in pink. Another creative use of the light bar was in *Grand Theft Auto V* where the controller would flash red and blue when the player was being pursued by police.

Other features included a 3.5 mm stereo headset jack (like the Xbox 360 controller's 2.5 mm jack), a mono speaker (like on the Wiimote), and a merged Start/Select button called "**Options**" to make room for the new "**Share**" **button** for players to upload screenshots and videos of their last 15 minutes of gameplay on social networking sites (Hsu, 2013, p. 2). The redesigned analog sticks featured convex dome caps and the L2 and R2 triggers (which were the only two buttons to retain pressure sensitivity) were curved inward like on Xbox controllers. Everything from the D-Pad,

to the spacing around the face buttons, to the curvature of the handles, was rethought and updated for the DualShock 4.

Tetsu Sumii designed the casing for the PS4. Sumii aimed to create "a simple object in the living room" that was "beautiful from all sides" (Codd, 2013, p. 2). Sony stayed with Blu-ray as its primary optical media, and while the PS4 could also play DVDs, it was not backward compatible with PS3 discs and could not play music CDs. As a first for home consoles, the PS4 required **mandatory installation** to the hard drive of all disc-based games, which could run 30–50 GB in size. This allowed the system to run games more efficiently with shorter load times, and gamers could play the initial stages of a game while the rest of the game downloaded in the background. The console could also be set up to download updates while in standby mode.

PS4's Orbis operating system was a modified version of the open-source FreeBSD 9, which was similar to Linux and included a **NetFront** browser. While similar in appearance to the PS3's XrossMediaBar, the PS4's **Dynamic Menu** was more visually oriented and much more intuitive. For example, when players inserted a game into the system, the menu placed the game's icon to the front of the list for easier access. Returning features included the PlayStation Store and **PlayStation Plus** subscription service (now required for online gaming). In 2014 Sony introduced a **cloud gaming** service called **PlayStation Now** where players could pay to download and play various PS3 games on PS4. Sony later integrated the service into its PlayStation Plus Premium subscription.

FIGURE 15.10   PS4 newspaper advertisement (2013) sponsoring the UEFA (soccer league).

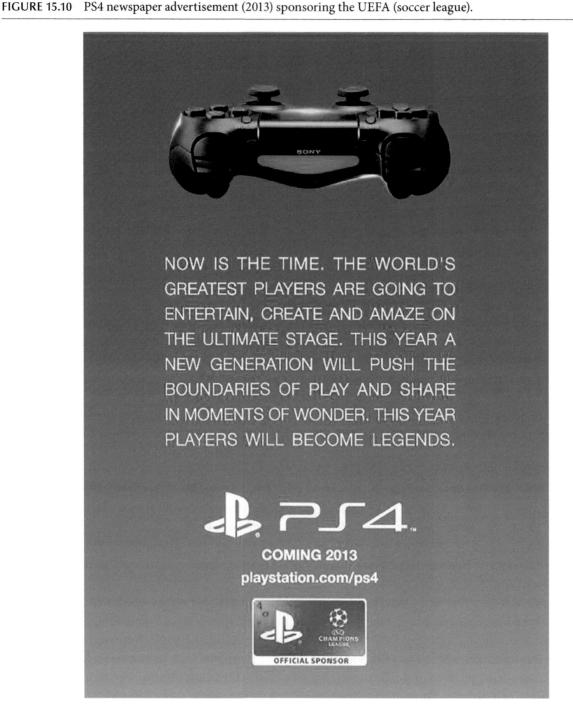

Social interaction and interconnectivity were also priorities for the system. In addition to allowing players to stream out gameplay online, its "**Share Play**" functionality allowed PlayStation Plus members to invite other members to play their games remotely or join them in multiplayer games for 60-minute sessions—whether the remote members owned a copy of the game or not (SIEE Ltd., 2017). While not a widely used feature on the PS3, Sony president **Shuhei Yoshida** mandated all PS4 games "to offer '**Remote Play**' on the PS Vita—that is, allow for PS4 games to be played on the Vita via a live video stream" (Rose, 2013, para. 2). This provided Vita owners with a feature similar to Off-TV Play on Wii U.

Beyond the typical peripherals such as alternative controllers, steering wheels, headsets, and charging docks—the two most innovative accessories for PlayStation 4 included the **PlayStation Camera** and **PlayStation VR**. The PlayStation Camera looked more like the Microsoft Kinect than a successor to the PlayStation Eye on PS3. The optional motion-sensing camera included two 1280×800-pixel lenses with an 85-degree field of view, which could precisely judge depth of space, sense the colors of the DualShock 4's light bar and **PlayStation Move** motion controllers, as well as allow users to log in to their PS4 using face recognition technology (Sony Computer Entertainment Inc., 2013, para. 7). The camera also included a four-channel microphone array that players could use for voice commands in certain games and hands-free navigation on the Dynamic Menu.

Formerly named "Project Morpheus" after *The Matrix* movie character, Sony joined the virtual reality movement with the PlayStation VR, which launched on October 13, 2016. For the introductory price of $399, the basic package included a VR Headset, Processor Unit, stereo headphones, and five required cables. The PlayStation VR could display 1,080p games at 960×1,080 per eye on its **OLED [organic light-emitting diode]** display. The unit ran "at either 90 Hz (meaning that the image refreshes itself 90 times per second) or at 120 Hz depending on the VR game or application" (Pino, 2017, p. 4).

It is important to note that the PlayStation Camera is necessary for the PS4 to play VR games—and while it is compatible with the DualShock 4, a pair of PlayStation Move controllers makes for a more immersive experience in games that support them. Recognizing this, Sony released a bundle with these accessories for $499, which was still the most affordable VR system of its time. Game development and early sales for the PlayStation VR were slow, taking approximately 6 months to reach 1 million sold. Sony would sell more than 5 million units by 2020 (Sony Interactive Entertainment, 2020).

Other major releases by Sony included the 40% smaller **PS4 Slim**, which debuted on September 15, 2016, and the larger **PlayStation 4 Pro** that launched worldwide on November 10 of that same year. The PS4 Slim retained most of the original system's features minus the optical audio output. Among other improvements, the PS4 Pro (codenamed "Neo") could output **4K** resolution (3840×2160p) on compatible displays and included a more powerful **911 MHz** GPU capable of **4.2 TFLOPS** (Porter, 2017).

▪ CONSOLE COMPARISON: PLAYSTATION 4 VS. WII U

As far as raw power went, there was little to discuss between the PlayStation 4 and Wii U with the PS4's 8-Core AMD x86-64 Jaguar CPU being leagues above the Wii U's Tri-Core Espresso chip. Sony's AMD GPU (codenamed "Pitcairn") was more than 30% faster at **800 MHz**, could process more than three times as many shaders, and could perform **1.84 TFLOPS** versus just 352 GFLOPS on the Wii U. See Table 15.5 for specs. While neither system could play audio CDs, only the PS4 doubled as a DVD and Blu-ray player. Sony's system also featured HDR10 high-dynamic-range

TABLE 15.5	PlayStation 4 Tech Specs
Manufacturer:	Sony Computer Entertainment & Foxconn
Launch price:	$399.99/£349.99
Release date:	11/15/13 (NA), 11/29/13 (JP), 11/22/14 (EU)
Format:	Blu-ray Disc (up to 50 GB) and DVD
Processors:	8-Core AMD x86-64 "Jaguar" CPU (1.6 GHz) AMD Radeon Graphics Core Next (800 MHz) with 1,152 shaders
Performance:	Up to 1080p and 1.84 TFLOPS
Memory:	8 GB GDDR5 + 256 MB DDR3 RAM and 500 GB hard drive
Sound:	7.1 Linear PCM and Bitstream (Dolby + DTS) with HDMI + Optical

color, four times the amount of RAM, larger internal storage with its **500 GB** hard drive, and more audio output options.

While it was not a technical powerhouse like the PlayStation 4, the Wii U provided free online play, backward compatibility with all Wii games, in addition to being more energy efficient. On the other hand, Wii U games were **region-locked**, meaning that NTSC consoles could not play PAL games and vice versa like the PS4. Another disadvantage was that the Wii U did not support cloud storage. Lastly, in what was basically a draw, Sony built the PS4 with a user-replaceable, non-proprietary SATA hard drive but did not support external USB storage like the Wii U.

HEAD-TO-HEAD

To compare the performance between PS4 and Wii U games, check out these titles released on both systems: *Assassin's Creed IV, Call of Duty: Ghosts, Child of Light, LEGO City Undercover, The Amazing Spider-Man 2,* and *Watchdogs.*

■ **KEY PLAYSTATION 4 TITLES**

Thanks to its support of indie and digital-only titles, well over 3,000 games were released for the PS4—including hundreds of exclusive games. Sony's consoles have always had an excellent number of elite titles and the PlayStation 4 was no exception. Among the best early retail releases were *Bloodborne* by *Dark*

Souls developer FromSoftware, *inFAMOUS: Second Son* by Sucker Punch, and Supermassive Games' *Until Dawn.* Console exclusives continued to roll out each year, such as Capcom's *Street Fighter V,* Insomniac's reboot of *Ratchet & Clank,* and SCE Japan Studio's long-awaited *The Last Guardian*—each released in 2016.

As if the system did not already encompass enough must-have Sony console exclusives, 2017 saw the releases of *Gravity Rush 2, Nioh, Horizon: Zero Dawn, Yakuza 0, NieR: Automata* (timed exclusive), and *Persona 5* (also on PS3). This was just a handful of a parade of titles introduced that year. See Figure 15.11 for five of the best PS4 games. Similar to what began as a customary practice on the PS3, the PS4 quickly became notorious for releasing updates of last-generation titles such as *God of War III Remastered,* Naughty Dog's *The Last of Us Remastered,* and *Uncharted: The Nathan Drake Collection.*

Naughty Dog released follow-ups to its Triple-A series with *Uncharted 4: A Thief's End, Uncharted: The Lost Legacy,* and *The Last of Us Part II.* Other key exclusive titles included *Marvel's Spider-Man, God of War* (reboot), *Shadow of the Colossus* (remake), *Ni No Kuni II: Revenant Kingdom,* Hideo Kojima's *Death Stranding, Final Fantasy VII Remake,* along with Quantic Dream's *Detroit: Become Human* and the beautiful *Ghost of Tsushima* by Sucker Punch Productions. Top PSVR titles included *Astro Bot Rescue Mission, Moss, Resident Evil 7, Until Dawn: Rush of Blood,* and *WipEout Omega Collection.*

FIGURE 15.11 Box art to five top PS4 titles: (a) *The Witcher 3: Wild Hunt,* (b) *God of War,* (c) *Uncharted 4: A Thief's End,* (d) *Persona 5 Royal,* and (e) *Horizon: Zero Dawn.*

(a)   (b)   (c)   (d)   (e)

KEY FACTS:

Lead architect and producer for PS4, PS5, and PlayStation Vita

Began career in video games at age 17 with Atari in 1982

MARK CERNY

PRO FILE

HISTORY:
• Born: August 24, 1964 in Alameda, CA

EDUCATION:
• Studied mathematics and physics at College Prep (1980)

CAREER HIGHLIGHTS:
• Programmer/Designer for *Millipede, Major Havoc, Marble Madness, California Games,* and more (1983-1991)
• Programmer/Designer for *Dick Tracy* (1990), *Kid Chameleon* (1991), and Producer for *Sonic the Hedgehog 2* (1992)
• Programmer and Designer for *Crash 'n Burn* (1993) and *Total Eclipse* (1994) on 3DO, and *Disruptor* (1996) on PS1
• Executive Producer and more for *Crash Bandicoot* series and *Spyro the Dragon* series on PS1 (1996-2000)
• Worked on *Jak series* and *Ratchet & Clank* series (2001-2007), *Resistance* series (2006-2008), *Uncharted: Drake's Fortune* (2007), *God of War III* (2010), *Killzone 3* (2011), *Knack* (2013), *The Last Guardian* (2016), *Knack 2* (2017), *Marvel's Spider-Man* (2018), *Death Stranding* (2019), and many more

RECOGNITION:
IGDA Lifetime Achievement Award (2004), AIAS Hall of Fame (2010), NAVGTR Honorary Award (2014), and others

■ HANDHELD SNAPSHOT: PLAYSTATION VITA

Codenamed "NGP" for Next Generation Portable, the **PlayStation Vita** (Figure 15.12) launched in Japan on December 17, 2011, and February 2012 in other regions. The standard Wi-Fi model cost $249 and an AT&T network 3G/Wi-Fi model was available for $299. More than two dozen titles were available at launch, including *BlazBlue: Continuum Shift Extend, Uncharted: Golden Abyss,* and *WipEout 2048.*

The Vita abandoned the Universal Media Discs (UMDs) from PSP in favor of **PS Vita Cards**, which were more similar to the game cards on Nintendo's handhelds. Players could also download titles from the PlayStation Network, including digital PSP titles. The original Vita model featured dual analog sticks, a 5-inch OLED touchscreen (Table 15.6), plus a **rear touchpad** for a whole new gaming experience.

The PS Vita was much more powerful than the Nintendo 3DS and its games looked similar to PS3 titles. The system's "LiveArea" graphical user interface (GUI) came pre-loaded with an Internet browser, email app, music player, photo app, video player, and a Content Manager app for sharing and managing data. Like the PSP, the handheld featured **Remote**

FIGURE 15.12 PlayStation Vita featuring *Gravity Rush*.

Play connectivity with PS3 and PS4, where players could link up wirelessly to view and play those consoles' games on the Vita—similar to the Wii U GamePad.

On the downside, the Vita did not include any internal storage and so users had to purchase a proprietary memory card to get the most out of the system. Sony released a thinner, **PCH-2000** model on October 10, 2013 (2014 in the West), with 1 GB of internal storage; however, the new model replaced the OLED touchscreen with a cheaper LCD screen.

Sony dropped the price of the Vita to $199 in 2013 and shifted its focus to the PS4. Fewer first-party titles released for the handheld, while an increase in third-party and indie games helped extend the lifespan of the system. Key indie games included *Guacamelee! Spelunky, Velocity 2X, Shovel Knight,* and *Axiom Verge.* Other titles such as *Lumines: Electronic Symphony, Killzone: Mercenary,* plus action RPGs *Soul Sacrifice* and *Freedom Wars* were Vita exclusives. See Figure 15.13 for five of the best games. With more than 1,300 titles available, Sony sold just over 15 million units of the Vita (VGChartz, 2022).

TABLE 15.6 PlayStation Vita Tech Specs

Format:	PS Vita Card/3.7 V 2210mAh lithium-ion battery (3–5 hours)
Processors:	Quad-core ARM Cortex-A9 and Power VR SGX543MP4+ GPU
Performance:	17 million colors, 444 MHz CPU, 166 MHz GPU, 6.4 GFLOPS
Memory:	512 MB system RAM and 128 MB VRAM
Resolution:	960 × 544 qHD/OLED touchscreen (5″ diagonal)
Sound:	Built-in stereo speakers and microphone/3.5 mm headphones jack

FIGURE 15.13 Box art to five top PlayStation Vita games: (a) *Gravity Rush*, (b) *LittleBigPlanet PS Vita*, (c) *WipEout 2048*, (d) *Tearaway*, and (e) *Zero Escape: Zero Time Dilemma*.

(a)   (b)   (c)   (d)   (e)

▪ XBOX ONE

Gamers and journalists often referred to Microsoft's next system as the "Xbox 720" prior to its release—however, its actual codename was "Durango" (Dutton, 2012, p. 1). Following its official title, **Xbox One** (Figure 15.14), the system underwent public scrutiny after the 2013 **E3 conference** where Microsoft's announcements left attendants unhappy. Among those announcements, the new console would require the (once optional) Kinect sensor to function and would need to connect to the Internet daily as part of a new **digital rights management** (**DRM**) system. The DRM scheme would bind each purchased game to the user's **Xbox Live** account, severely limiting the sharing or sale of preowned games—essentially eradicating the concept of renting physical titles (Bramwell, 2013, para. 5).

Microsoft quickly removed these restrictions after public backlash from its E3 announcements and shortly thereafter, president of Microsoft's Interactive Entertainment Business **Don Mattrick** announced he would be leaving Microsoft to become CEO of social game developer **Zynga**. Although no longer required, the Kinect remained bundled with the Xbox One at launch, resulting in a $499 price tag when the console debuted in North America and parts of Europe on November 22, 2013. The system would not reach Japan

TABLE 15.7 Xbox One U.S. Launch Titles

- *Angry Birds Star Wars*
- *Assassin's Creed IV: Black Flag*
- *Battlefield 4*
- *Call of Duty: Ghosts*
- *Crimson Dragon*
- *Dead Rising 3*
- *FIFA 14*
- *Fighter Within*
- *Forza Motorsport 5* (Figure 15.15a)
- *Just Dance 2014*
- *Killer Instinct* (Figure 15.15b)
- *Lego Marvel Super Heroes*
- *LocoCycle*
- *Madden NFL 25*
- *NBA 2K14*
- *NBA Live 14*
- *Need for Speed: Rivals*
- *Powerstar Golf*
- *Ryse: Son of Rome*
- *Skylanders: Swap Force*
- *Zoo Tycoon*
- *Zumba Fitness: World Party*

and other countries until September 2014. Despite the negative press, Microsoft saw its biggest Xbox launch, selling more than 1 million units during the console's first 24 hours on retail (Xbox Wire, 2013, p. 1). See Table 15.7 for launch titles.

The original bundle consisted of an Xbox One console with 500 GB hard drive, Kinect peripheral (shown

FIGURE 15.14 Xbox One console with original controller.

FIGURE 15.15   Screens of Xbox One launch titles: (a) *Forza Motorsport 5* and (b) *Killer Instinct*.

(a)   (b)

in Figure 15.16), wireless controller with two AA batteries, Xbox One **Chat Headset** with adapter, HDMI and power cables, and a free 14-day trial of Xbox Live Gold. **Carl Ledbetter** led the design of the new console, its **Kinect 2.0** accessory, and new controller. The system's bulky design (much larger than the original PS4) was stylized to complement existing home entertainment products. The casing featured a two-tone color scheme (referred to by Ledbetter as "liquid black") with each half measuring 16 × 9, consistent to the shape of a modern television screen. His team also implemented a large air vent to help the system run more quietly. Unlike the Xbox 360, the original Xbox One had to sit horizontally for optimal airflow and venting (Goldfarb, 2013, p. 1). On the plus side, Microsoft programmed the system to monitor its internal temperature and the console could increase the fan speed or cycle down its power usage to prevent overheating (Reisinger, 2013, para. 3).

FIGURE 15.16   Xbox One online ad featuring Kinect, console, and controller (2013).

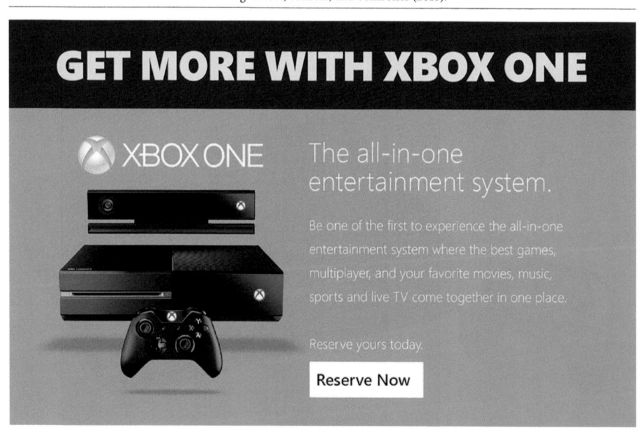

Ledbetter's team made more than 40 improvements to the controller, such as the micro-texture around the sides of the thumbsticks, refined D-Pad, finish of the buttons, and streamlined battery pack. They even gave the triggers the royal treatment, with each featuring separate rumble motors called "**impulse triggers**" that vibrate separately or together depending on the situation. The controller also had a micro-USB jack for connecting the gamepad to any PC running Windows 7 or later. In 2016, Microsoft added a 3.5 mm stereo headphones jack and later models featured Bluetooth connectivity.

Another unique and consistent feature on all three major devices includes "the 'white, magical' backlit Xbox logo on the console, [plus] Kinect and controller that knows to dim when the room is dark and shine brightly when it's not" (Warnick, 2014). Like Sony (and unknown to either company at the time), Microsoft chose AMD to design a custom APU based on its "Jaguar" architecture. Its eight-core CPU clocked at 1.75 GHz, complimented by an 853 MHz Radeon "**Bonaire**" GPU with 768 shaders, providing a peak theoretical power of 1.31 TFLOPS.

> ### ☀ DID YOU KNOW?
>
> For the Xbox One hardware, Carl Ledbetter and his industrial design team sketched and 3D-printed more than 75 iterations of the console, 100 versions of Kinect, and more than 200 models of the controller—which included more than 1,000 pairs of hands that went into assessing the different versions of the controller (Warnick, 2014).

The original Xbox One used **DirectX** 11.2 for its Application Programming Interface (API), along with three operating systems (including Windows) to run applications and games concurrently. This unique ability set the system apart from other consoles and is most apparent when using the system's split-screen multitasking functions with different applications. The console's "Snap" feature, which it borrowed from Windows 8, was similar to a more interactive version of **picture-in-picture** (**PiP**). Snap provided the player with multiple "panes," consisting of "1080p layers generated independently and displayed one on top of the other. These panes … allow a user to play full-fledged Xbox games while also seeing their fantasy football

app or Skype chat updating in an overlaid Windows pane" (Sakr, 2013, para. 3).

Microsoft's prelaunch slogan for the Xbox One was "All for one. Input one." Subsequent advertisements also emphasized the console's focus on being an all-in-one entertainment system that could be integrated with television programming, streaming, and social media applications. The console featured its own program guide called **OneGuide** and like the PlayStation Camera, players could use Kinect 2.0's improved motion tracking and voice recognition to navigate the system's **Dashboard** interface using hand gestures and voice commands. Also, like PS4, Xbox One featured a greater emphasis on cloud computing, live streaming, and sharing screenshots or video clips of gameplay with the **GameDVR** app.

Similar to PS4's Dynamic Menu, the original "Metro"-style UI for the Xbox One displayed recently used programs and games upon boot up. However, the interface was clearly made to utilize Kinect's voice commands, making navigation of the (often hidden) menus with the controller or motion gestures cumbersome (Rivington, 2017, p. 1). Microsoft completely overhauled the UI with an all-new user interface called the "**New Xbox One Experience**" as a system update on November 12, 2015. The updated, Windows 10-based firmware added a plethora of new features, including a new layout with more vertical navigation, a Snap overlay menu that players could quickly access by double clicking the Xbox button, and the "**Play Anywhere**" ability to stream Xbox One console games remotely to any PC or other device running Windows 10 (Veloria, 2015). The new UI also added backward compatibility with Xbox 360 games where users could insert an Xbox 360 disc into the Xbox One, which then authenticated the game and downloaded a digital copy to the system's hard drive.

Another new feature of the New Xbox One Experience was greater social integration with the new **Xbox App** (formerly Xbox One Smartglass). In its "**Clubs**" area, users could chat and play with other gamers in a public, private, or hidden (invitation-only) setting. While the new UI provided multiple improvements to the console, it also removed hand gesture control. According to Director of Program Management for Xbox **Mike Ybarra**, Microsoft removed the feature because hardly anyone used it (Graham, 2015, para. 5). In its place, the company added a new voice assistant named **Cortana** in 2016. Similar to Apple's Siri and Amazon's Alexa, Cortana added improved voice command functionality and better natural language recognition. Microsoft updated the Dashboard even further on March 29, 2017, featuring "a new Home screen, improved Guide menu, Beam streaming option, enhanced multitasking and deeper Cortana integration" (Hall, 2017, para. 1).

Among the many traditional accessories for the system, the most unique addition was the $150 **Elite controller** released in October 2015. The controller added "four interchangeable paddles around [the] back [to allow gamers to keep both thumbs on the thumbsticks at all times], Hair Trigger Locks for precise control in shooters, remappable buttons, and completely swappable components" (Welch, 2015, para. 1). In addition to releasing retail configurations of the Xbox One without the Kinect sensor, Microsoft debuted the **Xbox One Elite** (bundled with an Elite controller and a 1 TB solid-state hybrid drive) in November 2015 for $499.

The company followed the Elite with the 40% smaller, slightly faster **Xbox One S** model in August 2016, which like the PS4 Pro, supported 4K video resolution to bring the console up to par with the original PS4's HDR10 high-dynamic-range color. The Xbox One S added an internal power supply and the ability for users to position it vertically with a stand. The S model, however, required a USB adapter to attach the Kinect. Further enhancements to the S model included **Ultra HD Blu-ray** and **Bluetooth 4.0** support. Codenamed "Project Scorpio," a third major iteration released in late 2017 with the **Xbox One X**. This would be the most powerful Xbox One system, with even faster processors plus 50% more memory and bandwidth than the Xbox One S. Like Sony did with PlayStation Now (later PlayStation Plus Premium),

Microsoft offered an **Xbox Game Pass** subscription service on June 1, 2017, followed by its **Xbox Cloud Gaming** service (formerly Project xCloud) in 2020.

■ CONSOLE COMPARISON: XBOX ONE VS. PLAYSTATION 4

For those not interested in Kinect or the PlayStation Camera, the PS4 had the advantage at launch of being $100 cheaper and more powerful overall. Both systems contained an **x86-64 APU** by AMD with CPUs that were practically identical, other than Xbox One being clocked at **1.75 GHz** (Table 15.8) versus 1.6 GHz on the PS4. Both GPUs were based on Graphics Core Next (GCN) architecture with the Xbox One's **853 MHz** GPU clocking slightly higher than the 800 MHz GPU in the PS4. Otherwise, Xbox One's GPU contained just **12 compute units** (768 shaders) and a peak performance of **1.31 TFLOPS** versus the PS4's 18 compute units (1,152 shaders) and 1.84 TFLOPS of power—a 50% advantage.

That advantage extended even further with the PS4's 5,500 MHz GDDR5 RAM, which was twice as fast as the **2,133 MHz DDR3 RAM** found in Xbox One. "This leads to a massive bandwidth advantage in favor of the PS4. The PS4's CPU and GPU have 176 GB/s of bandwidth to system RAM, while the Xbox One has just **68.3 GB/s**. In Microsoft's favor, the Xbox One has **32 MB** of super-fast embedded SRAM (about 102 GB/sec in each direction, for a total of **204 GB/sec** of bandwidth)" (Lendino, 2015, para. 8). When used appropriately, this extra RAM could narrow the speed difference; however, cross-platform games typically ran at higher resolutions or fps on the PS4.

In other comparisons, both consoles could download updates while in standby mode and all games for each system required installation—a process that

---

TABLE 15.8 Xbox One Tech Specs

Manufacturer:	Flextronics & Foxconn
Launch price:	$499.99/£429.99
Release date:	11/22/13 (NA & EU), 09/04/14 (JP)
Format:	Blu-ray Disc (up to 50 GB), DVD, and Audio CDs
Processors:	8-Core AMD Custom Microsoft CPU (1.75 GHz) AMD Radeon "Bonaire" GPU (853 MHz) with 768 shaders
Performance:	Up to 1080p and 1.31 TFLOPS
Memory:	8 GB DDR3 + 32 MB eSRAM and 500 GB hard drive
Sound:	7.1 Linear PCM and Bitstream (Dolby + DTS) with HDMI + Optical

researchers have shown to take longer on Xbox One (Rivington, 2017, p. 2). Each console emphasized social media, sharing clips and screenshots, and users could connect both units to tablets and phones. While the PS4 could export the last 15 minutes of gameplay with its Share function, the Xbox One could only record the most recent 5 minutes of gameplay but could export the last 30 seconds of gameplay on the fly with the Kinect voice command, "Xbox, record that" (Grubb, 2013, para. 3–7).

Microsoft's 2015 firmware update provided notable benefits for the Xbox One, including a growing list of backward compatibility with Xbox 360 games. In comparison, Sony relied on its cloud gaming platform PlayStation Now (aka PlayStation Plus Premium) to provide playable PS3 games. This was more of a rental or subscription service because it required additional payment (Henderson, 2015, para. 14). Furthermore, the Xbox One's ability to stream games to Windows 10 devices was arguably more desirable than PS4's Remote Play integration with PlayStation Vita. Both systems charged for online gaming, with an annual subscription to Xbox Live Gold or PlayStation Plus costing $59.99.

HEAD-TO-HEAD

There were plenty of games that were released on both the Xbox One and PS4. Compare the gameplay and graphics to each system's version of *Battlefield 1, Grand Theft Auto V, Pro Evolution Soccer 2017, Resident Evil 7: Biohazard,* and *Titanfall 2.*

Both Xbox One and PS4 featured improved and more ergonomic controllers but only Sony's gamepad featured a touchpad, speaker, and motion controls. While an optional rechargeable battery pack was available, the Xbox One still required two AA batteries out of the box, compared to the built-in rechargeable lithium-ion battery pack in the PS4 controller. The PS4 controller was easier to charge with its mini-USB cable, which users could connect to while gaming, whereas the batteries tended to last around five times longer in the Xbox One controller.

In line with its greater emphasis on multitasking, the Xbox One was the only eighth-generation console that could play audio CDs. Both systems eventually supported MP3 format and **DLNA (Digital Living Network Alliance)**, which allowed users to stream media from a computer to their home console. While the original Xbox One lacked the Bluetooth and HDR10 high-dynamic-range color of the PS4, Microsoft added those features to the Xbox One S. With the growing trend of firmware updates and the release of more powerful iterations of existing systems (such as the Xbox One S, PS4 Pro, and Xbox One X), comparing consoles was becoming a constantly evolving process. Table 15.9 illustrates the key differences in performance among the different models of eighth-generation hardware introduced by Sony and Microsoft.

■ KEY XBOX ONE TITLES

More than 1,200 games released for the Xbox One, including dozens of exclusive titles. New Xbox-only titles included the hilariously fun *Sunset Overdrive*, puzzle platformer *Fru*, massive *Rare Replay* compilation, and **Remedy Entertainment**'s follow-up to *Alan Wake, Quantum Break* (also on PC). Returning first-party exclusives included *Gears of War 4* (now developed by Canadian studio **The Coalition**), new entries into the *Forza* series, and multiple *Halo* titles

TABLE 15.9 Xbox One and PS4 Console Versions Compared (Walton, 2017)

	PS4	Xbox One	Xbox One S	PS4 Pro	Xbox One X
CPU	8 cores @ 1.6 GHz	8 cores @ 1.75 GHz	8 cores @ 1.75 GHz	8 cores @ 2.1 GHz	8 cores @ 2.3 GHz
GPU	18 AMD GCN CUs @ 800 Mhz	12 GCN compute units @ 853 MHz	12 GCN compute units @914 MHz	36 AMD GCN CUs @ 911 Mhz	40 custom compute units @ 1172 MHz
Memory	8 GB GDDR5 and 256 MB DDR3	8 GB DDR3 and 32 MB ESRAM	8 GB DDR3 and 32 MB ESRAM	8 GB GDDR5 and 1 GB DDR3	12 GB GDDR5
Bandwidth	176 GB/s	68 and 204 GB/s	68 and 219 GB/s	218 GB/s	326 GB/s
Hard Drive	500 GB	1 TB/500 GB	1 TB/500 GB	1 TB	1 TB
Optical Drive	Blu-ray	Blu-ray	4K UHD and Blu-ray	Blu-ray	4 K UHD and Blu-ray

FIGURE 15.17 Box art to five Xbox One classics: (a) *Forza Horizon 4*, (b) *Red Dead Redemption 2*, (c) *Ori and the Blind Forest: Definitive Edition*, (d) *Metal Gear Solid V: The Phantom Pain*, and (e) *Rise of the Tomb Raider*.

| (a) | (b) | (c) | (d) | (e) |

including *Halo: Spartan Assault, Halo Wars 2*, and *Halo: The Master Chief Collection*.

Rise of the Tomb Raider (shown in Figure 15.17) was released exclusively for Microsoft systems and did not reach the PS4 for nearly a year later. Exclusives, however, were an issue for the system. *Halo: The Master Chief Collection*, which included remasters of *Halo 1–4*, was "plagued by match making issues since release, leading developers **343 Industries** to offer huge chunks of upcoming DLC (including the entirety of *Halo: ODST*) as free downloads to placate disgruntled owners"(Rivington, 2017, para. 17).

The game was so large that it occupied nearly all 45 GB of its Blu-ray disc and required a 20 GB **Day One Patch** to access its online multiplayer mode. Other highly anticipated exclusives were outright canceled by Microsoft, such as *Scalebound* and *Fable Legends*.

On the bright side, Microsoft acquired the rights to *Minecraft* after purchasing publisher/developer **Mojang** in late 2014. There were also countless cross-platform classics on Xbox One. Examples of other key titles from this generation included action-adventure games *Control* and *Batman: Arkham Knight*, RPGs *Dragon Quest XI: Echoes of an Elusive Age* and *Dragon Age: Inquisition*, zombie escapades *Dying Light* and *Resident Evil 2* (remake), and Rockstar's *Red Dead Redemption 2*. Among the most challenging games were *Dark Souls III* and *Sekiro: Shadows Die Twice*. Key indie titles included **Playdead**'s follow-up to *LIMBO* called *Inside* and the short but sweet *What Remains of Edith Finch*. For popular first-person shooters, there was *Apex Legends, Battlefield 1, Doom, Overwatch*, and *Call of Duty: Black Ops 4*.

■ NINTENDO SWITCH

After what would become the company's least successful hardware after the Virtual Boy, Nintendo parted ways with the Wii U to create an entirely new console. Codenamed "**NX**," the **Nintendo Switch** released worldwide on March 3, 2017, for $299. Two options were available at launch. One version came bundled with dark gray **Joy-Con** controllers and the other included red and blue Joy-Cons. Other than the controller color options, the packages were identical. Each console set included one Switch system, a left and right Joy-Con controller, two Joy-Con wrist straps, a Joy-Con grip, one dock to connect the unit to a television, an AC power adapter, HDMI cable, and paper manual. To keep costs down, the system did not include a pack-in title.

Nintendo built the Switch as a hybrid unit that would double as a portable handheld system and a home console when inserted into its docking station. The main unit is essentially a touchscreen tablet that accommodates two Joy-Con controllers that snap onto the sides of its 6.2-inch screen. This is the configuration to play the Switch in handheld mode. Users can also detach the Joy-Cons for multiplayer gaming. When detached, the screen can support itself on a small kickstand in what Nintendo refers to as "tabletop mode." Lastly, players can connect the unit to a TV by sliding the system into its dock—and assemble the Joy-Cons into a single controller configuration by attaching them to a "grip" accessory (as shown in Figure 15.18).

Nintendo struck gold by combining the best of handheld and console gaming into one affordable system.

FIGURE 15.18 Nintendo Switch in docked mode and Joy-Con controllers in grip configuration.

With flash storage coming down in cost, Nintendo was able to abandon optical media in favor of flash ROM cartridges (called "**game cards**") as its main form of physical media. Players can also download digital titles from the **Nintendo eShop**. The system only had 10 games available at launch (as seen in Table 15.10) but its unique functionality and *The Legend of Zelda: Breath of the Wild* was all it took for the Switch to fly off of store shelves. According to **SuperData Research**, the Switch sold over 1.5 million consoles in its first 2 weeks, along with the strong **attach rate** of an estimated 89% of Switch owners purchasing *The Legend of Zelda: Breath of the Wild* with the console (Dring, 2017, para. 1–4). The system outsold the Wii U (which had been on the market for 5 years) in just 10 months (Byford, 2018). Three years after its launch, the Switch would outsell the Xbox One, which had been on the market for more than 6 years.

TABLE 15.10 Nintendo Switch U.S. Launch Titles

- *1–2-Switch*
- *Fast RMX*[a] (Figure 15.19a)
- *I Am Setsuna*[a]
- *Just Dance 2017*
- *The Legend of Zelda: Breath of the Wild* (Figure 15.19b)
- *Shovel Knight: Specter of Torment*[a]
- *Shovel Knight: Treasure Trove*[a]
- *Skylanders: Imaginators*
- *Snipperclips*
- *Super Bomberman R*

[a] Digital-only.

The portability of the Switch was everything gamers wished the Wii U would have been and it was the company's experience with that console that led to its development. According to then-Nintendo of America President and COO **Reggie Fils-Aimé**, "Without Wii U, we would not have the Nintendo Switch, in terms of what we learned and, importantly, what we heard from our consumers. They told us, 'I want to play with this gamepad on the Wii U, but as soon as I get more than 30 feet away, it disconnects.' The core concept of taking it [anywhere], that was compelling" (Machkovech, 2018).

Marketing for the Switch console was simple. Television commercials showed all types of people using the system both docked and undocked. The brief Switch animation featuring the right Joy-Con snapping into place with a "click" sound was clean and simple. TV ads contained upbeat music and no complicated commentary whatsoever. Nintendo's ability to convey the console's features without a single word was appealing to the masses. Nintendo's use of the color red made the Switch logo and print advertisements stand out, as seen in Figure 15.20. To top it off, Fils-Aimé and Shigeru Miyamoto even appeared on *The Tonight Show Starring Jimmy Fallon* to debut the console to a national television audience on December 8, 2016.

Like its previous two consoles, the Switch focused on a new way of playing video games, rather than the raw power of Microsoft and Sony's systems. Unlike previous Nintendo consoles, the Switch was not

FIGURE 15.19 Screenshots of Switch launch titles: (a) *Fast RMX* and (b) *The Legend of Zelda: Breath of the Wild*.

(a)

(b)

region-locked, so gamers could play titles released in other countries without having to modify their systems in any way. This was one aspect where Nintendo made the Switch extremely user-friendly. The company was also able to keep costs down by adopting Nvidia's **Tegra X1** chipset, which manufacturers had commonly used in smartphones and other devices for years. This meant the Switch would already be compatible with existing game engines, making development for the console straightforward for programmers. The result was an increase in third-party development that was sorely lacking on the Wii U.

It also meant better battery life, with the original model (serial number starting with "XAW") lasting 2.5–6.5 hours and subsequent models lasting 4.5–9 hours (Nintendo of America, 2022). Users can charge the internal battery with a **USB-C** cable or by docking the system. For additional storage, the Switch can accommodate micro-SD cards as large as 2 TB. As for the size and weight of the unit, the Switch measures 6.81 in × 4.02 in × 0.55 in (173 mm × 102 mm × 13.9 mm) and weighs 10.5 oz (or 297 g). The 720p touchscreen features haptic feedback called "**HD Rumble**" from Immersion Corporation (Craddock, 2020, para. 2), as well as a 3.5 mm audio jack, stereo speakers, and a kickstand. See Table 15.11 for specs.

The Switch works with USB keyboards and amiibo figures. For peripherals, the system features an optional Joy-Con Wheel, Charging Grip, and AA Battery Pack. There is also a **Pro Controller**, GameCube controller, and a 4-port GameCube Controller Adapter available. One of the more interesting accessories for the system has been **Nintendo Labo**, introduced in April 2018.

Labo kits contain sheets of cardboard cut-outs and other materials that gamers can assemble around the Switch console and Joy-Con controllers. The combination of these stationary products with Switch hardware creates interactive peripherals the company refers to as "**Toy-Cons**." Examples of Toy-Cons include a cardboard fishing rod that uses both Joy-Cons, a piano stand which uses the Switch screen as its keyboard, a vehicle kit with three different cardboard steering wheels, and a VR kit where players can build a cardboard headset around the Switch console to view stereoscopic 3D images.

Nintendo released a handheld-only version of the Switch called **Switch Lite** on September 20, 2019, for $199. This model does not include detachable Joy-Cons, kickstand, or a dock since it cannot connect to a TV. The Switch Lite is compatible with all Switch titles and is an affordable alternative for gamers who just want to play handheld games. Two years later, on October 8, 2021, Nintendo released a higher-end version of the system with an **OLED** screen for $349. While not the souped-up "Switch Pro" gamers were anticipating, the OLED model features a clearer and larger 7-inch screen, twice the amount of on-board storage with 64 GB, enhanced speakers, and a better kickstand.

☼ DID YOU KNOW?

The Switch added a built-in controller finder with firmware update 3.0. Users can access the feature from the home screen by selecting the controller icon and then "Find Controllers" or "Search for Controllers" on later updates. This will display controller icons on the screen that when pressed, will make the controllers vibrate as long as they have battery life and are within Bluetooth range.

FIGURE 15.20 Nintendo Switch print ad showing local and portable play modes with blue and red Joy-Cons (2017).

TABLE 15.11 Nintendo Switch Tech Specs

Manufacturer:	Foxconn and Hosiden
Launch price:	$299.99 / £279.99
Release date:	3/03/17 (Worldwide)
Format:	Flash ROM cartridge/4,310 mAh Lithium-ion battery (2.5–9 hours)
Processors:	Nvidia Custom Tegra X1 with four ARM Cortex A57 CPU cores and four ARM Cortex A53 CPU cores (1.020 GHz) GM20B Maxwell CUDA GPU with 256 cores (307.2–768 MHz)
Performance:	Estimated more than 1 teraflop of (Takahashi, 2016, para. 11)
Memory:	4 GB LPDDR4 RAM/32 GB internal storage, expandable to 2 TB
Sound:	5.1 Linear PCM output/stereo speakers, with 3.5 mm jack

■ NO COMPARISON

Nintendo's decision to do their own thing and focus on affordable and innovative technology rather than expensive, powerful consoles dates back to the original Wii from 2006. By this point, it was clear that they were no longer in a hardware battle with Sony and Microsoft. Nintendo created the Switch to be a hybrid system that did not feature the same computing power as the PlayStation 4 or Xbox One. The Switch came with only 32 GB of internal storage (upgraded to 64 GB on the OLED model) versus the 500+ GB hard drives in Sony and Microsoft's offerings.

Its maximum resolution of **1920×1080p** in docked mode (1280×720p on its 6.2″ LCD screen) was comparable to the original PS4 and Xbox One but lower than the 4K-capable PS4 Pro and Xbox One S and X. For media, Nintendo chose **32 GB** flash ROM cartridges instead of 50 GB Blu-ray discs. As for audio, the Switch can output **5.1 channel surround** sound, while Sony and Microsoft's systems are capable of 7.1 surround. For Switch owners, the console's selling point has been more about its portability and unique library of games rather than hardware power.

■ KEY SWITCH TITLES

Nintendo had the killer app game at launch with *The Legend of Zelda: Breath of the Wild*. The company also had a clear strategy to developing the Switch library over the years. In addition to its must-have exclusives, Nintendo systematically ported its best Wii U titles to the Switch each year. At the end of 2017, the must-have exclusive was *Super Mario Odyssey* and the key Wii U port was *Mario Kart 8 Deluxe*. The year

2018 was a colossal year for Wii U ports, including *Bayonetta 2 + Bayonetta, Captain Toad: Treasure Tracker, Donkey Kong Country: Tropical Freeze, Hyrule Warriors: Definitive Edition, Shantae: Half-Genie Hero—Ultimate Edition*, and *Super Smash Bros. Ultimate*. Nintendo did not release many new titles that year aside from *Pokémon: Let's Go, Pikachu!* and *Let's Go, Eevee!*; however, developers supported the Switch with a parade of significant indie games such as *Undertale, Celeste, Inside, Bastion, Hollow Knight, Guacamelee! 2, Owlboy*, and *Iconoclasts*.

The following year saw the release of key Switch exclusives *Astral Chain, Fire Emblem: Three Houses, Luigi's Mansion 3, Super Mario Maker 2*, and a remake of the Game Boy classic *The Legend of Zelda: Link's Awakening*. To gamers' surprise, former PlayStation 3 exclusive *Ni no Kuni: Wrath of the White Witch* released for Switch in 2019, followed by the once-Xbox One console exclusive *Ori and the Will of the Wisps* in 2020. Other notable titles included *Animal Crossing: New Horizons* (a social simulator that became a bestseller during the pandemic), the isometric roguelike *Hades*, and *Metroid Dread*. The console saw new entries in the *Xenoblade Chronicles* series, as well as ports of *Xenoblade Chronicles: Definitive Edition* and *Super Mario 3D World + Bowser's Fury*. See Figure 15.21 for box art to five of the aforementioned titles.

■ NEXT GEN: XBOX SERIES X|S AND PLAYSTATION 5

When the Nintendo Switch first released, historians were undecided on whether to call it a ninth- or an eighth-generation machine. Due to its similar technology to PS4 and Xbox One, plus the extended

FIGURE 15.21 Box art to five key Switch titles: (a) *The Legend of Zelda: Breath of the Wild,* (b) *Super Mario Odyssey,* (c) *Animal Crossing: New Horizons,* (d) *Metroid Dread,* and (e) *Fire Emblem: Three Houses.*

   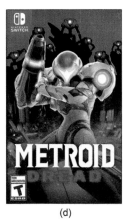 

(a)   (b)   (c)   (d)   (e)

lifecycle of those systems, the Switch would become the last major console of the eighth generation. Three years later, the purported "ninth generation" began with new systems by Microsoft and Sony who would release their consoles worldwide just 2 days apart. Microsoft debuted its **Xbox Series X|S** consoles on November 10, 2020, and Sony launched two versions of its **PlayStation 5** on November 12 (Figure 15.22).

Each publisher released two models of their systems: one with a **4K Ultra HD** Blu-ray reader and one without an optical drive. Sony Interactive Entertainment CEO **Jim Ryan** explained the disc-free options as a reflection of consumers moving more toward digital content over physical media (Makuch, 2020, para. 2). Microsoft and Sony deserve credit for providing consumers with these choices, as it will be the gamers who decide the future of physical gaming software.

One situation that will forever characterize the launch of these new systems was how they released in the midst of a global pandemic. Both Sony and Microsoft experienced ongoing supply issues and were unable to keep up with consumer demand for years. This led to inflated prices by **scalpers** who would buy and resell the system far above retail prices. On top of this, Microsoft discontinued production of all Xbox One systems by the end of 2020. Sony, meanwhile, announced they would continue producing PS4 [Slim] consoles through 2022 (Mochizuki & Wu, 2022, para. 1–2).

Sony's prolonged support for the PS4 went beyond its longer manufacturing lifecycle. Software titles the company had initially planned to be PlayStation 5 exclusives (like *Horizon: Forbidden West*) were released simultaneously on PS4. Aside from the controversial *Cyberpunk 2077* (which did not play well on older consoles), most cross-generation titles (like *Horizon Forbidden West*) looked and played exceptionally well on Sony's previous-generation system. Furthermore, Sony built the PS5 with backward compatibility for the vast amount of PS4 games.

Although Microsoft discontinued manufacturing the Xbox One two full years before Sony retired the PS4, the company continued to support the Xbox One in other ways. One such method was a new distribution framework called **Smart Delivery**. Games programmed with Smart Delivery are playable on both Xbox Series X|S and older Xbox One consoles. This feature pioneered **forward compatibility** with the Xbox One. Microsoft also designed the Xbox Series to be backward compatible with most Xbox One, Xbox 360, as well as original Xbox games. Xbox Series consoles can even upconvert older titles to a higher resolution and framerate. More than two-thirds of Xbox Series launch titles featured Smart Delivery (Table 15.12).

■ CONSOLE COMPARISON: XBOX SERIES X|S VS. PLAYSTATION 5

In previous generations, launch edition console options mainly came down to extra internal storage. This time consumers had a much greater decision to make between a higher-priced system with an optical drive, or a digital-only device at a lower cost. In this regard, consumers were not just choosing between Microsoft or Sony, but between a disc-based or disc-free console.

FIGURE 15.22 (Left) Xbox Series S and X; (Right) PlayStation 5 Standard and Digital Edition.

For the launch edition of the PlayStation 5, the only difference between models was the 4K Ultra HD Blu-ray drive. For the Xbox Series, Microsoft made noticeable differences between the Series X model and the 60% smaller S model. Aside from the lack of a disc drive, the S model features less processing power with less than half of the **compute units** (CUs) and only a third of the **teraFLOPS** (TFLOPS) of the X model. The S model also outputs at a lower resolution, has a third less RAM, and about half the internal storage of the Xbox Series X (Table 15.13).

Comparing the Xbox series X|S to the PlayStation 5 reveals surprising similarities between the consoles.

Each system features nearly identical core architecture with AMD Zen 2 CPUs and RDNA 2 GPUs. All consoles have solid-state drives (SSDs) and are capable of **ray tracing** (light rendering). Both optical disc units launched at $499 with 16 GB of GDDR6 RAM. All platforms are capable of 3D Audio with **Dolby Atmos**, **DTS:X**, as well as 7.1 surround sound. For other technical specifications, the PS5 finds itself in between the Series X and S for GPU speed with 10.28 TFLOPs and 36 CUs at 2.23GHz. Sony's 825 GB NVMe SSD is smaller than the 1 TB SSD in the Xbox Series X but runs at twice the speed. The PS5 also excels with its **DualSense controller** that features haptics, adaptive

TABLE 15.12 Xbox Series X|S and PlayStation 5 Launch Titles

Cross-Platform Launch Titles	Xbox Series X|S Launch Titles	PlayStation 5 Launch Titles
• *Assassin's Creed Valhalla*^	• *Bright Memory*	• *Astro's Playroom*
• *Borderlands 3*^	• *Enlisted**	• *Bugsnax**
• *Dead by Daylight*^	• *Evergate**	• *Concept Destruction*
• *Devil May Cry 5: Special Ed.*	• *The Falconeer*^	• *Demon's Souls*
• *DiRT 5*^	• *Forza Horizon 4*^	• *Godfall*
• *Fortnite*^	• *Gears 5*^	• *Goonya Fighter*
• *King Oddball*^	• *Gears Tactics*^	• *Marvel's Spider-Man: Miles Morales*
• *Maneater*^	• *Grounded*^	• *Marvel's Spider-Man Remastered*
• *NBA 2K21*^	• *Manifold Garden**^	• *The Pathless*
• *No Man's Sky*^	• *Ori and the Will of the Wisps*^	• *Sackboy: A Big Adventure*
• *Observer: System Redux*	• *Sea of Thieves*^	• *Undead Horde*
• *Overcooked! All You Can Eat*	• *Tetris Effect: Connected*^	• *Warsaw*
• *Planet Coaster*^	• *The Touryst**^	
• *Warhammer: Chaosbane*	• *Yakuza: Like a Dragon**^	
• *Watch Dogs: Legion*^	• *Yes, Your Grace*^	
• *WRC 9 FIA World Rally Championship*^		

* Timed exclusive (9th generation)
^ Smart Delivery supported

TABLE 15.13   Tech Specs for Xbox Series X|S and PlayStation 5

	Xbox Series X	Xbox Series S	PlayStation 5
Manufacturer:	Flextronics, Foxconn	Flextronics, Foxconn	Sony, Foxconn
Launch price:	$499 / £449	$299 / £249	$499 / £449 (Standard) $399 / £359 (Digital)
Release date:	11/10/20	11/10/20	11/12/20
Format:	UHD Blu-ray/Digital	Digital only	UHD Blu-ray/Digital or Digital only
Processors:	Custom 8-Core AMD Zen 2 (3.6–3.8 GHz) & Custom RDNA 2 GPU	Custom 8-Core AMD Zen 2 (3.4–3.6 GHz) & Custom RDNA 2 GPU	Custom 8-Core AMD Zen 2 (3.5 GHz) & Custom RDNA 2 GPU
Performance:	12 TFLOPS 52 CUs (1.825 GHz) Up to 120 fps; 4K up to 8K resolution	4 TFLOPS 20 CUs (1.565 GHz) Up to 120 fps; 1440p w/4K upscaling	10.3 TFLOPS 36 CUs (2.23 GHz) Up to 120 fps; 4K up to 8K resolution
Memory:	16 GB GDDR6 RAM 1 TB NVMe SSD	10 GB GDDR6 RAM 512 GB NVMe SSD	16 GB GDDR6 RAM 825 GB NVMe SSD
Sound:	Custom Project Acoustics 3D Audio Dolby Atmos & DTS:X 7.1 surround sound	Custom Project Acoustics 3D Audio Dolby Atmos & DTS:X 7.1 surround sound	Custom Tempest Engine 3D Audio Dolby Atmos & DTS:X 7.1 surround sound

triggers, and a built-in speaker. Other than PS4, the PS5 is the only current choice for **VR gaming** on a home console. In the end, the key comparison between these consoles will be the games.

💡 DID YOU KNOW?

Underneath all of their impressive features, there is no support for 3D discs, Super Audio CDs (SACDs), or DVD Audio discs on the Xbox Series X or PlayStation 5 consoles' 4K Blu-ray players (Archer, 2021).

▪ KEY XBOX SERIES X|S AND PLAYSTATION 5 TITLES

Many of the ninth-generation launch titles were already available on previous-generation systems. For the first 2 years, neither Xbox Series X|S nor PlayStation 5 would have a substantial number of exclusive titles that gamers could not play on an Xbox One or PlayStation 4. Examples of cross-generation Xbox console exclusives included *Forza Horizon 5, Forza Motorsport 8, Gears 5, Gears Tactics,* and *Halo Infinite.* Only a couple of titles were exclusive to the Xbox Series X|S (or PC), such as *Senua's Saga: Hellblade 2* and *State of Decay 3.* However, it is important to remember that the entire point of Microsoft's

Smart Delivery framework was to maintain cross-generational compatibility across the Xbox brand.

Key early PlayStation 5 games that also released on PS4 included *Gran Turismo 7, Horizon: Forbidden West, Kena: Bridge of Spirits,* and *Spider-Man: Miles Morales.* Sony would eventually release more titles that gamers could only play on the PlayStation 5. Examples of these exclusive PS5 titles included the *Demon's Souls* remake, *Destruction AllStars, Ratchet & Clank: Rift Apart, Returnal,* and *GhostWire: Tokyo* (also available on PC). Both Sony and Microsoft offer subscription gaming services where players can access a rotating catalog of games on PlayStation Plus and Xbox Game Pass.

▪ MARKET SUMMARY

The market saw key innovations that would define the modern era of video games. Console updates such as PS4 Pro and Xbox One S/X have extended the life cycles of those systems. Along with more digital games than ever being available for download, manufacturers are cutting costs of physical games by using game cases that use less plastic. In addition, most companies have discontinued including paper instruction manuals. China became a new market for video game systems when it lifted its 14-year-old console ban in 2014 and eliminated all sales restrictions in 2015.

After suffering one of its worst financial losses in 2014, Nintendo had to face the mobile landscape as a viable option for its beloved **intellectual properties (IPs)**. Following much hesitation by Nintendo president **Satoru Iwata**, Nintendo finally announced an alliance with Japanese mobile provider **DeNA** in March 2015 (Peckham, 2015, para. 3). The first titles to launch under the new partnership were *Miitomo* and *Super Mario Run* in 2016; however, a year before their release Iwata passed away from a bile duct growth on July 11, 2015 (Plunkett, 2015, para. 1). His successor was **Tatsumi Kimishima**.

As for the Wii U, one of Nintendo's biggest mistakes was with its marketing. "When the Wii U was originally announced, [Nintendo] put a lot of emphasis on the tablet controller, but near nothing was mentioned about the console itself" (Gittins, 2015, para. 4). It also did not help that the Wii U console looked just like a slightly larger, rounder Wii. Since the original Wii was known for its plethora of accessories, consumers viewed the Wii U Gamepad as another accessory for the original Wii and were not aware that the Wii U was a completely new console. Third-party support eventually died out and Nintendo struggled to release a substantial number of quality first-party games on a consistent basis. After just 4 years on the market, the Wii U became overshadowed by Nintendo's marketing of the Switch, and Nintendo officially discontinued the console on January 31, 2017 (Frank, 2017, para. 1).

Sony saw a major shift in its console development when the president of Sony's Worldwide Studios for SIE **Shuhei Yoshida** approved American software designer Mark Cerny as the lead architect for both the PlayStation Vita and PS4. Approaching the new hardware from a game developer's perspective was a way of correcting the difficulties the company faced with the PS3. The PS4 got off to a strong start before Sony even released it, thanks to Microsoft's blunders at E3 2013, which Sony was able to capitalize on. Sony received a standing ovation at their E3 conference after confirming "the PlayStation 4 would fully support used games, allow for easy lending and would have absolutely zero online requirements to play single player games" (Tassi, 2013, para. 7).

The PS4's $399 launch price was $100 less than an Xbox One and the system took off as the forerunner for the modern console generation. Just 2 years after its launch, Sony announced that the PlayStation 4

had sold more than 30.2 million units, making it the fastest-selling PlayStation console in that time period (Smith, 2015, para. 1). The console would maintain its lead in the years that followed, and by 2017 Sony had sold an estimated 53.4 million consoles (Sony Interactive Entertainment, 2017, p. 1). In 2022, Sony had sold more than 117 million PS4 units.

Microsoft recovered from E3 2013 by retracting features that led to its bad press, such as requiring the Kinect accessory, needing a daily online connection to play offline games, and restricting the usage of pre-owned games. The system's debut was the most successful launch for an Xbox console, although sales in Japan continued to remain poor. "The Xbox One sold a total of 23,562 units during its launch week in Japan [while] PlayStation 4, in comparison, opened to 309,000 sales, and Wii U to 308,000" (Romano, 2014, p. 1). Even the Xbox 360 fared better with 62,000 units sold in its first week when it debuted in Japan back in 2005.

Since around 2015, Microsoft stopped releasing sales figures for the Xbox One, although external sources such as SuperData Research, VGChartz, and other resources have helped paint a picture of how the console has sold over the years. A 2017 report from SuperData Research claimed that the Xbox One reached 26 million units sold and Microsoft stated that December 2016 was the company's "biggest month ever for Xbox One sales in the U.S.," which was "the top-selling console over the second half of 2016, following the announcement of Xbox One S at E3" (Makuch, 2017, para. 3).

Microsoft made a series of game developer acquisitions, purchasing Ninja Theory (*Enslaved, DmC: Devil May Cry, Hellblade*) in June 2018 and Obsidian Entertainment (*Star Wars: Knights of the Old Republic II, Neverwinter Nights 2*) in November of that year. The company then purchased Double Fine Productions (*Psychonauts, Brütal Legend, Broken Age*) in June 2019 and Bethesda Softworks-owned Zenimax Media (*The Elder Scrolls, Fallout*) and its subsidiaries between 2020 and 2021. Then on January 18, 2022, Microsoft announced it would be acquiring Activision Blizzard (*Call of Duty, Guitar Hero, World of Warcraft, StarCraft, Diablo*) for $68.7 billion in cash making Microsoft "the world's third-largest gaming company by revenue, behind Tencent and Sony" (Microsoft News Center, 2022, para. 2). In 2022, Microsoft had sold more than 50 million Xbox One units.

Until Nintendo released the Switch, Microsoft found itself in a solid second place—selling more than twice as many Xbox One systems compared to Wii U consoles, albeit only around half of the number of PS4s Sony was selling. Early sales of the Nintendo Switch were quite strong, exceeding the same number of total Wii U units sold in its first year alone. The Switch went on to surpass Microsoft's Xbox One in overall sales in just 3 years—and then outsold the PlayStation 4 at the end of 2022 as shown in Figure 15.23. For handhelds, Nintendo's 3DS line sold more than 75 million units—almost five times the number of PS Vitas, which sold approximately 15.5 million units.

The Switch even outsold the newer X|S and PS5 consoles into summer 2022 by a 2-to-1 ratio, reaching more than 109 million units sold. By this time, X|S lifetime sales had just exceeded 15 million units, while the PS5 had just surpassed 20 million units sold. Measured against the previous generation, "PS5 sales compared to the same week for the PS4 in 2015 [were] down by over 60,000 units, while the Xbox Series X|S compared to the same week for the Xbox One [were] up by nearly 58,000 units" (D'Angelo, 2022). Meanwhile, Sony acquired *Destiny* developer Bungie and German mobile game developer Savage Game Studios in 2022.

The company also reported development of a new PlayStation Studios Mobile Division, to "focus on creating games based on new and existing PlayStation IP. Sony says the new studio, which will operate independently from console game development, aims to reach new audiences and give gamers more ways to engage with its content" (Malik, 2022, para. 1).

Sony also announced the company would be raising the price of the PS5 in most countries due to global economic challenges such as high inflation rates. After 2 years on the console market, PS5 and X|S games only occupied about a quarter of retail shelf space compared to games for older hardware. With the mobile game market booming, chip shortages slowing production, and cross-generation gaming experiencing a longer lifespan than ever before, the video game industry had its hands full.

∎ MODERN GAMING BREAKTHROUGHS AND TRENDS

There were unique breakthroughs and trends that defined the modern era of video games. Here is a list of the top 10 features that defined the recent generations:

1. Console upgrades to extend the life cycle of existing game systems

2. 4K display resolutions (up to 3840×2160p via HDMI 2.0; and 8K via HDMI 2.1 on Xbox Series X|S and PS5)

3. Stronger GPUs (up to 4.2 TFLOPS on PS4 Pro and 6.0 on Xbox One X; to 4–12 TFLOPS on Xbox Series X|S and PS5)

4. Greater RAM (up to 8 GB on standard systems and 12 GB on Xbox One X; to 10–16 GB RAM on Xbox Series X|S and PS5)

5. Deeper integration with more apps and electronic devices

FIGURE 15.23 Modern generation console sales graph (as of January 2023).

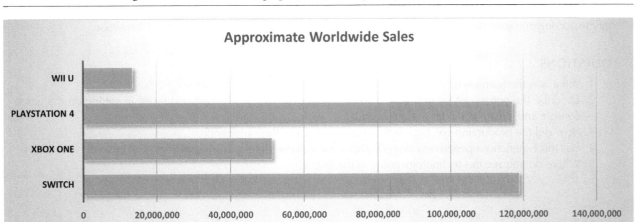

6. More intuitive, voice-controlled user interfaces

7. Emphasis on recording and sharing videos or pictures on social media

8. Augmented and virtual reality

9. Cloud-based gaming, subscription-based gaming, and disc-free consoles

10. Hybrid handheld/console gaming with Nintendo Switch

■ FINAL THOUGHTS

When the Wii U released in 2012, journalists deemed it the start of the next generation. The PlayStation 4 and Xbox One joined the market in the following year. These home consoles plus the Nintendo 3DS and PlayStation Vita handhelds became known as the "eighth generation" of video games. In addition to revised models of Sony and Nintendo's handheld units, Sony and Microsoft released upgraded, 4K versions of their home systems in 2016 with the PS4 Pro and Xbox One S and X. Nintendo followed up with the hybrid Switch console in 2017, at which point historians began to argue what generation it belonged in. Then came the handheld-only Switch Lite in 2019 and Switch OLED version in 2021. In the end, historians deemed the Nintendo Switch to be an eight-generation console and the ninth generation would begin in 2020 with brand new consoles by Microsoft and Sony.

With the strategy of updating existing consoles with more powerful versions, the lines between console generations are becoming less defined. There are even historians who believe the concept of a game console or "generation" may one day become obsolete. Since game consoles are essentially computers and vice versa, along with the way convergence continues to evolve, it may only be a matter of time until the platforms become one in the same. Regardless of how publishers label the technology or what their method of distribution, they will always be *video games* at heart. As the industry continues to grow, gamers can look forward to new and exciting experiences right around the corner. For this edition of *The Video Games Textbook:* Game Over!

Thanks for reading!

Dr. W

■ ACTIVITY: 15 MINUTES OF FAME

Twitch and YouTube Gaming have become major platforms for live streaming of gameplay including complete playthroughs of video game campaigns, multiplayer tournaments, eSports, and other webcasts. YouTube also allows live streaming and remains a popular platform for posting videos of game reviews, tutorials, and related videos.

GUIDELINES

Create an account with one of the major online video services listed above. Obtain a modern console and create your own live stream or 5- to 15-minute prerecorded video production of a video game review or other type of video using video game footage via the system's sharing capabilities. Use a microphone or headset to include a voiced commentary to accompany your video footage. You may use downloaded video game demos for this exercise.

QUESTIONS

1. What was the purpose of your video; what game did you select and why?
2. Describe the process of setting up an online account and any challenges you faced in setting up the game console and streaming and/or capturing video footage.
3. How did the production go? Explain the pros and cons of the experience.
4. Has this experience opened new doors for how you will use video game technology? Elaborate on your answer.
5. Where do you see this technology going in the future?

▪ CHAPTER 15 QUIZ

1. What is helping keep most arcade venues afloat today?
   a. The rise of casual games
   b. Video redemption or "videmption" games
   c. Food and beverage service
   d. All of the above

2. This company acquired all shares of Sega's arcade division:
   a. Genda, Inc.
   b. MadLab
   c. Play Mechanix
   d. Raw Thrills

3. Nintendo's Wii U was originally codenamed:
   a. Project Café
   b. Orbis
   c. Durango
   d. NX

4. Which of the following was *not* a key feature of the Nintendo Wii U GamePad?
   a. Asymmetrical, multiplayer gaming
   b. Ability to stream 3DS games
   c. Off-TV Play
   d. NFC (near-field communication) reader/ writer

5. This handheld system featured an autostereoscopic upper screen that could display stereoscopic 3D effects without 3D glasses:
   a. Nintendo 2DS
   b. Nintendo 3DS
   c. PlayStation Portable
   d. PlayStation Vita

6. This console's development was fronted by lead architect and producer Mark Cerny:
   a. Wii U
   b. PlayStation 4
   c. Xbox One
   d. Nintendo Switch

7. This gamepad includes a clickable, two-point capacitive touchpad and LED light bar:
   a. Wii U GamePad
   b. DualShock 4
   c. Xbox One controller
   d. Joy-Con

8. The PlayStation 4 function that allows PlayStation Plus members to share gameplay clips or invite other members to play their games remotely:
   a. Snap (PiP)
   b. Play Anywhere
   c. Remote Play
   d. Share Play

9. Which of the following was *not* one of the original plans for the Xbox One announced at the 2013 E3 conference?
   a. Kinect sensor required
   b. Daily Internet connection required
   c. Xbox Live account required
   d. Digital rights management (DRM) restricted preowned game usage

10. The design of the Xbox One console, Kinect 2.0, and Xbox One controller was led by:
    a. Don Mattrick
    b. Carl Ledbetter
    c. Mark Cerny
    d. Tetsu Sumii

11. Which was *not* a unique feature of the Xbox One console or controller?
    a. Snap (PiP)
    b. Separate rumble motors called "impulse triggers"
    c. OneGuide and GameDVR apps
    d. Options and Share buttons

12. The "New Xbox One Experience" user interface update added:
    a. a new layout with more vertical navigation and a Snap overlay menu
    b. backward compatibility with Xbox 360 games
    c. "Play Anywhere" to stream Xbox One games to other Windows 10 devices
    d. all of the above

13. Even though more than half of its early titles were released on other consoles, this system's 34 launch titles were the most ever for a home console:
    a. Wii U
    b. PlayStation 4
    c. Xbox One
    d. Nintendo Switch

14. The first home console with a CPU that utilized OOE (Out of Order Execution):
    a. Wii U
    b. PlayStation 4
    c. Xbox One
    d. Nintendo Switch

15. Like Activision's *Skylanders* series, _____ developed its own series of figurines called "amiibo" to play with certain games:
    a. Microsoft
    b. Nintendo
    c. Sega
    d. Sony

16. Similar to Apple's Siri and Amazon's Alexa, _____ on the Xbox One added improved voice command functionality and better natural language recognition:
    a. Beam
    b. Cortana
    c. Ybarra
    d. None of the above

17. The only console that did not contain a graphics processing unit (GPU) by AMD:
    a. Wii U
    b. PlayStation 4
    c. Xbox One
    d. Nintendo Switch

18. This handheld unit featured a *rear* touchpad and a front OLED touchscreen that was eventually replaced with a cheaper LCD screen:
    a. Nintendo 3DS
    b. Nintendo Switch
    c. PlayStation Vita
    d. WiiU GamePad

19. This console model featured less processing power and the lowest compute units and TFLOPS compared to other ninth-generation consoles by Sony and Microsoft:
    a. Xbox Series X
    b. Xbox Series S
    c. PlayStation 5
    d. PlayStation 5 Digital Edition

20. Went on a string of game developer acquisitions, purchasing Ninja Theory, Obsidian Entertainment, Double Fine Productions, and Bethesda Softworks-owned Zenimax Media:
    a. Nintendo
    b. Sony
    c. Microsoft
    d. None of the Above

True or False

21. Except for fighting games, the modern era of arcades implemented the business strategy of *not* porting arcade games to home consoles.

22. To run games more efficiently, the PS4 and Xbox One require mandatory installation to the hard drive of all disc-based games.

23. The PlayStation Camera is required for the PlayStation VR unit to play VR games.

24. The original Xbox One utilized a smaller air vent than the Xbox 360 to help the system run more quietly and to allow the console to sit both horizontally and vertically.

25. Historians consider the Nintendo Switch to be a ninth-generation console.

■ FIGURES

Figure 15.1 Screenshots of arcade hits (a) *Terminator Salvation* and (b) *Star Wars: Battle Pod.* (*Terminator Salvation,* courtesy of Raw Thrills, 2010; and *Star Wars: Battle Pod,* courtesy of Bandai Namco Games, 2014.)

Figure 15.2 Nintendo's Wii U console with touch-screen-enabled Wii U GamePad. ("Wii U Console and Gamepad transparent background" By Takimata (edited by: Tokyoship)— File: Wii U Console and Gamepad.jpg, CC BY-SA 3.0. Available at https://commons.wikimedia.

org/w/index.php?curid=23214469. Retrieved from https://en.wikipedia.org/wiki/Wii_U#/media/File:Wii_U_Console_and_Gamepad.png.) (Part of this image was used on the introductory page of this chapter.)

Figure 15.3 Wii U print advertisement showing Deluxe set with black hardware (2012). ("Wii U Releases in North America November 18th." Posted by Jason Nason, September 13, 2012. Retrieved from http://www.darkain-arts.com/gamers/wp-content/uploads/2012/09/wii_u_8gb.jpg.)

Figure 15.4 Screenshots of Wii U launch titles: (a) *New Super Mario Bros. U* and (b) *Nintendo Land.* (Courtesy of Nintendo, 2012.)

Figure 15.5 Box art to five Wii U hits including (a) *Super Mario 3D World,* (b) *Rayman Legends,* (c) *Super Smash Bros. for Wii U,* (d) *Bayonetta 2,* and (e) *Mario Kart 8.* (*Super Mario 3D World,* courtesy of Nintendo, 2013; *Rayman Legends,* courtesy of Ubisoft Montpellier/Ubisoft, 2013; *Super Smash Bros. for Wii U,* courtesy of Bandai Namco Games/Nintendo, 2014; *Bayonetta 2,* courtesy of Platinum Games/Nintendo, 2014; and *Mario Kart 8,* courtesy of Nintendo, 2014.)

Figure 15.6 Nintendo 3DS featuring *Super Mario 3D Land.* ("A Nintendo 3DS in Aqua Blue, photo taken during the 3DS launch event in NYC." By Evan Amos—own work, public domain. Available at https://commons.wikimedia.org/w/index.php?curid=14719223. Retrieved from https://en.wikipedia.org/wiki/Nintendo_3DS#/media/File:Nintendo-3DS-AquaOpen.png.) Screenshots of *Super Mario 3D Land,* courtesy of Nintendo, 2011.

Figure 15.7 Five 3DS hits: (a) *Super Mario 3D Land,* (b) *Pokémon Sun,* (c) *The Legend of Zelda: A Link Between Worlds,* (d) *Fire Emblem: Awakening,* and (e) *Metroid: Samus Returns.* (*Super Mario 3D Land,* courtesy of Nintendo, 2011; *Pokemon Sun,* courtesy of Game Freak/Nintendo, 2016; *The Legend of Zelda: A Link Between Worlds,* courtesy of Nintendo, 2013; *Fire Emblem: Awakening,* courtesy of Intelligent Systems/Nintendo, 2013; and *Metroid: Samus Returns,* courtesy of Mercury Steam/Nintendo, 2017.)

Figure 15.8 Sony PlayStation 4 with DualShock 4 controller. ("The PlayStation 4 (PS4) gaming console made by Sony: Released on 11-15-2013 in North America it is an eighth-generation system and competes with the Microsoft Xbox One and the Nintendo Wii U." By Evan Amos—Media: PS4-Console-wDS4.jpg. Public domain. Available at https://commons.wikimedia.org/w/index.php?curid=37808618. Retrieved from https://en.wikipedia.

org/wiki/PlayStation_4#/media/File:PS4-Console-wDS4.png.) (Part of this image was used on the introductory page of this chapter.)

Figure 15.9 Screenshots from PlayStation 4 launch titles: (a) *FIFA 14* and (b) *Resogun.* (*FIFA 14,* courtesy of EA Canada/EA Sports, 2013; and *Resogun,* courtesy of XDEV & Housemarque/SCEA, 2013.)

Figure 15.10 PS4 newspaper advertisement (2013) sponsoring the UEFA (soccer league). ("PS4 headed to Europe this year, according to an advertisement." By Dave Tach, May 24, 2013. Retrieved from http://www.polygon.com/2013/5/24/4362514/ps4-release-date-europe-2013.)

Figure 15.11 Box art to five top PS4 titles: (a) *The Witcher 3: Wild Hunt,* (b) *God of War,* (c) *Uncharted 4: A Thief's End,* (d) *Persona 5 Royal,* and (e) *Horizon: Zero Dawn.* (*The Witcher 3: Wild Hunt,* courtesy of CD Projekt Red Studio/Warner Bros. Interactive Entertainment, 2015; *God of War,* courtesy of SCE Santa Monica/Sony Interactive Entertainment, 2018; *Uncharted 4: A Thief's End,* courtesy of Naughty Dog/SCEA, 2016; *Persona 5 Royal,* courtesy of Atlus, 2020; and *Horizon: Zero Dawn,* courtesy of Guerrilla/Sony Interactive Entertainment, 2017.)

Figure 15.12 PlayStation Vita featuring *Gravity Rush.* ("The PlayStation Vita, a handheld gaming console by Sony released in 2012. The successor to the PlayStation Portable (PSP), the Vita has numerous improvements over the previous system." By Evan Amos—own work. Public domain. Available at https://commons.wikimedia.org/w/index.php?curid=45662069. Retrieved from https://en.wikipedia.org/wiki/PlayStation_Vita#/media/File:PlayStation-Vita-1101-FL.png.) Screenshot of *Gravity Rush* courtesy of SCE Japan Studio/SCEA, 2012.

Figure 15.13 Box art to five top PlayStation Vita games: (a) *Gravity Rush,* (b) *LittleBigPlanet PS Vita,* (c) *WipEout 2048,* (d) *Tearaway,* and (e) *Zero Escape: Zero Time Dilemma.* (*Gravity Rush,* courtesy of SCE Japan Studio/SCEA, 2012; *LittleBigPlanet PS Vita,* courtesy of Tarsier Studios & Double Eleven/SCEA, 2012; *WipEout 2048,* courtesy of Studio Liverpool/SCEA, 2012; *Tearaway,* courtesy of Media Molecule/SCEA, 2013; and *Zero Escape: Zero Time Dilemma,* courtesy of Chime/Aksys Games, 2016.)

Figure 15.14 Xbox One console with original controller. ("The Xbox One console, shown with the controller and the Kinect: Released in 2013 in North America and select markets, it is the third video game console made by Microsoft and succeeds the Xbox 360." By Evan Amos—own work. Public domain. Available at https://commons.wikimedia.

org/w/index.php?curid=31257131. Retrieved from https://en.wikipedia.org/wiki/File:Microsoft-Xbox-One-Console-Set-wKinect.jpg.) (Part of this image was used on the introductory page of this chapter.)

Figure 15.15 Screens of Xbox One launch titles: (a) *Forza Motorsport 5* and (b) *Killer Instinct*. (*Forza Motorsport 5,* courtesy of Turn 10/Microsoft Game Studios, 2013; and *Killer Instinct,* courtesy of Double Helix Games/Microsoft Game Studios, 2013.)

Figure 15.16 Xbox One online ad featuring Kinect, console, and controller (2013). ("New Xbox One Ad Shouts: '1080p/60, Adaptive A.I and Exclusive DLCs And More'" By Alex Smith, October 3, 2013. Retrieved from http://www.gamepur.com/news/12288-new-xbox-one-ad-shouts-1080p60-adaptive-ai-and-exclusive-dlcs-and-more.html.)

Figure 15.17 Box art to five Xbox One classics: (a) *Forza Horizon 4,* (b) *Red Dead Redemption 2,* (c) *Ori and the Blind Forest: Definitive Edition,* (d) *Metal Gear Solid V: The Phantom Pain*, and (e) *Rise of the Tomb Raider*. (*Forza Horizon 4,* courtesy of Playground Games/Microsoft Game Studios, 2018; *Red Dead Redemption 2,* courtesy of Rockstar Games, 2018; *Ori and the Blind Forest: Definitive Edition,* courtesy of Moon Studios/Microsoft Game Studios, 2016; *Metal Gear Solid V: The Phantom Pain,* courtesy of Kojima Productions/Publisher: Konami, 2015; and *Rise of the Tomb Raider,* courtesy of Crystal Dynamics/Square Enix, 2015.)

Figure 15.18 Nintendo Switch in docked mode and Joy-Con controllers in grip configuration. ("A Nintendo Switch video game console shown in docked mode and Joy-Con controllers in grip configuration." By Owen1962—own work. Public domain. Available at https://commons.wikimedia.org/w/index.php?curid=56950688. Retrieved from https://en.wikipedia.org/wiki/File:Nintendo_Switch_Console.png.) (Part of this image was used on the introductory page of this chapter.)

Figure 15.19 Screenshots of Switch launch titles: (a) *Fast RMX* and (b) *The Legend of Zelda: Breath of the Wild.* (*Fast RMX,* courtesy of Shin'en Multimedia, 2017; *The Legend of Zelda: Breath of the Wild,* courtesy of Nintendo. 2017.)

Figure 15.20 Nintendo Switch print advertisement showing local and portable play modes with blue and red Joy-Cons (2017). (From *Game Informer*, Issue 288, April 2017, page 25.)

Figure 15.21 Box art to five key Switch titles: (a) *The Legend of Zelda: Breath of the Wild,* (b) *Super Mario Odyssey,* (c) *Animal Crossing: New Horizons,* (d) *Metroid Dread,* and (e) *Fire Emblem: Three Houses.* (*The Legend of Zelda: Breath of the Wild,* courtesy of Nintendo. 2017; *Super Mario Odyssey,* courtesy of Nintendo, 2017; *Animal Crossing: New Horizons,* courtesy of Nintendo, 2020; *Metroid Dread,* courtesy of Mercury Steam/Nintendo, 2021; and *Fire Emblem: Three Houses,* courtesy of Intelligent Systems/Koei Tecmo (Kou Shibusawa)/Nintendo, 2019.)

Figure 15.22 (Left) Xbox Series S and X; (Right) PlayStation 5 Standard and Digital Edition. (Left) Xbox Series S and X image courtesy of Microsoft [Xbox[7] @Xbox]. (2020, September 17). Pre-order the Xbox Series X and Xbox Series S starting on September 22. [Tweet]. Twitter. https://twitter.com/xbox/status/1306716263796731905. Retrieved from https://twitter.com/Xbox/status/1306716263796731905/photo/1. (right) PlayStation 5 Standard and Digital Edition courtesy of Sony [PlayStation 5 News @PS5Console]. (2020, November 12). #PlayStation5 is now available in North America, Japan, Mexico, Australia, New Zealand, and South Korea. [Tweet]. Twitter. https://twitter.com/ps5console/status/1326796874754322432. Retrieved from https://twitter.com/PS5Console/status/1326796874754322432/photo/1; and Standing Sony PlayStation 5 with the new DualSense Wireless Controller on White Background. By Marco Verch. November 22, 2020. Retrieved from https://www.flickr.com/photos/160866001@N07/50632576407/ (CC BY 2.0). (Part of these images were used on the introductory page of this chapter.)

Figure 15.23 Modern generation console sales graph (as of January 2023). (Designed by Wardyga using data from VGChartz. (2023). Global Hardware Totals. Retrieved from http://www.vgchartz.com/.)

PRO FILE: Mark Cerny. Photo credit: By Katsura Cerny. Mark Cerny, CC BY-SA 3.0, https://commons.wikimedia.org/w/index.php?curid=9902481.

■ REFERENCES

Albert, A. (2013, February 3). *Wii U: The power of the fox.* Retrieved from http://wiiuconcepts.blogspot.com/.

Archer, J. (2021, February 2). PS5 Vs Xbox Series X 4K Blu-ray player showdown. Forbes. Retrieved from https://www.forbes.com/sites/johnarcher/2021/02/02/ps5-vs-xbox-series-x-4k-blu-ray-player-showdown/?sh=2489951083f1.

Ashcroft, B. (2021, June 6). Japanese gaming arcades are on their last life: Formerly hubs of human connection, arcades are now ghost towns. Japan Times. Retrieved from https://www.japantimes.co.jp/life/2021/06/06/digital/japanese-gaming-arcades-pandemic/

Bramwell, T. (2013, July 6). *Microsoft kills game ownership and expects us to smile: Last time they shipped a console that didn't work by accident. Here's one that doesn't work on purpose.* Retrieved from http://www.eurogamer.net/articles/2013-06-07-microsoft-kills-game-ownership-and-expects-us-to-smile.

Burns, M. (2012, September 26). *Here are the 23 Nintendo Wii U launch titles.* Retrieved from https://techcrunch.com/2012/09/26/here-are-the-23-nintendo-wii-u-launch-titles/.

Byford, S. (2018, January 31). *The Nintendo Switch has already outsold the Wii U.* Retrieved from https://www.theverge.com/2018/1/31/16954212/nintendo-switch-sales-earnings-q3-2017.

Codd, M. (2013, September 20). *Talking design with Tetsu Sumii, PlayStation 4 designer.* Retrieved from http://nzgamer.com/features/1244/talking-design-with-tetsu-sumii-playstation-4-designer.html.

Craddock, R. (2020, November 18). *The company behind Switch's HD rumble is also responsible for PS5 controller's haptic feedback: Thanks to the fittingly-named Immersion.* Retrieved from https://www.nintendolife.com/news/2020/11/the_company_behind_switchs_hd_rumble_is_also_responsible_for_ps5_controllers_haptic_feedback.

D'Angelo, W. (2022, June 27). *Switch tops 109M units, XS outsells PS5- worldwide hardware estimates for June 12–18- sales.* Retrieved from https://www.vgchartz.com/article/454165/switch-tops-109m-units-xs-outsells-ps5-worldwide-hardware-estimates-for-june-12-18/.

Dring, C. (2017, March 14). *Nintendo Switch has sold 1.5m worldwide - SuperData: And 9 out of 10 Switch owners bought Zelda with it.* Retrieved from http://www.gamesindustry.biz/articles/2017-03-14-nintendo-switch-has-sold-1-5m-worldwide-superdata.

Dutton, F. (2012, February 28). *New Xbox is codenamed Durango – report: Crytek dev lets cat out of the bag at London event.* Retrieved from http://www.eurogamer.net/articles/2012-02-28-new-xbox-is-codenamed-durango-report.

Frank, A. (2017, January 31). *Final Wii U models discontinued in Japan: RIP, Wii U.* Retrieved from https://www.polygon.com/platform/amp/2017/1/31/14452066/wii-u-discontinued.

Gittins, L. (2015, July 3). *Why the Wii U really failed.* Retrieved from https://videogamesuncovered.com/features/why-the-wii-u-really-failed/.

Goldfarb, A. (2013, May 4). *Xbox One 'intended to sit horizontally.'* Retrieved from http://www.ign.com/articles/2013/05/24/xbox-one-intended-to-sit-horizontally.

Graham, L. (2015, November, 12). *Xbox One console dumps Kinect hand gestures.* Retrieved from http://www.cnbc.com/2015/11/12/xbox-one-console-dumps-kinect-hand-gestures.html.

Grubb, J. (2013, November 19). *How Xbox One's video capturing is better and worse than PlayStation 4's.* Retrieved from https://venturebeat.com/2013/11/19/how-xbox-ones-video-capturing-is-better-and-worse-than-playstation-4s/.

Guinness World Records. (2015). *Guinness World Records: Gamer's Edition 2016.* Guinness World Records, New York, NY: Jim Pattison Group.

Hall, C. (2017, March 29). *Xbox One's new dashboard arrives today, here's what's included: New Home screen, improved Guide, Beam game streaming and Cortana multitasking.* Retrieved from http://www.polygon.com/xbox-one/2017/3/29/15113410/xbox-one-dashboard-update-guide.

Henderson, R. (2015, December 9). *Xbox One vs Wii U vs PS4: Which console should you buy?* Retrieved from http://www.pocket-lint.com/news/134392-xbox-one-vs-wii-u-vs-ps4-which-console-should-you-buy.

Hsu, D. (2013, October 24). *The PlayStation 4 controller: A close look at the touchpad, light bar, design, and everything else (part 4, exclusive).* Retrieved from https://venturebeat.com/2013/10/24/the-playstation-4-controller-a-close-look-at-the-touchpad-light-bar-design-and-everything-else-part-4-exclusive/2/.

Huffman, S. (2013, November 15). *PS4 and the history of lavish gaming system parties.* Retrieved from https://www.marketplace.org/2013/11/15/tech/numbers/ps4-and-history-lavish-gaming-system-parties.

Johann, C. (2021, March 29). *The current state of arcade gaming in Japan, and how it's dealt with COVID-19.* Retrieved from https://www.frontlinejp.net/2021/03/29/arcade-gaming-in-japan-before-and-after-covid-19/.

Leadbetter, R. (2013, May 2). *Wii U graphics power finally revealed: Hard facts on the Nintendo GPU emerge. So is it more powerful than PS3 and Xbox 360?* Retrieved from http://www.eurogamer.net/articles/df-hardware-wii-u-graphics-power-finally-revealed.

Lejacq, (2012, November 18). *Nintendo's Wii U aims to court casual and hardcore gamers.* Retrieved from http://blogs.wsj.com/speakeasy/2012/11/18/nintendos-wii-u-aims-to-court-casual-and-hardcore-gamers/.

Lendino, J. (2015, November 20). *Xbox One vs. PlayStation 4: Which game console is best?* Retrieved from https://www.extremetech.com/gaming/156273-xbox-720-vs-ps4-vs-pc-how-the-hardware-specs-compare.

Machkovech, S. (2018, October 3). *Nintendo president: "I compete for time," not against Xbox, PlayStation.* Retrieved from https://arstechnica.com/gaming/2018/10/nintendo-president-our-future-is-as-an-entertainment-company/.

Makuch, E. (2017, January 18). *Xbox One Sales Reach 26 Million - Report: Microsoft responds, saying it is focusing on "engagement" instead of hard sales numbers.* Retrieved from https://www.gamespot.com/articles/xbox-one-sales-reach-26-million-report/1100-6447023/.

Makuch, E. (2020, June 12). *Why Sony is releasing a disc-free PS5 Sony, like Microsoft before it, is releasing a digital-only PlayStation console--and now we know why.* Retrieved from https://www.gamespot.com/articles/why-sony-is-releasing-a-discfree-ps5/1100-6478354/.

Malik A. (2022, August 29). *Sony acquires Savage Game Studios, announces new PlayStation Studios Mobile Division.* Retrieved from https://techcrunch.com/2022/08/29/sony-acquires-savage-game-studios/.

Matthews, M. (2012, December 12). *The Wii U launch by the numbers.* Retrieved from http://www.gamasutra.com/view/news/183276/The_Wii_U_launch_by_the_numbers.php.

Microsoft News Center. (2022, January 18). *Microsoft to acquire Activision Blizzard to bring the joy and community of gaming to everyone, across every device.* Retrieved from https://news.microsoft.com/2022/01/18/microsoft-to-acquire-activision-blizzard-to-bring-the-joy-and-community-of-gaming-to-everyone-across-every-device/.

Mochizuki, T. and Wu, D. (2022, January 11). Sony is dealing with PlayStation 5 shortage by making more PS4s. *Bloomberg.* Retrieved from https://www.bloomberg.com/news/articles/2022-01-12/sony-tackles-playstation-5-shortage-by-making-more-ps4-consoles.

Moss, S. (2013, February 26). *AMD Talks PS4: "It is by far the most powerful APU we have built to date", "we have not built an APU quite like that for anyone else."* Retrieved from http://www.playstationlifestyle.net/2013/02/26/amd-talks-ps4-it-is-by-far-the-most-powerful-apu-we-have-built-to-date-we-have-not-built-an-apu-quite-like-that-for-anyone-else/.

Nintendo of America. (2022). *How long does the battery charge last?* Retrieved from https://en-americas-support.nintendo.com/app/answers/detail/a_id/46835/~/how-long-does-the-battery-charge-last%3F.

Peckham, M. (2015, March 18). Exclusive: Nintendo CEO reveals plans for smartphones. *Time Magazine.* Retrieved from http://time.com/3748920/nintendo-mobile-games/.

Pino, N. (2017, February 10). *PlayStation VR review: PlayStation VR is the promised land for virtual reality on consoles.* Retrieved from http://www.techradar.com/reviews/gaming/playstation-vr-1235379/review.

Plunkett, L. (2015, July 12). *Nintendo president Satoru Iwata dies at 55.* Retrieved from http://kotaku.com/nintendos-president-has-passed-away-1717386412.

Plunkett, L. (2016, July 27). *The Wii U has no games, a study.* Retrieved from http://kotaku.com/the-wii-u-has-no-games-a-study-1784419013.

Reisinger, D. (2013, August 14). *Xbox One knows when it's overheating, adjusts accordingly: The latest Xbox console will be aware of its temperature and will cycle down its power usage to cool itself off when needed.* Retrieved from https://www.cnet.com/news/xbox-one-knows-when-its-overheating-adjusts-accordingly/.

Rivington, J. (2017). *Xbox One review: The Xbox One is getting better with every firmware update.* Retrieved from http://www.techradar.com/reviews/gaming/games-consoles/xbox-one-1205739/review.

Romano, S. (2014, September 10). *Xbox One sells 23,000 during first week in Japan.* Retrieved from http://gematsu.com/2014/09/xbox-one-sells-23000-first-week-japan.

Rose, M. (2013, May 29). *Vita remote play mandatory for PS4 games.* Retrieved from http://www.gamasutra.com/view/news/193204/Vita_Remote_Play_mandatory_for_PS4_games.php.

Rougeau, M. (2014, June 19). *Destiny developer Bungie and Sony have been in bed longer than you think.* Retrieved from http://www.techradar.com/news/gaming/bungie-and-sony-have-been-in-bed-longer-than-you-think-1254114.

Sakr, S. (2013, May 21). *Xbox One runs three operating systems, including cut-down Windows for apps.* Retrieved from https://www.engadget.com/2013/05/21/xbox-one-runs-three-operating-systems/.

Smith, D. (2015, November 25). *The PlayStation 4 just made history.* Retrieved from http://www.businessinsider.com/playstation-4-just-made-history-2015-11.

Sony Computer Entertainment Inc. (2013, February 21). *Sony Computer Entertainment introduces wireless controller for Playstation®4 (Dualshock®4) and Playstation®4 Eye.* Retrieved from http://www.scei.co.jp/corporate/release/130221b_e.html.

Sony Interactive Entertainment. (2017). *Playstation®4 (PS4™) sells through 6.2 million units worldwide during the 2016 holiday season: PS4 software sell through 50.4 million over the same period, Uncharted 4: A Thief's End, reached a cumulative sell through of more than 8.7 million copies globally.* Retrieved from http://www.sie.com/en/corporate/release/2017/170105.html.

Sony Interactive Entertainment. (2020, January 7). *PlayStation network monthly active users reaches 103 million.* Retrieved from https://www.sie.com/en/corporate/release/2020/200107.html

Sony Interactive Entertainment Europe Limited. (2017). *Play together: Bring friends into play – even if they don't own the game.* Retrieved from https://www.playstation.com/en-gb/explore/ps4/features/share-play/.

Sutter, J. D. & Gross, D. (2011, June 7). *Nintendo unveils the Wii U system.* Retrieved from http://www.cnn.com/2011/TECH/gaming.gadgets/06/07/nintendo.e3.announcement/.

Takahashi, D. (2016, December 14). *Nintendo Switch specs: Less powerful than PlayStation 4.* Retrieved from https://venturebeat.com/2016/12/14/nintendo-switch-specs-less-powerful-than-playstation-4/.

Tassi, P. (2013, June 11). PS4's price and policies humiliate Microsoft's Xbox One at E3. *Forbes Magazine.* Retrieved from https://www.forbes.com/sites/insertcoin/2013/06/11/playstation-4s-price-and-policies-humiliate-microsofts-xbox-one-at-e3/#3d281e9f133f.

Veloria, L. (2015, November 3). *Everything that's changed in the new Xbox One user interface.* Retrieved from http://www.gamesradar.com/new-xbox-one-dashboard-update/.

Walton, M. (2017, April 6). *Xbox One Project Scorpio specs: 12GB GDDR5, 6 teraflops, native 4K at 60FPS: Release date and pricing yet to be announced—but expect it to be expensive.* Retrieved from https://arstechnica.com/gaming/2017/04/xbox-scorpio-hardware-specs/.

Warnick, J. (2014, January 20). *Carl Ledbetter: A designer's journey from arrowheads to Xbox One.* Retrieved from https://news.microsoft.com/stories/people/carl-ledbetter.html.

Welch, C. (2015, June 15). *Microsoft's Xbox One Elite Controller could be the ultimate console gamepad: Just take a look at that d-pad.* Retrieved from http://www.theverge.com/2015/6/15/8783211/microsoft-xbox-one-elite-wireless-controller-announced-e3-2015.

Wong, R. (2012, September 13). *Nintendo Wii U specs reveal large capacity discs and lots of ram.* Retrieved from http://bgr.com/2012/09/13/nintendo-wii-u-hardware-specs-revealed/.

Xbox Wire Staff. (2013, November 23). *Xbox One is biggest launch in Xbox history: More than one million consoles sold in less than 24 hours.* Retrieved from https://news.xbox.com/2013/11/23/xbox-one-biggest-launch-in-xbox-history/.

Index

Note: **Bold** page numbers refer to tables; *italic* page numbers refer to figures.

2.5D" games 42
2D sprite-generated polygons **220**
3DO Company 210
3DO Interactive Multiplayer 186, *210*,
        210–211, **211**, *211*
    vs. Atari Jaguar *215*, 215–216
    console comparison 212–213, **213**
    vs. Sega Saturn system 221
    tech specs **213**
    titles 213, *213*, 215
    U.S. titles **211**
3D audio 314
3D era, the *see* fifth-generation
3dfx 272
3dfx Interactive's Voodoo chipset 305
3D graphics accelerator 305
3D pad 220
3D polygon graphics 147, 166, 209
3DS XL 423
4G LTE 401
4K 427
4K resolution 403
4K Ultra HD 441
5G networks 406
007 Nightfire 263
The 7th Guest **304**
10NES 127
16-bit Era, the. *see* fourth-generation
18 Wheeler: American Pro Trucker 271
32X 159, 218–220
x86-64 APU 434
60 Minutes 191
130EX 99
343 Industries 436
360-degree joystick, Atari 75
1941-Counter Attack 147, 150
1943 Kai 152

A1200 110
A4000 110
AAR (After Action Review) 366
AC adapter 5
Accelerated Processing Unit (APU) 424
accelerometer 344, 389
Acclaim 192, 232
achievements 309, 331

achromatic color 41
Acorn Computers 106
action oriented games 172
Action Replay 187
Activision 132, 197
Activision Blizzard 404
activity feeds 406
ActRaiser 162, 165
Adam computer 72
Adobe Flash 306
"Adult Only" video compact discs
       (VCDs) 186
Advanced Television Systems Committee
       (ATSC) 37
Advanced Video System (AVS) 123, *124*
Adventure 61, *61*
Advertising Standards Authority
       (ASA) 393
After Burner 121, 147
After Burner II 152
After Burner Climax 329
Aiken, Howard 89
Aircars 216
Akumajō Dracula X: Chi no Rondo 152
Akumajou Dracula X: Gekka no
       Yasoukyoku 223
Aladdin 134
Alan Wake 334, 435
Alcorn, Al 10, 12
Aldynes 150
Alexa 434
Alex Kidd in Miracle World 134, *134*
Alien (movie) 152
Alien Brigade 136, 138, *138*
Alien Crush 152
Alien Raiders 68, *68*
Alien vs. Predator 218, *218*
Allard, J. 288, 331
Allen, Paul 287
Alleyway 155
Alpha Denshi Corporation (ADK) 167
Alphanumeric Television Interface
       Controller (ANTIC) 76, 96
alpha stage **246**
Altered Beast 154, *156*
Amateur Surgeon 368

Amaya, Daisuke 309
Amazon 401
Amazon Luna 318
Amazon Prime 338
AMD (Advanced Micro Devices)
       hardware 288
American Laser Games 211
American Psychological Association
       199
American Standard Code for Information
       Interchange (ASCII) graphics
       37, 37–38
America's Army 363, **363**
America's Army: Proving Grounds 363
Amiga 109, **109**, 301
Amiga 500 110
Amiga 1000 110
Amiga CD32 110
Amiga computer 210
Amiga series 103, 301
amiibo 421
Among Us 406, *406*, 408
Ampex 10
Amplitude 272
Amstrad CPC464 107, *108*
Amstrad CPC (Colour Personal
       Computer) **107**, 107–108, *108*
Amstrad GX4000 108
Amstrad Mega PC 108
amusement halls 3
analog control, Atari 5200 75
Analog Devices 344
analogous (color) 41
analytics 248
ancillary products 408
Anderson, Craig A. 199
Android 399
Android, Inc. 399
Android Market 399
Andy Capp's Tavern 10
Angry Birds 402, 407
Animal Crossing: New Horizons 440, *441*
Animal Crossing: Pocket Camp 405
Antarctic Adventure 73
anti-aliasing (edge smoothening)
       systems 229

ANTIC (Alphanumeric Television Interface Controller) 76, 96
AO (Adults Only) 187
Apex Legends **254**, 257, 317, 436
Appelbaum, Mark 372
Apple 397
Apple A5 401
Apple Arcade 318
Apple Computer Company 89, 154, 301, 308, 344
    early U.S. computer sales 111, *111*
Apple I *89*, 89–90
Apple II 89–90, *90*
    vs. Atari 8-bit family 96
    vs. Atari VCS (2600) 91, **91**
    magazine advertisement for *92*
    memory 91
    tech specs 90, 91, **91**
    titles *91*, 93, *94*
Apple II+ successors 93–94; *see also specific names*
Apple IIc 94
Apple IIe 94
Apple IIGS 94
Apple III 94
Apple III Business BASIC 94
Apple Lisa 94
Apple Music Synthesizer 90
Apple's CPU 91
application programming interfaces (APIs) 304, 433
application-specific integrated circuit (ASIC) chip 94
App Store 398
Arakawa, Minoru 56, 123, 125, 287
Arcade Card 151
arcade games; *see also specific names*
    decline and restructuring 271, *271*
    from Golden Age 55–56, **56**
    rail shooters 329, **329**
    revenue from 56
    revival of, in fourth generation 147, *147*
    update, seventh generation **329**, 330
arcade ports 70, 71, 78, 122
Arcade Racer 220
arcade scene 121, *121*
    modern 417–418
Arc Graphics 317
Arc System Works 341
Arena of Valor 406
Arm 399, 405
ARM9 397
Armor Battle 66
Armored Warriors 209
Arnold Palmer Tournament Golf 156, 157
artificial intelligence (AI) 247
artists **248**

Art mods 188
Art of Fighting 170
ArtX 281
ASCII Corporation 105
ASCII (American Standard Code for Information Interchange) graphics *37*, 37–38
ASCII keyboard controller 284
Ashida, Kenichiro 281, 344
ASIC (application-specific integrated circuit) chip 94
aspect ratio 36
Asterix games 134
Asteroids 37, 55
Astral Chain 440
Astro Bot Rescue Mission 428
Astrosmash 70
Astro Studios 332
Astro Warrior 131
Atari 10–12, 19, 37, 55, 121, *121*, 123, 147, 210, 285; *see also Pong*
    early U.S. computer sales 110–111
    financial crisis 123
    third-generation market summary 138–139, *139*
Atari, 400 94–96, **96**, *96*
Atari, 800 94–96, **96**, *96*
Atari, 5200 74–76, *75*, *76*, 134
    analog control 75
    automatic switchbox 75
    vs. ColecoVision 76–78
    360-degree joystick 75
    four controller ports 75, *75*
    magazine advertisement for *77*
    numeric keypad 75
    overlays 75
    radio frequency (RF) switch 75
    start, pause, and reset buttons 75
    tech specs 76, **76**
    titles 75, **75**, *76*, 78
    Trak-Ball controller 76
Atari 8-bit family (400 and 800) 94–96, **96**, *96*
    vs. Apple II 96
    vs. Commodore, 64 100–101
    controller ports (jacks) 96
    evolution of 99
    130EX 99
    magazine advertisement for *98*
    tech specs **96**
    titles 97, *97*, 99
    XE Game System (XEGS) 99, *99*
    600XL 99
    800XL 99
    1200XL 99
Atari 8-bit successors 97–99; *see also specific names*
Atari Corporation 121
Atari Falcon 110

Atari Games (division) 138
Atari generation 53–81
    Atari 5200
        vs. ColecoVision 76–78
        magazine advertisement for *77*
        tech specs 76, **76**
        titles 75, **75**, *76*, 78
    Atari VCS (2600) 56–59, **57**, *57*
        vs. ColecoVision 72–73
        console comparison **59**, 59–60, *60*
        vs. Magnavox odyssey 62–63
        vs. Mattel Intellivision 69–70
        titles 61, *61*
    breakthroughs and trends 80
    ColecoVision *71*, **71**, 71–72, *72*
        vs. Atari VCS and Intellivision 72–73
        titles *73*, 73–74
        two-page magazine advertisement for *74*
    Golden Age 55, 55–56, **56**
    Magnavox Odyssey 61–62, **62**, *62*, *63*
        vs. Atari VCS 62–63
        magazine advertisement for (1981) *64*
        vs. Mattel Intellivision 65–69
        tech specs 63, *63*
        titles 63–65, *65*
    market summary 79–80, *80*
    Mattel Intellivision 65, 65–69, **66**, *67*, *69*, *70*
        vs. Atari VCS and Odyssey 69–70
        vs. ColecoVision 72–73
        titles 70–71, *71*
    sales graph *80*
    timeline 54
    video game crash of, 1983 78–79, *79*
Atari Jaguar *215*, 215–216
    vs. 3DO *215*, 215–216
    magazine advertisement for *217*
    vs. Sega Saturn system 221
    tech specs 215, *215*, 216
    titles 218, *218*
Atari 2600 Jr. 135
Atari Lynx 161, *161*
    tech specs **161**
Atari MEGA STE 110
Atari Panther 215
Atari 7800 ProSystem 123, 134–135, **135**, *135*
    8-bit 6502C "SALLY" processor 136
    comic book advertisement for *137*
    MARIA, chip 136
    vs. NES 136, **136**, 138
    POKEY audio chip 136
    Proline controller 135, *135*
    vs. SMS 136, **136**, 138
    tech specs 136, **136**
    titles 138, *138*

U.S. launch titles **135**
Atari ST 109, **109**, *109,* 301
Atari STE 110
Atari TT 110
Atari Video Computer System (VCS)
 (2600) 56–59, **57**, *57,* 135, 184
 vs. Apple II 91, **91**
 vs. ColecoVision 72–73
 color palette 59
 console comparison **59**, 59–60, *60*
 vs. Fairchild Channel F 60
 features 57, *57*
 four colors per scan line 59
 magazine advertisement for (1981) *60*
 vs. Magnavox odyssey 62–63
 vs. Mattel Intellivision 69–70
 memory 59
 1.19 MHz 6507 processor 59
 vs. NES 127–129, **129**
 tech specs **59**
 titles 61, *61*
 U.S. launch titles **57**
Atari XL series 97
ATI (Array Technology Inc.) 281
Atic Atac 107
ATI Technologies 305, 307, 330
Atomiswave 329
ATSC (Advanced Television Systems
 Committee) 37
AT&T 397, 430
attach rate 437
audio card (sound card) 31, *31*
augmented reality (AR) 404, 423
automatic switchbox, Atari, 5200 75
autostereoscopic upper screen 423
Avalon Hill 359
avatar 311, 366
average cost 252
Ax Battler: A Legend of Golden Axe 168
Axiom Verge 317, 430
Ayaneo Next 319
AY-3-8500 chip 15
AY-3-8910 chip 105

Baca, Joe 197
Bachelor Party 184
Bachus, Kevin 287
Back to Skool 107
Back to the Future II 134
Back to the Future III 134
backward compatibility 130, 135, 282
Bad (album) 160
Baer, Ralph 5, 9, 12
Baffle Ball 3, *3*
Bagatelle 3, *3*
Baker, Troy 45, *45*
Baldur's Gate 42
The Ballad of Gay Tony 189
Ball 126, *126*

Ballblazer 136, 138
Bally 3
Bandai Namco 417
Banjo-Kazooie 232
The Bard's Tale 94
Barkley Shut Up and Jam! 188
Barlow, Sam 404
Barnett, Scott 361
Barr, Lance 123, 162
Baseball 8
Baseball Stars 169
Baseball Stars Professional (NAM-1975)
 169, *169,* 172
BASIC (Beginner's All-purpose Symbolic
 Instruction Code) 89, 287
Basic Input/Output System (BIOS) chip
 30, *30*
Bastion 309, 402, 404, 440
Batman: Arkham City **341**
Batman Returns 134
Battle Ace 150
Battle Field 167
Battlefield 1 435, 436
Battlefield 2042 255
Battle.net World Championship
 Series 261
Battle Royale (movie) 317
battle royale games 257, 317
Battle Squadron 109
Battlezone 37, *38,* 360
Bavelier, Daphne 373
Bayonetta 334
Bayonetta 2 422, *422,* 440
BBC Micro 106
beam 434
Beat 'Em & Eat 'Em 184
"beat 'em up"-style games 42
Beatmania 233, 271
Beat Saber 316
BEEP sound chip 107
Beginner's All-purpose Symbolic
 Instruction Code (BASIC)
 89, 287
Bejjanki, Vikranth 373
Bell & Howell 94
Bennett, John, Dr. 4
Ben's Game 370
Benton, Charles "Chuck" 183
Berkes, Otto 287
Bertie the Brain 4
Berzerk 44, 76
Betamax 223
beta stage **246**
Bethesda 308
bezel 147
Big Buck Hunter 329, *329*
Big Button Pad controller 339
big data 255
Big Fish Games 404

Bikkuriman World 147
binary code **32**, 32–33
Binary Runtime Environment for
 Wireless (BREW) 391
Bionic Commando 121
Bionic Commando: Elite Forces 233
BIOS (Basic Input/Output System) chip
 30, *30*
BioShock Infinite 42, **341**
BioWare 291, 306, 334
Birdo, character 188
bit (b) 32–33
bitmap 38
BlackBerry 389
BlackBerry 850 389
Blackley, Seamus 287, 288
Blades 331
blast processing 165
BlazBlue: Continuum Shift Extend 430
Blazing Lazers 152, *154*
Blazing Star 172
Blinn, Jim 42
Blinn–Phong reflection model 42
Blizzard Entertainment 308
BlizzCon 259
Block Buster 68, *68*
blockchain 312
Bloktopia 312
bloom (lighting) 42
Blue Lightning 161
Blue Sky Rangers 69
Bluetooth 391
Bluetooth 2.0 337
Bluetooth 4.0 434
Blum, Steve 45, *45*
Blu-ray console 336
Blu-ray Disc 223
Blu-ray Disc ROM (BD-ROM) 340
Bluth, Don 56
Bohemia Interactive 366
Bohemia Interactive Simulations
 (BISim) 366
Bomberman 105, 108, 152
Bonaire GPU 433
Bonk's Adventure 152, *154*
Boon, Ed 192
Borderlands: The Pre-Sequel! 189
Boulder Dash 97
Bounty Bob Strikes Back 97
Bowling 68
Bradford, Ron 62
Bradley Trainer 360, **360**
Braid **310**
Brain Dead 13 215
brain development 373–374, **374**
Brain Wave 8
Bran Stoker's Dracula 134
Breakout 61, 63, 68
Brennan, Martin 215

broadband 271
Broadband Adapter 279
Broken Age 246, 444
Bromberg, Irving 130
Bromley, Eric 72
Bromley, Martin 130
Brookhaven National Laboratory 4
Brownback, Sam 197
Brown, Bob 12
"Brown Box" 5
Brown, Jerry 198
"Brown v. Entertainment Merchants Ass'n" 198
Brütal Legend 444
bugs 248, 308
Bui Tuong Phong 41
bump mapping 39
Bump 'n' Jump 70
Bundy Manufacturing Company 301
Bundy, Willard 301
Bungie 425
Bungie Studios 289
BurgerTime 70, *70*
Burnout 3: Takedown 292
bus 31, 76
Bushnell, Nolan 4, 10, 55–58
Butler, Kevin 339
Buzz 339
byte (B) *32*, 32–33
ByteDance 408

cache memory 33
CA Law AB 1793 198
California bill AB1179 198
California Games 161
Call of Duty 42
Call of Duty 2 **331**
Call of Duty: Black Ops 4 436
Call of Duty: Black Ops: Cold War 255
Call of Duty Mobile 405, **405**
Call of Duty: Vanguard 255
Call of Duty: Warzone 317
Camouflage Combat 15
Candy Crush Saga **402**
Cannon, Tom 260
capacitive touchpad 425
Capcom 121, 147, 156, 160, 349
Capcom CPS2 209
capital and publishing layer 245
Captain Toad: Treasure Tracker 440
card readers 417
Carmack, John 194
cartridge slot 16
Casper 215
cassette deck 107
Castle of Illusion starring Mickey Mouse 168
Castlevania: Aria of Sorrow 282
Castlevania: Bloodlines 160

Castlevania X: Rondo of Blood 152
casual game/gaming 417; *see also* mobile game/gaming
   defined 389
   market summary 407–408
Catharsis theory 200
cathode ray tube (CRT) 4
cathode ray tube (CRT) monitor 36
   vector monitors 38
Cavalier 3
Cavanagh, Terry 402
Cawthon, Scott 403
CD-ROM 30, 165, 304; *see also specific names*
   background 150–151
Celeste 317, 440
Cell Processor 336
censorship 173
Centipede 138
central processing unit (CPU) 29, 91
Cerny, Mark 340, 424
Chase H.Q. **106**, 107
Chat Headset 432
Chess 10
Chiller 191
Chip's Challenge 161
chip shortage 250
chiptune 44
Choplifter 100, 101
chrominance (chroma) 41
Chrono Trigger 166
Chuck E. Cheese 55, 57, 271, 417
Chung, Anshe 311
CICS ChicagoQuest 377
Circle Pad Pro 423
circuit boards 3, 6
circuits 249
city-building games 109–110
citizen science 371
Civilization IV 47
Civilization series 101
Clash of Clans **402**
Clash Royale 404, 406
Classic Controller 347
click turning 314
Cliffe, Jess 307
Clinical Skills and Simulation Centers (CSSCs) 368
Clinton, Hillary 197
clock rate 33
clones, rise of, IBM and 301, **302**
Close Combat: The Bloody First 364
Close Combat: Gateway to Caen 364
Close Combat: Marines 364
closed-circuit television (CCTV) 197
cloud gaming 252, 318, 425
Club Nintendo 420
Clubs (on XBL) 433
The Coalition 435

coaxial digital 35
code freeze stage **246**
code release **246**
Coleco 13, 123
Coleco Adam Computer 123
Coleco Telstar 13–18, **15**, *15–17*, *18*
   cartridges 16, 18
   Combat! 15, *16*
   features 16
   magazine advertisement for *17*
   market summary 19
   Naval Battle 16, 18
   Road Race 16, *16*
   series releases **18**
   tech specs **15**
   Telstar Arcade 16, *16*
ColecoVision *71*, **71**, 71–72, *72*
   vs. Atari VCS and Intellivision 72–73
   12-button numeric keypad 71
   Expansion Module #1 71
   Expansion Module #2 71
   Expansion Module #3 71–72
   features 71, *71*
   Roller Controller 72, *72*
   Super Action Controller Set 72, *72*
   tech specs 72–73, **73**
   titles *73*, 73–74
   two-page magazine advertisement for *74*
   U.S. launch titles **71**, *72*
Collins, Karen 47
color
   layering 165, *165*
   and lighting 40–41
   overlays 37
   TV-Game series 18, **19**, *19*, 122
color identifiers 41
color palette 41
colors on screen 59
color wheel 41, *41*
Colossal Cave Adventure 93
Colour Clash 107
Columbine High School 194
Columns 101, 168
Combat! 15, *16*
comic book advertisement, for Atari 7800 ProSystem *137*
Comlynx Adapter 161
Commando 136, 138
commercial off-the-shelf (COTS) 376
Commodore, 16 103
Commodore, 64 99–100
   Amiga line 103
   vs. Atari, 8-bit 100–101
   magazine advertisement for *102*
   titles 101
Commodore, 128 103
Commodore Amiga 500 *109*
Commodore Amiga computer series 301

Commodore International 99
  early U.S. computer sales 111, *111*
Commodore PET (Personal Electronic
    Transactor) 99
Commodore Plus/4 103
Commodore 64 successors 101–103; *see
    also specific names*
community management 248
Compact Disc (CD) 223
CompactFlash (CF) 336
Compaq 301
Compile 105, 152
complementary color 41
component cable 343
composers, video game 44
composite cable 34
CompUSA 186
Compute! 109
computer-aided design (CAD) 307
computer-controlled opponent 57
Computer Entertainment Rating
    Organization (CERO) 193
Computer Gaming World 320
Computer Intro! 61
Computer Space 4–5, *5*
compute units (CUs) 442
Connect Four 68, *68*
Connecticut Leather Company 13
connectors, video game, visual reference
    guide **35**
console comparison; *see also* console
    gaming, modern
  PlayStation 4 (PS4) *vs.* Wii U *427,*
      427–428
  WII U *vs.* XBOX 360 and PS3 *421,*
      421–422
  Xbox One *vs.* PlayStation 4 (PS4)
      434–435, *435,* **436**
console gaming, modern
  about modern console gaming 418
  console comparison
    PlayStation 4 (PS4) *vs.* Wii U *427,*
        427–428
    WII U *vs.* XBOX 360 and PS3 *421,*
        421–422
    Xbox One *vs.* PlayStation 4 (PS4)
        434–435, *435,* **436**
  console timeline 416
  modern arcade scene 417–418
  PlayStation 4 (PS4) *424,* **424–426,**
      424–427
  PlayStation 5 440–441
  PlayStation 4 (PS4) titles 428,
      428–430
  Wii U console **418–419,** 418–421, *420,*
      421, 422
  Wii U titles 422, **422, 423**
  Xbox One *431,* **431–432,** 431–434
  Xbox One titles 435–436, *437,* **437**

Xbox Series X|S 440–441
console timeline 416
"console war" 66, 165
Consumer Electronics Show (CES) 123,
      258, **259**
Contra 129
Contra Hard Corps 160
control boxes 4
Controller Pak 231
controller ports 75
Control Program for Microcomputers 89
Control Program/Monitor (CP/M)
      operating system 103
control stick 124, 132
conventions, video game *258,*
      258–260, **259**
convergence 405
cooling fan 29
Cool Spot 159, 166
co-processors 33, 39–40
copy protection 211
copyrights 5
  infringement 12
Cordless Action Controller 279
cores (processing units) 33
Cortana 434
Counter-Strike 307
*Counter-Strike: Global Offensive
      (CS:GO)* 257
CPS (Capcom Power System) 147
CPS (hardware) 147
CPU (central processing unit) 29, 91, 307
Crash 'N Burn 210
Crazy Cross 209
Croft, Laura 189, 305
cross-platform gaming 405
cross-play 321, 405
crowdfunding 246
crowd-sourced science 371
Crowther, Will 93
CRT *see* cathode ray tube (CRT)
crunch time 245
Crystal Dynamics 213
Crystalis 167
Crystal Warriors 168
CTIA 96
Cuphead 317
Curiosity Inc. 282
Custer's Revenge 184, *184*
custom color 41
customizable character 189
cyberathletes 261
Cyber Lip 170
Cybermorph 215, 216, *216*
Cyberpunk 2077 441

Dabney, Ted 4, 10
Daglow, Don 69, 70
Dai Makai-Mura (Daimakaimura) 147, 150

Daisy chain concept 211
Dance Dance Revolution 225, 271, *271*
Darius Plus. 150
Dark Chambers 138, *138*
Darkstalkers 209
DARWARS 364–366, **365**
DARWARS Ambush! 365
Dashboard 331, 433
data cassette storage 90
Data East 121
Data research 255, **256**
DAUNTLESS 366
Dave & Buster's 417, 271
David, Keith 45, *45*
Day one patch 436
Days Gone 321
Daytona USA 2: Battle on the Edge 209
Dead Cells 317, *319*
Dead or Alive 190
Dead Rising 334
Deathloop 319
deathmatch 304
Death Race, violence and 191, *192*
DeCamp, Whitney 199
Decentraland 312
dedicated consoles 10
dedicated hardware 6
Defenders of Oasis 168
Defense Advanced Research Projects
      Agency (DARPA) 364
degrees of freedom (DoF) 314
Dell Streak 401
Demo disc 224
Demographic data, video game
      players 183
Demon Attack 63, 70, 79
Demon's Souls 443
DeNA 444
desensitization 200, 372
designer **248**
Destiny 425, 445
Destruction AllStars 443
Destruction Derby 224
developer(s) 245, 246
      example **248**
      independent 247
      in-house (first-party) 247
      second-party 247
      third-party 247
development team, role of 248
development, video game industry
      246–249, *247,* **248**
Dey, Alexander 301
Diablo III 253
Diamond Mine 101
Dickinson, Rick 107
diegetic sound 45
Dietz, Tracy 188
Dig Dug 56

DiGiovanni, Sundance 260
Digital Audio Tape (DAT) 223
Digital Bridges 391
Digital Chocolate 396
digital data pack (DDP) cassette 72
digital displays 3
digital distribution 250, 309
digital downloads 250
digital joystick controller 57, *57*
digital-only games 420
Digital Pictures 185
digital rights management (DRM)
          309, 431
digital signal processor (DSP) 165
digital signature 135
Digital Terrestrial Multimedia Broadcast
          (DTMB) format 37
Digital Theater Systems (DTS) 44
digital video broadcasting (DVB) 37, 339
Digital Visual Interface (DVI) **35**
digitized graphics 192
Direct3D 305
directional pad ("d-pad"), NES 124
Direct Memory Access (DMA) 166
DirectX 287, 304, 433
"DirectX Box" 288
Disco Elysium 317
Discord 317
Disgaea 42
Disk II 90, *90*
disk operating system (DOS) 89, 94,
          303, **303**
     gaming in 303
Disney Interactive 376
display port **35**
distribution layer 250
distribution, video game industry *250*,
          250–252
distributor 245
DK Bongos 284
DLNA (Digital Living Network
          Alliance) 435
DmC: Devil May Cry 341, 444
Dolby Atmos 44, 442
Dolby Digital 7.1 340
Dolby Laboratories 44
Dominick, J. R. 191
Donkey Kong 44, 55, *55*, 71, *72*, 73–75, 122,
          123, *123*, 125, 129, 138
Donkey Kong 3 126, *126*
Donkey Kong Country 166, *167*
*Donkey Kong Country: Tropical
          Freeze* 440
Donkey Kong Jr. 73, 122, *123*
Doom 218, *218*, 304
Doraemon 233
DOS *see* disk operating system (DOS)
Dota 2 **254**, 257, 262, 316
Double Dragon 42

Douglas, Alexander, Dr. 4
downloadable content (DLC) 257
D-pad controller 123, *124*, 131
Dragalia Lost 405
Dragon Age 189
Dragon Age: Inquisition 189, 436
Dragon Force 223
Dragoon Might 209
Dragon's Crown 190
draw distance 216
Dream Blaster 274
Dreamcast 34, 345
Dreameye 274
DreamHack 260, *260*
Driving Force GT steering wheel
          kit 279
Driv3r 282
Dr. Mario World 405
Dropzone 101
DrSim 368
DrumMania 271
DSi XL 335
DS Lite 335
DTS (Digital Theater Systems) 44
DTS:X 442
dual screen 335
DualSense controller 442
DualShock 2 276
DualShock 3 337
DualShock 4 424
DualShock controller 225
Duck Hunt 124, 130, 131
Duke controller 290
Duke Nukem 186
Dungeon Master 109, *110*
Dungeons & Dragons 62, 70, 93, 209
Durango 431
DVD remote control 277
DVDs (Digital Versatile Discs) 276
DVI (Digital Visual Interface) **35**
Dvorak, Robert 4
Dyer, Rick **56**
Dynamic Menu 425

EA Mobile 396
EA Play 318
early PC gaming 87–111; *see also* PC
          gaming
     Amstrad CPC **107**, 107–108, *108*
     Apple I *89*, 89–90
     Apple II 89–90, *90*
          vs. Atari 8-bit family 96
          vs. Atari VCS (2600) 91, **91**
          magazine advertisement for *92*
          titles *91*, 93, *94*
     Apple II successors 93–94
     Atari 8-bit family (400 and 800)
          94–96, **96**, *96*
          vs. Apple II 96

          vs. Commodore, 64 100–101
          evolution of *99*
          magazine advertisement for *98*
          titles 97, *97*, 99
     Atari 8-bit successors 97–99
     Commodore, 64 99–100, *102*
          vs. Atari, 8-bit 100–101
          magazine advertisement for *102*
          titles 101
     Commodore 64 successors 101–103
     Electronic Arts (EA) 93
     end of era 108–110
     market summary 110–111, *111*
     MSX *104*, 105, **105**
     NEC PC-98 *104*, 104–105, **105**
     overview 89
     timeline 88
     ZX Spectrum *106*, **106**, 106–107
early 1990s, PC gaming 303–304, **304**
early war games 359
Easter eggs 61, 129, 134
Eco-Box 249, *249*
E3 conference 431
eDRAM 333
EDSAC (Electronic Delay Storage
          Automatic Calculator) 4
Educator, 64 101
edutainment games 376
Edwards, Dan 4
effect sound 47
EGA (display) 301
Eisler, Craig 304
Electrocop 161
electromechanical relays 3
Electronic Arts (EA) 93, 149, 157, 186,
          210, 249, 275, 408
Electronic Delay Storage Automatic
          Calculator (EDSAC) 4
Electronic Entertainment Design and
          Research (EEDAR) 255, 406
Electronic Entertainment Expo (E3)
          220, 259
Electronic Sports League (ESL) 260
Electrotennis 12
Eliminate Down 160
Elite 101, 107
Elite controller 434
Embracer Group 408
Emergency Room 368
"Emotion Engine" 276
EndeavorRx 370
endless runner 402
end-users 253–255, **254**
"English control" 5
Engstrom, Eric 305
Enhanced Graphics Adapter (EGA) 301
enhancement chips 166
Enslaved 444
Enterbrain 253

Entertainment Software Association (ESA) 183, 190, 193, 253
Entertainment Software Rating Board (ESRB) 193
  rating labels with icon *194*
  regulation and 193
  video game ratings **193**
Entropia Universe 311
Epic Games 307
Epic Games Store 317
episodic gaming 310
Epoch 12
Erica 406
Eriksson, Stefan 397
'eroge' games 105, 184
ESA *see* Entertainment Software Association (ESA)
ESL Pro Tour 261
ESP Game 371
eSports *260,* 260–261, 306, 406
Espresso CPU 421
ESRB *see* Entertainment Software Rating Board (ESRB)
EST (Engagement Skills Trainer) 360
EteRNA 371
Eternal Darkness 285, *287*
Ethernet **35,** 279
E.T. the Extra-Terrestrial 61, 78
EverQuest 306, **307**
Evolution Championship Series (EVO) 260
Executive, 64 *see* SX-64
Exidy 191
The Exorcist: Legion VR 316
expansion cards 31
Expansion Module #1 71
Expansion Module #2 71
Expansion Module #3 71–72
expansion packs 254
Expansion Pak 231
expansion slots 31, 90
Explication de l'Arithmétique Binaire 32
explicit sexuality; *see also* sex/sexual themes, in video games
  game series known for **187**
exposure therapy 367
Extended RAM Cartridge 220, 225
The Extra-Terrestrial 61, 78
EyeToy 279, 333

Fable 189
Facebook 310
Factor 5 285
Fairchild Channel F 56
Fairchild Semiconductor 56
Falcon 110
falling block puzzle games 101
Fallout 305, 444
Famicom 122

Family Computer Disk System 122
Family Entertainment Protection Act (FEPA) 197
Far Cry 6 255
farming 311
Farmville 310
The Fast and the Furious 329, *396*
Fast RMX 438
Fatal Fury 170
Fatal Fury Special *172*
fatalities 173, 192
F.A.T.S (Firearms Training Simulator) 360
F Connector **35**
feature phone 389
Federal Trade Commission (FTC) 197
FEPA *see* Family Entertainment Protection Act (FEPA)
Ferguson, Christopher 199
Ferroni, Cameron 288
field exercises 359
FIFA 18 257
FIFA 22 255
fifth-generation (5G) 208–236, 403, 406
  arcades in flux 209, *209*
  Atari Jaguar *215,* 215–216
    titles 218, *218*
    vs., 3DO *215,* 215–216
  breakthroughs and trends 235
  3D era, the 210
  3DO Interactive Multiplayer *210,* 210–211, *211,* **211**
    vs. Atari Jaguar *215,* 215–216
    console comparison 212–213, **213**
    titles 213, *213,* 215
  Game Boy Color (GBC) 233, *233*
  market summary 234, *234,* 235, *235*
  Nintendo 64 (N64) 228–230, 228–231
    vs. Sony PlayStation **231,** 231–232
    titles 232, *232*
  Sega Saturn system 218–219, *219,* **220,** *221*
    changes 223
    vs. 3DO and Jaguar 221, *221*
    vs. Sony PlayStation 225, 226, 227, **227**
    titles 221, 223, *223*
  Sega 32X 218–219, *219*
  Sony PlayStation 223–225, **224,** *224, 225, 226, 227*
    vs. Nintendo 64 (N64) **231,** 231–232
    vs. Sega Saturn 225, 226, 227, **227**
    titles 227, *227*
  timeline 208
Fils-Aimé, Reggie 418, 437
Final Fantasy Adventure 155
Final Fantasy II 166
Final Fantasy III 167
Final Fantasy VII 227, *227*

Final Fight 42, 147, 173
Fire 126
Fire Emblem Awaking 423
Fire Emblem Heroes 404–405
Fire Emblem: Three Houses 440, *441*
Firemint 399
firmware 276
first 16-bit home video game system *see* Mattel Intellivision
first CD-ROM 150
first generation 1–20
  breakthroughs and trends 20
  Color TV-Game series 18, *19,* **19,** *19*
  earliest interactive computer games 4–18
    Coleco Telstar 13–18, **15,** *15–17,* **18**
    Computer Space 4–5, *5*
    Magnavox Odyssey 5–10, *6* (*see also* Magnavox Odyssey)
    Pong 10–13, *11–14*
    Spacewar! 4, *5*
    Tennis for Two 4, *4*
  market summary 19, *20*
  penny arcades to pinball 3, *3*
  pinball, evolution of 3, *3*
  timeline 2
first-party (in-house) developers 247
first-person perspective 42, *42*
first-person shooter (FPS) games 194, 196, 197, 303, 361
  Doom and 194, 196, *196,* 197
first-person shooter (FPS) titles 42
first playable stage **246**
five channels of mono sound 129
Flagman 126
Flame Zapper Kotsujin 105
Flare Technology 215
flash ROM cartridges 437
flat panel monitors 36
flight simulators 375
Flint, Charles Ranlett 301
flipper bumpers 3
"Flipper" graphics processor 281
floating point operations per second (FLOPS) 39–40, **40**
floating-point unit (FPU) 279
3.5" floppy disks 223
FLOPS (floating point operations per second) 39–40, **40,** 418
Flurry Analytics 255, 407
FM Sound Unit 131–132
FMV games *see* Full Motion Video (FMV) games
Folding@home 338
Foldit 371
Food Fight 138, *138*
Football 8
Football! 63
Football Frenzy 172

forced progression games 43
Forgotten Worlds 157
Fortnite 257, 261
Fortnite Battle Royale 317, *317*
Fortnite Mobile 405, 406, 409
forward compatibility 441
Forza Horizon 4 436
Forza Horizon 5 443
Forza Motorsport 8 443
fourth-generation (4G) 145–174
  arcade revival 147, *147*
  Atari Lynx 161, *161*
  breakthroughs and trends 173–174
  CD-ROM system 165
  Game Boy 155, *155*
  market summary 172–173, *173*
  NEC PC Engine 149, *149*
  sales graph *173*
  Sega Game Gear 168, *168*
  Sega Genesis 154, *156*, **156**, 156–159, **159**
    magazine advertisement for *158*
    titles 160, *160*
    vs. TurboGrafx-16 159, **160**
  Sega Mega Drive 154
  SNK Neo•Geo AES 167, *169*
    magazine advertisement for,
      1991 *171*
    vs. others 170
    titles 170, 172, *172*
  Super Famicom (SFC) 162, *162*
  Super Nintendo Entertainment
    System (SNES) *162*, 162–163,
    163, *163*
    vs. SEGA & NEC *165*, 165–166
  timeline *146*
  TurboGrafx-16 149–151, *150–151*, **152**
    magazine advertisement for *153*
    vs. NES 152, *154*
    vs. Sega Genesis 159, **160**
    titles 152, *154*
Fps (frames per second) 33
FPS games *see* first-person shooter (FPS)
  games
fragmentation 397
frame buffers 72
frame rate 33
frames per second (fps) 33
franchise 246
Franz, Martz 218
Freedom Wars 430
"freemium"model 257, 307, 309
free progression games 43
Frequency 33, 272
Freer, Carl 397
"free-to-play" (F2P) 257, 307
Friday the 13th movies 152
Fries, Ed 287
Frosthaven 246
Fujii 316

Fujitsu 104
Full Motion Video (FMV) games 159,
  185, 304
Full Spectrum Warrior (FSW) 364, **364**
funding, video game industry
  245–246, **246**
F-Zero 162, *163*

Gaiares 160
Galaga 135, 138, 329
Galaxian 55
Game After Ambush (GAA) 365
Game & Watch Gallery 2 233
game-based learning (GBL) 375
Game Boy 125, 155, *155*, 161, 168
  tech specs **155**
Game Boy Advance 282, **282**, *282*
Game Boy Color (GBC) 233, *233*
  tech specs **233**
Game Boy Player 31, 282, 284
Game Boy Pocket 155
game cards 5, 437
Game.com 233
GameCube 34, 344
GameCube-Game Boy Advance
  (GCN-GBA) cable 284
Game Developers Choice Awards 405
Game Developers Conference (GDC)
  258, **259**
GameDVR 433
game engine 248
Gamegun 211
Gameloft 391
Game Link Cable 155, 233
GamePad 419
"game paks," 125
GAME (retailer) 245
gamer card 330
Game Gear 168, *168*
gamer tag 330
GAMESbrief 199
Gamescom 259
GameStop 199, 253
game subscription 318
Gamevil 396
Game & Watch 122, 124–126, **126**, *126*
game with a purpose (GWAP) 371
GameWorks 418
gamification 376
Ganbare Goemon: Yukihime Kyūshutsu
  Emaki 165
Garena Free Fire 406
Garō Densetsu: Shukumei no Tatakai 170
Garriott, Richard 108, 305
Garry's Mod (GMod) 309
Gartner 255, 402
Gates, Bill 287, 301
Gate of Thunder 152
Gates of Zendocon 161

Gathering 186
The Gathering 260
Gattis, Bill 10
Gauntlet 121, 132
Gazzaley, Adam 374
GCC *see* General Consumer Corporation
  (GCC)
GCompris 376
GD-ROM (Gigabyte Disc) 273
Gears 5 443
Gears Tactics 443
Gears of War 188
Gears of War 2 **334**
GeForce 256 307
GeForce NOW 318
GeForce RTX 317
"Gekko" 281
Genda, Inc. 417
gender
  discrimination 191
  inequities in 190
  sex and violence in video games and
    188–191, *190*
General Consumer Corporation (GCC)
  134, 138
General Electric 10
General Instrument AY-3-8910 chip 105
General Instrument AY-3-8500 chip 15
General Packet Radio Service (GPRS) 391
Genesis 154
"Genesis does what Nintendon't" 157
Genesis Editor for Music and Sound
  effects (GEMS) 159
genlock 109
genre pioneers
  PC gaming (early 1990s) 303–304, **304**
Gerard, Manny 57
Get Dexter! 108, *108*
Gex 213
GFLOPS 339, 422
G.G. Shinobi titles 168
Ghostrunner 319
GhostWire: Tokyo 443
Ghouls 'n Ghosts 157, 160
Giant Interactive 408
gigaflops 276
Gizmondo 396–397, **397**
Gley Lancer 160
Global System for Mobile
  Communications (GSM) 391
G-Loc 168
Glorious Mission 364
Glove Controller 231
Glu Mobile 397
glyphs *see* color identifiers
Go 10
God games 108
God of War 188, 281, *281*
God of War: Ghost of Sparta **343**

Golden Age 19, *55*, 55–56, **56,** 121
Golden Axe 147
Golden Axe Warrior 134
Goldeneye 007 232
Gold master **246**
GoldStar (LG) model 211, *212*
Good, Berni 373
Google 399
Google Image Labeler 371
Google Play 399
Google Stadia 318
Goto, Teiyu 337
Gottlieb, David 3
Gouraud shading 226
Gourdin, Adam 190
GPU (graphics processing unit) 31, 307
Gradius 152
Gradius III 166
Graef, Ailin 311
Graetz, Martin 4
Grand Theft Auto III 279, *281*
Grand Theft Auto IV **334**
Grand Theft Auto: San Andreas 189, 197, *198*
Grand Theft Auto V **341**
Grand Theft Auto: Vice City Stories **343**
Gran Turismo 7 443
graphical adventure game 93
graphical MUDs 93
graphical user interface (GUI) 108–109, 331
graphics (GFX)
    ASCII 37–38, *38*
    digitized 192
    polygon *38,* 38–39, *39*
    raster *38,* 38–39
    rotation of 165
    vector 37–38, *38*
graphics card (video card) 31, *31*
Graphics Core Next (GCN) 317, 424
Graphics Display Controller (GDC) 104
graphics processing unit (GPU) 31, 231, 279, 307
Graphic Television Interface Adaptor (GTIA) 76
Gravity Rush 430
Greenberg, Arnold 13
Greenberg, Maurice 13
Griffiths, Mark D. 200
Grizzard, Andrew, Dr. 200
Grossman, Dave 196
Gryzor 108
GTA III 187
GTIA (Graphic Television Interface Adaptor) 76, 96
Guacamelee 189
Guacamelee! 317, 430
Guacamelee! 2 440
Guardian Heroes 223

GUI (graphical user interface) 108–109
Guide button 331
Guilty Gear 341
GuitarFreaks 271
Guitar Hero 272, 444
GunCon 225
GunCon, 2 277
Gunstar Heroes 160
The Guy Game 186, *186*
gyroscope 347

hack 188
Hades 440
Hagenuk MT-2000 390
Hair Trigger Locks 434
Hale, Jennifer 45, *45*
Half-Life 307, **307**
Half-Life: Alyx 315
Halo 3 **334**
Halo: Combat Evolved 289, *289,* 291, *292*
Halo Infinite 443
Hamster 233
Handball 15
HandCircus 399, **399**
Handler, Elliot 65
Hang-On 121, 131, *131*
hard disk drive (HDD) 279
Hard Drivin' 147
hardware (or virtual machine/software platform) layer 247
Harmonix 272
Harris, Eric 194
Harrison, Bill 5
Harrison, Phil 224
Harvard Mark I 89
Hase, Ted 287
Haunted House 8, *8*
Hawkins, Trip 93, 210, 396
HD Collection 341
HDMI *see* High-Definition Multimedia Interface (HDMI)
HDR10 high-dynamic-range color 427–428
HD Rumble 438
HDTV (High Definition Television) 37
HDV (High Definition Video) 37
Head Over Heels 107
headphones jack 211
heads-up displays (HUDs) 36
Hearthstone 260, 403, 406
Heavenly Sword 41
Heilig, Morton 314
Hellblade: Senua's Sacrifice VR Edition 316
Herman, Ben 173
H.E.R.O. 61
Hers Experimental Design Laboratory 332
hertz (Hz) **33,** 33–34

Hertz, Heinrich 33
Hewlett-Packard (HP) 301
hexgrids 359
High-Definition Multimedia Interface (HDMI) 31, 348
High Definition Television (HDTV) 37
High Definition Video (HDV) 37
high-fidelity game 405
high-fidelity patient simulations (HPS) 368
Higinbotham, William "Willy" 4, 36
History *see* early PC gaming; first generation; fourth-generation; second generation; third generation
Hitachi 104
Hitachi SH2 32-bit RISC CPUs 219
Hitachi SH4 processor 272
Hochberg, Josh 3
Hockey 13, 15
Hogan's Alley 124
Hollow Knight 317, *319,* 440
Holt, Rod 90
Home Arcade Systems 211
home port 61
home video game; *see also* Magnavox Odyssey
    evolution of 5–6
    Pong for Your Home TV 12–13
Honor of Kings 257, 405
Horizon: Forbidden West 441
"Hot Coffee" 187, *187*
The House of the Dead 4 329
HTC 315
HTC Dream 399
HTC Vive VR headset 315
HuCards 147, 149, 150
    vs. TurboChips 151
Hudson Soft 105, 147, 149
Hulu 338
human dimension modeling 366
Humble Bundle, Inc. 318
Humpert, James 130
Humpty Dumpty 3
Hyper Light Drifter 317
hypermasculine character 188, *188*
hypermasculinization of men 188, *188,* 200
HyperVerse 312
Hyrule Warriors 440

IBM (International Business Machines) 281, 301, 330
    and clones, rise of 301, **302**
    OS/2 2.0 304
IBM clones 301
IBM PC 5150 301, **302**
IBM PS/2 301

IBM Simon Personal Communicator 389
Iconoclasts 440
Ideaworks3D 394
Idestam, Fredrik 391
IDSA *see* Interactive Digital Software
    Association (IDSA)
id Software 194, 303
IEEE, 1394 276
IEEE-1394/firewire **35**
IK+ 103
Ikari Warriors 167
iMac computers 307
i-mode 390
Impossible Mission 103
impulse triggers 433
independent developers 247
Indie Fund 249
indie games 309–311, 389
inequities, in gender and race 190
Infogrames Entertainment SA (IESA) 320
Injustice 341
in-house (first-party) developers 247
input and output (I/O) devices 90
Inside 317, 440
Insomniac 341
Instant Game Collection 338
Institute of Play 377
Integrated Services Digital Broadcasting
    (ISDB) 37
Intel 8021 68
Intel Extreme Masters (IEM)
    tournaments 260
intellectual properties (IPs) 246, 444
Intellivision II 69; *see also* Mattel
    Intellivision
Intellivision Inc. (later INTV
    Corporation) 80
Intellivoice 69, *69*
"Intellivoice" adapter 45
Intel Pentium III processor 288
interactive component of video game 200
interactive computer games, earliest 4–18
    Coleco Telstar 13–18, **15**, *15–17*, **18**
    Computer Space 4–5, *5*
    Magnavox Odyssey 5–10, *6* (*see also*
        Magnavox Odyssey)
    Pong 10–13, *11–14*
    Spacewar! 4, *5*
    Tennis for Two 4, *4*
Interactive Digital Software Association
    (IDSA) 193, 196, 259
interactive entertainment industry 245;
    see also video game industry
Interactive Software Federation of Europe
    (ISFE) 183, 193
interchangeable games 16
interface music 47
interlaced scan 34, *34*
The *International* 260, *261*

International Age Rating Coalition
    (IARC) 194
International Game Developers
    Association (IGDA) 191
International Mobile Gaming Awards
    (IMGA) 405
International System of Units (SI) 33
Internet 31, 305
Interpolation 212
intrusion (hack) 337
Iomo 394
iPad 401
iPhone 397–399, **398**
    early games 399, **399**
    platforms 399–402
iPhone operating system (iOS) 398
iPod 308
iPod Touch 397
Irem 147
Iridion 3D 282
Ishikawa, Masami 154
isometric games 42, *42*
Ive, Jonathan 307
Iwadare, Kunihiko 149
Iwata, Satoru 287, 389, 444
Iwatani, Toru 55

Jackbox Games 405
Jackson, Michael 160
Jacobs, Jon 311
JagLink for local area network (LAN) 216
Jaguar CD 216
Jaguar CPU 424
JAMDAT Mobile 391
James 'Buster' Douglas Knockout Boxing 157
Japanese Amusement Machine
    Manufacturers Association
    (JAMMA) 121
Japanese role-playing game (JRPG) 134
Jarvis, Eugene 329
Java 2 Micro Edition (J2ME) 391
Jay, Miner 56
Jenkins, Henry, Dr. 197, 200
Jensen, Peter 5
Jet Grind Radio 275
Jet Set Willy 107
jewel case packaging 249, *249*
Jobs, Steve 89, 90, 307, 402
Joe Montana Football 157
John Madden Football 157
Joust 136, 138
Joy-Con 436
joystick controller 57
joysticks 15
JTS company 320
Judge 126
Jumpman Junior 73
Jump Pak 274
Jungle Hunt 56

Jurassic Park 134
Just Cause 189
Just Chatting 316

Kahoot! 376
Kalinske, Tom 157, 220, 258
Karate Champ 121
Karateka 94
Kassar, Ray 57–59, 123
Katana ZERO 317
Kates, Josef, Dr. 4
Katz, Michael 71, 157
Kawasaki, Eikichi 167
K.C. Munchkin! 65, *65*
K.C.'s Krazy Chase! 65, *65*
keep case (poly-box) 249
Keith Courage in Alpha Zones 150, *151*
Kena: Bridge of Spirits 443
Kent, Steve 162
kernel 31
Kickstarter 246
Kid Icarus Uprising 423
Killer Bees! 65, *65*
Killzone: Mercenary 430
kilobyte (KB) 33
Kimishima, Tatsumi 444
Kinect 333
Kinect 2.0 432
The *King of Fighters* 172
The *King of Fighters '98 172*
King of Glory 406
King's (company) 402
King's Quest 93, *93*
King's Valley II: The Seal of El Giza 105
Kirby's Adventure 130
Kirby's Dream Land 155
Kirby's Star Stacker 155
Klebold, Dylan 194
Knight Lore 107
Knights of the Round 147
Knowledge Adventure 376
Kōei 184
Kohl, Herb 193
Kojima, Hideo 341
Konami 105, 121, 160, 165, *165*, 178, 227,
    271, 329
Kondo, Koji 44
Königsspiel 359
Kordek, Steve 3
Korean e-Sports Association (KeSPA) 260
Koshiro, Yuzo 44, 159
Kotok, Alan 4
Kriegsspiel 359
Kühn, Simone 373
Kung Fu 121, *127*
Kutaragi, Ken 224, 276, 337

Lagettie, David 366
Lambert, Jerry 339

Lambert, Johann 41
Lambert lighting 41
LAN adapter 32
Lanier, Jaron 314
L.A. Noire: The VR Case Files 316
LAN parties 259
LANs *see* local area networks (LANs)
The Last Blade 172
The Last of Us **341**
The Last of Us Part II 189, 428
Las Vegas Poker & Blackjack 66, *66*
Latte GPU 421
The Lawnmower Man 314
LCD *see* liquid crystal display (LCD)
Le, Minh 307
leaderboards 406
League of Legends 257, **258**
League of Legends World Championship,
        the 261
LeapPad 376
Leapster 376
leap year bug 337
Ledbetter, Carl 432
Lee, Harold 12
Left 4 Dead 334
The Legend of the Mystical Ninja 165, *165*
The Legend of Zelda 122
*The Legend of Zelda: A Link Between
        Worlds* 405, 423, **423**
The Legend of Zelda: A Link to the Past
        166, **167**, 282
The Legend of Zelda: Breath of the Wild
        437, *437*, **438**, 440, **441**
*The Legend of Zelda: Link's
        Awakening* 155
The Legend of Zelda: Ocarina of Time
        232, *232*
*The Legend of Zelda: Ocarina of Time
        3D* 423
*The Legend of Zelda: Oracle of
        Seasons* 233
The Legend of Zelda: The Minish Cap 282
The Legend of Zelda: The Wind Waker
        285, *287*
The Legend of Zelda: Twilight Princess
        344, 349
Lehner, Steve 62
Leibniz, Gottfried 32
*Leisure Suit Larry in the Land of the
        Lounge Lizards* 184, *184*
Lemonade Stand 91
Leong, Tim **347**
lesbian, gay, bisexual, transgender, queer
        or questioning (LGBTQ)
        community 188, 189
level designer **248**
LG 399
licensed soundtracks 213
licenses 247

licensing 246
        policy 125
Lieberman, Joseph 193
Life & Death 368
Life & Death II: The Brain 368
Life Is Strange 189
LifeSigns: Surgical Unit 368
life simulation applications 375
Life with PlayStation 338
light bar 425
light-emitting diode (LED) displays 36
light gun 15
lighting 40–41
Limbo 40
Lincoln, Howard 123, 281
Lindbergh Yellow 329
Linden Lab 311
line scrolling 43
Linux 304, 337
Lipkin, Gene 12
liquid crystal display (LCD) 36
        viewing angle 36
live service games 258
Live Vision Camera 333
Llamas, Stephanie 257
Lobb, Ken 287
local area networks (LANs) 31, *32*
        JagLink for 216
localization 246
Lock 'N' Chase 70
locomotion 314
Logg, Ed 55
Logitech 211, 279
Lone Echo 316
"Longbox" keep case 249, *249*
Long-Term Evolution (LTE) 391
1944: The Loop Master 209
loot box 257
Lords of Midnight 107
Lords of Thunder 152
Lost Worlds 147
Lotus 1-2-3 301
Lovell, Nicholas 199
Lowe, Al 184
Lowenstein, Douglas (Doug) 193, 195,
        197, 255
LPCM (linear pulse code modulation) 340
Luckey, Palmer 314
Luigi's Mansion 284
Luis von Ahn 371
Luke, Horace 288
Lukin, Jarid 257
luminance (luma) 41
Lumines: Puzzle Fusion **343**
Lumines: Electronic Symphony 430
Lynx II 161

Macintosh "Classic" series 110
Macintosh computer 108, 301

Macintosh II 110
Macintosh 128K 94
Macintosh Plus 110
Mac OS X (Operating System X) 308
Mad Catz 420
Madden NFL 22 255
Madden NFL 97 221
Madden NFL 2002 289
MadLab 418
Madö King Granzört 150
Maeda, Takeshiro 149
magazine advertisement
        for Apple II *92*
        for Atari 5200 *77*
        for Atari 7800 *137*
        for Atari 800 computer *98*
        for Atari Jaguar *217*
        for Atari Video Computer System
                (VCS) *60*
        christmas catalog advertisement
                for Sears "Tele-Games" label
                (Pong) 14
        for Coleco Telstar *17*
        for ColecoVision *74*
        for Commodore, 64 *102*
        for Magnavox Odyssey
                1973 *7*
                1981 *64*
        for Magnavox Odyssey 2 *64*
        for Mattel Intellivision *67*
        for N64 *230*
        for Neo•Geo AES, 1991 *171*
        for Nintendo GameCube *286*
        for Nintendo Switch *439*
        for Nintendo Wii *346*
        for Nintendo Wii U *419*
        for Nokia N-Gage QD *395*
        for Sega Dreamcast *274*
        for Sega Genesis *158*
        for Sega Master System *133*
        for Sega Saturn system *222*
        for SNES, 1992 **164**
        for Sony PlayStation *225*
        for Sony PlayStation, 2 *280*
        for TG-16, 1992 *153*
Magical Drop 172
Magician Lord 169
Magic Knight RayEarth 223
Magnavox 5
Magnavox Odyssey 5–10, *6*, 12, 19
        Atari generation 61–62, **62**, *62*, 63
                vs. Atari VCS 62–63
                64 built-in characters 63
                color palette 63
                display 62
                magazine advertisement for
                        (1981) *64*
                vs. Mattel Intellivision 65–69
                memory 63

Magnavox Odyssey (*cont.*)
    party games 62
    tech specs 63, *63*
    titles 63–65, *65*
    U.S. launch titles **62,** *63*
    first generation
        magazine advertisement for
            (1973) *7*
        market summary 19
        series releases **10**
        tech specs **6**
        understanding games **6,** 6–10,
            7, 8
        U.S. launch titles 6, **6,** *8, 8*
    Odyssey 300 system 15
    Table Tennis 10, *12*
Main, Peter 229
Major League Gaming Inc. (MLG) 260
Mali-400 399
mandatory installation 425
Manhunt 197–199, *198*
Manic Miner 107
manufacturers **249,** 249–250
manufacturing **249,** 249–250
manufacturing plants 249
Marble Madness 121
MARIA, chip 136
Marine Doom 361, **363**
Mario Kart 7 423
Mario Kart 8 254
Mario Kart Tour 405
Mario's Picross 155
Mario the Juggler 126
market share 167
market summary
    early PC gaming 110–111, *111*
    fifth-generation 234, *234, 235, 235*
    first generation video games 19, *20*
    fourth-generation 172–173, *173*
    mobile and casual gaming
        407–408
    PC gaming 320–321, *321*
    second generation video games
        79–80, *80*
    seventh generation 349–350, **351**
    sixth generation 292–293, *293*
    third generation 138–139, *139*
Marks, Richard 279
Martech 184
Marvel's Spider-Man 428
Marvel's Spider-Man: Miles Morales
    189, 255
Marvel Super Heroes 209, 220, 223
Marvel vs. Capcom 2 271, *276*
Mascot Capsule 397
Mass Effect 189, *189*
Mass Effect 3 **334**
massively multiplayer online (MMO)
    games 257

"Massively Multiplayer Online Role-
    Playing Game" (MMORPG)
    108, 305
massively multiplayer online worlds
    (MMOWs) 311
"mass murder simulator" 196
Master Gear Converter 168
Master of Darkness 134
Master Strategy trilogy 62
Master System 131
Mastertronic 101, 108, 132
MasterType 376
matchmaking 309
match three game 402
Mathieson, John 215
Matrix World 312
Matson, Harold "Matt" 65
Matsushita Electric Industrial 281–282
Matsushita, Konosuke 210
Mattel 65, 157
Mattel Intellivision 65, *65*–69, **66,** *67,*
    69, 70
    vs. Atari VCS and Odyssey 69–70
    vs. ColecoVision 72–73
    directional disk 66
    features *65,* 65–66
    Intellivision II 69
    Intellivoice 69, *69*
    keyboard component 69
    magazine advertisement for, 1981 *67*
    numeric keypad 66
    overlays 66
    tech specs **70,** 70–71
    titles 70–71, *71*
Mattrick, Don 431
M2 Bradley 360
McCarthy, Dave 186
McDonald, Joel 404
Meade, Barry 402
medal games 417
Megablasters 108
megabyte (MB) 33
Mega-CD 157
Mega Drive Systems Inc. 154
Mega Man 6 43
Meier, Sid *46, 47,* 101
Melbits World 406
memory capacity 33
memory card 225
Memory Card Adaptor 339
memory controller 29
memory mapping 72
Memory Stick 336
Memory Track 216
Memory Unit 332
men
    as hypermasculine character 188,
        188, 200
    as video gamer 183

Menacer 157
Mercs 147
Messenger Kit 333
Metahero 312
Metal Gear 105, 130
Metal Gear Solid 227, *227, 233*
Metal Gear Solid: Peace Walker **343**
Metal Gear Solid 2: Sons of Liberty
    279, *281*
Metal Gear 2: Solid Snake 105
Metal Slug 172
Metal Slug X 172
Meta Quest 2 315
Metaverse 312
#MeToo movement 191
Metro 2033 334
Metroid 125, *129,* 130, 155
Metroid Dread 440, *441*
Metroid II: The Return of Samus 155
Metroid Prime 285
Metroid Prime 3: Corruption **349**
Metroid: Zero Mission 282
Mical, R. J. 210
Michael Jackson's Moonwalker 157
Mick & Mack as the Global Gladiators 159
Microsoft Corporation 93, 198, 287, 403
Microsoft Office 287
Microsoft's DirectX technology 287–288
Microsoft's Xbox 360 **330,** 330–333,
    331, *331*
    console comparison 333–334, *334*
    vs. PS3 *339,* 339–340
    tech specs 333–334, *334*
    titles 334, **334**
    U.S. launch titles *331*
    versions *332,* **332**
    vs. Wii *348, 348*
Microsoft Xbox 34, 287–290,
    288–290, **289**
    advertisement *290*
    vs. GameCube 290–291, **291**
    vs. PlayStation 2 290–291, **291**
    tech specs 290–291, **291**
    titles 291, *292*
    U.S. launch titles **289**
    Xbox Games Store 250
        12-month game sales curve *253*
microtransactions 248, 257, 309, 331
Microvision
    Block Buster 68, *68*
    cartridges 68, *68*
    tech specs 68, **68**
MIDI (Musical Instrument Digital
    Interface)-like format 43, 109
Midnight Mutants 138, *138*
Midway 55, 232
Midway Games 192
"Mii," character 345
Miiverse 420

Mike Tyson's Punch-Out!! 188
milestones (development stages), video
    game development cycle
    246, **246**
military exercises 359
Military Madness 152, *154*
military, science, and education 357–379
    America's Army 363, **363**
    Bradley Trainer 360, **360**
    brain development 373–374, **374**
    DARWARS 364–366, **365**
    early war games 359
    at ease (exposure therapy) 367
    Full Spectrum Warrior (FSW) 364, **364**
    games with a purpose **371**, 371–372
    Marine Doom 361, **363**
    military simulation 359–360, **360**
    *Multipurpose Arcade Combat
        Simulator (MACS)* 361, **361**
    negative side effects 372–373
    overview 359
    popular cots educational games
        376–377, *377*, **377**
    positive impact 373
    schools specializing in gaming
        377–379, *378*
    from science to education 374–376,
        375, **375**
    Serious games 367–370, **368, 369**
    Serious Games Showcase and
        Challenge 370, *370*
    video game research 372
    video games in science 367
    virtual battlefields 366–367, **367**
military simulation 359–360, **360**
Miller, Joe 218
millions of instructions per second
    (MIPS) 40
MILO (Multiple Interactive Learning
    Objectives) 360
Milton Bradley (MB) 68
Mindbuster 68, *68*
MineCon 259
Minecraft **310**, 377
Miner, Jay 218
minigame 187
MIPS (millions of instructions per
    second) 40
Mirror's Edge 41
Missile Command 61
Mitsubishi 18
Mitsubishi ML-8000 105
Mitsumi 122
Miyamoto, Shigeru 18, 55, 125, 128, 129,
    130, 283, 344
MK-80100 controller 220
MLB: The Show 21 255
mobile game/gaming 387–409; *see also*
    smartphone(s)

Apple iPhone 397–399, **398**
    competition 393–394
    defined 389
    gamer profile 406–407
    Gizmondo 396–397, **397**
    market summary 407–408, **408**
    merits 405
    milestones 402–404
    new millennium of mobile and
        391, *391*
    Nintendo 404–405
    Nokia N-Gage 391–393, *392,*
        392, 393
    origin 390, **390**
    other developments 394–396, **396**
    overview 389
    platforms 399–402
    recent trends 405–406
    usage trends **407**
Mobile Games Awards 405
Mobile Legends: Bang Bang 262, 406
Mobile VR 407
Mockingboard 91
modding 304
modem 32, 273
modern arcade scene 417–418
modern console gaming *see* console
    gaming, modern
modern gaming breakthroughs/trends
    445–446
Modern Times Group (MTG) 408
"Mode 7," SNES 165, *165*
mods 188
MOGA (Mobile Gaming) controller 402
Mojang 309, 436
Molyneux, Peter 108
monaural (mono) sound 43
monetization 248
monitors
    CRT monitor 36
    flat panel 36
    Hertz rating 33
    LCD 36
    LED displays 36
    OLED displays 36
    PDP 36
    refresh rate 33–34
    types of 36
    vector 38, 79
monochromatic color 41
monochrome 37
mono sound, five channels of 129
Monster Lair 151
Montezuma's Revenge 78
*Montezuma's Revenge: Featuring Panama
    Joe* 61
Monument Valley **403**
Moore, Peter 273, 332
Moppin 404

Morita, Akio 223
Mortal Kombat 147, *147*, 173, 188, 189,
    192, *192*
Mortal Kombat II 166, 173, 189
Mosaic (scrambling blocks) effects 165
Moss 316, 428
MOS Technology 99
MOS Technology 6502 56
MOS Technology MPS 7600-004 chip
    15–16
motherboard 29, *29*
motion blur 33
motion controller 339
motion estimation/motion compensation
    (ME/MC) processing 33
Motorola 68000 109, 121, 154, 159, 166
Motorola MC68000 RISC chip 217
Motorola RAZR 393
MPS 7600-004 chip 15–16
M-rated games 197
MS-DOS 287, 303, **303**
Ms. Pac-Man 56
MSX2 105
MSX2+ 105
MSX series *104,* 105, **105**
MSX TurboR 105
M.U.L.E 97, *97*
multicart 131
multicolor sprites 100
multicore chip 330
multicore processors 40
MultiMediaCards (MMCs) 392
Multimedia Messaging Service
    (MMS) 399
multiplayer adaptor 220
multiplayer gaming 304
multiplayer online battle arena (MOBA)
    game 257, 308
*Multipurpose Arcade Combat Simulator
    (MACS)* 361, **361**
Multi Screen 126
Multitap adaptors 225
multi-touch technology 399
Multi-User Dungeon (MUD) 93, 108
Munday, Rod 47
M.U.S.H.A. 160
Music 43–45
Musical Instrument Digital Interface
    (MIDI)-like formats 43, 109
Mutoscopes 3
Myst **304**
Mystery House 93, *93*
Mystic Quest 155
Mystique 184

N64 *see* Nintendo 64 (N64)
Nakayama, Hayao 157
Nakayoshi Cooking 233
Namco 55, 56, 121

Naka, Yuji 160, 223
NAOMI 275, 329
National Television Standards Committee (NTSC) 36
Naughty Dog 281, 341
Naval Battle 16, 18
navigation controller 339
NBA 2K7 **337**
NCsoft 310
NEC *see* Nippon Electric Company (NEC)
NEC VR4300 231
NEC PC-98 *104,* 104–105, **105**
NEC PC Engine 149, *149; see also* TurboGrafx-16 (TG-16)
    and PI-PD001 controller *149*
    redesigned (*see* TurboGrafx-16)
    tech specs 152, **152**
    vs. TurboGrafx-16 152, *154*
Need For Speed, the 213
Needle, Dave 210
negative side effects 372–373
Neo•Geo AES (SNK) 167, *169*
    magazine advertisement for, 1991 *171*
    vs. others 170
    tech specs **172**
    titles 170, 172, *172*
    U.S. launch titles **169**
Neo•Geo CD 170
Neo•Geo MVS (Multi Video System) 167, *169*
Neo•Geo Pocket 233
Neo•Geo Pocket Color 282
NES *see* Nintendo Entertainment System (NES)
NES Zapper 124, *125*
Netflix 338
NetFront 425
network adapter 32, 279
network card 32
networking methods 31; *see also* local area networks (LANs); wide area networks (WANs)
network interface controller (NIC) 32
Network Play service 279
NeuroRacer 374
Neutopia 154
Neverdie 311
Neverwinter Nights 2 444
Neville, Shane 394
Newell, Gabe 251
Newman, Garry 309
new millennium
    of mobile 391, *391*
    of PC gaming 308, *309*
New Nintendo 3DS 423
New Xbox One Experience 433
Newzoo 255, 406
NFC (near-field communication) 419
NFL 2K1 275

N-Gage platform 394
N-Gage QD 394
NHL Hockey 157
Nicolas, Gwénaël 282
Nielsen Media Research (NMR) 255
Night Battle 15
Night in the Woods 317
Night Life 184
NiGHTS into Dreams 223
Night Stalker 70, *70*
Night Trap 185, 186
Nimoy, Leonard 274
Nimrod 4
Ninja Gaiden 121, 130, 134
Ninja Gaiden 3 43
Ninja Gaiden Black 292
Ninja Golf 138, 138
Ni no Kuni: Wrath of the White Witch 341, 440
Nintendo 55
Nintendo 3DS 423
Nintendo 64 (N64) *228–230,* 228–231
    magazine advertisement for *230*
    NEC VR4300 processor 231
    vs. Sony PlayStation **231,** 231–232
    tech specs **231,** 231–232
    titles 232, *232*
Nintendo 64 Disk Drive (64DD) 235
Nintendo Advanced Video System (AVS) 123, *124*
Nintendo Color TV Game 19
    series releases **19**
Nintendo Co., Ltd. 122, 404–405
    Game Boy (*see* Game Boy)
    market summary 138–139, *139*
    Super Famicom (SFC) 162, *162*
Nintendo DS 330, 335, **335**
Nintendo Entertainment System (NES) 121, 123–127, *124, 125,* **127**
    vs. Atari 2600 (VCS) 127–129, **129**
    vs. Atari 7800 ProSystem 136, **136,** 138
    control stick 124
    directional pad ("d-pad") 124
    market summary 138–139, *139*
    NES Zapper 124, *125*
    redesigned 125
    Robot Operating Buddy (R.O.B.) 124, *125*
    vs. Sega Master System 132, **134**
    tech specs **129**
    titles *129,* 129–130
    vs. TurboGrafx-16 152, *154*
    U.S. launch titles **127**
Nintendo eShop 420, 437
Nintendo Famicom 122, *122,* 130
    redesign of 123, *124*
Nintendo Fun Club News 127
Nintendo GameCube 281–284, **283,** *283, 284,* 420

changes 287
    magazine advertisement for *286*
    vs. Microsoft Xbox 290–291, **291**
    vs. PlayStation 2 284, **285**
    tech specs 284, **285**
    titles 285, *287*
    U.S. launch titles **283**
Nintendogs + Cats 423
Nintendo Koppai 122
Nintendo Labo 438
Nintendo Network 420
Nintendo Power 127
Nintendo SNS-101 348
Nintendo Switch 436
Nintendo TVii 420
Nintendo Wii **344–347,** 344–348
    launch titles 345
    vs. PlayStation 3 and XBOX 360 348, *348*
    titles 349, **349**
    Wii Remote 345
Nintendo World 418
Nippon Electric Company (NEC) 104, 149, 229
NIS America 349
Nokia 6110 390
Nokia Corporation 391
Nokia N-Gage 391–393, *392,* **392, 393**
    advertisement for **395**
    competition 393–394
    titles 394
Nomad 233
non-diegetic sound 45
non-player characters (NPCs) 189
North American Video Game Crash of, 1983 78–79, *79,* 121
North, Nolan 45, *45*
Noughts and Crosses 4
NPCs (non-player characters) 189
NPD Group, Inc. 255
NTSC (National Television Standards Committee) 36
NTT DoCoMo 389–390
nudity; *see also* sex/sexual themes, in video games
    game series known for **187**
Nunchuk 345
numeric keypad 66, 71, 75
Nutting Associates 5
Nvidia 305, 336
Nvidia GoForce 397
Nvidia graphics chip 288
Nvidia's Tegra X1 chipset 438
Nvidia Turing 317
NXE (New Xbox Experience) 332

Oculus Quest 315
Oculus Rift 314–315
Oculus VR 314

Odyssey *see* Magnavox Odyssey
Odyssey² 61
Odyssey 300 system 15
Off-TV Play 419
Ohga, Norio 224
Ohshima, Naoto 160
Oil Panic 126
Okada, Satoru 155
Okawa, Isao 272
OLED (organic light-emitting diode) 427, 438
OneGuide 433
One on One: Dr. J vs. Larry Bird 93, 188
online social games 311
On-Line Systems 183
OnLive 318
OOE (Out of Order Execution) 421
open-ended game 101
OpenGL 305
OpenGL ES 396
open world games 279
Operation Rainfall campaign 349
optical audio output 332
options 425
The Orange Box 334, **334**
Orbis 424
The Oregon Trail 91, 94
organic light-emitting diode (OLED) 36
Ori and the Will of the Wisps 440, *442*
Orzack, Maressa Hecht 372
oscilloscope 4
OTS (over-the-shoulder) perspective 42
Outer Wilds 317
The Outer Worlds 189
Out of Order Execution (OOE) 40
OutRun 121, 147, 152
overhead games 42
oversexualization, of women 188, *188*, 200
over-the-shoulder (OTS) perspective 42
Overwatch 189, 257, 436
Owlboy 317, 440
OXO 4

Pachinko 3
packaging line 249
pack-in title 101, 344
Pac-Man 55, 78, 407
paddle controllers 57
Pajitnov, Alexey 101, 155
PAL (phase alternate line) 36
palette of 64 132
Palm, Inc. 389
PalmPilot 389
Panasonic 210, 211; *see also* 3DO Interactive Multiplayer
Panasonic FZ-10 *212*
Pandemic Studios 364

Pan-European Game Information (PEGI) 193, *196*
Panzer Dragoon 221, *221, 223*
Paperboy 121, 132
Paradroid 103
parallax scrolling 43, 147, 159
parallel processing 40
Parker Brothers 132
Parodius 105
patches 188, 248, 308
patents 5
Pat Riley Basketball 157
payment gateway 309
"Pay-outs" 3
"pay-to-win" (P2W) 257
PBS Kids 376
PC-98 series 111
PC/AT 301
PC-compatible systems 301
PC Engine 149
PC gaming 299–321; *see also* early PC gaming
    cloud gaming 318, *318*
    DOS (disk operating system) 303, **303**
    early 1990s 303–304, **304**
    genre pioneers (early 1990s) 303–304, **304**
    golden age of 305–307
    IBM and rise of clones 301, **302**
    indie games 309–311
    market summary 320–321, *321*
    modern VR pioneers 314–316
    new millennium of 308, *309*
    overview 301
    rise of 301
    social games 309–311
    Steam 309–311
    subscription 318, *318*
    timeline 300
    trends of 2010s 316–318
    virtual online worlds 311–312, *312*, **312**
    virtual reality 314
    Windows 95 and 3D graphics 304–305, **305–306**
PCH-2000 430
PCI (peripheral component interconnect) 31, *32*
PCjr 301
PC-9801-26K 104
PCM (pulse-code modulation) 44
PCs *see* personal computers (PCs)
μPD7220 Graphics Display Controller (GDC) 104
PDP *see* plasma display panel (PDP)
PDP-1 (Programmed Data Processor-1) computer 4
pdQ smartphone 389
Penguin Adventure 105
Penny Arcade Expo (PAX Prime) 259

penny arcades 3
Perfect Dark 232
peripheral component interconnect (PCI) 31, *32*
personal computers (PCs) 29, 109, 301
personal digital assistants (PDAs) 389
perspective *42, 42–43*, **43**
    axis 42–43
    "2.5D" games 42
    first-person 42, *42*
    isometric games 42, *42*
    over-the-shoulder (OTS) 42
    RPGs 42
    scrolling 43
    second-person 42
    stereoscopic 3D video games 43
    third-person 42, *42*
Pet Society 310
Phantasmagoria 186
Phantasy Star 132–133, 134, 160, *160*
Phantasy Star II 160, *160*
phase alternate line (PAL) 36
Philips 10, 79
Philips CD-i 173
Philips N.V. 165
Phillips, Howard 127
Phong lighting 41
Pick Axe Pete! 65, *65*
picture-in picture (PiP) 433
Pierce, Kenneth M. 184
Pikmin Bloom 405
Pilotwings 165
Pilotwings 64 229, *229*
Pilotwings Resort 423
Pinball Construction Set 94
pinball, evolution of 3, *3*
Pioneer LaserActive 173
PI-PD001 controller, NEC PC Engine and 149
pipelines 334
pirated games 211
Pitfall! 61, 73
Pitcairn 427
Pitfall II: Lost Caverns 61
Pit-Fighter 161
Pitrat, Julius E. 301
pixels 33
pixel shaders 333
plasma display panel (PDP) 36
plastic overlays 5
platform game genre 55
platforms, mobiles 399–402
Play Anywhere 433
Play Cable 220
Playdead 403, 436
PlayLink 405
Play Magazine 56
Play Mechanix 329, 417
The Playroom 424, *424, 425*

PlayStation 2 34
PlayStation 2 Slim 279
PlayStation 3 336
PlayStation 4 (PS4) 424, **424–426,**
        424–427; see also console
        gaming, modern
PlayStation 4 (PS4) vs. Wii U 427,
        427–428
PlayStation 4 (PS4) vs. Xbox One
        434–435, 435, **436**
PlayStation 4 (PS4) titles 428, **428–430**
PlayStation 4 Pro 427
PlayStation 5 440–441
PlayStation Camera 339, 424, 427
PlayStation Eyc 339
PlayStation Home 338
PlayStation Move 339, 427
PlayStation Network (PSN) 337
PlayStation Now 425
PlayStation PC 321
PlayStation Plus 338, 425
PlayStation Portable (PSP) 330, 343, **343**
PlayStation Store 250, 338
PlayStation Underground 224
PlayStation Vita 430
PlayStation VR (PSVR) 315, 427
Playtika 408
PlayTV 339
Plimpton, George 66, 67
Pober, Arthur, Dr. 193
Pocket Bomberman 233
Poison, character 188
Pokémon 155, 232, 248, 404, 423
*Pokémon: Brilliant Diamond/Shining
        Pearl* 255
Pokémon Crystal 233
Pokémon Emerald 282
Pokémon GO 404
Pokémon: Let's Go, Eevee! 440
Pokémon: Let's Go, Pikachu! 440
Pokémon Yellow 155
POKEY 96
POKEY (Pot Keyboard Integrated
        Circuit) sound chip 76, 96
Pole Position 56
Pole Position II 136, 136
Policenauts 105
poly-box (keep case) 249
polycarbonates 249
polygon count 39
polygon graphics 38, 38–39, 39, 186
        3D 147, 166
polygons per second (PPS) 275, 279
Pong 10–13, *11–14*, 19
        market summary 19
        Sears "Tele-Games" label 12, *13*
                christmas catalog advertisement
                        for *14*
        vs. *Table Tennis* 12, 12–13

tech specs **13**
        variations 13
        vendor print advertisement for *11*
Pong Doubles 13
Pong for Your Home TV 12–13
PopCap games 394
Popeye 56, 122, *123*
Popful Mail 105
Pop'n Music 271
popular cots educational games 376–377,
        377, **377**
Populous 103, 108
Portal 2 **319**
ports 31, *31*, 135, 247
positive impact 373
Postal 197
Pot Keyboard Integrated Circuit
        (POKEY) audio chip 136
Power Base Converter 156, 157, *157*
Powered Gear 209
Power Glove 127, 314
Power Pad 127
PowerPC Tri-Core "Espresso" 421
Power Strike II 134
Pridham, Edwin 5
Prince of Persia 108, 291, 396, **396**
Princeton Review 379
printed circuit board (PCB) 121
Pro Controller 216, 347, 438
product and talent layer 246
production and tools layer 247
pro gaming 260
Programmed Data Processor-1 (PDP-1)
        computer 4
programmer **248**
progressive scan 34, *34*, 272
Project Café 418
Project Gotham Racing 3 **331**
Project Scorpio 434
Proline controller 135, *135*
prosocial motive 199
protagonists 189
prototype 5, 165
Prune **403**
Psion Organiser 389
PSN outage 337
PSone 225, *227*
PSP Go 343
PS3 Slim 337
PS4 Slim 427
PS Vita Cards 430
Psychic World 168
Psychonauts 444
Psychonauts 2 **319**
Psygnosis 224
PTSD [post-traumatic stress disorder] 361
publisher 245
publishing 246
PUBG: Battlegrounds 254

PUBG Mobile 258, 262, 405, 406
pulse-code modulation (PCM) 44
push notification 406
Puyo Puyol 2 105
Puyo Puyol 105
Pyre 317

*Q*Bert* 56
Quad HD 403
Quake **306**
QuakeCon 259
Qualcomm 389
quality assurance (QA) standards 250
The Quest for the Rings! 63
Quest to Learn 377
Quest VR 315
Quinn, Tom 12, 375

race
        inequities in 190
        sex and violence in video games and
                188–191, *190*
        violence and Death Race 191, *192*
racial inequity 190
Radar Scope 55
Radeon DNA (RDNA) 317
Radeon graphics 307
radio frequency (RF) switch Atari 5200 75
radio-frequency (RF) switch 75
radio frequency (RF) switchbox 5
Rainbow Walker 97
Rains, Lyle 55
RAM (random access memory) 29–30,
        30, 91
Rapid Transit 3
Rare 232, 285
raster graphics *38*, 38–39
Ratchet & Clank 341
Ratchet & Clank: Going Commando 281
Ratchet & Clank: Rift Apart 443
Ratings of video games, ESRB **193**
Raven Software 197
Raw Thrills 329, 417
Rayman 218, *218*
Raymond Stuart-Williams 4
ray tracing 42, 317, 442
RCA 56
read only memory (ROM) 29–30, *30*, 91
Ready Player One 312
"Reality" co-processor (RCP) 228
Reality Synthesizer 336
real-time lighting effects 229
real-time strategy (RTS) 303
realtime tactics (RTT) game 364
Real Virtuality 2 engine 366
rear touchpad 430
Recreational Brainware 159
Rec Room 316
redbook audio 225

Red Dead Redemption 2 436, **436**
redemption games 271
red, green, and blue (RGB) component
    cables 34
RedLynx 394
"Red Ring of Death" 250, 332
refresh rates
    TVs and monitors 33
regional lockout components 211
region free 37, 211, 335
region-free systems 211
region-locked 428
Region protection 151
Regulation, ESRB and **193**
Remedy Entertainment 435
Remote Play 426, 430
Rendering Ranger: R2 166
Rendition 305
reprogramming 247
Rescue on Fractalus! 97, 101
research, video game 372
"reset" button 6
Resident Evil 227
Resident Evil 4 285, 287, *287*
Resident Evil 4 VR 316
Resident Evil 7 428, 435
Resident Evil–Code: Veronica 275, *275*
Resident Evil: Revelations 423
Resident Evil: Village 255
Resistance: Fall of Man **337**
retailers 245, 252
retail, video game industry *252*, 252–253
Retro Gamer Magazine 210
Retro Studios, Inc. 285
Returnal 443
Return of the Obra Dinn 317
The Revenge of Shinobi 159
Revenge of the Drancon 168
Rez Infinite 316
RGB (red, green, blue) color 41
rhythm game genre 271
Rick Dangerous 108
Ridge Racer 30, *225*
Ridiculous Fishing: A Tale of
    Redemption **403**
ring of light 331
Riot Games 191, *258*, 261, 316
Ripcord Games 97
River Raid 61, 70
Road Race 16, *16*
Road Rash 213
Robinett, Warren 61
Roblox 321
Robot Battle 15
Robot Operating Buddy (R.O.B.)
    124, *125*
Robotron: 2084 56, 78
Rock Band 272
Rocket Knight Adventures 160

Rockstar Games 187, 279
    and congressional bills 197–199, *198*
    Manhunt 197–199, *198*
Roebuck & Company 12
Rolando **399**
role-playing game (RPG) Dungeons &
    Dragons 93
role-playing games (RPGs) 42
RollerCoaster Tycoon 307
Roller Controller, ColecoVision 72, *72*
ROM (read-only memory) 29–30, *30*, 91
ROM BIOS 29, 30
Romero, John 194
Rong-Yu, Chen 373
Rosen, David 223
Rosen Enterprises 130
Rosser Jr., James 369
Ross, Steve 57
rotation of graphics 165
Roulette 8, *8*
Rovio Entertainment 399
royalties 12
royalty fees 246
R-Type 150, *151*
Rude Breaker 105
Rumble Pak 231
Running With Scissors 197
Rusch, Bill 5
Russell, Kent 169
Russell, Steve "Slug" 4, 5, 12, 36, 37
Rusty 105
Ryan, Jim 441
Ryder, Jared **347**
Rygar 161
Ryzen processor 317
R-Zone 233

Sadler, Matt 186
Safari Hunt 131, *131*
SAFE (Strategy and Force Evaluation) 359
Sakaguchi, Hironobu 334
Salamander 2 209
SALLY 76
Samantha Fox Strip Poker 184
Sammy 292
Sampson, Pete 4
Samsung 399
Samsung Galaxy Tab 401
Samsung Gear VR 314, 407
Samurai Shodown 147, 170, 172, **172**, 215
Samurai Spirits 172
sandbox 279
Sanders Associates 5, 12
Sanyo 3DO TRY 212, *212*
Satellaview 162
Sato, Hideki 130, 154, 219, 272
Saunders, Robert 4
Sawano, Kazunori 56
Sawyer, Ben 245

scale line blending 166
scaling (zooming) 165
scalpers 441
SCART *35*
Schmidt, Brian 291
Schmidt, Eric 399
schools, specializing in gaming
    377–379, *378*
Schwarzenegger, Arnold 198
science, video games in 367
    games with a purpose **371,** 371–372
score 47
scoring reels 3
screen burn-in 36
screen resolution 36
scrolling 43
Sculley, John 109
Sculptured Software 192
SD/Mini SD 336
Sea Duel 68, *68*
'Seal of Quality' 127
Sears "Quality Excellence Award" 3
Sears Super Video Arcade 66
Sears "Tele-Games" label 12, *13*, 57
    christmas catalog advertisement for *14*
Sears Video Arcade 57
SECAM (Séquentiel Couleur à Mémoire)
    36–37
second generation 56
second-level cache 284
Second Life 311, 375
second-party developers 247
second-person perspective 42
Secret of Mana 165
The Secret of Monkey Island 109,
    110, **110**
SECTER (Simulated Environment for
    Counseling, Training, Evaluation
    and Rehabilitation) 373
Sega 417
Sega Cards 130
Sega CD *29*, 31, 157, *157*
Sega Channel Adapter 159
Sega Dreamcast *272*, 272–275, **273,**
    344–345
    vs. fifth-generation consoles 275, **275**
    magazine advertisement for *274*
    vs. Sony PlayStation, 2 279, **279**
    tech specs 275, **275**
    titles *275*, 275–276
    U.S. launch titles **273**
Sega Enterprises 130, 157
Sega Game Gear 168, *168*
    tech specs **168**
Sega Games Co., Ltd. 130, 147, 163, 329
    changes at 223
    market summary 138–139, *139*
    R&D (Research and Development)
        team 154

Sega Genesis 154, *156*, **156,** 156–159, **159,** 218
  "Genesis does what Nintendon't" 157
  magazine advertisement for *158*
  Power Base Converter 156, 157, *157*
  Sega CD 157, *157*
  tech specs 159, **160**
  titles 160, *160*
  vs. TurboGrafx-16 159, **160**
  U.S. launch titles **156**
Segale, Mario 56
Sega Light Phaser 131
Sega Mark III 130, *130*
  tech specs 132, **134**
Sega Master System *131,* 131–132, *133,* 154
  magazine advertisement for *133*
  vs. NES 132, **134**
  tech specs 132, **134**
  titles 132–134, *134*
Sega Mega Drive 154; *see also* Sega Genesis
  tech specs 159, **160**
SegaNet 273
Sega NetLink 220
Sega Rally 2 209
Sega Sammy Holdings Inc. 292
Sega Saturn system 218–219, *219,* **220,** 221
  changes 223
  vs. 3DO and Jaguar 221, **221**
  magazine advertisement for *222*
  vs. Sony PlayStation 225, 226, 227, **227**
  tech specs 221
  titles 221, 223, *223*
  U.S. launch titles **220**
"SegaScope 3-D glasses" 131
Sega SG-1000 130, *130*
Sega Sports Pad 132
Sega's R&D (Research and Development) team 154
Sega Virtua Processor (SVP) chip 157
Sega 32X 218–219, *219*
Seiken Densetsu 3 166
Self Determination Theory (SDT) 373
semiconductor 250
Sengoku 172
Sensor Bar 345
The Sentinel 101, 108
Senua's Saga: Hellblade 2 443
Sepso, Mike 260
Séquentiel Couleur à Mémoire (SECAM) 36–37
serious games 367–370, **368, 369**
Serious Games Showcase and Challenge 370, *370*
Service Games 130
seventh generation 327–351
  arcade apocalypse 329, **329**
  breakthroughs and trends 350–351
  market summary 349–350, **351**

Nintendo DS 330, 335, **335**
Nintendo Wii **344–347,** 344–348
  vs. PlayStation 3 and XBOX 360 348, *348*
  PlayStation Portable (PSP) 330, 343, *343*
  titles 349, **349**
Sony PlayStation 3 *336,* 336–339, **336–339,** *338*
  titles 341, *342*
  vs. XBOX 360 339–340, *340*
  timeline 328
Xbox 360 **330,** 330–333, **331,** *331*
  console comparison 333–334, *334*
  titles 334, **334**
Sewer Shark 159, 213, 215
sex/sexual themes, in video games; *see also* violence, in video games
  Custer's Revenge 184, *184*
  effects of 200
  gender and race 188–191, *190*
  Grand Theft Auto series *187,* 187–188
  The Guy Game 186, *186*
  highlighted games timeline 183
  Leisure Suit Larry in the Land of the Lounge Lizards 184, *184*
  Night Trap and other FMV games *185,* 185–186, **187**
  overview 183
  regulation and the ESRB 193, **193,** *194*
  Softporn Adventure 183–184
SFC *see* Super Famicom (SFC)
shader architecture 333
shaders **39,** 39–40, *40*
Shadow of the Beast 109, 161
Shadow of the Colossus 281, *281*
Shadows of the Damned 189
Shadow Warriors 121
Shanghai 149
Shantae: Half-Genie Hero 440
Shaq Fu 188
"Share" button 425
Share Play 426
shareware distribution method 304
Sharp 104
Sheff, David 374
Sherry, John L. 374
Shining Force III 223
Shining Force: The Sword of Hajya 168, **168**
Shining the Holy Ark 221–223
Shin Nihon Kikaku (SNK) Corporation 167
Shinobi 132, *134*
Shinobi II: The Silent Fury 168
Shinobi III 160
shoot 'em ups 42
Shooting Gallery 8
Shooting Star 68

short-term aggression 199
Shovel Knight 317, 422, 430
Shovelware 78
SID 6581 (Sound Interface Device) **100,** 101
side-scrolling "platformer" games 129
sidetalking 394
Sid Meier's Pirates! 101, *103*
Sierra On-Line 186
signifiers 41
Silent Scope 2: Dark Silhouette 271
Silicon Graphics, Inc. (SGI) 229, 281, 305
Silicon Knights 285
SimCity 103, 110
SIMNET 360
Simogo 403
Sinclair, Clive 106
The Simpsons 147
The Sims Online 311
Sinclair, Clive 106
Sinclair Research 106
Sinclair User 107
Siri 434
Sixaxis controller 337
sixth generation 269–294
  arcade decline and restructuring 271, *271*
  Game Boy Advance 282, **282,** *282*
  market summary 292–293, *293*
  Microsoft Xbox 287–290, 288–290, **289**
    vs. GameCube 290–291, **291**
    vs. PlayStation 2 290–291, **291**
    titles 291, *292*
  Nintendo GameCube 281–284, **283,** *283, 284*
    changes 287
    vs. Microsoft Xbox 290–291, **291**
    vs. PlayStation 2 284, **285**
    titles 285, *287*
  Sega Dreamcast *272,* 272–275, **273**
    vs. fifth-generation consoles 275, **275**
    vs. Sony PlayStation, 2 279, *279*
    titles *275,* 275–276
  Sony PlayStation, 2 *276,* 276–279, *277,* **277**
    vs. Dreamcast 279, **279**
    vs. Microsoft Xbox 290–291, **291**
    titles 279–281, *281*
  timeline 270
Ski 8, *8*
skins 333
Skool Daze 107
Skyrim VR 316
slowdown 166
slow load times 172
Smart Boards 376
Smart Delivery 441
"Smart" devices 389–390, **390**

smartphone(s) 389
Smith, Jay 68
Snail Maze 134
Snap 433
snap turning 314
Snatcher 152
SNES *see* Super Nintendo Entertainment System (SNES)
SNK *see Shin Nihon Kikaku*
Snyder, Dan 361
soap opera effect 33
social features 406
social games, online 310, 311, 401
social network 310
Society for Simulation in Healthcare (SSH) 368
Softporn Adventure 183–184
Soldier of Fortune 197
Somnium Space 312
Sonic Adventure 273, 275, 285
Sonic & Knuckles 160
Sonic Team 223
Sonic the Hedgehog 157, 160, *160*, 163, 168, *168*, 172
Sonic the Hedgehog 2 172
Sonic the Hedgehog Spinball 160
Sonic the Hedgehog: Triple Trouble 168
"Sonic Tuesday" 172
Sony Computer Entertainment (SCE) 224
Sony Corporation 165, 223
    marketing strategy 224
Sony Ericsson 397
Sony Online Entertainment 306
Sony PlayStation 223–225, **224**, *224, 225, 226, 227*
    magazine advertisement for *225*
    12-month game sales curve *253*
    vs. Nintendo 64 (N64) **231**, 231–232
    vs. Sega Saturn 225, 226, 227, **227**
    tech specs 225, **227**
    titles 227, *227*
    Underground disc series 224
    U.S. launch titles 224
Sony PlayStation, 2 *276,* 276–279, *277,* **277**
    vs. Dreamcast 279, **279**
    vs. GameCube 284, **285**
    magazine advertisement for *280*
    vs. Microsoft Xbox 290–291, **291**
    Network Play service 279
    tech specs 279, **279**
    titles 279–281, *281*
    U.S. launch titles **277**
Sony PlayStation 3 *336,* 336–339, **336–339,** *338*
    titles 341, *342*
    U.S. launch titles *345*
    versions *338*
    vs. Wii 348, *348*
    vs. XBOX 360 339–340, *340*

Sony SPC700 165
Sony Walkman 223
Sord (Toshiba) 104
SoulCalibur 273, 275
Soul Calibur series 190
Soul Sacrifice 430
sound 43–45
SoundBlaster card 303
sound card (audio card) 31, *31*, 301
sound channels 44
sound effect 62
sound engineer **248**
sound theory 45–47, **47**
Space Ace 215
Space Dungeon 78, *78*
Space Harrier 121
Space Harrier II 154, *156*
Space Invaders 43, 55, *55,* 61, *61,* 62, 79
Space Manbow 105
Spacewar! 4, 5, *5,* 12, 36, 37
"Speccy" 106
spectator modes 406
Spectrum HoloByte 101
Speedway! **62,** *63*
Spelunky 309, 430
Spider-Man: Miles Morales 189, 255, *442*, 443
Spindizzy 108
Splatterhouse 152, *154*
SpotPass data systems 423
sprite-generated polygons 220
sprite rotation 147
sprites 38
sprite scaling 147
sprite technology 38
Spy Hunter 100, 101
Squaresoft 227
S-SMP audio processing unit 165
SSX 277, 277
standalone architecture (SA) 406
Standard Games 130
Star Control II 213
Stardew Valley **319**
Star Fox 166
Star Ocean 166
Star Raiders 97, *97*
Star Trek: Phaser Strike 68
Star Wars 55, 134, *248*
Star Wars Arcade 218
Star Wars Battlefront II 257
Star Wars: Knights of the Old Republic 291, *292*
Star Wars Rogue Leader: Rogue Squadron II 284
State of Decay 3 443
static random-access memory (SRAM) 165
statista 255
Steam 254, 309–311

Steam app 310
Steam Deck 319
Steam online 363
SteamVR platform 315
Steel Media 405
Stella, chip 56
stereophonic (stereo) sound 44
stereoscopic 3D technology 39
stereoscopic 3D video games 43
stereotypical 188, 200
Stern Electronics 44
St. GIGA 162
St. John, Alex 304–305
Stockburger, Axel 47
Stockburger's sound objects 47, **47**
Stolar, Bernie 224, 272
stream processors 422
street date 172
Street Fighter 188
Street Fighter Alpha 209
Street Fighter II: Champion Edition 152, 160
Street Fighter II: Special Champion Edition 160
Street Fighter II: The World Warrior 147, *147*, 152, 170
Street Fighter IV 341
StreetPass data systems 423
Streets of Rage 2 160
Streets of Rage 3 188
Streets of Rage 44, *44,* 159, 160, 168, 189
Strider 157
Strider Hiryu 152
strings 32
Stroop Effect test 373
Stuart-Williams, Raymond 4
studio 247
Studio II 56
Stunner light gun 220
S.T.U.N. Runner 161
Stunt Race-FX 166
ST-V (SegaTitan Video) 209
stylus 335
Submarine 8
Subnautica 317
Sugar, Alan 107
Sumii, Tetsu 425
Summer Game Fest 259
Sun Microsystems' Java 306
Super Action Controller Set, ColecoVision 72, *72*
Super Blockbuster 68, *68*
Super Breakout 75, 97
Super Castlevania IV 163
Supercell 402
Super Columns 168
SuperData Research, Inc. 255, 437
Super Famicom (SFC) 162, *162*
SuperFX chip 166

Super Game Boy 155
Super Ghouls 'n Ghosts 163
SuperGrafx 150, *151*
Super Hang-On 156
Super Mario 18
Super Mario 64 229, *229*, 232
Super Mario Bros. 38, 43, 125, *127*, *129*,
    129–131, 136, 154, 188
Super Mario 3D Land 423, **423**
Super Mario 3D World 255, 422, **422**
Super Mario 3D World + Bowser's
    Fury 440
Super Mario 64 DS 335, 373
Super Mario Galaxy **349**
Super Mario Land 155, **155**
Super Mario Land 2: 6 Golden Coins
    155, *155*
Super Mario Maker 2 440
Super Mario Odyssey 440, **441**
Super Mario World 162, *163*, **163**, 166, 282
Supermassive Games 406
Super Metroid 166
Super Nintendo Entertainment
    System (SNES) *162,* 162–163,
    163*, 163*
    color layering 165, *165*
    magazine advertisement for **164**
    "Mode 7" 165, *165*
    vs. SEGA & NEC 165-166, *165* 146,
        148, *148*, **148**
    tech specs 166, **166**
    U.S. launch titles **163**
Super Pong 13
Super Puzzle Fighter 2 Turbo 209
Super Scope (Nintendo) 157
Super Slim 338
Super Smash Bros **349**
Super Smash Bros. Melee 285
Super Smash Bros. Ultimate 420, 440
Super Street Fighter II 209, 213, **213,** 215,
    221, 260
Super Street Fighter II Turbo 213
Super System Card 151
Super Thunder Blade 154
The Surgeon 368
Surgeon Simulator 368
surround (multichannel) sound 44
Sutherland, Ivan 314
Suzuki, Yu 121, 147, 148
S-video **35**
Switch Lite 438
SX-64 101
Symbian 389
Symbian OS 6.1 391
sync generator 10
Syndicate 42
system 274
System 16 121
System 246 329

system bus 30, *30*
System Link cables 289
Syzygy Engineering 4–5

Table Tennis 10
    vs. *Pong 12,* 12–13
Tactical Engagement Simulation
    (TES) 360
Tactical Iraqi 365
Tactical Language & Culture Training
    System (TLCTS) 365
Taiko: Drum Master 329
Tails' Adventures 168
Taisen Puzzle-Dama 209
Taito 55, 56, 121, 209
Takeshiro Maeda 149
Take-Two Interactive 408
Tallarico, Tommy 47
Tales of Arise **319**
Tales of Phantasia 166
TandyVision model 66
Target: Renegade 107
Taylor, John 424
Team Tap adapter 216
Tech Model Railroad Club 4
technology 27–47
    ASCII and vector graphics 37–38, *38*
    BIOS 30, *30*
    bits and bytes *32,* 32–33
    color and lighting 40–41
    CPU 29
    graphics and sound cards 31
    hertz and frame rate **33**, *33*–34
    interlaced scan 34, *34*
    local area networks (LANs) 31, *32*
    monitors, types of 36
    motherboard 29, *29*
    overview 29
    peripheral component interconnect
        31, *32*
    perspective *42,* 42–43, **43**
    polygon graphics *38,* 38–39, *39*
    ports 31, *31*
    progressive scan 34, *34*
    raster graphics *38,* 38–39
    shaders, flops, and cores **39**, *39*–40,
        40, *40*
    sound and music 43–45
    sound channels 44
    sound theory 45–47, **47**
    video formats 36–37
    wide area networks (WANs) 31, *32*
Technōs Japan 121, 147
Tecmo 121
Tectoy 132
Teenage Mutant Ninja Turtles 147
Tekken 209, *209,* 227
Tekken Tag Tournament 277, *277*

Tele-Communications, Inc. (TCI) 159
Tele-Games 12
teleportation 314
teleprinters 90
Television Interface Adaptor (TIA)
    56, 135
Telltale Games 310
Telstar Arcade 16, *16*
Telstar Colormatic 15
Telstar Gemini 15
Telstar Ranger 15
Tempest 2000 216, 218, **218,** 221
Tencent 408
Tennis 15
Tennis for Two 4, *4,* 36
terabytes (TB) 420
The Terminator 134
Terranigma 166
tester **248**
Tetris 101, 155, *155*
Tetris DX 233
Tetris Effect Connected **319**, *442*
Texas Instruments 73
    SN76489AN sound card 73
    SN76499N chip 15
    TMS1100 68
text adventure games 93
texture mapping 39, *39*
TG-16 *see* TurboGrafx-16 (TG-16)
The Learning Company 376
"The Voice" 62
Thexder 105
third generation (3G) 391
    arcade scene 121, *121*
    Atari 7800 ProSystem 123, 134–135,
        135, *135*
        comic book advertisement for *137*
        vs. NES 136, **136,** 138
        titles 138, *138*
    breakthroughs and trends 139
    market summary 138–139, *139*
    Nintendo Entertainment System
        (NES) 121, 123–127, *124,*
        125, **127**
        vs. Atari 2600 (VCS) 127–129, **129**
        vs. Atari 7800 ProSystem 136,
        136, 138
        vs. Sega Master System 132, **134**
        titles *129,* 129–130
    Nintendo Famicom 122, *122,* 130
    Sega Mark III 130, *130*
    Sega Master System *131,* 131–132, *133*
        vs. NES 132, **134**
        titles 132–134, *134*
    timeline 120
    United States 123, *124*
third-party developers 247
third-person titles 42, *42*
Thompson, Jack 199

THQ Wireless 396
Thumper 316
TIA (Television Interface Adaptor) 135
Tiger Electronics 126
Tiger Telematics 396
tilt mechanisms 3
Time (magazine) 184, 185
Time Crisis 209
timeline
    Atari generation 54
    console 416
    early PC gaming 88
    8-bit era 120
    fifth-generation 208
    first generation 2
    fourth-generation 146
    PC gaming 300
    sixth generation 270
Time Soldiers 167
"time-to-solution" 40
Time Warner Cable 159
TitanIM 367
T-Mobile 406
TMS9928A video display processor 73
TMS9918 video processor 105
Tobias, John 192
Todd's Adventure in Slime World 161
toggle circuit 90
Tomb Raider 188, 227, *227*, **305**
*Tom Clancy's Splinter Cell: Chaos
    Theory* 292
Tommy Lasorda Baseball 157
Tomohiro Nishikado 55
Tonka 139
Toon Blast 408
top-down games 42
Top Gear Rally 282
Topheavy Studios 186
Toshiba 276, 336
Toslink/optical **35**
Total Eclipse (1988) 108, *211,* **211,** 213,
    218, *224*
touchscreen 335, 389
Toy Blast 408
Toy-Cons 438
Trak-Ball controller, Atari 5200 76
Tramiel, Jack 99, 100, 134, 138
Transfer Pak 231
Transparency 226
Trauma Center 345, 368
Treasure 232
Trevor McFur in the Crescent Galaxy.
    216, *216*
Trophy system 337
Trubshaw, Roy 93
true 3D games 42–43
Turbo 71, *73*
TurboChips 150, 151
    vs. HuCards 151

TurboDuo 151
TurboExpress 151
TurboGrafx-16 (TG-16) 149–151, *150–151,*
    152; see also NEC PC Engine
    8-bit central processing unit (CPU) 152
    16-bit graphics processing unit
        (GPU) 152
    8-bit Hu6820 processor 152
    localization 150
    magazine advertisement for *153*
    vs. NES 152, *154*
    vs. Sega Genesis 159, **160**
    tech specs 152, **152**
    titles 152, *154*
    TurboChips 150
    TurboPad controller and 150, *150*
    turbo switches 150
    TurboTap 150
    U.S. launch titles **152**
TurboGrafx-CD 151, *151*
TurboPad controller 150, *150*
turbo switches 150
TurboTap 150
Turbo Technologies, Inc. (TTI) 172
TurboVision 151, 168
Turing architecture 317
Turtle Entertainment 260
Turtles! 65, *65*
TV Control button 420
TVs
    Hertz rating 33
    refresh rate 33–34
TV Tuner 168
Twitch 261, 316, 427

Ubisoft 349
Ubisoft+ 318
Ubisoft Entertainment SA 191
Uematsu, Nobuo 44
Uemura, Masayuki 122, 162
Ultima I: The First Age of Darkness 94
Ultima IV - Quest of the Avatar 134
Ultima Online **306**
Ultima series 101, 108
Ultra HD Blu-ray 434
ultra HD (4K/8K) 37
Ultra Pong 13
UMD (Universal Media Disc) 343
Uncharted 2: Among Thieves **341**
Uncharted: Golden Abyss 403
*Uncharted Legacy of Thieves
    Collection* 321
Undertale 317, 440
United States
    NES in 123–124
    Nintendo Famicom in 122, *122*
Universal Media Disc (UMD) 343
Universal Serial Bus (USB) 31, 276
    micro **35**

mini **35**
Universal Studios 209
Unreal Engine 307, 363
Unreal Engine 5 317
Until Dawn: Rush of Blood 428
Untitled Goose Game 317
Unwired Planet 390
U.S. Army Training Doctrine and
    Command (TRADOC) 360
USB *see* Universal Serial Bus (USB)
USB-C cable 438
user interfaces (UI) 247

Valeski, Terrence 80
value chain, game industry 245, *245*
Valve Corporation 254, 334, 307
Valve Index 315
Vampire 108, 209
Vampire Killer 105
Van Elferen, Isabella 47
Vanguard 167
VBS1 (Virtual Battlespace 1) 366
VBS2 366
VBS3 366
VBS4 367
VBS Blue 367
VCR (Video Cassette Recorder) 123
vector graphics 37–38, *38*
vector monitors 79
vector processing units (VPU0 and
    VPU1) 279
Vectrex 37, 79
Velocity 2X 430
Venture 71, *73*
Vermin 126
vertex shaders 333
"vertically scrolling" games 43
VES *see* Video Entertainment
    System (VES)
VGA (Video Graphics Array) **35,** 301
VGA Box 275
VGChartz 255, **256**
VIC-20 computer 99
videmption 417
Video8 223
video card (graphics card) 31, *31*
videocarts 56
Video Cassette Recorder (VCR) 123
video compact discs (VCDs) 210
    "Adult Only" 186
video display processors (VPDs) 221
Video Entertainment System (VES) 79
video formats 36–37
    HDTV 37
    HDV 37
    NTSC 36
    PAL 36
    SECAM 36–37
    ultra HD/4K format 37

video game addiction 372
video game crash, 1983 78–79, *79*, 121
video game industry 243–263
    as big business 255–258, *257*, **258**
    big data 255
    conventions *258*, 258–260, **259**
    data research 255, **256**
    development 246–249, *247*, **248**
    distribution *250*, 250–252
    end-users 253–255, **254**
    eSports *260*, 260–261
    funding 245–246, **246**
    manufacturing **249**, 249–250
    overview 243
    publishing 246
    retail *252*, 252–253
    value chain 245
video game players, demographic
    data 183
video game research 372
Video Games Live (VGL) 47
Video Graphics Array (VGA) **35,** 301
VideoLogic PowerVR 305
VideoLogic PowerVR2 card 272
Video Toaster 109
Vid Grid 216
viewing angle 36
violence, in video games **197**; *see also*
    sex/sexual themes, in video
    games
    Death Race and 191, *192*
    Doom and FPS games 194, 196,
    196, 197
    effects of 199–200, *200*
    gender and race 188–191, *190*
    Grand Theft Auto series *187*, 187–188
    highlighted games timeline 183
    Mortal Kombat 192, *192*
    overview 183
    regulation and the ESRB 193, **193,** *194*
    Rockstar games and congressional
    bills 197–199, *198*
VirTra 360
VIRTSIM 366
"*Virtua*" 147
Virtua Cop 209
Virtua Fighter 2 221, **223**
Virtua Fighter 3 209
Virtua Fighter 5 329
Virtua Fighter 147, *221, 223*
virtual battlefield 365
Virtual Battlespace (VBS) 366
Virtual Boy 228, *228*
Virtual Console 345, 420
Virtual Dental Implant Trainer 369, **369**
virtual items 311
virtuality 314
virtual online worlds 311–312, *312,* **312**
virtual reality (VR) 312, 314, 366

virtual reality therapy (VRT) 373
virtual worlds 311
Virtua Racing 157, 209, *209*
VisiCalc 110
Visual Concepts 275
Visual Memory Unit (VMU) 273
visual reference guide, video game
    connectors **35**
Viva Group 249
Vive Cosmos 315
Vive Focus 315
Vive Focus 3 315
Vive Pro 315
Vive Pro 2 315
Vive Pro Eye 315
Viverse 321
Vivid Interactive 186
vocalization 45
voice actors 45
Voice Recognition Unit (VRU) 231
voice synthesis 44
Voodoo 3 card 272
Voodoo chipset 305
VPDs *see* video display processors
    (VPDs)
VRAM bandwidth 166
VR gaming 443

The Walking Dead 189
*The Walking Dead: Saints and
    Sinners* 316
Walkman 223
Wall, Jack 47
Walton, Brett 255
WAN card 32
WANs *see* wide area networks (WANs)
Warcraft: Orcs & Humans 304
Wardynski, Casey 363
war games, early 359
Wario Land 3 233
WarioWare: Twisted! 282
Warlords 61
Warner Communications 56, 57, 79,
    134, 138
Warshaw, Howard Scott 59, 61
WaveBird 284
Way of the Warrior 213, 215
WebTV team 330
Western Electric Company 149
Westwood, Jim 106
What Remains of Edith Finch 317, 436
Whitaker, Andrew 218
Whyte, Ronald M. 198
wide area networks (WANs) 31, *32*
Wi-Fi 331
Wi-Fi adapter 32
Wii 344; *see also* Nintendo Wii
Wii Balance Board 347
Wii Family Edition 347

Wii Menu 345
Wii Mini 348
Wiimote 344
Wii MotionPlus 347
Wii Remote 344
Wii Remote Plus 347
Wii Shop Channel 345
Wii Speak microphone 347
Wii Sports 345
Wii U **418–419,** 418–421, *420,* **421,**
    422; *see also* console gaming,
    modern
Wii U GamePad 419
Wii U Pro Controller 420
Wii U titles 422, **422, 423**
Wii U *vs.* PlayStation 4 (PS4) *427,*
    427–428
WiiWare 345
Wii Wheel 347
Wii Zapper 347
Wild Gunman 124
Williams Electronics 56
Williams, Harry 3
Williams, Ken 93
Williams, Roberta 93, 186
Wilson, Barbara J. 199
Windows 287
Windows 3.0 303
Windows 7 320
Windows 95 304
Windows 10 Mobile 403
Windows OS 304
Windows 95 OS 287
Windows Phone 401
Windows Phone Store 401
Windows XP 308
WipEout 2048 430, **430**
WipEout 224
WipEout Omega Collection 428
WipEout Pure **343**
Wireless Application Protocol
    (WAP) 390
Wireless Gaming Receiver 333
Wireless Keypad 339
Wireless Network Adapter 331
The Witcher 2: Assassins of Kings 334
The Witcher III: Wild Hunt 189
Wizardry 233
Wolfenstein 3D 194, 218, *218,* 303
women
    in game characters 188
    as oversexualized character 188,
    188, 200
    as sex objects in video games 188
    as video gamer 183
Wonder Boy in Monster World 134, *134*
WonderSwan 233
World Championship Soccer 156
World Cyber Games (WCG) 260

Worlds of Wonder 125
World War II 130
Wozniak, Steve "Woz" 89, 90, *95*
Wright, Will 110, 311

X axis 43
Xbox *see* Microsoft Xbox
Xbox 360 330
Xbox App/Smartglass 433
Xbox Cloud Gaming 318, 434
Xbox 360 Dashboard (GUI) 332
Xbox 360 E 332
Xbox Game Pass 434
Xbox Games Store 250
Xbox Live 289, 330, 431
Xbox Live Gold 432
Xbox One *431*, **431–432**, 431–434; *see* also
     console gaming, modern
Xbox One Elite 434
Xbox One S 434
Xbox One titles 435–436, *437*, **437**
Xbox One *vs.* PlayStation 4 (PS4)
     434–435, *435*, **436**
Xbox One X 434

Xbox 360/PS3 *vs.* WII U *421,* 421–422
Xbox 360 S 332
Xbox Series X|S 440–441
XE Game System (XEGS) *99*, *99*
Xenoblade Chronicles **349**
Xenon 333
Xenon 2: Megablast 109
Xenophobe 138, **161**
Xenos 330, 340
Xevious 135, 138
X-Forge 3D 391
X86-64 "Jaguar" 424
X-Men 147, 209, 233
Xperia Z5 Premium 403
XrossMediaBar (XMB) 337
Xseed Games 349
Xyphoes Fantasy 108

Yamamoto, Tatsuo 272
Yamaha VDP graphics chip 166
Yamaha YM2203 104
Yamaha YM3812 301
Yamauchi, Hiroshi 123, 125, 287
Yamauchi, Fusajiro 122

Yannes, Bob 101
Yars' Revenge 59, 61, *61*
Y axis 43
Ybarra, Mike 433
Yee, Leland 198
Yokoi, Gunpei 55, 124–126, 130, 155, 228
Yoshida, Shuhei 426, 444
YouTube 316, 345
Yie Ar Kung-Fu 121

Z axis 42
Zaxxon 71, *72*
Zelda 18, 155
Zillion 134, *134*
Zilog Z80 121, 154
Zilog Z80A CPU 106
Zilog Z80 CPU 103, 105
zone sound 47
*Zork I: The Great Underground
     Empire* 91
ZX Spectrum *106,* **106,** 106–107
ZX Spectrum+ 107
ZX Spectrum128 107
Zynga 310, 401, 431

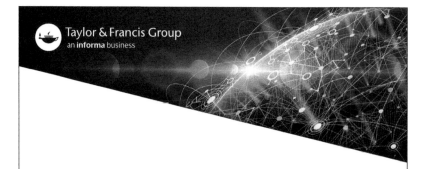